REVELATION

Smyth & Helwys Bible Commentary: Revelation

Publication Staff

Publisher and President
Cecil P. Staton

Executive Vice-President
David Cassady

Vice-President, Editorial
Lex Horton

Senior Editor
Mark K. McElroy

Art Director
Jim Burt

Assistant Editor
Erin Smith

Editorial Assistance
Jennifer W. Becton, Kelley Fuller, Laura Shuman, Bryan Whitfield

Smyth & Helwys Publishing, Inc.
6316 Peake Road
Macon, Georgia 31210-3960
1-800-747-3016
© 2001 by Smyth & Helwys Publishing
All rights reserved.
Printed in the United States of America.

The paper used in this publication meets the minimum
requirements of American National Standard for Information
Sciences—Permanence of Paper for Printed Library Materials.
ANSI Z39.48–1984 (alk. paper)

Library of Congress Cataloging-in-Publication Data

Reddish, Mitchell Glenn, 1953-
Revelation / Mitchell G. Reddish.
p. cm. — (Smyth & Helwys Bible Commentary)
Includes bibliographical references and index.
ISBN 1-57312-087-1
1. Bible. N.T. Revelation—Commentaries.
I. Title. II. Series.

BS2825.3 .R43 2001
228'.077—dc21

Library of Congress Control Number: 2001020092

SMYTH & HELWYS BIBLE COMMENTARY

REVELATION

MITCHELL G. REDDISH

SMYTH&HELWYS
PUBLISHING, INCORPORATED · MACON, GEORGIA

PROJECT EDITOR
R. SCOTT NASH
Mercer University
Macon, Georgia

OLD TESTAMENT
GENERAL EDITOR
SAMUEL E. BALENTINE
Baptist Theological Seminary
at Richmond, Virginia

NEW TESTAMENT
GENERAL EDITOR
R. ALAN CULPEPPER
McAfee School of Theology
Mercer University
Atlanta, Georgia

AREA
OLD TESTAMENT EDITORS
MARK E. BIDDLE
Baptist Theological Seminary
at Richmond, Virginia

AREA
NEW TESTAMENT EDITORS
R. SCOTT NASH
Mercer University
Macon, Georgia

KANDY QUEEN-SUTHERLAND
Stetson University
Deland, Florida

RICHARD B. VINSON
Averett College
Danville, Virginia

KENNETH G. HOGLUND
Wake Forest University
Winston-Salem, North Carolina

ART EDITOR
HEIDI J. HORNIK
Baylor University
Waco, Texas

ADVANCE PRAISE

Reddish's commentary is based on solid research and is clearly written, bridging many of the gaps that separate historical meaning from contemporary church life. The author knows both sides of the bridge and how to bring them together. One can only hope that the book will be widely read in church study groups.

—*M. Eugene Boring*
Briscoe Professor of New Testament
Brite Divinity School
Fort Worth, Texas

Enlightened and enlightening—Reddish's commentary is a reliable guide to an often misunderstood book—the product of over two decades of grappling with apocalyptic literature in general and the Apocalypse of John in particular.

—*Edgar V. McKnight*
William R. Kenan Jr. Professor Emeritus of Religion
Furman University
Greenville, South Carolina

Mitchell Reddish has given us a remarkably well-written and cogent explanation of the Apocalypse. He has balanced a careful reading of the text, provocative dialogue with other scholars, and an honest struggle with the ethical and theological issues the Apocalypse raises for modern readers. His reading is sharp, multidimensional, and sensible. This is a splendid introduction to John's Apocalypse.

—*David L. Barr*
Professor of Religion
Wright State University
Dayton, Ohio

Though a plethora of commentaries and monographs on Revelation exists, few of them are as readable as Reddish's recent effort. His presentation of the material is well researched and carefully nuanced, reflecting a wide reading on the subject. Of the midlevel commentaries on this challenging book, Reddish's must rank among the best for pastors and teachers who want an accessible point of entry to discussing Revelation.

—*Ben Witherington III*
Asbury Theological Seminary
Wilmore, Kentucky

Reddish combines careful scholarship with thoughtful reflection, helping readers grasp the images Revelation's first readers would have envisioned and, most importantly, hear Revelation's message. While readers of Revelation commentaries rarely agree with any one on every detail, this commentary reflects the mainstream of contemporary Revelation scholarship and a happy alternative to the common "pop" prophetic speculation plaguing our era.

—*Craig S. Keener*
Professor of New Testament
Eastern Baptist Theological Seminary
Wynnewood, Pennsylvania

CONTENTS

ABBREVIATIONS USED IN THIS COMMENTARY

Books of the Old Testament, Apocrypha, and New Testament are generally abbreviated in the Sidebars, parenthetical references, and notes according to the following system.

The Old Testament

Genesis	Gen
Exodus	Exod
Leviticus	Lev
Numbers	Num
Deuteronomy	Deut
Joshua	Josh
Judges	Judg
Ruth	Ruth
1–2 Samuel	1–2 Sam
1–2 Kings	1–2 Kgs
1–2 Chronicles	1–2 Chr
Ezra	Ezra
Nehemiah	Neh
Esther	Esth
Job	Job
Psalm (Psalms)	Ps (Pss)
Proverbs	Prov
Ecclesiastes or Qoheleth	Eccl Qoh
Song of Solomon or Song of Songs or Canticles	Song Song Cant
Isaiah	Isa
Jeremiah	Jer
Lamentations	Lam
Ezekiel	Ezek
Daniel	Dan
Hosea	Hos
Joel	Joel
Amos	Amos
Obadiah	Obad
Jonah	Jonah
Micah	Mic

Nahum	Nah
Habakkuk	Hab
Zephaniah	Zeph
Haggai	Hag
Zechariah	Zech
Malachi	Mal

The Apocrypha

1–2 Esdras	1–2 Esdr
Tobit	Tob
Judith	Jdt
Additions to Esther	Add Esth
Wisdom of Solomon	Wis
Ecclesiasticus or the Wisdom of Jesus Son of Sirach	Sir
Baruch	Bar
Epistle (or Letter) of Jeremiah	Ep Jer
Prayer of Azariah and the Song of the Three	Pr Azar
Daniel and Susanna	Sus
Daniel, Bel, and the Dragon	Bel
Prayer of Manasseh	Pr Man
1–2 Maccabees	1–2 Macc

The New Testament

Matthew	Matt
Mark	Mark
Luke	Luke
John	John
Acts	Acts
Romans	Rom
1–2 Corinthians	1–2 Cor
Galatians	Gal
Ephesians	Eph
Philippians	Phil
Colossians	Col
1–2 Thessalonians	1–2 Thess
1–2 Timothy	1–2 Tim.
Titus	Titus
Philemon	Phlm
Hebrews	Heb
James	Jas
1–2 Peter	1–2 Pet
1–2–3 John	1–2–3 John
Jude	Jude
Revelation	Rev

Other commonly used abbreviations include:

BC	Before Christ
(also commonly referred to as BCE = Before the Common Era)	
AD	*Anno Domini* ("in the year of the Lord")
(also commonly referred to as CE = the Common Era)	
v.	verse
vv.	verses
C.	century
c.	*circa* (around "that time")
cf.	*confer* (compare)
ch.	chapter
chs.	chapters
d.	died
ed.	edition or edited by or editor
eds.	editors
e.g.	*exempli gratia* (for example)
et al.	*et alii* (and others)
f./ff.	and the following one(s)
gen. ed.	general editor
ibid.	*ibidem* (in the same place)
i.e.	*id est* (that is)
LCL	Loeb Classical Library
lit.	literally
n.d.	no date
rev. and exp. ed.	revised and expanded edition
sg.	singular
trans.	translated by or translator(s)
vol(s).	volume(s)

Additional written works cited by abbreviations include:

1QM	*War Scroll*
2–3–4 Bar.	*2–3–4 Baruch*
1–2–3 En.	*1–2–3 Enoch*
4QTest	*Testimonia*
Alex.	Lucian, *Alexander (Pseudomantis), Alexander the False Prophet*
Ant.	Josephus, *Jewish Antiquities*
Ascen. Isa.	*Ascension of Isaiah*
CD	*Damascus Document* (Cairo)
CEV	Contemporary English Version of the Bible
Civ.	Augustine, *De civitate Dei, The City of God*

Conf.	Augustine, *Confessionum libri XIII, Confessions*
Dial.	Justin, *Dialogus cum Tryphone, Dialogue with Trypho*
Dom.	Suetonius, *Domitianus*
Ep. Tra.	Pliny the Younger, *Epistulae ad Trajanum, Epistles to Trajan*
Epist.	Jerome, *Epistulae*
Haer.	Hippolytus, *Refutatio omnium haeresium (Philosophoumena), Refutation of All Heresies*
Haer.	Irenaeus, *Adversus haereses, Against Heresies*
Hist. eccl.	Eusebius, *Historia ecclesiastica, Ecclesiastical History*
Hist. rom.	Dio Cassius, *Historia romana, Roman History*
JSNTSup	Journal for the Study of the New Testament: Supplement Series
Jub.	*Jubilees*
KJV	King James Version of the Bible
LXX	Septuagint
m. Ketub.	Mishnah tractate *Ketubbot*
Mart. Pol.	*Martyrdom of Polycarp*
NAB	New American Bible
NIV	New International Version of the Bible
NPNF	*Nicene and Post-Nicene Fathers*
NRSV	New Revised Standard Version of the Bible
PMich	Michigan Papyrus
REB	Revised English Bible
RSV	Revised Standard Version of the Bible
Sib. Or.	*Sibylline Oracles*
T. Jud.	*Testament of Judah*
T. Levi	*Testament of Levi*
TDNT	*Theological Dictionary of the New Testament*
Tract. ep. Jo.	Augustine, *In epistulam Johannis ad Parthos tractatus, Tractates on the First Epistle of John*
Vesp.	Suetonius, *Vespasianus*

DEDICATED WITH GRATITUDE TO
MY PARENTS, WARREN AND JUANITA REDDISH,
AND TO
THE ALTERNATIVE CLASS AT
FIRST BAPTIST CHURCH, DELAND, FLORIDA

PREFACE

In *The City of God*, Augustine wrote, "Now in this book called the Apocalypse there are, to be sure, many obscure statements, designed to exercise the mind."[1] Most modern readers would agree with Augustine's assessment. This writing by John of Patmos is the strangest and most puzzling literature in the New Testament. It is a work that teases and tantalizes the imagination, a work that often obscures as much as it reveals. Yet if Revelation is the most enigmatic of the New Testament writings, it is also one of the New Testament's most powerful works. It challenges its readers to be faithful servants of God, demanding unswerving loyalty to the God "who is, who was, and who is to come, the Almighty." John's visions contain strong words of warning and judgment, reminding readers of the stringent demands placed upon those who would be followers of the Lamb. At the same time, Revelation presents a message of comfort, offering images of hope and assurance in the midst of uncertainty and despair.

Like many readers, ancient and modern, I too have been captivated by John's dizzying array of symbols, images, and visions. No other work in the canon has intrigued and challenged me as has the book of Revelation. It has ignited my imagination, exhilarated my spirit, indicted my complacency, and sustained my hope. I have found my faith in God enriched, expanded, and reshaped by the eloquent visions of the Apocalypse. If this commentary can help others experience the profundity and power of John's Revelation, then my labor will not have been in vain.

This commentary on Revelation, while written by an individual, is in many ways a community product. Various academic communities and faith communities have shaped my understanding of John's Apocalypse. In addition, particular individuals have contributed in significant ways to the production of this work. In this modest way, I wish to pay tribute to them. With deepest appreciation, I acknowledge my indebtedness and gratitude to the following: to Stetson University for providing partial funding for travel to the cities of Revelation; to James Ridgway, Jr., of Educational Opportunities and Ünver Gazez of Azim Tours for their assistance in my research in Turkey and on Patmos; to Necdet (Net) Özeren, a good friend and excellent guide in Turkey; to Clyde Fant, my colleague and fellow traveler "to the seven churches that are in Asia" and beyond; to my colleagues in the Department of Religious Studies, Stetson University, for their encouragement; to my wife, Barbara, and our children, Tim, Beth, and Michael, for their patience, support, and understanding; and to Professor James R. Blevins, who more than two decades ago helped me appreciate the drama and creativity of the Apocalypse. A word of gratitude is also due to the special editors of this commentary project for their assistance, Scott Nash, Alan Culpepper, and Heidi Hornik, as well as to the publication staff at Smyth & Helwys (particularly Lex Horton, Jim Burt, and Erin Smith) who worked diligently to bring this work to completion.

Special acknowledgments are due to those to whom I dedicate this commentary: my parents, Warren and Juanita Reddish, who first nurtured me in the faith and introduced me to that "great multitude that no one could count, from every nation, from all tribes and peoples and languages"; and the Alternative Class at First Baptist Church, DeLand, Florida, who have graciously allowed me to serve as their teacher, have opened my eyes to new meanings and insights, and have helped keep me honest in dealing with the Scriptures.

NOTE

[1] *Civ.* 20.17, trans. Henry Bettenson; ed. David Knowles (New York: Penguin, 1972), 929.

SERIES PREFACE

The *Smyth & Helwys Bible Commentary* is a visually stimulating and user-friendly series that is as close to multimedia in print as possible. Written by accomplished scholars with all students of Scripture in mind, the primary goal of the *Smyth & Helwys Bible Commentary* is to make available serious, credible biblical scholarship in an accessible and less intimidating format.

Far too many Bible commentaries fall short of bridging the gap between the insights of biblical scholars and the needs of students of God's written word. In an unprecedented way, the *Smyth & Helwys Bible Commentary* brings insightful commentary to bear on the lives of contemporary Christians. Using a multimedia format, the volumes employ a stunning array of art, photographs, maps, and drawings to illustrate the truths of the Bible for a visual generation of believers.

The *Smyth & Helwys Bible Commentary* is built upon the idea that meaningful Bible study can occur when the insights of contemporary biblical scholars blend with sensitivity to the needs of lifelong students of Scripture. Some persons within local faith communities, however, struggle with potentially informative biblical scholarship for several reasons. Oftentimes, such scholarship is cast in technical language easily grasped by other scholars, but not by the general reader. For example, lengthy, technical discussions on every detail of a particular scriptural text can hinder the quest for a clear grasp of the whole. Also, the format for presenting scholarly insights has often been confusing to the general reader, rendering the work less than helpful. Unfortunately, responses to the hurdles of reading extensive commentaries have led some publishers to produce works for a general readership that merely skim the surface of the rich resources of biblical scholarship. This commentary series incorporates works of fine art in an accurate and scholarly manner, yet the format remains "user-friendly." An important facet is the presentation and explanation of images of art, which interpret the biblical material or illustrate how the biblical material has been understood and interpreted in the past. A visual generation of believers deserves a commentary series that contains not only the all-important textual commentary on Scripture, but images, photographs, maps, works of fine art, and drawings that bring the text to life.

The *Smyth & Helwys Bible Commentary* makes serious, credible biblical scholarship more accessible to a wider audience. Writers and editors alike present information in ways that encourage readers to gain a better understanding of the Bible. The editorial board has worked to develop a format that is useful and usable, informative and pleasing to the eye. Our writers are reputable scholars who participate in the community of faith and sense a calling to communicate the results of their scholarship to their faith community.

The *Smyth & Helwys Bible Commentary* addresses Christians and the larger church. While both respect for and sensitivity to the needs and contributions of other faith communities are reflected in the work of the series authors, the authors speak primarily to Christians. Thus the reader can note a confessional tone throughout the volumes. No particular "confession of faith" guides the authors, and diverse perspectives are observed in the various volumes. Each writer, though, brings to the biblical text the best scholarly tools available and expresses the results of their studies in commentary and visuals that assist readers seeking a word from the Lord for the church.

To accomplish this goal, writers in this series have drawn from numerous streams in the rich tradition of biblical interpretation. The basic focus is the biblical text itself, and considerable attention is given to the wording and structure of texts. Each particular text, however, is also considered in the light of the entire canon of Christian Scriptures. Beyond this, attention is given to the cultural context of the biblical writings. Information from archaeology, ancient history, geography, comparative literature, history of religions, politics, sociology, and even economics is used to illuminate the culture of the people who produced the Bible. In addition, the writers have drawn from the history of interpretation, not only as it is found in traditional commentary on the Bible but also in literature, theater, church history, and the visual arts. Finally, the *Commentary* on Scripture is joined with *Connections* to the world of the contemporary church. Here again, the writers draw on scholarship in many fields as well as relevant issues in the popular culture.

This wealth of information might easily overwhelm a reader if not presented in a "user-friendly" format. Thus the heavier discussions of detail and the treatments of other helpful topics are presented in special-interest boxes, or Sidebars, clearly connected to the passages under discussion so as not to interrupt the flow of the basic interpretation. The result is a commentary on Scripture that focuses on the theological significance of a text while also offering the reader a rich array of additional information related to the text and its interpretation.

An accompanying CD-ROM offers powerful searching and research tools. The commentary text, Sidebars, and visuals are all reproduced on a CD that is fully indexed and searchable. Pairing a text version with a digital resource is a distinctive feature of the *Smyth & Helwys Bible Commentary.*

Combining credible biblical scholarship, user-friendly study features, and sensitivity to the needs of a visually oriented generation of believers creates a unique and unprecedented type of commentary series. With insight from many of today's finest biblical scholars and a stunning visual format, it is our hope that the *Smyth & Helwys Bible Commentary* will be a welcome addition to the personal libraries of all students of Scripture.

The Editors

HOW TO USE
THIS COMMENTARY

The *Smyth & Helwys Bible Commentary* is written by accomplished biblical scholars with a wide array of readers in mind. Whether engaged in the study of Scripture in a church setting or in a college or seminary classroom, all students of the Bible will find a number of useful features throughout the commentary that are helpful for interpreting the Bible.

Basic Design of the Volumes

Each volume features an Introduction to a particular book of the Bible, providing a brief guide to information that is necessary for reading and interpreting the text: the historical setting, literary design, and theological significance. Each Introduction also includes a comprehensive outline of the particular book under study.

Each chapter of the commentary investigates the text according to logical divisions in a particular book of the Bible. Sometimes these divisions follow the traditional chapter segmentation, while at other times the textual units consist of sections of chapters or portions of more than one chapter. The divisions reflect the literary structure of a book and offer a guide for selecting passages that are useful in preaching and teaching.

An accompanying CD-ROM offers powerful searching and research tools. The commentary text, Sidebars, and visuals are all reproduced on a CD that is fully indexed and searchable. Pairing a text version with a digital resource also allows unprecedented flexibility and freedom for the reader. Carry the text version to locations you most enjoy doing research while knowing that the CD offers a portable alternative for travel from the office, church, classroom, and your home.

Commentary and Connections

As each chapter explores a textual unit, the discussion centers around two basic sections: *Commentary* and *Connections*. The analysis of a passage, including the details of its language, the history reflected in the text, and the literary forms found in the text, are the main focus of the *Commentary* section. The primary concern of the *Commentary* section is to explore the theological issues presented by the Scripture passage. *Connections* presents potential applications of the insights provided in the *Commentary* section. The *Connections* portion of each chapter considers what issues are relevant for teaching and suggests useful methods and resources. *Connections* also identifies themes suitable for sermon planning and suggests helpful approaches for preaching on the Scripture text.

Sidebars

The *Smyth & Helwys Bible Commentary* provides a unique hyperlink format that quickly guides the reader to additional insights. Since other more technical or supplementary information is vital for understanding a text and its implications, the volumes feature distinctive Sidebars, or special-interest boxes, that provide a wealth of information on such matters as:

- Historical information (such as chronological charts, lists of kings or rulers, maps, descriptions of monetary systems, descriptions of special groups, descriptions of archaeological sites or geographical settings).

- Graphic outlines of literary structure (including such items as poetry, chiasm, repetition, epistolary form).

- Definition or brief discussions of technical or theological terms and issues.

- Insightful quotations that are not integrated into the running text but are relevant to the passage under discussion.

- Notes on the history of interpretation (Augustine on the Good Samaritan, Luther on James, Stendahl on Romans, etc.).

- Line drawings, photographs, and other illustrations relevant for understanding the historical context or interpretive significance of the text.

- Presentation and discussion of works of fine art that have interpreted a Scripture passage.

Each Sidebar is printed in color and is referenced at the appropriate place in the *Commentary* or *Connections* section with a color-coded title that directs the reader to the relevant Sidebar. In addition, helpful icons appear in the Sidebars, which provide the reader with visual cues to the type of material that is explained in each Sidebar. Throughout the commentary, these four distinct hyperlinks provide useful links in an easily recognizable design.

Alpha & Omega Language

This icon identifies the information as a language-based tool that offers further exploration of the Scripture selection. This could include syntactical information, word studies, popular or additional uses of the word(s) in question, additional contexts in which the term appears, and the history of the term's translation. All non-English terms are transliterated into the appropriate English characters.

Culture/Context

This icon introduces further comment on contextual or cultural details that shed light on the Scripture selection. Describing the place and time to which a Scripture passage refers is often vital to the task of biblical interpretation. Sidebar items introduced with this icon could include geographical, historical, political, social, topographical, or economic information. Here, the reader may find an excerpt of an ancient text or inscription that sheds light on the text. Or one may find a description of some element of ancient religion such as Baalism in Canaan or the Hero cult in the Mystery Religions of the Greco-Roman world.

Interpretation

Sidebars that appear under this icon serve a general interpretive function in terms of both historical and contemporary renderings. Under this heading, the reader might find a selection from classic or contemporary literature that illuminates the Scripture text or a significant quotation from a famous sermon that addresses the passage. Insights are drawn from various sources, including literature, worship, theater, church history, and sociology.

Additional Resources Study

Here, the reader finds a convenient list of useful resources for further investigation of the selected Scripture text, including books, journals, websites, special collections, organizations, and societies. Specialized discussions of works not often associated with biblical studies may also appear here.

Additional Features

Each volume also includes a basic Bibliography on the biblical book under study. Other bibliographies on selected issues are often included that point the reader to other helpful resources.

Notes at the end of each chapter provide full documentation of sources used and contain additional discussions of related matters.

Abbreviations used in each volume are explained in a list of abbreviations found after the Table of Contents.

Readers of the *Smyth & Helwys Bible Commentary* can regularly visit the Internet support site for news, information, updates, and enhancements to the series at <**www.helwys.com/commentary**>.

Several thorough indexes enable the reader to locate information quickly. These indexes include:

• An *Index of Sidebars* groups content from the special-interest boxes by category (maps, fine art, photographs, drawings, etc.).

• An *Index of Scriptures* lists citations to particular biblical texts.

• An *Index of Topics* lists alphabetically the major subjects, names, topics, and locations referenced or discussed in the volume.

• An *Index of Modern Authors* organizes contemporary authors whose works are cited in the volume.

INTRODUCTION

No other writing in the New Testament evokes the wide range of reactions and emotions that the last book, the book of Revelation, does. This work (also called the Apocalypse) has offered comfort to the grieving, encouragement to the oppressed, hope to the downtrodden, and warning to the complacent. It has inspired painters (Albrecht Dürer, Jan van Eyck, and Michelangelo), musicians (George Handel, Olivier Messiaen, Pëtr Tchaikovsky), and writers (John Milton, William Blake, and Ernesto Cardenal). It has provided the texts for several of the great hymns of the church, including "Holy, Holy, Holy," "For All the Saints," and "Lo, He Comes with Clouds Descending."

On the other hand, teachers and preachers, as well as ordinary readers, often avoid dealing with this work. Some find Revelation too confusing and difficult to understand. It seems to be poorly arranged; it uses strange symbols and images; and in spite of its name, it often conceals more than it reveals. Many readers would agree with the assessment of Jerome in the fourth century when he said, "Revelation has as many mysteries as it does words."[1] [Acceptance of Revelation]

Some readers are repulsed by what they find in the book of Revelation, citing the work's violent imagery, bloodshed, militaristic symbols, and cries for vengeance. This is, after all, a work that has given us the graphic imagery of the four horsemen of the Apocalypse and the martyrs under the altar who cry out to God in vengeance, "How long will it be before you judge and avenge our blood on the inhabitants of the earth?" (6:10). This is the book that describes the aftermath of God's wrathful judgment with the gory description that "blood flowed as high as a horse's bridle, for a distance of about two hundred miles" (14:20) and depicts Rome as a great prostitute, the

---

Acceptance of Revelation

The book of Revelation has a checkered history in the church. Even though it was read and accepted as authoritative in some areas as early as the 2d century, the book just as quickly had its opponents. Marcion, the 2d-century church leader who was eventually declared heretical, rejected Revelation (as well as the entire Hebrew Bible and much of the New Testament). In the 4th century, Eusebius listed it as one of the "disputed" books. Churches in the eastern part of the empire frequently rejected the authority of Revelation, while churches in the West generally accepted it. The official decrees of the church at the end of the 4th century and later did include Revelation as an authentic part of Scripture. Later, during the Protestant Reformation, Martin Luther found the work objectionable, as did many other leaders of the Reformation. John Calvin wrote a commentary on every book of the New Testament, except the book of Revelation. For many modern Christians, the book is canonical in theory only. They seldom, if ever, read and study it.

mother of whores, "drunk with the blood of the saints" (17:6). The work seems to revel in the pain and suffering inflicted on others, inviting the reader to celebrate at the downfall of mighty Rome. It is no wonder that some readers have characterized Revelation as sub-Christian and even antithetical to the teachings of Jesus.

Still other Christians shy away from the book of Revelation because of its popular use as a source for futuristic scenarios. Sometimes sincere but misguided readers have distorted John's message by turning it into a sensationalist game of "Match the Prediction," in which events happening today are understood as literal fulfillment of events supposedly foretold in detail by the author of Revelation. Self-proclaimed "prophecy" experts warn of the signs of Armageddon, the mark of the beast, the antichrist, and the great tribulation. Some are even so brash as to predict the dates when certain "prophecies" will be fulfilled, usually couched in language vague enough to allow "reinterpretations" when events do not happen as predicted. Rather than be falsely identified with such embarrassing misreadings and abuses of the biblical texts, some people in the church avoid dealing with the book of Revelation at all. Functionally, it becomes a nonexistent part of their canon.

Why should the church be concerned about the book of Revelation, a work D. H. Lawrence described as "the most detestable of all these books of the Bible"?[2] Would we not be better off distancing ourselves from this book that has been the fertile field for fundamentalist soothsayers, that helped fuel the fires at the Branch Davidian compound near Waco, Texas, and that to some people seems more of an embarrassment than a work to be taken seriously? One of the most obvious reasons that the church, and especially its leaders, needs to be reading the book of Revelation is that this work is a part of the church's Bible. If we take seriously the claim that all the works in the canon function as bearers of the word of God, then we have a responsibility to read and understand this work, as well as to preach and teach from it.

Even more than simply for this formalistic reason, the church needs to embrace the Apocalypse because it is a powerful presentation of the message of our faith. Here is a work that challenges us to be faithful servants of God, regardless of the difficulties we may face. Here is a work that overwhelms us with its portrayal of a God "who is and who was and who is to come, the Almighty," while at the same time comforting us with a picture of a God who cares for God's people and who "will wipe every tear from their eyes." Here is a work that holds before us a vision of the world as God intended it to be, and ultimately will be—and that challenges us to be involved in bringing that world into reality now. [Preaching from Revelation]

Because the book of Revelation is different from other works in the New Testament, it may require more background studies and more serious grappling with the text itself than do other New Testament writings. Nevertheless, the reader who will spend the time and energy necessary to enter the world of the Apocalypse and to mine its treasures will be amply rewarded. Like no other work in the canon, the book of Revelation is filled with symbols and images that will titillate the imagination and cause the spirit to soar. It is a creative masterpiece that can invigorate, challenge, and inspire us. "Blessed are those who hear and who keep what is written in it" (1:3).

Preaching from Revelation

"There is little [in Revelation] for the preacher who is in a hurry to get 'something for Sunday.' . . . But for the preacher who will linger in the text until the eyes adjust to the brilliant obscurity, the ears discern the words in trumpet blasts, and the heart is no longer a stranger amid terrible splendor, there is much to be seen and heard and to be proclaimed from the pulpit."

Fred B. Craddock, "Preaching the Book of Revelation," *Interpretation* 40/3 (July 1986): 271.

Literary Genre

What kind of writing is the book of Revelation? That is a question that many readers would like answered. This work contains strange visions, gruesome monsters, perplexing numbers, and confusing repetitions. Readers familiar with the Gospels or the Letters in the New Testament soon discover that one cannot read the Apocalypse in the same way that one reads the other material in the New Testament. To a large degree, the seeming strangeness of the book of Revelation is due to its literary genre. According to most scholars, this work belongs to the category of writings known as apocalypses. Whereas apocalyptic ideas and images influenced other books in the New Testament, no New Testament writing other than Revelation belongs to the literary genre of an apocalypse. (The only example in the Hebrew Bible of an apocalypse is the book of Daniel.) Thus when readers encounter the book of Revelation, they are dealing with a type of writing that is generally unfamiliar to them.

The word "apocalypse" comes from the opening word in the Greek text of Revelation, *apokalypsis*, which means "revelation." Apocalyptic literature, then, is revelatory literature; that is, it is literature that claims to reveal cosmic secrets to a human recipient. These secrets usually involve information about otherworldly regions (heaven, hell, the places of the dead, the outer regions of the earth) and/or events of the final days (the destruction of the world, the Last Judgment, rewards for the righteous, and punishments for the wicked). Typically, apocalypses contain an otherworldly figure (such as an angel) who serves as a mediator of the revelation given to the earthly recipient. This otherworldly mediator sometimes delivers the revelation orally, sometimes discloses it through dreams or visions, sometimes interprets the dreams or visions for the recipient, and sometimes serves as a guide to lead the recipient on a journey to otherworldly regions. In Revelation, the Son of Man figure (the exalted Christ), angels, and an elder function as otherworldly mediators. [Definition of an Apocalypse]

In most apocalypses, the human recipient of the revelation is supposedly some important figure from the past (Abraham, Enoch, Daniel, Ezra, Adam, Elijah). In actuality, however, the author came later in history and wrote under an assumed name. The purpose of this literary technique of pseudonymity was to lend the writing more credibility. By assuming the name of some venerable figure from antiquity, the writer gave the appearance that the work came from some respected, authoritative individual. As we shall see, the book of Revelation does not make use of pseudonymity.

Although the social and historical settings of many apocalypses are not known, in many cases apocalypses seem to have been written in response to some crisis, either real or imagined. The crisis may have been social, political, theological, or existential. For this reason, apocalyptic literature has often been described as crisis literature. The purpose of apocalypses was to give comfort and hope to people who were overwhelmed, confused, frightened, and beleaguered. The intended readers often suffered from "cognitive dissonance," meaning their preconceived notions about the world and reality did not match the actual situation as they experienced it. For example, the intended readers of Daniel were Jews living under the persecution of the Syrian ruler, Antiochus IV. Their theological understanding of the world was that God was dominant, not Antiochus. Their personal experience, however, was just the opposite—Antiochus appeared to be the supreme power as he persecuted and killed those who were faithful to God. The purpose of apocalyptic literature was to provide an alternative way of

Definition of an Apocalypse

AΩ One of the most widely accepted definitions of an apocalypse is that proposed by John J. Collins and other members of the Apocalypse Group of the Society of Biblical Literature's Genres Project. Their definition of an apocalypse states:

"Apocalypse" is a genre of revelatory literature with a narrative framework, in which a revelation is mediated by an otherworldly being to a human recipient, disclosing a transcendent reality which is both temporal, insofar as it envisages eschatological salvation and spatial insofar as it involves another, supernatural world.

John J. Collins, "Introduction: Towards the Morphology of a Genre," *Apocalypse: The Morphology of a Genre*, ed. John J. Collins, *Semeia* 14 (1979): 9.

understanding the world, a different worldview. Apocalyptic writings assured their readers that indeed God was ultimately in control of history and the universe, in spite of current appearances. Eventually God would intervene to defeat the wicked and reward the righteous. [Sources for Understanding Apocalyptic Literature]

Apocalyptic writings not only offered hope and comfort, but they also served as protest literature. They were a protest against the prevailing worldview of the dominant culture. Apocalyptic writers encouraged their readers not to accept the beliefs and lifestyles of the world around them, but to remain true to their own convictions. They encouraged their readers not to become subservient to human rulers or institutions, but to remain faithful to God. Because of their beliefs that history was in God's hands and that human action could do little to change that, apocalyptic writers did not call for social or political action. Yet their works were still forms of protest. They refused to accept the present social and historical reality. The transcendent world that had been revealed to them presented clear evidence that in God's ultimate design, evil, pain, suffering, violence, and injustice do not belong. Through their visionary writings, the apocalyptic authors encouraged their readers to resist any worldview that was in conflict with God's ultimate goal for the world.

Apocalyptic thought apparently arose within Judaism following the sixth-century Babylonian exile of the Jewish people. Although the book of Daniel is the only complete example of an apocalypse in the Hebrew Bible, other

 Sources for Understanding Apocalyptic Literature

Collections of Primary Sources

Charles, R. H., ed. *The Apocrypha and Pseudepigrapha of the Old Testament*. 2 vols. Oxford: Clarendon, 1913.

Charlesworth, James H., ed. *The Old Testament Pseudepigrapha*. Vol. 1: *Apocalyptic Literature and Testaments*. Garden City NY: Doubleday & Co., 1983.

Hennecke, Edgar. *New Testament Apocrypha*. Vol. 2: *Writings Relating to the Apostles; Apocalypses and Related Subjects*. Edited by Wilhelm Schneemelcher. English translation edited by R. McL. Wilson. Rev. ed. Louisville: Westminster/John Knox, 1992.

Reddish, Mitchell G., ed. *Apocalyptic Literature: A Reader*. Nashville: Abingdon, 1990. Reprint. Peabody MA: Hendrickson, 1995.

Sparks, H. F. D., ed. *The Apocryphal Old Testament*. Oxford: Clarendon, 1984.

Helpful Studies on Apocalyptic Literature

Collins, Adela Yarbro, ed. *Early Christian Apocalypticism: Genre and Social Setting*. Semeia 36 (1986).

Collins, John J., ed. *Apocalypse: The Morphology of a Genre*. Semeia 14 (1979).

_____. *The Apocalyptic Imagination: An Introduction to the Jewish Matrix of Christianity*. New York: Crossroad, 1984.

Hanson, Paul D. *The Dawn of Apocalyptic*. Rev. ed. Philadelphia: Fortress, 1979.

_____. *Old Testament Apocalyptic*. Interpreting Biblical Texts. Nashville: Abingdon, 1987.

McGinn, Bernard, Stephen J. Stein, and John J. Collins. *The Encyclopedia of Apocalypticism*. 3 vols. New York: Continuum, 1998.

Minear, Paul. *New Testament Apocalyptic*. Nashville: Abingdon, 1981.

Morris, Leon. *Apocalyptic*. Grand Rapids: Eerdmans, 1972.

Rowland, Christopher C. *The Open Heaven: A Study of Apocalyptic in Judaism and Early Christianity*. New York: Crossroad, 1982.

Russell, D. S. *Apocalyptic: Ancient and Modern*. Philadelphia: Fortress, 1978.

_____. *Divine Disclosure: An Introduction to Jewish Apocalyptic*. Minneapolis: Fortress, 1992.

_____. *The Method and Message of Jewish Apocalyptic, 200 BC–AD 100*. Philadelphia: Westminster, 1964.

_____. *Prophecy and the Apocalyptic Dream: Protest and Promise*. Peabody MA: Hendrickson, 1994.

The Fall 1984 issue (4/3) of *Quarterly Review*, a journal for ministers published by the United Methodist Church, was devoted to apocalypticism.

passages contain ideas that are either apocalyptic or similar to apocalyptic thought. Examples would include Zechariah 9–14, Ezekiel 38–39, and Isaiah 24–27. Apocalyptic literature flourished within Judaism between the third century BC and the second century AD. At least fourteen nonbiblical Jewish apocalypses were produced during this time. After the two disastrous revolts of the Jews in Palestine against the Romans (AD 66–74 and AD 132–135), both of which were at least partially fueled by apocalyptic expectations, apocalyptic literature fell into disfavor within Judaism.

Apocalyptic thought had a tremendous influence on the New Testament and Christianity. The ideas of a final judgment, resurrection, future rewards and punishments, destruction of the forces of evil, conflict between good and evil forces, angels, and demons are all ideas drawn from apocalyptic thought. In addition to the book of Revelation, Christian writers produced more than twenty apocalypses in the early centuries of the Christian church. [Apocalyptic Writings]

Apocalyptic Writings

Even though the Bible contains only two complete apocalypses (Daniel and Revelation), many Jewish and Christian works of this genre were produced. The dates given for these works are, in many cases, only approximate.

Jewish Apocalypses
1. The "Book of the Watchers" (*1 En.* 1–36)—3rd century BC
2. The "Book of the Heavenly Luminaries" (*1 En.* 73–82)—3rd century BC
3. The "Animal Apocalypse" (*1 En.* 85–90)—2d century BC
4. The "Apocalypse of Weeks" (*1 En.* 93:1-10; 91:11-17)—2d century BC
5. *Jubilees* 23—2d century BC
6. The *Testament of Levi* 2–5—2d century BC
7. The *Testament of Abraham*—1st century BC–2d century AD
8. The *Apocalypse of Zephaniah*—1st century BC–1st century AD
9. The "Similitudes of Enoch" (*1 En.* 37–71)—1st century AD
10. *2 Enoch*—1st century AD
11. *4 Ezra*—1st century AD
12. *2 Baruch*—1st century AD
13. The *Apocalypse of Abraham*—1st–2d century AD
14. *3 Baruch*—1st–2d century AD

Christian Apocalypses (Gnostic Christian works are not included in this list.)
1. The *Shepherd of Hermas*—1st or 2d century
2. The *Book of Elchasai*—2d century
3. The *Ascension of Isaiah* 6–11—1st or 2d century
4. The *Apocalypse of Peter*—2d century
5. 5 Ezra 2:42-48
6. *Jacob's Ladder*—2d century?
7. The *Testament of the Lord* 1:1-14—3rd century?
8. The *Questions of Bartholomew*—3rd century?
9. The *Apocalypse of Sedrach*—2d–4th century?
10. The *Apocalypse of Paul*—4th century
11. The *Testament of Isaac* 2-3a—1st–5th century?
12. The *Testament of Isaac* 5-6—1st–5th century?
13. The *Testament of Jacob* 1-3a—2d–5th century?
14. The *Testament of Jacob* 2-5—2d–5th century?
15. The *Story of Zosimus*—3rd–5th century
16. The *Apocalypse of St. John the Theologian*—2d–9th century?
17. The *Book of the Resurrection of Jesus Christ by Bartholomew the Apostle* 8b-14a—3rd–6th century?
18. The *Book of the Resurrection of Jesus Christ by Bartholomew the Apostle* 17b-19b—3rd–6th century?
19. The *Apocalypse of the Virgin Mary*—4th–9th century?
20. The *Apocalypse of Esdras*—5th–9th century?
21. The *Apocalypse of the Holy Mother of God Concerning the Punishments*—4th–11th century?
22. The *Apocalypse of James, the Brother of the Lord*—pre-11th century
23. The *Mysteries of St. John the Apostle and Holy Virgin*—pre-11th century

Whereas the dominant literary genre of Revelation is that of an apocalypse, the work exhibits characteristics of other literary genres as well. Elements of typical Hellenistic-Roman letters appear, such as the greeting (1:4-5a), blessing or thanksgiving (1:5b-6), body (1:7–22:20), and closing (22:21). Chapters 2 and 3 contain messages to seven churches that are cast in the

Island of Patmos
A view across the island of Patmos.
(Credit: Mitchell Reddish)

form of imperial decrees. In addition, Revelation is similar to prophetic literature. The author himself refers to the work as a prophecy (1:3; 22:7, 10, 18, 19) and refers to the prophets as his fellow servants (22:9). Some scholars have even proposed that Revelation was written in the form of an ancient drama and have arranged the text accordingly.[3] Although their arguments for reading the Apocalypse as an actual drama are not persuasive, they do point to the highly dramatic and creative aspects of this work. Furthermore, envisioning the work as a staged production helps the reader enter the visual and imaginative world of the Apocalypse.

Provenance and Social Setting

John, the author of Revelation, claimed that he was on the island of Patmos, located in the Aegean Sea off the coast of western Asia Minor, when he received the revelation that he recorded in the Apocalypse (1:9). [Island of Patmos] The seven churches that were the recipients of the messages in chapters 2 and 3 were all located in cities of western Asia Minor. For these reasons, the place for the writing of Revelation was almost certainly in Asia Minor. This area, which today is part of Turkey, was an important center of culture, commerce, and agriculture in the ancient world. Asia Minor contained several major cities, including Ephesus, Smyrna, Pergamum, Laodicea, Aphrodisias, Perga, Tarsus, and Sardis. In fact, during the first century AD, Ephesus was likely the fourth largest city in the Roman world. The city of Pergamum boasted one of the largest libraries in the ancient world, reportedly containing more than 200,000 volumes. The setting out of which Revelation came, then, was no cultural backwater, but was at the crossroads of the ancient world.

By the end of the first century (apparently the time when Revelation was written), Christianity was well established in western Asia Minor. The book of Acts mentions several cities in Asia Minor in conjunction with the travels of Paul. (Paul's hometown of Tarsus, according to Acts, was also in Asia Minor.) Included among these would be Lystra, Derbe, Troas, Antioch (in Galatia), Ephesus, and Miletus. One of Paul's Letters was sent to the churches of Galatia, a region in Asia Minor. The New Testament contains a letter to the church at Colossae, also. This city in Asia Minor was likely the home of Philemon and his runaway slave Onesimus (see Col 4:9 and Phlm 10). The Letter to the Colossians mentions Christians in Laodicea and Hierapolis as well (4:13, 15-16). The Letter of 1 Peter is addressed to Christians throughout Asia Minor (1:1); apparently 2 Peter was intended for the same people (3:1). The three Letters of John, and possibly the Gospel of John, likely originated in Asia Minor. Two of the Pastoral Letters (1 and 2 Timothy) suggest a connection with Asia Minor (1 Tim 1:3; 2 Tim 4:13). The book of Revelation, then, is addressed to Christians in an area that was rich with Christian tradition. [Map: First-Century Christian Churches]

The evidence that we have about the situation of the Christian communities in Asia Minor during this period suggests that Christians, for the most part, were assimilated into the larger society with few problems. There seem to have been no systematic

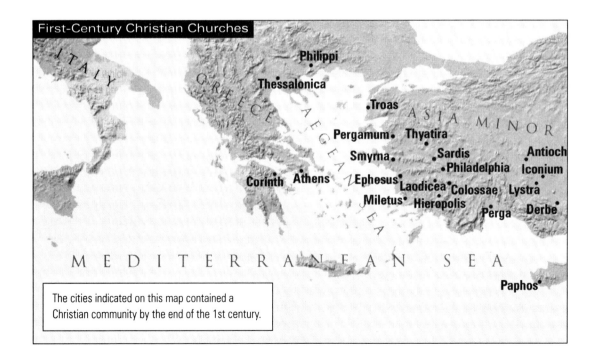

First-Century Christian Churches

The cities indicated on this map contained a Christian community by the end of the 1st century.

persecutions of Christians nor widespread ostracism of them. Christians were a minority in Asia Minor, but not an oppressed and persecuted minority. Occasionally some conflicts with local magistrates or Roman authorities would occur, and some Christians lost their lives. Such situations seem to have been the exception rather than the norm. After examining the ancient sources, Leonard Thompson has concluded, "Sources other than the Book of Revelation portray Christians, for the most part, as sharing peacefully in urban Asian life alongside their non-Christian neighbors."[4] On the basis of New Testament texts and evidence in non-Christian writers, Thompson claimed that Christians in Asia Minor represented almost all social classes.

He cited, for example, the words of Pliny the Younger (c. AD 112) in one of his letters to the emperor Trajan that Christians were "of every age and class, both men and women" (*Ep. Tra.* 10.96.9).[5] Some were wealthy enough to own slaves, host house churches, and travel extensively. The book of Revelation portrays some of the members of the church at Laodicea as saying, "I am rich, I have prospered, and I need nothing" (3:17). On the other hand, some of the early Christians were slaves, and some were poor (Rev 2:9). The Christians in Asia Minor did not form separate communities or conventicles. They participated in the Hellenistic and Roman social world of which they were a part.

Importance of Asia Minor in Church History

The area of Asia Minor was one of the most important areas for the development of the Christian church. In addition to its importance because of its connection to New Testament figures and writings, many important early church leaders were from Asia Minor, including Polycarp (bishop of Smyrna), Irenaeus (raised in Smyrna), Melito (bishop of Sardis), Polycrates (bishop of Ephesus), Marcion (born in Sinope), and Papias (bishop of Hierapolis). Ignatius traveled through the region on his way to his death in Rome, writing letters along the way to Polycarp and the churches in five cities in Asia Minor. Justin Martyr lived for a while in Ephesus before he went to Rome. The important councils of Nicea (325) and Chalcedon (451) were in Asia Minor.

In spite of this picture of general assimilation to their culture, the early Christians experienced certain tensions between their beliefs and practices and those of the larger society. Their rigid monotheism meant that they could not participate in the worship of any of the state or local deities that permeated the world of their day. Even their belonging to civic associations and trade guilds was problematic because these were usually under the patronage of a particular god or goddess. Public banquets, festivals, and celebrations also had at least a veneer of religious tradition. Likewise, the veneration and homage that the people of the empire were expected to render to the emperor, if such were couched in divine terms, were serious issues for Christians. [Importance of Asia Minor in Church History]

Literary evidence suggests that some residents of the Roman Empire viewed their Christian neighbors with suspicion and distrust because they saw the Christians as being antisocial and even dangerous. Non-Christians (except Jews, of course) could not understand the exclusive, monotheistic belief of the Christians. Worship of the Christian God was acceptable, but why not worship the other gods as well? Failure to pay proper respect to all the gods and goddesses rendered the individual and the state vulnerable to divine displeasure and punishment. For this reason, the Christians were accused of atheism. In addition, their neighbors sometimes suspected the Christians of illegal activities. Misunderstandings of the Christian celebration of the Lord's Supper led to accusations of cannibalism, whereas misunderstandings of their love-feasts (or *agapē* meals) and their custom of calling each other "brother" and "sister" caused some of their neighbors to accuse the Christians of incest and immorality. Such suspicions and disdain for Christians are reflected in the oft-quoted remarks of the Roman writer Tacitus, who said they were "loathed for their vices" and were guilty of "hatred of the human race" (*Annals* 15.44 [Jackson, LCL]). Similarly, Suetonius called Christianity a "mischievous superstition" (*Nero* 16.2 [Rolfe, LCL]).

These suspicions of Christians, however, did not lead to any prolonged, governmental persecution of the first-century church (see discussion below on emperor worship and persecution). Christians may have been in danger from the state if their neighbors denounced them for illegal activities. Even this danger, however, we should not exaggerate. Evidence of actual instances of persecution of Christians in the first century is scarce.

One of the major concerns for Christians in Asia Minor, as throughout the empire, was assimilation to the culture around them. How far could the church go in adapting and accepting the prevailing culture without losing its own distinctiveness and identity? New Testament writers answered that question in different ways. Paul was rather receptive to accepting cultural traditions, as long as they were not obvious violations of Christian principles (cf. 1 Cor 8; Phil 4:8). The author of 1 Peter also appeared to call for adaptation of cultural norms ("accept the authority of every human institution," 2:13-17; follow the household codes, 2:18–3:7). The author of Revelation, on the other hand, had a very harsh view of his cultural world. He saw the Roman Empire and the society of Asia Minor as basically antithetical to the Christian faith. He tended to view the world in rather rigid categories. The Roman Empire was the evil empire. It was the instrument of Satan and was to be resisted. John saw little room for compromise. In his view, cultural accommodation by Christians endangered their standing as a part of the people of God. In the messages to the seven churches in chapters 2 and 3, the issue of cultural accommodation is paramount. John wrote to those individual churches to warn them of the dangers of their involvement with this "demonic" culture. His message throughout the book in regard to Christians and society is

"Come out of her, my people,
  so that you do not take part in her sins,
and so that you do not share in her plagues." (18:4)

Emperor Worship and Persecution

Persecution and emperor worship are often cited as the primary problems addressed in Revelation. More precisely, these issues are specific instances of the larger problem of cultural accommodation. The cult of the emperor developed slowly in the Roman Empire. Emperor worship involved the offering of divine honors, including sacrifices, to the emperors, either living or dead. The early emperors were rather cautious in allowing much direct worship or divine honors, especially in Rome, during their lifetimes because Roman thought normally did not blur the distinction between humans and gods. The emperors were revered as superior to ordinary humans, but not divine. In the Hellenistic east, these same emperors were more accepting of such worship and adulation because in the East the rulers were often viewed as the earthly manifestations of the gods. (The Hellenistic ruler Antiochus IV, e.g., proclaimed himself Antiochus Epiphanes, meaning the "manifest one." He asserted that he was the earthly manifestation of the god Zeus.)

Even in Rome, however, the understanding of the status of the emperor began to change. Although during his lifetime the emperor Augustus had tried to retain the old Roman distinction between human and divine, after his death he was officially declared divine by the Roman Senate, and a temple with its attendant priests was built in Rome. [Augustus] Tiberius, his successor, attempted to follow the lead of Augustus, resisting divine honors

Augustus

This marble bust of Caesar Augustus represents the portrait type used during the early Imperial period. The curly hair reflects more the style of Roman portraiture than a personal attribute of the emperor.

Augustus. 1st C. Marble. (Credit: Mitchell Reddish)

for himself. In contrast, the next emperor, Caligula, demanded that his statue be set up in temples of other gods throughout the empire. He claimed that he was the incarnation of the god Jupiter.

The situation with the emperors during the rest of the first century varied. Claudius, successor to his nephew Caligula, followed the practice of Augustus and Tiberius of discouraging divine accolades. Nero, his step-son, who became emperor after Claudius was poisoned by his own wife (the mother of Nero), was more willing to accept and believe the divine praises and honors bestowed on him by the public. Vespasian, on the other hand, joked about the belief in the divine status of the emperors. Poking fun at the practice of declaring the emperors divine after their death, Vespasian reportedly remarked on his deathbed, "Alas, I think I am becoming a god" (Suetonius, *Vesp.* 23.4 [author's translation]). Titus likewise downplayed divine claims.

The situation with the emperor Domitian (AD 81–96) is more difficult to assess. Certain later Roman writers, specifically Suetonius and Dio Cassius, presented Domitian as a ruler who, more than any before him, furthered the cult of emperor worship. For example, Dio Cassius described Domitian by saying, "He even insisted upon being regarded as a god and took vast pride in being called 'master' and 'god' " (*Hist. rom.* 67.4.7 [Cary, LCL]). The traditional view of Domitian's role in the propagation of the imperial cult is summed up by Kenneth Scott, who wrote,

> Domitian himself became the object of worship. Such reverence of the reigning monarch was not new, for it was already manifest under Julius Caesar and Augustus. What Domitian did was to permit and encourage to an excessive degree homage which had been shown— generally with more restraint—to his predecessors. In other words, his reign marks a departure from the moderation of Augustus, Tiberius, Claudius, Vespasian, and a return to the ways of Caligula and to some extent of Nero.[6]

Recently, scholars have begun to reassess these ancient descriptions of Domitian, pointing out that the ancient writers who described Domitian in these terms appear to have been trying to ingratiate themselves with his successors Trajan and Hadrian by portraying Domitian in extremely negative terms. Even though ancient writers claimed that Domitian demanded to be called "our lord and god," it is significant that "the latter title has not been found on any coin, inscription, or manuscript."[7]

A judicious reading of the evidence, then, suggests that at the end of the first century, emperor worship was widely established in the

Roman Empire, and particularly strong in Asia Minor. Yet this does not mean that there was any empire-wide enforcement of participation in the imperial cult. Where pressure was exerted on individuals to participate, such coercion was likely a local matter. Overzealous local officials, perhaps in an attempt to impress the emperor, may have emphasized emperor worship. There would certainly have been social pressure to participate, and in cases in which Christians were brought before the local authorities on other charges, they may have been required to offer a sacrifice to the emperor or to the Roman gods.

A letter from a provincial governor in Asia Minor early in the second century provides evidence for the precarious situation of Christians. Around AD 112, Pliny was sent by Trajan to Bithynia-Pontus in northwestern Asia Minor as governor, with the assigned task of setting in order the affairs of the province. In one of his letters to the emperor, Pliny inquired about the proper procedures to follow in the prosecution of Christians who were brought before him. He stated that his policy had been to give the accused a chance to renounce their faith and to make an offering to the emperor. Anyone who refused was to be executed. Trajan responded to Pliny that his practice seemed fair, requiring that he not seek out Christians, but when any were brought to his attention to deal with them in the prescribed manner.

[Roman Emperors of the First Century]

Roman Emperors of the First Century

Augustus (27 BC–AD 14)
Tiberius (14–37)
Caligula (37–41)
Claudius (41–54)
Nero (54–68)
Galba (June 68–January 69)
Otho (69)
Vitellius (69)
Vespasian (69–79)
Titus (79–81)
Domitian (81–96)
Nerva (96–98)
Trajan (98–117)

In the book of Revelation, the problem of emperor worship is most evident in chapter 13, in which the Roman Empire is pictured as a beast that demands to be worshiped and that exterminates those who refuse. Persecution of Christians for failure to honor the emperor may not have been widespread in John's day. Yet John was aware of some instances of persecution. He himself had been exiled to Patmos "because of the word of God and the testimony of Jesus" (1:9). Antipas had been martyred in Pergamum (2:13). John warned the church of impending imprisonment and testing for some of its members (2:10), and saw martyrs under the heavenly altar crying out for vindication (6:9-11). Furthermore, Rome is described as the great whore, "drunk with the blood of the saints and the blood of the witnesses to Jesus" (17:6). These situations were likely sporadic, local instances of persecution and martyrdom. But for John, these few instances were enough to cause him to sound the alarm to the churches of Asia Minor. John expected the slow trickle of martyrs' blood to become soon a flowing river.

In actuality, how prevalent was governmental persecution of the church during the first century? Contrary to popular belief, no empire-wide persecution against Christians occurred in the first century. The first instance of any major persecution took place during the reign of Nero (54–68). When a fire broke out in Rome, popular opinion blamed Nero for the fire because it occurred in an area of the city that Nero had targeted for demolition and re-building. In order to shift blame away from himself, Nero blamed the Christians for the fire. As punishment, he had numerous Christians arrested and executed in rather gruesome ways. The details given by Tacitus are as follows:

> First, then, the confessed members of the sect were arrested; next, on their disclosures, vast numbers were convicted, not so much on the count of arson as for hatred of the human race. And derision accompanied their end: they were covered with wild beasts' skins and torn to death by dogs; or they were fastened on crosses, and, when daylight failed were burned to serve as lamps by night. Nero had offered his Gardens for the spectacle, and gave an exhibition in his Circus, mixing with the crowd in the habit of a charioteer, or mounted on his car. Hence in spite of a guilt which had earned the most exemplary punishment, there arose a sentiment of pity, due to the impression that they were being sacrificed not for the welfare of the state but to the ferocity of a single man. (*Annals* 15.44 [Jackson, LCL])

As horrendous as this experience was for the church, it was a very limited persecution, both in its duration and its scope. It apparently did not last long, and it affected only Christians in Rome. Nero did not institute an empire-wide persecution of the Christian church. According to ancient Christian tradition, Peter and Paul both were martyred during the reign of Nero.

Popular thought made Emperor Domitian the next persecutor of the church. The fourth-century church historian Eusebius described Domitian as "the successor of Nero's campaign of hostility to God. He was the second to promote persecution against us" (*Hist. eccl.* 3.17 [Lake, LCL]). The idea that Domitian was one of the first persecutors of Christianity is widespread. Evidence for such treatment by Domitian, however, is surprisingly scant. At most, one can point to isolated situations in which a few people were persecuted. The evidence suggests, however, that any Christians who were persecuted suffered this treatment because they in some way came into conflict with Domitian or his policies, not simply because they were Christians. The portrayal of

Domitian as a cruel despot by Roman and early Christian writers is likely due more to bias and imagination than to historical fact. [Domitian]

Both the New Testament and other writings (Christian and non-Christian) mention persecution of Christians during the first and early second centuries. None of these references, however, provides evidence of any systematic, prolonged attack against the church. Even the evidence from the letters of Pliny and Trajan indicates that only when Christians were brought to the attention of the authorities were they to be punished. The early persecutions, then, were apparently isolated and few in number.

As noted above, the book of Revelation indicates that John expected a fresh onslaught of persecution to break out soon against the church that would be more severe than any the church had yet encountered. Whether a major persecution was actually imminent is beside the point. John perceived persecution to be a threat to the church and wrote his Apocalypse

Domitian
The right profile portrait both reveres and identifies the figure as Domitian, who reigned from AD 81–96. The inscription, IMP.CAES.DOMIT.AVG.GERM.P.M.TR.P.OTV, and appearance of the laureate are in keeping with the customary coin of the first century.

Domitian. Coin. AD 85, Rome (silver 5-denarius piece). British Museum. BMCRE 85. London, England. (Credit: ©The British Museum)

from that perception. Reality is a matter of perspective, and from the perspective of John and his audience, persecution was a present experience and a future threat. Although all Christians in Asia Minor likely did not view the social and historical situation as life-threatening, John certainly did. Elisabeth Schüssler Fiorenza has made the valid point that how we answer the question of whether or not the threat of persecution was real during John's time depends

on whose perspective we adopt. One could argue from the perspective of well-to-do white Americans that no harassment, denigration, discrimination, or oppression of blacks existed at the time of Martin Luther King, Jr., even though King was assassinated. The perspective and experience of blacks would be quite different! Similarly, the author of Rev. had adopted the "perspective from below" and expressed the experiences of those who were powerless, poor, and in constant fear of denunciation.[8]

Date

The most widely accepted date for the writing of Revelation is during the reign of Domitian (AD 81–96). The statement of Irenaeus (c. AD 140–c. 202) that the vision of Revelation was seen at the end of the reign of Domitian is the earliest external evidence attesting the date of Revelation (*Haer.* 5.30.3). Several writers in the following centuries also supported a Domitianic dating for the book. Other early writers mentioned the reigns of Claudius, Nero, and Trajan as the setting for Revelation. Internal evidence lends additional support to the claim of Irenaeus. In Revelation, "Babylon" is used as a symbolic name for Rome (14:8; 16:19; 17:5; 18:2, 10, 21), a practice that would have been appropriate only after AD 70. As Babylon had destroyed Jerusalem in the sixth century BC and had persecuted the people of God, so Rome had also destroyed Jerusalem (AD 70) and was now persecuting God's people. A further indication of dating appears in the use of the Nero *redivivus* myth in chapters 13 and 17. This belief in the return of Nero was popular during the last half of the first century, following the death of Nero in AD 66. Since the internal evidence coheres with Irenaeus's dating of the book during the time of Domitian, most scholars place its composition around AD 95.

Some modern scholars still argue for dates other than during the reign of Domitian for the writing of the book. The times of Nero, Galba, Vespasian, and Trajan all have their proponents. Of these possibilities, the reign of Nero has the most supporters. In many cases the argument for dating the work is based on the enigmatic passage in 17:7-11, which describes the beast with seven heads. The seven heads symbolize Roman emperors; on this much there is agreement. A consensus disintegrates, however, concerning who the seven emperors were that are depicted. Most arguments are circular. Each interpreter sets out to prove that certain emperors were intended and, by manipulating the list of emperors, ends up with the anticipated individuals. Whereas John's early audience may have understood his symbolism, it has become too ambiguous for the modern reader. J. P. M. Sweet has suggested that even John's intended readers likely could not have identified the seven emperors. He said they "were as unlikely to have known the succession of emperors as readers now are unlikely to know that of the Presidents of the United States."[9] Some commentators have argued that the number seven, in this instance as frequently elsewhere in the book, is to be understood symbolically and not literally. What becomes clear when one reads all the scholarly arguments for the identification of the seven "heads" is that any attempt to date the book on this basis is unreliable.

The same holds true for arguments for dating the writing based on the persecution setting presupposed in the work. Some scholars have argued that the persecution mentioned in the book refers to the Neronic attack on the church in Rome. Others have seen the supposed persecution by Domitian as the backdrop for John's writing. As noted above, however, not only is evidence for a Domitianic persecution of the church virtually nonexistent, but the reality of any major persecution affecting the church during John's day is questionable. When all the evidence is weighed, a date near AD 95 appears most likely.

Authorship

In contrast to most apocalypses, the author of Revelation did not claim to be some venerable figure from the past. Four times in the book he identified himself as John (1:1, 4, 9; 22:8). There is no valid reason to doubt that John was the actual name of the author. The question is, which John? As early as the second century, Christian writers identified the author as John, the son of Zebedee, one of the disciples of Jesus. Justin Martyr was the earliest witness to this tradition. Writing c. AD 155, he said,

> There was a certain man with us whose name was John, one of the apostles of Christ, who prophesied by a revelation that was made to him, that those who believe in our Christ would dwell a thousand years in Jerusalem; and that thereafter the general, and in short, the eternal resurrection and judgment of all men would likewise take place. (*Dial.* 81.4)

Various writers from the second century and later repeated this identification.

According to Eusebius, Dionysius of Alexandria challenged this view of authorship during the third century, arguing on the basis of language and stylistic differences that the writer of Revelation could not have been the same person as the one who wrote the Gospel of John and the Letters of John (whom he assumed was John the disciple). After suggesting and then rejecting the idea that the author might have been John Mark, the one-time traveling companion of Paul (see Acts 13:5, 13; 15:37-38), Dionysius concluded that the author of the Apocalypse was another, now unknown, John (*Hist. eccl.* 7.25 [Oulton, LCL]).

In the fourth century, Eusebius also disagreed with the attribution of authorship to the disciple John. Eusebius (*Hist. eccl.* 3.39.2-4 [Lake, LCL]) claimed that the author was a different John, called John the elder, basing his identification on a statement attributed to the early second-century church leader Papias of Hierapolis. In this statement, Papias appears to have differentiated between the Apostle John and "John the elder." Many modern scholars have argued, however, that Eusebius misunderstood the statement of Papias and that Papias was not distinguishing two different people named John. Rather, he was describing the disciple John as an elder as well. Even if we were to accept Eusebius's identification of the author as John the elder, we would be no better off, for absolutely nothing is known about this "elder" John. (Any connection with "the elder" mentioned in 2 John 1 and 3 John 1 is highly speculative.) [Prochorus]

As this brief survey has indicated, the only viable, known candidate as author is the disciple John. This identification is almost certainly ruled out, however, by clues from the writing itself. In 21:14, the author referred to the twelve apostles whose names were written on the foundations of the new Jerusalem. The writer was looking back on a venerated group of heroes of the faith. This description would have been an odd way for the disciple John (if he were the author) to refer to himself. Furthermore, the author never claimed apostolic authority for his writing. He described his writing as a prophecy and himself simply as "I, John, your brother who share with you in Jesus the persecution and the kingdom and the patient endurance" (1:9).

The author, then, is best understood as an unknown John living in Asia Minor in the closing years of the first century.[10] The authority with which he wrote indicates that he was obviously well known to the Christians in Asia Minor and knew the churches and their backgrounds intimately. Since he referred to his message as a prophecy (1:3), he viewed himself as a Christian prophet and had possibly functioned in this role among the Christians in Asia

---

Prochorus

According to a legendary 5th-century writing known as the *Acts of John by Prochorus*, John was accompanied to Asia Minor by Prochorus, one of the seven people chosen by the Jerusalem church to assist in the daily distribution of food (Acts 6:5). In addition to describing other events in the life and work of John, this work narrates John's exile to Patmos. Prochorus accompanied him there and served as his scribe, recording the visions dictated to him by John that became the book of Revelation. Although the story of Prochorus is likely nonhistorical, the traditions are strongly followed in some churches, particularly on the island of Patmos. The memory of Prochorus is celebrated on June 28 in Orthodox churches. For further information about the Prochorus legends, see R. Alan Culpepper, *John, the Son of Zebedee: The Life of a Legend* (Columbia SC: University of South Carolina Press, 1994), 206-23.

John Dictating His Vision

This mosaic is located above the door of the monastery enclosing the cave that is the traditional site where John received his revelation on Patmos. The style is reflective of the Byzantine period with its flattened forms, striated drapery, and black outlines. The scene depicts John dictating his vision to his legendary assistant, Prochorus.

John on Patmos. Mosaic. Monastery of the Apocalypse. Patmos. (Credit: Mitchell Reddish)

Minor, perhaps as an itinerant prophet. His extensive use of the Hebrew Bible and the many Semitisms (Hebrew or Aramaic idioms expressed awkwardly in Greek) in the book suggest that he was a Jewish Christian, likely originally from Palestine. As an outspoken leader in the churches, John apparently ran into trouble with the government authorities and as a result was banished or exiled to the island of Patmos where he received a revelation from God. The duration of his stay on Patmos is unknown. Early Christian writers assigned various lengths of time to his exile, ranging from eighteen months to fifteen years. Christian tradition also claims that John was released from exile after the death of Domitian and returned to Ephesus (see, e.g., Eusebius, *Hist. eccl.* 3.20.8-9 [Lake, LCL]). The reliability of these traditions is questionable, however.[11] [John Dictating His Vision]

Literary Structure

To many readers, one of the most perplexing problems in understanding the book of Revelation is trying to understand its organization and arrangement. The novelist John Hersey, for example, described his impression of the text:

> There remains a sense that the work, after it is introduced by the letter to the churches, has been broken into halves by two strong voices, and that parts within the two sections have been sewn together, sometimes with crude stitching.[12]

New Testament scholars, also, have been perplexed by the structure of John's work. Some scholars have found the arrangement of materials so confusing that they have used this as a major point in their argument that the book, as it presently exists, is a compilation from different sources or the product of multiple redactions or rewrites. R. H. Charles, for instance, claimed that most of the material in 1:1–20:3 was from John and that 20:4–22:21, along with some interpolated sections in the first part, came from a later editor.[13] J. Massyngberde Ford, on the other hand, saw a three-stage development behind the Apocalypse: Chapters 4–11 (in oral form) came from the circle of John the Baptist; 12–22 originated from the disciples of John the Baptist; and 1–3 and 22:16a, 20b, 21 were added later by a Jewish-Christian disciple of John the Baptist who had come to a more accurate knowledge of Jesus.[14] (Neither of these proposals has won many adherents among scholars.) Most recently, David Aune has proposed that Revelation reached its present form in two major stages. The "First Edition," as he called it, consists of approximately 1:7-12a and 4:1–22:5. The "Second Edition" adds 1:1-6, 1:12b-3:22, 22:6-21, and "several expansions or interpolations in the earlier sections of the text."[15]

All commentators recognize the importance of the number seven as a structuring device in the book—seven messages, seven seals, seven trumpets, seven bowls. How are these series of sevens related? The seven messages in 2:1–3:22 have sometimes been viewed as disconnected from the remainder of the work. A close examination, however, reveals otherwise. The clearest example of such connections occurs in the introductions to each of the seven messages, which borrow phrases from the description of the exalted Christ in chapter 1. Furthermore, the themes of persecution, faithfulness, endurance, rewards for the righteous, and the new Jerusalem, which are prominent in the seven messages, are also the major topics in the remainder of the book.

Some interpreters see the four series of sevens as consecutive series; that is, John presents in chronological order his vision of coming events. A progression is certainly intended in the events described, as evidenced by the opening of the seventh seal, which introduces the seven trumpets. Yet the progression is not strictly linear. Rather, later events sometimes retell earlier events. For example, the plagues and calamities of the seven trumpets describe in a new way the punishments and judgments of the end times depicted by the seven seals. This view of the arrangement of the material in Revelation is called recapitulation and is the approach to understanding the work that is followed in this commentary. Instead of a straight linear progression, the structure of Revelation presents a movement that is spiral. Earlier events are presented in different forms and use different images. Various analogies have been used to explain this arrangement of the material in Revelation. In one sense, it is like looking through a kaleidoscope in which one sees the colors and shapes arranged in a certain pattern. As one turns the kaleidoscope, the pieces rearrange themselves in a different pattern, presenting the viewer with a different perspective on the same objects. Reading Revelation is also like listening to a musical composition in which certain themes of the piece are repeated, but with variations and new interpretations, each variation moving the piece forward. [The Power of Revelation]

John structured the book of Revelation in a similar manner. The writing presents visions of judgment and destruction, as well as scenes of hope and reward, in a variety of ways. Each new scene provides the reader/hearer a different and fuller picture of John's message, while at the same time moving forward in the telling of John's story. In Revelation, the movement of the work is from John's historical situation to the arrival of the new Jerusalem, the fulfillment of God's ultimate plan for creation. Within that overall forward movement, however, are numerous instances of overlapping and parallel scenes.

A part of the reason for John's use of recapitulation in structuring the book of Revelation was likely due to the auditory nature of this work. Contrary to the manner in which most people today encounter the Apocalypse, the original recipients of John's message heard the text read aloud. They did not have a copy to read themselves. Thus by repeating his message in new images, John reinforced what his audience heard and remembered. Repetition functioned as an aid to understanding as well as to memory.

The Power of Revelation

"Exegetes and theologians still have to discover what artists have long understood: the strength of the language and composition of Rev. lies not in its theological argumentation or historical information but in its evocative power inviting imaginative participation. The language and narrative flow of Rev. elicit emotions, reactions, and convictions that cannot and should not be fully conceptualized and phrased in propositional-logical language."

Elisabeth Schüssler Fiorenza, *The Book of Revelation: Justice and Judgment* (Philadelphia: Fortress, 1985), 22.

Finally, Revelation operates impressionistically rather than logically. John attempted to convey his message through imagination, symbols, and metaphors. The reader should remember that this is revelatory literature, presented as visions. It is not tightly organized, rational arguments. For the modern reader to analyze and dissect the work, instead of experiencing it, is to do an injustice to the work. We should avoid the temptation to impose too rigid a structure or order on John's writing. The accompanying outline suggests one way in which the reader may understand the arrangement of the Apocalypse. [Outline of Revelation]

Theological Themes and Emphases

Preachers and teachers who avoid the book of Revelation are missing a rich resource of theological treasures. As powerful and influential as the images and motifs of Revelation have been for artists, writers, and musicians, these do not explain the persistent popularity of this writing throughout the centuries. Rather, the Apocalypse has maintained its appeal because its powerful words and images speak to some of the deepest fears, joys, and yearnings of the human spirit. The book of Revelation is a book of hope, warning, encouragement, critique, and motivation. The following paragraphs will briefly highlight some of the more important theological issues that Revelation addresses. The commentary will explore these themes more fully. [Transcendent World]

1. *The sovereignty of God.* Of all the themes in Revelation, none is more central to John's theology than his conviction that God is the ultimate power in the universe. God's sovereignty is comprehensive, for God is "Alpha and Omega," the creator of the world and the one who will bring it to completion. Modern theologians and philosophers have strongly attacked the idea of the sovereignty of God, claiming that this belief has fostered patriarchal domination, violence, and abuse of power. A careful reading of the Apocalypse, however, reveals that, for John, God's control over the universe is exemplified in the sacrificial, suffering work of the Lamb, not in coercive domination.

Transcendent World

AΩ "The language of the apocalypses is not descriptive, referential newspaper language, but the expressive language of poetry, which uses symbols and imagery to articulate a sense or feeling about the world. Their abiding value does not lie in the pseudo-information they provide about cosmology or future history, but in their affirmation of a transcendent world. Even if the physical universe were to endure forever, there is no doubt that the social and cultural worlds we inhabit are constantly crumbling. Christianity inherited from the Jewish apocalypses a way of affirming transcendent values, those things we should affirm even when the world around us collapses. Beyond the thresholds of life and of this world we can only see as in a glass darkly. The apocalyptic revelations are symbolic attempts to penetrate the darkness, which provide ways of imagining the unknown, not factual knowledge."

John J. Collins, *The Apocalyptic Imagination: An Introduction to the Jewish Matrix of Christianity* (New York: Crossroad, 1984), 214.

OUTLINE OF REVELATION

The Book of Revelation

I. Prologue—1:1-8

II. The Vision of the Son of Man—1:9–3:22
  A. The Commissioning of John—1:9-20
  B. The Messages to the Seven Churches—2:1–3:22
    1. Ephesus—2:1-7
    2. Smyrna—2:8-11
    3. Pergamum—2:12-17
    4. Thyatira—2:18-29
    5. Sardis—3:1-6
    6. Philadelphia—3:7-13
    7. Laodicea—3:14-22

III. Visions of the Future—4:1–22:5
  A. The Heavenly Throne Room—4:1–5:14
    1. The Throne of God—4:1-11
    2. The Lamb and the Scroll—5:1-14
  B. The Seven Seals—6:1–8:5
    1. The First Four Seals—6:1-8
    2. The Fifth Seal—6:9-11
    3. The Sixth Seal—6:12-17
    4. Interlude—7:1-17
      a. The Sealing of the 144,000—7:1-8
      b. The Multitude from Every Nation—7:9-17
    5. The Seventh Seal—8:1-5
  C. The Seven Trumpets—8:6–11:19
    1. The First Four Trumpets—8:6-13
    2. The Fifth Trumpet—9:1-12
    3. The Sixth Trumpet—9:13-21
    4. Interlude—10:1–11:14
      a. The Mighty Angel and the
        Little Scroll—10:1-11
      b. The Temple and the Two Witnesses—11:1-14
    5. The Seventh Trumpet—11:15-19

  D. The Great Conflict—12:1–14:20
    1. The Vision of the Great Dragon—12:1-18
    2. The Two Beasts—13:1-18
    3. Interlude—14:1-20
      a. The 144,000 with the Lamb—14:1-5
      b. The Messages of the Three Angels—14:6-13
      c. The Harvests of the Earth—14:14-20
  E. The Seven Bowl Plagues—15:1–16:21
    1. Introduction of the Seven Angels—15:1
    2. The Martyrs on the Heavenly Shore—15:2-4
    3. The Seven Angels with Bowls—15:5-8
    4. The Pouring of the Seven Bowls—16:1-21
  F. The Fall of Babylon—17:1–19:10
    1. The Great Whore—17:1-18
    2. Laments on Earth—18:1-24
    3. Celebration in Heaven—19:1-10
  G. The Final Victory—19:11–20:15
    1. The Triumphant Christ—19:11-21
      a. The Rider on the White Horse—19:11-16
      b. The Defeat of God's Enemies—19:17-21
    2. The Millennial Reign and the Defeat
      of Satan—20:1-10
      a. The Imprisonment of Satan—20:1-3
      b. The Millennial Reign—20:4-6
      c. The Final Conflict—20:7-10
    3. The Last Judgment—20:11-15
  H. The New Jerusalem—21:1–22:5
    1. New Heaven and New Earth—21:1-8
    2. The Holy City—21:9-27
    3. The River of Life—22:1-5

IV. Epilogue—22:6-21

2. *Radical monotheism.* A corollary to John's belief that all of history and the universe is under the control of God is his staunch commitment to the idea that no power on earth or heaven is worthy of ultimate allegiance but God alone. This is not simply an abstract theological concept for John, but a belief that has strong pastoral relevance. It is the basis for John's warnings about participation in emperor worship and entanglement in the quasireligious practices of his day. This belief serves as a reminder to all readers of the

Apocalypse that all institutions, people, systems, and power structures are relativized by the reality of the one true God. Governments, economic systems, occupations, and even religious organizations stand under the judgment of God. Christians might render partial allegiance to these entities, but such allegiance must always be secondary and subservient to one's ultimate allegiance to God.

3. *Exalted Christology.* The book of Revelation presents an exalted view of Christ that few New Testament writings match. John applied several of God's titles to Christ (Alpha and Omega, the beginning and the end, Lord). Christ shares the heavenly throne with God and, like God, is the object of heavenly and earthly worship. God and the Lamb (Christ) receive almost identical words of praise in chapters 4, 5, and 7. Furthermore, Revelation states that just as salvation belongs to both God and to the Lamb (7:10), so does divine judgment (6:16-17). John applied imagery to Christ's defeat of God's enemies that the Hebrew Bible had reserved for God alone (19:11-21). Clearly, in Revelation, the work and nature of God and Christ are closely intertwined. What Christ does, God does. But in spite of this close identification of God and Christ, John never called Jesus "God." John's thoroughgoing monotheism does not allow the idea of two separate deities for the Christian church. Jesus carries out the will and desires of God; he reveals in himself the true nature of God; he acts on behalf of God. John might well have affirmed that Christ partakes of the very nature or being of God. Yet he stopped short of identifying Christ with God. We may wish that John had written with more clarity or specificity about the relationship between Christ and God. But there is no Nicene Creed in Revelation. That will come a few centuries later. [Imagery in Revelation]

4. *Salvation.* For many people, the word "apocalyptic" has a harsh ring to it, connoting judgment, destruction, and punishment. While such events do comprise a part of most apocalyptic writings, they are only a part of the message of apocalypses and definitely are not the primary focus of Revelation. John presents God, through Christ, as actively bringing salvation to the world. The description of Jesus in the opening chapter of Revelation is the one "who loves us and freed us from our sins by his blood" (1:5). The primary image of Christ in Revelation is the slain Lamb, a reminder of the sacrificial, atoning work of Christ. The hymns in chapters 7, 11, and 19 praise God specifically for God's saving activity. The God of

Imagery in Revelation

"The images [in Revelation] should be taken seriously as images. One should not rush to a commentary to decode the images and focus on their probable historical referents alone. Rather, one should take the time to feel the impact of the image and to adopt a receptive attitude in which feelings play as great a role as thinking."

Adela Yarbro Collins, " 'What the Spirit Says to the Churches': Preaching the Apocalypse," *Quarterly Review* 4/3 (Fall 1984): 79.

the Apocalypse cares for the world and its inhabitants and yearns to provide health, wholeness, peace, and security—in short, salvation—for all of creation. The visions of the new heaven and new earth (ch. 21) and the new Jerusalem (ch. 22) are ample evidence of this. Whereas these visions describe the eschatological dimension of salvation, John views God's salvific work as operative in the present as well. The Son of Man figure in chapter 1 already stands among the lampstands (the churches), signifying the presence of Christ with God's people in their present situation.

5. *Judgment and warning.* From the messages to the seven churches in chapters 2 and 3 to the final judgment scene in chapter 20, John warns his readers that all the universe comes under the judgment of God. Although the God of Revelation is a God who loves us, shepherds us, comforts us, and provides for us, God also stands in judgment over our failures and sins. The Apocalypse serves as a powerful warning that those who would be the people of God must be obedient to God. John's imagery of the lake of fire, reserved for eternal torment for the opponents of God, is as much figurative, nonliteral language as his description of Christ as a Lamb and the new Jerusalem as streets of gold and gates of pearls. The truth of the imagery, however, is that God and evil cannot coexist in God's ultimate design for the world.

6. *Nonviolent lifestyle.* The book of Revelation can function as a call to a nonviolent lifestyle. That may seem like a strange statement, given the extensive use of militaristic and even violent imagery in the book itself. Yet one must distinguish between texts that use language and imagery to encourage or endorse violence and those that use traditional imagery to subvert violence. The Apocalypse belongs in the latter category. The book of Revelation exhibits a creative transformation of traditional symbols and language, what Austin Farrer has called a "rebirth of images."[16] In the Apocalypse, Jesus is indeed the mighty conqueror, the warrior on the white horse (19:11-21). He conquers not by violence, however, but by his own death, for John sees Christ's robe dipped in blood. The blood is likely Christ's own blood, a visual reminder that he conquered by his own death. His weapon was not a sword, but a cross. John's interplay of lion-lamb imagery in chapter 5 is also a reminder that Christ's conquering is martyrological. Through this imagery, John declares that the only "conquering" that is consistent with the values of God is conquering that occurs through self-sacrifice and love, not through violence.

7. *Hope.* One of the ways that the book of Revelation has spoken most forcefully to its readers through the years has been to offer a message of hope. John's confident assertions that God is in control, that evil will be defeated, that death will not have the last word, and that God will always be present with God's people have provided the necessary assurances to allow people to face the most difficult and demanding situations in life. John did not take a "Pollyanna" approach to life. He knew that all too often suffering and pain wreak havoc with human lives. He had himself suffered persecution. In spite of those experiences, John was confident that ultimately "death will be no more; mourning and crying and pain will be no more, for the first things have passed away" (21:4). John reassures us that the way things are is not the way that things always will be.

The reader will notice that missing from this list of important ideas in the book of Revelation is any discussion about specific end-time events. That omission is intentional. The book of Revelation addressed the concerns of its original readers. John's purpose was to help them live as faithful Christians in the present world, not to provide them with details about the future. That is still the way the Apocalypse functions today. Any use of the book of Revelation to fill out charts and timetables of the future, to predict the date or time of the end of the world, or to prove the fulfillment of biblical "prophecies" in contemporary happenings in the world (Russia, the Gulf War, the European Community, etc.) is a gross misuse and distortion of John's message. Its vision of God's ultimate goal for history uses not descriptive, but evocative language. It is intended to evoke hope and comfort, not because it can predict the events of the future, but because it is certain of the one who is in charge of that future.

Interpreting Revelation

As early as the end of the second century, people began writing commentaries on the book of Revelation. Melito, bishop of Sardis (one of the cities addressed in Revelation), wrote a work on the Apocalypse c. AD 175. Unfortunately, all that has survived is a brief reference to it in Eusebius.[17] A century later, Victorinus of Pettau (d. c. 304) produced a commentary on Revelation, portions of which are still extant today. Since those early years, there has been no shortage of works attempting to explain the meaning of John's visionary writing. As one might suppose, a book as mysterious as

Revelation has spawned numerous, sometimes contradictory, even absurd, interpretations.[18] [Recommended Resources on Revelation]

One of the most widely popularized approaches today to interpreting Revelation understands the messages to the seven churches

---

🔍 **Recommended Resources on Revelation**

Aune, David E. *Revelation 1–5*. Word Biblical Commentary. Dallas: Word Books, 1997.

_____. *Revelation 6–16*. Word Biblical Commentary. Dallas: Word Books, 1998.

_____. *Revelation 17–22*. Word Biblical Commentary. Nashville: Thomas Nelson, 1998.

Bauckham, Richard. *The Theology of the Book of Revelation*. New Testament Theology. Cambridge: Cambridge University Press, 1993.

Beale, G. K. *The Book of Revelation: A Commentary on the Greek Text.* New International Greek Testament Commentary. Grand Rapids: Eerdmans, 1998.

Beasley-Murray, George R. *The Book of Revelation*. New Century Bible. Greenwood SC: Attic, 1974.

Beckwith, Isbon T. *The Apocalypse of John*. Macmillan, 1919. Reprint. Grand Rapids: Baker, 1979.

Blevins, James L. *Revelation*. Knox Preaching Guides. Atlanta: John Knox, 1984.

_____. *Revelation as Drama*. Nashville: Broadman, 1984.

Boesak, Allan A. *Comfort and Protest: Reflections on the Apocalypse of John of Patmos*. Philadelphia: Westminster, 1987.

Boring, M. Eugene. *Revelation*. Interpretation: A Bible Commentary for Teaching and Preaching. Louisville: John Knox, 1989.

Caird, G. B. *A Commentary on the Revelation of St. John the Divine.* Harper's New Testament Commentaries. New York: Harper & Row, 1966.

Charles, R. H. *A Critical and Exegetical Commentary on the Revelation of St. John*. 2 vols. The International Critical Commentary. Edinburgh: T. & T. Clark, 1920.

Collins, Adela Yarbro. *The Apocalypse*. New Testament Message. Wilmington DE: Michael Glazier, 1979.

_____. *Crisis & Catharsis: The Power of the Apocalypse*. Philadelphia: Westminster, 1984.

Fiorenza, Elisabeth Schüssler. *The Book of Revelation: Justice and Judgment*. Philadelphia: Fortress, 1985.

_____. *Revelation: Vision of a Just World*. Proclamation Commentaries. Minneapolis: Fortress, 1991.

Ford, J. Massyngberde. *Revelation*. Anchor Bible. Garden City NY: Doubleday & Co., 1975.

González, Catherine Gunsalus and Justo L. González. *Revelation*. Westminster Bible Companion. Louisville: Westminster/John Knox, 1997.

Harrington, Wilfrid J. *Revelation*. Sacra Pagina. Collegeville MN: Liturgical, 1993.

Jeske, Richard. *Revelation for Today: Images of Hope*. Philadelphia: Fortress, 1983.

Ladd, George Eldon. *A Commentary on the Revelation of John*. Grand Rapids: Eerdmans, 1972.

Mounce, Robert H. *The Book of Revelation*. The New International Commentary on the New Testament. Rev. ed. Grand Rapids: Eerdmans, 1998.

Murphy, Frederick J. *Fallen Is Babylon: The Revelation to John*. The New Testament in Context. Harrisburg PA: Trinity, 1998.

Richard, Pablo. *Apocalypse: A People's Commentary on the Book of Revelation*. Maryknoll NY: Orbis Books, 1995.

Rogers, Cornish R. and Joseph R. Jeter Jr. *Preaching Through the Apocalypse: Sermons from Revelation*. St. Louis: Chalice, 1992.

Roloff, Jürgen. *The Revelation of John: A Continental Commentary*. Continental Commentaries. Translated by John E. Alsup. Minneapolis: Fortress, 1993.

Sweet, J. P. M. *Revelation*. Westminster Pelican Commentaries. Philadelphia: Westminster, 1979.

Swete, Henry Barclay. *Commentary on Revelation*. Grand Rapids: Kregel, 1977; reprint of the 3rd ed. published by Macmillan, London, 1911, under the title, *The Apocalypse of St. John*.

Talbert, Charles H. *The Apocalypse: A Reading of the Revelation of John*. Louisville: Westminster/John Knox, 1994.

Thompson, Leonard L. *The Book of Revelation: Apocalypse and Empire*. New York: Oxford University Press, 1990.

Wainwright, Arthur W. *Mysterious Apocalypse: Interpreting the Book of Revelation*. Nashville: Abingdon, 1993.

Issues of two journals designed at least partially for ministers were devoted to the book of Revelation:

Word & World: Theology for Christian Ministry 15/2 (Spring 1995).

Interpretation: A Journal of Bible and Theology 40/3 (July 1986).

(chs. 2–3) not as actual messages to churches in the first century but as descriptions of and warnings to the church in general during seven specific periods of its history. The first church (Ephesus) represents the apostolic period. The remaining churches represent the succeeding stages of church history, with the last church (Laodicea) representing the present situation of the church. According to this view, the remainder of the Apocalypse describes the events that are to occur during the very last years of world history. The proponents of this approach to Revelation always locate their present time as immediately prior to the final events supposedly depicted in Revelation. According to them, the world is currently at the edge of the last days. By creative manipulation of texts from Revelation and elsewhere in the Bible (especially Daniel and Ezekiel), these interpreters are able to "prove" how events taking place today were predicted in the Bible. Wars, earthquakes, political troubles, and economic disasters are interpreted as events foretold in the Bible. The fulfillment of these "prophecies" is evidence that we are the "final generation" before Armageddon takes place and the world is brought to an end.

This understanding of the book of Revelation has been popularized by the Scofield Reference Bible, Hal Lindsey, John Walvoord, and a host of radio and television evangelists. Such an approach has a strong appeal to many people because it appears to be biblically based; it provides a framework for understanding the events and condition of the world today; and it claims to give information about the future. Unfortunately, it is merely an attempt at "biblical" fortune-telling. This approach to Revelation is based on a misuse of biblical texts and a failure to understand the nature and function of apocalyptic writings.

While differences of opinion will always exist among interpreters of Revelation, a proper understanding of the Apocalypse must take into consideration the sociohistorical setting of the work and its literary genre. Written to Christian communities in Asia Minor at the end of the first century, Revelation was intended to address the needs and concerns of those believers. To interpret Revelation as primarily concerned with end-time events is to divorce it from its first-century context. The work then becomes incomprehensible and meaningless to the very people to whom it was originally addressed. Furthermore, to interpret the work as detailed prophecies waiting to be fulfilled some two thousand years later is to misunderstand the nature of apocalyptic literature. Apocalyptic literature is not predictive literature in the sense that it offers detailed scenarios for the distant future. Apocalyptic writings deal with their contemporary situations by means of the general affirmation that the future belongs to God.

To read and appreciate the book of Revelation, one must be aware of how the language and symbols of Revelation function. The book of Revelation uses visions, symbols, and ancient myths to convey its message. The language of the book is primarily pictorial, symbolic language. It is not the language of science or logic. Rather, it is evocative, powerful, emotive language, at times more akin to poetry than to prose. Like the language of poetry, the language of Revelation sometimes is mysterious and slippery, teasing its reader to make connections and see possibilities that one has never made or seen before. The language of Revelation "works" not by imparting information, but by helping the reader to experience what John experienced. The reader is taken up with John, sees the visions, hears the commands, smells the incense. By the end of the work, John's revelation has become our revelation. With the "Hallelujah Chorus" still ringing in our ears, we feel as if we have been in the very throne room of God.

To understand the Apocalypse, one must read it imaginatively—with eyes, ears, and mind wide open. Revelation is a fantasia of sights, sounds, smells, and action. In addition, the work has a strong dramatic quality to it. It is no wonder that artists of all types have been inspired by this work. The reader would do well to heed the advice of one commentator who wrote that anyone "who has not, or has and refuses to use, a fertile imagination, will do well to leave this book alone."19

The book of Revelation does not have one meaning, or even a list of meanings that when comprehended exhausts the value of this work. Revelation is open-ended. It continues to speak in fresh ways to different readers. That is the beauty and power of its symbols and images. It addresses us anew as the word of God, reminding us that the beasts of Revelation are continually rising up in our lives and in our society. The beasts of pride, idolatry, greed, hatred, and abuse of power may take on new forms and new identities, but they are still manifestations of evil. Revelation challenges us to name those beasts and to resist them. Even more importantly, the voices of hope and assurance that reverberate throughout the Apocalypse still echo in our lives to remind us that in spite of what difficulties we might face, "the Lord our God the Almighty reigns." With the heavenly host, we can then sing, "Amen! Hallelujah!"

NOTES

[1] *Epist.* 53.8. Cited by Bernard McGinn, "Revelation," *A Literary Companion to the Bible*, ed. Robert Alter and Frank Kermode (Cambridge MA: Belknap, 1987), 523.

[2] D. H. Lawrence, *Apocalypse*, in *Apocalypse and the Writings on Revelation*, The Cambridge Edition of D. H. Lawrence, ed. Mara Kalnins (Cambridge: Cambridge University Press, 1980), 61.

[3] See John Wick Bowman, *The First Christian Drama* (Philadelphia: Westminster, 1955); and James L. Blevins, *Revelation as Drama* (Nashville: Broadman, 1984).

[4] Leonard L. Thompson, *The Book of Revelation: Apocalypse and Empire* (New York: Oxford University Press, 1990), 172.

[5] Ibid., 128.

[6] Kenneth Scott, *The Imperial Cult Under the Flavians* (New York: Arno, 1975), 89.

[7] Brian W. Jones, "Domitian," *The Anchor Bible Dictionary*, ed. David Noel Freedman, 6 vols. (New York: Doubleday & Co., 1992), 2:221.

[8] Elisabeth Schüssler Fiorenza, *The Book of Revelation: Justice and Judgment* (Philadelphia: Fortress, 1985), 9.

[9] J. P. M. Sweet, *Revelation*, Westminster Pelican Commentaries (Philadelphia: Westminster, 1979), 257.

[10] A rather strange, subsidiary argument against the disciple John being the author is given by Jürgen Roloff. He has written, "One must consider, moreover, that John of Zebedee would have had to be ninety years old at the time Revelation was written. With its dazzling colors and sharp contrasts, this powerful book does not bear traces of a work of old age" (*The Revelation of John: A Continental Commentary*, Continental Commentaries, trans. John E. Alsup [Minneapolis: Fortress, 1993], 11).

[11] That John was released after the death of Domitian is not in itself improbable. David Aune (*Revelation 1–5*, Word Biblical Commentary [Dallas: Word Books, 1997], 77) has pointed out that "those banished by a particular emperor could be recalled or given amnesty upon that emperor's death."

[12] John Hersey, "The Revelation of Saint John the Divine," *Incarnation: Contemporary Writers on the New Testament*, ed. Alfred Corn (New York: Viking, 1990), 349.

[13] R. H. Charles, *The Revelation of St. John*, The International Critical Commentary, 2 vols. (Edinburgh: T. & T. Clark, 1920), 1:l-lv.

[14] J. Massyngberde Ford, *Revelation*, The Anchor Bible (Garden City NY: Doubleday & Co., 1975), 3-4, 50-57.

[15] Aune, *Revelation 1–5*, cxx-cxxxiv.

[16] Austin M. Farrer, *A Rebirth of Images* (Boston: Beacon, 1949).

[17] *Hist. eccl.* 4.26.2.

[18] For good summaries of the four major "schools" of interpretation of Revelation, see M. Eugene Boring, *Revelation,* Interpretation: A Bible Commentary for Teaching and Preaching (Louisville: John Knox, 1989), 47-51; and Wilfrid J. Harrington, *Revelation*, Sacra Pagina (Collegeville MN: Liturgical, 1993), 14-17. A book by Arthur W. Wainwright (*Mysterious Apocalypse: Interpreting the Book of Revelation* [Nashville: Abingdon, 1993]) provides a very readable account of the history of interpretation and uses of the book of Revelation.

[19] Ray Summers, *Worthy Is the Lamb* (Nashville: Broadman, 1951), 51.

PROLOGUE AND THE COMMISSIONING OF JOHN

1:1-20

COMMENTARY

Prologue, 1:1-8

The author of the last book of the Bible begins by declaring that his writing is a revelation, an *apokalypsis*, the Greek word from which the term "apocalypse" is derived. At the very outset, John alerts the reader that this is a different type of writing. This work is not a letter, although it does exhibit some characteristics of ancient letters. It is not a gospel; the writer shows no interest in the life and teachings of the earthly Jesus. It is not historical writing, although John was well informed about the events and situations of the Christian churches in Asia Minor. John informs us (warns us, maybe?) from the beginning that this work is an apocalypse; that is, it contains information that God revealed to him.

As we shall see, John claims to have seen visions and heard voices. Take note, then, of John's opening words—"the revelation." Readers could avoid much misunderstanding about the nature and purpose of John's writing if they took seriously those opening words. This book is apocalyptic literature, not history, not a letter, not a gospel. It should not be read like those genres of literature. Rather, it is to be read with imagination, with sensitivity, and with eyes and ears wide open to experience the fascinating creativity of the writer. When reading Revelation, to "literalize" is to trivialize. "Let anyone who has an ear listen" to what John is saying. Furthermore, let anyone who has an imagination experience what John is disclosing. This is a revelation, John says, so don't miss it!

Martin Marty, the "dean" of American religious life and professor of church history at the University of Chicago, wrote about a letter a pastor received from a junior high student seeking help for a sermon about the book of Revelation. The pastor wondered how Marty might respond to the student's inquiry. A portion of Marty's answer follows:

Notice that the Book of Revelation is at the end of the Bible. It barely made it into the scriptures. It's one of the two or three biblical books that calls itself a vision, a dream, yet it's a book that many people seem to take more literally than they do the non-dream books. Try interpreting your dreams and you'll see why people expound weird ideas based on this book.[1]

The message that John delivered is not his own; it is a "revelation of Jesus Christ" (contrary to the title of the work given in some Bibles—"The Revelation of St. John the Divine"). [Outline of 1:1-8] Whereas grammatically this construction could be understood to mean either a revelation *from* Jesus or a revelation *about* Jesus, the former understanding is primary here. Jesus is the source of the information that John

> **Outline of 1:1-8**
> 1. Introduction—1:1-3
>   a. Title—1:1-2
>   b. Benediction—1:3
> 2. Epistolary Salutation—1:4-5a
>   a. Sender—1:4a
>   b. Recipients—1:4b
>   c. Greetings—1:4c-5a
> 3. Doxology—1:5b-6
> 4. Prophetic Pronouncement—1:7
> 5. Divine Declaration—1:8

passes on to his audience. Like the prophets of the Hebrew Bible, John claimed divine inspiration for his message. Because of the centrality of the Christ event, however, John declares that what he received is not simply "the word of the Lord," but also a word from Jesus Christ. John describes a chain of communication: the revelation originated with God, was given to Jesus, then mediated by an angel to John. The use of angels as mediators of divine revelation is a common literary device in Jewish and early Christian apocalyptic literature.

As with most apocalyptic writers, John wrote with a sense of urgency. He believed that the events he described "must soon take place" (v. 2) because "the time is near" (v. 3). [Nearness of the End] From John's perspective, evil was becoming so dominant in the world that surely God would intervene soon. In his view, the justice of God demanded that wickedness not be allowed to triumph much longer. By claiming that "the time is near" when God would be victorious over evil, John offered his readers hope and encouragement. They must persevere only a short while longer.

> **Nearness of the End**
> "There is . . . something for the modern reader to receive from the early church's expectation of the near end of history: Without sharing their chronology, we can share their sense of urgency, the sense that our generation is the only generation we have in which to fulfill our calling."
>
> M. Eugene Boring, *Revelation*, Interpretation: A Bible Commentary for Teaching and Preaching (Louisville: John Knox, 1989), 73.

What were these events that "must soon take place"? As his work makes clear, John expected the destruction of Rome to be one of the components of the final events of history. The Roman emperors, with their claims to divine status, were a part of the forces of evil that would soon be defeated. These and other events that "must soon take place" comprised the end of the world, the end of this age. Like other apocalyptic writers, John viewed history in two phases, this age and the age to come. God would bring this age, or this world, seemingly dominated by the power of evil, to a cataclysmic end. Following its dissolution, the old age would be superseded by a new age, a new world.

Ultimately Rome did fall (although not in the manner in which John stated), and its downfall was not one of the final events of history. What do we say, then, about John's belief that "the time is near"? Obviously the world did not come to an end. John, like other apocalyptic thinkers, was wrong in tying the events of his day so closely to the end of the world. His mistaken expectation of the imminent end of the world does not invalidate his message for the church, however. The importance of John's message lies not in chronology, but in theology. The enduring message of Revelation is John's confident assurance that God is ultimately in control of the universe. In the end God will reign triumphant over the forces of evil.

After the opening two verses, which serve as a title to the book, v. 3 pronounces a blessing upon the reader and the hearers of John's message, which he calls a prophecy. [Prophets and Prophecy] John intended his work to be read aloud, most likely as Christians were gathered together for worship. The blessing is effective, however, not for those who only hear, but for those who hear and obey ("keep") the message. The claim that "the time is near" adds an urgency to the need to respond positively to John's message.

Adapting the format of a typical Greek letter of his day, John identifies himself and the recipients of his writing in v. 4 and then includes a greeting. [Ancient Letters] The "seven churches that are in Asia" are identified specifically in v. 11 and later addressed in chapters 2 and 3. [Asia Minor] The one "who is and who was and who is to come" is a reference to God, adapted from Exodus 3:14. The last part of this description is not what one would expect ("who is and who was and who will be"). Instead of a future form of the verb "to be," John switches to the verb "to come," perhaps to emphasize that God is not static,

Prophets and Prophecy

AΩ John considered his writing to be a "prophecy" (1:3; 22:7, 10, 18, 19) and likely saw himself as a prophet. For modern readers, "prophecy" often connotes predictions of the future, at times bizarre and titillating. Unfortunately, Revelation is also often viewed in those terms. The biblical understanding of prophecy and prophets, however, does not concentrate on the future. Rather, a prophet was one who served as a spokesperson for God, interpreting the current situation from a divine perspective and delivering a word from God to that situation. At times, future events, either punishments or blessings, comprised the message of the prophets. Their major focus, however, was on the present.

Asia Minor

AΩ In Revelation, as generally elsewhere in the New Testament, "Asia" refers to the Roman province by that name in western Asia Minor, located in what is modern Turkey. This province, whose western edge bordered the Aegean Sea, was one of the richest Roman provinces and one of the most hellenized provinces in Asia Minor. Worship of the Roman emperor became particularly strong in this region during the 1st century AD. Christianity was introduced to this region early, for according to the book of Acts, the Apostle Paul visited this area during his second and third missionary journeys.

Ancient Letters

The book of Revelation is somewhat similar in format to ancient Greek letters, which followed a rather fixed structure. A typical Greek letter began with the name of the writer, the name of the recipient, and a greeting, usually in the form "A to B, greetings." Following this opening salutation, the writer often expressed praise, gave thanks, or offered a prayer on behalf of the recipient. Then, after the main body of the letter, the writer concluded the letter, often with additional greetings or a benediction. A good example of an ancient Greek letter is the following letter written in the 2d century AD by a young soldier to his mother.

Apollinarius to Taesis, his mother and lady, many greetings. Before all I pray for your health. I myself am well and make supplication for you before the gods of this place. I wish you to know, mother, that I arrived in Rome in good health on the 25th day of the month Pachon and was posted to Misenum, though I have not yet learned the name of my company; for I had not gone to Misenum at the time of writing this letter. I beg you then, mother, look after yourself and do not worry about me; for I have come to a fine place. Please write me a letter about your welfare and that of my brothers and of all your folk. And whenever I find a messenger I will write to you; never will I be slow to write. Many salutations to my brothers and Apollinarius and his children and Karalas and his children. I salute Ptolemaeus and Ptolemais and her children and Heraclous and her children. I salute all who love you, each by name. I pray for your health. (Addressed) Deliver at Karanis to Taesis, from her son Apollinarius of Misenum.

As did the Apostle Paul, John altered the Greek letter style in several ways, including changing "greeting" (*chairein*) to "grace" (*charis*) and adding the familiar Semitic "peace" (*eirēnē*). Not only does Revelation begin with the elements of a salutation (1:4-5a), it also ends with words typical of the conclusions of ancient letters, particularly of New Testament letters (22:21). Recognition of the quasiletter format of Revelation is important for interpreting John's writing. One should not see the book of Revelation as a general treatise, unconnected to any specific situation. Rather, like the letters of Paul, the book of Revelation functions as a pastoral letter, written to 1st-century Christians in Asia Minor who were dealing with specific historical, theological, and sociological crises.

PMich VIII490. A. S. Hunt and C. C. Edgar, trans., *Select Papyri* (LCL; Cambridge MA: Harvard University Press, 1932), 1:303-304.

but active. The God who is and who has been is the same one who will continue to be active in world history and in the lives of God's servants. God is continually coming into human history. John's vision proclaims that God will come decisively in the future to bring justice and righteousness and to eliminate evil.

The "seven spirits who are before his throne" likely symbolize the divine presence and activity in the world (compare Zech 4:2, 10). Thus this symbol is roughly equivalent to the Holy Spirit. Some commentators have suggested that the seven spirits also refer to the tradition found in some Jewish literature about seven archangels who serve at God's disposal. [Seven] The description of Jesus as "the faithful witness, the firstborn of the dead, and the ruler of the kings of the earth" (1:5; the latter two adapted from Ps 89:27) would have been particularly significant for the original recipients of John's message, who were facing persecution and possible martyrdom. Like Jesus, they too were to be "faithful witnesses," even if their faithfulness cost them their lives. Even in death, Jesus, the "firstborn of the dead," will be with them. Faced with persecution and discrimination, John's audience may have felt discouraged and fearful, believing that the powers of oppression and tyranny were in control. John states otherwise, however, reminding them that Jesus Christ is the one who is "the ruler over the kings of the earth."

The doxology in vv. 5b-6 offers praise to Jesus for three activities—loving us, freeing us from our sins, and making us into a new community, a "kingdom." The latter two activities are specific examples of the first: Jesus has demonstrated his love for us through his liberating death on the cross and by his incorporating us into God's new family. These two activities do not exhaust his love for us, however. John states that Jesus "freed" us (past tense) and "made" us a kingdom (past tense), but he "continues to love" us (present tense). Those who are members of God's community are given a task: They are to be priests to God, serving God by serving God's creation. The followers of Christ are to be mediators between God and humanity.

The imagery of kingdom and priesthood is derived from Exodus 19:6 (see also Isa 61:6), in which the Israelites were told that they were to be "a priestly kingdom and a holy nation." Like other New Testament writers (see especially 1 Pet 2:5, 9), John proclaims the followers of Christ to be a part of God's chosen people. This description is the first of many instances in the book in which the author borrows images and themes from the exodus and wilderness traditions of Israel. A new Pharaoh has arisen, in the guise of the Roman emperor, to enslave God's people. In the midst of cataclysmic destruction and punishments reminiscent of the Egyptian

Seven

AΩ The number seven is important both structurally and symbolically in the book of Revelation. Structurally, John organized his writing around the number seven. Obvious examples of this are the messages to the seven churches (chs. 2–3), the seven seals (chs. 6–8), the seven trumpets (chs. 8–11), and the seven bowls (chs. 15–16). Other explicit uses of the number seven include the seven spirits (1:4; 5:6), the seven angels of the churches (1:20), the seven stars (1:16, 20; 2:1), the seven lampstands (1:12, 20; 2:1), the seven torches (4:5), the seven thunders (10:3-4), the Lamb with seven horns and seven eyes (5:6), the seven-headed dragon (12:3), and the seven-headed beast (13:1).

In the ancient world, the number seven was sometimes considered a sacred number. Rituals or objects associated with the divine often occurred in groups of seven. In Judaism, seven had special significance because the seventh day was the Sabbath, the day of rest and God's holy day. Seven was also seen as a number that denoted completeness or perfection, perhaps derived from the observation of seven planets in the sky. In Revelation, the number seven often appears to carry this symbolic significance. Thus, for example, the "seven spirits who are before his throne" (1:4) likely represent the totality of the spirit of God.

For further information on the ancient significance of the number seven, see M. H. Pope, "Seven, Seventh, Seventy," *Interpreter's Dictionary of the Bible*, ed. George Arthur Buttrick, 4 vols. (Nashville: Abingdon, 1962), 4:294-95; and Jöran Friberg, "Numbers and Counting," *The Anchor Bible Dictionary*, ed. David Noel Freedman, 6 vols. (New York: Doubleday & Co., 1992), 4:1139-45. On the other hand, Adela Yarbro Collins ("Numerical Symbolism in Jewish and Early Christian Apocalyptic Literature," *Aufstieg und Niedergang der römischen Welt*, ed. Hildegard Temporini and Wolfgang Haase [Berlin: Walter de Gruyter, 1984], II.21.2:1221-87) has argued that there is little evidence to support the belief that seven was symbolic of completeness.

plagues, God's people will again be marked for protection and will pass safely through their own Red Sea.

Verse 7 contains a prophetic pronouncement that combines elements from Daniel 7:13 and Zechariah 12:10. The combination of these two texts from the Hebrew Bible is likely not John's own creation, but a part of early Christian tradition because the same combination, although in reverse order, occurs also in Matthew 24:30. The first part of the pronouncement attributes to Jesus the description from Daniel of a human-like figure ("one like a son of man") who descends from heaven with the clouds and is given "dominion and glory and kingship" (Dan 7:14). In Daniel, this mysterious figure is likely a reference to the archangel Michael, who in one sense represents the faithful people of God. For John, as for other early Christian thinkers, Jesus is the one who will fulfill this role. John draws upon this same imagery from Daniel elsewhere in Revelation (1:13; 14:14). John envisioned this appearance of Jesus to be of such magnitude that "every eye will see him, even those who pierced him." Language such as this is not to be taken literally. This is poetic language. It is John's way of saying that God's rule over the world, effected through Jesus, will not be a minor, local event, but an event of universal significance. [Delay of Christ's Coming]

Delay of Christ's Coming

The early church believed that the resurrected Jesus would return very soon to complete the coming of the kingdom of God, whose inauguration he announced during his ministry. Paul apparently expected the return of Jesus shortly. As the years passed and the anticipated event did not occur, the early Christians dealt with this delayed return in several ways. Some reacted with fear and concern about Christians who had already died (1 Thess 4:13-18); some claimed that the day of Christ's return had already occurred or was occurring (2 Thess 2:1-2); some reinterpreted the meaning of "soon," claiming that "with the Lord one day is like a thousand years, and a thousand years are like one day" (2 Pet 3:8). For John, the gravity of his present situation led him to conclude that surely the end must be near. God would not allow the world to continue much longer. He interpreted the events of his day as signs that Christ would return soon to establish God's justice and righteousness.

The appearance of the once crucified Jesus affects even those responsible for his death. All people join in mourning. The text does not specify whether the people's remorse is based on their contrition and repentance (as in the Zechariah text) or whether it is a reaction of guilt and fear. Elsewhere in Revelation, John intimates that all the world will eventually be drawn under the influence and power of the mercy of God (see 15:3-4; 21:24; 22:2). Perhaps John intended that here as well.

The theme of reversal is prominent throughout the book of Revelation. The slain Lamb is the victorious Lamb; those who have been oppressed and persecuted are vindicated; the powerful become powerless. Here, those who brought about the death of Jesus now grieve over their actions. The focus in this scene is not on the mourners, however. The central figure is the one who comes on the clouds, the triumphant Jesus. This is a scene of vindication.

John reminds his readers that the drama of God's dealing with the world did not end with the crucifixion of God's faithful witness, for the last act is yet to be performed. When the final curtain does fall, those who have opposed God will be surprised at the ending. Even those who were responsible for the death of Jesus will lament their deed. The visions of the Apocalypse are John's attempt to portray in symbolic language the astounding truth that all evil and injustice will ultimately bow before the indomitable power of God. The last chapter of Revelation ends with John yearning for this event to take place, crying out "Come, Lord Jesus!" (22:20). John underscores the importance of this pronouncement by adding a double confirmation, "So it is to be [literally, "yes"]. Amen."
[The Coming of Christ]

God's response in v. 8 is a validation of John's message. Only twice in the entire book does God speak directly (see also 21:5-8). Near the beginning and near the end of the work, the voice of God intrudes into the story. These divine proclamations serve to authenticate the revelation. John attributes three self-designations to God in v. 8. The first phrase identifies God as the Alpha and Omega, the first and last letters of the Greek alphabet. This description occurs twice more in Revelation. In 21:6, John once more applies it to God and expands it by the phrase "the beginning and the end." In 22:13, Christ says, "I am the Alpha and the Omega, the first and the last, the beginning and the end." [Alpha and Omega] These descriptive expansions explain the meaning of "Alpha and Omega." God is the one who was "in the beginning" (Gen 1:1) and who will be at the end. As all creation owes its existence to God, so all creation finds its ultimate meaning and purpose in God. Creation and eschatology are united in God. What God began in creation, God will bring to completion at the eschaton, the last days.

The second self-designation by God in v. 8, "who is and who was and who is to come," repeats John's description of God from v. 4.

The Coming of Christ

The Advent hymn, "Lo, He Comes with Clouds Descending," whose text was written by Charles Wesley, borrows from Rev 1:7. Verses 1–2 state,

Lo, He comes with clouds descending,
  Once for favored sinners slain;
Thousand thousand saints attending
  Swell the triumph of His train:
Alleluia, alleluia!
  God appears on earth to reign.

Ev'ry eye shall now behold Him,
  Robed in splendor's majesty;
Those who set at naught and sold Him,
  Pierced and nailed Him to the tree,
Deeply wailing, deeply wailing,
  Shall the true Messiah see.

Alpha and Omega

The use of *alpha* (α/Α) and *omega* (ω/Ω) as symbols for God was likely influenced by the words of God in Isa 44:6, "I am the first and I am the last" (see also Isa 41:4; 48:12). In later Jewish writings the rabbis spoke of keeping the Law in its entirety as keeping the Law from *aleph* (א) to *tau* (ת), the first and last letters of the Hebrew alphabet. To speak of God as the alpha and the omega is not to restrict God to only the beginning and the end, but is to proclaim the entirety of God's sovereignty and power. God rules not only the beginning and the end of history, but all that lies in between.

St. John on Patmos

This is often considered the masterpiece by Memling, a Northern Renaissance artist. It is the right panel of a triptych (three-part altarpiece). According to the original inscription on the frame, it was completed in 1479. It was originally intended for the high altar of St. John's hospital church and was paid for by two brothers and two sisters of the hospital. It is the largest triptych painted by Memling.

Hans Memling (1433–1494). *Saint John the Evangelist on Patmos,* from the *Altarpiece of Saint John the Baptist and Saint John the Evangelist.* 1474–79. Oil on wood, 68 x 31 in. Memling Museum, Saint John's Hospital, Bruges, Belgium. (Credit: Erich Lessing/Art Resource)

This phrase, like Alpha and Omega, John uses later in the work as descriptions of both God and Christ (4:8; 11:17; 16:5). The third self-designation, "the Almighty," is John's favorite title for God (see 4:8; 11:17; 15:3; 16:7, 14; 19:6, 15; 21:22). The Greek term used here, *pantokratēr*, is the usual Septuagint translation of the Hebrew phrase normally translated as "lord of hosts." The emphasis in this title is that God is the supreme ruler. For John's readers, such an affirmation would have been a powerful encouragement. In the minds of many Christians, the Roman rulers, political systems, and institutions appeared to be the ones who were in charge, the "almighty ones." John reminds his audience, however, that in reality God is the one who is sovereign over the universe.

The Vision of the Son of Man, 1:9–3:22

The first vision in the Apocalypse presents the powerful Son of Man figure who calls John and commissions him to deliver this revelation to the churches of Asia Minor. Even though the entire section is a part of John's vision, the major portion of this section, chapters 2–3, is an auditory revelation rather than a visual one.

The Commissioning of John, 1:9-20

One of the literary characteristics of works belonging to the genre of apocalypses is that the revelation mediated to the author of the work is set in a narrative framework. Verses 9-20 function in that manner for Revelation, helping to delineate the narrative setting of John's visions. These verses also provide important information about the writer himself. As discussed in the introduction to this

Patmos

Patmos, one of the Sporades Islands in the Aegean Sea, is ten miles long and six miles wide. Located off the coast of Asia Minor, the island is approximately thirty-seven miles southwest of Miletus. It is a rocky, volcanic island whose primary significance is due to early Christian tradition that John was banished to the island. Banishment was a form of punishment used on occasion by the Roman authorities, although scholars have debated whether the Romans ever used Patmos for such purposes. Whereas the Roman writer Tacitus *(Annals* 3.68, 4.30) stated that three of the islands in the Sporades (Gyarus, Donusa, and Amorgus) were used for places of exile or banishment, Patmos is never so mentioned. (Many modern commentators mistakenly claim that Tacitus mentioned that Patmos was used as a place of punishment. He did mention the island, but only to give its physical description.) Perhaps, as later Christian tradition claimed, the Romans used Patmos also for this purpose. If, as seems likely, John's statement that he was on Patmos because of the testimony of Jesus means that he was exiled there for his Christian faith, then Revelation provides evidence for the use of Patmos as a place of banishment.

commentary, the identity of this "John" is unknown, apart from the information given in the book. Although virtually all Jewish apocalypses, as well as many Christian apocalypses, were written pseudonymously, there is no reason to assume that "John" is a pseudonym. [St. John on Patmos] The writer was apparently well known to the Christians in Asia Minor, perhaps having served as an itinerant prophet in the region. John was careful to establish a connection with his readers. He was not a disinterested observer of their situation, but was their "brother and partner in Jesus in the tribulation and kingdom and patient endurance" (v. 9). He shared with them not only the privileges and responsibilities of being a part of the kingdom of God, but also the suffering that at times accompanies those who endure patiently as faithful witnesses to Jesus.

John says that he was on the island of Patmos [Patmos] when his visionary experience occurred. Although his claim that he was on Patmos "because of the word of God and the testimony of Jesus" could be understood to mean that he had gone to the island to preach to the people there, the more likely meaning is that he was banished to Patmos as punishment for his Christian faith. In Revelation, the Greek word *dia* ("because of") always indicates the result of an action, not the purpose of the action. Thus John was on Patmos not for the purpose of bearing witness to Jesus, but because he had already been a faithful witness. Twice in Revelation (6:9; 20:4), the phrase "on account of the word of God and the testimony of Jesus" is explicitly connected to persecution and death. Moreover, John states that he is a partner in suffering with his readers. A reasonable conclusion, then, is that John was on Patmos not of his own choice, but because he had been banished to the island because of his faithfulness to the call of Christ.

The Lord's Day

AΩ John says that his revelation came to him "on the Lord's day" (1:10). This phrase likely refers to Sunday, the first day of the week. Because the resurrection of Jesus occurred on the first day of the week, this day soon became the day Christians gathered to worship. The phrase "the Lord's day" occurs nowhere else in the New Testament, although Acts 20:7 and possibly 1 Cor 16:2 refer to Christians assembling on this day. The *Didache*, an early Christian handbook on ethics and church practices (dated to the late 1st or the 2d century), commands that Christians are to assemble "on the Lord's Day" (14:1). It is fitting that Revelation, a work so filled with liturgical elements, should have its origin on the day set aside for Christian worship.

The revelation given to John occurred as an ecstatic experience ("in the spirit," v. 10) involving both auditory and visual effects: he heard a voice and saw a vision. [The Lord's Day] This scene is similar to commissioning episodes of some of the Hebrew prophets, particularly Ezekiel and Isaiah, and functions in that manner for John. The scene is indebted even more, however, to revelatory moments in other apocalypses, especially the book of Daniel.

The text does not indicate why John singles out these particular seven churches to receive special messages. That he wrote to them with such authority is a clear indication that he was well known to them, perhaps having served among them. Scholars have often noted that the cities in which these churches were located were connected by roadways, forming an inner circle in Asia Minor. [Map: The Seven Cities of Revelation] An ancient traveler, beginning at Ephesus, could have followed the route of these seven cities, stopping at the church in each city to read John's message to the Christians there. The choice of exactly seven churches was likely intentional, given the structural and symbolic importance of the number seven to the author. By addressing his message to seven churches, John intends all churches to hear his message ("Let anyone who has an ear listen to what the Spirit is saying to the churches," 2:11).

John's description of his vision is filled with images borrowed from the Hebrew Bible, especially from the description of the Ancient of Days in Daniel 7 and the mighty angel in Daniel 10. The seven golden lampstands are adaptations of Zechariah's vision (4:1-14). Contrary to the NRSV translation, John probably did not use a title ("the Son of Man") to identify the figure in his vision. Rather, "one like a son of man" (author's translation) means, as it does in Daniel 7:13, "one in human form" (cf. Dan 10:5). The sword protruding from the mouth of this mighty figure symbolizes the

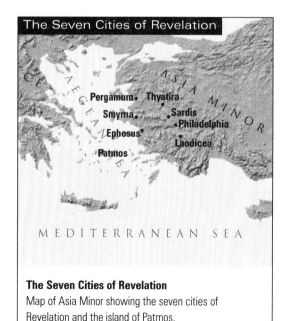

The Seven Cities of Revelation
Map of Asia Minor showing the seven cities of Revelation and the island of Patmos.

judgment of God. In biblical tradition, the word of God can be both creative and destructive, comforting and judging. Here, Christ stands as the eschatological judge. As we shall see, all people stand under the judgment of Christ, both the churches (chs. 2–3) and the nations (ch. 19).

Although noting in detail the sources of John's imagery is instructive, excessive attention to John's sources can dilute the force of the passage.

The Cave of the Apocalypse
The interior of the cave on the island of Patmos that, according to local legend, is the location where John received and wrote down his visionary experience. (Credit: Mitchell Reddish)

The scene is to be experienced, not analyzed. There is an accumulation here of images of power, majesty, and judgment—snowy hair, fiery eyes, powerful legs, roaring voice, mighty sword, radiant face. This passage, like all of the Apocalypse, should be heard imaginatively. The visual and auditory components of John's vision should overwhelm the reader/hearer, just as they did John, who "fell at his feet as though dead" (1:17).

[The Cave of the Apocalypse]

John's reaction to the appearance of the glorified Christ is one of fear and reverence. Whereas this scene is modeled primarily after Daniel 10, John's response is similar to that of other biblical figures when faced with a theophany or christophany (cf. Isa 6:5; Ezek 1:28; Dan 8:18; Matt 28:8-9; Luke 5:8). Christ reassures John by placing his hand upon him and speaking to him. In describing himself as "the first and the last" (v. 17; cf. Isa 44:6; 48:12), Christ applies to himself a phrase equivalent to the description of God as Alpha and Omega. (In 22:13, both phrases describe Christ.) John does not hesitate to apply to Christ certain attributes that his sources applied to God, for in John's understanding, one encounters God in the risen Christ, who possesses the power and majesty of God and executes judgment on God's behalf. Revelation has an exalted Christology.

The emphasis in v. 18 is on life and the conquering of death. For John's readers, faced with persecution and martyrdom, the claims of Christ to be the living one who now controls death and Hades would have been powerful words of assurance. Even death, this last enemy of humanity, holds no threat to those who are followers of

Death and Hades

AΩ   The keys of Death and of Hades (1:18), which Jesus possesses, indicate the extent of his authority and control—he has power even over death. Hades is the realm of the dead, the underworld, where the shades or shadows of former living individuals continued on (cf. Sheol in Hebrew thought). As the view of resurrection developed, Hades or Sheol was seen as the temporary dwelling place of the dead until the time of the resurrection. (Contrary to the KJV translation, Hades is not hell, the place of eternal punishment.) The risen Christ has the power to open the gates of Hades and release the dead to new life. Here and elsewhere in Revelation (6:8; 20:13, 14), Death and Hades personify the forces of evil that are arrayed against God and God's people. They are no match, however, for Christ, who not only can release those who are captive to them, but also ultimately defeats and destroys them (20:14).

the risen Christ. Through his own death and resurrection he has conquered the power of death. As John well knew, such assurance did not mean that faithful witnesses would be spared persecution and death. In fact, the very act of their being faithful would at times culminate in their deaths. But the Christ who holds the key to death and is "alive forever and ever" will set them free from the constraints of death. [Death and Hades]

The command in v. 11 to write down what is revealed is reiterated in v. 19. The seemingly tripartite command ("Write what you have seen, what is, and what is to take place after this") is not, as some have suggested, a structuring device indicating three sections of the Apocalypse (1:9-20; 2:1–3:22; 4:1–22:5), but a formula indicating the totality of the contents of John's vision.

In apocalypses, otherworldly figures often appear to interpret bewildering aspects of the vision or speeches of the revelation. Usually angels act as such interpreters. Here, Christ serves as the interpreter, explaining to John the symbolism of the seven stars and the seven lampstands that John saw. The meaning given to the lampstands is clear: they represent the seven churches to which John is to send his message. The symbolism of the seven stars is more obscure. Although Christ declares that the stars represent "the angels of the seven churches," who are these angels? Scholars have proposed various interpretations, including the following: seeing the angels as the messengers who are delivering John's messages to the churches, messengers sent to John from each of the churches, the leaders of the churches, or the guardian angels of the churches. None of these solutions is satisfactory, however, because in chapters 2–3 the messages are not directed to individuals, but to the congregations.

The interpretive key is found in other apocalyptic literature in which earthly realities are viewed as having heavenly counterparts. Struggles in the supernatural realm mirror the struggles of the faithful on earth. Part of this worldview was the belief that nations or kingdoms had a patron angel. One of the clearest examples of this is in Daniel 10, where Michael, the patron angel (or "prince") of the Jewish people, joined forces with the angel Gabriel to do battle against the patron angels of Persia and Greece. In Daniel, to speak of heavenly conflict is a way of speaking about earthly conflict. The patron angels represent the people as a whole. A similar idea is likely behind the "one like a human being" (son of man) figure in Daniel 7. He is the heavenly counterpart to the people of God. His receiving the kingdom represents the faithful people of God receiving the kingdom. Thus in Revelation the angels of the churches are the heavenly counterparts of the earthly churches. The messages addressed to the angels are words intended for Christ's followers.

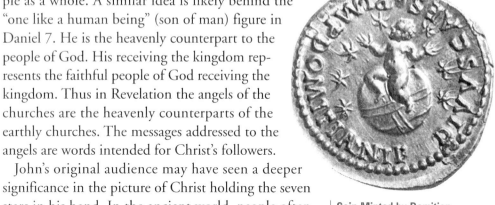

Coin Minted by Domitian

Reverse (shown here) depicts the son of Domitian holding or playing with the seven stars.

Domitian Coin. AD. 81–84, Rome. Gold. British Museum. BMCRE 62. London, England. (Credit: ©The British Museum)

John's original audience may have seen a deeper significance in the picture of Christ holding the seven stars in his hand. In the ancient world, people often viewed heavenly bodies as being divine and controlling the events on earth. This was particularly true of the sun, moon, and the five planets that one could observe with the naked eye (Jupiter, Venus, Saturn, Mercury, and Mars). On a gold coin minted during Domitian's reign, the seven stars surround a baby boy seated on a globe. The coin commemorates Domitian's son (portrayed on the coin as the infant Jupiter), who died as an infant and whom Domitian proclaimed to be divine. The child straddling earth and heaven rules the cosmos. [Coin Minted by Domitian] For John such claims were false claims. All power and authority belong to God and his Christ.

CONNECTIONS

1. The opening verses of Revelation are filled with rich theological treasures. At the beginning of Paul's letters in the New Testament, in what is called the thanksgiving section of each letter, Paul normally signals to the observant reader the major themes that are addressed in the body of the letter. In a similar way, the first eight verses of Revelation contain several of the key themes that surface in the remainder of the book. Two of those themes are hope and worship.

As clues in Revelation indicate, John perceived the current political and social situations to be perilous. Whether his perception was accurate or not, John believed that his readers were in danger due to governmental persecution, particularly related to emperor worship (see ch. 13). Anxiety, fear, and despair likely characterized his readers. What hope could John offer individuals in such a situation? John reminds his readers of the ultimate source of power and strength in the world—God Almighty, the one who is, and who was, and who is to come. The God who had been with them in the past would not forsake them now nor in the future. Further hope is to be found in Jesus, who as the "firstborn of the dead" has triumphed over Death itself and made possible new life for his followers, both in the present and beyond.

Modern readers of the book of Revelation usually are not confronted with the same perils or dilemmas as were the original recipients of the work. Anxiety, fear, and despair—whether personal, financial, or social—are still common conditions, however. John's words of assurance and hope still powerfully address our present-day situation. The task of the teacher and preacher is to help people understand that even in today's world, God still reigns supreme. Domestic violence, terrorism, world hunger, poverty, AIDS—these and a host of other problems often make claims of God's sovereignty seem foolish. God seems to be absent or powerless. The book of Revelation offers an alternative view of reality. It declares for modern readers as it did for its first hearers that in spite of appearances, God is supreme. The one who is Alpha (the Creator) is also Omega (the consummator of history). [The Second Coming]

The Second Coming

"Christian faith always lives 'as if' the second coming were just around the corner, for it is so certain of its vindication."

R. H. Fuller, *Preaching the New Lectionary: The Word of God for the Church Today* (Collegeville MN: Liturgical, 1974), 453.

In addition to encouraging his readers, John also wrote to challenge them. Christ has "made us to be a kingdom, priests serving his God and Father." To be a part of the kingdom of God carries a responsibility, the obligation to be priests. John does not elaborate on what being a priest involves, except to say that it means serving God. In the Hebrew Bible, a priest was one who served as a mediator between God and the people. The priest represented the people before God and God before the people. One of the primary activities of the priest was to lead the people in the worship of God. An important fulfillment of our priestly task is to offer praise and thanksgiving to God in worship. Worship dominates the book of Revelation. Angels, the twenty-four elders, the four living creatures, and multitudes of people are described as worshiping God. Hymns and liturgies abound in the book. The prominence of worship in Revelation is no accident. John knew what many believers throughout the centuries have discovered also, which is that a period of crisis or despair is not the time to abandon worship. Rather, those difficult times—when the situation looks hopeless or God seems absent—are often when worship is most meaningful.

2. The opening scene (1:9-20) in the Apocalypse is a powerful one. The reader should not pass over it too quickly, for to do so is to blunt the force of John's work. Visualize the scene: The opening credits of 1:1-8 roll from the screen as the camera focuses on John, situated on a small island in the Aegean Sea. A thunderous voice speaks, and John, startled, turns to see an imposing figure standing among seven lampstands. It is Christ, the representative of God. Out of all the imagery associated with this figure, John gives explanations for only two symbols—the seven lampstands and the seven stars—thus pointing to the importance of these two images. Both are images of assurance. Christ standing among the lampstands represents Christ among his people. Christ has not forgotten or abandoned them. In this scene, John gives a visual representation of the words of Jesus in Matthew, "And remember, I am with you always, to the end of the age" (28:20).

What does it mean to say that Christ is with us, that in and through the risen Christ, God is present among us? Is that nothing more than a pious saying, or is there real substance in that promise? Those of us in the church have spouted such phrases too quickly and too glibly; as a result, we are often not heard anymore. [Hope]

But that message of hope and assurance is the very core of John's Apocalypse. Over and over in Revelation he will remind us that even in the bleakest moments, God is still present. John does not offer us a philosophical argument about the existence of God; he does not give us a well-reasoned defense of a just and merciful God in the midst of human suffering and agony. Instead of logic, John gives us images. Visual imagery fills the book of Revelation. Therein lies the enduring power of this work, for its evocative images are more powerful and convincing than any words could be. Christ is with us! He stands in our midst, a powerful figure: long robe, golden sash, white hair, eyes blazing with fire, feet of bronze, with a thunderous voice more powerful than a two-edged sword. We do not face life's

Hope

J. Christiaan Beker, commenting on Bonhoeffer's critique of "cheap grace," warned,

We should be equally critical of cheap hope, a simple imposition of biblical verses and visions on the human predicament today as if they are self-explanatory or a bandage for bloodied souls. Cheap hope will not be able to speak a redemptive word either to the profound and new questions about the meaning of suffering today or to the projects of hope which our culture produces. Our Christian task today is to find an answer to the double question: What constitutes authentic Christian hope? Is authentic Christian hope able to respond to our questions about suffering in all its enormity and complexity and its seemingly tragic dimensions? In short, is there any hope to be had?

J. Christiaan Beker, *Suffering & Hope: The Biblical Vision and the Human Predicament* (Grand Rapids: Eerdmans, 1994), 30.

difficulties alone. That message needs to be heard as much today as it did in the first century.

John knew what many of us who teach and preach these texts need to be reminded of—symbolic language and sensory imagery are often more effective and more powerful forms of communication than is rational speech. Too often, in dealing with image-rich texts, we feel compelled to try to explain and decipher every detail, to remove the language of symbol and replace it with the language of logic. Yet, as any poet knows, suggestive language is often more effective than analytical language, for suggestive language is more open-ended and allows more connections and possibilities of meaning. Image-oriented speech evokes emotions and elicits responses in ways that rationalistic speech cannot. Note how Jesus' teaching and preaching were saturated with image-oriented language. The parable, a classic example of metaphorical speech, was Jesus' favorite teaching technique. As Clyde Fant has noted,

> When we speak of God or the things of God, we stand at the boundaries of language itself. We must then describe what we cannot define; we must sketch what we cannot calculate. This preaching sticks in the mind. It opens new horizons; it awakens dreams.[2]

Apocalyptic writings were almost always written pseudonymously in the name of some authoritative, venerated figure of the past—Abraham, Enoch, Baruch, Isaiah, Ezra. This was a literary device intended to lend authenticity and authority to the writing. John apparently chose to write under his own name. "What then is his authority?" the reader might ask. "Why should he be trusted?" The biographical sketch of John in 1:9 serves to answer those questions. The one who through his images claims that Christ is always among us has earned the right to make such claims. He has shared with his readers the difficulties of life. He has known persecution and patient endurance. Like Job, John has experienced the dark side of life. Thus his claim that Christ stands with his people is no hollow assertion. In the same way that we can hear and accept the words of a Mahatma Gandhi, or a Dietrich Bonhoeffer, or a Martin Luther King Jr., or a Nelson Mandela because they have forged their words in the crucible of suffering, we can hear these words of John and know that they are authentic words.

Both John and Christ are symbols of solidarity with the people in the churches of Asia Minor. John, through his experiences similar to theirs (he is their "brother" who shares in their suffering), and Christ, through his continual presence with the people (standing among the lampstands), are united with John's readers.

The vision of Christ among the lampstands conveys more than assurance, however. The presence of Christ brings judgment as well as comfort. The church that welcomes the presence of Christ must also be willing to stand under the intense scrutiny of the penetrating gaze of the one with "eyes like a flame of fire" (1:14). As the messages to the seven churches in chapters 2–3 make clear, the word from God can be painful as well as consoling.

The other part of this vision that John interprets for the reader is Christ holding the seven stars in his hand. John says that the stars are the angels of the churches, the heavenly counterpart to the Christians. Thus the image of Christ holding the stars in his hand portrays Christ holding the churches. He supports them and keeps them secure in the midst of the chaos of life. One can hear the power of this symbolism in the African American spiritual "He's Got the Whole World in His Hands." ["To God"]

"To God"
by Robert Herrick

Do with me, God! As Thou didst deal with John,
(Who writ that heavenly *Revelation*)
Let me (like him) first cracks of thunder hear;
Then let the harp's enchantments strike mine ear;
Here give me thorns; there, in thy Kingdom, set
Upon my head the golden coronet;
There give me day; but here my dreadful night:
My sackcloth here; but there my stole of white.

Robert Atwan and Laurance Wieder, eds., *Chapters into Verse: Poetry in English Inspired by the Bible* (Oxford: Oxford University Press, 1993), 2:339.

NOTES

[1] Martin E. Marty, "M.E.M.O.: A Revelation," *The Christian Century* 114/16 (14 May 1997): 495.

[2] Clyde E. Fant, *Preaching for Today*, rev. ed. (San Francisco: Harper & Row, 1987), 247.

THE MESSAGES TO THE
FIRST FOUR CHURCHES

2:1-29

The Messages to the Seven Churches, 2:1–3:22

Chapters 2 and 3 form a distinct unit, composed of messages for the seven churches mentioned at the end of the preceding chapter. Some readers have wondered if these chapters originated independently of the rest of the work because they seem so different. The style of these chapters is more mundane and less esoteric or symbolic than the other chapters in the book. Furthermore, these chapters address the current situation in Asia Minor, whereas the emphasis in chapters 4–22 seems to be on future, even eschatological, events. Yet the messages to the seven churches are an integral part of John's work. They are closely tied to the first chapter of the book by means of the repetition of the descriptions of the risen Christ as the sender of the messages. They are also intimately connected to the remainder of the work, both by the repetition of select words or phrases here and in later chapters and by similar emphasis of major themes. Examples of words and phrases that occur here and elsewhere in the book include "the second death" (2:11; 20:14), "the morning star" (2:28; 22:16), "the book of life" (3:5; 13:8; 17:8; 20:12, 15), and "the new Jerusalem" (3:12; 21:2). Major themes that recur are persecution, faithfulness to God, endurance, the reign of Christ, and rewards for those who are faithful to God. [Asia Minor and Christianity]

While the observation is true that, compared with the rest of the work, the focus of chapters 2 and 3 is more on the present situation of the first-century readers than on future events, eschatology is a

---

Asia Minor and Christianity

"Asia Minor, specifically the western part of Asia Minor where John and his audience were located, was one of the most significant geographical areas in the development of early Christianity. In the fifties of the first century the apostle Paul carried on missionary work in this area. The author of 1 Peter writes to the churches of Asia and other provinces in Asia Minor. New Testament writings associated with John—the Gospel and the three letters as well as the Book of Revelation—also, according to tradition,

originated in Asia at the city of Ephesus. At the beginning of the second century Ignatius of Antioch writes letters to five churches in Asia as he travels to die in Rome. Through these writings we know of Christian groups in at least eleven cities of the Asian province by the beginning of the second century AD. Moreover, these churches are associated with major apostolic figures such as Paul, Peter, and John."

Leonard L. Thompson, *The Book of Revelation: Apocalypse and Empire* (New York: Oxford University Press, 1990), 11-12.

Son of Man among the Candlesticks

St. John Among the Candlesticks is one of Albrecht Dürer's fifteen woodcuts on the book of Revelation. The *Apocalypse* is the first of three religious books Dürer made during the period 1496–1501. In these works of art, Dürer liberated the technique of woodcut from book illustration. This is the first set of prints that contain biblical text in letterpress on the back. The increased size also furthered the woodcut technique. The Apocalypse print series was widely circulated and contributed greatly to establishing Dürer's international reputation. Here, Christ is shown as the glorious Son of Man among the seven candlesticks, while John kneels in reverence and fear.

Albrecht Dürer (1471–1528). *St. John Among the Candlesticks* from the *Apocalypse of St. John*. 1496–1498. Woodcut. (Credit: Dover Pictoral Archive Series) strong component of these chapters also. The rewards that are promised to the faithful at the close of each message to the churches are eschatological rewards. Furthermore, the claim that the remainder of Revelation is totally future-oriented is misleading. Although the scenes in the remaining chapters primarily describe end-time events, the present situation of the readers is always in the foreground. John presents visions of the future for the sake of the present. The purpose of the work is to give meaning to the present life of the readers, not simply to offer hope for the future. While the emphasis may vary, the material both in chapters 2 and 3 and in the later chapters holds in tension the present and the future. [Son of Man among the Candlesticks]

Any claims, then, that chapters 2 and 3 are unconnected to the rest of Revelation are misguided. These chapters are an integral part of John's vision and are properly understood only as a part of this larger work. The entire work, from the first chapter to the last, is intertwined with themes and images that reinforce and reinterpret each other.

The contents of chapters 2 and 3 are often referred to as letters. Whereas a brief glance at the material might lead one to concur that these messages are in letter form because they each begin with an identification of the intended recipient and the sender, a closer examination suggests otherwise. These messages are more akin to prophetic pronouncements (compare the oracles of judgment against the nations in Amos 1:3–2:16) or royal proclamations. [Example of an Imperial Edict] The introductory formula "these are the words of" (*tade legei*, literally "this is what . . . says") found in each of the messages is synonymous with the introductory formula used in the prophetic writings of the Hebrew Bible, as well as in the introductory words of Near Eastern royal edicts. The messages of chapters 2 and 3, then, are not simply letters, but divine pronouncements. The words that John delivered to the churches are not his words, but God's words, spoken through the risen Christ. They demand to be heard and obeyed. [Outline of the Messages to the Seven Churches]

Example of an Imperial Edict

The messages to the seven churches are similar to imperial edicts, as illustrated by the opening lines of an edict from the emperor Claudius cited by the 1st-century Jewish historian Josephus:

> Tiberius Claudius Caesar Augustus Germanicus, of tribunician power, speaks [*legei*]: "Since I have known [*epignous*] from the beginning that the Jews in Alexandria called 'Alexandrians' were joint-colonizers with the Alexandrians."

Josephus, *Ant.* 19 §280-81. Cited by David E. Aune, *The New Testament in Its Literary Environment* (Philadelphia: Westminster, 1987), 242-43.

Outline of the Messages to the Seven Churches

With a few exceptions, each of the messages to the churches follows a similar pattern:

1. Identification of the addressee, in the form of a command to John to write to the angel of that church
2. Identification of the sender of the letter, described in terms borrowed from the description of the son of man figure in ch. 1
3. Words of commendation or praise for the church, introduced by the formula, "I know"
4. Admonitions or criticisms for the churches' failures
5. An exhortation to faithfulness
6. An appeal to listen: "Let anyone who has an ear listen to what the Spirit is saying to the churches"
7. A promise to the one who is faithful, the one "who conquers"

(In the final four messages the last two components above are reversed.)

Map of Asia Minor showing the seven cities
of Revelation and the island of Patmos.

MEDITERRANEAN SEA

The Seven Churches

 For further study of the messages to the seven
churches and their settings:

Hemer, Colin J. *The Letters to the Seven Churches of Asia in
Their Local Setting.* Journal for the Study of the New
Testament Supplement Series 11. Sheffield: Sheffield
Academic Press, 1989.

Ramsay, W. M. *The Letters to the Seven Churches.* Edited by
Mark W. Wilson. Updated edition. Peabody MA:
Hendrickson, 1994.

Yamauchi, Edwin M. *New Testament Cities in Asia Minor.*
Grand Rapids: Baker Book House, 1980.

The messages that John delivered to
the churches are personalized for each situation, revealing an intimate knowledge
of the condition of the churches and
their communities, not only their present
situation, but also their past. Each message contains intriguing allusions to the
local settings of the churches, allusions
that the original hearers of John's work
would certainly have noted. Although
these messages have specific warnings
and commendations for each congrega-
tion, they are in actuality circular pronouncements for all the
churches. These messages never existed independently, but only as
a part of the whole work. John likely intended that his entire
Apocalypse be taken from church to church in Asia Minor and read
to the Christians gathered in worship. Each congregation would listen in on the message to the other recipients ("Let anyone who has
an ear listen to what the Spirit is saying to the churches," 2:7, 11,
17, 29; 3:6, 13, 22). The warnings to one congregation would then
become warnings to all the congregations. Likewise, the commendations, when appropriate, became universal commendations. As
modern readers of these messages, we interact with the text in a
similar manner, being challenged and corrected by the warnings
and exhortations and finding comfort in the words of praise. [Map:
Seven Cities 1] [The Seven Churches]

COMMENTARY

The Message to Ephesus, 2:1-7

The church at Ephesus was a fitting recipient of the first message, for Ephesus was the most important city of Asia Minor in terms of commerce and culture. [Ephesus] Although the city is now landlocked, located approximately six miles inland from the Aegean Sea, during the time of the New Testament the city was a major seaport. Situated at the mouth of the Cayster River, where it emptied into the sea, Ephesus was plagued by silt deposits from the river, which eventually clogged its harbors and turned the coast into a marshy region. Not only its busy harbors, but also its location along a major highway through Asia Minor contributed to the commercial and economic success of Ephesus. According to Acts 19:8-10, Paul preached in Ephesus for more than two years, where he ran into trouble with the silversmiths who made statues of the goddess Artemis. Ephesus contained a major temple, the Artemision, to Artemis. Later tradition associated John the disciple and Mary the mother of Jesus with Ephesus. [Outline of the Message to Ephesus]

Christ praises the Ephesian Christians for their works, their labor, and their endurance. As an exemplary group who took their Christian responsibilities seriously, their faithfulness was particularly evident in their resistance to false teachers or false apostles. These "false apostles" were possibly itinerant prophets who traveled from community to community, peddling their religious wares and seeking monetary support from the religiously gullible. Such religious charlatans were well known in the ancient world, both within Christian circles and without. Paul had to deal with false apostles at Corinth, criticizing the church there for being duped by these people who proclaimed a "different gospel" and apparently lived off the support of the church (2 Cor 11–12). The *Didache*, a church "instructional manual" dating from the late first century or early

Ephesus
Curetes Street in Ephesus, with the Library of Celsus in the background. (Credit: Mitchell Reddish)

Outline of the Message to Ephesus
1. Identification of the Addressee—2:1a
2. Identification of the Sender—2:1b
3. Words of Praise—2:2-3, 6
4. Words of Criticism—2:4
5. Exhortation—2:5
6. Appeal to Listen—2:7a
7. Promise to the Faithful—2:7b

second century, warns its readers about false teachers, apostles, and prophets. The writing tells the churches to be wary of individuals who teach false doctrines, who stay more than two days, who ask for money when leaving, or whose behavior does not cohere with their own teachings.[1] Although John gives no details about the false apostles at Ephesus, they were possibly connected with the people labeled "Nicolaitans" (2:6, 15).

In addition to problems from false leaders within the church, the Christians at Ephesus were also suffering from unnamed external threats. Christ praises them for their patient suffering and endurance, qualities that are lauded frequently in Revelation (2:13; 3:10; 13:10; 14:12).

Praise quickly turns to criticism as Christ rebukes the Ephesians for their loss of love in dealing with others. Their zeal for orthodoxy and their struggle to remain faithful under pressure exacted too heavy a cost: they forgot that their primary obligation as Christians was to act in love. Like the elder brother in the Parable of the Prodigal Son (Luke 15:11-32), they were so consumed with being right and obedient, that they lost proper perspective. Love and joy were replaced with censoriousness. As Paul so eloquently stated in 1 Corinthians 13, any act, no matter how well intentioned, that is done without love is inadequate.

Artemis of Ephesus
Artemis. 2d C. Ephesus Museum. Selçuk, Turkey.
(Credit: Mitchell Reddish)

Christ commands the Ephesian church to repent, to return to the love and compassion that formerly characterized their lives. Failure to repent and to return to the love that they had earlier would result in disciplinary action—"I will come to you and remove your lampstand from its place" (2:5). This is not an eschatological threat, but a present warning. Christ will come in judgment upon the church. To have its lampstand removed means that the church would no longer exist. The people would still have the outward trappings of a church, but they would be spiritually dead. Before they reached that point, however, Christ called them to change their ways and recover the spirit of love that once belonged to them. [Artemis of Ephesus]

The term "conquerors," used for the faithful, reflects the apocalyptic worldview that sees the world engaged in a cosmic struggle between the forces of good and evil— God versus Satan. Even though Christ has already won the decisive battle, the conflict continues daily in humanity's struggle to be faithful to God. Those who are obedient to God and resist the powers of evil contribute to the victory that will ultimately occur. The reward promised to the Ephesian Christians—"to eat from the tree of life that is in the paradise of God" (2:7)—is a reference to the garden of Eden story in Genesis 2–3 and draws on a theme found frequently in Jewish apocalyptic works, the idea that the end time will be a return to the beginning, to the paradise of Eden (cf. *1 En.* 24:4-6; *T. Levi* 18:11). Whereas the book of Genesis claims that God did not allow Adam and Eve to eat from the tree because if they had they would have lived forever (Gen 3:22), the privilege of eating from the tree and thus enjoying eternal life is now extended to those who are faithful to God.

The Message to Smyrna, 2:8-11

The ancient city of Smyrna (modern Izmir), which according to some reports was the birthplace of Homer, enjoyed a prestigious and prosperous reputation. The city was commercially successful due to its harbor and its location (approximately thirty-five miles north of Ephesus) at the end of a major route through Asia Minor. The people of Smyrna had a long history of loyalty to Rome. In 195 BC, the city built a temple to Roma, the goddess of Rome. The Roman Senate rewarded the city for its loyalty by giving the city the privilege (in AD 26) of constructing a temple in honor of the emperor Tiberius. [Outline of the Message to Smyrna]

The origins of Christianity at Smyrna are unknown. The city earned a spot in Christian history, however, when Ignatius, bishop of Antioch in Syria, stopped at Smyrna while being transported to Rome for execution around AD 107. While there, Ignatius met with Christian leaders from Asia Minor and wrote letters to several congregations. Later during his journey, he sent a letter back to the church at Smyrna and one to their bishop, Polycarp. Polycarp, like Ignatius, also suffered a martyr's fate, being executed in Smyrna around AD 156. [Map: Distances between Cities]

> **Outline of the Message to Smyrna**
> 1. Identification of the Addressee—2:8a
> 2. Identification of the Sender—2:8b
> 3. Words of Praise—2:9
> 4. Words of Criticism—(Missing)
> 5. Exhortation—2:10
> 6. Appeal to Listen—2:11a
> 7. Promise to the Faithful—2:11b

The message to the church at Smyrna is free of criticisms. The church received only praise, warning, and encouragement. Although the city of Smyrna was commercially prosperous, its Christian inhabitants apparently did not share in its wealth. The cause of their poverty is not mentioned. The church at Smyrna may have drawn its adherents from the poorer class, or

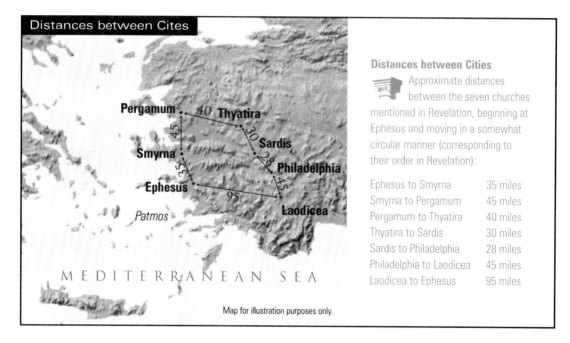

Distances between Cites

Pergamum   *40* Thyatira
         45   *30*
                     Sardis
Smyrna   *28*
         35   Philadelphia
   Ephesus   *45*
             95
   Patmos   Laodicea

MEDITERRANEAN SEA

Map for illustration purposes only.

Distances between Cities

Approximate distances between the seven churches mentioned in Revelation, beginning at Ephesus and moving in a somewhat circular manner (corresponding to their order in Revelation):

Ephesus to Smyrna	35 miles
Smyrna to Pergamum	45 miles
Pergamum to Thyatira	40 miles
Thyatira to Sardis	30 miles
Sardis to Philadelphia	28 miles
Philadelphia to Laodicea	45 miles
Laodicea to Ephesus	95 miles

their poverty may have resulted from economic discrimination against the Christians by the inhabitants of Smyrna. Materially poor as they were, they were nonetheless spiritually rich (2:9). [Travel and Communication in New Testament Times]

The major problem confronting the church at Smyrna was antagonism from the Jewish population of the city. The tone of the message indicates that the antagonism was severe. Jewish violence against the church apparently continued into the next century, as evidenced by the second-century letter from the church at Smyrna describing the death of Polycarp. This letter, known as *The Martyrdom of Polycarp*, states that the Jews of Smyrna joined with their neighbors in cheering for the death of Polycarp, even helping to gather wood for the fire for his execution.

This conflict with the Jews in Smyrna called forth a harsh verbal attack. In John's eyes, such people were not true Jews, but were a "synagogue of Satan" (2:9). They forfeited the right to be called Jews because of their attacks on the church. They claimed to be a synagogue of God, but in reality they were servants of Satan. The reader must be careful not to generalize this invective as a blanket condemnation of all Jews. John condemns the Jews at Smyrna (as well as those at Philadelphia, 3:9) for their persecution of the church, not because they are

Travel and Communication in New Testament Times

Whereas the Roman government had a reliable postal system for conveying official messages throughout the Roman Empire, the imperial post was normally not available for private use. Ordinary citizens had to rely on private couriers to carry their messages, or they imposed on friends, travelers, or merchants to convey their letters or other news. Private travelers on horseback might cover 25–30 miles in a day; pedestrians might cover 15–20 miles.

F. F. Bruce, "Travel and Communication (NT World)," *The Anchor Bible Dictionary*, ed. David Noel Freedman, 6 vols. (New York: Doubleday & Co., 1992), 6:648-53.

Smyrna
Ruins of the ancient Roman agora in Smyrna (modern Izmir). (Credit: Mitchell Reddish)

Jews. In the eyes of the government officials, as well as most of the populace at large, Jews and Christians were often viewed as belonging to the same group. Since Judaism was a legally protected religion, Christians, as long as they were thought to be a part of Judaism, enjoyed the privileges and protection afforded to Jews. By denouncing the Christians to the authorities as non-Jews, the Jews rendered Christians vulnerable to official persecution (for example, if they failed to offer sacrifices to the emperor). John warns the church at Smyrna that such persecution will soon intensify. John pulls back the curtain and reveals the true force—Satan—that is behind the persecution that the church will face. [Smyrna]

As difficult as this time of tribulation may have been, John interpreted the experience constructively. The persecution would be a time for the testing of the church's faith. The time of affliction would be brief ("ten days," that is, an indeterminate, short period) but may result in death for some of the faithful. They were not to fear, however, because Christ will reward the faithful with eternal life ("the crown of life"; cf. 1 Cor 9:25; Jas 1:12). Those so rewarded will escape "the second death" (2:11), that is, exclusion from participation in God's final kingdom (cf. 20:6, 14). [Crown of Life]

Crown of Life

Crowns were used for a variety of purposes in the Roman world. They were awarded to the victors in athletic and military contests. Politicians and priests wore them for processionals and important occasions. Brides sometimes wore crowns at their weddings, as did also the guests at the wedding feasts. The crowns were variously signs of joy, respect, honor, and victory. Often they were made of intertwined ivy, laurel, olive, or oak leaves. Some were more elaborate, made of gold and precious stones. The crown of life promised to the faithful at Smyrna (2:10) is the victor's crown. Because they remained true to their faith, even until death, they were victorious and received the crown as their reward. The crown is a symbol of the eternal life that God granted to them.

Walter Grundmann, "στέφανος, στεφανόω," *Theological Dictionary of the New Testament*, ed. Gerhard Kittel, Gerhard Friedrich, trans. Geoffrey W. Bromiley, 10 vols. (Grand Rapids: Eerdmans, 1971), 7:615-36.

The Message to Pergamum, 2:12-17

Located approximately forty-five miles north of Smyrna, Pergamum became an important military and political center during the third century BC when it was the center of the Attalid kingdom of western Asia Minor. One of its early rulers, Attalus I, entered into a military alliance with the Romans. The city of Pergamum came under Roman control in 133 BC when its king, Attalus III, died with no heirs to the throne. According to his will, the Attalid kingdom was to be given to the Romans, who created the province of Asia out of this territory. [Outline of the Message to Pergamum]

> **Outline of the Message to Pergamum**
> 1. Identification of the Addressee—2:12a
> 2. Identification of the Sender—2:12b
> 3. Words of Praise—2:13
> 4. Words of Criticism—2:14-15
> 5. Exhortation—2:16
> 6. Appeal to Listen—2:17a
> 7. Promise to the Faithful—2:17b

A large acropolis dominated the city of Pergamum, upon which were constructed various imposing buildings, including a temple of Athena, a temple of Demeter, a temple of Dionysus, a large library (second only to the one in Alexandria), a theater, a gymnasium, and a monumental colonnaded altar to Zeus (reconstructed and housed today in the

Great Altar of Zeus at Pergamum
The altar of Zeus is located in the center of a rectangular court surrounded by an Ionic colonnade. The colonnade is located on a base 100 feet square. The altar at Pergamum was the most elaborate of all the Ionian altars and the one that has the most surviving portions. The frieze covering the base is 400 feet long and over 7 feet tall.

The west front of the Great Pergamum Altar (restored). Staatliche Museen zu Berlin, Preussicher Kulturbesitz, Antikensammlung.

Great Altar
Location of the Great Altar
of Zeus in Pergamum.
(Credit: Mitchell Reddish)

Pergamum Museum in Berlin). [Great Altar of Zeus at Pergamum] [Great Altar] Various other shrines, altars, and temples were located at Pergamum. One of the most famous was the Asclepieion, the sanctuary of Asclepius, the god of healing. [Sanctuary of Asclepius]

Not only was Pergamum a center of traditional religions, but during Roman times it became a center for the imperial cult as well. In 29 BC, Caesar Augustus allowed Pergamum to build a temple dedicated to the deified emperor and to Rome. As a consequence, Pergamum became the focal point for emperor worship throughout the province of Asia.

In Revelation, the Christians in Pergamum are said to be located "where Satan's throne is" (2:13). This phrase has spawned several interpretations, all of which are feasible: (a) It refers to the magnificent altar of Zeus. (b) It refers to Pergamum as the center of imperial worship. (c) It alludes to Pergamum's role as the seat of Roman government in the province. (d) It refers to the temple of Asclepius, whose symbol was a snake. (e) It alludes to the acropolis that towered over the city and on which were located temples to various gods and goddesses.

Although the exact nature of the difficulties is not clear, it is evident from the text that the church at Pergamum was in a precarious situation. The language of v. 13 indicates that the Christians had experienced and were still experiencing persecution and suffering. In the face of such attacks, whether it was official persecution or the result of mob violence, the Pergameme Christians "held fast" and did not deny their faith. One of their colleagues, Antipas (otherwise unknown), had paid the ultimate

Sanctuary of Asclepius
Part of the Sanctuary of Asclepius in Pergamum, which
included a temple, a theater, and healing rooms.
(Credit: Mitchell Reddish)

price for his faithfulness by becoming a martyr for the sake of
Christ. Antipas is the only named victim of persecution in
Revelation.

The description of Antipas—"my witness, my faithful one"—is
modeled after the description of Jesus in 1:5 and 3:14, "the faithful
witness." Antipas demonstrated his loyalty to Christ by following
him even to death. The parallel between the titles given to Jesus
and Antipas is not accidental. Rightly understood, this parallelism
is a paradigm of John's exhortation to the churches. As Jesus was
the faithful witness, all believers are called to be faithful witnesses
like Antipas. This parallelism illustrates the call to endurance that
resounds throughout the book. The faithful witness is the one who
endures, who "holds the testimony," even at the cost of his or her
life. The *imitatio Christi* motif is at work here. Not only will
believers share in Christ's kingdom, but they must also share in his
sufferings. They are called to witness even as he did—sometimes
through suffering and death. [Witness/Martyr]

Even though they were strong in resisting the external threat of persecution, the
Christians in Pergamum were weak in
resisting internal threats to their faith.
Within the Pergamum church were individuals spreading false teachings, "the

Witness/Martyr

AΩ The Greek words *martys* ("witness") and
martyria ("testimony" or "witness") occur five
times and nine times respectively in Revelation. Being a
faithful witness is an important theme of the book. From
the Greek word *martys* was derived the English "martyr,"
denoting someone who is a faithful witness even to the
point of death.

teaching of Balaam" (2:14). According to Numbers 22–24, Balaam was a non-Israelite "seer" (prophet) who was enlisted by Balak, king of Moab, to pronounce a curse upon the Israelites. Balaam, however, refused to curse them, but instead followed the instructions of God and blessed the Israelites. Juxtaposed to this story in Numbers is the account in chapter 25 of the sexual involvement of Israelite men with foreign women and the participation of the Israelites in worship of foreign gods. Although in chapter 25 Balaam is not associated with these immoral and idolatrous acts, Numbers 31:16 explicitly places the blame on Balaam. The false teachers at Pergamum were new manifestations of Balaam because they led others to "eat food sacrificed to idols and practice fornication" (2:14). [Nicolaitans]

Eating meat that had been ritually slaughtered and dedicated to other gods was a problem the early church faced. Such meat was sold in the public markets that were often attached to pagan temples and was served at public feasts and private gatherings. Was it wrong to eat such meat? Was one implicitly participating in the worship of other gods by buying and eating such meat? Paul faced this problem in Corinth (1 Cor 8–10) where his view was that eating such meat was permissible as long as doing so did not harm the faith of those who were less mature in their understanding. Even Paul, however, acknowledged the dangers involved in this practice. The line between viewing the meat as simply food and participating in pagan worship could be easily blurred. For this reason, even though Paul allowed his Corinthian readers to eat idol meat, he thought it best that they abstain from the practice.

John was even less accommodating than was Paul. He viewed the eating of such meat as a grave violation of one's commitment to God. In a persecution setting, the dangers of accommodation to the beliefs and practices of the larger society are more severe than

---

Nicolaitans

AΩ The term "Nicolaitans" is used to describe problematic groups in Ephesus (2:6) and Pergamum (2:15). Even though "Jezebel" and her followers at Thyatira are not labeled Nicolaitans, their teachings and practices were similar to those of the Nicolaitans at Pergamum. "Jezebel" was perhaps a Nicolaitan prophet. The origin of the name "Nicolaitan" is unknown. Later church writers (Irenaeus, *Haer.* 1.26.3; Hippolytus, *Haer.* 7.24; Eusebius, *Hist. eccl.* 2.29.1-3) connected the term with Nicolaus, one of the seven men chosen in the book of Acts to help supervise the distribution of goods to the widows in the Jerusalem church (Acts 6:5). There is no evidence, however, that this Nicolaus

or his followers had any connection with the groups mentioned in Revelation.

Another suggestion for the origin of the name "Nicolaitans" draws upon the possible etymology of the Greek word *Nikolaitōn*, explaining it as derived from two Greek words *nika laon*, meaning "he has conquered the people." If this derivation is correct, it likely arose because of the comparison of the Nicolaitans to Balaam (2:14), whose name was sometimes explained to mean "he has consumed the people." The name "Nicolaitans" would then be the Greek version of "Balaamites." This explanation for the origin of the name is possible, but it is equally plausible that the group was named for one of its leaders.

they are in a more benign situation. The different contexts likely explain the differences in the attitudes of John and Paul to this problem. Faced with the danger of Christians who might compromise their beliefs in order to avoid persecution or suffering, John took a rigorous stand against entanglements with other cults.

The charge against the Pergameme Christians, that they practiced fornication, is probably metaphorical and not to be understood literally as sexual immorality. Biblical writers often use sexual imagery to describe religious unfaithfulness (Exod 34:16; Lev 20:5; Jer 3:1-10; Ezek 16:15-43; 23:1-49; Hos 1:2; 5:3). To be unfaithful to God is to commit religious adultery. John uses sexual imagery in this way elsewhere in Revelation (17:2, 5; 18:3, 9). The heretical group in the church at Pergamum was similar to the group at Ephesus. Both are called Nicolaitans. The difference lies in the churches' response to these people. The Ephesian church was diligent in resisting the menace of the Nicolaitans, whereas the church at Pergamum permitted their practices. The church at Pergamum needed to repent and see the danger in what they were doing. Their lax attitude was endangering the integrity of their faith and would result in a visit from Christ in judgment upon the Nicolaitans.

Those who are faithful will receive hidden manna and a white stone with a new name inscribed upon it. Both of these symbols carry eschatological meanings. Jewish tradition claimed that the miracle of manna provided to the Israelites during their wilderness wanderings would be repeated for God's people in the messianic kingdom (see *2 Bar.* 29:4-8). White stones (as opposed to black ones) were used by jurors in antiquity to vote for acquittal of an accused. White stones were also used as entrance tickets to plays and banquets. Either of these explanations could apply, the former indicating that the faithful are acquitted in the final judgment, the latter symbolizing their entrance into the messianic banquet. Some commentators have suggested that the white stone serves as an amulet whose significance is in the new, secret name that it bears. Especially in magic, names were considered powerful. Thus the name is kept secret and is not revealed. The "new name" is probably a new name for the faithful, symbolizing their new character and status, and not the secret name of God or Christ, as some interpreters have suggested. The color white is common in Revelation as a symbol of victory.

The Message to Thyatira, 2:18-29

Thyatira has been described as "the least known, least important and least remarkable" of the seven cities addressed in Revelation.[2] The city was located in the region of Lydia in western Asia Minor, about thirty-five miles inland from the Aegean Sea. Situated at the intersection of several trade routes, Thyatira was home to a large number of trade guilds that functioned as social and religious clubs or organizations. The wool and textile

> **Outline of the Message to Thyatira**
> 1. Identification of the Addressee—2:18a
> 2. Identification of the Sender—2:18b
> 3. Words of Praise—2:19
> 4. Words of Criticism—2:20-23
> 5. Exhortation—2:24-25
> 6. Appeal to Listen—2:29
> 7. Promise to the Faithful—2:26-28

industries were particularly strong in Thyatira, as was also the production of purple dye. The book of Acts describes Paul's encounter in Philippi with Lydia, a native of Thyatira, who was a seller of purple cloth (16:14-15). [Outline of the Message to Thyatira]

The church at Thyatira received strong praise, being lauded for its "love, faith, service, and patient endurance" (2:19). Unlike the church at Ephesus, which was guilty of abandoning the love it initially had, the church at Thyatira was a growing and maturing

Thyatira
These marble ruins, dated to the 2d and 4th centuries AD, are portions of the arches and pillars from the monumental entrance to the marble colonnaded street at Thyatira (Akhisar) in Turkey. (Credit: Mitchell Reddish)

church, one whose "last works are greater than the first" (2:19). The problem at Thyatira was the church's toleration of a "false" prophet and teacher, a woman symbolically called "Jezebel." An infamous character from the Hebrew Bible, Jezebel was a foreign wife of King Ahab of Israel. According to 1 and 2 Kings, Jezebel was a promoter of Baal worship and a persecutor of the prophets of Yahweh. Because the biblical tradition often used sexual imagery to describe idolatry, Jezebel was accused of being guilty of "many whoredoms" (2 Kgs 9:22). This metaphorical use of sexual imagery explains the charge of fornication leveled against the Thyatiran "Jezebel." She is a seducer who leads the people astray with her false teachings, causing them to "commit adultery with her" (2:22).

The clue to the erroneous teaching of this woman is in the additional charge that she leads the people "to eat food sacrificed to idols" (2:20). As with the message to the church at Pergamum, this charge refers to the practice of eating meat that had been ritually offered to other gods. The problem would have been particularly acute in a place like Thyatira with its numerous trade guilds that were themselves often associated with particular deities. At the feasts of the guilds, meat that had been offered to the gods was served. What was a Christian to do? Did eating such meat involve one in the worship of these other gods? [Thyatira]

The dilemma faced by these early Christians was one of assimilation to their culture. To what extent could one participate and not compromise one's faith? As already noted, this is not the only place where the New Testament addresses this problem. Paul also dealt with the issue in 1 Corinthians 8–10 (cf. the "Apostolic Decree" in Acts 15:20, 29). Paul, "Jezebel," and John have different responses to this issue. "Jezebel" was more accepting of the cultural practices around her, embracing and perhaps even encouraging them. Paul took a moderating stance, conceding that participating in certain

Gnosticism

The theological problems confronting the churches in Asia Minor are sometimes viewed as a form of Gnosticism. The term "Gnosticism" refers to a variety of religious systems in the ancient world that offered salvation through knowledge. (The Greek word for "knowledge" is *gnōsis*.) Gnostic systems viewed the physical world as evil. A person gained salvation by acquiring the knowledge that the material world, created by a lesser god, is evil and transient and that the spiritual realm is the true goal of the enlightened. Salvation involved a deliverance from the evil of the physical body. Some gnostics taught avoidance of the physical world and its pleasures through asceticism; others took the opposite approach, advocating a libertine lifestyle. They argued that since the material world was not important, one could do whatever one chose with the physical body as long as one was properly attuned to the spiritual world.

The Nicolaitans and followers of "Jezebel" mentioned in the messages to Ephesus, Pergamum, and Thyatira were guilty of eating food sacrificed to idols and "practicing fornication" (2:14, 20). Their argument, like that of some gnostics, could have been that their physical behavior was inconsequential. They had achieved the higher knowledge ("the deep things," 2:24), that is, the knowledge that the true child of God was concerned only with spiritual realities.

cultural activities was not in itself wrong, but at the same time worrying about its damaging effects on weaker Christians. John, however, took a very hard-line approach. He allowed no room for compromise. To eat meat that had been offered to other gods was tantamount to worshiping these gods. The only choice for faithful Christians, in his view, was to abstain totally from such practices.

The unacceptable teachings and practices of "Jezebel" and her followers are characterized as "what some call 'the deep things of Satan' " (2:24). This can be understood in two ways. On the one hand, "Jezebel" could have been claiming a more mature, even esoteric spiritual insight for herself and her followers, what she would have referred to as "the deep things of God." John sarcastically labels her beliefs for what they really are—"the deep things of Satan." On the other hand, the phrase "the deep things of Satan" could have come from "Jezebel" herself. She could have claimed that to participate in the guild feasts or cultic meals was indeed to enter the domain of Satan and, consequently, to learn his secrets and possibly gain power over him. Yet she and her followers were above danger because of their more mature faith or special knowledge. [Gnosticism]

"Jezebel" had been warned previously about her false teachings and practices, but she refused to change her ways (2:21). Because of her refusal, she was punished. "Throwing her on a bed" likely means a sickbed. (The Greek word *klinē* can mean a bed, a dining couch, or a sickbed.) Thus the punishment is that God would strike her with an illness. The phrase has a double meaning, however, suggesting a sexual implication. She liked the bed so much that Christ would throw her into it. But this bed is not one of sexual (idolatrous) pleasures, but one of pain and suffering. This is an example of "measure-for-measure" punishment in which the punishment suits the offense. The woman's followers would also be punished, being thrown "into great distress" or even killed (2:22-23).

No other task was given to the faithful except that they hold fast to the way they have been following. Adapting a passage from Psalm 2, Christ promises to the faithful that they will share in his power and authority (2:26-27). They will also be given "the morning star" (2:28). Since the text describes Christ as "the bright morning star" in 22:16, this may be only a promise to the believers of the abiding presence of Jesus, which is with them. On the other hand, the morning star is Venus, in ancient times often the symbol of sovereignty. Thus, to receive the morning star may be a poetic restatement of the promise of authority and power in vv. 26-27.[3]

CONNECTIONS

The Christians of Asia Minor were struggling with how to live out their Christian faith in their political, social, and economic situations. Too often, people read the book of Revelation as a document dealing with future events, unrelated to the present circumstances of life. The contents of these seven messages, however, anchor the book firmly in the everyday realities of life. Here are men and women asking, "To what extent can we be involved in our society and still maintain our commitment to Christ? Can we join with our neighbors in the public feasts and celebrations? Can we belong to the civic clubs and the professional organizations that sometimes have practices that we find unacceptable? What if our jobs and even our lives are at risk if we do not participate?" The modern reader will not have to listen long before hearing the echoes of these same questions in the lives of church members today.

Cultural accommodation is the issue that surfaces in these verses. How much compromise with non-Christian beliefs and practices is acceptable? To use the terminology of the Apostle Paul, to what extent can one be a part of the world without being "conformed to this world" (Rom 12:2)? Paul is apparently more lenient in his answer to this question than is John of Patmos. Is John's stricter attitude the correct one? [Guilds and Associations in the Roman World]

The danger that John sees is a real threat to Christian life. It is easy to be so accepting of the beliefs and lifestyles of others that one loses the distinctiveness of the Christian faith. "Openness" and "acceptance" can degenerate into a laissez-faire attitude that does not take seriously the church's calling to be "a kingdom, priests serving his God and Father" (1:6); that is, the church is not the same as society. It must be distinct, set apart.

The use of sexual imagery in the letters is appropriate. The temptation to compromise one's beliefs is often very seductive and alluring. Like sexual desires, the desire to be liked, to be successful, or to "fit in" with everyone else is a powerful desire. John clearly saw, however, that faithfulness to God demands a choice.

Cultural accommodation is as much a danger in modern society as it was in the first century, perhaps even more so. Whereas John's

Guilds and Associations in the Roman World

"Clubs and associations afforded opportunities of common worship, enjoyment of social intercourse, and in some cases the satisfaction of holding office. These societies further promoted a spirit of comradeship and mutual aid in time of difficulty. Most of them tended to funerary responsibilities and provided tombstones. Associations formed the natural organization for foreigners and foreign worship entering a city. Clubs were associated with a deity, often met in a temple, offered libations and sacrifices, and ate meat from idol temples.... Political, economic, and family life and public entertainment were organized around the pagan deities; so also were the ordinary social groupings."

Everett Ferguson, *Backgrounds of Early Christianity,* 2d ed. (Grand Rapids: Eerdmans, 1993), 136.

readers could readily perceive a difference between their beliefs and practices and those of the larger Roman society, modern culture (particularly in the United States) is often seen as being "Christian," or at least sympathetic to Christianity. As such, the institutions and structures of society are viewed as "Christian" institutions and structures. Democracy and capitalism are viewed as biblical ideals. America itself becomes the new "promised land." To fight for Western values and ideals is equated with fighting for Christian values. In such a setting, the danger of Christianity losing its "otherness" is very strong.

The challenge for the church is to find a way to be a part of the society in which it lives without losing its own identity. In the churches of Asia Minor, John saw two equally troubling situations. On the one hand, the church at Ephesus was so adamant in maintaining its theological correctness that it became rigid and unloving. On the other hand, the church at Thyatira had become so lax and accommodating that it was in danger of losing its Christian voice. In his classic work *Christ and Culture*, H. Richard Niebuhr explained the various approaches that the Christian church has taken throughout its history to the problem of cultural accommodation. These approaches he labeled "Christ Against Culture," "The Christ of Culture," "Christ Above Culture," "Christ and Culture in Paradox," and "Christ the Transformer of Culture." Although Niebuhr viewed the last approach as the best, he discussed the problems and values of each approach, noting that each has a contribution to make to the church's struggle of working out a proper relation between Christ and culture. He wrote, "No Christian thought can encompass the thought of the Master, and that as the body is one but has many members so also the church."[4] That early Christians (such as John of Patmos and Paul) as well as modern ones arrived at different answers to these questions should caution the interpreter from too hastily reaching a conclusion.

NOTES

[1] The *Didache* 11–13.

[2] Colin J. Hemer, *The Letters to the Seven Churches of Asia in Their Local Setting* (Sheffield: Sheffield Academic Press, 1989), 106.

[3] George R. Beasley-Murray, *The Book of Revelation*, New Century Bible (Greenwood SC: Attic, 1974), 93-94.

[4] H. Richard Niebuhr, *Christ and Culture* (New York: Harper & Row, 1951), 229.

THE MESSAGES TO THE OTHER THREE CHURCHES

3:1-22

COMMENTARY

The Message to Sardis, 3:1-6

During the seventh and sixth centuries BC, Sardis was the capital of the Lydian Empire in Asia Minor, two of whose famous kings were Gyges and Croesus. Sardis was legendary for its great wealth in antiquity due to the gold in the region. During the sixth century, Cyrus of Persia captured Sardis and made it a part of his empire, ending the city's role as the capital of an independent empire. Later, on separate occasions, both Alexander the Great and Antiochus III captured the city. During the time of John of Patmos, the city was under Roman control. In AD 17, Sardis, along with several other cities in Asia Minor, suffered a devastating earthquake, but with the help of funds from the emperor Tiberius, the city was able to rebuild. Because of its location at the intersection of major roads through Asia Minor, Sardis enjoyed success as a commercial center. Josephus indicated that the city contained a sizable population of Jewish residents (*Ant.* 14 §259-261; 16 §166, 171). [Temple of Artemis] [Map: Seven Cities 2]

Temple of Artemis
Temple of Artemis at Sardis, with the acropolis in the background. (Credit: Mitchell Reddish)

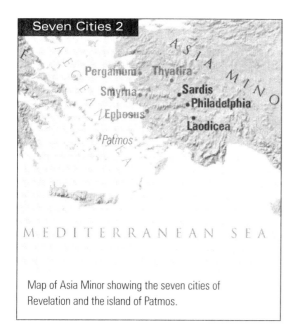

Map of Asia Minor showing the seven cities of
Revelation and the island of Patmos.

Outline of the Message to Sardis
1. Identification of the Addressee—3:1a
2. Identification of the Sender—3:1b
3. Words of Praise—3:4
4. Words of Criticism—3:1c
5. Exhortation—3:2-3
6. Promise to the Faithful—3:5
7. Appeal to Listen—3:6

The speaker of this message is identified as the one "who has the seven spirits of God and the seven stars" (3:1), descriptions drawn from 1:4, 16, and 20. Christ holds in his hands not only the churches themselves ("the seven stars"), but also the spirit of God ("the seven spirits") that is sent to those churches. [Outline of the Message to Sardis]

John uses five imperatives in this address to the church at Sardis. The people are told to "wake up," to "strengthen," to "remember," to "obey" and to "repent." The Greek word in vv. 2-3, translated in the NRSV as "wake up" (*grēgoreō*), can also mean "be alert." Both meanings fit the context well. A "dead" church needs to wake up from its death-like sleep if it is going to function. On the other hand, a church that does not want to be caught unprepared by the sudden appearance of Christ must be watchful and alert. The church at Sardis is in critical condition. It is so far gone that it can be described as already dead. Drastic action is required if the church is going to recover from its near-fatal condition. It must strengthen the weakened relationship with God that it has. The remedy for the church's recovery will lie in its ability to remember what it used to be and to return to that early commitment, to remember the teachings and traditions it had received and to obey them. The people must change their current practices ("repent"). Only by returning to the true message of the gospel and obeying it can the church survive.

Christ accuses the church at Sardis of not having any "works perfect in the sight of my God" (v. 2). *Peplērōmena* can mean "completed" as well as "perfect." The church is guilty of not fulfilling its calling. It has stopped short of completing its role as God's people. Apparently they had done a good job of fooling everyone—including themselves—that they were faithful followers of Christ. Their outward appearance does not deceive Christ, however, who recognizes the inadequacy and failures of the church. [Judgment]

The text does not provide the reader with any specifics about the situation at Sardis. Obviously the original recipients of this message would have known the cause of their spiritual near-death existence. Perhaps the church at Sardis, like the believers at Ephesus, Pergamum, and Thyatira, had compromised its faith through accommodation to society to such an extent that the church barely existed anymore. To those outside the church, it still seemed alive, perhaps even thriving, because it readily accepted and involved itself in the cultural, social, and political activities of the larger society. Measured by the standards of the prevailing culture, the church was vibrant. Measured by the standards of Christ, however, the church was for all practical purposes dead. Any church—ancient or modern—that gauges its health only by the measures of society (popularity, membership size, financial resources, social prestige, and acceptance) is in danger of mistaking sick religion for a vital faith. [Cowper's Sardis]

After providing instructions for how the church at Sardis can change its present situation and bring life back to its corpse-like state, Christ issues a warning to them. If they do not change, he will come to them "like a thief, and you will not know at what hour I will come to you" (3:3), imagery that occurs several times in the New Testament to describe the unexpected arrival of Christ (cf. Matt 24:42-44; Luke 12:39-40; 1 Thess 5:2; 2 Pet 3:10). As is the case in the warnings to the churches at Ephesus, Pergamum, and Thyatira, this warning refers to Christ's coming in judgment on the churches during the present situation, not at the end of time. John has here taken imagery used elsewhere in the New Testament to refer to the eschatological return of the Son of Man and adapted it to Christ's judgment within history. The people at Sardis would have heard in this warning a historical allusion to the two times in their past when the city of Sardis, almost impregnable because of its location on a high acropolis, was overtaken when the

Judgment

"Why did John not simply shower the churches with love and praise? Because John was a prophet and prophets have very high standards. But also because people and churches, then and now, who become morally lax and spiritually lazy, who abandon the faith journey for a self-satisfied dwelling place veneered with the pretense of religion, and who continue to be told how wonderfully perfect *they are,* tend to sink in the mire of their own lethargy and sin."

Joseph R. Jeter Jr., "I Have This Against You," *Preaching Through the Apocalypse: Sermons from Revelation,* ed. Cornish R. Rogers and Joseph R. Jeter Jr. (St. Louis: Chalice, 1992), 71.

Cowper's Sardis
"Sardis" by William Cowper

"Write to Sardis," saith the Lord,
    And write what he declares,
He whose Spirit and whose word,
    Upholds the seven stars:
"All thy works and ways I search,
    Find thy zeal and love decayed:
Thou art called a living church,
    But thou art cold and dead.
"Watch, remember, seek, and strive,
    Exert thy former pains;
Let thy timely care revive,
    And strengthen what remains:
Cleanse thine heart, thy works amend,
    Former times to mind recall,
Lest my sudden stroke descend,
    And smite thee once for all.
"Yet I number now in thee
    A few that are upright:
These my Father's face shall see,
    And walk with me in white,
When in judgment I appear,
    They for mine shall be confessed;
Let my faithful servants hear,
    And woe be to the rest!"

Robert Atwan and Laurance Wieder, eds., *Chapters into Verse: Poetry in English Inspired by the Bible* (Oxford: Oxford University Press, 1993), 2:341-42.

Sneak Attacks

Twice in its history, enemy armies captured the city of Sardis due to the lack of diligence by the city. During the 6th century BC, Cyrus of Persia laid siege to Sardis and was successful in capturing the city when one of his soldiers was able to climb up the acropolis at an unguarded spot and enter the city. Over three centuries later, Antiochus III was also able to capture the city due to the negligence of its defenders.

soldiers became lax in their watchfulness. [Sneak Attacks]

A few in the church in Sardis have remained faithful. They are the faint heartbeats in the nearly dead body of the Sardis church. Apart from their steadfastness and endurance in faith, the church would have been completely lifeless, only a corpse. Since they have not "soiled their clothes" (v. 4), they will be allowed to walk with Christ dressed in white robes, the symbol of purity, celebration, and victory. [White Robes] If the others in the church at Sardis heed the warning and repent, they too will become conquerors and will receive the white robe as a sign of their righteousness. Additionally, those who conquer will not have their names removed from the Book of Life, that is, the registry of those who belong to the people of God. The converse of this assurance to the faithful, though not stated, is certainly implied— those who are not faithful will have their names expunged from the Book of Life and will lose their place in God's fellowship. This is a sobering wake-up call to those who take their relationship to God for granted. As Wilfrid Harrington has noted, "While one cannot earn the right to have one's name in this book, one can forfeit it."[1] Furthermore, Christ will personally acknowledge and claim as true children of God those who are faithful (cf. Matt 10:32-33; Luke 12:8-9). [Nominal Christianity]

White Robes

AΩ White is a common symbol of purity or holiness. The contrast between the robes that have been soiled through sinfulness and the white robes that are given to the faithful indicates that purity and holiness are at least a part of the symbolism intended here. The connection of white to purity and holiness is likely the reason that white is the color associated with the clothing of God (Dan 7:9) and heavenly beings (Matt 28:3; Mark 16:5). When Jesus was transfigured, his clothes became a dazzling white, symbolizing his glorification (Mark 9:3; Matt 17:2; Luke 9:29). White robes were also associated with times of celebration and victory. White robes, therefore, are an appropriate symbol of eternal life.

The word "name" appears four times in the message to Sardis— vv. 1, 4 ("persons" [NRSV, v. 4] is literally "names" in the Greek), and twice in v. 5. This word-play on "name" emphasizes the problem at Sardis. They have become a church in name only. They have a name for being alive, but their name or reputation is false. Because of their faithlessness, they will lose even their names when they are blotted out of the Book of Life and their names are not

Nominal Christianity

"A church is alive only when it is moved by the life of Jesus Christ and, in concrete life experience, authenticates the salvation it has received. Christianity in name only falls under the judgment of the Lord to whose name it falsely appeals."

Jürgen Roloff, *The Revelation of John: A Continental Commentary,* Continental Commentaries, trans. John E. Alsup (Minneapolis: Fortress, 1993), 58.

confessed or recognized. Those whose names are true will have their names kept in the Book of Life and their names (themselves) welcomed by God. [Book of Life]

The Message to Philadelphia, 3:7-13

The city of Philadelphia, located approximately thirty miles southeast of Sardis, was named for Attalus Philadelphus, the Attalid king from 159–138 BC. Because of his loyalty to his brother Eumenese II, who preceded him as king (197–159 BC), Attalus earned the nickname "Philadelphus," meaning brotherly love. Either Eumenese or Attalus was responsible for founding the city. The area in which Philadelphia was located was very fertile land, especially good for growing grapes. Unfortunately, the area was also subject to frequent earthquake activity. The devastating earthquake that hit the area in AD 17 and destroyed Sardis also did extensive damage to Philadelphia. Like Sardis, Philadelphia received an imperial exemption from taxation for five years in order to aid the city in rebuilding. Early in the second century, Ignatius, bishop of Antioch in Syria, passed through Philadelphia as a prisoner on his way to his martyrdom in Rome. Farther along on his journey, while at Troas, he wrote a letter to the church at Philadelphia encouraging them to remain united and to support their bishop and other church leaders. [Outline of the Message to Philadelphia]

The self-identification of the speaker of the message to the church at Philadelphia is different from that in the other messages. In the other messages, the descriptions of the speaker are drawn from the description of the exalted Christ at the end of chapter 1 or from earlier descriptions of Jesus in chapter 1 (in the case of the message to Laodicea). The description of Christ in 3:7, however, does not draw directly from imagery in the preceding chapter. Here we find a fresh description, using terms taken from the Hebrew Bible. Jesus is "the holy one, the true one." Writers in the Hebrew Bible often applied the word "holy" to God or the things of God. In the book of Isaiah particularly, "the holy one" is used as a title for God (e.g., 1:4; 5:19; 40:25). Likewise, the Septuagint (the Greek version of the Hebrew Bible) describes God as being *alēthinos*, the word translated here as "true," meaning faithful or dependable (Exod 34:16; Num 14:18; Isa 65:16). As elsewhere in

Book of Life

AΩ The idea of a heavenly "book of life" that contains the names of the living is found in the Hebrew Bible (Exod 32:32; Ps 69:28; Isa 4:3) as well as in other ancient Near Eastern texts. Later writings speak of a book that serves as a registry of those destined for eternal salvation, thus a heavenly roll book of the citizens of God's kingdom (Dan 12:1; Phil 4:3; *1 En.* 108:3; cf. Luke 10:20; Heb 12:23).

Outline of the Message to Philadelphia
1. Identification of the Addressee—3:7a
2. Identification of the Sender—3:7b
3. Words of Praise—3:8-10
4. Words of Criticism—(Missing)
5. Exhortation—3:11
6. Promise to the Faithful—3:12
7. Appeal to Listen—3:13

Philadelphia
Ruins of a Byzantine church in Philadelphia (modern Alaşehir), Turkey. (Credit: Mitchell Reddish)

Revelation, here a description normally applied to God is applied to Jesus (in 6:10, God is called "holy and true"). The designation of Jesus as the one who holds the "key of David" and "who opens and no one will shut, who shuts and no one opens" is also drawn from the Hebrew Bible. In Isaiah 22:22, God confers "the key of the house of David" upon Eliakim, King Hezekiah's steward, symbolizing the authority to grant admittance and exercise control over the palace. That the exalted Christ possesses the key of David indicates his authority to grant or deny access to God's kingdom. The mention of the key that Christ possesses should perhaps be connected also with the statement in 1:18 that he has "the keys of Death and of Hades," for to be granted entrance into God's kingdom is to be granted life; to be denied entrance is to experience death (cf. Matt 16:19).

Like the message to Smyrna, the message to Philadelphia contains no words of criticism or judgment on the church. Both churches receive only praise and encouragement. Both seem to be experiencing problems from the Jewish people in their communities, and both contain the same polemical invective directed at the

Jewish community ("synagogue of Satan"). Furthermore, both congregations are described as being marginalized in some way: the church at Smyrna is physically poor, and the church at Philadelphia has little power. [Philadelphia]

The body of the message to Philadelphia continues the door imagery contained in the opening description of Christ. In v. 8, Christ declares, "Look, I have set before you an open door, which no one is able to shut." Some commentators have looked to other New Testament uses of the imagery of an open door (1 Cor 16:9; 2 Cor 2:12; Acts 14:27) to help interpret the meaning of the imagery in this passage. Elsewhere in the New Testament the open door represents an opportunity for evangelism, a chance for the church to share the gospel message. Here, however, the context suggests another meaning. The problem facing the church at Philadelphia has arisen from "those who say that they are Jews and are not, but are lying" (v. 9). The church has apparently been suffering at the hands of the Jewish community in Philadelphia. The situation may have been a political/social crisis in which the Christians were denounced publicly as being a group separate from Judaism and thus not under the privileges and protections afforded the Jews by the Roman government. If such were the case, the Christians were vulnerable to hostility and persecution. [John's Letters to the Seven Churches]

On the other hand, the problem may have been theological. The Jews in Philadelphia may have claimed that they and they alone were the true people of God. They may have excluded the Christians from participating in synagogue life. Shut out by the Jews, the Christians are instead now comforted by Christ, who reassures them that he holds the key to fellowship with God. He has opened the door to the kingdom of God for this church, and no one, not even the Jews in Philadelphia, is able to close this door. By their exclusion of the Christians and their rejection of Jesus, the Jews in Philadelphia have shut the door on themselves. They are no longer truly Jews, that is, God's people. They have instead become partners with Satan. As a result, they will be forced to "come and bow down before your feet," a reference to an idea expressed several times in Isaiah (45:14; 49:23; 60:14) that ultimately the Gentiles will bow down in subjection to the people of God. Here the scenario is reversed. The Jews are the ones who must bow down. They will be forced to admit that the church is indeed the true people of God.

In spite of its difficulties, the church at Philadelphia is praised by Christ for its loyalty and trustworthiness. The Christians have

John's Letters to the Seven Churches

In this scene from the *Douce Apocalypse,* John is preparing to write messages to the seven churches. He has picked up his penknife in his left hand and has turned his head to hear the messages being given to him. To his right can be seen the seven churches, each containing the angel of that church.

The Seven Churches from the *Douce Apocalypse.* MS Douce 180, p. 2. Bodleian Library. Oxford, England. (Credit: The Bodleian Library, University of Oxford)

remained strong and have not denied their allegiance to Christ. They may be small in political or social power ("little power," v. 8), but their endurance and faithfulness are strong. Because they have been so strong in their commitment to Christ, he will reward them with special protection during the coming time of trial. A play on words occurs here in Greek. As they have "kept" his word, he will "keep" them from the difficulties that lie ahead. As they were faithful to him, he will likewise be faithful to them. To "keep" them from the coming trials does not mean that the church will be exempt from the difficulties. Rather, this is a promise of Christ's abiding presence with the church that will strengthen and sustain it regardless of the trials ahead.

What is the "hour of trial" that is to come? John describes it as one that will "test the inhabitants of the earth" (v. 10). A common idea in apocalyptic literature was that a series of eschatological woes would precede the end of the world (see Mark 13; 2 Esd 5:1-13; 6:11-28; 8:63–9:13; *2 Bar.* 25:1–27:15; 32:6; 70:1–71:1). These would include a severe time of testing for the people on the earth. For the wicked, these events would be a means of punishment; the faithful, however, would be protected by God during these terrible calamities. This time of tribulation is different from the impending "ten days" of affliction about which Christ has warned the church at Smyrna (2:10). The warning to the church at Smyrna concerned a limited period of persecution that was about to break out against the church. The "hour of trial" (3:10), on the other hand, is a part of God's punishment against the wicked of the earth.

The promise of the exalted Christ that he is "coming soon" (v. 11) can be understood as a reference to his eschatological return or to his coming to the church within history. Elsewhere in the messages to the churches, the references to Christ's coming appear in most cases to designate his coming in judgment upon the historical situations of the churches (2:5, 16, 22-23; 3:3). Their unfaithfulness will not go unnoticed. They will be punished for their disobedience and sinfulness. Here in the message to Philadelphia, however, the promise of Christ's coming is not a threat, but a word of hope, a hope that will be realized when Christ returns. Christ tells those who are faithful that they will not have to endure much longer because he will come soon to usher in God's final kingdom. Their task in the interim is to "hold fast" (3:11; cf. 2:25) and not give up their faith. By remaining faithful they will not lose their crowns, here a symbol of victory and celebration (cf. 2:10).

Christ promises two rewards to those who conquer. First, they will be made pillars in the temple of God; and second, they will have special names inscribed on them. Being a pillar in the temple of God is a metaphor for a place of honor and security in the presence of God. (The temple in Jerusalem was no longer standing, the Romans having destroyed it in AD 70.) This promise is not a contradiction of John's vision of the new Jerusalem in chapters 21–22 where no temple is to be found. John's language here is figurative language. As a pillar represents a firm support for a building, John assures the faithful that their presence among God's people is firm and secure. Not only is their position in God's kingdom secure, but it is an exalted position. They will be pillars, the same metaphor used in Galatians 2:9 for Peter, James, and John as foundational leaders of the early church. The pillars as symbols of strength, along with the words of reassurance that those who will be placed in the temple as pillars "will never go out of it," are often interpreted in light of the history of earthquakes in Philadelphia. For people who have experienced firsthand the instability and impermanence of buildings during a severe earthquake and who at times have had to flee their homes and city to keep from being injured or killed by tumbling buildings, the promise that they will be a pillar (of strength) and will never have to go out of the temple will indeed be good news.

While the geological history of the community may have affected how the original readers heard the promise given here, the tensions between the church and the synagogue may also have colored their hearing of this promise. If the Jewish Christians had been excluded from the synagogue and told that they were not a part of the people of God, then the promise that they "will never go out of" the temple of God would have been heard as assurance that even though they might be excluded from the synagogues ("of Satan"), they would not be excluded from the true community of God.

Christ declares that three names will be written on the faithful "pillars": the name of God, the name of God's city, and Christ's new name. Inscriptions on pillars in ancient temples were common as a way of indicating to whom the temple was dedicated or who was being honored by the pillar. Here, bearing the name of God and God's city indicates ownership. They will be God's people, God's own possession, enrolled as citizens of the heavenly Jerusalem. The new name of Christ that will also be inscribed on the "pillars" is not stated. That is a part of the mystery not yet revealed. To keep the name secret is a part of John's artistry as a writer. He tantalizes the reader with revelations still unrevealed. To bear the name of Christ is a high honor. This reward is especially fitting for the people at Philadelphia. They are the ones who did not deny Christ's name, even in the face of opposition. Now those who kept "the name" will be inscribed with the name. The image of being marked with the name of God and Christ will appear again in 14:1-5.

The Message to Laodicea, 3:14-22

The final message is addressed to the church at Laodicea, a city located in the Lycus River valley, approximately forty miles southeast of Philadelphia and one hundred miles east of Ephesus. The city of Colossae, known to New Testament readers because one of

Laodicea
Unexcavated Hellenistic theater at Laodicea. (Credit: Mitchell Reddish)

the letters in the New Testament was addressed to the church there, was also located in the Lycus Valley, only about ten miles from Laodicea. Laodicea was established in the middle of the third century BC by the Seleucid king, Antiochus II, who named the city after his wife Laodice (whom he divorced soon after). Earlier settlements on this site were called Diospolis and Rhoas. Situated at the intersection of the main east-west highway connecting Ephesus with the western area of Asia Minor and the north-south highway connecting Pergamum and Sardis with the southern coast, the city grew in importance and by the first century AD had surpassed Colossae as the leading city of the area.

Laodicea was famous for its banking industry, its textile production, and its medical school. All three of these aspects of the city's reputation are reflected in the message to the church located there, as will be seen in the discussion that follows. During the first century AD, the city was economically prosperous. When an earthquake destroyed the city in AD 60, the city refused imperial assistance, instead opting to rebuild the city out of its own financial resources. [Laodicea]

Among the many gods and goddesses honored and worshiped at Laodicea, the main god worshiped was Zeus. Indirect evidence from ancient sources points also to a sizable Jewish population in Laodicea. The New Testament provides some hints about the spread of Christianity to Laodicea. Likely, associates of Paul established the church, perhaps during Paul's period of ministry at Ephesus (Acts 19). Paul himself had apparently not visited Colossae or Laodicea (Col 2:1). The Letter to the Colossians mentions Epaphras as the leader and likely founder of the Colossian church (1:7), as well as one who "has worked hard for you and for those in Laodicea and in Hierapolis" (4:13). Epaphras probably spread the Christian message throughout the cities of the Lycus Valley, including Laodicea. (Even if Paul did not actually write Colossians, but one of his followers wrote it at a later date, the letter still represents a strong tradition concerning the origin of the Laodicean congregation.) According to Colossians 4:16, the churches at Colossae and Laodicea were instructed to exchange the letters that had been sent to each of them. [Outline of the Message to Laodicea]

Outline of the Message to Laodicea
1. Identification of the Addressee—3:14a
2. Identification of the Sender—3:14b
3. Words of Praise—(Missing)
4. Words of Criticism—3:15-17
5. Exhortation—3:18-20
6. Promise to the Faithful—3:21
7. Appeal to Listen—3:22

The opening verse of this message identifies the speaker as "the Amen, the faithful and true witness, the origin of God's creation" (3:14). The description of Christ as "the Amen" reflects the Masoretic Text of Isaiah 65:16, which uses the Hebrew word *'āmēn*, meaning "truly" or "verily," to describe God (NRSV: "faithfulness"). In both Judaism and the early church, "amen" was used as a way of signifying what was true and valid. Individuals and communities in worship uttered the "amen" after prayers, doxologies, and blessings as a way of confirming and joining themselves to what had been said. Jesus is the ultimate "Amen," the epitome of truth and faithfulness. This is reinforced by the following words applied to him, "the faithful and true witness." Both meanings of faithful—obedient and trustworthy—are appropriate here. Jesus is faithful in that he has been obedient to God. He was the faithful witness throughout his entire earthly existence as he bore testimony to God. Even when his witness cost him his life, he remained faithful. Yet he is faithful also in the sense of being dependable. His word is true and reliable. The promises he gives in these messages to the churches (as well as the words of warning) are not empty assurances. Christ can be trusted to do what he says. [Amen]

Amen

AΩ Some commentators have suggested another meaning for "Amen" in 3:14, claiming that it is the transliteration of a different Hebrew word (*'āmôn*), meaning "a master worker." This word appears in Prov 8:30 as a metaphor for wisdom, which is described as the first of God's creations and as God's assistant who is beside God during creation (8:22). This suggestion is tempting because of the final designation of Christ in 3:14, "the origin of God's creation," an idea similar to Prov 8:22. The problem with this suggestion, however, is that it presumes that the intended readers (or hearers) of Revelation would have known Hebrew and would have made the connection between the Greek *amēn* and the Hebrew *'āmôn* (used in Prov 8:30). That presumption is not realistic.

The last title applied to Christ in 3:14 identifies him as "the origin [or "beginning"] of God's creation." A similar description of Christ appears in Colossians 1:15-20 (cf. John 1:2-3; Heb 1:2). If indeed the church at Colossae had exchanged letters from Paul with the church at Laodicea (see Col 4:16), then the Laodiceans would have been familiar with this image of Christ. This phrase may have been a part of an ancient confession of faith or hymn to Christ. The idea is that Christ is the source of God's creation, the agent through whom God created the world. Ultimately behind this imagery is an adaptation of Hebrew wisdom speculation, which personified the wisdom of God and claimed that God's wisdom was present and active in the creation of the world (see Prov 3:19; 8:22-31). As the source of creation, Christ speaks with authority to the churches.

The message to the Laodicean church begins with the familiar words, "I know your works" (v. 15). By now the reader has come to realize that these words can presage either comfort or condemnation. Unfortunately for the church at Laodicea, the latter is the case here. Christ condemns the church for being neither cold nor hot. They are merely lukewarm. This is a picture of a complacent and apathetic community. They have no zeal or intensity. Christ does not accuse them of any major heresy or immoral practices. Rather, Christ describes them as a church that is spiritually indifferent and smugly self-sufficient. In a graphic picture, Christ says that he will spit them out of his mouth in disgust. "Spit" is really too mild a translation. The Greek word *emeō* really means "to vomit" (cf. the English word "emetic"). The self-satisfied complacency and half-hearted commitment of this congregation are enough to make Christ sick! The Laodicean Christians are ineffective and useless. The reference to cold, hot, and warm water would have had special significance for the people in Laodicea. Six miles away in Hierapolis, hot water springs bubbled up and cascaded over the cliffs, leaving behind snowy white deposits of calcium carbonate. These white cliffs were easily visible from Laodicea. The hot springs in Hierapolis (and elsewhere in the Lycus Valley) were valued for their medicinal benefits. At Colossae, on the other hand, was a stream that perennially furnished clear, cold water that was excellent for human consumption. At Laodicea,

Hot and Cold

 Pablo Richard has suggested a slightly different meaning for the hot-cold imagery:

The cold-hot dichotomy is not expressing merely a psychological attitude of indifference or enthusiasm, but rather two opposed historical categories. The cold symbolizes the indifference of the pagan and rich world toward Christians. The hot symbolizes the apocalyptic indignation of poor Christians toward the oppressive structures of the Roman empire. The Laodiceans want to be both rich (cold) and Christian (hot) and thereby end up lukewarm. They want to live simultaneously as rich Romans and as Christians, and in the end they are neither one nor the other. They are like the Nicolaitans (gnostics), who seek to live a spiritualistic, individualistic, and ahistorical Christianity apt for living as part of the Roman empire. They seek to "inculturate" Christianity into the oppressive structures of the empire and end up being neither true followers of the beast nor true followers of Jesus.

Pablo Richard, *Apocalypse: A People's Commentary on the Book of Revelation* (Maryknoll NY: Orbis Books, 1995), 62.

however, the water supply was not good. The water that was available was barely drinkable, lukewarm, and apparently had an emetic quality. Like the water at Laodicea, the church is useless. [Hot and Cold]

The church at Laodicea suffers from the same spirit of self-sufficiency that caused the city earlier to spurn offers of imperial assistance to rebuild after the earthquake of AD 60. They are rich and need nothing—not even Christ! In some ways, the Laodicean congregation is the opposite of that at Smyrna. At Laodicea the church is materially prosperous, but spiritually bankrupt. At Smyrna the church is spiritually rich, but materially poor. Christ sees the church as it really is. It may think it is rich and important. In reality it is "wretched, pitiable, poor, blind, and naked." They need what Christ can give them: moral purity ("gold refined by fire" and "white robes"), salvation ("white robes"), and spiritual vision (salve for their eyes). All three of these items probably have special significance for the Laodicean readers. As a banking center, Laodicea dealt with much gold and money. The white robe likely alluded to the textile industry of the area, and the eye salve is possibly a reference to an eye ointment that was used at the medical school in Laodicea. [Wealth and Poverty]

In spite of the failures of the church at Laodicea and Christ's harsh criticisms of the people there, he still speaks of them as people whom he loves. In fact, that love is the basis for his words of warning and his threatened discipline of the church. He punishes not from anger, but from compassion (cf. Prov 3:12).

Wealth and Poverty

Recent literary studies have emphasized that the historical, political, and social context of an individual reader shapes how that reader hears and understands a particular text. Middle- and upper-class North American readers of the book of Revelation (particularly white males) approach the text, usually unconsciously, from a position of power, wealth, and social standing. Fresh insights can be gained by viewing the text through the lens of people in other contexts.

Pablo Richard, a Chilean priest and theologian living in Costa Rica, has approached the study of Revelation from, in his words, "the standpoint of the oppressed: the poor, indigenous people, blacks, women, young people, the cosmos and nature, and all those who endure the discrimination of the oppressive and idolatrous system." Richard has identified the problem at Laodicea as being related to a lifestyle based on exploitation of others. Commenting on vv. 17-18, he has written,

A very common but false interpretation of this text is that the church in Laodicea is materially rich but spiritually poor and that Jesus is advising it to be also spiritually rich. . . . In this false interpretation the important thing is spiritual poverty or wealth, and material poverty or wealth means nothing. What Revelation is really demanding of the church in Laodicea is that it stop being lukewarm, gnostic, and Nicolaitan, that is, that it stop being rich like the idolatrous and oppressive Romans, that it not become rich by exploiting others, and that it cease being haughty and self-sufficient. If it is rich in this fashion it will be (materially and spiritually) wretched, pitiable, poor, blind, and naked. Jesus is not simply urging it to be spiritually rich, but to strive (materially and spiritually) for a wealth that is not acquired by exploiting others . . . that its behavior not be idolatrous, . . . that its conscience be clean.

Pablo Richard, *Apocalypse: A People's Commentary on the Book of Revelation* (Maryknoll NY: Orbis Books, 1995), 62-63.

The well-known image of Christ standing at the door knocking (captured in the famous Holman Hunt painting, *The Light of the World*) is a message of assurance that no one who is receptive to the invitation of Christ will be denied fellowship with him. [I Am Standing at the Door, Knocking] Although often understood in individualistic terms, this promise is perhaps best understood as a corporate promise addressed to the church. If the church at Sardis (or any other church) will open the door and invite Christ in, he will enter and be a part of that fellowship. A church that—through its complacency, accommodation with society, false practices, or lack of love—shuts Christ out of its presence has ceased to be a church. It has become a corpse instead of the living body of Christ. The reader cannot help hearing eucharistic overtones in the promise that Christ will come in and eat with whoever invites him in, for in the sharing of the bread and wine, Christ is supremely present with his people. The Eucharist, however, is a foretaste of the heavenly banquet that the faithful will share with Christ in the coming age, the marriage

I Am Standing at the Door, Knocking
William Holman Hunt was one of the three founders, along with John Everett Millais and Dante Gabriel Rossetti, of the Pre-Raphaelite Brotherhood in September 1848. This group of English painters was active from 1848–53. They sought a freshness in painting that was reminiscent of Italian pictures prior to Raphael (d. 1520). Holman Hunt experienced a conversion during the painting of this picture. He wrote of this experience in a letter to a friend, Thomas Combe, in August 1853. This picture became one of the most popular Protestant paintings of the 19th century, as it was known through engravings and replicas. Christ is depicted knocking at the door (Rev 3:20). The title of the work is from John 12:46.

William Holman Hunt (1827–1910). *The Light of the World*. 1853. Oil. Oxford, Keble Collection. (Credit: By permission of the Warden and Fellows of Kebel College, Oxford)

Christt Knocking at the Door

The figure of Christ knocking at the door and the promise of a meal for those faithful who open the door is likely an adaptation of the parable of the watchful servants in Luke 12:35-38. The Lukan parable, as well as the scene in Rev 3:20, is an assurance of eschatological communion with God.

supper of the Lamb (19:9; cf. Matt 26:29; Luke 13:29; 22:18, 30). This promise, then, of fellowship with Christ is a promise that looks forward to its future fulfillment. Now fellowship with Christ is an anticipatory communion that will find its perfection in God's final kingdom. The future orientation of these verses does not diminish the significance of Christ's presence with the church in the current situation. On the contrary, it suffuses the present experience with Christ with a deeper meaning. [Christ Knocking at the Door]

The promise given in v. 21 to the conqueror—"a place with me on my throne"—is similar to the words of Jesus in Luke 22:28-30. Those who are faithful—who conquer as Christ conquered—will share in his heavenly kingdom. The message to the church at Laodicea ends with the same formulaic statement found at the end of each of the other messages: "Let anyone who has an ear listen to what the Spirit is saying to the churches." The danger in the statement being repeated over and over is that exactly the opposite will happen—it will not be heard; ears will become dulled to the claim of the words on the reader. The command to hear these words challenges the reader to apply these messages to her or his own situation. They may be ancient words, but they still have a modern message for the reader who will listen with discriminating ears. The word that proceeds from the mouth of Christ is a sharp, two-edged sword that penetrates and dissects even our modern situation, offering our churches, like the seven churches, words of criticism and words of praise. As Wilfrid Harrington translated this command, "You have ears—so listen to what the Spirit is saying to the Churches!"[2]

CONNECTIONS

The messages to the churches of Smyrna and Sardis contain harsh statements about the Jews in the communities to which the letters are addressed (2:9; 3:9). Interpreters of Revelation have a theological and ethical obligation to help their audiences properly understand these remarks. If not understood within the social and religious world of the first century, these statements could unfortunately be used to foster anti-Jewish attitudes and polemics. William Barclay, the New Testament scholar whose popularized studies on the New Testament have been widely used by clergy and laity alike,

Prophetic Ministry

Teachers and preachers of the gospel today, if they are faithful to the task to which God has called them, must at times, like John, speak a word of judgment to their own congregations. Joseph R. Jeter Jr. has written,

We have been called to ministry, the whole ministry. And part of that is the prophetic ministry, the ministry of "no" to things as they are, the ministry of afflicting the comfortable, the ministry of God's judgment and grace. Let us not shrink from this task that John has modeled for us so well. How shall we do it? "You are children of Christ that I love. Do not be afraid, because the new reign of God is coming. In between, and in order that you might both claim your heritage and stretch toward your destiny, I take a deep breath and speak in God's name, because you must know that 'I have this against you.' "

Joseph R. Jeter Jr., "I Have This Against You," *Preaching Through the Apocalypse: Sermons from Revelation,* ed. Cornish R. Rogers and Joseph R. Jeter Jr. (St. Louis: Chalice, 1992), 74.

was guilty of using irresponsible language when interpreting these passages from Revelation. For example, when discussing the situation in Smyrna, he wrote, "The Jews were strong in Smyrna; they had the ear of the authorities. Such was their envenomed bitterness that they would even plead concern for the pagan gods, and even join with the hated Gentiles, if by so doing they could bring death to the Christians."3 [Prophetic Ministry]

John's harsh language against the Jewish community arose out of a situation of conflict. During the last quarter of the first century, Jews and Christians both were involved in an identity crisis. Jews living outside Palestine had over the centuries learned how to live with their non-Jewish neighbors. Some of the beliefs and practices of Judaism made them appear strange or even suspicious to their neighbors. Observance of the Sabbath, food laws, circumcision, and their rigorous monotheism often left their neighbors puzzled. In spite of the suspicions they aroused, the Jews had earned certain privileges from the Roman government, among them exemption from military service and emperor worship, the right to observe the Sabbath, the right to assemble for worship, and even a certain degree of self-governance in their own communities. As long as Christians were understood as a part of Judaism, they enjoyed the same privileges as the Jews did.

Jews and Christians both claimed to be the legitimate heirs of Abraham, each to the exclusion of the other. The early church saw itself as the new Israel and appropriated the imagery and symbols of Jewish tradition for its own use (cf. the description of the church in 7:4-8 as being composed of twelve thousand "out of every tribe of the people of Israel"). Christians denounced the Jews who failed to accept the Christian claim of Jesus' messianic status, considering them no longer the children of God. The Jews, on the other hand,

God's Judgments

The warnings to each of the churches are reminders "that the judgment of God is exercised constantly upon the Church. The history of the Church is the history of judgments executed, *hic et nunc* by God (as upon his people Israel)."

Jacques Ellul, *Apocalypse: The Book of Revelation* (New York: Seabury, 1977), 127.

argued that they were the true Israel. Christians had no right to usurp the Jewish identity. A part of the hostility reflected in the messages to Smyrna and Sardis possibly arose from situations in which Jewish Christians were excluded from the synagogue and denounced to the government authorities as being non-Jewish. Such action could result in social and legal sanctions against Christians. [God's Judgments]

This context of theological and, to some extent, social rivalry between Jews and Christians helps explain the harsh language of John. The privileged Jewish community was at times willing to denounce the Christians in order to deny Christians the privileges they enjoyed and to bolster their own positions of influence. The reaction of John and other Christians to such treatment is understandable, but not excusable and certainly not commendable. Christians today should denounce the vitriolic language of John toward the Jews as being not only unacceptable, but even

Sardis
A view of the reconstructed bath-gymnasium complex, completed in the 2d century AD at Sardis. Adjacent to the structure was the largest non-Palestinian synagogue ever found, dating to the 2d or 3d century AD. (Credit: Mitchell Reddish)

sub-Christian. Particularly in worship, one must use with extreme caution these and similar texts in the New Testament that contain harsh and condemnatory language against Jews. The teacher and preacher must make it clear that hatred, even when dressed in religious garb, is still hatred. This type of rhetoric too easily becomes the fuel for the fires of hatred, persecution, and violence of individuals and groups. In his denunciations of the Jews at Smyrna and Sardis, John himself seems to be guilty of the very sin of which Christ accuses the church at Ephesus. He has "abandoned the love" that is at the heart of a true relationship with God. [Sardis]

NOTES

[1] Wilfrid J. Harrington, *Revelation*, Sacra Pagina (Collegeville MN: Liturgical, 1993), 68.

[2] Ibid., 67.

[3] William Barclay, *Letters to the Seven Churches* (Philadelphia: Westminster, 1957), 36.

THE THRONE OF GOD

4:1-11

Visions of the Future, 4:1–22:5

In Jewish and Christian apocalyptic literature, revelations are mediated to the human recipient in one of two ways. The first way is through dreams, visions, or direct discourse with otherworldly beings. Usually an angel or some other heavenly figure appears as the mediator of the revelation, either as interpreter of the dreams and visions or as the one who delivers the message of the revelation. The first revelatory section of Revelation (1:9–3:22) belongs to this first category of apocalypses. John receives the divine message through the vision of the exalted Son of Man figure who speaks directly with John and imparts the message to him (cf. the visions of Daniel in Dan 7:2 in which an angel, usually Gabriel, serves as the interpreter of Daniel's visions). The second way in which revelations are disclosed is through otherworldly journeys, sometimes called "rapture" experiences. In these instances, the recipient claims to have been taken away to another world—heaven or hell, or other places of reward or punishment, or to the outer ends of the earth, that is, places not accessible to the average person. (In 2 Cor 12:2, Paul refers autobiographically to such an experience when he mentions a person who "was caught up to the third heaven." Paul only mentions that such an event happened; he does not describe the actual experience.) Apocalyptic literature that contains these otherworldly journeys is often exceedingly graphic in describing the sights that were shown to the recipient and telling how the recipient was transported from one place to another to be shown various things normally not revealed to humans.

The material in Revelation 4:1–22:5 is similar to apocalypses with otherworldly journeys. In chapter 4, John says that a voice invited him up to heaven to be shown the heavenly throne room. A large part of the book apparently takes place in this setting in which John sees numerous visions of events that will soon occur. Unlike most other apocalypses with otherworldly journeys, the journey motif is not carried through in Revelation. Whereas in other apocalypses of this type the recipient is typically led from one place to another in the otherworldly regions, in Revelation that seldom occurs. The only other indications of a journey are in 17:3 when John is carried away "in the spirit into a wilderness" to see the great whore, and in 21:10 when he is carried away in the spirit "to a great, high mountain" from which he sees the new Jerusalem. Because the journey motif is so muted in Revelation, some scholars would classify this work as one without an otherworldly journey. [Otherworldly Journeys]

Otherworldly Journeys

Examples of Jewish apocalypses that contain otherworldly journeys are the *Apocalypse of Abraham*, the "Book of the Watchers" (*1 En.* 1–36), the "Book of the Heavenly Luminaries" (*1 En.* 72–82), the "Similitudes of Enoch" (*1 En.* 37–71), *2 Enoch*, *3 Baruch*, and the *Testament of Abraham*. Examples of early Christian apocalypses with otherworldly journeys include the *Ascension of Isaiah* 6–11, the *Apocalypse of Paul*, and the *Apocalypse of Esdras*. This motif of a journey to heaven or hell or to another region beyond normal human bounds is probably best known today through Dante's use of a similar literary technique in *The Inferno*.

Regardless of whether the work fits the otherworldly journey type, the call of John in 4:1 to "come up here" signals a major shift in the work. The first part of John's revelation consists of his vision of the Son of Man and the messages to the seven churches. The second major section begins in chapter 4 and continues almost to the end of the book. The setting for these two sections is different. John claims that he was on the island of Patmos when he received the first vision. He remains on the island in the presence of Christ, who dictates the messages that John must send to the seven churches. For the second part, he is taken up to heaven to the very throne room of God. Whereas the first section focuses primarily on the present situation of the churches in Asia Minor, the second part reveals eschatological scenarios that involve the entire world. The two sections are tied together, however, by the one who speaks directly to John in both parts—the exalted Christ. In the first vision, the exalted Christ stands among the lampstands and declares his messages to the churches. At the outset of the second section it is this same exalted Christ who invites John to "come up here" so that he might see the unfolding of God's plan for the world. The central role of Christ in these visions is a fulfillment of the opening words of the book, "The revelation of *Jesus Christ* [emphasis added], which God gave him to show his servants." [The Heavenly Throne Room]

As the first vision consists of several distinct scenes (the vision of the "one like the Son of Man," and the seven vignettes of the churches of Asia Minor), likewise the second section contains multiple visions, including visions of the heavenly throne room, the seven seals, the seven trumpets, the great red dragon and the two beasts, the seven bowl plagues, the fall of Babylon, the triumphant Christ, and the new Jerusalem. As discussed in the introduction to this commentary, one should not interpret the various scenes in 4:1–22:5 in a historic or chronological sequence. John is not attempting to present a blueprint for the future, a road map for the eschatologically minded. His approach is not logical and sequential. He does not attempt to convince the reader through reason and well-ordered argumentation. Rather, John's approach is more creative. His visions are variations on a few related themes, themes that will become clearer as the reader hears and sees these themes being presented in ever more imaginative and compelling ways.

The Heavenly Throne Room

Dürer shows John before the seated figure of God the Father and surrounded by the 24 elders. The seven candlesticks are visible above God. The buildings on earth are typical to contemporary Nuremberg architecture.

Albrecht Dürer (1471–1528). *St. John Before God in the Heavenly Throne Room* from the *Apocalypse of St. John.* 1496–1498. Woodcut, 15 x 11 in. (Credit: Dover Pictorial Archive)

The book of Revelation (and particularly the visions of 4:1–22:5) is a work that needs to be experienced, more than it needs to be dissected. The reader needs to allow the visual and auditory images of John's visions to overwhelm the senses and to take control of the imagination. For that reason, the reader should read the entire section of 4:1–22:5 without stopping for explanations. By so doing, one begins to experience the grandeur and power of John's Apocalypse. In some ways, these visions of John's are like a good joke—if they have to be explained, they are not worth it! Unfortunately, the cultural, temporal, social, and political distance between the modern and ancient reader at times make explanation and clarification necessary. The reader would do well, however, to step back and view these visions of John in their entirety, rather than in detail. As with a painting, if one inspects it in excessive detail, one may gain an understanding of certain aspects of the work, but lose an overall perspective on what the artist is trying to convey.

The Heavenly Throne Room, 4:1–5:14

References to the heavenly throne appear throughout Revelation (7:9-17; 11:15-19; 19:4-8; 20:11-15; 22:3). The scene in chapters 4 and 5 presents the most detailed and vivid description of God's throne of any passage in the book. [Parallel Structures] The prevalence of the heavenly throne in the book points to the significance of this imagery for John. The throne represents the power and rule of God. By emphasizing the throne, John is pulling back the curtain and showing his readers the true locus of the world's power. The emperor may sit on his throne in Rome, but his throne is no match for God's throne. In spite of his lofty claims and grandiose pronouncements, the emperor is not in control of the universe. That power resides with God. The struggle in Revelation can be viewed as a struggle between these two thrones, the throne of God and the throne of Rome (which is also the throne of Satan). Revelation demands a choice on the part of the reader. One must choose before whose throne one will bow. For John the answer is simple. Because God is the one before whom all other powers must fall, only God is worthy of human worship, adoration, and praise.

Parallel Structures

Charles Talbert has pointed out the parallel structures of chs. 4 and 5:

Revelation 4 (God)	Revelation 5 (The Lamb)
God's glory (4:2b-8a)	The Lamb's glory (5:5-7)
Worship of God (8b-11)	Worship of the Lamb (8-12)
First hymn (8b)	First hymn (9-10)
Narrative (9-10)	Narrative (11-12a)
Second hymn (11)	Second hymn (12b)

Charles H. Talbert, *The Apocalypse: A Reading of the Revelation of John* (Louisville: Westminster/John Knox, 1994), 26-27.

The placement of this heavenly scene at the beginning of John's series of visions of coming judgments is critical. John reassures his readers at the outset that in spite of the calamities and punishments that may strike the earth, the faithful are not to worry. Even though chaos and confusion may seem to be rampant, John asserts that the heavenly throne is not empty—God is in control. A part of the purpose of the book of Revelation is to provide its hearers with an alternative worldview, a different way of viewing reality. Whereas to John's readers the situation may appear hopeless, John claims otherwise. To John's readers, God no longer seems in control. Satan and his cohorts are the dominant forces in the universe. Evil, not good, is triumphant. Rome is viewed as the monstrous beast who had authority "over every tribe and people and tongue and nation" (13:7). Elisabeth Schüssler Fiorenza has described well the crisis that must have confronted John's readers:

> [The] experience of harassment, persecution, and hostility challenged Christians' faith in Christ as Lord. Their experience of hunger, deprivation, pestilence, and war undermined their belief in God's good creation and providence. Christians experienced painfully that their situation in no way substantiated their faith conviction that they already participated in Christ's kingship and power.[1]

Through the Apocalypse, and specifically this vision of the heavenly throne room, John seeks to lead his readers to a deeper understanding of reality to help them see that the power structures of the world were illusory and temporal. The true course of history resides in the one "who is and who was and who is to come, the Almighty" (1:8; 4:8). [The Heavenly Throne]

Visions of the heavenly throne are quite common in apocalyptic literature (cf. *1 En.* 14:8–16:4; 39:1–40:10; 71:1-17; *T. Levi* 5:1) as well as in the Hebrew Bible (cf. 1 Kgs 22:19; Isa 6:1-13; Ezek 1:4-28; Dan 7:9-14). John's description of the heavenly throne room is heavily indebted to Ezekiel's vision. As with his other uses of the Hebrew Bible, however, John does not simply borrow images from Ezekiel. As we shall see, he greatly transforms them.

The Heavenly Throne
"The great throne dominates Revelation: a constant reminder that God rules even in our chaotic world."

Wilfrid J. Harrington, *Revelation*, Sacra Pagina (Collegeville MN: Liturgical, 1993), 82.

COMMENTARY

The Throne of God, 4:1-11

The second major section of the Apocalypse begins with the words, "After this I looked" (4:1), a phrase that occurs four other times in Revelation (7:1, 9; 15:5; 18:1; cf. 19:1; see also Dan 7:6). Each time this phrase is used it introduces a new vision in the book. "After this" should not be taken in a strictly chronological sense, as if these visions actually came to John one after the other. The phrase serves as a structuring device in the book, calling attention to a new revelation that John has received. One should be careful, also, in taking too literally John's claims that these revelations came to him through visions, as if he actually saw the events he describes.

Divine revelation mediated through dreams and visions is a stock literary device of apocalyptic literature. John uses this device as a literary vehicle to convey his theological message to his readers. [Thrones]

John claims that he saw an open door in heaven, indicating that access to the heavenly world was granted to him and that revelation from heaven was possible. The voice that calls to him is identified as the same voice that spoke to him earlier, the "first voice . . . like a trumpet" (4:1; cf. 1:10). The one who invites John up to heaven, then, is Christ. Like the recipients of revelations in other apocalypses, John is taken on a journey to the dwelling place of God, the heavenly throne room. The description of the throne room reflects ancient Near Eastern monarchies in which a ruler sat in his royal court surrounded by a variety of attendants. The one seated on the heavenly throne is obviously God. John's depiction of God is very sparing, using impressionistic rather than realistic terms. God "looks like jasper and carnelian" (4:3), precious stones. In addition, a rainbow that looks like an emerald surrounds the throne. The individual stones John mentions are not what is important here. One should not look for special significance in the types of stones or in their colors. Rather, the jewels suggest the brilliance and splendor of God. This entire scene functions to overwhelm and awe the reader with a sense of the majesty and mysteriousness of God.

Thrones

Readers often overlook the political symbolism of the throne in Revelation. Elisabeth Schüssler Fiorenza has aptly noted,

The central theological symbol of the book is the throne signifying divine or demonic power. While the Christians are the representatives and agents of the power and empire of God and Christ here on earth, the universal Roman empire and its imperial powers are the agents of the demonic and destructive power of Satan. Revelation is thus a deeply political-theological book.

Elisabeth Schüssler Fiorenza, *Invitation to the Book of Revelation* (Garden City NY: Image Books, 1981), 27.

Readers familiar with the Genesis story of Noah and the flood cannot help associating the rainbow that surrounds the throne with the rainbow that appeared after the flood as a sign that God would not destroy the earth again by a flood (Gen 9:8-17). Accordingly, some commentators interpret the rainbow as a symbol of God's mercy. G. B. Caird understood the rainbow in this way, commenting, "This rainbow is second in importance only to the throne. It tells us that there is to be no triumph for God's sovereignty at the expense of his mercy, and it warns us not to interpret the visions of disaster that follow as though God had forgotten his promise to Noah."[2] The source for John's imagery of precious stones and a rainbow is Ezekiel's vision of God's throne-chariot. In Ezekiel's vision, the prophet used a variety of precious stones to describe what he saw in the heavenly court. John modifies Ezekiel's imagery and uses the stones to symbolize the presence of God, rather than the accouterments of the throne room. The splendor that surrounded the entire throne, Ezekiel said, was "like the bow in a cloud on a rainy day" (1:28). [Precious Stones]

Surrounding the throne, John sees twenty-four other thrones, each occupied by an elder dressed in white and wearing a golden crown. The identity of these twenty-four elders is not clear. Scholars have proposed several possibilities for the significance of the number twenty-four. One of the most common suggestions derives the number from the twelve patriarchs of Israel (i.e., the twelve sons of Jacob) combined with the twelve disciples of Jesus. This view is supported by a reference to 21:12-14, John's description of the wall of the new Jerusalem, which states that "on the gates are inscribed the names of the twelve tribes of the Israelites" and on the twelve foundations of the wall "are the twelve names of the twelve apostles of the Lamb." An ancient suggestion similar to the one previously stated saw the number twenty-four as being derived from the twelve tribes of Israel. In John's vision, the number is doubled, representing "the Jewish and Gentile believers who

---

Precious Stones

AΩ John describes God and God's throne in terms of three gem stones. Jasper is "a precious stone found in various colors, mostly reddish, sometimes green, brown, blue, yellow, and white. In antiquity the name was not limited to the variety of quartz now called jasper, but could designate any opaque precious stone." In 21:11, however, a jasper is said to be as "clear as crystal," prompting some to conjecture that a diamond is meant.

"Carnelian" is the translation for *sardion*, which is a red or deep orange-red precious stone. The word *smargdinos*, translated as "emerald," denotes a precious stone of green color, possibly green feldspar or green turquoise. The term could denote an emerald, but such stones are rare in archaeological excavations.

"ἴασπις," Walter Bauer, William F. Arndt, F. Wilbur Gingrich, and Frederick W. Danker, eds., *A Greek-English Lexicon of the New Testament and Other Early Christian Literature*, 2d ed. (Chicago: University of Chicago Press, 1979), 368.

were one in Christ."[3] The imagery then symbolizes the totality of the church. Some commentators have looked for astrological significance in the number twenty-four, pointing out that "the Babylonian zodiac was ruled by twenty-four gods of the stars."[4] Others have suggested that the twenty-four elders represent the twenty-four orders of priests in the Jerusalem temple (see 1 Chr 24:1-19), functioning somewhat as priests in their continual worship of God and in their offering to God the prayers of the people (5:8). Jürgen Roloff argued for a simpler explanation, claiming that "the number twenty-four is most easily explained as a reference to the number of hours in the day; accordingly, the elders represent before God the fullness of time and their purpose is to praise God ceaselessly, day and night."[5]

In addition to the significance of the number twenty-four, another question concerning the identity of the elders is whether they represent human or angelic beings. They wear crowns and white robes like the faithful people of God elsewhere in Revelation (2:10; 3:4-5, 11, 18; 6:11; 7:9-14; 19:8-9). Furthermore, like the faithful, the twenty-four elders are seated on thrones (3:21; 20:4). On the other hand, human beings seem out of place in this heavenly scene amidst the throne of God and the four living creatures. The elders are probably best understood as angelic attendants for God. To pose the question as an either/or question is likely the wrong approach, however. In apocalyptic literature, angels sometimes represent earthly realities. John earlier uses imagery in this way when he describes the seven stars as being the seven angels of the churches (1:20). The angels are not totally separate from the churches. They are the heavenly representatives of the earthly churches. Likewise, in this vision the image is fluid. The twenty-four elders are on one level angelic courtiers for God. They function in the vision, however, also as representatives of God's people. The crowns symbolize their kingly role, while their offering of incense and prayers to God symbolizes their priestly role. [Golden Crown]

Golden Crown

A crown made of gold, designed to look like a wreath of oak leaves.

Amphipolis Archaeological Museum. Amphipolis, Greece. (Credit: Mitchell Reddish)

The imagery here is drawn from ancient royal courts in which a variety of personal and official attendants surrounded the ruler and his throne. David Aune has pointed to the similarities between John's description of the heavenly throne room and the Roman imperial court, in which the emperor dispensed justice and received emissaries. Surrounding the emperor would be his friends and advisors who assisted him in hearing cases and deciding issues of justice.[6] This transference to God of characteristics of earthly rulers is a part of the tradition that John inherited from Judaism. The idea of a heavenly council of supernatural beings who are part of God's heavenly court is found several places in the Hebrew Bible (Gen 1:26; 1 Kgs 22:19-23; Job 1:6; 2:1; Ps 89:7; Dan 7:10; Isa 6:1-13).

More important than the identification of the elders is the function that they serve in John's vision. The elders participate continually in the worship and praise of God, prostrating themselves, offering prayers and incense, and playing their harps to provide music for the heavenly liturgy. They are heavenly exemplars of the pure worship of God, models for the churches on earth to follow. They serve also as a contrast to the worship that is occurring elsewhere on earth, the worship of the emperor. The only one truly deserving of worship is the one who sits enthroned in the heavens.

The flashes of lightning and rumbles of thunder that John associates with the presence of God are typical characteristics of theophanies in the Hebrew Bible (cf. Exod 19:16; Ps 18:7-19). [Thunder and Lightning] Thunder and lightning were conventional imagery used for the Semitic storm god. In John's vision, the thunder and lightning add to the sense of mystery, awe, and transcendence of God. John's readers/hearers who were Jewish Christians or who were familiar with the symbols of Judaism would likely have seen in the "seven flaming torches" a similarity to the seven-branched lampstand (menorah) in the Jerusalem temple. John identifies the seven torches as "the seven spirits of God," which the reader encountered previously in chapter 1 (1:4). As noted there, they represent at the same time the seven archangels who serve God as well as the spirit of God that is at work in the world (cf. Ezek 1:13, which describes "coals of fire, like torches moving to and fro among the living creatures" around God's throne). [The Seven Archangels]

The "sea of glass, like crystal" that appears before the throne is perhaps an adaptation of the ancient idea of a heavenly sea. Ancient Hebrew cosmology conceived of waters below the earth

---

Thunder and Lightning

ΑΩ The association of thunder and lightning with the appearance of God in the Hebrew Bible is likely derived from their connection with the Semitic god of storms and rain. Lightning was his weapon and thunder his voice. Called "Hadad among the Amorites and Arameans, Adad among the Mesopotamians, and Haddu among the Canaanites," he is referred to as Baal in the Hebrew Bible. He is sometimes depicted in artwork as "wearing a headpiece with horns protruding from the front and grasping the thunderbolt."

Walter A. Maier III, "Hadad," *The Anchor Bible Dictionary*, ed. David Noel Freedman, 6 vols. (New York: Doubleday & Co., 1992), 3:11.

The Seven Archangels

AΩ Jewish tradition frequently thought of the various supernatural beings who served God as being arranged hierarchi-
cally. Although much diversity exists in Jewish literature concerning who and what the various beings were and
how they were ranked, one tradition claimed that there were seven special angels who performed important duties for God.
In Tob 12:15, for instance, the angel Raphael said, "I am Raphael, one of the seven angels who stand ready and enter
before the glory of the Lord." The names and responsibilities of the seven archangels are given in *1 En.* 20:1-7. The text
reads,

And these are the names of the holy angels who keep watch. Uriel, one of the holy angels, namely (the angel) of thunder and of tremors. Raphael, one of the holy angels, (the angel) of the spirits of men. Raguel, one of the holy angels,
who takes vengeance on the world and on the lights. Michael, one of the holy angels, namely the one put in charge of
the best part of mankind, in charge of the nation. Saraqael, one of the holy angels, who (is) in charge of the spirits of
men who cause the spirits to sin. Gabriel, one of the holy angels, who (is) in charge of the serpents and the Garden
and the Cherubim.

This list contains only six archangels. One ancient manuscript of *1 Enoch* adds: "Remiel, one of the holy angels, whom
God put in charge of those who rise. Seven names of archangels."
   While angels appear occasionally in the Hebrew Bible, they are mentioned frequently and in detail in nonbiblical Jewish
literature from around the 3rd century BC and later. Some works provide names for the angels, assign them tasks (as God's
messengers, protectors of the righteous, controllers of the universe, heavenly attendants, enforcers of divine punishment),
attribute the origin of evil to fallen angels, see evil angels as the source of human temptations, and envision heavenly
armies of angels in conflict with evil angels or demons. For further information on the development of angelology in
Judaism, see Carol Newsom and Duane F. Watson, "Angels," *The Anchor Bible Dictionary*, ed. David Noel Freedman, 6 vols.
(New York: Doubleday & Co., 1992), 1:248-55; and D. S. Russell, *The Method and Message of Jewish Apocalyptic*, Old
Testament Library (Philadelphia: Westminster, 1964), 235-62.

and above the firmament (the dome covering the earth; cf. Gen
1:7). Early Hebrew creation myths, likely adapted from Babylonian
and Canaanite myths, spoke of the sea as a monster that had to be
tamed as a part of God's creative activity (cf. Job 26:12-13; Pss
74:13-14; 89:10; Isa 27:1; 51:9-10). The sea thus represented
chaos, evil, the untamed part of creation. It is significant that the
formidable beast of chapter 13 rises out of the sea. We will return
to the symbolism of the sea when we examine that passage. If the
sea represents chaos and evil, why does John describe the sea as
being present in God's heaven? Perhaps this is John's way of calling
attention to the persistence and stubbornness of evil in the world.
Evil, chaos, and destruction are still a part of the created order.
They have been subdued, but continue to break
loose at times. They will not be finally destroyed
until the creation of the new heaven and earth in
which the sea no longer exists (21:1). In heaven
the sea is under control, for the moment at least.
John sees not a tumultuous sea, but one that is
calm, looking like glass (4:6). [The Sea of Glass]

The Sea of Glass

"The glassy sea stands before the
throne as a mute reminder that the
whole creation is affected by the taint of evil."

G. B. Caird, *A Commentary on the Revelation of St. John the
Divine*, Harper's New Testament Commentaries (Harper & Row,
1966), 68.

The prophet Ezekiel described four living creatures, part human and part animal, who accompanied God's chariot throne (cf. the seraphs in Isa 6:1-8). These are variations of the cherubim that are mentioned several places in the Hebrew Bible (Gen 3:24; Exod 25:18; Num 7:89; 1 Sam 4:4; 2 Kgs 19:15; Pss 80:1; 99:1; Ezek 10:1-22). [Cherubim and Seraphim] John modifies Ezekiel's imagery, describing the four living creatures as each having a different form—three with animal forms (a lion, an ox, and an eagle) and one with a human face. In Ezekiel, each of the creatures has four faces (those of a lion, an ox, an eagle, and a human). As in Isaiah 6, the creatures each have six wings. They are covered with eyes inside and outside (cf. Ezek 1:18, in which the rims of the wheels associated with the creatures are covered with eyes).

Clearly, John has borrowed and modified the imagery of the four living creatures, so the specific types of animal forms mentioned are not original to him. Yet he feels free to modify his sources to suit his message. Is there a deeper significance intended by the specific animal forms listed (lion, ox, eagle, and human)? An intriguing parallel occurs in later rabbinic literature that names these specific creatures as the mightiest species of

---

Cherubim and Seraphim

AΩ Cherubim (or cherubs) are mentioned several places in the Hebrew Bible. They stood guard over the way to the tree of life in the garden of Eden (Gen 3:24). They were a part of the adornment of the Jerusalem temple, including two enormous ones carved of olive wood and overlaid with gold whose outstretched wings filled the Holy of Holies and overarched the ark of the covenant (1 Kgs 6:23-28; 2 Kgs 7:28-36). God flew through the heavens mounted on cherubim (2 Sam 22:11; Ps 18:10) and his throne-chariot is supported by cherubim (Ezek 1:4-14; cf. 10:1-22). Seraphim (or seraphs) are mentioned only in Isa 6. Both cherubim and seraphim are drawn from ancient Near Eastern mythology that viewed these winged, animal/human creatures as part of the divine landscape, serving as functionaries of the gods or as minor deities themselves. In later Jewish literature, the cherubim and seraphim are considered different classes of angels. A passage in *1 En.* 61:10, for example, lists the various orders of the angels as cherubim, seraphim, ophannim, the angels of power, and the angels of the principalities.

The physical descriptions of the cherubim are not uniform, except that they are winged creatures. They are often portrayed as having a combination of different animal features or animal and human features. The modern depiction of "cherubs" as cute, plump children is a far cry from the biblical and ancient Near Eastern concept of the cherubim.

God's creation. The specific saying, attributed to Rabbi Abahu (c. AD 300), states, "There are four mighty creatures. The mightiest among the birds is the eagle, the mightiest among domestic animals is the ox, the mightiest among wild animals is the lion, the mightiest of them all is man; and God has taken all these and secured them to his throne."[7] If such a tradition already existed during John's time and he was aware of it, then the choice of these specific creatures may have symbolized the entire created order of God—birds, wild animals, domestic animals, and humans. All creation joins in the heavenly worship of God. While this interpretation is theologically attractive, it is exegetically doubtful. The four creatures do not have that meaning in Ezekiel, and there is no evidence that the view reflected in rabbinic literature was known as early as the first century. The four living creatures in the

The Four Living Creatures and the Four Evangelists

Church tradition as early as the middle of the 2d century began to see the four living creatures in Revelation (adapted from Ezekiel) as symbols of the four Gospel writers. The traditional iconographic representations for the four evangelists are: the face and/or figure of a human is Matthew; the lion is Mark; the ox is Luke; and the eagle is John. For a discussion of the various identifications of the four creatures with the four evangelists, see R. Alan Culpepper, *John, the Son of Zebedee: The Life of a Legend* (Columbia SC: University of South Carolina Press, 1994), 167-68.

Beneath each iconographic symbol is the gospel writer's name written in Latin. Christ is placed in a mandorla or almond shape, typical of the Romanesque period. Note the letters (A) and (ω) on one page of the book that Christ is holding.

Christ in Glory. Westminster Psalter (ROY.2.A.XXII). 12th C. Manuscript illumination. British Library. London, England. (Credit: By Permission of The British Library)

Apocalypse are better understood as representations of the highest order of angels, those who stand closest to the throne of God and lead in worshiping God "day and night without ceasing" (4:8) [The Four Living Creatures and the Four Evangelists]

The song of praise sung by the four living creatures is adapted from Isaiah 6:3. This "trisagion" (thrice-holy) hymn appears in modified form in several other apocalyptic works (*1 En.* 39:12; *2 En.* 21:1; *3 En.* 1:12; 40:2). Like the prophet Isaiah, John emphasizes the holiness of God, God's "otherness" and awesome transcendence. John's major alteration of the Isaiah text is the replacement of the last line with the phrase, "who was and is and is to come," a phrase used several times in Revelation, affirming both God's transcendence over time and God's authority throughout all time. This is the first of many hymns that appears in the book of Revelation, bearing testimony to the early church's extensive use of hymns in worship. The New Testament also contains other hymns

and confessions of faith from the early
Christians (Eph 5:14; Phil 2:6-11; Col 1:15-20;
1 Tim 3:16; Heb 1:3; 1 Pet 1:18-21; 2:21-25;
3:18-22). [Holy]

The twenty-four elders join in the worship of
the one who is seated on the throne. Their pos-
ture—falling down before the throne—is an act
of submission as well as worship. Whereas the
Gospels provide numerous examples of people
falling down before Jesus in worship, the background for John's imagery here is likely the
Roman imperial court in which visitors pros-
trate themselves as an act of honor and submission to the emperor.
David Aune has connected the elders' offering of their golden
crowns with imperial court practice, citing examples from antiquity
to show that the presentation of gold crowns was a tradition associated with Hellenistic kingship that the Romans inherited. He has
noted that "the Roman emperor was customarily presented with
gold crowns by the senate (and provincial cities) on the occasions
of accessions, consulships, victories and anniversaries."8

The song of the four living creatures barely ends before the
twenty-four elders take up the notes and continue the heavenly
praise of God. Perhaps John hears this singing in an antiphonal
pattern, with the elders answering the praise of the creatures. In
John's vision, heaven rings with the glorious music of praise to
God, a never-ending liturgy. The reason that God is deserving of
such praise is because God is the creator of all things. The biblical
affirmation of God's creation of and responsibility for the world is
here taken up in song. The praise of God as creator is not an incidental doctrine that John happens to include only in passing. God's
creative activity is at the heart of God's sovereignty. God is sovereign over the world because this is *God's*
world. God is the one who said, "Let there
be," and there was. The claims to power and
sovereignty by the Roman emperors are false
claims. They are mere pretenders, trying to
usurp the power that belongs to God.
Furthermore, because God is creator, the one
who began the whole process, God is also the
one who will bring the present order to its
ultimate goal. As the Alpha and the Omega,
God holds together the creation and the consummation of the universe. [God as Creator and
Redeemer]

Holy

AΩ The Hebrew word for "holy" is apparently derived from a root word meaning
separate, or set apart. God is holy because God is
separate from, different from, everything else. To
call God holy is to recognize God's distinctiveness.
People and even objects can be considered holy
when they are set apart or dedicated to God for
the service of God. Holiness is only secondarily an
ethical or moral quality. Since sinfulness is abhorrent to God, those who are set apart for God
distance themselves from sin.

God as Creator and Redeemer

Barclay Newman has highlighted the two
themes of God as creator and redeemer that
occur in Rev 4 and 5. He claimed that the purpose of
this section "is to make explicit what is implicit in his
every characterization of God; that is, the *oneness of
Creator and Redeemer*. For orthodox Jews or
Christians this was a well-known axiom, but for persons who differentiated between Creator and
Redeemer, as in gnosticism, this would be a stringent
rebuttal."

Barclay Newman, *Rediscovering the Book of Revelation* (Valley Forge
PA: Judson, 1968), 57.

The doctrine of creation also forces a problem for theology. If, as John asserts, God created all things and by his "will they existed and were created," how does one deal with the problem of evil and suffering in the world? Is God responsible for these also? We will have to come back to this question later after John has shared the rest of his visions with us. He does not stop now to deal with this problem. The choirs are singing and must not be interrupted!

The words "our Lord and God" used in the hymn by the elders perhaps contain a polemical jab directed at the worship of the emperor. The Roman writer Suetonius tells that Domitian sent out a letter in the name of his procurators that began "Our Master and our God bids that this be done" (*Dom.* 13.2 [Rolfe, LCL]). Dio Cassius, another Roman writer, reports similar claims to divinity by Domitian (*Hist. rom.* 67.4.7 [Cary, LCL]). Since some scholars have questioned the reliability of these ancient traditions about Domitian, we must be cautious about using them to understand John's language.

CONNECTIONS

No other work in the canon has such a strong emphasis on the transcendence of God. To experience John's Apocalypse is to be brought in touch with the awesome majesty and mystery of the God of the universe. God is holy, the four living creatures remind us, as they sing "Holy, Holy, Holy" to the one seated on the throne. Like the prophet Isaiah, John declares the radical otherness of God. God is distinct from creation. ["Holy, Holy, Holy"]

> **"Holy, Holy, Holy"**
>
> The classic Christian hymn, "Holy, Holy, Holy," whose words were written by Reginald Heber and are based largely on this text, captures some of the power and majesty of John's vision. The words of the second verse, which is particularly indebted to the Apocalypse, state:
>
> Holy, holy, holy! all the saints adore Thee,
> Casting down their golden crowns around the glassy sea;
> Cherubim and seraphim falling down before Thee,
> Who wert, and art, and evermore shalt be.

This emphasis on the transcendence of God is evident in the liturgical sections that undergird the entire Apocalypse. For John, the community of faith is a worshiping community. Worship is not an option or an addendum to the Christian life. Worship is at the heart of the people of God. John's vision of the heavenly throne room is a worship setting. The twenty-four elders and the four living creatures offer prayers and words of praise to God day and night without ceasing. It is from within this worship setting that the majority of the book takes place. The visions of chapters 4–22 all originate from the throne room of God, while in the background the four living creatures and twenty-four elders continue their worship in song and adoration. They provide a never-ending heavenly chorus of praise that quietly sustains the movement of the Apocalypse, but that occasionally breaks forth in the book in an extended "Hallelujah." It is no wonder that the lofty and inspiring music of Handel's *Messiah*, and especially his "Hallelujah Chorus," derives its text from the book of Revelation. Because John, like other apocalyptic writers, sees the events in heaven as models of earthly realities, the heavenly worship serves as a paradigm for the earthly worship of God. [Proper Worship]

The church is sometimes tempted to downplay the importance of worship, perhaps not explicitly, but implicitly in a variety of ways. Worship is demoted when little time is spent on careful planning of the church's worship gatherings. Quality corporate worship seldom happens by itself. It requires serious planning and coordination by the individuals who lead the congregation in worship. Worship is devalued when the focus of the service is not on God. Although an important part of being the body of Christ is the shared community with other believers, the focus in worship should not be on the participants, but on the praise and adoration of God. Note the wonderful hymnic sections throughout the book of Revelation. They all direct one's gaze and one's adoration to God. The hymns are themselves an offering from the worshiper to God. Frequently, present-day worship is treated as entertainment. Music and sermons are chosen on the basis of their appeal to the worshipers, rather than on their ability to transport the worshiper to the throne of God. Congregational applause of choral music or solos (a practice becoming more common) is inappropriate because it shifts the focus from God to the performers. Music in worship is for the glorification of God, not for the entertainment of the congregation.

Worship is devalued also when it is not allowed to give voice to the full range of human feelings toward God. Granted, worship is

---

Proper Worship

"While edification and instruction always occur when the Christian community gathers for worship, the primary purpose of our worship is always praise and prayer which are directed to God, not edification and instruction directed to the community. In our Protestant, Sunday morning 'preaching service,' there is a great need to examine the focus, purpose, and direction of our worship. Whenever that service is *used* to motivate the congregation to respond to the denomination's latest program, or the pastor's own crusade, or social action, or personal commitment—or to educate, titillate, soothe, excite, coerce—or any other often worthwhile purpose, then it is safe to say that the worship of God has been perverted into a means of achieving our own human purposes rather than an occasion to respond to God's purposes. This is less than full Christian worship."

William H. Willimon, *Word, Water, Wine and Bread* (Valley Forge PA: Judson, 1980), 123.

primarily praise, thanksgiving, and adoration. Those themes should dominate both our private and corporate worship of God. But there are times when cries of anguish, despair, and even doubt are appropriate in worship. In Revelation 6:9-11, the souls of the martyrs under the heavenly altar cry out in agony to God, "How long?" Such cries have a rightful place in worship. Readers of the Hebrew Bible know that cries of lament, anger, and despair are often raised to God (cf. the books of Job, Psalms, Lamentations, and Jeremiah). In fact, the book of Psalms contains more psalms of lament than it does any other category of psalm. A faithful worshiping community is able to gather all its experiences and troubles and offer them up to God, confident that God will hear their cries of pain as readily as God will hear their hymns of praise.

Worship is so important in the book of Revelation because John rightly understood that worship is a political act. Through worship one declares one's allegiance, one's loyalty. Through repeated acts of worship, one reconfirms that commitment. The reason public versus private worship, corporate rather than individual, is crucial is because worship is a statement to the world that the church will bow to no other gods, but to God alone. In the context of the churches of first-century Asia Minor, the struggle for loyalty was intense. Whereas some in the early churches could apparently with a clean conscience participate in the imperial cult and in the religious rituals associated with the various trade and professional guilds, John saw those actions as acts of treason against God. To participate in the worship of the emperor would have been to give assent to the claim that all power lay with Rome and the emperor. John's message is that only God deserves ultimate allegiance. In the narrative world of the Apocalypse, even John forgets this central truth, for on two occasions he falls down to worship his angel guide, only to be rebuked by the words, "You must not do that! Worship God!" The message is clear: If even the angels are not worthy of worship, then certainly no human, including the emperor, is deserving of such allegiance.

The current context of readers of the Apocalypse may seem distant from that of the original recipients of John's message. After all, not too many people are tempted to bow down in worship before the governors and presidents of our day. Yet perceptive readers of the Apocalypse have seen that John's warnings are still valid. One of the most insightful applications of the book of Revelation in the last two decades has been the book by Allan Boesak, *Comfort and Protest: Reflections on the Apocalypse of John of Patmos.* Boesak, who was one of the leading spokespersons against apartheid in South

Africa and who was imprisoned because of his activities, wrote this work when South Africa was still in the grips of its official policy on apartheid. Boesak saw the parallels between the beasts of Roman power and the beasts of the South African government. He labeled the power structure what it really was—the beast from the sea that demanded worship and that killed any who refused to accept and participate in its claims. [Worship in Revelation]

Worship in Revelation

"Revelation invites the reader to sing, to pray, and to praise God. The book is primarily liturgical. Before planning a single sermon from this text, let the preacher read through Revelation in one or two sittings, marking every shout, every doxology, every prayer, every hallelujah, every benediction, every song. Clearly it was composed for use in the worship service of the church, and it would be shorn of much of its power and effect were those who teach and preach to offer its relevant themes apart from a liturgical setting."

Fred B. Craddock, "Preaching the Book of Revelation," *Interpretation* 40/3 (July 1986): 278.

In a less graphic and more subtle way, American culture lays claim to the allegiance of the church. Patriotism becomes entwined with religious faith. American flags are placed in the churches; churches hold patriotic rallies. Capitalism is seen as a divinely ordained economic system. Caesar demands to be worshiped, and too readily the church obeys. As a result, the message of the gospel is subverted, and the church becomes a willing participant in the deification of nationalism. To this situation, also, the book of Revelation declares, "You must not do that. Worship God!"

NOTES

[1] Elisabeth Schüssler Fiorenza, *The Book of Revelation: Justice and Judgment* (Philadelphia: Fortress, 1985), 194.

[2] G. B. Caird, *A Commentary on the Revelation of St. John the Divine* (New York: Harper & Row, 1966), 63

[3] Henry Barclay Swete, *Commentary on Revelation* (1911; reprint, Grand Rapids: Kregel Publications, 1977), 69. Swete attributed this interpretation to Victorinus, a 3rd-century bishop who produced the earliest Latin commentary on the Apocalypse.

[4] Jürgen Roloff, *The Revelation of John: A Continental Commentary*, Continental Commentaries, trans. John E. Alsup (Minneapolis: Fortress, 1993), 69. Roloff mentioned this view, but rejected it.

[5] Ibid., 70.

[6] David E. Aune, "The Influence of Roman Imperial Court Ceremonial on the Apocalypse of John," *Biblical Research* 28 (1983): 8-9.

[7] Cited by George R. Beasley-Murray, *The Book of Revelation*, New Century Bible (Greenwood SC: Attic, 1974), 117.

[8] Aune, "Influence of Roman Imperial Court Ceremonial," 12.

THE LAMB AND THE SCROLL

5:1-14

COMMENTARY

The Lamb and the Scroll, 5:1-14

John's description of the heavenly throne room continues in chapter 5. Whereas in the previous chapter the focus of the vision has been on the throne of God and its surroundings, in chapter 5 the focus is on Christ, depicted as a lamb. In fact, Christ has not even appeared in chapter 4. It is appropriate that John presents first his description of God, followed by his description of Christ, for Christ is God's agent, the one who puts into action God's plan for creation. [Outline of 5:1-14]

> **Outline of 5:1-14**
> 1. The Sealed Scroll—5:1-5
> 2. The Slain Lamb—5:6-7
> 3. The First Song of Praise—5:8-10
> 4. The Second Song of Praise—5:11-12
> 5. The Third Song of Praise—5:13-14

As the scene opens, a scroll catches our attention, a scroll that is "written on the inside and on the back, sealed with seven seals." Both of these characteristics mark the scroll as unusual. [Books] Scrolls in antiquity were normally written on only one side. Some commentators have looked for examples from antiquity of types of documents that might have been written on both sides of the material. Legal documents (including deeds, marriage contracts, and debts) were often written on one side of the material, folded with the writing on the inside, sewn together and sealed, with a summary of the contents written on the outside. Some scholars have argued that the presence of the seven seals is a further clue to the identity of this scroll,

---

Books

AΩ In the KJV, the Greek word *biblion* is translated in Revelation as "book." The document that John had in mind was a scroll, that is, a book in roll form. Books as we know them today, consisting of bound sheets, were not widely used for Christian writings in the 1st century. As in Judaism, the earliest Christian Scriptures were written on scrolls made of papyrus (made from the papyrus plant; the English word "paper" is derived from "papyrus") or parchment (made from the skins of cattle, sheep, goats, or antelopes). These books in roll form were usually no longer than approximately 30 feet. Scrolls longer than that were too unwieldy for use. Because of the inconvenience of rolling and unrolling scrolls and the difficulty of locating specific passages in them, the use of folded and sewn together sheets of papyrus and parchment developed. Known as codices (sg. codex), these bound books became popular in the Christian community by the early 2d century and replaced the use of scrolls for the Christian Scriptures.

pointing to some evidence that testaments or wills in the ancient world were sealed in this manner. Understood in this way the scroll represents the kingdom of God that is conveyed by deed or testament to humanity, a kingdom "made possible through the death of the Lamb of God and his exaltation to the throne of God."[1] While these are attractive possibilities, the presence of scrolls or books in other apocalyptic writings suggests those traditions as the source for John's imagery (cf. Dan 10:21; *1 En.* 81:1-3; 93:1-3; 103:1-3; 106:19). In these works, similar heavenly scrolls or tablets contain descriptions of the future course of the world. Likewise, in Revelation the sealed book contains the destiny of the world, the purposes and plans of God for all creation. As this scene makes clear, God's plans for the world are effected through Jesus, the slain Lamb.

Seals in Antiquity

In antiquity, wet clay or wax was applied to secure the closures of containers or documents. Seals were then used to make an impression in the clay or wax to identify the source of a document or object, to guarantee the work's authenticity, or to safeguard the document or object from tampering. Seals might contain an individual's name or profession; they might be decorated with scenes; or they might consist of both.

An impression from a seal found at the city of Megiddo in Israel. Dated to the 8th century BC, the seal was inscribed with the Hebrew words, "to Shema, servant of Jeroboam."

Seal of Jeroboam, King of Israel. Copy of lost original. 1000 BC. Reuben & Edith Hecht Collection, Haifa University. Haifa, Israel. (Credit: Erich Lessing/Art Resource, NY)

The immediate source for John's description of the scroll may be the scroll given to the prophet Ezekiel, which also was described as being written on the front and back (2:10). As in Ezekiel, so in Revelation the writing on both sides may be simply an indication that the message was so long that it continued from the front of the scroll to the back. The seven seals indicate the secure nature of the scroll. This scroll will not be opened by accident or by one who does not have the proper authority. It is sealed tightly—seven times!

The scroll is sealed to guarantee its authenticity and to keep its contents secret. [Seals in Antiquity] "Who is worthy to open the scroll and break its seals?" asks an angel (5:2). Therein lies the dramatic tension in this scene. No one among the heavenly assembly is able to open the scroll. Furthermore, no one in all the universe ("in heaven or on earth or under the earth," cf. Phil 2:10) can break the seals and reveal the contents of the book. In disappointment and despair, John weeps at the news that no one is worthy to open the book and bring God's plans to fruition. This literary technique of apparent failure because no one is able to accomplish the task at hand, common in folk tales, serves not only to heighten the dramatic tension of the scene, but also to increase the stature of the one who finally is able to accomplish the seemingly impossible task.

The heavenly assembly knows what John does not know: there is indeed one who is able to open the scroll. One of the elders announces the good news to John. Success has already been achieved; the victory has been won because "the Lion of the tribe of Judah, the Root of David, has conquered" (5:5). He can open the sealed book. The two images used by the elder, "the Lion of the tribe of Judah" and "the Root of David," are drawn from the Hebrew Bible. "The Lion of the tribe of Judah" (Gen 49:9-10; see also *T. Jud.* 24:5 and 2 Esd 12:31-32) and "the Root of David" (Isa 11:10, "root of Jesse"; cf. the use of the phrase the "Branch" [of David] in Isa 11:1; Jer 23:5; 33:15; Zech 3:8; 6:12) were used in these writings to refer to a coming king of the line of David. As the *Testament of Judah*, *4 Ezra*, and Romans (15:12) indicate, certain segments of first-century Judaism understood these titles messianically.

But the reader who searches, as John did, for a fierce, conquering lion will be surprised. In place of a lion, John sees a lamb. [The Lamb] This is a startling transformation. The reader is told that a lion, a fierce creature of the wild, has conquered. What the reader finds, however, is that the lion is in reality a lamb—but not any ordinary lamb. It bears the marks of its execution, "standing as if it had been slaughtered" (5:6). This lion-lamb is clearly Jesus, the one "who loves us and freed us from our sins by his blood" (1:5). "Lamb" is the most prominent christological title in Revelation. The word appears twenty-eight times as a metaphor for Jesus. The source of John's imagery for Jesus as a lamb is uncertain. Suggestions have included the lambs that were offered as sacrifices in the temple every morning and evening, the Passover lamb, the Suffering Servant of Isaiah 53, and the conquering lamb of *1 Enoch* 89–90. Rather than seeing the lamb imagery in Revelation as being drawn from only one source or having only one meaning, a better approach is to acknowledge the multivalent character of this powerful symbol. John has drawn on several ideas associated with the lamb image, shaping his materials and creating a new symbol—a victorious figure who conquers by self-sacrifice, who willingly gives up his life to become "the faithful and true witness."

The seven horns on the lamb symbolize the power and strength of the lamb. [Horns] He is no helpless victim, but a powerful,

> **The Lamb**
>
> Occurring 28 times in Revelation, "Lamb" is John's favorite christological title. Apart from Revelation, the imagery of a lamb is applied to Jesus only four places in the New Testament (John 1:29, 36; Acts 8:32; and 1 Pet 1:19). In each of these instances, a different Greek word, *amnos*, is used instead of the word *arnion* used by John.

Horns

Animal horns are an obvious symbol of strength and power since horns function as weapons for many animals. The author of the book of Daniel used horned animals to portray various earthly rulers. The breaking of the animals' horns symbolized the rulers' defeat (cf. Dan 7 and 8). The seven horns on the Lamb in Revelation symbolize complete power held by the Lamb.

conquering lamb. The seven eyes, John explains, represent God's spirits sent forth into the world. They are symbols of God's presence and knowledge. The Lamb thus acts with the authority of God. He is filled with God's power and God's insight. John's depiction of Christ as a slaughtered lamb with seven horns and seven eyes combines images of death and defeat with symbols of power and authority. Through this imagery John declares that the only "conquering" that is consistent with the values of God is conquering that occurs through self-sacrifice and love, not through violence.

By taking the scroll from God, the Lamb receives authority and lordship from God. Jesus is the only one who is worthy and able to bring to completion God's plans and purposes for the world. Recognizing this, the four living creatures and the twenty-four elders fall down in reverence and worship before the Lamb. Each of the heavenly beings holds two objects related to worship—harps and bowls of incense. (Even though the syntax of the sentence would imply that the four living creatures as well as the elders hold these objects, some interpreters view these as belonging to the elders alone, arguing that only the elders play a priestly role.)

Incense

Incense was widely used in ancient worship among people of various cultures. In Israel, the burning of incense was a regular part of temple worship, following the instructions given in Exod 30. The aroma of the burning incense was thought to be a pleasant sensation for God. The pleasing odor would help to appease divine wrath against human sinfulness and thus help effect atonement. Various aromatic gums and spices were used in the making of incense (see Exod 30:34-38).

Harps, along with other musical instruments, had been a regular feature of temple worship in Jerusalem. Musicians' guilds formed choirs and orchestras that provided music as a part of the temple worship. John portrays a heavenly worship scene modeled after, but even more resplendent than, earthly worship. In the Hebrew Bible, harps were instruments of praise to God and accompanied the singing of psalms (Pss 33:2; 43:4; 147:7; 149:3). Here they provide musical accompaniment for the new song that the heavenly chorus sings.

The "golden bowls full of incense" call to mind the incense that the priests offered to God every morning and evening in the temple. [Incense]The purpose of this incense offering in the temple was "to secure the presence of God and his attention to man's prayer.

The incense smoke carries the prayer to God, who is hopefully appeased when he smells the fragrant odor of the delicious incense."[2] For John, the prayers themselves are the incense that is offered to God. The imagery of prayers as incense is a graphic portrayal of the prayers of the people wafting up to God and a reminder to the readers that their prayers are not in vain. God will hear and respond to their cries. For John's readers, faced with persecution, social ostracism, and ridicule—as well as for modern readers confronted with life's difficulties—the assurance that God hears their prayers is a powerful comfort. John says that these are the prayers of the "saints." In the New Testament, the word "saints" does not denote a special class of elite Christians. The word "saints" or "holy ones" refers to all faithful followers.

The activity of the heavenly beings as bearers of the prayers of the people suggests a priestly role. This is similar to what is found in some Jewish literature where angels serve as mediators for the people, presenting their prayers to God. In Tobit 12:12, 15, the angel Raphael identified himself as one of the seven angels "who stand ready and enter before the glory of the Lord." One of the specific tasks he performed was to bring the prayers of the people to God (cf. *T. Levi* 3:5-7; *3 Bar.* 11).

The four living creatures and the elders, who previously had sung their praises to God, now join together to sing a new song to the Lamb. [A New Song] The reference to a "new song" is found often in the book of Psalms (33:3; 40:3; 96:1; 98:1; 144:9; cf. Isa 42:10). In Revelation, the song is new not only in the sense that it appears for the first time. Rather, it is new because it is qualitatively different. It celebrates God's decisive act of salvation enacted through the sacrificial death of Jesus. The song declares a three-fold reason why Jesus is worthy of praise and adoration: He has been slaughtered; he has ransomed the saints; and he has made them a kingdom and priests. The word used to describe Jesus' death, "slaughtered" (*esphagēs*), is a violent term, often used in association with an animal that is slaughtered for sacrifice. Accordingly, the use of this term here may suggest an interpretation of the death of Jesus as the Passover lamb. Through his death (his "blood") he has ransomed or purchased the people for God, an economic metaphor that reflects the practice of buying the freedom of slaves or prisoners of war. The death of Christ was an act of liberation. It has freed people from their bondage to sin and from the

A New Song

"The death of Jesus has created a new situation, so the elders sing *a new song*. The death of Jesus is a cosmic turning point. It marks the beginning of the defeat of Satan."

Adela Yarbro Collins, *The Apocalypse*, New Testament Message 22 (Wilmington DE: Michael Glazier, Inc., 1979), 42.

Kingdom and Priests

"John does not think of Christ as having withdrawn from the scene of his earthly victory, to return only at the Parousia. In and through his faithful followers he continues to exercise both his royal and his priestly functions."

G. B. Caird, *A Commentary on the Revelation of St. John the Divine*, Harper's New Testament Commentaries (New York: Harper & Row, 1966), 77.

powers of evil that oppress and enslave. As in the exodus event when God had liberated the Hebrew slaves from Egyptian control and had created them as a special nation for God (Exod 19:6), now God in a greater way has created a new community through Christ. This new, liberated community is to be "a kingdom and priests serving our God" (5:10; cf. 1:6). They are to be mediators between God and God's creation, helping to bring into reality the redemption and reconciliation effected by Christ. Christ has already brought about this liberation and this new community. It is a present reality. Those who belong to this new "kingdom" do not presently exercise their full royal role, however. That will be realized in the end time, when all of God's creation is redeemed and the faithful "will reign on earth" (5:10). [Kingdom and Priests]

This new community is a universal community. Christ has redeemed people "from every tribe and language and people and nation" (5:10). The people of God are drawn from every station and walk of life. This vision of a universal community echoes the message of Paul to the Galatians: "There is no longer Jew or Greek, there is no longer slave or free, there is no longer male and female; for all of you are one in Christ Jesus" (3:28). The emphasis here on the communal aspect of the work of Christ—making people into a new "kingdom"—should serve as a corrective to an excessively individualistic understanding of salvation that persists in the thinking of some Christians. God has created a "new people," not simply new individuals.

After the hymn by the four living creatures and the elders, a chorus of angels lifts their voices in praise to the Lamb. They, too, sing a song extolling the worthiness of the Lamb. The throng of angels is innumerable. The Greek word *myrias* (myriad) can mean ten thousand, but can also be used to refer to a countless throng. The latter is intended here. The imagery of the innumerable band of heavenly attendants surrounding the throne is drawn from Daniel 7:10. Whereas earlier God has been recognized as being worthy because, as creator, God is the source of all things (4:11), the Lamb is declared worthy because of his act of redemption (5:9, 12). The sacrificial death of the Lamb, through which God's salvation of the world has been made possible, is the basis for the outburst of praise directed to the Lamb. [Worthy Is the Lamb]

Worthy Is the Lamb

This scene in ch. 5 of the praise of the Lamb has been the inspiration for several Christian hymns, including "Worthy Is the Lamb," "All Hail the Power of Jesus' Name" and " 'Tis the Church Triumphant Singing." The text of this last hymn, written by John Kent (1766–1843), is particularly indebted to this scene of the adoration of the Lamb. The hymn states,

'Tis the church triumphant singing, Worthy the Lamb!
Heav'n thro'out with praises ringing, Worthy the Lamb!
Thrones and pow'rs before Him bending, Odors sweet with voice ascending
Swell the chorus never ending, Worthy the Lamb!

Ev'ry kindred, tongue and nation—Worthy the Lamb!
Join to sing the great salvation; Worthy the Lamb!
Loud as mighty thunders roaring, Floods of mighty waters pouring,
Prostrate at His feet adoring, Worthy the Lamb!

Harps and songs for ever sounding Worthy the Lamb!
Mighty grace o'er sin abounding; Worthy the Lamb!
By His blood He dearly bought us; Wand'ring from the fold He sought us;
And to glory safely brought us: Worthy the Lamb!

Sing with blest anticipation, Worthy the Lamb!
Thro' the vale of tribulation, Worthy the Lamb!
Sweetest notes, all notes excelling, On the theme for ever dwelling,
Still untold, tho' ever telling, Worthy the Lamb!

The praise of the Lamb continues to expand in an ever-widening circle, moving from the four living creatures and the twenty-four elders to the angels in heaven, finally encompassing "every creature in heaven and on earth and under the earth and in the sea" (5:13). [Biblical Cosmology] All creation bursts forth in adoration of God and the Lamb. The scene reaches its climax when the four living creatures and the elders, who had begun this praisefest in the throne room of God, burst forth with an "Amen!" and fall down and worship both God and the Lamb. Heaven and earth reverberate with the joyous hymns of praise and the echoes of "Amen!" Chapter 5 opens on a somber and disappointed note; it ends in celebration.

The scene of heavenly worship serves an important function in the overall structure of the Apocalypse. Through this scene, John assures his readers that God is in

Biblical Cosmology

New Testament writers inherited the ancient Hebrew understanding of a three-storied universe: heaven above, the earth in the middle, the underworld (*Hades* or *Sheol*) below. Heaven contained the storehouses of wind, snow, and hail. It was also the dwelling place of God. Separating earth from heaven was a dome-shaped covering or canopy, the firmament, which was supported by pillars and contained windows through which rain fell to the earth. Under the earth was the place of the dead, variously called *Hades* or *Sheol*. As water surrounded the earth above the firmament, so water also surrounded the earth beneath, gushing up at times in springs and floods.

The Lamb Opening the Book

In this manuscript illumination, God and the Lamb are seated together on an embroidered throne. The Bruges tapestry tradition is reflected in the patterning of the painted throne. The symbols of the four evangelists (eagle, angel, ox, and lion) and the kneeling elders surround the throne. The artist portrays John kneeling in the foreground.

The Lamb Opening the Book from the *Commentary on the Apocalypse*. 15th C. Flemish. Manuscript on Vellum. The Pierpont Morgan Library, New York. (Credit: The Pierpont Morgan Library/Art Resource, NY)

control of the universe and that the Lamb has successfully brought God's plans and purposes to fulfillment. Before revealing the coming scenes of judgment, suffering, and destruction, John reminds his readers of the centrality of the throne of God in heaven. The one seated on that throne holds sway over the universe because the one on the throne is the same one who created the universe. The outcome of God's plans are not in doubt because the Lamb has already conquered. Regardless of what else John's vision may entail, the reader can face life with assurance, knowing that the ultimate outcome of the world is not in doubt. [The Lamb Opening the Book]

Furthermore, by portraying the worship in which all creation has taken part, John invites the reader to join in this paean of praise also. In so doing, the reader experiences in the present moment the reality of God's eschatological triumph. One celebrates that final victory that is presently assured but yet to be completed. True worship has the power to move the worshiper beyond his or her present experience into a different dimension. It gives one a different place to stand and from which to view reality. The world and its problems look different because one sees reality in a new light. Leonard Thompson has explained:

> In both Revelation and the churches of Asia Minor, worship realizes the kingship of God and his just judgment; through liturgical celebration eschatological expectations are experienced presently. Hymns, thanksgivings, doxologies, and acclamations realize in the context of worship the eschatological message. Worship, then, becomes a context that integrally relates the visions in Revelation with John's original revelatory experience and the re-presentation of John's experience in the life of the worshipping community. The Book of Revelation, by functioning in communal worship of Asia Minor as heavenly worship functions in the book itself, links heaven and earth. The work mediates its own message.[3]

CONNECTIONS

1. Through the image of the sealed scroll that contains God's plan for the world and through the picture of God and Christ seated on the throne, ruling over the world, this heavenly throne room scene asserts that God is in control of the universe. [God and the Lamb] The theological term for this belief is *providence*. This affirmation is a source of deep comfort. It assures us that in spite of all the chaos, confusion, and misdirection of the world, God is still in control. The God who created the world sustains, guides, and ultimately brings it to completion. This is a major theme of the book of Revelation, indeed of all apocalyptic writings. This theme is probably the most important reason for the continued popularity of apocalyptic theology. Even when people might not be able to formulate in precise words why apocalyptic texts are so appealing, deep down they are attracted by the unyielding certitude that ultimately everything is going to be all right.

God and the Lamb

"The throne symbolizes God's power and the Lamb slain symbolizes God's vulnerability, God's self-offering for our sakes. The throne says that God *can*; all things are possible with God. The Lamb slain says that God *will*; all that must be done will be done for the redemption of creation."

Fred B. Craddock, "Preaching the Book of Revelation," *Interpretation* 40/3 (July 1986): 276.

But is that still a viable belief today? Can the modern reader claim with integrity that God is in control of the universe? Those are questions with which any interpreter of this text must be willing to grapple, not because such questions are an interesting intellectual exercise, but because those are the questions that people in the pews and the classrooms are already asking—the parents who have recently buried their teenage daughter who was killed by a drunk driver, the family that has been torn apart by charges of sexual abuse, the wife who must learn to cope with a husband who is progressively debilitated by Alzheimer's. These are but a few examples of the people to whom we must be accountable if we assert with John that God sits on the throne and is in control of the universe.

The doctrine of providence is difficult, particularly for an age that has witnessed the atrocities of the Holocaust and the slaughter in Bosnia and Rwanda. Easy, glib answers are an insult to our congregations and to God. We must be willing to struggle with the seeming absence at times of God in our world and in our own lives. One approach to dealing with the question of providence is to state clearly which views on providence are unacceptable. One such example would be the belief, heard quite often, that everything that happens has been determined in advance by God. This view is more correctly labeled fatalism, for it allows no role for human freedom and ultimately absolves people of any responsibility for their choices and actions. A deterministic, mechanical understanding of God's providential care of the world robs human life of any real meaning or significance, for then human thoughts and actions are merely acted-out roles in a cosmic script.

The view of providence that is implicit in the book of Revelation respects human freedom—the freedom to do evil or to do good. [Assurance] The consequences of human evil are sometimes overwhelming. John does not paint a rosy picture of a world in which God's people are spared all pain and suffering. Rather, John sees a world that persecutes and kills the people of God, a world that is enamored with power and wealth, a world that sells humans like merchandise (18:13). Yet in spite of what he sees, John is still confident that God's purposes are being worked out in the world. John sees beyond the present situation to the ultimate goal of God—a universe that recognizes the sovereignty of God, a universe in which all evil has been eradicated. John does not reach this conclusion on the basis of evidence that he sees. In fact, as people throughout the centuries have pointed out, an observation of how the world operates would lead one to argue that there is no divine providence at work in the world. Yet John sees the world through eyes of faith. John bases his belief in the providence of God more on eschatological vision than on present perceptions. Because of John's belief that God is Alpha and Omega, the one who stands at

Assurance

John of Patmos faced persecution and possibly even death. His readers faced a similar precarious future. John was a realist. He knew that life was not simple or easy. But John was convinced that God would not abandon him, regardless of the difficulties. The vision of God seated on the throne provided hope and assurance. Another individual who, like John, confronted the beasts of pride, oppression, and dehumanization and was sustained by the presence of God was Martin Luther King Jr. In one of his writings, he described the source of stability and assurance that strengthened him through all his ordeals:

One of the most dedicated participants in the bus protest in Montgomery, Alabama, was an elderly Negro whom we affectionately called Mother Pollard. Although poverty-stricken and uneducated, she was amazingly intelligent and possessed a deep understanding of the meaning of the movement. After having walked for several weeks, she was asked if she were tired. With ungrammatical profundity, she answered, "My feets is tired, but my soul is rested."

On a particular Monday evening, following a tension-packed week which included being arrested and receiving numerous threatening telephone calls, I spoke at a mass meeting. I attempted to convey an overt impression of strength and courage, although I was inwardly depressed and fear-stricken. At the end of the meeting, Mother Pollard came to the front of the church and said, "Come here, son." I immediately went to her and hugged her affectionately. "Something is wrong with you," she said. "You didn't talk strong tonight." Seeking further to disguise my fears, I retorted, "Oh, no, Mother Pollard, nothing is wrong. I am feeling as fine as ever." But her insight was discerning. "Now you can't fool me," she said. "I knows something is wrong. Is it that we ain't doing things to please you? Or is it that the white folks is bothering you?" Before I could respond, she looked directly into my eyes and said, "I don told you we is with you all the way." Then her face became radiant and she said in words of quiet certainty, "But even if we ain't with you, God's gonna take care of you." As she spoke these consoling words, everything in me quivered and quickened with the pulsing tremor of raw energy.

Since that dreary night in 1956, Mother Pollard has passed on to glory and I have known very few quiet days. I have been tortured without and tormented within by the raging fires of tribulation. I have been forced to muster what strength and courage I have to withstand howling winds of pain and jostling storms of adversity. But as the years have unfolded the eloquently simple words of Mother Pollard have come back again and again to give light and peace and guidance to my troubled soul, "God's gonna take care of you."

Martin Luther King Jr., *Strength to Love* (New York: Harper & Row, 1963), 116-17.

the end as well as at the beginning of history, he is confident that God will draw the world to its appointed end.

The theologian Paul Tillich described providence as God's "directing creativity." God is continually creating the universe to conform it to God's designs. God does not override human freedom or remove all difficulties and obstacles in life. God does not coerce. God works through humanity's failures and resistance, as well as through the horrors and calamities of the natural world. God, the creator of the universe, is still at work creating as God directs and drives the entire universe to its appointed end. Tillich wrote:

> Providence is not interference; it is creation. . . . Providence is a *quality* of every constellation of conditions, a quality which "drives" or "lures" toward fulfillment. . . . The man who believes in providence does not believe that a special divine activity will alter the conditions of finitude and estrangement. He believes, and asserts with the courage of faith, that no situation whatsoever can frustrate the fulfillment of his ultimate destiny, that nothing can separate him from the love of God which is in Christ Jesus (Rom 8).[4]

An unswerving belief in the sovereignty of God is what provides John with the resounding hope that sustains the Apocalypse. Over and over again, the assurance of hope reverberates throughout the book of Revelation. Here in the throne room scene in chapters 4 and 5, heaven and earth break forth in anthems of praise because all of creation has seen who sits on the heavenly throne. The occupier of the throne is not the Roman emperor or any other earthly ruler. The one who sits on the throne is God. For that reason, John is certain that ultimately everything will be all right—certainly not now, but one day.

Is John correct? Or is he whistling in the dark, trying to calm his own fears and convince himself as well as others? Speaking to this issue, Eugene Boring has written:

> From the midst of my cool, jaded affluence, I can give you twenty reasons why John is a fool. And in the midst of the loneliness and absurdity of his unjust situation, he paints a picture larger than the world that says, "Go ahead and celebrate. Everything is going to be all right." Heaven already joins in the song of celebration. Finally all creation will. We are given permission not only not to cry, but to join in the singing. And we can say to each other, not as a banal nonstatement but as life-giving word: everything is going to be all right.[5]

2. The singing of hymns of jubilation and praise occurs frequently in Revelation. The author of Psalm 137 described a different experience. For the psalmist, as well as for many other inhabitants of Jerusalem who had been taken in exile as captives of the Babylonians, there was nothing to sing about. All hope seemed vanquished. There was no reason to sing. It was the time for despair and mourning. The psalmist lamented,

By the rivers of Babylon—
    there we sat down and there we wept
    when we remembered Zion.
On the willows there
    we hung up our harps.
For there our captors
    asked us for songs,
and our tormentors asked for mirth, saying,
    "Sing us one of the songs of Zion!"
How could we sing the LORD's song
    in a foreign land? (137:1-4)

But John sees the world differently. In spite of life's pains and trouble, in spite of oppression and persecution, singing still breaks forth. [Hymns in Early Christian Worship] Allan Boesak described a similar experience in South Africa during the terrible days of apartheid when Blacks were being cruelly mistreated, imprisoned, injured, and even killed. Writing prior to the downfall of apartheid, Boesak said,

Hymns in Early Christian Worship

 Music is prominent in the Apocalypse. Hymns and songs appear in 4:8, 11; 5:9-10, 12, 13; 7:12; 11:17-18; and 15:3-4. These hymns, along with others scattered throughout the New Testament (Luke 1:46-55, 68-79; 2:29-32; Eph 5:14; Phil 2:6-11; 1 Tim 3:16; 6:15-16; 2 Tim 2:11-13; and Titus 3:4-7), suggest that the early church was a singing church. The New Testament contains specific statements about singing hymns and songs (1 Cor 14:26; Eph 5:19; Col 3:16). External evidence that the early Christians expressed their faith through music is found in the words of the Roman governor of Bithynia and Pontus, Pliny the Younger, who in one of his letters to the emperor Trajan described the activities of the Christians of his day (c. 110). Pliny wrote that the Christians "met regularly before dawn on a fixed day to chant verses alternately among themselves [or "to sing a hymn antiphonally"; the Latin phrase may mean to recite any set form of words] in honour of Christ as if to a god."

Pliny, *Ep. Tra.* 10.96.7, trans. Betty Radice, Loeb Classical Library (Cambridge MA: Harvard University Press, 1969).

Black people in South Africa have made freedom songs part of the struggle; in fact, the struggle is inconceivable without them. Marching down the streets, facing the police and army troops of the South African government, they sing. In jail, they sing—songs of defiance and faith and freedom. . . . We sing because we believe, we sing because we hope. We sing because we know that it is only a little while, and the tyrant shall cease to exist.[6]

NOTES

[1] George R. Beasley-Murray, *The Book of Revelation*, New Century Bible (Greenwood SC: Attic, 1974), 123.

[2] Kjeld Nielsen, "Incense," *The Anchor Bible Dictionary*, ed. David Noel Freedman, 6 vols. (New York: Doubleday & Co., 1992), 3:407.

[3] Leonard L. Thompson, *The Book of Revelation: Apocalypse and Empire* (New York: Oxford University Press, 1990), 72-73.

[4] Paul Tillich, *Systematic Theology,* 3 vols. (Chicago: University of Chicago Press, 1951), 1:267.

[5] M. Eugene Boring, "Everything Is Going to Be All Right," *Preaching Through the Apocalypse: Sermons from Revelation*, ed. Cornish R. Rogers and Joseph R. Jeter Jr. (St. Louis: Chalice, 1992), 82.

[6] Allan A. Boesak, *Comfort and Protest: The Apocalypse from a South African Perspective* (Philadelphia: Westminster, 1987), 60-61.

THE FIRST SIX SEALS

6:1-17

The Seven Seals, 6:1–8:5

In Revelation, three different seven-fold series depict a variety of calamities that are to strike the earth—the seven seals, the seven trumpets, and the seven bowls. [The First Seal] A fourth series, the seven thunders, is mentioned, but John is forbidden to disclose the contents of that series (10:4). These three series exhibit several similarities, both in form and in content. How is the reader supposed to understand these three series of calamities? Are they different events, one occurring after the other? Or do the three series portray in different imagery the same events? In attempting to understand John's vision, the reader must avoid a rigid, chronological interpretation of the imagery of Revelation. Apocalyptic literature is more impressionistic than descriptive, which means that the reader should

The First Seal

In this manuscript illumination, the artist shows the Lamb in the upper right corner with its foot placed in the pages of the book. The rider carries a bow and wears a crown. He is placed on the white horse as John describes in 6:2. The artist adds an angel who delivers the written message to John on an extended scroll.

The Opening of the First Seal from the *Commentary on the Apocalypse*. 15th C. Flemish. Manuscript on Vellum. The Pierpont Morgan Library, New York. (Credit: The Pierpont Morgan Library/Art Resource, NY)

The Second Seal

Henri Rousseau began painting after retiring from his position of customs collector. Although he received no formal training, he is revered by Picasso as an inspiration for modern painting. Even this picture of the opening of the second seal, showing the figure of War on horseback, reflects a folk style often associated with his more famous work, *The Dream*, located in the Museum of Modern Art, New York. Rousseau's War is clothed in white, in contrast to the darkness of the horse behind him. The vultures have already descended and begun to eat the corpses strewn along the front of the picture plane.

Henri Rousseau (1844–1910). *War.* 1984. Oil. Musee d'Orsay. Paris, France. (Credit: Réunion des Musées Nationaux/Art Resource, NY)

not expect a clear and precise, or even logical, presentation of the writer's message. The language of the Apocalypse is more poetic than scientific. The three series of judgments that John portrays are three different ways to present the same or similar ideas. John's method here has often been compared to a musical composition in which the composer gives three variations of the same musical theme. In one scene, John uses the imagery of seven seals being broken; in another, he uses seven trumpets; in yet a third, he writes about seven bowls of wrath being poured upon the earth. Each time John describes these scenes of catastrophe and destruction some variation occurs, but basically John is portraying the same idea.

In the series of seven seals, as also in the trumpet and bowl series, John is drawing upon traditional apocalyptic expectations of judgment and catastrophes that will precede the end of the world. [The Second Seal] Apocalyptic writings often contain descriptions of cataclysmic events that are to happen prior to the final events of history. Scholars often refer to these end-time calamities as eschatological woes or messianic woes, the latter description indicating that they occasionally precede or accompany the arrival of a messianic figure in the last days. The eschatological woes may include earthly events (earthquakes, wars, famines, persecutions) and cosmic disturbances (stars falling, the sun shining at night, and the moon shining in the day). The eschatological woes are a time of intense suffering and tribulation for the inhabitants of the earth. Much variety existed among apocalyptic writers concerning the purpose and duration of this time of extreme distress and tribulation. In some apocalypses, the eschatological woes affect only the wicked. As such, they serve as God's judgment upon the earth and punishment for the wicked. In other writings, the woes fall on both the wicked and the righteous. The righteous are sometimes given divine protection from the effect of the calamities. In other works, the righteous are tested by the eschatological woes.

For Christian readers, the best-known example of such end-time events is the listing in Mark 13 and its parallels (Matt 24:1-44; Luke 21:5-38). In Mark, the series of eschatological woes includes wars, earthquakes, famines, persecution, and disturbances of the sun, moon, and stars. Matthew's list is nearly identical to Mark's, whereas Luke's is slightly different. R. H. Charles compared the lists in all three Synoptic Gospels with the events in Revelation 6 and 7. His arrangement of the events in the Synoptic Gospels and

 Eschatological Woes

Matthew 24:6, 7, 9a, 29
1. Wars
2. International Strife
3. Famines
4. Earthquakes
5. Persecutions
6. Eclipses of the sun and moon; falling of the stars; shaking of the powers of heaven

Mark 13:7-9a, 24-25
1. Wars
2. International strife
3. Earthquakes
4. Famines
5. Persecutions
6. Eclipses of the sun and moon; falling of the stars; shaking of the powers of heaven

Luke 21:9-12a, 25-26
1. Wars
2. International strife
3. Earthquakes
4. Famines
5. Persecutions
6. Signs in the sun, moon, and stars; men fainting for fear of the things coming on the world; shaking of the powers of heaven

Revelation 6:2-17; 7:1
Seal 1. War
Seal 2. International Strife
Seal 3. Famine
Seal 4. Pestilence (Death and Hades)
Seal 5. Persecutions
Seal 6. (6:12–7:3) Earthquakes; eclipse of the sun; ensanguining of the moon; falling of the stars; men calling on the rocks to fall on them; shaking of the powers of heaven; four destroying winds

R. H. Charles, *A Critical and Exegetical Commentary on the Revelation of St. John*, The International Critical Commentary, 2 vols. (Edinburgh: T. & T. Clark, 1920), 1:158.

Revelation is given below. [Eschatological Woes] John of Patmos is clearly dependent on the Synoptic accounts or on an independent version of the same tradition that underlies the Synoptic accounts of the eschatological woes. The similarity of the Gospel accounts to lists of eschatological woes found in earlier Jewish apocalypses indicates that such eschatological events were stock motifs of apocalyptic literature.

COMMENTARY

The First Four Seals, 6:1-8

As each of the first six seals is opened, a new scene unfolds. [Outline of 6:1-17] Commentators have been puzzled by John's visual imagery here. Strictly speaking, a scroll that is sealed with seven seals cannot be opened until all seven seals are broken. Yet John describes action breaking forth each time a seal is broken, apparently implying that the action bursts forth from the scroll as the seal is opened. Some commentators have tried to salvage John's presentation by arguing that the breaking of the seals does not reveal information from the scroll itself. Rather, the actions that take place when the seals are broken represent preliminary events to those contained in the scroll. While such a reading removes the problem of ascertaining the contents of a scroll before all its seals are broken, it also creates a bigger problem. Unless the breaking of the seals reveals the contents of the scroll, the contents remain unknown because the scroll is not mentioned again. Such an understanding is unacceptable given the high value placed on the scroll and its contents in chapter 5. The opening of the scroll is of major concern to John. It is unlikely that he would fail to disclose its contents. The better approach is to allow John some creative freedom in his use of images. The breaking forth of a new activity with the opening of each seal is a part of John's dramatic and creative artistry. In a work in which a lion is a lamb (with seven horns and seven eyes!) and the sun turns black and the moon like blood, the release of information when seals are broken does not require an excessive stretch of the imagination.

Outline of 6:1-17
1. The First Four Seals—6:1-8
   a. The First Seal: The Rider on the White Horse—6:1-2
   b. The Second Seal: The Rider on the Red Horse—6:3-4
   c. The Third Seal: The Rider on the Black Horse—6:5-6
   d. The Fourth Seal: The Rider on the Pale Horse—6:7-8
2. The Fifth Seal: The Souls under the Altar—6:9-11
3. The Sixth Seal: Cosmic Disturbances—6:12-17

The first four seals form a distinct group. The opening of each of
these seals unleashes a horse and rider who thunder across the
stage, presenting one of the most memorable scenes from the book
of Revelation, "the four horsemen of the Apocalypse." Each horse is
a different color—white, red, black, and pale green. [Horses]
The source of the four horsemen imagery is Zechariah 1:7-17 and
6:1-8. Zechariah 1:7-17 describes a vision
of several horsemen (the exact number is
not stated) on red, sorrel, and white horses
who have been sent out by God on a
reconnaissance patrol of the earth. The
vision proclaims a message of assurance
that the temple in Jerusalem (destroyed by
the Babylonians in 587 BC) will soon be rebuilt, and Jerusalem will
again be God's chosen city. Although not stated, the vision also perhaps implies judgment on the nations that have made God angry
by their treatment of the people of Judah. The second text
describes four chariots, each drawn by horses of a different color
(red, black, white, and dappled gray), sent out on patrol in all four
directions over the earth. They represent messengers from the
divine council who will establish peace and justice in the world.

Horses

Horses were not widely used for transportation in the ancient world. That role was played more often by the donkey or camel. Horses were primarily mili-tary animals, used to pull chariots or for mounted cavalry.

John has borrowed his imagery of horsemen and colored horses
from these two visions, but in his typical fashion he has altered the
imagery and made it his own. For John, the four horsemen are not
messengers of assurance or world order, but rather they symbolize
the cataclysmic destruction that will precede the end. As each seal is
broken, John hears one of the four living creatures around the
throne cry out, "Come!" On the one hand, this cry serves a practical purpose of calling each rider onto the stage. More importantly,
however, it connects with the anticipated coming of Christ in 22:7,
12, 17, 20. The coming of the four horsemen brings judgment and
punishment. But this, too, is a part of the coming of Christ (cf.
19:11-21). The events set in motion by the opening of the scroll
and the cries of "Come!" are both bad news and good news, judgment and grace.

The rider on the white horse is a symbol of military conquest. He
carries a bow, a weapon for defeating his enemies. The crown he is
given symbolizes his victory over his enemies. The color of his
horse is also significant, for white was the color of victory. In order
that the hearer/reader not miss the symbolism, John explicitly
states that the purpose of the horseman is to conquer. Due to the
description of Christ in 19:11-21 as a rider on a white horse, some
commentators have sought to identify the first horseman of chapter

6 also as representing Christ. His conquering, then, refers to the universal proclamation of the gospel. This interpretation has scant support, however. The only similarity between the two horsemen is the color of their horses. Furthermore, the first horseman of chapter 6 joins with the horsemen of the other three seals to depict images of destruction and death. To interpret the rider of the white horse in 6:2 as Christ or the spread of the gospel does violence to the context in which the imagery occurs.

Whereas the Zechariah texts provided the raw materials for John's imagery, the picture of mounted archers was possibly dependent also on a contemporary reality. The Parthians, renowned in the ancient world for their skill as archers on horseback, were a formidable rival to the Romans. Lying to the east of Rome, the Parthian Empire stretched from the Euphrates River to the Indus River. On various occasions the Romans and Parthians had engaged each other in battle. In 53 BC, the Roman general Crassus suffered a major defeat in Mesopotamia at the hands of the Parthians. In 40 BC, the Parthians had invaded Palestine, driven out the rulers installed by the Romans (including the young Herod), and placed a native Jewish ruler in power. (Three years later the Romans regained control and placed Herod in charge.) In 36 BC, the Parthians thwarted Mark Antony's invasion of Parthia. As recently as AD 62 the Parthians had decisively defeated a Roman army that was attempting to invade Parthia. Although peaceful relations between Rome and Parthia characterized most of the latter half of the first century, Parthia was still remembered as a military threat. The depiction of Parthia as a victorious army marching across the world stage would have been a frightening image for John's readers.

Denarius

A silver denarius stamped with the head of the emperor Gaius (Caligula).

Denarius. AD 40, Roman. British Museum. BMCRE 23. London, England. (Credit: ©The British Museum)

The breaking of the second seal unleashes a rider on a red horse who shatters peace with the slaughter of war. The results from the second horseman are similar to the those of the rider on the white horse. The first horseman clearly symbolizes external attacks and defeat. The horrors of the rider on the red horse may include internal strife, civil war, and anarchy, as well as international conflict. Whatever the cause, the result is disastrous, as the inhabitants of the earth "slaughter one another" (6:4). Red, the color of blood, is an appropriate color for this bearer of human slaughter. The aftermath of the first two horsemen is similar to the initial eschatological calamities listed in the Gospels—"wars and rumors of wars" (Mark 13:7).

When the Lamb opens the third seal, a rider on a black horse gallops across the stage. He carries in his hand a pair of balance scales, used by merchants for weighing various products, including food. An unidentified voice from the midst of the four living creatures interprets for the reader the significance of the scales, "A quart of wheat for a day's pay, and three quarts of barley for a day's pay" (6:6). The "day's pay" is literally "a denarius," which was the typical daily wage earned by a common laborer. [Denarius] The prices that are announced are exorbitant, estimated by scholars as between eight and sixteen times the normal prices at that time for wheat and barley. Since a quart of wheat was normally considered the daily amount needed for one individual, the situation is one in which a common laborer would have to work all day to provide enough food for himself, with nothing left for his family. The alternative would be to spend the day's wages to buy three quarts of barley to make inferior bread in hopes of providing enough food to sustain his family. The scourge of the third seal, then, is famine, which appropriately follows in the wake of the war and bloodshed of the first two seals. [Wheat and Barley]

Wheat and Barley

AΩ In the Bible, "references to bread usually are to wheat bread, thought to be superior to that made from barley. Barley's lower gluten content, low extraction rate, taste, and indigestibility made it the staple of the poor in Roman times. Both the Old Testament (2 Kgs 7:1, 16, 18) and the authors of the Mishnah (*m. Ketub.* 5:8) assume wheat meal to be twice the value of barley meal."

Bruce J. Malina and Richard L. Rohrbaugh, *Social-Science Commentary on the Synoptic Gospels* (Minneapolis: Fortress, 1992), 62.

The famine conditions affect the wheat and barley—basic foodstuffs—but the olive oil and wine are not to be damaged. Olive oil and wine, although common in the Mediterranean world, were not necessities of life. [Oil] They symbolize the luxury and extravagant lifestyle of the wealthy. John envisions the final days as a time when the poor are starving while the rich are unaffected by the shortages. It is a vision of greed and selfishness among the "haves" who exhibit no concern for the "have-nots." [Wine]

The fourth horse is pale green in color. (The Greek word is *chlōros*, from which the word "chlorine," a pale, yellowish-green gas, is derived.) The sickly, pallid, yellowish-green color is a fitting color to represent Death, who is explicitly named as the fourth horseman. The Greek word *thanatos* can mean "pestilence" as well

Oil

Olive oil was used for a variety of purposes in the ancient world: for fuel in lamps, for cooking, for sacrifices, for cosmetic purposes (to soften the skin or to mix with spices to make perfumes), for religious anointing, and for medical purposes.

Wine

Wine was usually made from fermented grape juice, although in some places in the ancient world wine was produced from dates and pomegranates as well. Often diluted with water, wine was a common, everyday drink throughout the Mediterranean world. Because of its importance at feasts and banquets, wine was a symbol of celebration and luxurious living.

The Fourth Seal

This tapestry and several others illustrated in this book are examples from the largest extant group of historiated tapestries from Europe in the 14th century. The production of these tapestries is very well documented. The designs were made by Jan Boudolf for Louis I, Duke of Anjou. Boudolf was in the employ of the Duke's brother, King Charles V. The Parisian tapestry designer, Nicolas Bataille, was given the task of weaving the tapestries. This was done between 1373 and 1382. The tapestries, illustrating 84 scenes from the Apocalypse, were woven in six pieces, each piece over 23 meters long and 4.5 meters high. It is believed that beneath each tapestry was an inscribed panel with the corresponding text from Revelation.

Jan Boudolf and Nicolas Bataille. *The Fourth Seal: Death on a Pale Horse and Hell Scene* from the *Apocalypse of Angers*. 1373–1382. Musee des Tapisseries. Angers, France. (Credit: Scala/Art Resouce, NY)

as "death." [The Fourth Seal] (In 18:8, the NRSV translates *thanatos* as "pestilence.") Perhaps John intends this ambiguity: the fourth horseman represents Death in all its forms as well as the specific form of pestilence. Death is followed by Hades, the dwelling place of the dead. Artists have often depicted Hades in this scene as a ravenous mouth following along behind the fourth horseman, swallowing everything in its path. That presents a vivid picture of John's scene in which Death and Hades move across the landscape, consuming their victims in a multitude of ways. As v. 8 makes clear, the fourth horseman and Hades bring death not only by pestilence, but also in all the ways already enacted by the first three riders. John has obviously borrowed from Ezekiel 14:21 the list of "sword, famine, and pestilence, and by the wild animals of the

Opening of the Fifth Seal

The illuminator depicts the moment in which the martyrs are under the heavenly altar. Christ stands to the left of the scene, holding up his right hand with all five fingers outstretched. This signifies the fifth seal. The lamb above holds a closed book with five of the seals "opened" and two still closed. Two fingers of Christ's left hand are positioned downward. One martyr is being handed the white robe by the angel. There are two other groups of figures. The group in the background reaches toward the angels to receive their robes. The foreground group shows two sleeping figures, perhaps martyrs already told they must continue to wait.

Opening of the Fifth Seal from the *Douce Apocalypse.* Original c. 1270. Manuscript on Vellum. MS Douce 180, p. 17. Bodleian Library. Oxford, England. (Credit: The Bodleian Library, University of Oxford)

earth" (6:8; cf. Jer 14:12; 15:3). These were typical ways of describing the accompanying horrors of war. This destruction by the four horsemen is not the final scene, however, for their efforts result in only one-fourth of the earth's inhabitants being killed.

The Fifth Seal, 6:9-11

The opening of the first four seals revealed scenes of bloodshed and death on the earth. [Opening of the Fifth Seal] With the opening of the fifth seal, a new scene unfolds situated not on earth, but in heaven. John sees under the heavenly altar the souls of the martyrs who cry to God for vindication. These are people who, like Antipas at

Souls under the Altar

The location of the souls of the martyrs under the altar possibly suggests an honored and privileged position. Beasley-Murray (*Revelation*, 135) cited a saying attributed to Rabbi Akiba.

He who is buried in the other countries (other than Babylonia and Palestine) is as if he were buried in Babylon; and he who is buried in Babylon is as if he were buried in the land of Israel; and he who is buried in the land of Israel is as if he were buried beneath the altar, for the whole land of Israel is appropriated for the altar; he who is buried beneath the altar is as if he were buried beneath the throne of glory.

Pergamum (2:13), were faithful witnesses for God. They were willing to sacrifice their lives rather than perjure themselves by falsifying their testimony. Although this scene is in heaven, it is the result of actions that have occurred on earth, the place where the martyrs were persecuted and killed. This scene continues the description of the eschatological woes depicted in the opening of the first four seals. Mark 13 (and parallels) also includes persecution as one of the end-time terrors.

Why are the martyrs under the heavenly altar? This imagery was likely suggested by Leviticus 4:7, which states that the blood of the sacrificial bull is to be poured out at the base of the altar. In Hebrew thought, the life or soul (*nepeš*) was in the blood (Lev 17:11); thus the "souls" of the martyrs who have been sacrificed to God lie under the heavenly altar. Underneath the altar also likely represents a place of prestige and honor; they are near God. [Souls under the Altar]

To those who did not have the spiritual insight of John, the deaths of the faithful Christians appeared only as meaningless losses of life. John sees beyond the surface, however, and interprets their deaths as meaningful sacrifices offered to God. Eugene Boring noted, "The chopping-block of the Roman executioner has become a cosmic altar. Christians who refused to sacrifice to the image of the emperor are nonetheless Christian priests who sacrifice themselves on the true altar of God."[1]

The cry of the martyrs for vindication in v. 10 has been labeled sub-Christian by some readers who interpret it as a cry for personal vengeance. Although R. H. Charles may have been correct in his assertion that "the note of personal vengeance cannot be wholly eliminated from their prayer," more than simply a cry of personal vindictiveness is expressed in these verses.[2] Their cry is more a cry for the vindication of God and God's justice. To the world it looked as if the martyrs had died in vain. Their God was powerless to save them. The forces of evil had conquered. The prayer of the martyrs is that God will reverse the judgment of the world so that the purpose of their dying, as well as the sovereignty of God, might be revealed.

The cry "How long?" is similar to the cry heard often in the psalms of lament in the Hebrew Bible (cf. Pss 6:3; 13:1-2; 35:17;

74:9-10; 79:5; 80:4; 89:46; 90:13; 94:3). In Zechariah's vision of the horsemen sent on patrol, which was the source for John's imagery of the four horsemen, the angel also raises the question, "How long?" (1:12). The closest parallel for this scene in Revelation is found in a Jewish apocalyptic work that was written around the same time as the book of Revelation. Contained in 2 Esdras 4:33-37 is not only the cry "How long?" but also an answer that is somewhat similar to the one that the martyrs under the altar receive. The answer that Ezra received in 4:35-36 is, "Did not the souls of the righteous in their chambers ask about these matters, saying, 'How long are we to remain here? And when will the harvest of our reward come?' And the archangel Jeremiel answered and said, 'When the number of those like yourselves is completed.' " This idea of a predetermined number of righteous who must die before the end arrives is also found in an earlier Jewish writing, *1 Enoch* 47:3-4. (In *2 Bar.* 23:1-7 is a related idea, that before the end can come, a predetermined number of people must be born.) [Cry for Vindication]

Cry for Vindication

Gen 4:10, the blood of Abel crying for vindication, is the source of this idea of the dead crying out for vindication. In the New Testament, this idea is found in the words of Jesus in Matt 23:29-36, which accuse the religious leaders of murdering God's prophets, wise men, and scribes, with the result that "upon you may come all the righteous blood shed on earth, from the blood of innocent Abel to the blood of Zechariah the son of Barachiah."

Whether John took literally this idea of a fixed number of martyrs who must die before God intervenes is not clear. The freedom he exhibits elsewhere to adapt and modify ancient traditions and to cast ideas in symbolic forms leads one to suspect that here also he is using a traditional apocalyptic idea in a nonliteral way. This motif expresses three important ideas. First, it is a message of assurance. God has not forgotten those who are the faithful witnesses. Ultimately their deaths would be vindicated. The world may seem out of control, and God may appear to ignore the cries of the righteous. In the words of the psalmist, it may seem that God has "cast us off forever" (74:1). But John knows otherwise. He is convinced that God is still in control of the world and history. At the appropriate time, God will act.

Second, John does not believe that the church of his day has seen the end of persecution. It would have perhaps been easier for John to have told his readers, "The worst is over. Everything will soon be all right." But John did not believe that to be the case. He was afraid that the few cases of martyrdom of which he was aware were not isolated instances, but were the first raindrops of a major storm that was about to break over the church. The martyrs under the altar would be joined by many more before the great beasts of evil were finally vanquished. John writes to warn and prepare his readers for the dark days that lie ahead.

Third, this scene serves to give meaning to the suffering and death that John expected many of his readers to face. He was telling them that their faithfulness to God, even when such faithfulness included death, was not wasted or forgotten. Their deaths help fulfill the predetermined number and thus hasten the coming of the end when God's justice will be accomplished. John is telling the prospective martyrs that their deaths are a necessary part of God's plan for conquering evil. The final victory will occur when the last martyr has given her or his witness in death. As G. B. Caird explained, "The death of the martyrs is the means by which God is to win his victory over the powers of evil, and only total victory can bring about the consummation of God's purpose."[3] John has already made clear that God's victory over evil has been accomplished by the death of the Lamb. Now he shows that the deaths of the faithful also contribute to victory.

In addition to receiving the message to wait, the martyrs also receive white robes. As in 3:5, the white robes are symbols of purity and victory. The martyrs may appear to the world to be victims of defeat, but in reality they are the true victors. The white robes, symbolizing the victory of the faithful over evil and death, also symbolize the eternal life which God has bestowed on them.

Sackcloth

Sackcloth was a fabric made from goat hair or camel hair, usually dark in color. Clothing made from it was normally worn as a sign of mourning or penitence, either because of its dark color or perhaps because it was rough and uncomfortable. The dark color of sackcloth explains the statement in Isa 50:3,

I clothe the heavens with blackness,
    and make sackcloth their covering.

The Sixth Seal, 6:12-17

The opening of the sixth seal brings even more cataclysmic events. John follows the typical apocalyptic pattern (cf. Mark 13) in which wars, famine, and pestilence are followed by earthquakes and cosmic disturbances. The magnitude of the eschatological woes has intensified—not only the earth, but the entire cosmos is shaken by the horrendous events. The depiction of unnatural events occurring as a part of these calamities (such as the sun becoming black as sackcloth, the moon like blood, and stars falling to the earth) is common in apocalyptic writings. [Sackcloth] The author of 2 Esdras, for example, described this as a time when

The sun shall suddenly begin to shine at night,
    and the moon during the day.

Blood shall drip from wood,
> and the stone shall utter its voice;
the peoples shall be troubled,
> and the stars shall fall. (5:4-5)

Even earlier, the prophet Joel had used similar language to describe the coming "day of the LORD," the day when God would appear on earth to punish God's enemies. Joel 2:30-31 states, "I will show portents in the heavens and on the earth, blood and fire and columns of smoke. The sun shall be turned to darkness, and the moon to blood, before the great and terrible day of the LORD comes." Clearly the apocalyptic idea of eschatological woes is an adaptation of the prophetic expectation of a future day of God's visitation for judgment upon the wicked.

Obviously John's description of these events is not to be taken literally. The cosmic disturbances are John's way of depicting the awesome results of God's judgment on the world. In the Hebrew Bible, the appearance of God was usually accompanied by thunder, lightning, and fire. Here, the reactions to God's appearance are intensified. The day of God's final judgment is coming. It is an "earth-shattering" event. The whole world trembles and shakes at the presence of God; the sky is rolled up (cf. Isa 34:4), and the mountains and islands are removed. As impressive as the reactions of the cosmos are, the real focus of the scene is on the people and their reaction to the presence of God. So terrified are they at the prospect of facing the judgment of God that they cry out to the mountains and rocks to fall on them and hide them from what is about to occur (cf. Luke 23:28-31).

While the text indicates that all people will suffer the judgment of God, particular emphasis is placed on the wealthy and the powerful—the kings, the magnates, the generals, the rich, and the powerful. The singling out of the power elite is appropriate. They are likely the ones primarily responsible for the martyrs under the altar in the previous scene. Their actions have led to the deaths of God's faithful and have caused the martyrs to lament, "How long?" Their cry for vindication is being answered as the wicked face God's justice. The anticipated wrath of God and the Lamb is so great that the people cry out in terror, asking, "Who is able to stand?" (6:17).

The "wrath of the Lamb" has struck some commentators as a paradoxical phrase. A lamb is a meek, nonviolent animal. Furthermore, the Lamb in Revelation is a slain lamb—he has conquered by his death, not by violence toward others. Is this another example of John's transformation of images? John's understanding of the way in which Christ achieves his victory in the world will become clearer later in the book, but several points can be stressed already. First, the wrath of God and the Lamb is real. God takes sin and evil seriously. They are not minor infractions of a celestial rule book, as we have so often trivialized them. Rather, they are enemies of God because they have distorted and even destroyed God's creation. The results of sin and evil are evidenced in the opening of the first four seals, which display human pride, greed, and arrogance, unleashed on the world in the form of wars, bloodshed, famine, and death. Human evil has resulted in the deaths of God's faithful, leading them to cry out to God for vindication. Divine justice requires that God not disregard these cries. The "wrath" of God is God's certain response to the destructive effects of evil in the world.

Second, God's response to human evil and sinfulness is not vindictive. God acts out of love for a world that God has created and nurtured. The vision of the heavenly throne in chapter 4 reminds us that the God who sits enthroned is the God who brought the world into existence. God's "wrath," unleashed on the world, is somehow a part of God's creating power still at work, conforming the creation to God's ultimate intentions.

Third, the "wrath" of God is defined by the cross of Christ. Since the "wrath" of God is the "wrath" of the Lamb, the slaughtered Lamb becomes the clue for how God effects salvation and judgment. God's purposes are ultimately achieved through self-sacrificial love. Eugene Boring commented, "With one exquisitely paradoxical phrase John calls before the imagination of his hearer-readers both the terror of the coming judgment and the glad tidings that the judge is the One who has already paid the supreme penalty in behalf of the world. Though it is no less wrath for being so, the wrath is 'the wrath of the Lamb' (6:16)."[4]

CONNECTIONS

1. Few scenes from the book of Revelation have ingrained themselves in the popular imagination as deeply as has the scene with the four horsemen of the Apocalypse. Countless artists from antiquity to the present have tried to capture the mood and the power of this scene. The most famous representation of this scene is probably the haunting woodcut by Albrecht Dürer that depicts the four riders galloping across the earth, so intent on their mission of destruction that they are not mindful of the people trampled under

the hooves of their horses. The fourth rider, Death, is portrayed as an emaciated individual whose bones are clearly visible underneath his skin. Following Death are the gaping jaws of Hades, consuming its victims. This rendering of the opening of the first four seals captures in a powerful way the terror and destruction unleashed by the four horsemen. [The Four Horsemen]

Why has this scene captivated artists and readers alike? Possibly because we recognize in this scene the horrors of human history with which we are all too familiar—World War I and World War II, the Korean Conflict, Vietnam, the Gulf War, Bosnia, starvation in North Korea. The hoofbeats of death and destruction continue to reverberate across the stage of history. One modern artist has painted his version of the four horsemen of the Apocalypse and titled it *Again and Again*, recognizing that the horrors that John describes are not unique to any age. In that sense, the four horsemen do ride again and again. In keeping with that view, some commentators have argued that for John the calamities that occur when the seals are opened are nothing more than reminders of the terrors that continually confront the world. As attractive as that interpretation may be, it does not do justice to this scene. This is an eschatological scene. John is portraying in typical apocalyptic language the catastrophes that will precede the end time. The scene is so terrifying because it is a scene of God's judgment upon the earth.

The preacher or teacher should not stop with the first four seals, however. The fifth seal, even though in form and content distinct from the first four, belongs with them as a crucial part of this scene. To end after the opening of the first four seals is to hear the message of doom and terror alone. But John wants his readers to hear the message of comfort contained in the opening of the fifth seal. The martyrs, those who perhaps have been victims of the bloodshed of the initial seals, are reassured that ultimately God will triumph, and evil will be defeated. Their cries for God's help will not go unheeded. Here is possibly a point of contact with the vision for the modern reader. Confronted by a world in which the four horsemen seem already to be let loose (they stampede nightly into our living rooms via the evening news!), this vision is a forceful reminder that God has not and will not abandon the world to the forces of evil. The scene is eschatological, but it has a modern relevance. As God provides comfort and assurance to those under the heavenly altar, God's presence is also offered to reassure and sustain in the midst of the darkest moments of life. The world is not spinning wildly out of control with no one at the helm. Remember that prior to opening the seals of the scroll, John

The Four Horsemen

The Four Horsemen is the most famous work by Dürer, and as the Apocalypse woodcuts were circulated throughout Europe in 1498, it made him instantly famous. This scene reflects Dürer's full understanding of the body, which is an aspect of artistic training that he learned through the study of Italian artists. The woodcut is given extensive detailing and line, which elevates it to a true graphic art. The iconography of the four horsemen is also anti-Catholic, for among those being trampled is a bishop. Famine swings scales and War wields a sword. Conquest, the rightmost figure, draws his bow.

Albrecht Dürer (1471–1528). *The Four Horsemen* from the *Apocalypse of St. John*. 1497–1498. Woodcut. (Credit: Dover Pictoral Archive) showed us the heavenly throne room in which God and the Lamb are the central focus. That arrangement of the text is intentional. The heavenly vision provides the lens through which all the remaining scenes in the Apocalypse are to be viewed. Even when violence, terror, and death touch us personally, we continue in faith, knowing that God and the Lamb are still on the throne. [Injustice and Oppression]

Injustice and Oppression

"God takes up the cause of the poor and the oppressed precisely because in this world their voices are not heard—not even by those who call themselves Christians. God even has to take up the cause of the poor *against* 'Christians.' Christians who enjoy the fruits of injustice without a murmur, who remain silent as the defenseless are slaughtered, dare not become indignant when the suffering people of God echo the prayers of the psalms and pray for deliverance and judgment."

Allan A. Boesak, *Comfort and Protest: Reflections on the Apocalypse of John of Patmos* (Philadelphia: Westminster, 1987), 72-73.

2. Modern readers of the Apocalypse are apt to be uncomfortable with the cry for justice from the martyrs under the altar. Even if the cry is correctly understood as a cry for divine justice and the vindication of God's honor, rather than a vindictive cry for personal vengeance, the scene is still unsettling. We may be able to understand and even identify with the feelings expressed by the martyrs, for who among us has not at some time also cried out in anguish and despair to a God who seems slow to respond to the injustice and cruelty, not only in the world at large, but in our very own experiences? Yet that still does not make the lament any easier to accept, particularly when that cry occurs in a context of worship, as it does in Revelation. (Remember, the martyrs are under the altar of the heavenly temple when they cry out. Furthermore, the entire book of Revelation emanates from a liturgical setting, as John reminds us at the very outset by saying that this revelation overpowered him "on the Lord's day" [1:10], the Christian day of worship.)

Yet the most appropriate place for such a cry is in the context of worship. Here is where the book of Psalms has much to teach the modern worshiper. The ancient Israelites knew that lament as well as praise belonged in worship, both private and corporate. As noted earlier, the book of Psalms contains more psalms of lament than it does any other type of psalm. The psalmists realized that God was not threatened or offended by their honest cries of pain, despair, and discouragement. "Why, O LORD, do you stand far off? Why do you hide yourself in times of trouble?" the psalmist asked (10:1). Another psalmist cried out in pain and agony,

How long, O LORD? Will you forget me forever?
  How long will you hide your face from me?
How long must I bear pain in my soul,
  and have sorrow in my heart all day long?
How long shall my enemy be exalted over me? (13:1-2)

An amazing thing happens in most of the psalms of lament in the Bible. By the end of the psalm, the victim's cries of anger and despair have been transformed into words of praise and trust. The author of Psalm 13, for example, concluded with the words,

> But I trusted in your steadfast love;
>   my heart shall rejoice in your salvation.
> I will sing to the LORD,
>   because he has dealt bountifully with me. (13:5-6)

In fact, some form critics have argued that the songs of trust and songs of thanksgiving in the Psalter were outgrowths of the psalms of lament. In the experience of voicing a complaint to God, the psalmist moves from lament to praise. As some scholars suggest, the form of the psalms of lament may point to a liturgical explanation for this move from despair to trust. In the context of Israelite worship, after the individual voiced her or his complaint to God, an officiant (priest or prophet, perhaps) uttered an assurance of God's grace and salvation. In response to this pronouncement, the worshiper then expressed confidence in and praise to God.

Whereas this explanation may correctly explain the way the psalms of lament functioned in a worship setting, the deeper reason that the psalms of lament conclude with an expression of trust in God is that cries to God are themselves acts of faith. [Honest Worship] The person who, along with the martyrs, cries "How long, O Lord?" is expressing her faith in a God who can act decisively and bring relief. The seeming absence of God hurts so badly because the presence of God is so meaningful in our lives. Bernhard Anderson, talking about the psalms of lament, explained how our cries "out of the depths" of despair are also expressions of trust. He wrote,

Honest Worship

"A church that goes on singing 'happy songs' in the face of raw reality is doing something very different from what the Bible itself does."

Walter Brueggemann, *The Message of the Psalms,* Augsburg Old Testament Studies (Minneapolis: Augsburg, 1984), 52.

These protests, however, are all based on one grand conviction: the God who is supremely worthy of worship, and to whom people cry out even in the time of "the eclipse of God," is the faithful God, the God of *ḥesed*. That basic premise of trust, which is found in all the psalms of lament, releases people to expostulate with God, as was the case with Abraham (Gen 18:22-33), Moses (Exod 32:7-14), Jeremiah (Jer 15:15-18), Job, and other heroes of faith. In the psalms of lament, then, we do not find people shaking their fists in protest at a cold and brassy heaven or resigning themselves grimly to impersonal fate, but people who testify, even in times when they walk through the valley of dark shadow, that God is faithful and concerned and therefore hears their cry. It would be a mistake to overemphasize the element of petition in the psalms of lament and to disregard the element of trust.

Laments, then, are praises in the time of God's absence, when God's "face" (presence) is hidden. These poignant human outcries express a faith that dares to question and even to wrestle with God in situations of suffering and distress. Perhaps there is something therapeutic in prayer of this kind. It is a trait of human nature to want the simple answers, the packaged doctrines, the secure orthodoxy; but the psalmists display the kind of faith that is honest to God and that boldly seeks for the meaning and purpose of life.[5]

Planners and leaders of corporate worship would do well to remember this insight from the psalmists. Laments such as those found in Revelation 6:10, the Psalms, Job, and Jeremiah have an important role to play in public worship. Life is not all celebration. Sometimes the church must sing songs in a minor key. Faith—and worship—loses touch with reality when it allows no room for the experiences of pain, loneliness, and despair that are so much a part of us. And that is where the laments have so much to teach us. They remind us that God is larger than our frustration, our anger, our doubts. Indeed, God invites them. [Martyrs under the Altar]

Martyrs under the Altar

The image of the martyrs under the heavenly altar provided the idea for the text of the second verse of the hymn, "O God, Our Help in Ages Past" by Isaac Watts. The words of that verse state:

Under the shadow of Thy Throne
Thy saints have dwelt secure;
Sufficient is Thine arm alone,
And our defense is sure.

NOTES

[1] M. Eugene Boring, *Revelation,* Interpretation: A Bible Commentary for Teaching and Preaching (Louisville: John Knox, 1989), 125.

[2] R. H. Charles, *A Critical and Exegetical Commentary on the Revelation of St. John*, The International Critical Commentary, 2 vols. (Edinburgh: T. & T. Clark, 1920), 1:175.

[3] G. B. Caird, *The Revelation of St. John the Divine,* Harper's New Testament Commentaries (New York: Harper & Row, 1966), 87.

[4] Boring, *Revelation*, 127.

[5] Bernhard W. Anderson, *Out of the Depths: The Psalms Speak for Us Today* (Philadelphia: Westminster, 1983), 103-104.

AN INTERLUDE

7:1-17

The first six seals have been opened. The narrative tension mounts as
we await the opening of the last seal, which should usher in the final
events that John has told us "must soon take place" (1:1). Is this only
a Hitchcock-like "word from our sponsor," intended to tease us by
heightening the suspense prior to the unveiling of the final scene?
While John's technique certainly adds to the dramatic effect of the
work, a more important reason underlies his pause at this point in
the action. The opening of the first six seals has unleashed events
much more horrific than the aftermath of the opening of Pandora's
box. Scenes of slaughter, destruction, famine, and terror have played
out before our eyes. The cry of the masses at the end of chapter 6 is
the question that most readers/hearers are apt to be asking: "The
great day of their wrath has come, and who is able to stand?" Many
of John's intended hearers, some of whom were already feeling alienated and oppressed and likely felt that the cataclysms of the end had
already begun, would have been wondering who could survive such
terrible calamities. The interlude of chapter 7 provides an answer to
that question. Prior to revealing additional scenes of tribulation, John
pauses to offer words of assurance and comfort for the faithful. This
interlude consists of two scenes: 7:1-8, the sealing of the 144,000;
and 7:9-17, an innumerable throng of people from every nation. The
setting of the first scene is on earth; the second scene is set in heaven.

COMMENTARY

The Sealing of the 144,000, 7:1-8

The opening words of v. 1, "After this I saw," indicate a new and
important vision that John has. They demarcate this vision from the
one that precedes it (see 4:1) and the one following it (7:9). When
John speaks of a four-cornered earth (cf. Isa 11:12; Ezek 7:2), one
should be cautious about assuming that John meant this literally.
Since there are four cardinal directions, one corner for each wind is
perhaps only poetic language (see also Dan 7:2 for a reference to the

Angels of Destruction

AΩ Several Jewish writings describe angels in charge of punishments or destruction. In *1 En.* 66:1-2, angels were in charge of the waters of judgment and destruction that were to be let loose upon the earth during the time of Noah. The writer of *2 Baruch* described four angels, each with a burning torch, standing at the four corners of Jerusalem immediately prior to the city's destruction by the Babylonians (6:1–7:1). The angels had been sent by God to destroy the city walls to prevent the Babylonians from boasting that they were the ones who destroyed the dwelling place of God. Another angel came from heaven to command the four angels to delay their burning until he was able to remove the sacred objects from the temple and hide them in the earth.

four winds). Obviously, like his contemporaries, John held to a flat earth cosmology. In an early Jewish apocalyptic text, often called the "Book of the Heavenly Luminaries" (*1 En.* 72–82), the author described twelve openings in the sky from which the winds blow across the earth, three from each of the four cardinal directions. From four of the openings blow winds of blessing; from twelve blow winds of pestilence, which will "destroy the whole earth, the water upon her, all those who dwell upon her, and all those which exist in the waters and the dry land" (76:4). Other apocalyptic texts describe angels who are in charge of the winds (*Jub.* 2:2; *1 En.* 60:11-21). [Angels of Destruction]

The destructive winds represent the eschatological woes that are ready to be unleashed upon the earth. How is the reader to understand these destructive winds in relationship to the eschatological woes that appear in chapter 6? The winds are possibly another way of describing the same events. John has given us a picture of eschatological destruction with the opening of the seals. The focus there was on the calamities. Now he stops and describes the coming destruction using different imagery. This time the focus is not on the punishment of the wicked, but on the status of the faithful. The reader/hearer is likely to be asking, "What about the people of God? Will they, too, suffer the wrath of God and the wrath of the Lamb?" This time John emphasizes that they will be protected by God.

John sees an angel coming from the east ("from the rising of the sun") with instructions from God to delay the blowing of the winds until the faithful "servants of God" are protected. In the midst of all the catastrophic events, God is still in control. That is an important part of the message of this interlude. God halts the process long enough to provide for the safety of the faithful. John notes that the winds have the ability to damage earth, sea, and, surprisingly, trees. Why does he single out the trees for special mention? Likely it is because trees are especially vulnerable to storm damage. [The Angel from the East]

The angel comes bringing "the seal of the living God" (7:2). The seal mentioned here is different from the seven seals on the scroll. (In Greek as in English the same word is used.) The seal in 7:2

likely denotes a signet ring worn by a king or other authoritative official. The seven seals refer to the impression in clay or wax that is made by such a signet ring or a cylinder seal. By possessing God's seal, the angel acts with God's authority. The purpose of the seal is to stamp or imprint an image on an object, thus signifying ownership of the object or protecting the contents within from being altered or examined. Both functions of seals are appropriate here. On the one hand, to be stamped with the seal of God is to be marked as God's possession, God's people (cf. 1 Pet 2:9). [Marked with God's Seal] To be the people of God involves both privileges and responsibilities. In the messages to the seven churches in chapters 2–3, John challenged the churches to live up to their responsibilities, pointing out ways in which they had failed to be God's people. To bear the seal of God signifies that one's ultimate allegiance and commitment are to God, not to any person, human institution, belief system, or personal goals.

On the other hand, to be marked with the seal of God signifies divine protection. It is this idea that is primary here. Placing a seal on a document or a container guaranteed the authenticity of the contents. They could not be altered or removed without breaking the seal. Thus the contents were secure. In chapter 7, John pauses in the midst of the eschatological woes to reassure the faithful that they will be sealed (protected) by God. The eschatological woes will

The Angel from the East

Why does John present the angel as coming from the east ("from the rising of the sun," 7:2)? The direction may have no significance, providing only colorful detail to John's description. On the other hand, some commentators have suggested that John is drawing from Ezek 43:2-4 in which the glory of the LORD comes from the east and enters the restored temple by the eastern gate. Other interpreters have pointed to the expectation of a messiah from the east (*Sib. Or.* 3:652; cf. Matt 2:1-2).

Marked with God's Seal

To be marked with the seal of God means that one belongs to God, and thus that one has dignity, worth, and status. For John's readers, as well as for many people today struggling with low self-esteem and despair, to be reminded that they are God's people is a powerful message. Howard Thurman, the great African American minister and educator, told in his autobiography of listening to his grandmother tell stories from her childhood as a slave. She would often tell of the slave preacher from a neighboring plantation who was permitted once or twice each year to come over and preach to the slaves. He would end each sermon with a grand retelling of the death and resurrection of Jesus. Thurman wrote:

At the end, he would be exhausted, but his congregation would be uplifted and sustained with courage to withstand the difficulties of the week to come. When the slave preacher told the Calvary narrative to my grandmother and the other slaves, it had the same effect on them as it would later have on their descendants. But this preacher, when he had finished, would pause, his eyes scrutinizing every face in the congregation, and then he would tell them, "You are not niggers! You are not slaves! You are God's children!"

When my grandmother got to that part of her story, there would be a slight stiffening in her spine as we sucked in our breath. When she had finished, our spirits were restored.

Howard Thurman, *With Head and Heart: The Autobiography of Howard Thurman* (San Diego: Harcourt Brace & Co., 1979), 20-21.

The Sealing of the 144,000

In this scene, also known as the *Angels Restraining the Four Winds* and *Four Angels Staying the Wind*, the four winds appear as four faces blowing in the upper portion of the print. Four angels appear with swords in the lower left corner. Another angel holds a chalice in his left hand and moves to mark the forehead of a kneeling man. All the people surrounding that figure, who maintains the position of a communicant, also kneel in anticipation of their turn. Dürer emphasizes this eucharistic tone.

Albrecht Dürer (1471–1528). *Sealing of the 144,000* from the *Apocalypse of St. John*. 1497–1498. Woodcut. (Credit: Dover Pictoral Archive Series) serve as punishment on God's enemies, but the faithful will be protected. [The Sealing of the 144,000]

Several passages from the Hebrew Bible likely form the background for John for this imagery of sealing. In Genesis 4:15, God places a mark on Cain to protect him from people who might try to kill him. In Exodus 12:1-28, the Israelites mark the doorposts and lintels of their houses as a protection against the tenth plague, the death of the firstborn throughout the land of Egypt. The closest parallel to this act of sealing in Revelation is in Ezekiel 9:1-11. Before sending out six executioners to destroy the wicked of Jerusalem, God sends out a seventh individual to put a mark upon the foreheads of the righteous (those who groan over the wickedness of the city) in order that they might be spared.

Some commentators have understood the sealing as a reference to baptism or the bestowal of the Holy Spirit (cf. 2 Cor 1:22; Eph 1:13; 4:30). While such an interpretation may be attractive (and even have value for exposition), there is no justification for seeing that as John's intention. The sealing is a mark of protection and security. We are not told what the mark is; in 14:1, however, the 144,000 are identified as those who have the name of the Lamb and the name of God written on their foreheads.

It is crucial that the reader understand this protection that is granted the people of God. John does not envision literal, physical protection for the faithful. As the scene of the martyrs under the altar indicates, John expects that fidelity to the cause of Christ may cost a person his or her life. God's people are not exempt from trouble and suffering. In fact, in typical apocalyptic fashion, John expects persecution of the faithful to become even more severe during the last days. John has no special "rapture" theology whereby the faithful are exempt from the pains and sufferings of the world. The Lamb who conquers is victorious through the path of suffering. The way of the Lamb is the way of the cross. Those who would be faithful to the Lamb cannot expect that their treatment should be any better than his. No, the protection afforded the faithful is spiritual protection. In spite of what happens, the people of God are secure in the arms of God. As Eugene Boring has commented, "Faithful Christians are preserved through (not from!) the great persecution that is about to be unleashed upon them."[1]

John does not describe the actual sealing of the faithful, but he hears how many are sealed. The number of those sealed is 144,000, composed of 12,000 from each of the twelve tribes of Israel. Several points need to be noted. First, the number 144,000 is not to be taken literally. As a multiple of both ten and twelve, numbers that often signified completeness, 144,000 is a symbol of completeness. It represents a vast throng of people. Second, the description of the group as being drawn from the twelve tribes of Israel has led some interpreters to argue that the 144,000 are Jews or Jewish Christians, whereas the group mentioned in 7:9-17 are Gentile Christians. If John is adapting a Jewish or Jewish-Christian source here, then in his source the 144,000 might have referred to Jews or Jewish Christians. Such cannot be the function of this group in Revelation, however. John does not make a distinction between Jewish and Gentile Christians. Instead, the imagery depicts the church as the new people of God, the new Israel (cf. Jas 1:1). The entire church is the new Israel in which racial or ethnic distinctions play no part.

Third, does the group represent the complete church or a special group within the church? Many commentators are content to understand the symbolism as referring to all faithful believers. The vision of the sealing then becomes a word of comfort and assurance for all the people of God. Another interpretation of the symbolism of the 144,000 is possible, however. The number does not depict the completeness of the church, but the completeness of a special group within the church, i.e., the martyrs (see also 14:1-5). Caird argued, "If the tribes of Israel represent the whole church, then twelve thousand from each tribe can mean only a proportion of the

---

Twelve Tribes of Israel

ΑΩ The traditional view holds that ancient Israel was organized into twelve tribes, based on the twelve sons of Jacob (Israel). Some variation occurs, however, in virtually every listing in the Hebrew Bible, whether in the names, the order of the names, or even the number of the tribes. Some tribes were incorporated into other tribes and were replaced by new tribal groups (e.g., the tribe of Joseph is replaced in some lists by Manasseh and Ephraim, two of the sons of Joseph). The following chart presents the lists found in Gen 49; Num 1:20-43; Deut 33; and Judg 5.

Genesis 49	Numbers 1:20-43	Deuteuronomy 33	Judges 5
Reuben	Reuben	Reuben	Ephraim
Simeon	Simeon	Judah	Benjamin
Levi	Gad	Levi	Machir
Judah	Judah	Benjamin	Zebulun
Zebulun	Issachar	Joseph	Issachar
Issachar	Zebulun	Zebulun	Reuben
Dan	Ephraim	Issachar	Gilead
Gad	Manasseh	Gad	Dan
Asher	Benjamin	Dan	Asher
Naphtali	Dan	Naphtali	Naphtali
Joseph	Asher	Asher	
Benjamin	Benjamin		

church marked out by God's seal for special service."2 This interpretation of the 144,000 does justice to the importance of the
theme of martyrdom in the Apocalypse. Since the martyrs are those
who pay the ultimate price for their faithfulness, John singles them
out for special mention and special encouragement.

If the 144,000 are identified as the martyrs, then 7:1-8 can be
understood as a response to the martyrs' cry in chapter 6, "How
long?" The martyrs under the altar are told that they must wait for
vindication until the number of martyrs is complete. Chapter 7, in
a symbolic way, shows the completed number of the martyred
saints—144,000.

Lists of the tribes of Israel appear approximately twenty times in
the Hebrew Bible, with variations of which tribes are included and
in the order of the tribes. [Twelve Tribes of Israel] Reuben, being the oldest son of Jacob, often appears first. In this list Judah occurs first,
perhaps because that was the tribe from which the messiah was to
come (cf. 5:5, "the Lion of the tribe of Judah"; in other biblical lists
in which Judah appears first, the list is arranged geographically
from south to north. That is not the case here, however.). Dan is
absent from this list, with his place being taken by Manasseh, one
of the sons of Joseph. [Tribe of Dan]

The Multitude from Every Nation, 7:9-17

The setting of the second vision of chapter 7 shifts from earth to
heaven, specifically to the heavenly throne room described in chapters 4 and 5. The vision in 7:9-17 is a proleptic vision. John sees
the redeemed in heaven not at the present time, but in the future
when God has brought the divine plan to completion and all the
redeemed stand united as the people of God. "After this I looked"
(v. 9) indicates that a new vision is being introduced. This time,
instead of seeing 144,000 from the tribes of Israel, John sees

Tribe of Dan

AΩ Dan was the fifth son of Jacob and the ancestor of the tribe that bore his name. Although
initially assigned land north of Judah and west of the Benjamin tribe, the tribe of Dan
eventually moved to the very northern area of Israel and settled there. They conquered the city of
Laish and renamed it Dan. Two instances of religious unfaithfulness are associated with the city of
Dan. Judg 18 describes the people of Dan capturing an idol and setting it up in the city. According
to 1 Kgs 12:25-33, Jeroboam, king of the northern kingdom of Israel, established an illegitimate
sanctuary at Dan. Likely because of these episodes, later traditions viewed Dan with disfavor. The
Testament of Dan (c. 2d century BC) states that the prince of Dan is Satan and predicts that "in the
last days you will defect from the Lord" (5:4-6). The 2d-century Christian writer Irenaeus claimed
that Dan is omitted from the list of tribes in Revelation because the antichrist is to come from the
tribe of Dan (*Haer.* 5.30.2).

The Lamb Worshiped by the Great Multitude
The lower central panel of the interior of the *Ghent Altarpiece* by Jan van Eyck, showing the adoration of the Lamb.

Jan van Eyck (c. 1390–1441). *Adoration of the Mystic Lamb*, detail from the *Ghent Altarpiece*. Cathedral St. Bavo. Ghent, Belgium. (Credit: Scala/Art Resource, NY)

"a great multitude that no one could count, from every nation, from all tribes and peoples and languages." This vision is a fulfillment of the Abrahamic promise in Genesis, in which God told Abraham that he would become a great nation and through him "all the families of the earth shall be blessed" (12:2-3). Abraham's offspring would eventually become as numerous as the stars in the sky, the dust of the ground, and the sand on the seashore (Gen 13:16; 15:5; 22:17; 26:4; 28:14). In the spiritual descendants of faithful Abraham, that promise has now been fulfilled, for they constitute a throng that is beyond counting. This innumerable crowd is inclusive, encompassing people from every racial, ethnic, political, and linguistic background. [The Lamb Worshiped by the Great Multitude]

Right from the start, this is a scene of joyous celebration. John does not envision a small gathering of a select few. God has thrown a party, and the attendees are packed wall to wall! This is in stark contrast to the view expressed in another apocalyptic writing that was likely penned within five to ten years of the writing of Revelation. In 2 Esdras, the writer expressed the view that the number of the saved will be very small. God has "made this world for the sake of many, but the world to come for the sake of only a few" (8:1). Because they are few, they are more precious to God, just as precious metals are more valuable because they are less abundant (7:52-58). John's vision of a God who welcomes a massive crowd of faithful servants is reminiscent of Jesus' joy-filled parables of the lost coin, the lost sheep, and the lost son (Luke 15).

The great crowd of the faithful has joined the heavenly throng who surround the throne of God and the Lamb. They are robed in white, the color of victory, celebration, and purity. The palm branches that each person holds indicate the festive nature of this gathering, for palm branches were symbols of celebration and victory (see 1 Macc 13:51; 2 Macc 14:4; John 12:13). The great multitude breaks out in a loud song of praise to God and the Lamb:

> "Salvation belongs to our God who is seated on the throne, and to the Lamb!" (7:10) [Palm Branch]

Palm Branch

A marble relief from a small gymnasium in Pergamum depicting a victorious rooster with a palm branch, symbol of victory.

Rooster with Palm Branch. 1st C. Marble. Bergama Archaeological Museum. Bergama, Turkey. (Credit: Mitchell Reddish)

The Greek word *sōtēria*, translated here as "salvation," can also mean deliverance or safety. This song is a song of victory. God has rescued the faithful by bringing them safely through "the great ordeal" (7:14). These people have "fought the good fight" (2 Tim 4:7) and have triumphed. They have not succumbed to the pressures and demands of the beast of chapter 13. They have been victorious over persecution and even death. They are the "conquerors" (see chs. 2 and 3) who have held fast to their faith and have not compromised their commitment to God. As the redeemed recognize, however, this salvation that they celebrate is the salvation that belongs to God and the Lamb. The faithful have not achieved their own victory. They have become partakers of God's victory and salvation. The victory is the victory of the Lamb, achieved in his self-sacrificial death. Furthermore, salvation, in all the richness of the meaning of that term—victory, wholeness, well-being—belongs to God and the Lamb and not to imperial Rome or any other human construct. As Elisabeth Schüssler Fiorenza has commented, "The official source of such a total well-being, peace, and salvation was supposed to be the Roman emperor. Here those who stand before the throne acknowledge God and the Lamb as the ultimate sources of all well-being and salvation."[3] To sing the song of the great multitude is to affirm not only that all power belongs to God, but also that all blessings and benefits ultimately derive from God.

In antiphonal response to the song of the great multitude, all the angels, the elders, and the four living creatures cry out, "Amen!" Their song to God and the Lamb is a seven-fold elaboration of the succinct praise of the great multitude. To attribute salvation to God is to recognize that God is the legitimate source of all power and blessing. The song the heavenly attendants offer in adoration to God lists almost the identical elements as those in the song to the Lamb in 5:12.

In apocalyptic works, a typical literary technique is the use of an angelic guide or interpreter who explains the visions and revelations to the recipient. In Daniel, the angel Gabriel filled the role of interpreting angel. In 2 Esdras, Uriel explained the events to Ezra. Here, John utilizes this technique in the dialogue with one of the elders (cf. 5:5). The elder raises the question of the identity of this great multitude in vv. 9-10. John's response to him is modeled after Ezekiel's response to God in 37:3, "You know."

The people dressed in white are the ones who have come through the "great ordeal" (or "great tribulation"). Apocalyptic writings frequently describe a time of intense persecution or suffering that will occur in the last days. Daniel 12:1 says, "There shall be a time of anguish, such as has never occurred since nations first came into existence." In Mark 13:19, Jesus said, "For in those days there will be suffering, such as has not been from the beginning of the creation that God created until now, no, and never will be." John has already mentioned this time of extreme persecution and suffering in the message to the church at Philadelphia (3:10). The faithful in Philadelphia were assured that they would be kept from this "hour of trial" that would come upon the whole world. From this vision in chapter 7 we see more clearly what that promise to the Philadelphians entailed. To be "kept from the hour of trial" did not mean that they would be spared persecution and possibly even death. Rather, it was the promise, seen here in its fulfillment, that God would see them through the ordeal to victory. God would keep them secure and bring them safely into God's eternal kingdom.

In rather startling imagery, the elder states that the faithful have "washed their robes and made them white in the blood of the

Lamb." How can a bath of blood render their garments white? Here is another example of John's paradoxical use of language. The idea of the cleansing effect of the blood of Christ appears elsewhere in the New Testament (see Heb 9:11-22; 1 John 1:7). John has already depicted the effects of sin as dirty or stained clothing (3:4; cf. Isa 64:6; Zech 3:3-4). Thus clean clothing represents a cleansed or purified life that is acceptable before God. The background for the concept of blood as a means of atonement is obviously the sacrificial system, in which blood represented the life of the victim. Leviticus 17:11 explains, "For the life of the flesh is in the blood; and I have given it to you for making atonement for your lives on the altar; for, as life, it is the blood that makes atonement." The ritual of the purification offering required that the blood of the sacrificed animal be daubed on the horns of the altar and then poured out at the base of the altar. This act purified the altar (Lev 4:1-35; 8:14-17). Lepers were rendered ritually clean in part through the use of sacrificial blood (Lev 14:1-57).

The "blood of the Lamb" is a reference to the death of Jesus. Through his sacrificial death Jesus defeated the forces of evil and made possible the victory of the faithful (cf. 1:5; 5:9). These individuals have been "washed in the blood," meaning that they have participated in the life and death of Jesus. For some of the faithful, their commitment to the way of Christ leads to martyrdom. Their blood is mingled with the blood of the Lamb. For others, the demands of discipleship may take different forms, but they too share in Christ's sacrifice when they align themselves unreservedly with him and refuse to yield to the demands and allures of the power structures and culture around them. Notice that salvation is made possible by the work of Christ—it is his blood, his sacrifice, that "whitens." Yet faithfulness on the part of the believers is also required. "They have washed their robes," which is a way of saying that they have aligned themselves with the cause of Christ and made his faithfulness, even unto death, their faithfulness as well. Only those whose clothes are thus "washed in the blood of the Lamb" will have access to God's final kingdom (22:14). [Salvation]

Salvation

"The lesson from Revelation [7:9-17] has something significant to say about the understanding of salvation by the first Christians. The universal testimony of all who are saved is that 'Salvation belongs to our God who sits upon the throne, and to the Lamb!' That is to say, humility is the mark of those who have been saved: all is God's; nothing is ours. Although those who rejoice in heaven have washed their robes, it was not their washing which made their robes white. At the hands of human beings, the robes of the martyrs become red with blood; it is only the blood of the Lamb that turns the red blood of death into the white sign of victory. God alone gives salvation."

Edgar Krentz and Arthur A. Vogel, *Proclamation 2: Aids for Interpreting the Church Year,* Easter, Series C, ed. Elizabeth Achtemeier, Gerhard Krodel, and Charles P. Price (Philadelphia: Fortress, 1980), 38.

The elder's identification of the multitude may have been sufficient for John, but it has left subsequent readers of the work puzzled. Who are these people that no one could count? What relationship do they have to the 144,000 who are sealed in 7:1-8? Numerous suggestions have been made, none completely satisfactory. As one commentator observed, "No explanation can be offered to which at least plausible objections may not be made."4 The most common interpretations include the following: (1) The first vision represents faithful Jews or Jewish Christians, and the second vision describes Gentile Christians. (2) The first group represents the martyrs, and the second group is the complete people of God. (3) Both groups represent the martyrs. (4) Both groups depict the church in its entirety.

As already stated (see above on the 144,000), the first option is without support in the book of Revelation and is thus a less likely interpretation. The other three are plausible views, however. Good arguments can be made for seeing the two visions as different presentations of the same group (either the martyrs or the universal church). As is evident in the Apocalypse, John is certainly willing and capable of presenting the same idea using new and different imagery. Yet, a more appealing interpretation is to view the visions as representing different realities. The first vision depicts the martyrs under the image of 144,000. The second vision portrays the entire church, all the faithful, of which the martyrs are a part. This understanding makes sense of the apparent contrast between the 144,000 and the multitude "which no man could number" and the contrast between those drawn from the twelve tribes of Israel versus those "from every nation, from all tribes and peoples and languages." Furthermore, this view coheres with John's interest in Revelation to offer special encouragement and hope to the martyrs. He pays special attention to those who are called upon to pay the greatest price for their faithfulness. Yet the entire church must face the great tribulation, not the martyrs alone. Thus all believers are in need of assurance and encouragement. The second vision accomplishes this. John sees all the faithful as victorious. They reside in safety and comfort in God's presence.

Regardless of how one identifies the two groups in chapter 7, the purpose of John's vision remains the same. He pauses in the opening of the seals to assure the faithful that they are secure. This interlude announces that in spite of how severe circumstances may become, even if martyrdom is the outcome, God's people will be preserved.

The closing verses of chapter 7 elaborate on the future status of the redeemed. They will stand before the throne of God where they will never cease to worship God day and night "within his temple." Such worship is the appropriate response in gratitude and thanksgiving for one who has brought them safely through their great ordeal. The Greek word *latreuō* (NRSV: "worship") basically means "service." In the New Testament, it denotes any service or ministry offered to God. Here, worship in the strict sense is likely what is intended. Since their service to God occurs in the heavenly temple, their role as priests (see 1:6; 5:10) is especially in mind.

The first of the promises given to the redeemed is that God will shelter them (7:15). The imagery of the Greek text is that God's tent or tabernacle will be put over them, providing protection and security. For the readers/hearers familiar with the story of the Israelites' wandering in the wilderness, this imagery evokes memories of God's abiding presence with the Israelites in the wilderness when the pillar of fire by night and the cloud by day accompanied the Hebrew people. In the wilderness, the Israelites carried with them the tabernacle of God, symbolizing God's presence in their midst. Now, John says God will spread a tabernacle over the people. No longer will there be any distance between God and God's people.

The other blessings that will be enjoyed by the faithful are drawn almost verbatim from Isaiah 49:10 and 25:8, passages which describe the anticipated blessings awaiting the returning exiles from Babylon. Thirst, hunger, and scorching sun will no longer be problems for God's people. Here, these blessings are promises of eschatological protection, comfort, and fulfillment that will be realized in God's final kingdom. All of these will be made possible because the Lamb will serve as their shepherd. Once more, John uses a surprising transformation of images. The Lamb becomes the shepherd! As in Psalm 23, the shepherd provides food, water, and protection for the sheep. Jesus, the Good Shepherd (cf. John 10:11-18), the one who has brought the faithful through the great tribulation, will lead and nurture and protect his own. Their earthly ordeal may have been filled with pain and sorrow; such experiences will no longer trouble them, however, for "God will wipe away every tear from their eyes" (7:17). [Worship in Tribulation]

Worship in Tribulation

"In the very midst of her tribulations on earth, the martyr church already sings the songs of victory in her liturgy."

Reginald H. Fuller, *Preaching the New Lectionary: The Word of God for the Church Today* (Collegeville MN: Liturgical, 1974), 88.

CONNECTIONS

1. One of the first tasks confronting the preacher or teacher dealing with chapter 7 of Revelation may well be helping people understand what the text *does not* say. The imagery of the 144,000 has received a wide array of interpretations in popular writings (e.g., the view that there will be 144,000 Jewish evangelists during the "Tribulation Period" who will convert many of the unbelievers to Christianity). Unfortunately, many of these interpretations bear little resemblance to the actual meaning of the text. Sometimes merely reading the text and seeing what is actually there (as opposed to relying on what one has been told the text says) can be a major step in gaining a valid interpretation of the passage. In a college class, students were assigned to read the entire book of Revelation and then to write a reaction paper. One student wrote,

> After reading the book of Revelation all the way through, I wondered where the rest of the information was located. From what I have heard in and around church, I expected more or maybe just different text. One example of my misconceptions is that I understood from my religious background that after Jesus returns to earth and resurrects the saved that 144,000 more Jews would become saved. However, after reading Revelation I think this concept is incorrect.

In chapter 7, as throughout the Apocalypse, John is not interested in presenting a blueprint for the future that contains details of events that will be literally fulfilled. Rather, John is using pictorial language to offer comfort and hope to Christian communities that are struggling to maintain their commitment to God during difficult circumstances. John expects the situation to worsen before it got better. The interlude of chapter 7 is John's way of reassuring his readers that God will protect and sustain them throughout any and all ordeals that they must face. That is the message that surfaces most clearly from this text. Even though John casts his message in eschatological imagery and believes that the end times will be a time of special difficulties for the church, his message of hope and assurance is a message directed to the church living out its faith in its current time and place. God will sustain them not only in the future, but in the present as well. Here is the connection of this text with the modern reader: This text assures us of God's protection and security in all of the "tribulations" of life. [Encouragement]

What about those situations, however, when God does not seem to protect, when the forces of evil seem overwhelming? Two responses are appropriate. First, note that John never promises the faithful that they will not suffer hardship, persecution, or even martyrdom. In fact, he expects the ultimate test of faith commitment—martyrdom—to be required of many of the members of the churches of Asia Minor. What John promises his readers is that God will not abandon or forsake them regardless of how difficult their situation might become. The seal that is placed on them is a reminder that they are

Encouragement

"John intended to bring a word of encouragement and hope to his original audience, and any use of John's writing to frighten people and to increase their anxieties, especially by means of speculative predictions, is a misuse of John's writing. The good news of the one who died and now lives offers hope, not anxiety. John's message is that through the most tragic of human circumstances God's offer of life and hope is still good."

Richard L. Jeske, "The Book of Revelation in the Parish," *Word and World* 15/2 (Spring 1995): 192.

God's possession, and because of that, they are secure. The power structures of this world might harass, intimidate, persecute, and even execute, but those who bear the mark of God will ultimately be victorious. Assurance based on this conviction provides the strength necessary to face life's toughest moments.

Second, even in times of difficulty, when God does not protect or deliver us in the way that we would like, faith in God is the appropriate response. One of the most popular stories from the book of Daniel is the tale of the three young men who refused to follow King Nebuchadnezzar's order that all were to worship a large golden statue. Because of their refusal, they were condemned to death in the fiery furnace. When brought before the king, they courageously replied to him, "If our God whom we serve is able to deliver us from the furnace of blazing fire and out of your hand, O king, let him deliver us. But if not, be it known to you, O king, that we will not serve your gods and we will not worship the golden statue that you have set up" (3:17-18). Writing during the time of the persecution of the Jews by the Syrian king, Antiochus IV, the author of Daniel was well aware that for many of his readers, faithfulness did not mean exemption from persecution and death. Like John, he too knew of instances of martyrdom. (See 2 Macc 6:18–7:42 for martyr stories from this period.) By including these words from the three young men, the author of Daniel was reminding his readers that faith in God should not be dependent on the outward circumstances of our lives. True faith persists through times of crisis as well as times of ease.

2. The vision in Revelation 7:9-17 of a great multitude "from every nation, from all tribes and peoples and languages" provides an opportunity for the teacher/preacher to deal with the issue of the inclusiveness of the church. Appropriately, this passage is one of the

lectionary texts for World Communion Sunday. John envisions the redeemed community in heaven to be a group composed of people from every racial and ethnic background. Here is a real picture of the Reverend Jesse Jackson's "Rainbow Coalition"! In religious circles we often talk about the need to be inclusive and accepting of all peoples. Even in society at large, multiculturalism and diversity have become fashionable topics. College faculty alter their curricular requirements to include perspectives and insights from a variety of ethnic, racial, and social groups. Corporations hold workshops and seminars to help their employees become more sensitive to gender and minority issues. But in reality, how open and inclusive are we, especially in our churches? Is it still true that the most segregated hour in American life is 11:00 A.M. on Sunday mornings? John's vision of the community of God composed of people from every background and group becomes for the church of today both a standard by which to measure ourselves and a prod to goad us to bring that vision into reality. We are forced to ask if we have truly become the inclusive fellowship envisioned by John, or if we are racial, ethnic, and class ghettos. Have we taken to heart Paul's statement that in Christ "there is no longer Jew or Greek, there is no longer slave or free, there is no longer male and female" (Gal 3:28)? Even in the best of congregations there is much yet to be done. [An Inclusive Community]

An Inclusive Community

Archbishop Desmond Tutu of South Africa has described his experience at St. Mary's Cathedral in Johannesburg, prior to the abolishment of the policy of apartheid in his country. He has written,

There is no question whatever that our Cathedral is thoroughly prayed in and by all kinds of people—Black people, White people, big people, little people, representatives of the variegated family of God find a warm welcome. . . .

. . . I will always have a lump in my throat when I think of the children at St. Mary's, pointers to what can be if our society would become sane and normal. Here were children of all races playing, praying, learning and even fighting together, almost uniquely in South Africa. And as I have knelt in the Dean's stall at the superb 9:30 High Mass, with incense, bells and everything, watching a multi-racial crowd file up to the altar rails to be communicated, the one bread and the one cup given by a mixed team of clergy and lay ministers, with a multi-racial choir, servers and sidesmen—all this in apartheid-mad South

Africa—then tears sometimes streamed down my cheeks, tears of joy that it could be that indeed Jesus Christ had broken down the wall of partition and here were the first fruits of the eschatological community right in front of my eyes, enacting the message in several languages on the noticeboard outside that this is a house of prayer for peoples of all races who are welcome at all times.

St. Mary's has made me believe the vision of St. John the Divine: "After this I looked and saw a vast throng, which no one could count, from every nation, of all tribes, peoples, and languages, standing in front of the throne and before the Lamb. They were robed in white and had palms in their hands, and they shouted together:

'Victory to our God who sits on the throne, and to the Lamb!' And all the angels stood round the throne and the elders and the four living creatures, and they fell on their faces before the throne and worshipped God, crying: 'Amen! Praise and glory and wisdom, thanksgiving and honour, power and might, be to our God for ever and ever, Amen!' " (Revelation 7:9-12, [Tutu's rendition]).

Desmond Tutu, *Hope and Suffering* (Grand Rapids: Eerdmans, 1984), 134-36.

3. Part of the imagery John uses in this chapter may need special attention for modern readers. John says that the multitude makes their robes white by washing them "in the blood of the Lamb." Such language is John's shorthand for the life and death of Christ. For John's original audience, blood imagery was more easily understood than it is for readers today. Even though the Jerusalem temple, with its attendant sacrificial system, was no longer in existence at the time of the writing of Revelation, animal sacrifices were a prominent part of the worship rituals of other religions of John's world. [Blood and Sacrifice] In addition to this common type of ritual sacrifice, another connection first-century readers might have made with blood imagery was the use of blood in certain popular religions of the day. In the cult of Cybele (the Great Mother) and Attis, a ritual known as the taurobolium was practiced, in which the priest or the initiate was placed in a pit. A bull was slaughtered over the pit and the individual below would be bathed in the blood from the slaughtered bull. The blood of the sacrificial victim was understood to purify and cleanse from sin. The origin of this practice seems to have been in Asia Minor. One must be cautious, however, about using this ritual to understand John's description of washing in the blood of the Lamb. The strongest extant evidence for the practice comes from the second century AD and later, although the rite was probably in existence during the first century as well.

> **Blood and Sacrifice**
>
> AΩ "Neither in the Old Testament nor among Jews of the New Testament period was it believed that the mere slaughter of a victim was the essential ritual which effects the purpose of sacrifice. 'Once the blood has reached the altar, the owners are forgiven,' said the rabbis. The sprinkling on the altar is the important moment. So then, although slaying is presupposed, the reference in sacrifice is primarily not to death but to the sprinkling of blood."
>
> Nigel Turner, "Blood: (1) Shedding of Blood," *Christian Words* (Nashville: Thomas Nelson, 1981), 53.

John's language likely communicated with his original audience. Today such imagery is more apt to leave readers puzzled or even repulsed. Worship leaders must be sensitive to the ability of language to conceal as well as to reveal meaning. The "blood hymns," still popular in some circles, sound rather barbaric to people who have not been acclimated to the sacrificial language of the church. Hymns such as "Are You Washed in the Blood" "There Is Power in the Blood," "Nothing But the Blood," "There Is a Fountain (Filled with Blood)," whose texts were derived or inspired at least in part from this passage in Revelation 7, are prime examples of worship materials that may sound strange to modern ears. If churches continue to use these hymns, worship leaders have a responsibility to educate their congregations on the symbolism involved in these words. Blood imagery, along with other sacrificial terminology, is only one way in which New Testament writers attempted to understand the redemptive significance of the life and death of Jesus. Other images were drawn from the law courts (justification), from slavery and the market place (redemption), and from personal relationships (reconciliation, adoption). All of these images need to be understood, not as objective realities, but as metaphors used to comprehend what is almost beyond human comprehension—God's loving embrace and acceptance of the world through Jesus Christ.

NOTES

[1] M. Eugene Boring, *Revelation*, Interpretation: A Bible Commentary for Teaching and Preaching (Louisville: John Knox, 1989), 128.

[2] G. B. Caird, *The Revelation of St. John the Divine*, Harper's New Testament Commentaries (New York: Harper & Row, 1966), 96.

[3] Elisabeth Schüssler Fiorenza, *Invitation to the Book of Revelation: A Commentary on the Apocalypse with Complete Text from the Jerusalem Bible* (Garden City NY: Doubleday & Co., Image Books, 1981), 92-93.

[4] Isbon T. Beckwith, *The Apocalypse of John* (Macmillan, 1919; reprint, Grand Rapids: Baker Book House, 1979), 106.

THE SEVENTH SEAL AND
THE FIRST FOUR TRUMPETS

8:1-13

COMMENTARY

The Seventh Seal, 8:1-5

The two-part interlude of chapter 7 has ended. John has paused long enough in the action to reassure the faithful that they will not suffer God's wrath during the final acts of judgment and destruction. The reader is now ready for the climactic opening of the seventh seal, which will presumably usher in God's final kingdom. [Outline of 8:1-13] The opening of the seventh seal will mean that the sealed scroll is completely open. When the Lamb finally opens the seventh seal, however, we are met not by a vision of the end, but by an eerie silence. Why silence? Primarily, this is good dramatic effect. All heaven waits breathlessly for the final events to unfold. The heavenly beings who have been lavishing God and the Lamb with songs of praise now stand quietly in hushed anticipation. G. B. Caird noted, "It is as though there is one bar's rest for the whole orchestra and choir of heaven before they launch on the second of John's symphonic variations."[1]

> **Outline of 8:1-13**
> 1. The Seventh Seal—8:1-5
>   a. The Seal Is Opened—8:1
>   b. The Seven Angels—8:2
>   c. The Altar of Incense—8:3-5
> 2. The First Four Trumpets—8:6-13
>   a. The Seven Angels—8:6
>   b. The First Trumpet—8:7
>   c. The Second Trumpet—8:8-9
>   d. The Third Trumpet—8:10-11
>   e. The Fourth Trumpet—8:12
>   f. The Eagle in Midheaven—8:13

The silence perhaps carries a deeper significance, however. Some scholars have noted the passage in 2 Esdras 7:26-44 that describes the events of the end time. After the end of the messianic kingdom on earth, "then the world shall be turned back to primeval silence for seven days, as it was at the first beginnings" (7:30). As a period of silence preceded the first creation (cf. 2 Esd 6:39; *2 Bar.* 3:7), a period of silence will precede the new creation by God. Supposedly John is adapting a similar tradition and thus arranges for a brief period of silence before God's creation of the new heavens and new earth. Such an understanding of the silence would be more

The Silent Pause

"The pause, as some have argued, is dramatic and effective. But it is more. It is as if all of heaven and earth is holding its breath before the final revelations of the scroll. It is a moment of reverent silence, of realization that the events of history do not just 'happen,' driven by some grim predetermined force. Somehow, in and through these events, God is there, shaping and challenging, confronting and undermining, subverting and changing human history, working towards the fulfillment of his kingdom."

Allan A. Boesak, *Comfort and Protest: Reflections on the Apocalypse of John of Patmos* (Philadelphia: Westminster, 1987), 75.

compelling, however, if in Revelation the period of silence were followed by the new creation. That does not happen, though. The period of silence is followed by scenes of destruction and punishment. The new heavens and earth must wait until the end of the book. [The Silent Pause]

Another suggestion has been that the period of silence is so that God might hear the prayers of the saints that are offered up to God (8:3-4). R. H. Charles explained, "The praises of the highest orders of angels in heaven are hushed that the prayers of all the suffering saints on earth may be heard before the throne. Their needs are of more concern to God than all the psalmody of heaven."[2] This understanding is plausible and fits the context. Moreover, the scene in vv. 3-5 is set in the heavenly throne room, which contains an altar. Thus this is a worship setting. John may have had in mind the command of Habakkuk 2:20, "But the LORD is in his holy temple; let all the earth keep silence before him!" (cf. Zeph 1:7; Zech 2:13). [Silence in Heaven]

The silence is only for a brief time—"about half an hour." There is apparently no significance to the length of time mentioned. It is an inexact period—about half an hour. Although relatively brief, it stops the action long enough to create a noticeable dramatic pause.

The seven angels John sees are described as the ones "who stand before God" (8:2). These are the archangels, or the "angels of the presence" (cf. *Jub.* 1:27, 29; 2:1-2, 18; 15:27; 31:14; Tob 12:15. See also Isa 63:9 which, according to some readings of the text, speaks of "the angel of his presence."). They are the seven archangels of Jewish tradition, listed in some texts of *1 Enoch* 20 as Suruel (Uriel), Raphael, Raguel, Michael, Saraqael, Gabriel, and Remiel. Although the passage in *1 Enoch* assigns various tasks to the archangels, in this scene in Revelation they inaugurate the eschatological judgments by blowing the trumpets given to them. The use of the impersonal passive voice to describe the trumpets that were given to the angels is a common technique of biblical writers when God is intended as the subject. To say that the trumpets "were given to them" means that God gave them the trumpets.

Silence in Heaven

"There are times in history, taken on every scale, from that of the individual man to that of the whole world, when men and nations, groups of God's people or the church at large, hold their breath, as it were, to watch for the bursting forth of new judgement."

C. Anderson Scott, *Revelation,* The Century Bible (New York: Henry Frowde, n.d.), 198.

The text of Revelation seems jumbled at this point. After introducing the seven angels and their trumpets in v. 2, the text leaves
them aside and describes another scene, the heavenly throne room.
The seven angels are not taken up again until v. 6. Because of this
awkwardness of the text, R. H. Charles argued that v. 2 originally
stood after v. 5 instead of in its present location. It was later misplaced by a redactor or editor of Revelation.[3] A rearrangement of
the text along these lines certainly makes the text flow better. One
must resist the temptation to "improve" John's writing for him,
however, especially since no ancient manuscript contains the verses
rearranged in the manner suggested by Charles.

The insertion of the heavenly throne room scene in vv. 3-5 is significant. Prior to the opening of the seven seals that unleashed
eschatological divine judgments on the earth, John showed his
readers the throne of God (chs. 4–5) as a reminder that in spite of
the calamities that would occur, God was still in charge. Similarly,
prior to the blowing of the trumpets and the destruction that they
will set in motion, John shows us once again the heavenly throne
room. This scene also serves as a reminder that God is in control.
The events let loose by the blowing of the trumpets are not hap-
hazard or chaotic; they are a part of the divine plan. Equally
significant, both heavenly throne room scenes (chs. 4–5 and 8:3-5)
are settings of heavenly worship.

"Another angel," an unnamed one who is not a part of the seven
archangels, appears holding a golden censer, a container in which
incense is burned. The altar that is mentioned throughout vv. 3-5
(called "the golden altar" in v. 3) is not the altar of burnt sacrifices
(which seems to be the one in mind in 6:9), but the incense altar.
In the Jerusalem temple, the altar of burnt sacrifices stood in the
courtyard in front of the building that housed the Holy Place and
the Holy of Holies. The altar of incense was located in the Holy
Place and in some texts in the Hebrew Bible was described as overlaid with gold (1 Kgs 6:22). John sees the heavenly altar as being
located in front of God's throne. Either John envisions two different altars (the incense altar and the altar for burnt sacrifices) or he
has combined the two into one.

The angel functions as a priest, offering incense which is mingled
with the prayers of the saints. The smoke from the incense carries
aloft the prayers of the people and lifts them up to God. This language is a poetic way of affirming that the prayers of God's people
are not in vain; God hears their prayers. The Christian community
as John knew it was a worshiping community, offering up its
praises, thanksgivings, and intercessions to God. John does not

show us the earthly church at worship. Rather, he shows the effects of that worship. The prayers of God's people rise to the very throne of God where they are mingled with incense from the altar. One of the purposes of incense was to provide a sweet aroma that would be pleasing to God and render God more accepting of human pleas. Here, the mingling of incense with the prayers of the people assures their reception by God. [Incense Altar]

What was the content of these prayers? John does not say. In 5:8, John described golden bowls full of incense "which are the prayers of the saints," but failed to tell the contents of those prayers. For the reader, the cries of the martyrs under the altar in 6:9-11 come readily to mind. Such cries are probably not far from the content of these prayers. These prayers are the sincere yearnings for God's justice, God's sovereignty, and God's will. They are ultimately prayers for God's kingdom. They are the prayers of a people trying to be faithful to God in the midst of difficult circumstances, calling on God for help, for comfort, for strength, and for understanding. Some of these prayers would have been prayers like that of Psalm 22:1, "My God, my God, why have you forsaken me?" Others would have been closer to the words of Stephen, "Lord, do not hold this sin against them" (Acts 7:60). Still other prayers, voiced by individuals struggling to maintain their faith in a society that did not understand and sometimes despised such faithfulness, would have echoed the words of the distraught father who cried, "I believe; help my unbelief!" (Mark 9:24).

Incense Altar
An ancient cultic stand, likely an incense altar, from Jerash in modern Jordan.
(Credit: Mitchell Reddish)

When the worshiping church today prays the Lord's Prayer, its prayers become a part of this same yearning of "Thy kingdom come, Thy will be done, on earth as it is in heaven." God's people join together to voice their concerns over a world of injustice, hatred, discrimination, and oppression. Their prayers are pleas for God to act, to bring this world into conformity with God's ultimate designs. The plea of John at the end of the book is a similar prayer, "Come, Lord Jesus!" (22:20).

The prayers that are offered up have their desired effect. The angel takes the censer, fills it with fire from the altar, and throws the fire upon the earth, symbolizing God's judgment on a world that has failed to live up to God's standards. (John's imagery of coals from the altar thrown upon the earth was perhaps borrowed from Ezek 10:2.) The punishment is not separate from that unleashed by the blowing of the trumpets in the following scene, but is the prelude or warning sign of God's judgment. John portrays the divine judgment in images that are typically associated with the appearance of God—"thunder, rumblings, flashes of lightning, and an earthquake" (8:5; cf. 4:5; Exod 19:16-19).

The Seven Trumpets, 8:6–11:19

After this scene of heavenly worship in 8:1-5, John returns to the seven angels to whom the trumpets had been given. They are standing ready, waiting for the command to blow their trumpets. The structure of this section parallels that of the seven seals. As with the seals, the first four events in the series are grouped together, followed by the fifth and sixth events. Prior to the seventh event of the series, an interlude occurs, which in both series consists of two parts. The seventh and final event in each series reveals a scene set in the heavenly throne room. [Parallel Structure of Seals and Trumpet Plagues]

Like the seven seals, the seven trumpets set into motion divine judgments upon the earth. As already noted, these events should be understood not as completely new calamities, but as different ways to portray God's eschatological judgments upon the world. The two series overlap rather than follow one another chronologically. The trumpet judgments depict an intensification of the divine judgments. Whereas the destruction brought about by the opening of the seals was primarily limited to humans, the destruction from the trumpet blasts affects the entire universe: the earth (8:7), the oceans (8:8-9), fresh water (8:10-11), the heavenly bodies (8:12), and people (9:1-20). A further intensification occurs in the number of people affected by the punishments. Whereas the opening of the fourth seal resulted in the death of one-fourth of the inhabitants of the earth, the blowing of the sixth trumpet causes the death of one-third of humanity. In neither case should John's language be taken literally. This is poetic, dramatic language, rather than the language

---

🔍 Parallel Structure of Seals and Trumpet Plagues

First Four Seals—6:1-7	First Four Trumpets—8:6-13
Fifth Seal—6:9-11	Fifth Trumpet—9:1-12
Sixth Seal—6:12-17	Sixth Trumpet—9:13-21
Interlude—7:1-17	Interlude—10:1–11:14
The Sealing of the 144,000—7:1-8	The Angel and the Little Scroll—10:1-11
The Multitude from Every Nation—7:9-17	The Two Witnesses—11:1-14
The Seventh Seal—8:1-5	The Seventh Trumpet—11:15-19

⌕ **The Trumpets, the Bowls, and the Egyptian Plagues**

The Trumpet Plagues	The Egyptian Plagues	The Bowl Plagues
1. Hail, fire, and blood—Rev 8:7	7. Thunder and hail—Exod 9:13-35	7. Thunder, lightning, earthquake, and
2. Sea turns to blood—Rev 8:8-9	1. Nile turns to blood—Exod 7:14-25	hail—Rev 16:17-21
3. Fresh water becomes bitter—	1. Nile turns to blood—Exod 7:14-25	2. Sea turns to blood—Rev 16:3
Rev 8:10-11		3. Fresh water turns to blood—
		Rev 16:4
4. Sun, moon, and stars darkened—	9. Darkness—Exod 10:21-29	5. Darkness, pains, and sores—
Rev 8:12		Rev 16:10-11
5. Locusts—Rev 9:1-12	8. Locusts—Exod 10:1-20	
6. Invading cavalry—Rev 9:13-21		
7. Throne room scene—Rev 11:15-19		
	6. Boils—Exod 9:8-12	1. Painful sores—Rev 16:2
		4. Scorching by the sun—Rev 16:8-9
	2. Frogs—Exod 8:1-15	6. Three foul spirits like frogs—
		Rev 16:12-16

---

of mathematical precision. As Eugene Boring has stated, "John works with the imagination, not calculators."[4] The increase from one-fourth to one-third adds to the dramatic tension of the story and indicates that the end is drawing nearer. The reader senses the forward movement in this eschatological drama.

The events heralded by the trumpets are modeled after the Egyptian plagues described in the book of Exodus. In this regard they are similar to the seven bowl plagues of chapters 15 and 16. [The Trumpets, the Bowls, and the Egyptian Plagues] An exodus motif figures prominently in the Apocalypse, for John recognizes in the Roman emperor a new Pharaoh who has enslaved and oppressed the people of God. As the journey from Egypt was preceded by divine plagues of judgment against the land of Egypt, a new series of plagues will bring God's judgment upon a disobedient and recalcitrant world.

The First Four Trumpets, 8:6-13

The blowing of the first trumpet brings hail, fire, and blood, reminiscent of the seventh plague of Exodus 9:22-26 in which thunder, hail, and fire rained down on crops, people, and livestock that were out in the fields. The addition of "blood" to the trumpet plague is possibly due to borrowing from one of the signs of the end in Joel 2:30. The first trumpet blast affects the vegetation of the earth, burning up one-third of the trees and grass. [Trumpets in Antiquity]

The blast of the second trumpet sends a burning mass, "something like a great mountain," into the sea, turning the water to blood and killing its fish. The similarity to the first Egyptian plague

Trumpets in Antiquity

Trumpets in the ancient Greek, Roman, and Jewish worlds were primarily used as heralds of important events rather than as musical instruments. They were used as military instruments—to sound an alarm, gather the troops, pass on orders, inspire courage, terrify the enemy, and herald victory. They were used in religious ceremonies to announce special feasts or fasts, to secure the attention of the gods, and to accompany various acts of worship. In the Jerusalem temple, trumpets sounded daily to announce the opening of the temple gates and the time of the morning and evening sacrifices. In Jewish tradition, the blowing of trumpets was associated with eschatological events, also. In Joel 2:1, the command is given to "blow the trumpet in Zion . . . for the day of the LORD is coming, it is near." Zeph 1:14-16 describes the day of the LORD as "a day of trumpet blast and battle cry." In 2 Esd 6:23, the sounding of the trumpet is one of the signs of the last days. The eschatological association with trumpets is found in the New Testament writings as well (Matt 24:31; 1 Cor 15:52; and 1 Thess 4:16).

(Exod 7:20-21) in which the Nile turned to blood and its fish were killed is obvious. Going beyond the Egyptian plague, John adds that the ships were also destroyed. This calamity, like the one associated with the first trumpet, is partial, resulting in a third of the water, fish, and ships being affected. Commentators have suggested several possibilities for John's imagery of the mountain burning with fire. [Star Falling from Heaven]One suggestion is that John is following a tradition represented in *1 Enoch* that describes seven stars of heaven that were "like great, burning mountains" (18:13). Another suggestion is that Jeremiah 51:25 provides the imagery. This text describes Babylon as a "destroying mountain" that God will turn into a "burned-out mountain." A third suggestion looks to a historical event in the first century as the source for John's imagery. In AD 79, Mount Vesuvius erupted, wiping out the cities of Pompeii and Herculaneum. The explosive force of the volcano shot flames and ashes into the sky and sent lava cascading down its sides. Writing fewer than twenty years after this event, John may have been adapting this memorable event for his imagery. Whatever the source of John's imagery, the burning mountain graphically depicts destruction and judgment. [The Second Trumpet]

Star Falling from Heaven

Some commentators have seen in the great star falling from heaven a reference to Isa 14:12-21, which depicts the downfall of the king of Babylon. Drawing upon ancient Canaanite mythology, the Babylonian king is described as the Day Star (likely Venus) that falls to the depths of Sheol. The possibility of this interpretation is enhanced by Revelation's prediction in later chapters of the destruction of Rome, the new "Babylon." If this interpretation is correct, then John is here giving a preview of what he will describe in detail in 17:1–19:10.

The third trumpet plague has no direct parallel in the Egyptian plagues, although it could be seen as a variation of the water turning to blood because the third trumpet blast also involves a transformation of the waters of the earth. Whereas the second trumpet blast affected the salt water, the third affects the fresh

The Second Trumpet

As described on page 128, this work of art is part of an extremely valued grouping of tapestries. Altogether the 84 scenes from the Apocalypse form a 130-meter long narrative. St. John appears to the side of each composition. Here, he looks saddened by the blowing of the second trumpet (Rev 8:8). As the text describes, a burning mountain is seen in the sky, heading toward the sea. One of the two visible ships is destroyed.

Jan Boudolf and Nicolas Bataille. *The Second Trumpet: the Shipwreck* from the *Apocalypse of Angers*. Tapestry. 1373–87. Musée des Tapisseries. Angers, France. (Credit: Giraudon/Art Resource, NY)

waters of the earth. A great star, named Wormwood, falls into the water, turning the water poisonous. [Wormwood] The imagery of a star polluting the water indicates that this is punishment from heaven, that is, divine punishment. Wormwood is the popular name of several related plants. The wormwood mentioned several places in the Bible (Deut 29:18; Prov 5:4; Jer 9:15; 23:15; Lam 3:15, 19; Amos 5:7) is probably a small shrub with hairy, gray leaves that was known for its extremely bitter taste. In the Bible, wormwood is often used figuratively to refer to bitterness and sorrow, particularly as those characteristics are associated with the aftermath of divine judgment. Although the plant is not poisonous, John uses his literary license to enhance the effect of this bitter plant. Turning fresh water into bitter or poisonous water is perhaps intended as a reversal of the activity of God during the Israelite's wandering in the Sinai wilderness. At a place called Marah, the

Israelites could not drink the water because it was bitter. Following God's instructions, Moses tossed a piece of wood into the water and the water became sweet, that is, drinkable (Exod 15:22-25).

The judgments following the first three trumpets have brought devastation to the land, the seas, and the fresh water. Now with the blowing of the fourth trumpet the heavenly bodies—sun, moon, and stars—are brought within the scope of the divine wrath. These sources of light (or in the case of the moon, reflected light) are struck and lose part of their light, thus bringing partial darkness on the earth. This scene parallels the ninth plague in Exodus 10:21-23 in which darkness covered the land of Egypt. John continues the pattern of the first three trumpets in which the calamities affect only one-third of their targets. This is John's way of saying that God's judgment is not complete yet. It will be soon, but this scene is not the final act of judgment. That is yet to come. These are the preliminary judgments of God, whose purpose is to warn the people and bring them to repentance (cf. 9:20-21). [Imagery of Divine Judgment]

Darkness is frequently a sign of the judgment of God, both in apocalyptic and nonapocalyptic texts (cf. Rev 6:12-13). The prophet Amos described the coming day of the LORD as a day of "darkness, not light, and gloom with no brightness in it" (5:20). On that day God "will make the sun go down at noon, and darken the earth in broad daylight" (8:9). Joel 3:15 describes the coming day of the LORD as a time when,

> The sun and the moon are darkened,
>   and the stars withdraw their shining.

Isaiah also used this imagery (13:10). It is found as well in Mark 13:24-25 and Matthew 24:29.

John's description of the effects of the sun, moon, and stars being struck is a good example of the absurdity of trying to read

Wormwood

AΩ The wormwood plant mentioned in the Bible is likely the plant bearing the scientific name *Artemisia herba-alba Asso.* It is a small shrub with hairy, gray leaves. Although it has a bitter taste, it is not poisonous. Goats and camels eat its leaves, and bedouins make a strong tea from its dried leaves. Among its many uses in folk medicine is as a treatment for intestinal worms, which likely explains the popular name for the plant. (Photo Credit: Mitchell Reddish)

Imagery of Divine Judgment

In the plagues of the seven trumpets and seven bowls, "John has taken some of his contemporaries' worst experiences and worst fears of wars and natural disasters, blown them up to apocalyptic proportions, and cast them in biblically allusive terms. The point is not to predict a sequence of events. The point is to evoke and to explore the meaning of the divine judgment which is impending on the sinful world."

Richard Bauckham, *The Theology of the Book of Revelation*, New Testament Theology, James D. G. Dunn, gen. ed. (Cambridge: Cambridge University Press, 1993), 20.

the book of Revelation literally. John envisions that when the sun loses a third of its light, the day will become one-third shorter, rather than that the intensity of the light will be diminished. Likewise, the partial darkening of the moon and stars will shorten the night, according to this scenario. John is not concerned with scientific accuracy. He is once more exercising his creative imagination. The reader/hearer needs to visualize the Apocalypse more than he or she needs to analyze it. Such scenes are a part of John's "special effects." A generation of people that has grown up with Disney animation and *Star Wars* wizardry should have no problem appreciating John's creative mind!

The first four trumpets have sounded. Now there is a brief pause in the action as a new sight and a new voice break into the scene. A bird flies across midheaven blaring forth a foreboding message: "Woe, woe, woe to the inhabitants of the earth, at the blast of the other trumpets that the three angels are about to blow!" (8:13). The NRSV translates *aetos* as "eagle." The word may mean either "eagle" or "vulture" (cf. Luke 17:37 where the same word is used). Because the Romans used the eagle as an insignia, the eagle was a frequently used symbol for Rome (cf. 2 Esd 11:1–12:39). Here, the eagle does not symbolize Rome. Rather, if "eagle" is the correct interpretation, the emphasis is on the bird's strength and swiftness. It serves as a powerful proclaimer of the message of doom. As a fierce predator, the eagle imparts also a sense of trepidation and even fear to this scene. In modern parlance, this is no single-engine propeller plane towing a banner behind it. This is a fighter jet, screaming its warning across the skies.

Some commentators have argued for the translation of *aetos* in v. 13 as "vulture." If that is correct, the imagery is one of doom and destruction. As vultures hover over a decaying carcass, the presence of this vulture would be a warning sign of the destruction that is about to occur on the earth.

Regardless of whether the bird is understood as an eagle or a vulture, its presence is an ominous sign, which is confirmed by the message that the bird announces. The three-fold repetition of "woe" corresponds to the three trumpets that are yet to blow. The judgments upon the wicked that are set in motion by these trumpet blasts will be worse than those unleashed by the earlier trumpets. When read aloud in Greek, the effect of this cry in midheaven is even more chilling, for the Greek word for "woe" is onomatopoetic, creating the screeching sound of the animal's call: *ouai, ouai, ouai!* The announcement functions for the readers as a preview of what is to come, as well as serving in the context of

Angel or Eagle

AΩ The KJV follows another textual tradition and says in 8:13 that what John heard was an angel, instead of an eagle (as in NRSV). Although some ancient Greek manuscripts contain the word "angel" rather than "eagle," textual critics are convinced that "eagle" is what was originally written. A scribe likely changed "eagle" to "angel" because the proclamation of divine judgment seemed more appropriate for an angel than an eagle. The appearance in 14:6 of an angel flying in midheaven announcing judgment probably contributed to this textual change.

John's vision as a warning to the inhabitants of the earth. The first four trumpets have unleashed their punishments, but even more terrifying are the calamities that will accompany the remaining three trumpets. This announcement is a dramatic technique that heightens the suspense of John's vision. [Angel or Eagle]

CONNECTIONS

1. The opening of the seventh seal (8:1) results in a brief period of silence in heaven during which all the heavenly creatures are silent before God. [Silence] This silence occurs in the context of worship. Whereas in this scene the silence serves primarily a dramatic function, it also has rich theological significance. Hymns of praise and adoration, as well as prayers, are important, even essential parts of corporate worship. These are some of the ways that people express their dependence upon God, their gratitude to God, their reverence and admiration of God, and their petitions to God. Both individual and corporate worship, however, should provide periods of silence, at least occasionally. While it is true that, at its core, worship is an offering of ourselves to God, worship is also a time when we open ourselves most fully to the presence of God. It is a time to listen for the voice of God, a time to be directed by the spirit of God, a time to be touched and healed and comforted by God.

Silence

📖 "What deadens us most to God's presence within us, I think, is the inner dialogue that we are continuously engaged in with ourselves, the endless chatter of human thought. I suspect that there is nothing more crucial to true spiritual comfort . . . than being able from time to time to stop that chatter including the chatter of spoken prayer. If we choose to seek the silence of the holy place, or to open ourselves to its seeking, I think there is no surer way than by keeping silent."

Frederick Buechner, *Telling Secrets* (San Francisco: HarperSanFrancisco, 1991), 105.

Worship services that are continually "busy" may not be conducive to these possibilities. They may, in fact, hamper or interfere with worshipers' needs to be open to the presence of God. A period of silence, on the other hand, may allow for hearing the "still, small voice" of God. A time of silence can provide a needed break from the clutter and congestion of our lives and help us focus on our relationship to God and on God's communication with us.

It provides a time to "be still, and know that I am God" (Ps 46:10). A period of silence can allow worshipers to focus on their own individual needs and concerns that they want to share with God. It can become a powerful, intimate experience between the worshiper and God.

Unfortunately, we are uncomfortable with silence. Our lives are constantly filled with noise and activities. Radios, televisions, and CD players are our constant companions, allowing little time for silence. Silent meditation and contemplation are alien to our lifestyles. With the exception of Quaker worship, this is true in corporate worship as well. We quickly become restless and anxious during times of silent prayer. Even when the liturgy includes a period of "silent mediation," soft music often plays in the background to reduce our unease in the absence of talk.

In Revelation 8:1, the silence is a silence of awe and reverence before the sovereign Lord of the universe. It is a "pregnant" silence, filled with expectancy and anticipation of what God is yet to do. Those two attitudes—awe and expectancy—are desirable in any situation of worship.

2. For some readers, 8:3-5 may raise the question of the efficacy of prayer. Is prayer useless? Is it nothing more than a collection of words that never rise above the ceiling? This text in Revelation says "No" to both questions. John believes that the prayers of God's people are heard and acted upon by God. Like pleasing incense wafting heavenward, the prayers of the people rise to God, who hears and responds to the pleas of the people. The judgment of God against the oppression and wickedness of the world is in part a response to the cries of God's people who pray that God's will might be enacted on earth.

Even though John sees prayer as being effective, prayer is not itself the cause of what happens. Prayer is the means by which the people bring their concerns and pleas before God, but prayer does not force God or put God under any obligation. God is still sovereign. The prayers of the saints in Revelation are effective because those prayers are in harmony with the ultimate will of God.

Because of the way it is written, the book of Revelation invites the reader to identify with John and the people of God. The prayers that are offered up are in a sense our prayers, too. To join, however, in the prayers asking for God's justice and God's will on earth is a dangerous venture. To ask God to judge those who abuse and oppress others may be to invite God's judgment on ourselves. Even though we may not readily see ourselves as guilty of oppression or fostering injustice, we may be partially to blame. Through our actions (or our failure to act) do we perpetuate a system that discriminates against people of other races, against women, against the poor, or against people of different ethnic backgrounds? Do we enjoy a higher standard of living than others in our community or in our world because we are exploiting cheap labor? Do we care about the physical and psychological damage done to millions because of hunger, homelessness, and poverty? If we sincerely pray for justice and God's will to be done, perhaps we will become more sensitive to the ways in which we are in opposition to God's kingdom. In seeking to remove those hindrances, we align ourselves with God's kingdom.

3. The exodus motif that is so prominent in this section (and elsewhere in the book as well) is a powerful metaphor for the human predicament and God's salvation. The exodus story is a story of oppression, enslavement, and ultimately freedom. It is a story of a people liberated from bondage and set free in a new land. This story is what Marcus Borg has called one of the three "macro-stories" of the Bible, stories that shape the entire Jewish and Christian Scriptures.[5] Each of these "macro-stories" seeks to portray the human condition or human predicament and to present the solution to that dilemma.

These stories are so potent because, even though rooted in history, they are timeless stories. They are stories of the present as well as stories of the past. When we read and tell the exodus story, we are recounting not only the story of the ancient Israelites, but our story also. We know what it means to be in bondage and to seek liberation. We yearn for true freedom, for escape from the "Pharaohs" of our own lives. As Borg has said, the exodus story

> provocatively images the human condition as bondage, an image with both cultural-political and psychological-spiritual dimensions of meaning. It invites us to ask, "To what am I in bondage, and to what are we in bondage?"
>
> The answer for most of us is "Many things." We are in bondage to cultural messages about what we should be like and what we should pursue—messages about success, attractiveness, gender roles, the good life. We are in bondage to voices from our own past, and to addictions of various kinds.
>
> The Pharaoh who holds us in bondage is inside of us as well as outside of us. Who is the Pharaoh within me who has me enslaved and will not let me go? What instruments of fear and oppression does

Trumpets

This relief sculpture reveals the items carried back from the Jerusalem temple. Among them are the menorah and the trumpets visible in the right-hand corner.

Spoils from the Arch of Titus. Relief in passageway, Arch of Titus, Rome. AD 81. Marble, h. 7'10". (Credit: Mitchell Reddish)

he use, this Pharaoh who tries everything to remain in control? What plagues must strike him?

If the problem is bondage, the solution of course, is liberation. . . . Liberation involves coming out from under the lordship of Pharaoh and the lordship of culture.[6]

Why does John use exodus imagery? Because as he surveys the landscape of the churches of his day, he sees Christians who have become enslaved to culture, to political and economic systems, and ultimately to their own self-preservation. He recognizes in the cultural accommodation of many of the first-century Christians an allegiance to a new Pharaoh. John's vision of the trumpet plagues is a reminder to God's people that they must separate themselves from all false powers and loyalties. [Trumpets]The plagues bring judgment upon the world and ultimately upon all its enslaving systems and powers. The "Pharaohs" of this world—whoever or whatever they may be, along with their support systems—are ultimately doomed. The people of God must be willing to journey forth, to leave the "fleshpots" of Egypt (Exod 16:3), and to seek a "new land." To remain behind is to bring oneself under the wrath of God.

The plagues are also a word of hope and encouragement to the Christians who are struggling to remain faithful to God. In spite of the hardships they are enduring, the word of John is that liberation and salvation are a part of God's plan that will not be thwarted. "In each of the trumpet blasts God is saying to the Pharaoh of the new Egypt, 'Let my people go!' And at the same time he is saying to the Christians, 'When all this begins to happen, breathe again and hold your heads high, because your rescue is at hand' (Luke 21:28)."[7] For the church or for individual Christians today who are trying to remain faithful to the calling of God, but feel alienated, overwhelmed, or even oppressed, this message of assurance can be a powerful, sustaining force in their lives. The demand of God, "Let my people go!" can no more be resisted by the new Pharaohs of our world and culture than it could by the Pharaoh of ancient Egypt. That is the good news contained in the trumpet plagues.

NOTES

[1] G. B. Caird, *The Revelation of St. John the Divine*, Harper's New Testament Commentaries (New York: Harper & Row, 1966), 106.

[2] R. H. Charles, *A Critical and Exegetical Commentary on the Revelation of St. John*, The International Critical Commentary, 2 vols. (Edinburgh: T. & T. Clark, 1920), 1:224. Charles pointed to a somewhat analogous idea in the Talmudic tractate *Hagiga* 12b that states that in the fifth heaven are angels who sing praises at night but are silent during the day because of Israel's glory, meaning they are silent so that the prayers or praises of Israel may be heard.

[3] Ibid., 221-24.

[4] M. Eugene Boring, *Revelation*, Interpretation: A Bible Commentary for Teaching and Preaching (Louisville: John Knox, 1989), 135.

[5] Marcus J. Borg, *Meeting Jesus Again for the First Time: The Historical Jesus and the Heart of Contemporary Faith* (San Francisco: HarperSanFrancisco, 1994), 121-37. The other two "macro-stories" are the story of the exile and return from Babylon and the priestly story of temple, sin, and sacrifice.

[6] Ibid., 124.

[7] Caird, *Revelation*, 116-17.

THE FIFTH AND SIXTH
TRUMPETS

9:1-21

COMMENTARY

The Fifth Trumpet, 9:1-12

The first four trumpet plagues have primarily affected the world of nature, destroying portions of the trees and the grass, turning one-third of the sea and the fresh water to blood, killing marine life, and darkening the sun, moon, and stars. Humanity has been affected only indirectly, as some people have suffered and even died from the effects of the plagues on the natural world. The cry of the eagle has warned that three woes are yet to come. Now the plagues are going to become even worse for the people of the earth; for with the next two trumpet blasts, humankind will be the direct targets of the plagues. [Purpose of the Plagues]

Purpose of the Plagues

Elisabeth Schüssler Fiorenza, in discussing the function of the trumpet plagues in Revelation, has commented:

Revelation functions neither as an accurate transcript of divine information nor as a factual prediction of future eschatological events. Instead, it must be read as a rhetorical work of vision written in the language of image and myth. As such, it could be likened to today's literature warning against ecological and atomic destruction.

Present-day futuristic accounts portraying atomic warfare, ecological devastation, or scientific cloning do not intend to predict or accurately describe the future. Rather, they offer a fictional projection of what might be if the industrialized nations do not halt their military expansion or their technological exploitation of the earth. The terrible visions of such literature that portray a totally manipulated and dehumanized future seek to shock us out of our current lethargy. They are based on our present knowledge of the destructive potential of nuclear power, and they envision the worst possibilities for devastation. Their rhetoric seeks to spur us on to cut military spending and to stop nuclear deployment.

In a similar fashion, Revelation's mythological rhetoric represents the repulsive and grotesque powers of Satan and the abyss in order to shock the audience to repent from idolatry and to reject completely destructive powers. At the same time, Revelation's rhetoric seeks to engender trust and confidence in God's justice and powers of well-being even though experience and evidence seem to mock such hope and faith.

Elisabeth Schüssler Fiorenza, *Revelation: Vision of a Just World,* Proclamation Commentaries (Minneapolis: Fortress, 1991), 72-73.

The star John sees, which has fallen from heaven to earth (9:1), is an angel. In Jewish tradition, stars were often equated with supernatural beings or powers, especially angels. Note that this star had already fallen (past perfect tense). The imagery here is different from the star called Wormwood that John sees fall in 8:10-11. This star (angel) who is given the key to the bottomless pit is also different from the angel in 20:1 who comes down from heaven to imprison Satan in the bottomless pit. In 20:1, the angel is a messenger of God coming to earth to complete this task for God. In 9:1, the angel is apparently one of the fallen angels. The notion of fallen angels has a long history in Jewish thought. Genesis 6:1-4 contains a strange tradition about supernatural beings ("sons of God") who, being enamored by human women, came to earth and took wives for themselves from among the women. Their offspring "were the heroes that were of old, warriors of renown" (6:4). The book of Genesis does nothing more with this story. The author/compiler of this portion of the Genesis material apparently used this part of the tradition to depict the extent of wickedness on the earth—now even heavenly creatures are engaging in sin and disobedience.

Later Jewish writers were intrigued by this story, however, and elaborated upon it. One of the best examples of such expansion of the biblical tradition is in the first section of *1 Enoch*, usually called the "Book of the Watchers." The "Watchers" is the name used in this work (as well as in other Jewish writings) for the disobedient angels who came down to earth, took wives from among the earthly women, and taught them practices and ideas that corrupted the earth. As a result of the angels' disobedience, God imprisoned them in a place full of fire that "had a cleft reaching to the abyss" (*1 En.* 21:7). The author of *Jubilees* stated that these rebellious angels were bound "in the depths of the earth" where they were isolated (5:6). In the New Testament, the author of 2 Peter referred to this tradition when he said that "God did not spare the angels when they sinned, but cast them into hell [Greek: Tartarus] and committed them to chains of deepest darkness to be kept until the judgment" (2:4; cf. Jude 6).

John is apparently adapting this Jewish tradition of fallen angels. Here, the fallen angel is given a key to the shaft of the

Bottomless Pit

ΑΩ "Abyss" is a transliteration of the Greek word *abyssos*, which literally means "without a bottom." The bottomless pit is the place from which "the beast" of Rev 11:7 (cf. 17:8) arises and the source of demons (cf. Luke 8:31). During the millennial reign of Christ, Satan will be locked away in the abyss (Rev 20:1-3), from which he will be released at the end of the thousand-year period (Rev 20:7).

abyss (NRSV: "bottomless pit"). [Bottomless Pit] The abyss is the
reservoir of evil, the place where the disobedient angels have
been locked away. To open the abyss is to unleash a new plague
of evil on the earth. Because the abyss is frequently pictured as
a place of fire and continuous burning, when the angel opens
the shaft, a large cloud of smoke billows out of the abyss, darkening the air. John is a skilled storyteller. The suspense of this
scene continues to build—from the warning of the eagle, to
the angel with the key, the opening of the
shaft, and now the dense smoke.

    The smoke and darkness are not the real
plague, however. Out of the smoke
appears a horde of demonic locusts who
inflict torture upon the people of the
earth. Swarms of locust were well-known
terrors to people in the Mediterranean
world. [Locusts] Locusts are used in the
Bible as symbols of destruction and divine
punishment (Deut 28:42; 1 Kgs 8:37;
2 Chr 6:28; 7:13; Pss 78:46; 105:34; Nah
3:15). Two particular biblical texts likely
provided the background for John's use of
locust imagery. Obviously the eighth
Egyptian plague (Exod 10:1-20) is the primary source for John's imagery because, as
with several other trumpet plagues, the
fifth trumpet plague is an adaptation of the plagues on Egypt.
An additional source for John is probably the book of Joel,
which in an extended passage uses swarms of locusts as powerful symbols of God's punishment of the people (cf. Joel 1–2).

    The locusts of John's vision are not normal locusts. John
demonstrates his creative imagination in his description of
these surreal locust monsters. They are a marauding army of
voracious locusts whose physical appearance is terrifying.
Beasley-Murray commented, "The description of the locusts
reads like a verbal picture, besides which Picasso pales."[1]
Drawing from Joel, John describes the locusts as looking "like
horses equipped for battle" (9:7; cf. Joel 2:4). The book of Joel
also contributed the description that the locusts' teeth were like
lions' teeth (9:8; cf. Joel 1:6), a graphic way of portraying the
ravenous appetite of the locusts, and that they sounded like
"the noise of many chariots with horses rushing into battle"
(9:9; cf. Joel 2:5). The features of the locusts are part human as

Locusts

AΩ Locusts are a type of insect related to grasshoppers. In contrast to grasshoppers, locusts
seasonally reproduce in large numbers, gather in huge
swarms, and migrate en masse. When they swarm into
an area, they are capable of destroying almost all the vegetation in the area. Thus swarms of locust were (and still
are) greatly feared because of the extensive damage they
can do to natural and cultivated vegetation. In ancient
times, locusts were sometimes eaten as food, as they still
are among certain bedouin groups. According to Lev
11:21-22, locusts were one of the few insects permissible
for food for the Israelites. They are eaten dried, roasted,
raw, and cooked. Sometimes they are ground up and
added to other foods. They are rich in protein (75 percent)
and low in fat (3. 4 percent).

Yaaqov Palmoni, "Locust," *The Interpreter's Dictionary of the Bible,* 4 vols.
(Nashville: Abingdon, 1962), 3:146.

well. They wear what look like crowns of gold, have human faces, and have "hair like women's hair." This mixing of animal and human characteristics heightens the terror that these demonic creatures create.

Even more terrifying than their looks is the damage that these locust monsters inflict. Rather than harm vegetation, like normal locusts, these locusts wreak havoc on humanity. They have "tails like scorpions" (9:10) with which they inflict torture on their victims. [Scorpions] Specifically, they are allowed to torture those "who do not have the seal of God on their foreheads" (9:4), a reference to the faithful of 7:1-8. So horrible is the torture that the victims yearn for death rather than suffer the pain. There will be no easy escape for them, however, for "death will flee from them" (9:6).

The limitation of the torture of the locusts to five months is puzzling. Some commentators see this as a reference to the typical life span of the locust. Others understand it as a lengthening of the normal duration of locust plagues and thus an intensification of suffering. (Since locusts swarm and migrate, they would not remain in one place for five months.) A more likely interpretation, however, is that the five-month period is intended to show that the effect of the plague is partial, similar to the earlier trumpet blasts whose plagues affected only one-third of the targeted elements.

Although Proverbs says that locusts have no king (30:27), this swarm of locusts is different. It is a demonic horde that does have a king—"the angel of the bottomless pit" whose name is Abaddon. The word "Abaddon" is a transliteration of a Hebrew word that means "destruction" or "ruin." The word appears three times in Job (26:6; 28:22; 31:12), twice in Proverbs (15:11; 27:20), and once in the book of Psalms (88:11). In these passages, Abaddon is a companion and parallel to Sheol or Death. John has borrowed this term that personifies death and destruction and applied it to the leader of the demonic locusts, a powerful force of destruction. Earlier John has spoken of Hades (1:18; 6:8) as the companion of Death. For John, Death, Hades, and Abaddon all represent the same idea. They are personifications of the power that destroys life. As the destroyers of what God has created, they are the antitheses and enemies of God and ultimately will be destroyed

Scorpions

AΩ A scorpion belongs to the arachnid category (as do spiders, mites, and ticks). Most scorpions have a poisonous stinger at the tip of their tail by which they paralyze their prey. Although not fatal to humans, the venomous sting of the scorpion can be extremely painful. The author of Sir 39:30 included the scorpion as one of God's means of punishing the ungodly.

by God. For now, however, John sees Abaddon as an instrument used by God to bring punishment upon a disobedient humanity. [Locusts as Delicacy]

In order that no one should fail to understand the significance of this demonic king, John gives a Greek rendering of his name—"Apollyon." The Greek word that John uses to translate Abaddon, however, is not the word that is consistently used in the Septuagint to translate Abaddon (*apōleia*), but a variation of the term. What is interesting about John's variation is that it is similar to the name "Apollo," the ancient Greek god whose name was often linked in ancient writings with the Greek word for destruction. The worship of Apollo was widespread throughout the Mediterranean world. One of the symbols of the god Apollo was the locust. By identifying the angel of the abyss as Apollyon, John may have been taking a swipe at the Apollo cult. [Temple of Apollo] Even more intriguing is the possibility that John's use of the name Apollyon may have been directed at the emperor Domitian, who liked to claim that he was the living embodiment of the god Apollo. If the use of Apollyon was John's intentional pun on Domitian's divine claims, then John was inviting his readers to see the true identification of the Roman emperor who claimed to be the incarnation of Apollo. The emperor of Rome was in reality the king of evil, the leader of destruction.

No sooner has the terrifying swarm of locusts passed from view than the reader is reminded that this is only the first woe that is to strike the earth (9:12). Two more woes are yet to appear. Structurally, this announcement serves to tie the preceding and succeeding scenes more closely together. It reminds the reader that the locust plague is part of a special series of calamities that has been announced. Dramatically, the announcement increases the sense of foreboding and terror. If the first woe is this terrible, what will the two

Locusts as Delicacy
Artist's rendering of an Assyrian relief showing Assyrian attendants carrying skewers of locusts and pomegranates.

(Credit: Jim Burt)

Temple of Apollo
Ruins of the temple of Apollo at Side in modern Turkey.

(Credit: Mitchell Reddish)

remaining woes be like? John the consummate storyteller is at work!

The Sixth Trumpet, 9:13-21.

The sixth trumpet plague has no direct parallel in the Egyptian plagues. In one respect, however, it is parallel to the final plague in Exodus. The tenth plague on Egypt results in the death of the firstborn throughout the land. That is the only plague in which humans die. Likewise with the trumpet plagues, the only plague that causes death among the people of the earth is the sixth trumpet plague. The first four plagues directly affect the earth; people are only indirectly targeted. The locusts of the fifth plague do attack and torture sinful humanity, but they are prohibited from killing them. In the sixth plague, however, death comes to the human population.

The immediate result of the blowing of the sixth trumpet is that John hears a voice from the heavenly altar. The identity of the voice is not stated, but its origin from the heavenly altar indicates that the voice, if not actually that of God, speaks with divine authority. [Ancient Altar] This altar is the incense altar upon which the prayers of the people are offered and from which the fire is thrown upon the earth (8:3-5). That the voice comes from the altar is an indication that the actions resulting from the trumpet blast are at least in part an answer to the prayers that have been offered. [Horns on the Altar]

The voice commands the sixth angel to release "the four angels who are bound at the great river Euphrates" (9:14). In contrast to the other trumpet plagues, in this plague the angel participates in the action of the plague rather than simply initiating the plague with a trumpet blast. The four angels "bound

---

Horns on the Altar

ΑΩ Ancient Israelite altars (as well as altars of various other peoples in the ancient world) contained projections or "horns" at the corners of the altars, the purpose of which is not clear. The presence of these horns is supported both by biblical descriptions (Exod 27:2; 30:2-3; 37:25-26; 38:2; Ps 118:27; Ezek 43:15) and by archaeological discoveries. Some scholars have suggested that originally they may have been designed to help tie down the objects to be sacrificed. Others have suggested that they symbolized God (cf. Num 23:22; 24:8). In ancient Israel, part of the blood from sacrificed animals was smeared or dabbed on the horns of the altar (Exod 29:12; Lev 4:7, 18, 25, 30, 34; 8:15; 9:9; 16:18). A person guilty of an unintentional crime could apparently seek sanctuary or safety by grasping the horns of the altar (cf. Exod 21:12-14; 1 Kgs 1:50-53; 2:28-34).

Ancient Altar
This is a copy of a large reconstructed stone altar (c. 63 inches high), from c. 9th–8th centuries BC, that was located at Beer-sheba in Israel. Note the "horns" on the four corners of the altar. (Credit: Clyde E. Fant)

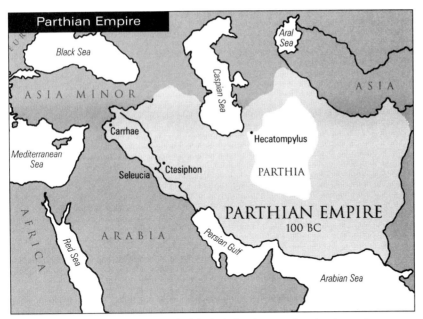

The Parthians controlled a large empire in Asia, including the area of modern Iran and Afghanistan. The Euphrates River, which was the western limit of the Parthian Empire, served as the boundary between the Parthian and Roman Empires.

at the great river Euphrates" are not the same as the four angels in 7:1-3 who stand at the four corners of the earth holding back the four winds. In the latter case, the angels are divine functionaries, carrying out the tasks assigned to them. In the scene in chapter 9, however, these angels are bound, like the evil angels of Jewish tradition. These are demonic forces whose destructive power God uses for divine purposes. The command to release them portends grave danger.

Why are the angels bound at the Euphrates River? [Map: Parthian Empire] The Euphrates River is located in the Mesopotamian region, the area of modern Iraq. In biblical tradition, this was the place of Israel's enemies, for from this area came the Assyrians, the Babylonians, and the Persians. The prophet Isaiah warned that God would use the Assyrians, who are "beyond the River," as instruments of punishment against Israel (7:20; cf. 8:5-8). This was the place from which "the enemy from the north" would come to inflict punishment and destruction on Jerusalem. As Caird noted, "All the scriptural warnings about a foe from the North, therefore, find their echo in John's blood-curdling vision (Isa 14:31; Jer 1:14f.; 6:1, 22; 10:22; 13:20; 25:9, 26; 46:20, 24; 47:2; Ezek 26:7; 38:6, 15; 39:2)."[2] John updates this idea, saying that once again God will let loose the enemies that are beyond the Euphrates, and they will serve as instruments of divine punishment.

The Euphrates River likely had an ominous sound to John's audience for another reason as well. John is drawing upon the deep-seated fears of the people of the Roman Empire. The Euphrates River was generally the eastern boundary of the Roman Empire. Beyond it lay threatening nations, particularly the Parthians. As discussed above in the comments on 6:2, the Parthians were the dreaded enemies of the Romans. To say that these angels of terror were let loose at the boundary of the empire would have tapped into a reservoir of fear and anxiety among the people of John's day. The effect would be similar to announcing to modern Israelis that the armies at the Syrian border had been let loose. John is not literally predicting an invasion by the Parthians (or any other army), but he is using the Roman dread and paranoia to create a scene of terror and devastation.

The release of the four angels sets loose a terrifying cavalry that sweeps across the river and invades the land. The statement that the angels had been held ready for this event—"the hour, the day, the month, and the year"—serves to emphasize that God is in control of this scene. Apocalyptic literature typically operates with a deterministic worldview. All that happens occurs within the predetermined plan of God. John utilizes that idea here. The size of the invading horde is almost unfathomable—twice ten thousand times ten thousand, or two hundred million (9:16). As if the sheer number of the invaders were not terrifying enough, the physical appearance of this army is shocking. The riders (or the horses, or both; the Greek text is ambiguous) have breastplates the color of fire and of sapphire (or hyacinth) and of sulfur.

Sapphire

AΩ The Greek term that the NRSV translates as "sapphire" is the adjective form of *hyakinthos*, the word from which the English "hyacinth" is derived. In antiquity, *hyakinthos* could denote one of several varieties of flowers or a precious stone (either the jacinth, a yellow-red stone that is a form of zircon, or the sapphire, a dark blue stone). The KJV uses the translation "jacinth" here, although that is not likely what is meant. The colors of the breastplate (9:17) are intended to represent the destructive elements coming from the mouths of the lion-horses (9:18). The dark blue color of the sapphire would represent the blue-gray smoke.

[Sapphire] Like the locusts of the previous trumpet blast, these horses are hideous hybrid monsters. Their heads are like lions' heads, and their tails are like serpents. Both their heads and tails are dangerous weapons. From their mouths issue fire, smoke, and sulfur, all of which are symbols of punishment, destruction, and terror (cf. the destruction of Sodom and Gomorrah by sulfur and fire and the accompanying smoke in Gen 19:24, 28; see also Deut 29:23; Job 18:15; Ps 11:6; Isa

30:33; 34:9; Ezek 38:22; Luke 17:29).
These are no ordinary horses. They are
fire-breathing monsters, "an army straight
from the jaws of hell."[3] They are a part of
the chaos let loose on the world, manifestations of the Leviathan monster of
ancient myth (Job 41). [Brimstone]

Brimstone

AΩ The KJV translates *theion* as brimstone. The
word "brimstone" (likely derived from words
meaning "burning stone") is an archaic term for sulfur.

The serpent-like tails of these monstrous lion-horses conjure
up associations with Satan, "that ancient serpent" (12:9). John
is possibly drawing upon historical associations here as well.
The Parthians were renowned archers on horseback. Not only
did they shoot their arrows as they advanced toward their
enemy, but as the archers went past, they turned around back-
wards on their horses and fired a volley of arrows from the rear.
Many commentators have suggested that this Parthian practice
provided the image for John of horses whose power was "in
their mouths and in their tails" (9:19). Whatever the source of
John's imagery, he has succeeded in creating a terrifying scene
of an invading army of millions of grotesque and deadly monsters who attack the world.

This monster army may be overwhelming, but its power is
limited. It is allowed to kill only a third of humankind, symbolizing both that this is not yet the final act of God's
judgment and that God's mercy has limited the extent of this
destructive plague. In the final Exodus plague, death did not
strike all the Egyptians, but only the firstborn of each
household.

As horrendous as the effect of this plague is, John says that
those who survive still do not repent. [Immorality] Like the recalcitrant Pharaoh of Egypt, humanity remains stubborn and
obstinate, unchanging in its rebellion against God. "The works
of their hands" (9:20) means their actions, their deeds. A person's true loyalties are evidenced by what he or she does, not by
what he or she says. Unrepentant humanity, John says, continues to make its own petty gods and idols, not realizing that
these "gods" made of gold, silver, bronze, stone, and wood are

Immorality

H. B. Swete has commented that the people who survived the sixth plague "were no
less unwilling to repent of their immoralities than of their idolatries. . . . Primitive
Christianity was a protest, not only against polytheism, but against the moral condition of the
pagan world. The Seer voices this protest, and enforces it with a terrific description of the
vengeance which threatened the world unless it should repent."

Henry Barclay Swete, *Commentary on Revelation* (1911; reprint, Grand Rapids: Kregel Publications, 1977), 125-26.

powerless. [Worshiping Demons] They cannot hear or walk, much less offer life, hope, and salvation. The words of the prophet designated as Second Isaiah (Isa 40–55) serve as an appropriate commentary on this text. "All who make idols are nothing," says the prophet, "and the things they delight in do not profit; their witnesses neither see nor know. And so they will be put to shame. Who would fashion a god or cast an image that can do no good?" (44:9-10). In words of biting satire, the prophet ridiculed the carpenter who used part of a tree for fuel and made an idol out of the rest of it, to which he bowed down and worshiped, praying "Save me, for you are my god!" (44:17) The prophet said,

Worshiping Demons

As did Paul (1 Cor 10:20-21), John considered demons to be the supernatural reality behind idols and other false gods. Thus to worship these idols or gods is in reality to worship demons.

> They do not know, nor do they comprehend; for their eyes are shut, so that they cannot see, and their minds as well, so that they cannot understand. No one considers, nor is there knowledge or discernment to say, "Half of it I burned in the fire; I also baked bread on its coals, I roasted meat and have eaten. Now shall I make the rest of it an abomination? Shall I fall down before a block of wood?" He feeds on ashes; a deluded mind has led him astray, and he cannot save himself or say, "Is not this thing in my right hand a fraud?" (44:18)

Yet, like the people in Second Isaiah's time, John says that humanity, in its blindness and stubbornness, will continue to worship that which is not only useless, but also dangerous. Such idolatry John sees as the root cause of human wickedness, including murder, sorceries, fornication, and theft. [Sorceries] Each of these, as well as other acts of human sinfulness, is evidence of human rebellion against God, of humanity turning to its own petty gods and goddesses. Like Paul (cf. Rom 1:18-25), John sees the world's depravity as symptomatic of idolatry—

Sorceries

AΩ The word "sorceries" (9:21) refers to the practice of magic. Magic in the ancient world was not parlor games or stage acts for entertainment. Magic was a way of gaining control over or influencing supernatural beings or of affecting the outcome of certain events. Through the use of incantations, rituals, spells, or charms, one could force the gods or the evil spirits to act in a certain manner and accomplish what one desired. The use of magic was widespread in the ancient world.

According to David Aune, "Ancients had an ambivalent attitude toward magic. . . . Magic was both feared for its malevolent effects, necessary for protection, and a means for achieving antisocial ends (without anyone being the wiser)." In Acts, Philip converted a man named Simon, who had been a magician (8:4-13). Later, Paul and Barnabas encountered the Jewish magician Bar-Jesus (also called Elymas) on the island of Cyprus (13:4-12).

David E. Aune, *The New Testament in Its Literary Environment,* Library of Early Christianity (Philadelphia: Westminster, 1987), 149.

the failure to worship the true God. The author of the Wisdom of Solomon likewise saw idolatry as the root of human sinfulness, claiming, "For the idea of making idols was the beginning of fornication, and the invention of them was the corruption of life" (14:12).

In the world of John's day, plenty of alternative gods and goddesses were worshiped. In the cities of Asia Minor he could easily see temples to Artemis, Apollo, Cybele, Aphrodite, Zeus, Demeter, Dionysus, Asclepius, and many others. [Temple of Aphrodite] In addition, the cult of the emperors was widespread and popular in Asia Minor, with many of the major cities containing one or more temples to the various emperors. Participation in the trade guilds and civic associations, as well as public feasts and other events, involved ceremonial acknowledgment and homage of patron gods and goddesses. In John's view, human allegiance to these false gods is ultimately the cause of these plagues that wipe out a third of humanity. Yet people remain unchanged, even in the face of such horrors. They cling to their powerless gods and in so doing bring about their own destruction.

Temple of Aphrodite
Remains of the temple of Aphrodite in Aphrodisias, Turkey. (Credit: Mitchell Reddish)

CONNECTIONS

1. How do we make sense of these hybrid demon locusts who inflict pain and torture on humanity? What is John doing with this scene? Many readers would likely agree with the assessment of T. F. Glasson, who wrote, "Few commentators have been able to find much of spiritual or literary value in this chapter. We have the impression that the writer has to fill out his numerical scheme of sevens somehow; and so horror is piled upon horror."[4] Perhaps it would be best at first to say what we should *not* do with the imagery of this fifth trumpet plague. One approach to this text that obviously should be avoided is the temptation to take John's picture language literally. John is not predicting a literal swarm of mutant locusts who will inflict terror and suffering on the earth. This is no B-grade science-fiction movie come to life! Likewise, one should not understand this scene to be a veiled prediction of events occurring in the twentieth century, as if John were pulling back the curtain on time and revealing in coded language the events of the future. For example, Hal Lindsey, the popularizer of sensationalist readings of apocalyptic texts, when writing in the early 1970s, implied that John's description of these flying locusts who have stingers in their tails was an allusion to the use of Huey Cobra helicopters during the Vietnam War!

Another approach to the text is to view the plagues as ever-present manifestations of evil in the world. This approach views the locust plague (as well as the other plagues in Revelation) not as an eschatological event, but as a timeless assault of evil against the world. Such an understanding of the locust plague is appealing, especially for the teacher or preacher who is concerned about the modern relevance of this passage. Understood in this light, the locust plague is said to represent moral decay that eats away at the fiber of society[5] or the locusts "may represent to us memories of the past brought home at times of Divine visitation, which hurt by recalling forgotten sins."[6]

As enticing as such interpretations may be, they do not seem to be warranted by the text. In order to have a clear vision of what John is doing in the Apocalypse, the reader periodically needs to step away from the details of the text and view the larger context of an individual scene. One can easily get lost in the details and lose sight of the larger purpose of the text. The locust plague is one of the trumpet plagues, all of which are a part of John's portrayal of the cataclysmic events that are to precede the end. These events are a part of God's judgment on a disobedient and rebellious world. These plagues are to be viewed in their totality, rather than interpreted individually as specific events that are to occur. They are John's way, using traditional apocalyptic formulas, to remind his readers that evil has no place in God's ultimate design. The trumpet plagues (like the seals and bowl plagues) are not actual events that have already occurred or that will take place in the future. Rather, they are symbolic representations of divine judgment.

At the risk of allegorizing the text, we should perhaps take notice of one interesting detail that John gives in his description of the demonic locusts. He states that "their faces were like human faces" (9:7). This detail is perhaps nothing more than John's monstrous hybridization of animal and human elements to construct a terrifying figure of evil. G. B. Caird, however, pointed to an interesting possibility when he commented, "Evil may take many sinister forms and ramify far beyond the immediate implications of individual sin; but in the last analysis it has a human face, for it is caused by the rebellion of human wills against the will of God."[7] Whereas what are normally called "natural" disasters are usually beyond the control of humans, most evil that threatens our world is ultimately of our own creation. We may blame systems, institutions, society at large, or even try to project our guilt onto some Satan figure, but behind the greed, corruption, abuse, and hatred that infects our world is a human face. Even the disastrous effects of so-called natural calamities may be worsened because of human sinfulness. Pablo Richard explained that these events

are not "natural" disasters but rather direct consequences of the structure of domination and oppression: the poor die in floods because they are pushed out of safe places and forced to live alongside rivers; in earthquakes and hurricanes the poor lose their flimsy houses because they are poor and cannot build better ones; plagues, such as cholera and tuberculosis, fall primarily on the poor who are malnourished, uneducated, and lacking in sanitation infrastructure. Hence the plagues of the trumpets and bowls in Revelation refer not to "natural" disasters, but to the agonies of history that the empire itself causes and suffers; they are agonies of the beast caused by its very idolatry and lawlessness. Today the plagues of Revelation are rather the disastrous results of ecological destruction, the arms race, irrational consumerism, the idolatrous logic of the market, and the irrational use of technology and of natural resources.[8]

The human face of evil makes this plague even more terrifying. God uses humanity's own corruption and evil as the means of its punishment. The evil that the world has created has finally turned against it. Other apocalyptic writings also depict human evils as part of the eschatological woes that will afflict the earth. A part of the end-time events listed in 2 Esdras, for example, is that "all friends shall conquer one another . . . and unrighteousness and unrestraint shall increase on earth" (5:9-10).

2. A major theological problem with the fifth trumpet plague is the picture of God that it paints—a God who allows, even instigates, the torture of humankind. This problem is not limited only to this scene, however. Throughout the book of Revelation, violence, torture, suffering, and pain are attributed to God or Christ. It is largely for this reason that many readers have condemned the Apocalypse as being sub-Christian. The Christ of Revelation often seems far-removed from the Jesus of the Gospels. Martin Luther, for example, disliked the book, claiming that "Christ is not taught or known in it."[9]

We will need to address this issue more fully after we have examined all of John's Apocalypse, but a few preliminary remarks are needed here. First, the reader should keep in mind that the plague of locusts, like the other scenes in Revelation, is not a description of an actual event. John is not literally predicting what will occur. Rather, he is using imaginative language to convey theological concepts. This kind of language is impressionistic rather than descriptive; it is emotive language. It produces its desired effect by creating impressions and stirring emotions and feelings in the reader, not by means of rational argumentation. That is why the details in John's visions are not as important as the overall presentation. The reader of John's Apocalypse needs to be asking, "What is the message that is being communicated by this imagery? What is the purpose of this scene?" In the case of the plagues, including the locust plague, the primary message is that sinfulness, which is contrary to the will of God, will ultimately come under the judgment of God. The horrific images that John uses to convey that idea are intended to impress upon the reader the seriousness of human sinfulness and evil.

Second, images of warfare, conquest, punishment, and violence are stock items in apocalyptic literature. By choosing to use the genre of an apocalypse as the vehicle for his message,

John has to some extent bought into the language and imagery of this genre. Thus the imagery may be due more to the genre than to John's own ideas. Third, the controlling image in Revelation for how God and Christ operate is the slain Lamb of chapter 5. God conquers not by force or violence, but by the sacrificial death of Jesus. All other images of God's judgment, punishment, and victory must be evaluated in light of this powerful and surprising image of the nature and activity of God.

3. Modern moviegoers are familiar with films that feature monstrous space aliens, ravenous mutant species, terrifying "creatures from the black lagoon," and other beastly horrors. These movies "work" when they succeed in creating in their audiences feelings of fear, dread, and horror. The purpose of these films is entertainment. Only the most ill-informed or misguided moviegoer would mistake these works for newscasts, documentaries, or nature programs. When encountering monstrous beasts in the Apocalypse, readers need to remind themselves of the type of literature they are reading and to ask what purpose these monstrous characters serve. As with horror movies, apocalyptic literature is not factual, either concerning the present or the future. It is imaginative, surrealistic literature. Contrary to horror movies, however, apocalyptic literature in general, and Revelation specifically, was not written for entertainment purposes. It was written to convey an important message, from John's perspective a message of life and death. Its purpose was not so much to provide information as to convince its readers/hearers to act in an appropriate manner. As Adela Yarbro Collins has noted, "On the deepest level, the Apocalypse expresses an interpretation of reality and exhorts its audience to live in a way that is an appropriate response to that interpretation."[10]

John has a different perspective on the world than most of the people of his day. He sees it as a world that has turned its back on God, that has followed its own desires, that has allowed evil to run rampant throughout society. A part of the function of the Apocalypse, and especially its visions of judgment and destruction, is to convince its readers to change, to repent, in order that they might avoid such calamities. In this regard John's task is much like that of the prophets of the Hebrew Bible who warned the people of God's coming judgment—judgment that was always conditional upon the people's failure to repent.

As the messages to the seven churches in chapters 2 and 3 indicate, John knows that there is plenty of room in the churches as well as in the larger society for repentance and change of lifestyle. He presents the various scenes in Revelation partially to serve as a wake-up call to Christians who have become complacent in their commitment to God and who have become too acculturated to their society. [Spiritual Blindness]

> **Spiritual Blindness**
>
> "Verses 20-21 express the prophet's conviction that the people of his day were so alienated from the creator that no crisis could move them to repentance. Events in which the faithful would see divine providence and justice are simply acts of blind fate to others."
>
> How spiritually perceptive are we? Do we see God's acts of warning and grace in our world and our lives, or are we blind to the activity of God?
>
> Adela Yarbro Collins, *The Apocalypse*, New Testament Message 22 (Wilmington DE: Michael Glazier, 1979), 63.

NOTES

[1] George R. Beasley-Murray, *The Book of Revelation*, New Century Bible (Greenwood SC: Attic, 1974), 162.

[2] G. B. Caird, *The Revelation of St. John the Divine*, Harper's New Testament Commentaries (New York: Harper & Row, 1966), 122.

[3] Ibid.

[4] T. F. Glasson, *The Revelation of John*, The Cambridge Bible Commentary on the New English Bible (Cambridge: Cambridge University Press, 1965), 59.

[5] James L. Blevins, *Revelation*, Knox Preaching Guides (Atlanta: John Knox, 1984), 48.

[6] Henry Barclay Swete, *Commentary on Revelation* (1911; reprint, Grand Rapids: Kregel Publications, 1977), 118.

[7] Caird, *Revelation*, 120.

[8] Pablo Richard, *Apocalypse: A People's Commentary on the Book of Revelation* (Maryknoll NY: Orbis Books, 1995), 86.

[9] This quotation is from the preface of the 1522 edition of Luther's German translation of the New Testament. In his 1530 edition he omitted these disparaging remarks, having softened his views toward the Apocalypse. Cited by Bernard McGinn, "Revelation," *A Literary Guide to the Bible*, ed. Robert Alter and Frank Kermode (Cambridge MA: Harvard University Press, 1987), 529.

[10] Adela Yarbro Collins, "Reading the Book of Revelation in the Twentieth Century," *Interpretation: A Journal of Bible and Theology* 40/3 (July 1986): 242.

THE MIGHTY ANGEL
AND THE LITTLE SCROLL

10:1-11

Interlude, 10:1–11:14

As happened after the opening of the sixth seal, a break in the action occurs after the blowing of the sixth trumpet. The reader is ready for the final trumpet blast, but John interrupts the trumpet plagues with an interlude. [Outline of 10:1–11:14] As with the interlude after the sixth seal, the interlude here consists of two parts: the angel and the little scroll (10:1-11) and the two witnesses (11:1-13). These pauses in the action allow the reader to catch his or her breath after the furious onslaught of the plagues, and they increase the dramatic tension of the work. Instead of hearing the final trumpet blast, the reader must wait a while longer. From a rhetorical standpoint, part of the purpose of the interlude is to offer reassurance to the faithful that in spite of the horrible devastation that will be unleashed, they will be protected. The interlude, particularly the scene of the two witnesses in chapter 11, describes the role of the faithful during the time of troubles and persecution.

> **Outline of 10:1–11:14**
> 1. The Mighty Angel and the Little Scroll—10:1-11
>   a. The Angel and the Seven Thunders—10:1-7
>   b. The Little Scroll—10:8-11
> 2. The Temple and the Two Witnesses—11:1-14
>   a. The Measuring of the Temple—11:1-2
>   b. The Two Witnesses—11:3-14

COMMENTARY

The Mighty Angel and the Little Scroll, 10:1-11

The phrase "I saw" (10:1) occurs more than forty times in the Apocalypse. It is an indication of the overwhelming visual nature of this work. The reader who wants to enter the narrative world of John's writing must attempt to enter the visual world with him. One needs to read the work with visual imagination, watching the scenes unfold as John elaborately describes them.

Not surprisingly, the first scene in this two-chapter interlude borrows imagery from several passages in the Hebrew Bible, most heavily from Daniel and Ezekiel. For readers familiar with the Hebrew Bible, John's borrowing and adapting of these images enriches the message of Revelation, providing multiple layers of meanings and associations. The visions of the book tantalize the imagination, inviting the reader to explore the various allusions and backgrounds of the imagery. The angel of chapter 10 is a prime example of John's multi-layered imagery, for the description of the angel is reminiscent of the Son of Man figure of chapter 1, of God seated on the throne in chapter 4, and of the angel Gabriel in Daniel 8:15-17; 10:2-9; 12:5-13, and his actions recall the commissioning of the prophet Ezekiel (Ezek 2:1–3:11). John describes this angel as "another mighty angel." The angel in 5:2 and the one in 18:21 are also called "a mighty angel." John gives no clear identification of this angel who appears in chapter 10. He remains anonymous. [The Mighty Angel]

The Mighty Angel

AΩ The angel in the book of Daniel after whom this mighty angel of ch. 10 is modeled is named Gabriel. Some commentators have suggested that John intended a wordplay on the name Gabriel since in Hebrew the name Gabriel is related to the Hebrew word *gibbôr*, which means "mighty."

John's perspective changes with this vision. Beginning in chapter 4, John had described his visions as if he were in the heavenly throne room and viewing the scenes as they unfolded. In 10:1, John writes that he sees the angel "coming down from heaven," thus indicating that he is on earth when he sees this vision. The cloud that envelops the angel is a symbol of divine presence (cf. Exod 16:10; 1 Kgs 8:10). This detail not only indicates the heavenly source of the angel, but also adds to the angel's mystique. Furthermore, clouds are often the means by which God or other heavenly beings travel (cf. Pss 68:4; 104:3; Dan 7:13; Mark 13:26; Acts 1:9; Rev 1:7; 14:14). The rainbow over his head is a reminder of the rainbow in the heavenly throne room in chapter 4, which harks back to the description of God in Ezekiel 1:28. Like the face of Christ in 1:16, the angel's face shines like the sun. The "legs like pillars of fire" is imagery borrowed from Ezekiel 1:27 and possibly Daniel 10:6 ("legs like the gleam of burnished bronze"; cf. Rev

Interpretations of the Angel

The angel of ch. 10 has spawned various interpretations through the years. A few commentators have suggested that this figure is Christ because the description that his "face was like the sun" echoes the description of Christ in 1:16. That is a weak reason for such an identification, however. Ancient commentators who identified the characters in Revelation with historical people claimed variously that this angel was the emperor Justin, the emperor Justinian, the monk Benedict, St. Francis of Assisi, or a coming saintly pope. (For citations of the ancient interpretations, see Arthur W. Wainwright, *Mysterious Apocalypse: Interpreting the Book of Revelation* [Nashville: Abingdon, 1993], 54, 57.)

1:15). The reference to the cloud that surrounds the angel and to the legs like fire may be intended as allusions to the cloud and fire that accompanied the Israelites in the wilderness. This connection would be appropriate in light of the extensive use of exodus imagery in the Apocalypse. If the exodus allusion is present in these two references, they serve as symbols for the presence of God, further emphasizing that this angel is a divine emissary. [Interpretations of the Angel]

This is, indeed, a powerful angel that John sees. When he speaks, he roars! [Roar of a Lion] He speaks with authority because, as the various elements of his description make clear, he is a messenger sent from the presence of God. His description functions to create a sense of power and awe for the reader. The massive size of this angelic figure is indicated by his stance—he has one foot on the sea and the other on the land (a modification of Dan 12:5, in which Daniel saw two angels, "one standing on this bank of the stream and one on the other"). [One Foot on the Sea]

> **Roar of a Lion**
>
> AΩ Some texts in the Hebrew Bible speak of God roaring like a lion. Examples would include Jer 25:30; Hos 11:10; Joel 3:16; Amos 1:2; 3:8.

The most important attribute of this angel is the object that he carries—"a little scroll open in his hand" (10:2). Before telling us anything more about the scroll, however, John says that the angel gave a great shout that caused the seven thunders to sound. The reader, aware of John's predilection for series of sevens, expects a new series of seven to begin here, just as earlier John has described the contents of the seven messages, the seven seals, and the seven trumpets. Having heard the message of the seven thunders, John is about to write their message down when a voice from heaven prevents him from doing so. The idea of thunder as the voice of God is found several times in the Bible (1 Sam 2:10; 7:10; 2 Sam 22:14; Job 37:4-5; 40:9; Pss 18:13; 29:3; John 12:29). The idea is that John has received a new revelation, apparently another series of calamities that is about to break forth on the earth. But we can only guess what the contents of this new revelation are, for we are not told. The voice from heaven commands John to seal up what the seven thunders said and not to write it down. The reader who is bound to literal consistency encounters a problem with this command. How could John seal up (as a scroll was sealed to prevent its contents from being read or tampered with) the words that he had not yet written

> **One Foot on the Sea**
>
> 📖 "The Angel plants his right foot on the sea, as if to defy its instability. The sea is ever present to the mind of the Seer (5:13; 7:1ff.; 8:8f.; etc.); to the exile in Patmos there must have been a peculiar attraction in the thought of the strong Angel to whom the Aegean was as solid ground."
>
> Henry Barclay Swete, *Commentary on Revelation* (1911; reprint, Grand Rapids: Kregel Publications, 1977), 127.

down? Obviously the wording is not to be pressed here. What John means is that he was prohibited from divulging the message of the thunders. It was to be "sealed," or kept secret, in that sense. [Heavenly Secrets]

What is the purpose of this scene with the seven thunders? Why does John tell us about the seven thunders only to refuse to describe their contents? Commentators have suggested several possibilities: (1) This is John's way of saying that the end is near. By eliminating the seven thunders, God has shortened the time until the end. The words of Mark 13:20 are sometimes cited as support for this view: "And if the Lord had not cut short those days, no one would be saved; but for the sake of the elect, whom he chose, he has cut short those days." The sealing up of the seven thunders, then, is an act of mercy on God's part. The message that the angel delivers to John in 10:6, "There will be no more delay," makes this interpretation of the sealing of the thunders even more attractive. The problem with this view, as appealing as it may be, is that John *does* give us another seven-fold series of plagues, the bowl plagues. If the sealing up of the seven thunders indicates that God has shortened the time, this scene would be more appropriately placed after the bowl plagues.

(2) The seven thunders may be simply a literary device deployed by John to add to the dramatic tension of the work. We have already encountered John's use of certain techniques for dramatic effect—the insertion of interludes prior to the seventh seal and the seventh trumpet, and the period of silence that followed the opening of the seventh seal. Mentioning the seven thunders, yet refusing to disclose their contents, may be John's way of teasing his audience. The secrecy motif heightens the drama. While the episode of the seven thunders adds a dramatic flair to John's work, a more significant purpose for its presence is likely.

(3) The command not to reveal the message of the thunders is a way of saying that humankind is not privy to all the secrets of God. Some divine secrets are not to be revealed. To know God completely is beyond human capacity. Keeping the message of the thunders secret preserves part of the mystery of God. As Jesus told his disciples, "But about that day or hour no one knows, neither the angels in heaven, nor the Son, but only the Father" (Mark 13:32), so John here informs his readers that some parts of God's plan are known only to God.

Heavenly Secrets

John's not being allowed to write down and thus disclose the message of the seven thunders is sometimes compared with Paul's experience described in 2 Cor 12:2-4. Paul speaks of "a person in Christ" (almost certainly an autobiographical reference) who "was caught up into Paradise and heard things that are not to be told, that no mortal is permitted to repeat."

The Angel with the Scroll

This print somewhat modifies Rev 10. The text states that John is given a small scroll by a mighty angel, wrapped in a cloud with a halo around his head; his face was like the sun and his legs were like pillars of fire. The angel raises his right hand to heaven as stated in the text. Dürer maintains the vivid description of the angel but further dramatizes the narrative with the replacement of a small scroll with a large book.

Albrecht Dürer (1471–1528). *St. John Devouring the Book Given by the Angel* from the *Apocalypse of St. John*. 1497–1498. Woodcut. (Credit: Dover Pictorial Archive Series)

The mighty angel, standing astride the sea and the land, lifts his hand to heaven and swears an oath. [The Angel with the Scroll] Raising the hand was a standard gesture for taking an oath. (Compare the similar practice today of people raising their right hand when they are sworn into office or sworn to tell the truth.) The key to understanding this passage is the scene in Daniel 12:5-10, which was the model for this scene in Revelation. The text in Daniel reads:

> Then I, Daniel, looked, and two others appeared, one standing on this bank of the stream and one on the other. One of them said to the man clothed in linen, who was upstream, "How long shall it be until the end of these wonders?" The man clothed in linen, who was upstream, raised his right hand and his left hand toward heaven. And I heard him swear by the one who lives forever that it would be for a time, two times, and half a time, and that when the shattering of the power of the holy people comes to an end, all these things would be accomplished. I heard but could not understand; so I said, "My lord, what shall be the outcome of these things?" He said, "Go your way, Daniel, for the words are to remain secret and sealed until the time of the end. Many shall be purified, cleansed, and refined, but the wicked shall continue to act wickedly. None of the wicked shall understand, but those who are wise shall understand."

John has combined the three figures in the Daniel text into one angelic figure. Like the man in linen in Daniel, the mighty angel in Revelation raises his hand to heaven and swears "by him who lives forever." John fills out the oath of the angel by adding "who created heaven and what is in it, the earth and what is in it, and the sea and what is in it" (10:6). Throughout the book of Revelation, John has emphasized that the God who will bring the world to its conclusion is the same God who created the world. The beginning and the end are tied together by God, who holds them both in God's power. God has the authority to conclude history because God is the one who started history.

The question of one of the figures in Daniel is the unspoken question of this scene in Revelation as well: "How long shall it be until the end of these wonders?" (Dan 12:6). When will the end occur? The author of Daniel provided an answer: "a time, two times, and half a time" (12:7). That is, three and a half years must pass. For the author of Daniel, a short interval (three and a half years probably is not literal, but figurative, for a brief period) of persecution and suffering under Antiochus IV had to pass before the end would occur. This question "How long?" has already been asked in Revelation by the martyrs under the heavenly altar (6:10).

The answer given to them was to wait; the time was not right. Now a different answer is given. The decisive act of God is at hand, for the angel announces, "There will be no more delay" (10:6). [No More Delay] The clue that the end is at hand will be the blowing of the seventh trumpet, for that will bring about the conclusion of God's plans for the world. [Olivier Messiaen]

The focus of the remaining part of this scene shifts from the angel and the seven thunders to the scroll that the angel holds in his hand. This scroll is specifically described as an open scroll. Furthermore, the Greek word used for the scroll in 10:2, 9, and 10 is a diminutive form of the word, thus meaning "little scroll."

What is the connection between this "little scroll" of chapter 10 and the sealed scroll that is opened by the Lamb in chapters 5–6? Scholars have proposed numerous possibilities. Some interpreters place a major emphasis on the different Greek words used for "scroll" in chapter 5 (*biblion*) and chapter 10 (*biblaridion*). Furthermore, the scroll of 5:1 is sealed, and the scroll of 10:2 is opened. Because of one or both of these contrasts, some scholars argue that two different scrolls are meant. The usual interpretation is that the little scroll of 10:2 contains the events described in 11:1-13. The larger scroll of 5:1 is seen to contain either all of God's eschatological plans or specifically the events of 6:1–8:5.

No More Delay

According to the NRSV, the words of the mighty angel in v. 6 are "There will be no more delay," a translation followed by most English editions of the Bible. A few versions, however, (including the Douay Version and the KJV) translate the Greek phrase as "there shall be no more time" (cf. the opening line of the hymn "When the Roll is Called Up Yonder," which states, "When the trumpet of the Lord shall sound, and time shall be no more"). This understanding of the Greek text—that the angel is declaring that ultimately time will cease to exist—was also the one accepted by several ancient commentators. Whereas both translations are possible, the remainder of the angel's statement in v. 7, as well as the passage in Dan 12 on which this text is modeled, makes clear that the idea is that the time of waiting is over. There will be no further delay.

Olivier Messiaen

This chapter in Revelation was the inspiration for a major musical composition by the French composer, Olivier Messiaen, who was captured by the Germans in 1940 and sent to a prisoner of war camp in eastern Germany. Fascinated by this angel who announced "the end of time" (the translation with which Messiaen was familiar used this phrase instead "there shall be no more delay"), Messiaen wrote *Quartet for the End of Time* while a prisoner. He has described the writing of the work in these words:

While I was a prisoner, the lack of food gave me colored dreams: I saw the Angel's rainbow and strange swirlings of color. But the choice of the "angel who announces the end of time" rested on somewhat more serious reasons.

As a musician I had worked with rhythm. Essentially, rhythm is change and division. To study change and division is to study Time. Time—measured, relative, physiological and psychological—is divided in a thousand ways, of which the most immediate for us is the perpetual transition of the future into the past. In eternity, these things do not exist. What problems! I posed them in my *Quartet for the End of Time*. . . .

In the name of the Apocalypse, my work has been criticized for its calm and its concern with detail. My detractors forget that the Apocalypse contains not only monsters and cataclysms, but also moments of silent adoration and marvelous visions of peace.

Olivier Messiaen, jacket cover for the album, *Quartet for the End of Time*.

Another view (which still considers the scrolls as being distinct) is that of G. B. Caird, who said, "The great scroll contained the purposes of God in so far as they were to be achieved by the Lamb. The little scroll contains a new version of those same purposes in so far as they are to be achieved through the agency of the church."[1]

Other scholars argue that the two scrolls are identical. The diminutive force of the word *biblaridion* is not to be pushed because diminutive forms of words in Greek often function without their diminutive meaning. Furthermore, even in chapter 10, *biblaridion* (10:2, 9, 10) is used interchangeably with *biblion* (10:8). The scroll in chapter 10 is described as opened because it is the previously sealed scroll of chapter 5 that has now been opened. Both references are to the same scroll, a scroll that contains God's eschatological plans for the world.

What then are we to understand about the little scroll and its contents? One is tempted to settle for the comment by Morris Ashcraft: "It may be futile to inquire about the content of a book which no one read before John ate it."[2] The clue for the meaning of this little scroll, however, is found in the source that John is borrowing here. John says that the voice from heaven directed him to take the scroll from the hand of the angel. When John takes the scroll, he is instructed further to eat the scroll. Readers familiar with the call and commissioning of the prophet Ezekiel in the Hebrew Bible will recognize immediately the source of this episode. John has adapted the story in Ezekiel 2:1–3:3 that describes God's commissioning of Ezekiel to be a prophet. Ezekiel was instructed to take a scroll that was open before him and to eat the scroll. The eating of the scroll symbolized Ezekiel's taking in the message that God would have him deliver. In internalizing the message, Ezekiel became the messenger for God. The word of God became his own words that he had to deliver to the people. In Revelation, John is presenting, in imagery drawn from Ezekiel, his own commission to be a prophet. This scene presents another view of what John described in 1:9-20, that is, his being called to be a witness and messenger for Christ.

Thus, attempts to determine the relationship between the contents of the little scroll of 10:2 and the larger scroll of 5:1 are misdirected. The two are conveying different ideas. The importance of the scroll of 5:1 is its contents—it contains God's plans for the world. The importance of the scroll of 10:2 is found in John's actions in regard to it—he eats the scroll. As Beasley-Murray stated, "The handing of the scroll to John is not the passing on of a note for communication to the churches, but the imparting to him of a prophetic commission, like that which Ezekiel had when he became a prophet."3

For Ezekiel, the scroll contained "words of lamentation and mourning and woe" (2:10). These were "funeral words," words of grief over Israel's failure to repent and over the destruction that will follow. Surprisingly, when Ezekiel ate the scroll it "was as sweet as honey" (3:3), perhaps a reflection of the words of the psalmist who said,

> How sweet are your words to my taste,
>   sweeter than honey to my mouth! (119:103)

The prophet Jeremiah described in picturesque language similar to Ezekiel's his experience of receiving the message of God: "Your words were found, and I ate them, and your words became to me a joy and the delight of my heart" (15:16).

The experience of eating the scroll is different for John than it was for Ezekiel. Whereas Ezekiel tastes only the sweetness of the message of God, John tastes both sweet and bitter aspects of the message. "It was as sweet as honey in my mouth, but when I had eaten it, my stomach was made bitter" (10:10). The scroll is sweet because John's task as God's prophet is to proclaim the good news that in Christ the victory has been won. The Lamb through his sacrifice has brought salvation to the world. John's message is one of hope, comfort, and assurance. The message is made even sweeter by the announcement John has heard from the angel, "There will be no more delay." The time of God's salvation is at hand.

Bittersweet Scroll

"The duality of joy and pain applies equally to the word for the Church as it does to the word for the world. For the Church must learn the weight of the cross before she participates in the glory of the kingdom, and the world must learn the reality of judgment before it experiences the grace of the kingdom."

George R. Beasley-Murray, *The Book of Revelation*, New Century Bible (Greenwood SC: Attic, 1974), 175.

But there is a bitter side to this message that John has received, bitter in at least two ways. [Bittersweet Scroll] First, John knows from personal experience that to be a messenger for God is a costly experience. He has already tasted the bitterness of exile on the island of Patmos because of his testimony to Christ. Antipas (2:13) has tasted the bitterness of martyrdom because he, too, has been willing to be a faithful and true witness. John expects even more outbreaks of persecution to engulf the church of his day. The Lamb may have won the victory, but many skirmishes are yet to be fought by the faithful. The cost will be high for those who refuse to compromise their commitment to God. The sweetness of God's salvation is diluted for John by the realization of the bitter cost that it will entail for many in the church. God's salvation may be near, but the road to the "promised land" lies through dangerous ground.

Second, the scroll is bitter because John's message is not completely a message of salvation. It also contains a message of judgment against those who refuse to repent and turn to God. John believes in a holy God, a God who is opposed to evil, a God who expects obedience and righteousness from the people of the earth. As the seven seals and seven trumpet blasts have already made clear, those who reject God's call to faithfulness and ignore God's gracious offer of mercy are left with God's judgment.

After eating the scroll, John hears a voice (or voices) speaking to him again. ["They"] Once more, the identity of the speaker is not given. It could be the angel, or more likely it is the heavenly voice of v. 8, which is the voice of God or Christ. The command puts in words the message conveyed by the symbolic eating of the scroll. John is told, "You must prophesy again about many peoples and nations and languages and kings." John's commission as a prophet is being renewed and reinforced. He has already been functioning as God's prophet, declaring God's message to the churches in chapters 2 and 3 and sharing the subsequent visions he received. His task is not finished, however. Once more ("again") he must speak the word of God to the world, a word of judgment and mercy. This recommissioning of John to be a prophet does not mean that he is given an entirely new message. As we will see, John's message in the remainder of the book will in many ways be a reformulation of what he has already proclaimed. John will pick up some of the threads of his earlier message and weave them together into a new tapestry, announcing God's message to all the people of the earth.

"They"

AΩ The use of the plural pronoun "they" in 10:11 is odd. Who is the speaker or speakers? Two speakers have appeared in this chapter—the voice from heaven and the mighty angel. Some interpreters have understood the plural to be a reference to both of these speakers. They now in unison issue the prophetic commission to John. That understanding fits the grammatical structure of the sentence, but it seems somewhat awkward to have the angel joining in with the heavenly voice. Accordingly, many scholars understand the plural pronoun to be an example of "the plural of indefinite statement," which according to R. H. Charles is "an idiom sometimes found in Hebrew, and frequent in Biblical Aramaic." If, as seems likely, one speaker is intended, the identity of that speaker is still not clear. Perhaps the commission to be the spokesperson for God would be more fitting coming from the heavenly voice (God or Christ) than from the angel.

R. H. Charles, *A Critical and Exegetical Commentary on the Revelation of St. John,* The International Critical Commentary, 2 vols. (Edinburgh: T. & T. Clark, 1920), 1:269.

This restatement of John's call to be God's spokesperson functions not simply as a reaffirmation for John. It serves also as a reminder to the reader of the source of John's visions and his revelation that he is declaring. This is not merely his own message he is delivering. It is "the revelation of Jesus Christ" that has been entrusted to John to make known to the churches. As the Hebrew prophets prefaced their message with the words

Prophesy

John's commission to prophesy is similar to that given to the ancient prophets of Israel. Compare especially the words to Jeremiah in Jer 1:10.

"thus saith the LORD" as a declaration of their authority to speak to the people, so John by this recommissioning scene reminds us that he, too, speaks as a divinely appointed messenger. [Prophesy]

CONNECTIONS

1. The title of this last book of the Bible is Revelation, a reminder that the understanding of God that John communicates is one that God has given to him, has revealed to him. Humanity does not discover God; God reveals God's self to the world. The etymological meaning of *apokalypsis*, the Greek word for "revelation," is uncovering that which is hidden. God chooses to uncover or disclose God's self to the world. The command by the heavenly voice telling John not to record the message of the seven thunders serves as a reminder that there are some aspects of God that remain hidden or undisclosed to humanity. In an age in which human knowledge is rapidly expanding and information is power, to be told that some areas of knowing are beyond our grasp may strike some people as preposterous. Human comprehension and learning seem limitless.

To pursue knowledge is certainly a part of our God-given ability as human beings. The abilities to question, probe, experiment, and reason are all a part of what makes us human. To use those gifts is to be good stewards of who we have been created to be. Yet failure to recognize that we are not the fount of all knowledge is a failure to recognize the distinction between the Creator and the created. The Genesis account of the Tower of Babel presents that truth in story form. Humans are finite creatures. We may continue to expand our knowledge of ourselves and our world exponentially, but ultimately there is a limit to what we can know and understand.

The age in which we live has been called the information age. Not only have we increased our knowledge in the arts, sciences, medicine, and technology, but the advancements in computer science have provided us the means to manipulate and store this data in ways that would have been unthinkable only a few decades earlier. In our quest for more and more education and increased knowledge, we must not forget the lesson learned by the author of Ecclesiastes, who said,

> I said to myself, "I have acquired great wisdom, surpassing all who were over Jerusalem before me; and my mind has had great experience of wisdom and knowledge." And I applied my mind to know wisdom and to know madness and folly. I perceived that this also is but a chasing after wind.
>   For in much wisdom is much vexation,
>   and those who increase knowledge increase sorrow. (1:16-18)

The author of Ecclesiastes found that although wisdom is definitely better than folly, it is not the answer to the ultimate meaning of life. Human understanding has its limits. This is also part of the realization that comes to the character Job. After complaining that life (and God) is not fair because the wicked prosper while the righteous suffer, Job demands that God appear in order to "justify the ways of God to man" (*Paradise Lost*, I.50.1). When God does speak to Job out of the whirlwind, God makes clear to Job that Job's insight and knowledge are limited. The ways of God are sometimes beyond human understanding. (One could certainly debate whether our lack of full comprehension is due to God's concealing some aspects of God, as the sealing of the seven thunders seems to imply, or whether it is due to the innate limits of the human condition. Regardless of the cause, the result is the same— God remains partially hidden and mysterious.) [The Mystery of God]

The Mystery of God

ΑΩ Heavenly mysteries or secrets are an important part of apocalyptic writings. The purpose of apocalyptic literature was the revealing of these heavenly secrets that were disclosed to the writers through visions, signs, or otherworldly journeys. According to Günther Bornkamm, in apocalyptic traditions the term "mystery" refers to "divinely ordained future events whose disclosure and interpretation is reserved for God alone." This eschatological meaning of "mystery" is also found in the New Testament (cf. Rom 11:25; 1 Cor 15:51; 2 Thess 2:7). In Rev 10:7, "the mystery of God" is thoroughly eschatological, referring to God's final plan for the world that God has created.

Günther Bornkamm, "Μυστήριον," *TDNT*, 4:814-15.

What does this limited revelation of God mean in practical terms for us? At a minimum, two insights spring from this realization. First, it means that all our efforts to speak of and understand God will be partial at best. This realization should lead to humility in any of our attempts to say what the will of God is in a particular situation. While those of us who teach and preach in the service of the church must attempt to understand and interpret God for our world, we should do so with humility and with openness to dialogue with those whose understanding of God and faith is different from our own.

Second, the mystery of God should be a part of our worship experience. God is "other" than we are. When worship is allowed to become too "chummy" with God, the result is likely to be a downsizing of God. Rather than standing in awe and reverence before the one who always transcends us, we begin to conceptualize God as our "cosmic pal," as one who is like us, only on a grander scale. In doing so, we have cheated ourselves, for we have reduced God to something that is within human grasp. Granted, the heart of the Christian faith is the affirmation that, in Christ, God has come near to us. But that awareness of the divine presence in and through Christ, as well as the abiding presence of God through the Holy Spirit, does not mean that all of God is reduced to human understanding and experience. God is still "other" than we are. The ideas of God's transcendence and God's immanence must always be held in tension.

The rich variety of biblical images and descriptions of God exhibits this interplay between God's transcendence and God's immanence. On the one hand, God is described as being distant from us (in the heavens); God is the king over the universe; or God is the divine warrior. On the other hand, God is like a shepherd caring for his sheep; or God is like a mother nursing her child; or God is like a parent who lovingly teaches the child how to walk and picks the child up when he or she falls. Even the two creation accounts in Genesis 1 and 2 portray God in different terms. In the first account, God is like an all-powerful monarch who commands and orders are carried out. In Genesis 2, however, God is like an artist who molds and shapes humans into existence.

Rudolf Otto, in his well-known work *The Idea of the Holy* (English title), spoke of God as *mysterium tremendum et fascinans*. God is "wholly other," according to Otto. There is and will remain a mystery, an unknown, about God that humanity will never be able to comprehend. This mystery both repels and attracts us; it creates in us a sense of our unworthiness before the overpowering majesty of God, yet at the same time fascinates us, attracts us, and allures us. While our worship should be a time of experiencing the presence of God and celebrating God's love and care for us, our worship should also be designed to remind us of the mystery of God, to inspire in us an awareness of the awesome majesty, splendor, and otherness of God.

Prophetic Task

Concerning the bittersweet message that John must deliver, Eugene Boring has written,

Every person who struggles to preach and teach the word of God knows this taste, this satisfaction, and this sickness in the stomach.

M. Eugene Boring, *Revelation*, Interpretation: A Bible Commentary for Teaching and Preaching (Louisville: John Knox, 1989), 142.

Divine Calling

John is told that he *must* (Greek: *dei*) prophesy (10:11). Individuals who have been called by God to perform a task can identify with this sense of necessity or compulsion. The prophet Jeremiah, describing his experience of being given a message to proclaim, said,

If I say, "I will not mention him,
    or speak any more in his name,"
then within me there is something like a burning fire
    shut up in my bones;
I am weary with holding it in,
    and I cannot. (Jer 20:9)

2. Being a spokesperson for God is a heavy responsibility. In language adapted from the prophet Ezekiel, John speaks of his calling as being both bitter and sweet. [Prophetic Task] The task of the teacher and preacher is to proclaim the good news of Jesus. That message is why the scroll that John eats tastes sweet. The message of the gospel is a joyous message because it is a life-giving message, a message of hope and comfort, a message of God's ultimate triumph. It is a message that proclaims God's sovereignty, God's grace, and at times God's judgment. The message that we proclaim, if we are true spokespersons (true prophets and not false prophets), is both gift and demand, grace and responsibility. And that's the problem. This message is not one that is always received gladly, even by those in the church, because at times the word of God addresses us as a word of judgment, even condemnation. Those, however, who would be faithful teachers and preachers must also be willing to speak clearly that negative word from God. [Divine Calling]

NOTES

[1] G. B. Caird, *The Revelation of St. John the Divine*, Harper's New Testament Commentaries (New York: Harper & Row, 1966), 126.

[2] Morris Ashcraft, "Revelation," *The Broadman Bible Commentary*, ed. Clifton J. Allen, 12 vols. (Nashville: Broadman, 1972), 12:301.

[3] George R. Beasley-Murray, *The Book of Revelation*, New Century Bible (Greenwood SC: Attic, 1974), 172.

THE TEMPLE, THE TWO WITNESSES, AND THE SEVENTH TRUMPET

11:1-19

COMMENTARY

The Temple and the Two Witnesses, 11:1-14

Chapter 11 in Revelation has been a difficult one for both interpreters and readers. [Outline of 11:1-19] The first difficulty is the structure of the chapter, specifically the structure of the first part of this chapter (vv. 1-14). Are

> **Outline of 11:1-19**
> 1 The Temple and the Two Witnesses—11:1-14
>   a. The Measuring of the Temple—11:1-2
>   b. The Two Witnesses—11:3-14
> 2. The Seventh Trumpet—11:15-19

there two sections to this part of John's interlude or only one? If there are two sections, where does the break occur, between vv. 2 and 3 or between vv. 3 and 4? What is the connection between these two sections? Readers should keep in mind that chapter and verse divisions, paragraphs, punctuation marks (including quotation marks), and capitalization are not a part of the earliest Greek manuscripts. All such reader helps are editorial additions to the text. Thus one should view these additions as scholarly suggestions for how to read and interpret the text but not as definitive interpretations of the text. (Note, for example, the variety in paragraphs in this section in English versions of the Bible. The reader should be aware of how these divisions subtly influence one's reading of the text.) The position taken here is that 11:1-14 consists of two different, but joined, scenes. The first (vv. 1-2) describes the measuring of the Jerusalem temple; the second (vv. 3-13) presents the church as two end-time witnesses. Verse 14 serves as a transitional verse between the sixth and seventh trumpet plagues.

The second difficulty with this section is the source of John's imagery used here. Verses 1-2 have been particularly problematic. The scene describes the temple in Jerusalem being measured, thus assuming that the temple is still standing. As argued in the introduction to this commentary, John likely wrote the book of Revelation

History of the Jerusalem Temple

First Temple	Second Temple	Herodian Temple
Built by Solomon c. 960 BC	Built by Zerubbabel c. 515 BC	Built by Herod the Great; begun in 20 BC; not completed until 50–90 years later
Destroyed by Babylonians in 587 BC	Dismantled by Herod the Great in 20 BC	Destroyed by the Romans in AD 70

around AD 95. By that time, the temple in Jerusalem was nothing more than a memory, having been completely destroyed by the Roman army in AD 70. [History of the Jerusalem Temple] The only part of the temple that survived was a portion of its western wall. Because this passage assumes the existence of the temple, some scholars have argued that the entire book of Revelation was written prior to AD 70. Others have suggested that perhaps this section, along with other portions of the book, may have been written prior to AD 70 and was later incorporated into the final product. A specific version of this latter view is that underlying this scene in vv. 1-2 is an earlier Jewish source that John has reworked. According to this view, behind 11:1-2 is a Jewish oracle that originated among the Zealots, who had control of the temple immediately prior to its destruction by the Romans. This oracle was a prediction by some Zealot prophet that although the Romans would conquer the outer portion of the temple, God would prevent them from capturing the inner part of the temple and would thus preserve the faithful remnant inside. (If such were the source of John's imagery, the original oracle was greatly in error, for the Romans destroyed the entire temple in Jerusalem.) Somehow this Zealot oracle survived, even after having been proven false, and was adapted by John.[1] [Jerusalem Temple]

G. B. Caird completely rejected this idea of a Zealot oracle, calling it "improbable, useless, and absurd."[2] He argued instead that John is responsible for this imagery. Whether there ever was a Jewish or Jewish-Christian oracle that underlay this scene or not, in its present setting the imagery of the temple is clearly to be understood symbolically, not literally. John is not concerned with an actual measuring of the Jerusalem temple (which no longer existed when he wrote). [Measuring Rod] Either through his own originality or his reuse of an earlier source,

Measuring Rod

AΩ The common reed, *Phragmites communis*, is a bamboo-like cane whose woody-jointed stems are hollow. Found along river banks in Israel and elsewhere in the Middle East, it grows to a height of 4–10 feet and is ½–1 inch thick. Among its many uses in antiquity was its use as a measuring rod. In Ezek 40:5, from which John borrowed the measuring rod imagery, the measuring rod is described as being "six long cubits" in length, that is, approximately 3 meters, or slightly over 10 feet, long.

Jerusalem Temple
Model of the Jerusalem temple during the time of Herod the Great.

Model of the Herodian Temple and Jerusalem at the Time of the Temple. c. AD 50. Holy Land Hotel. Jerusalem, Israel. (Credit: Erich Lessing/Art Resource, NY)

John has adapted the temple tradition to offer comfort to the Christians of his day.

Given a measuring rod, John is told to measure "the temple of God." The temple that John is told to measure is the earthly temple in Jerusalem, not the heavenly temple that is mentioned elsewhere in Revelation (3:12; 7:15; 11:19; 14:15, 17; 15:5, 6, 8; 16:1, 17). This is clear from the statement that the court of the temple will be given over to the nations (11:2). The imagery of measuring the temple is likely derived (either by John or his source) from Ezekiel 40:1–42:20 and Zechariah 2:1-5. In neither of these two passages from the Hebrew Bible is the measuring explained as representing the protection or safety of the temple, although in the Zechariah text the measuring of the city of Jerusalem immediately precedes an assurance that God will protect the city. In the Revelation passage, however, the protective purpose of the measuring is made explicit by the statement that the part of the temple that is not measured, the outer court, will be "given over to the nations" (11:2). Whereas the purpose of the measuring is clear, the identification of the

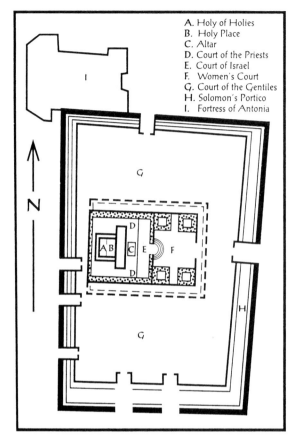

A. Holy of Holies
B. Holy Place
C. Altar
D. Court of the Priests
E. Court of Israel
F. Women's Court
G. Court of the Gentiles
H. Solomon's Portico
I. Fortress of Antonia

N

The Temple Courts

A sketch of the Jerusalem temple and its courtyards during the time of Herod the Great. (Credit: Elizabeth C. Clark)

measured and unmeasured parts is not so certain.

The Jerusalem temple consisted of three inner courts—the court of the women, the court of the Israelites, and the court of the priests—and a large outer court, the court of the Gentiles. [The Temple Courts] The part of the temple that is measured ("the altar and those who worship there") represents the inner part of the temple, specifically the court of the priests (where the altar stood) and possibly also the other two inner courts. The court that is not measured is the court of the Gentiles. The inner courts represent (for John) the church, the faithful people of God. They are guaranteed divine protection during the coming days of punishments and calamities. This protection is not protection from physical harm, but it is protection from spiritual harm. As we have seen already in Revelation, John expects that the church will have to pay a terrible price of suffering and persecution in the days ahead. Yet through all their difficult times, God will offer them strength and spiritual protection. The measuring of the temple, then, serves the same purpose as the sealing of the 144,000 in chapter 7. Both scenes are reassurance to God's people that even though pain, suffering, and persecution may engulf them, God will not abandon them. God will preserve them through their worst ordeals.

The identification of the inner courts as the faithful people of God is accepted by almost all interpreters. The identity of the outer court, however, is not as clear. Several possibilities have been argued: (1) The outer court represents faithless Christians for whom the time of suffering is intended as redemptive, to bring them back to faithfulness.[3] (2) The outer court represents the church in its engagement with the world in which the church will face persecution (be trampled), whereas the inner court represents the church from another perspective, its spiritual protection by

God.[4] (3) It symbolizes the unbelieving world that will feel the full effects of God's punishment during the time of the eschatological woes.[5] Although persuasive arguments can be given for each of these views, the last suggestion seems the most natural reading of the text. The portion of the temple that is measured and thus protected represents the faithful people of God. The part that is not measured and given over to the nations represents the world that is opposed to God. The objection to this interpretation on the grounds that the rebellious world cannot be both the ones trampled (the outer court) and at the same time the ones trampling (the nations) is not convincing because it fails to consider the fluid nature of apocalyptic imagery. As will be seen later in the book, John is not concerned with such seemingly illogical imagery. For example, in chapter 19 the church seems to be both the bride of the Lamb and simultaneously the wedding guests. Furthermore, a common biblical idea is that God sometimes uses the unfaithful nations as instruments of divine punishment against others who are faithless.

"The holy city" (11:2) refers to Jerusalem. Even though John no longer sees Jerusalem as God's special city (see comments on 11:8), he refers to it here as the holy city because he is using traditional material. A saying of Jesus in Luke 21:23-24 reflects the popular apocalyptic expectation that Jerusalem would be overrun and trampled by its enemies in the last days: "For there will be great distress on the earth and wrath against this people . . . and Jerusalem will be trampled on by the Gentiles, until the times of the Gentiles are fulfilled." John has taken this expectation and modified it. His concern is not with Jerusalem, but with the temple in Jerusalem as a symbol for the people of God who will be protected by God during the terrible ordeal that is to come. [Forty-Two Months]

Forty-Two Months

AΩ The duration of the trampling of the city is given as forty-two months, that is, three and a half years (cf. 1,260 days in 11:3). This number is borrowed from the book of Daniel in which three and a half years is given as the duration of the persecution of Antiochus IV Epiphanes, an event that the author of Daniel interpreted eschatologically (Dan 7:25; 12:7). When John wants to refer to the outbreak of violence by the wicked against the persecution of the faithful, he borrows the Danielic period of three and a half years. The number is symbolic of a period of persecution. Some scholars have suggested an additional significance for the duration of the suffering. Since seven is the perfect or complete number, half of seven (three and a half) represents an incomplete or limited period of time.

John uses forty-two months and one thousand two hundred and sixty days interchangeably. Assuming a thirty-day month, forty-two months (or three and a half years) would equal one thousand two hundred and sixty days. Although a year containing twelve thirty-day months does not quite equal either a solar year (containing 365 ¼ days) or a lunar year (containing 354 ½ days), thirty days was used as the approximate length of a month (cf. Num 20:29; Deut 34:8; Esth 4:11; and Dan 6:7, 12).

Announcement of Reversal

Elisabeth Schüssler Fiorenza has said that Rev 11:1-2 is "best understood as a prophetic announcement of reversal. Christians who *now* suffer the oppressions and persecutions of the nations will be eschatologically protected in the end while the nations will suffer the eschatological plagues and punishments of God's wrath."

Elisabeth Schüssler Fiorenza, *Revelation: Vision of a Just World*, Proclamation Commentaries (Minneapolis: Fortress, 1991), 77.

Two Witnesses

The presence of two witnesses validates the message they proclaim, for according to Deuteronomic law, at least two witnesses were necessary in judicial proceedings to corroborate each other's testimony (cf. Deut 19:15). Elisabeth Schüssler Fiorenza has suggested that the number of witnesses comes from Luke 10:1 in which Jesus sends the disciples out in pairs and assures them that nothing will harm them.

Elisabeth Schüssler Fiorenza, *Revelation: Vision of a Just World*, Proclamation Commentaries (Minneapolis: Fortress, 1991), 78.

The vision of the seven seals and the vision of the seven trumpets have presented scenes of great destruction, calamity, and judgment, events that are known as the messianic woes or eschatological woes. These punishments have been primarily directed at the unfaithful. Along with these terrors, John has also disclosed scenes of persecution and martyrdom of the faithful. How do these two ideas (eschatological woes and persecution) fit together? Much variety exists in Jewish and Christian apocalypses concerning the nature and extent of the eschatological woes and suffering of the faithful.[6] Persecution of the faithful is often seen as a part of the events that will happen at the end time. It is one of the traditional signs that the end is near. John appears to adopt this viewpoint as well. The last days will be times of intense suffering and persecution for the faithful. Even though the wicked may torture and punish God's people, God assures the faithful of spiritual protection. [Announcement of Reversal]

The speaker in v. 3 is either God or an angel. Likely, it is an angel who speaks on behalf of God. John is told that two witnesses will prophesy for one thousand two hundred sixty days, the same period as the forty-two months of v. 2 (42 months of 30 days each, as in a lunar calendar). Their period of witnessing coincides with the time when persecution and suffering of the faithful will be at its worst. The task of these two individuals is to bear faithful testimony to the world about God, that is, "to prophesy." They are to be God's spokespersons to a world that does not want to hear God's message. The garb of the two witnesses is likely an indication of the content of their message. Since sackcloth is worn as a sign of mourning and penitence, the message of the two witnesses is a call to repentance. [Two Witnesses]

John borrows imagery from Zechariah 4:3, 14 to describe further these prophet-witnesses as "the two olive trees and the two lampstands" (11:4). For Zechariah, the two olive trees represented Zerubbabel, the governor of Jerusalem, and Joshua, the high priest, both of whom were viewed as messianic figures. The two olive trees stood on each side of the lampstand (John has doubled the

Moses

Michelangelo depicted Moses with horns due to a variant translation of the Hebrew word for "shining" as "was horned."

Michelangelo (1475–1564). *Moses*. 1513–16. Marble. Church of San Pietro in Vincoli. Rome, Italy. (Credit: Mitchell Reddish)

lampstand) and provided fuel for it. Whereas for Zechariah, Zerubbabel and Joshua represented respectively a kingly and a priestly messiah, that is not John's concern here. These two prophet-witnesses symbolize the church in its mission to the world. John has already used the imagery of the lampstands to represent the churches (1:12-20). That imagery is picked up again in this passage. Here, however, only two lampstands are mentioned, instead of the seven that appear in chapter 1. This perhaps implies that only a portion of the church is in view, specifically the portion of the church that through its faithful witness experiences martyrdom (11:7). In Judaism, the tradition had developed that to be a true prophet often led one to martyrdom. The role of prophet involved rejection and death. Even Jesus reflected this view (cf. Matt 23:29-39). It is not surprising to find John sharing in this outlook. The true prophet, the one who holds to the testimony of Jesus, can expect no better treatment than that received by the earlier prophets and indeed even by Jesus himself. To be a prophet means to be a martyr.

The powers that the two witnesses possess identify them as Moses and Elijah figures. Like Moses, they possess power to turn water into blood and to strike the earth with plagues (Exod 7:14–12:32). [Moses] Like Elijah, they are able to destroy with fire and to cause the cessation of rain (1 Kgs 17–18). [Elijah] Certain strands of Jewish and Christian eschatological belief expected that Moses and Elijah would return to usher in the final kingdom of God. For John, the church itself will play this role of the end-time

Elijah

Located on Mt. Carmel in Israel, this statue depicts the prophet Elijah defeating the prophets of Baal.

(Credit: Mitchell Reddish)

Unburied Corpses

Allowing corpses to lie unburied and exposed was a common way of showing extreme contempt and ridicule, or even additional punishment, for the dead person. An unburied corpse would be vulnerable to wild animals and birds. In the book of Tobit, Tobit displayed his compassion and piety by secretly burying the bodies of people who had been killed by the Assyrian king and left unburied (see Tob 1:16–2:10).

prophets for God. The task of the entire church is to be faithful witnesses for God, to bear witness not only *to* the world but also *against* the world. For some the cost of such faithfulness will be death.

The two witnesses experience the awful truth that many before them learned—the world is not receptive to the message of God. To challenge the power structures of the world is to invite death. At the conclusion of their testimony, the witnesses are confronted by "the beast that comes up from the bottomless pit" (11:7). Although John will identify this beast more fully in the following chapters, its source already indicates its nature. It comes from the bottomless pit, the reservoir of evil. Not content with killing the witnesses, the beast adds to his attack on them by leaving their bodies exposed in the street, an act of extreme shame and contempt. [Unburied Corpses]

The place where the witnesses are killed is identified as "the great city that is prophetically called Sodom and Egypt, where also their Lord was crucified" (11:8). The latter part of that statement is a clear reference to Jerusalem. For John, Jerusalem (like Sodom and Egypt) represents places that were opposed to God. Jerusalem, God's city, has now become a symbol of rebellion against God. John is following certain traditions of the Hebrew Bible here in condemning Jerusalem for its disobedience to God and its rejection of God's spokespersons. Jesus reflected a similar sentiment when he exclaimed, "Jerusalem, Jerusalem, the city that kills the prophets and stones those who are sent to it!" (Matt 23:37). Obviously for John, Jerusalem is even more a symbol of rebellion against God because it is the city where Jesus met his death. One should not limit this referent to the historical city of Jerusalem, however. Sodom, Egypt, and Jerusalem are symbolic of all the world that resists God. They represent any place where God's witnesses face opposition and death.

The death of the witnesses will be cause for rejoicing and partying by the people of the world. This will be a victory celebration, for it will seem that the beast and his followers have won. Their celebration will be short-lived, however ("three and a half days"). God will not allow his prophets to die in vain. In language borrowed from Ezekiel 37 (the vision of the valley of dry bones), John describes the resurrection of the two witnesses: "the breath of life from God entered them, and they stood on their feet" (11:11). A strong *imitatio Christi* motif runs throughout the Apocalypse. The followers of the Lamb are to be imitators of him. As he was a faithful witness, they too are to be faithful witnesses. Like him they must expect persecution and suffering. [Suffering] At times that faithfulness will demand a martyr's death. In death as in life, however, the imitation motif continues, for those who are God's faithful will be resurrected to share in God's eternal kingdom. As Christ was vindicated through his resurrection, so too will God's faithful be vindicated.

At the command of a heavenly voice, the two witnesses ascend into heaven in the sight of their enemies. Their ascension, reminiscent of Christ's ascension, is also a further echo of the Elijah and Moses motif. Elijah was carried off to heaven in a whirlwind (2 Kgs 2:11), and Jewish tradition claimed that Moses also was taken out of sight of the people by a cloud (Josephus, *Ant.* 4§326). After the ascension of the two witnesses, a great earthquake strikes the city, destroying a tenth of the city and killing seven thousand people. [A Tenth of the City] The earthquake is divine punishment on the city for its mistreatment of God's messengers. The combination of the resurrection of the two witnesses along with the devastating earthquake strikes fear in the people who survive. John says that the people "gave glory to the God of heaven" (11:13). The response of the people of the city has been interpreted differently by various commentators. Some argue that the response of the people is simply one of terror and dread. Others have understood their reaction in more positive terms. The fear of the people is not abject terror, but reverential fear. That their fear leads them to give glory to God suggests that the response of the people is repentance. The people have turned from their rebellion against God and are converted. In support of this latter view, Beasley-Murray noted that in Joshua 7:19 and in Jeremiah 13:16, "to give glory to God means to confess sin and repent of it."[7]

Suffering

"For the church, the experience of being called into God's heavenly world is no escapist 'rapture'; in John's revelation Christians go to the presence of God through tribulation and martyrdom, not instead of it."

M. Eugene Boring, *Revelation,* Interpretation: A Bible Commentary for Teaching and Preaching (Louisville: John Knox, 1989), 148.

A Tenth of the City

Rev 11:13 states that because of the great earthquake, one tenth of the city was destroyed, killing seven thousand people. The significance of the number seven thousand is not clear, likely meaning a large number. Even though John likely did not know the size of the Jerusalem population, interestingly, seven thousand people is close to one tenth of the estimated population of Jerusalem at that time. During the Roman period, the population of Jerusalem is estimated at around 80,000 people or more.

Philip J. King, "Jerusalem," *The Anchor Bible Dictionary,* ed. David Noel Freedman, 6 vols. (New York: Doubleday & Co., 1992), 3:753.

The work of the two witnesses, then, produces results. They are protected by God until they are able to give their testimony. This testimony, which culminates in their deaths, helps to bring about conversion. In the words of Allison Trites,

> John is saying that the testimony of the witnesses is not in vain. Despite widespread impenitence in the face of the punitive judgments of God (9:20-21; 16:9, 11), their witness in life and death is effective, for through it an innumerable company respond to God by revering his name and paying homage. Here is a classic illustration of the familiar adage, "the blood of the martyrs is the seed of the church."[8]

This section closes with an ominous pronouncement: "The second woe has passed. The third woe is coming very soon" (11:14). The second woe was comprised of the events that followed the blowing of the sixth trumpet (9:13-21).

The Seventh Trumpet, 11:15-19

After the lengthy interlude of 10:1–11:14, John returns to the series of seven trumpet blasts. Six trumpet blasts have sounded already; the seventh trumpet is waiting to be blown. The results of the blowing of the seventh trumpet are unlike the resultant events from the blowing of the first six trumpets. The first six trumpet blasts unleashed various judgments of God upon the earth; cataclysmic destruction, pain, and death followed in their wake. The blowing of the seventh trumpet, however, unleashes a heavenly chorus proclaiming the universal sovereignty of God. The mood shifts from fearfulness to celebration. A second difference between the first six trumpets and the last trumpet is the setting. The first six depict the situation on earth; the seventh trumpet reveals a scene in the heavenly throne room.

One interpretation problem with 11:15-19 concerns its relationship to the three impending woes that were announced in 8:13. The three woes were to be the final three trumpet blasts. The fifth and sixth trumpet blasts coincide with the first two woes, as 9:12 and 11:14 make clear. But what about the third woe? As noted, the events following the blowing of the seventh trumpet are not woeful events, but celebration and praise. Accordingly, some commentators have argued that the third woe is not found in chapter 11 but is contained in the seven bowl plagues of chapters 15 and 16. Other scholars have suggested that the attack of the beasts on the church in chapters 12 and 13 comprises the third woe. Others have suggested that John has omitted the third woe. To be sure, John does not specifically designate any event as the third woe. Rather than looking for the third woe later in the book, however, or assuming that John has either intentionally or unintentionally omitted it, one is likely on safer ground in identifying the third woe with the events of 11:15-19. Even though the seventh trumpet blast describes the joyous finale of God's triumph, this consummation scene also includes a message of judgment. The hymn sung by the twenty-four elders declares that God's "wrath has come" and also the time "for destroying those who destroy the earth" (11:18). The third woe is not described in detail, but is mentioned. It is God's defeat of evil and God's judgment against all powers and forces that oppose the plans and purposes of God.

The seventh trumpet vision is located in the heavenly throne room, a setting that occurs also at 4:1–5:14; 7:9-17; 8:1-5; 14:2-3; 15:2-8; 19:1-10; 21:3-8. John does not identify the "loud voices" who break forth in heavenly praise in 11:15. They are obviously a part of the heavenly court that includes angels, the four living creatures, and the twenty-four elders. These voices celebrate the fulfillment of God's ultimate plan for the universe, the "mystery of God" announced at 10:7. This "mystery" is the universal recognition of God's sovereignty. Whereas God has always been "the Alpha and the Omega," "the Almighty," God's lordship has not been recognized by all people. Now the heavenly chorus exclaims that the entire universe has come under the sovereignty of God. The petition that is prayed as a part of the Lord's Prayer—"Thy kingdom come. Thy will be done, on earth as it is in heaven"—has now become reality. The kingdom of God has been completed; the final triumph of God has occurred. [Kingdom of God] No longer is there any question about who is in charge of the universe. All earthly rulers and powers, including the Roman emperor, have been subjugated to the reign of God. John thinks in dichotomous terms—God versus the powers of the world. Thus he can lump together all the forces who are opposed to God's rule and refer to them as "the kingdom of the world" (11:15; KJV erroneously makes "kingdom" plural). The book of Revelation uses the word "world" (*kosmos*) in a manner similar to that of the Johannine and Pauline writings in the New Testament. The "world" represents the universe, both humanity and creation, in rebellion against God. "The κόσμος [kosmos] is the sum of the divine creation which has been shattered by the fall, which stands under the judgment of God."[9] John envisions a day when the world that has been broken by sin and rebellion will be healed, a day when all opposition and resistance to God will

Kingdom of God

AΩ The phrase "kingdom of God" does not refer to a place or a territory. It is not a spatial concept. Rather, the kingdom of God means the sovereignty or rule of God in the lives of people and over all of creation.

Messiah

$A\Omega$ The word "messiah" is a transliteration of a Hebrew word meaning "anointed one." In ancient Israel, anointing (by pouring oil on the head) was a way of consecrating someone for special service. Kings especially, but on occasion also priests and even prophets, were anointed. The king was God's anointed one because the king was God's representative on earth. Whereas present kings were sometimes described as God's anointed, the anointed one, or "messiah," came to be used for the future ideal Davidic king. The early followers of Jesus saw Jesus as fulfilling the role of God's anointed one and thus ascribed the title Messiah (or "Christ," in Greek) to him.

---

cease, a day when God's ultimate design for creation will finally be realized. With the sounding of the seventh trumpet, the heavenly chorus joyously proclaims that finally that day has arrived.

The close identification of God and Christ is evident in the claim by the heavenly chorus that

> "The kingdom of the world has become the kingdom of our Lord and of his Messiah." (11:15)

"Our Lord and of his Messiah" is wording borrowed from Psalm 2:2 ("the LORD and his anointed"), a passage referring to God and the king of Israel. [Messiah] The psalmist viewed the earthly king of Israel as God's representative, God's client-king, ruling over Israel on behalf of God. Modifying this idea, John can say that Christ rules along with God. The kingdom of God *is* the kingdom that Christ has been establishing. Jesus in the Gospel of John can proclaim, "The Father and I are one" (10:30) and "I am in the Father and the Father is in me" (14:10). John of Patmos likewise sees that there are not two authorities or two kingdoms, a kingdom of God and a kingdom of Christ. Rather, they are one and the same. As further evidence of John's high Christology, note the use of the singular pronoun in the final clause of v. 15, "and he will reign forever and ever." Although the previous clause has referred to "the kingdom of our Lord and of his Messiah," John writes that "*he* will reign." Questioning whether the "he" refers to God or Christ is

---

Unity of God and Christ

Commenting on John's use of a singular verb or pronoun in reference to God and Christ, Richard Bauckham has said,

It is not clear whether the singular in these cases refers to God alone or to God and Christ together as a unity. John who is very sensitive to the theological implications of language and even prepared to defy grammar for the sake of theology (cf. 1:4), may well intend the latter. But in either case, he is evidently reluctant to speak of God and Christ together as a

plurality. He never makes them the subjects of a plural verb or uses a plural pronoun to refer to them both. The reason is surely clear: he places Christ on the divine side of the distinction between God and creation, but he wishes to avoid ways of speaking which sound to him polytheistic. The consistency of his usage shows that he had reflected carefully on the relation of Christology to monotheism.

Richard Bauckham, *The Theology of the Book of Revelation*, New Testament Theology (Cambridge: Cambridge University Press, 1993), 60-61.

futile because the reign of God and Christ is one and the same. Grammatical correctness has given way to theological insight. [Unity of God and Christ]

After the declaration of God's sovereignty by the unnamed heavenly chorus, the twenty-four elders fall down in obeisance to God, adding their song of thanksgiving to the heavenly celebration. Their description of God is striking in what it omits. Earlier in Revelation, God is described as the one "who is and who was and who is to come" (1:4, 8; 4:8). Now the elders address God as you "who are and who were." No longer is God the one "who comes." The last element is no longer needed because the long-anticipated coming of God has arrived. The kingdom of God has finally been realized; God has taken God's "great power and begun to reign" (11:17).

This eschatological victory hymn describes the results of the actualization of God's rule: judgment, destruction, and salvation. The world will face the judgment of God; those who "destroy the earth" will themselves be destroyed, while those who are God's servants will be rewarded. [Those Rewarded] Surprisingly, John does not give any details about these events. The effect of the seventh trumpet blast is announced, but not described. We have reached the finale; the curtain has dropped. The chorus bursts into jubilant celebration. The reader who is expecting fire and brimstone, Armageddon, and a new Jerusalem is apt to be puzzled, if not disappointed. The finale is certainly anti-climactic, following in the wake of the vivid descriptions of the events of the seven seals and first six trumpets. As we shall see, however, John is not finished yet. The remainder of the Apocalypse will give in more detail much of what has only been sketched in outline here. In the latter half of Revelation, for example, John will clarify who are "those who destroy the earth"—the dragon, the beasts, and those who follow them.

> **Those Rewarded**
>
> The song of the twenty-four elders proclaims that at the time of judgment God will reward God's servants. Three specific groups of people are singled out for reward: the prophets, the saints, and all who fear the name of God (11:18). By "prophets" John likely has in mind inspired Christian spokespersons who addressed the church as well as the world with the message of God. The "saints" would include all Christians, that is, those who have been set apart for God. The last group, "all who fear your name," perhaps refers to those outside the church who have turned to God in repentance (cf. 11:13).

That the end has occurred at the midpoint of John's work is clear evidence that the events in Revelation are not to be taken in strict chronological order, as if one could construct a detailed timetable or chart of the events of the end time. The structure of Revelation is not linear. The structure is more akin to a spiral that loops back

Although greatly disputed, according to some scholars this relief carving from a 4th-century AD synagogue in Capernaum depicts the Israelite ark of the covenant being carried on a wagon.

(Credit: Mitchell Reddish)

Ark of the Covenant

AΩ The ark of the covenant (or ark of Yahweh, ark of God, ark of the testimony) was a wooden chest or box, overlaid with gold (according to some biblical descriptions). The tablets of the law received at Mount Sinai were supposedly kept in the ark. The ark served as a visual representation of the presence of God with the people. During the time of the settlement of the Hebrew people in Canaan and during the early monarchical period, the ark was carried into battle with them, with the idea that the presence of the ark guaranteed the presence of God with the Hebrew people and thus assured them of victory over their enemies. When Solomon built the temple in Jerusalem, the ark was placed in the most sacred part of the temple, the Holy of Holies. The ark was considered God's throne in the temple. The ark also had atoning significance, for on top of the ark was a covering of pure gold (the "mercy seat"). On the yearly Day of Atonement, the priest would sprinkle blood from the sacrificed bull onto this covering of the ark.

upon itself, restating themes that have been introduced earlier and moving forward with them.

Chapter 11 closes with a glimpse of the heavenly temple, counterpart to the Jerusalem temple. Inside the temple John can see the ark of the covenant, which in ancient Israel represented the presence of God in the midst of the people. During the time of the Solomonic temple, the ark stood in the innermost part of the temple, the Holy of Holies. Only the High Priest was allowed to enter this inner sanctum, and then only on the Day of Atonement. The ark disappeared sometime around the period of the Babylonian exile of the Jews. A likely possibility is that the ark was destroyed or taken as a spoil of war by the Babylonians when they captured Jerusalem and the temple in 587 BC. Several traditions arose in Judaism about the fate of the ark. One tradition, found in 2 Maccabees, claims that the prophet Jeremiah hid the ark in a cave on Mount Nebo where it was to remain hidden "until God gathers his people together again and shows his mercy" (2 Macc 2:7; cf. a variant tradition in *2 Bar.* 6:1-9). John is perhaps drawing upon this belief that the ark would be restored in the last days. The presence of the ark in the temple, then, is a further indication that indeed the end time has arrived and God has gathered God's people. [Ark of the Covenant]

Sight of the Ark

"When the prophet John sees the ark in the heavenly temple, it is the ultimate promise that God's love is steadfast and that the Kingdom is coming."

Charles H. Talbert, *The Apocalypse: A Reading of the Revelation of John* (Louisville: Westminster/John Knox, 1994), 47.

Some commentators have suggested another possible meaning for the open temple with the ark visible inside. The ark serves as a reminder of the promises of God and specifically the faithfulness of God in fulfilling God's covenant promises. The ark is therefore not a sign of eschatological consummation, but a sign of assurance to the faithful that God will always be with them and protect them. Robert Mounce has commented, "For the days of wrath that lie immediately ahead, believers will need the assurance that God will bring his own safely to their eternal reward."[10] [Sight of the Ark]

The phenomena accompanying the heavenly temple are typical cosmic signs associated with divine appearances. These events not only add to the visual and audio effects of John's dramatic vision, but also serve as reminders of the mystery and power of God.

CONNECTIONS

1. The measuring of the temple is a reminder of God's presence and support in the midst of all of life's difficulties and uncertainties. The specific context for this promise is the persecution that John expected to occur against the church in the last days. But there is a broader principle at work here. John is convinced that God does not abandon God's people. Other New Testament writers expressed in their own words the truth that John is conveying by means of this imagery. In the Gospel of Matthew, the Gospel writer recorded the words of Jesus: "Remember, I am with you always, to the end of the age" (28:20). Paul, in his writing to the Christians at Rome, in some of the most eloquent language in all of his letters, wrote,

What then are we to say about these things? If God is for us, who is against us? He who did not withhold his own Son, but gave him up for all of us, will he not with him also give us everything else? Who will bring any charge against God's elect? It is God who justifies. Who is to condemn? It is Christ Jesus, who died, yes, who was raised, who is at the right hand of God, who indeed intercedes for us. Who will separate us from the love of Christ? Will hardship, or distress, or persecution, or famine, or nakedness, or peril, or sword? As it is written,

"For your sake we are being killed all day long;
we are accounted as sheep to be slaughtered."

No, in all these things we are more than conquerors through him who loved us. For I am convinced that neither death, nor life, nor angels, nor rulers, nor things present, nor things to come, nor powers, nor height, nor depth, nor anything else in all creation, will be able to separate us from the love of God in Christ Jesus our Lord. (Rom 8:31-39)

The confidence of Paul that nothing in life or death can separate us from the love of God is the same assurance voiced by John. Even if persecution, suffering, or martyrdom afflicts the faithful, God will not abandon them. The teacher or preacher of this text needs to be sure that the text is not misunderstood to mean that the people of God are exempt from the kind of troubles and problems that are common to individuals and families. This text offers no support for a "success and prosperity gospel," that is, a belief that people who follow the will of God lead lives that are trouble-free and prosperous. John knows from personal experience and from observation of others that the people of God are not exempt from suffering. In fact, John is convinced that the opposite is true. Those people who are "faithful witnesses" are the ones who encounter the most resentment and mistreatment. Those who resist the beasts of society are often trampled by the beasts. But John has also come to realize that in the midst of such suffering, God is always present.

Such claims run the risk of sounding hollow, of being empty promises. Is it really true that God is present in the midst of human suffering? Do people of faith truly find strength from God to help them endure situations of despair, pain, and suffering? Does God actually sustain people of faith during times of crisis? When we teach or preach such ideas, there will be people in the audience who question such statements. If we are honest, at times we too raise such questions. From his own experience and observation of the experience of others, John is able to answer "yes" to these questions. God does provide "protection," that is, comfort and strength in the midst of difficult situations. The teacher or preacher dealing with this text can offer no more "proof" that this claim is true than what John had to offer—personal experience. People who minister to others during times of crisis have often witnessed the amazing strength and security that people of deep faith exhibit. These

people can testify with the psalmist that, "even though I walk through the darkest valley, I fear no evil; for you are with me; your rod and your staff—they comfort me" (Ps 23:4). Thus the assurance that this scene of measuring the temple conveys is not simply an eschatological promise, but is one that is being fulfilled in the present time in the lives of God's people.

Westminster Abbey
Statues of ten 20th-century martyrs on the west façade of Westminster Abbey.
(Credit: J. T. Faircloth)

2. The focus of 11:3-7 is on the two witnesses who are called to prophesy to the people and, as a result of their prophesying, are killed. If, as argued above, the two witnesses represent not the entire people of God, but only a portion, this identification does not mean that only a part of God's people are called to be witnesses. As is clear throughout the Apocalypse, all people are called to be faithful witnesses, to bear testimony to the world about the message of God. The two witnesses, however, serve as a reminder that for some who are faithful, the cost of faithfulness is extremely high—their lives.

Christian martyrdom is not unknown in the modern world. In many countries, to profess faith openly and practice one's Christian faith is still dangerous, more dangerous than is realized by "comfortable" Christians today. In fact, some people have argued that the twentieth century has been the most deadly century in the history of the church in terms of the cost of Christian witness. As a tribute to and reminder of the ultimate price paid by faithful believers, in July 1998 Westminster Abbey in London unveiled statues of ten Christian martyrs of the twentieth century. [Westminster Abbey] These statues, placed in the ten vacant niches over

Twentieth-Century Martyrs

Two of the martyrs memorialized in Westminster Abbey are Manche Masemola and Maximilian Kolbe. These two individuals represent the diversity of situations in which Christians have been forced to pay the ultimate price for their faithfulness to God. Manche Masemola was born around 1913 in the village of Marishane in the Transvaal province of South Africa. Masemola's parents were not Christian; they adhered to the customs and practices of the Pedi society to which they belonged. When as a teenager Masemola began to be interested in Christianity, her parents tried to dissuade her and to thwart her efforts to convert to Christianity. Her parents' opposition became more and more hostile and violent; they repeatedly beat her. Masemola, determined to pursue this new religious devotion, told her cousin, "Even if they kill me, I am ready." Those words would soon ring true. A month later (February 1928), her parents, convinced that there was no way to prevent their daughter from abandoning her family's beliefs and traditions, led her out to an isolated area and beat her to death.

The story of Maximilian Kolbe takes place on a different continent, almost a decade and a half later. Kolbe was a Polish Franciscan priest who was arrested and imprisoned at the Auschwitz concentration camp during World War II. As a prisoner, Kolbe defied orders to the contrary and gave away portions of his food to other prisoners, heard confessions, and even celebrated mass. In July 1941 a fellow prisoner escaped from Cell Block 14 of the concentration camp. In retaliation, the authorities ordered that ten other inmates would be sentenced to death by starvation. One evening during roll call, the ten were selected and called forward. One of the men begged not to be chosen since he had a wife and child. Courageously, Kolbe stepped forward and volunteered to go in his place. Of the ten men placed in the starvation cell, six died within two weeks. Kolbe persisted longer but was executed on August 14, 1941, by a lethal injection of phenol. Kolbe followed in the footsteps of Jesus by giving his life for someone else. In his sacrificial act he fulfilled the words of 1 John 3:16: "We know love by this, that he laid down his life for us—and we ought to lay down our lives for one another."

Mandy Godhals, "Imperialism, Mission and Conversion: Manche Masemola of Sekhukhuneland" and Roman Komaryczko, "Auschwitz: Maximilian Kolbe of Poland," in *The Terrible Alternative: Christian Martyrdom in the Twentieth Century,* ed. Andrew Chandler (London: Cassell, 1998), 28-65.

the door of the West Front of the Abbey, commemorate not only these specific martyrs, but all faithful believers who have given their lives in witness to their faith. The ten people memorialized with the statues are Maximilian Kolbe, Manche Masemola, Janani Luwum, Elizabeth of Russia, Martin Luther King Jr., Oscar Romero, Dietrich Bonhoeffer, Esther John, Lucian Tapiedi, and Wang Zhiming. [Twentieth-Century Martyrs] Some of these names are familiar to many readers; most of them are probably unknown. All of these people in one way or another paid with their lives for their religious convictions. They include martyrs from China; the United States; Poland; El Salvador; Pakistan; Germany; Uganda; South Africa; Papua, New Guinea; and Russia. Some were killed by oppressive governments, others by violent militants.

For the comfortable, established church member in America, the stories of these martyrs and others like them are interesting, perhaps even inspirational, but often seem more like oddities. What connection can we make with martyrdom, living in a culture that still wears a veneer of Christianity? What message can we derive from John's vision of the two witnesses? The first point that needs to be made is that John is not issuing a call for martyrs. In many instances in the later church, Christians began to exhibit a perverse craving for martyrdom. This morbid attitude concerning martyrdom is even seen in the letters of Ignatius of Antioch, who encouraged the Christians to entice the wild beasts to tear him to shreds. For some victims, martyrdom became more a way for personal glorification than a means for the furtherance of the gospel. The martyr died not for the sake of Christ, but for the glory of self. This yearning for martyrdom is not found in the book of Revelation. John extols the virtues and rewards of martyrdom, to be sure, but nowhere does he encourage the Christians to seek the martyr's death. John never lets his readers forget that martyrdom is not pleasant. Those who must die the death of a martyr will need all the endurance and courage they can muster. In the eyes of their persecutors, the martyrs' lives are cheap and their deaths are intoxicating (17:6). The cries from underneath the altar (6:10) are not cries of rejoicing and jubilation, but the yearning cries of the martyrs who seek divine vindication for their deaths. The Apocalypse, then, while seeking to encourage and strengthen prospective martyrs by glorifying martyrdom, nevertheless is realistic in its assessment of the cost of this ultimate act of witnessing. John does not seek to entice prospective martyrs through a misrepresentation of the reality of martyrdom. [Martyrs of the Church]

John does, however, call for all people to be faithful witnesses. This idea is the second point that needs to be heard. To be true to one's calling as a follower of Christ is demanded of all believers. Few of us live up to that responsibility. It is easier to compromise our principles and our beliefs. John knew that truth first-hand as he looked at the situation of the churches in Asia Minor and saw people in the churches who had become too acculturated. They had lost the ability or the willingness to distinguish between the ways of God and the ways of the larger culture. [Witnesses and Martyrs]

The word "witnessing" is one of those words that has been taken over by the church and in the process has lost some of its potency. "To witness" frequently means to go door-to-door inviting people to church or to stand on the street corner passing out religious tracts. Little danger is involved in those activities—embarrassment,

Martyrs of the Church

"Whenever we remember the martyrs of the church, some good questions are: What would we have to do, as Christians, to get ourselves killed? If we devoted ourselves entirely to being God's friends, what kind of enemies might we make? Should we be sad or thankful that our opportunities for martyrdom are so few?

I never know how to end a sermon on a martyr's day. I look out at those good, ordinary people—one of whom, I know, spends eight hours a day sitting with her homebound mother, another of whom drives his wife to another county for radiation therapy five days a week. What should I say to them? 'God wants more of you! We must all find something worth dying for!'

I cannot say that. The best I can manage is, 'May we all find that which is worth living for, giving ourselves to it with heart, body and mind, and refusing, under any circumstances, to be parted from it.' That is how all the martyrs started out, as best I can tell. They did not go hunting around for some way to die. They simply stumbled onto the way of life and decided never to forsake it, no matter what. The rest was out of their hands."

Barbara Brown Taylor, "Faith Matters: The Great Tribulation," *The Christian Century* 115/22 (12-19 August 1998): 758.

Witnesses and Martyrs

The book of Revelation was written to a 1st-century audience, addressing the particular needs of those Christians, some of whom were facing persecution and martyrdom, others of whom were compromising their faith for personal gain. Even though the circumstances of the modern reader may differ, the demand for faithful witnesses remains the same. In some situations today, as in John's day, fidelity may require a martyr's death. Other situations, less severe, may not demand death, but faithfulness is still essential. As R. H. Charles rightly noted,

Real faithfulness to Christ demands in all ages some measure of the martyr's courage and endurance. Indeed the worst martyrdoms are not always, or even generally, those which terminate in a speedy and violent death.

R. H. Charles, *A Critical and Exegetical Commentary on the Revelation of St. John,* The International Critical Commentary, 2 vols. (Edinburgh: T. & T. Clark, 1920), 1:370.

---

discomfort, perhaps even humiliation, but not persecution. Those are rather benign, "safe" activities. Authentic witnessing involves not only witnessing "to," but witnessing "against." The true witness is the one who is willing to confront the power structures and the power brokers, to challenge the system when it demoralizes, demeans, and crushes the innocent. The true witness is willing to declare "thus saith the LORD" in the face of injustice and evil. Such authentic witnessing is indeed dangerous witnessing. The "principalities and powers" do not like to be challenged. Look at what happened to Martin Luther King Jr. when he challenged a racist American society and bore witness against it as God's messenger. Or look at Daniel Berrigan, who spoke and acted against the horror and injustice of war and the military and was imprisoned. The power structures do not like to be challenged; true witnesses must be silenced. John knew well that the world does not like to hear the voice of God's witness. Such a voice is an annoyance and even a threat. For that reason "the inhabitants of the earth will gloat over them and celebrate and exchange presents, because these two prophets had been a torment to the inhabitants of the earth" (11:10).

We seldom experience discomfort, much less persecution and martyrdom, because we are not a "torment to the inhabitants of the earth." Society has domesticated the Christian witness and made it palatable. To be authentic witnesses, the church needs to be a "holy people" in the original sense of the term "holy," that is, a people distinct, set apart for God. To witness for God will at times involve bearing testimony against the world as we know it. Where in our communities does an authentic Christian voice need to be heard? Who will be willing to confront the beasts of modern society with the message of God? [The Task of the Church]

3. The sounding of the seventh trumpet is the event that we, as readers, have been waiting for. We have heard the cries of the

oppressed; we have watched as evil was let loose upon the world; and we have seen God's judgments upon the earth. Now John partially pulls back the curtain and lets us hear and see the victory party celebrating God's triumph over all the oppressive and recalcitrant forces of the world. Move back the furniture; bring out the party hats; turn on the music! It's time to celebrate! God reigns! Hallelujah! But wait. Such wild celebration is untimely and somewhat premature. How can we celebrate that which has not happened yet? Evil, in its multiplicity of forms and disguises, has not been eradicated. We live in a world in which the brokenness of creation is more readily apparent than is the wholeness, or salvation, of creation. Yet on the basis of this proleptic vision in chapter 11, John calls us to celebrate. And that is exactly what we must do as the people of God. We are a community that sees the world differently from the way others see it. Where others see brokenness, we see wholeness. Where others see death, we see life. Where others see hatred, we see love. Where others see a world in rebellion, we see a world transformed. Even when the events around us seem to argue against any belief that God will triumph, we keep singing our victory songs, confident that the love and mercy of God will ultimately bring healing to a fractured creation. The power of such a vision is its ability to create hope, to overcome despair, and to transform lives.

> **The Task of the Church**
>
> "The passage [11:1-13] shows that the Church has something more important to do than simply to survive. It is set in the world to bear witness to men, even when the witness is resisted with force. The darker the hour, the more need for the Churches to be what they are: lamps, through which Christ's light shines."
>
> George R. Beasley-Murray, *The Book of Revelation,* New Century Bible (Greenwood SC: Attic, 1974), 181.

Are we simply deluded dreamers, following a misguided visionary? Maybe. That is always a possibility. But the church is founded on such wild and seemingly foolish ideas. We have chosen to cast our lots with people like John of Patmos, Martin Luther King Jr. and Mother Teresa—people who refused to accept the view of the world that others held, people who saw a different world with a different set of values, and who lived their lives on the basis of that alternative vision of reality.

As the church, not only do we see the world through different lenses, but we are also called to be different from "the world." The sovereignty of God over all the world, for which we yearn and pray and which we proleptically celebrate, should already be manifesting itself within our midst. The church should be a place where justice and equality are valued and promoted; where barriers of race, social class, economic status, ethnic diversity, and gender orientation are broken down; where brokenness—of spirit, of body, of relationship—is healed; and where grace, love, and forgiveness flow freely.

"The kingdom of the world has become the kingdom of our Lord and of his Messiah," proclaims the heavenly chorus in John's vision. Can we join our voices to that joyous song? Is the church the place where "the kingdom of the world" is to be found, or "the kingdom of our Lord and of his Messiah"?

Certainly the church is not identical with the kingdom of God. We are still flawed creatures, waiting for the final realization of God's new reign. But we are flawed creatures who have been transformed by the grace of God and in whom the love of God should be active and evident. We—the church—are not the kingdom of God, but we are on the way to the kingdom. In the words of Paul, "Not that I have already obtained this or have already reached the goal; but I press on to make it my own, because Christ Jesus has made me his own" (Phil 3:12). As the theologian Hans Küng has stated,

> The Church is not the kingdom of God, but it looks toward the kingdom of God, waits for it, or rather makes a pilgrimage toward it and is its herald, proclaiming it to the world. . . .
>
> Thus the Church as the eschatological community of salvation lives and waits and makes its pilgrim journey under the reign of Christ, which is at the same time, in Christ, the beginning of the reign of God. Thus the promises and powers of the coming reign of God are already evident and effective, through Christ, in the Church, which so partakes in a hidden manner in the dawning reign of God. Thus the Church may be termed the fellowship of aspirants to the kingdom of God. . . .
>
> The Church is not a preliminary stage, but an *anticipatory sign* of the definitive reign of God: a sign of the reality of the reign of God

---

Psalm 2

In Rev 11:15-18, John draws heavily from Ps 2. This insight was not lost on George Handel. In his magisterial oratorio *Messiah*, Handel (or his friend Charles Jennens who compiled the text) preceded the words of Rev 11:15 with selections from Ps 2. The following chart displays the direct borrowings from Ps 2.

Revelation 11	**Psalm 2**
"of our Lord and of his Messiah" (v. 15)	"the LORD and his anointed" (v. 2)
"the nations raged" (v. 18)	"Why do the nations conspire" (v. 1)
"your wrath has come" (v. 18)	"he will speak to them in his wrath (v. 5; cf. v. 12)

More than simply borrowing these specific phrases, John has adapted the idea of Ps 2, which tells of God's promise to establish universal rule through his anointed king. In the vision of Rev 11:15-18, John proleptically announces that universal sovereignty has been accomplished by God and his Anointed One.

already present in Jesus Christ, a sign of the coming completion of the reign of God.[11]

In the church we celebrate in anticipation what should already be at work among us—the transforming of "the kingdom of the world" into the kingdom of God. [Psalm 2] The Lord's Prayer, which is so often glibly and mindlessly recited in worship, is in reality a dangerous request on our part. "Thy kingdom come. Thy will be done, on earth as it is in heaven." To pray this prayer is to ask God to bring God's sovereignty into reality—in our lives as well as throughout the rest of the world. To pray this prayer is to place ourselves under the rule of God. As Eugene Boring has noted, "One cannot pray this prayer without committing one's own will and action to fulfilling the will of God in the present."[12] The church—meaning us—is too much a part of "the kingdom of this world." We are not willing to relinquish our own claims to power, prestige, or dominance. Our situation is like that of Augustine, who in his struggle with rampant sexual pleasures prayed to God, "Make me chaste and continent, but not yet" (*Conf.* 8:7).[13]

To make "the kingdom of this world . . . become the kingdom of our Lord and of his Messiah" is not our task. That is God's job. Our task, however, is to open our lives and our community of faith to the rule of God, to allow God's sovereignty to be at work, already, within us. We celebrate with John this eschatological vision, not only because we yearn for its fulfillment in the future, but also because we have already experienced a foretaste of it in the present. [God's Sovereignty]

God's Sovereignty

"In one sense God's sovereignty is eternal: he entered on his reign when he established the rule of order in the midst of primaeval chaos (Ps 93:1-4); he has reigned throughout human history, turning even men's misdeeds into instruments of his mercy; and above all he reigned in the Cross of Christ (12:10). But always up to this point he has reigned over a rebellious world. A king may be king *de jure*, but he is not king *de facto* until the trumpet which announces his accession is answered by the acclamations of a loyal and obedient people."

G. B. Caird, *A Commentary on the Revelation of St. John the Divine,* Harper's New Testament Commentaries (New York: Harper & Row, 1966), 141.

NOTES

[1] For a well-reasoned argument for the plausibility of 11:1-2 originating from a Jewish oracle prior to AD 70, see George R. Beasley-Murray, *The Book of Revelation*, New Century Bible (Greenwood SC: Attic, 1974), 176-77.

[2] G. B. Caird, *The Revelation of St. John the Divine*, Harper's New Testament Commentaries (New York: Harper & Row, 1966), 131.

[3] Charles H. Talbert, *The Apocalypse: A Reading of the Revelation of John* (Louisville: Westminster/John Knox, 1994), 44-45.

[4] Caird, *Revelation*, 132; Robert H. Mounce, *The Book of Revelation*, The New International Commentary on the New Testament, rev. ed. (Grand Rapids: Eerdmans, 1998), 213-14.

[5] Beasley-Murray, *Revelation*, 182.

[6] For a good summary of the various views, see Talbert, *Apocalypse*, 31-33.

[7] Beasley-Murray, *Revelation*, 187.

[8] Allison A. Trites, *The New Testament Concept of Witness* (New York: Cambridge University Press, 1977), 170.

[9] Hermann Sasse, "κόσμος," *Theological Dictionary of the New Testament*, ed. Gerhard Kittel, 10 vols. (Grand Rapids: Eerdmans, 1965), 3:893.

[10] Mounce, *Revelation*, 228.

[11] Hans Küng, *The Church*, trans. Ray and Rosaleen Ockenden (New York: Sheed and Ward, 1967), 95-96.

[12] M. Eugene Boring, "The Gospel of Matthew: Introduction, Commentary, and Reflections," *The New Interpreter's Bible*, 12 vols. (Nashville: Abingdon, 1995), 8:204.

[13] *Conf.* 8.7, trans. Rex Warner (New York: New American Library, 1963), 174.

THE VISION OF
THE GREAT DRAGON

12:1-18

The Great Conflict, 12:1–14:20

Chapter 12 begins a new section of Revelation. Christopher Rowland has called the beginning of chapter 12 "one of the most abrupt transitions in Revelation."[1] Similarly, Jürgen Roloff has noted that "a large caesura lies between 11:19 and 12:1."[2] The preceding chapters have brought to an end the seven seals and the seven trumpet plagues. Indeed, 11:15-19 appears to bring John's entire eschatological, cosmic vision to an end—the messianic woes have occurred; God's kingdom has arrived; God's enemies have been defeated; the final judgment has been pronounced; punishments have been dispensed; and rewards have been bestowed. All that is lacking is the final "Amen!"

But John is not ready to let the final curtain fall. He has a new revelation to present, signaled by the words of 12:1—"a great portent appeared in heaven." To use imagery drawn from the theater, the curtain has fallen on one act in John's apocalyptic drama; now the curtain rises on a new act. Or, in imagery familiar to moviegoers, John as director of this "film" cuts away from the previous action to provide us a new scene. The sequences are not related chronologically, but thematically. The struggle between God and evil, which is depicted in earlier scenes in Revelation, is here shown in a new way. Recognizing the break that occurs at 12:1 can help one avoid the mistake of reading chapters 12 and those following as chronological successors to the preceding events.

Viewed in light of the overall structure of the Apocalypse, 12:1–14:20 functions as a break in the action, a pause to present a close look at the assault on the people of God by the forces of evil. These chapters serve as John's "great parenthesis . . . inserted to illuminate the struggle between the Church and the forces of darkness."[3] John has presented the reader with images of eschatological destruction and judgment through the visions of the seven seals and seven trumpets. Before returning to that theme with another seven-fold series, the seven bowl plagues, John portrays in graphic imagery the life-and-death struggle that confronted the church of his day. The specific manifestation of this struggle with evil with which these chapters deal is the conflict between the church and the Roman Empire. For John and his readers, the Roman emperor, with his claims to divinity, has become the incarnation of evil. With keen insight, John has realized that the conflict between the church and the empire is not simply a political or even a religious conflict. Rather, it is a cosmic conflict as old as the created order. For that reason, John adopts mythological language and imagery in order to convey to his readers the seriousness of the struggle in which they are engaged. John wants them to know that the evil powers of the universe have always been in rebellion against God; chaos has always tried to overturn the created order. Their struggle to remain faithful, as seen in their endurance against emperor worship, is a part of the cosmic conflict between the forces of evil and the forces of God. The primeval chaos monster has reared its ugly head again, this time in Roman dress. By painting their problems on a cosmic canvas, John is giving added meaning and significance to their struggles. Theirs is no minor or inconsequential skirmish, but another battle in the ongoing conflict that has existed since primeval times. By their faithfulness to God, they are helping to defeat the powers of evil. Thus their persecution and martyrdom are not in vain.

Perhaps more than any other passage in Revelation, chapters 12–14 have been grossly misinterpreted, misused, and abused. Such confusion and puzzlement over the text is understandable. Nowhere else in the work does John draw so heavily from Jewish and pagan myths and from the contemporary political situation as he does in this section. The heavy use of strange, even bizarre, images and numbers demands a careful reading (or hearing) by those who want to comprehend John's message to the churches. Two dangers should be avoided in this section. The first is getting so involved in trying to uncover the sources of John's images and the historical and political referents underneath the symbolism that one fails to see the overarching vision that John is presenting. One may dissect the text to such an extent that one ends up with a cadaver rather than a living text that continues to inspire, challenge, and embrace the reader. The text invites, even requires, a creative engagement of the imagination by the reader. Furthermore, as helpful as identifying the historical and political backgrounds of John's symbols is, such identifications do not exhaust the meaning of John's symbols. The beasts and dragons recur throughout history in ever new forms.

The second danger is the antithesis of the first, that is, the temptation to make the symbols of chapters 12–14 mean whatever the reader wants them to mean. The history of the interpretation of Revelation is littered with examples of grotesque and untenable speculations about the meaning of the beasts and numbers of Revelation. Ancient traditions upon which John drew and the political and historical situation against which he was writing must be allowed to serve as correctives on any reading of the visions of these chapters. Understanding the text will require "imaginative participation on the part of the hearers/readers,"[4] but an imagination that is grounded in the text itself and in the world in which John lived.

The Vision of the Great Dragon, 12:1-18

Myths are forceful conveyors of truth. They express some of humanity's deepest insights, experiences, and yearnings. At times they speak more eloquently and powerfully than any language of logic, science, or theology. Apparently John knows the power of mythological language, for he creatively engages the myths of the ancient world and makes them vehicles for his Christian message. In chapter 12, John has borrowed an ancient combat myth that was well known in various forms in many cultures of the ancient world. The Romans, the Greeks, the Egyptians, the Persians, the Babylonians—all of them told a story of conflict between the gods and goddesses, a cosmic struggle between good and evil that affected the earth. This cosmic combat myth was a way of talking about the struggle between light and darkness, good and evil, chaos and order. John does not seem to have borrowed directly from any one version of this myth. Rather, his story in chapter 12

> **Outline of 12:1-18**
> The Vision of the Great Dragon
> 1. The Woman, the Dragon, and the Child—12:1-6
> 2. Michael and the Dragon—12:7-12
> 3. The Pursuit of the Woman—12:13-18

draws upon elements that come from several ancient combat myths. In fact, there is reason to believe that John is making use of a Jewish tradition that has already adapted these ancient myths to express the idea of God's defeat of the forces of evil (see comments on 12:5, 7-12). [Outline of 12:1-18]

The closest parallel to John's story in chapter 12 of a woman who gives birth and is attacked by a dragon who tries unsuccessfully to destroy her and her child is a Greek version of this international myth adapted to tell the story of the birth of Apollo. [Apollo] The goddess Leto became pregnant by Zeus. The great dragon, Python, after learning that this soon-to-be-born child of Leto would one day kill him, sought to kill the unborn Apollo and his mother. Poseidon, the god of the sea, intervened and protected Leto by carrying her to safety to the island of Delos. He hid Leto by sinking the island under the sea. Unsuccessful in his search for the pregnant woman, Python ended the search and went away. Poseidon then raised the island, and Leto gave birth to Apollo, who pursued the dragon Python and killed him.

John recasts this ancient myth in Christian dress. The hero who defeats evil is not Apollo or any other god or goddess, but Jesus. Initially, this revamped ancient myth might seem far removed from the Jesus tradition of the Gospels. Yet this is nothing more than "the old, old story" told in a new form. In the Gospels, Jesus must struggle against evil (the temptations in the wilderness, the exorcisms), ultimately defeating the forces of evil in his death and resurrection. In chapter 12, John is telling that same story, but doing it through myth rather than through Gospel narratives.

For John's original hearers/readers, this revamped myth may have also carried political significance. Several of the Roman emperors utilized the Apollo myth for their own propaganda purposes, presenting themselves as Apollo, the destroyer of evil. The goddess Roma, the deity of Rome, was seen as the mother goddess, the Queen of Heaven. Eugene Boring has noted,

> A grateful citizen of the Roman world could readily think of the story as a reflection of his or her own experience, with the following cast: the woman is the goddess Roma, the queen of heaven; the son is the emperor, who kills the dragon and founds the new Golden Age; the dragon represents the power of darkness . . . that oppose[s] the goodness of life.[5]

Apollo

This figure is from the 4th century BC. The Romans favored and copied these pieces brought to Rome from Greece. In many cases, Greek artists were also imported to make the copies. The Roman copies were made of marble, and the original bronze was melted down for other uses. The style reflects a naturalness, emotion, and movement that the earlier Archaic and Classical Greek styles did not.

Apollo Belvedere. Roman marble copy of a Greek bronze original of the late 4th C. BC. Height 7'4". Musei Vaticani, Museo Pio Clementino, Cortile Ottagono, Città del Vaticano, Rome. (Credit: Mitchell Reddish)

John's reuse of this ancient myth challenges the divine claims and arrogant presumptions of the imperial cult. Christ, not the emperor, is the real victor over the malevolent forces of chaos, darkness, and wickedness. John unmasks the Roman power for what it truly is—a tool of Satan, and not a god worthy of worship.

COMMENTARY

The Woman, the Dragon, and the Child, 12:1-6

The first spectacle (portent, or sign) John sees in the sky is a woman with attributes that would suggest her identity as the cosmic queen, or Queen of Heaven ("clothed with the sun, . . . the moon under her feet, . . . a crown of twelve stars"). Various sources have provided different aspects of this description, including goddesses of ancient myths (particularly Isis) and astrological speculation. For example, the crown of twelve stars likely originated as a reference to the twelve signs of the zodiac. To readers from a Jewish or Christian context, however, the twelve stars would suggest the twelve tribes of Israel (cf. Gen 37:9). This woman is pregnant [Woman in Labor] and soon gives birth to a son, one "who is to rule all the nations with a rod of iron" (12:5), the latter clause an adaptation of a passage from Psalm 2 describing the rule of the king of Israel over the other nations of the world. Within both Judaism and early Christianity, this psalm was interpreted as a reference to the Messiah. By adding this line from Psalm 2, John (or a Jewish tradition from which he borrows) has modified the pagan myth into a story of triumph by the Messiah. In John's presentation of this ancient myth, the identity of the child is clear—he is Jesus, who in his ascension after his death was "snatched away and taken to God and to his throne" (12:5). By raising Jesus from the dead and exalting him to heaven, God thwarted the attempt of Satan to "devour" him (12:4).

The reader who is too rigid and unimaginative may have severe problems dealing with this text. "The details of chapter 12 do not all fit the story of Jesus," one might say. "How, for example, could a child who is taken away to heaven represent the ascension of

Woman in Labor

AΩ The image of a woman in labor is used in several passages in the Hebrew Bible to portray Israel (Isa 26:17-18; 66:7-9; Mic 4:10). The Isa 26 passage is particularly interesting, for not only does the text speak of Israel as a pregnant woman, but the verses of the following chapter also describe God's defeat of Leviathan. Isa 27:1 states,

On that day the LORD with his cruel and great and strong sword will punish Leviathan the fleeing serpent, Leviathan the twisting serpent, and he will kill the dragon that is in the sea.

Heaven

AΩ The Greek word for "heaven" (*ouranos*) can also be translated as "sky." In the Bible, "heaven" is used to describe both a physical part of the universe (where the stars, planets, sun, and moon are located) and the dwelling place of God. In 12:1, 3, "sky" is perhaps a better translation than "heaven," for the location of these signs is different from the location of the heavenly throne room of 4:1ff. (Note 15:1, however, which does seem to refer to the heavenly throne room and uses the same expression used in 12:1, 3.)

Jesus as an adult? Where in this story is his ministry and, more importantly, his death on the cross?" An approach such as this fails to recognize that John is not starting from scratch, but he is "Christianizing" ancient pagan myths in order to tell the story of God's triumph over evil. As John stretches the Christian story over the frame of the pagan myth, the fit will not be exact. Furthermore, this chapter uses the language of mythology, not the language of a historical narrative. Mythological language is evocative, not descriptive.

In addition to the woman, another sign appears in the sky— "a great red dragon, with seven heads and ten horns, and seven diadems on his heads" (12:3). [Heaven] This dragon is Python from the Leto myth; he is also Tiamat, the seven-headed monster of the deep in Babylonian mythology; as well he is Leviathan, the serpent-like monster in Hebrew folklore (cf. Ps 74:14); further, he is the deceitful serpent of the garden of Eden story; and he is also Satan, "the deceiver of the whole world" (12:9). [Leviathan] He is each of these—and all of them combined—for he is the representation of all that is evil and chaotic and in opposition to God. The seven heads of the dragon are a traditional description of the chaos monster in ancient mythologies. His ten horns are symbols of his strength (cf. Dan 7:7, 20), while the seven diadems symbolize his authority and dominion. In his awesome ferocity he swings his mighty tail, knocking down a third of the stars of heaven and throwing them to earth. This is no wimpish creature to be taken lightly. Evil is real, John wants us to know, and we would be well advised to take it seriously.

Leviathan

AΩ Leviathan is the name of a mythological sea monster, usually in the form of a serpent or dragon. Leviathan appears in several passages in the Hebrew Bible (Job 3:8; 41:1-34; Pss 74:14; 104:26; Isa 27:1) and in later Jewish texts (2 Esd 6:49-52; *2 Bar.* 29:3-8; *1 En.* 60:7-9, 24). Leviathan is the monster of chaos, defeated by God at creation. In some Jewish texts, Leviathan is the eschatological monster who will be defeated at the end time. Leviathan is the same as Lotan (or Litan) in the Ugaritic texts found at Ras Shamra. Linguistically, "Leviathan" and "Lotan" share the same Semitic root. (Ugarit was a kingdom, located in the northwest of modern Syria along the Mediterranean coast, that flourished during the second millennium BC. The extant Ugaritic texts date mostly from the 14th century BC.) In the Ugaritic texts, Lotan is described as a twisting serpent with seven heads who is defeated by the god Baal or his consort, the goddess Anat. (In Ps 74:14, Leviathan is also mentioned as being multiheaded.)

Michael

AΩ In Jewish tradition, Michael was one of the seven archangels. In Dan 10:13, 21; 12:1, Michael is described as the patron angel of Israel who fights on their behalf against the patron angels of the other nations. In *1 En.* 54:6, Michael is one of the four archangels who casts the fallen angels into the furnace of fire on the day of judgment. In the Dead Sea Scrolls, Michael is the Prince of Light who will lead the army of angels and the faithful people of God ("the sons of light") in the eschatological battle against Belial ("the Angel of Darkness"), his wicked angels, and the unrighteous of the earth (cf. *War Scroll* 13:10-12; 17:6-8; *Community Rule* 3:20–4:1).

Michael and the Dragon, 12:7-12

Surprisingly, the hero of this heavenly battle against evil is not Christ, but Michael, one of the archangels of Jewish tradition. [Michael] (This is evidence that John is reworking an old Jewish story here.) John sees a fierce battle being waged in heaven. Michael and his angelic army mount an attack against the dragon, who fights back with his own angelic army rather than surrender. The dragon's fight is in vain, however, for the rebellious dragon/Satan and his angels are defeated, cast out of heaven, and thrown to the earth.

Before trying to hear what John is saying with this story, the reader should perhaps be clear as to what John is not saying. This passage is not describing the primeval overthrow of Satan. As will be clear from the following verses, the defeat of Satan occurs at the death of Christ, not at some point in prehistory. John is not interested in explaining the origin of evil in the world. John takes the reality of evil for granted. He is not concerned with its origin, but with its defeat. Unfortunately, too many readers approach this passage in Revelation by means of John Milton's *Paradise Lost* and thus understand these verses as describing Satan's primeval expulsion from heaven because he and his band of rebel angels attempted a coup against the throne of God. [Paradise Lost] That is not what is taking place in John's vision. (In fact, such a story of Satan is found nowhere in biblical literature. One has to go to *Paradise Lost* to find this account.)

The key to John's understanding of this scene is found in the hymnic pronouncement from heaven in vv. 10-12. In these verses, the overthrow of Satan is celebrated as the arrival of God's salvation, power, and kingdom, and

Paradise Lost

In Milton's epic poem, *Paradise Lost,* the rebellion and defeat of Satan are described as follows:

Th' infernal Serpent; hee it was, whose guile
Stirr'd up with Envy and Revenge, deceiv'd
The Mother of Mankind; what time his Pride
Had cast him out from Heav'n, with all his Host
Of Rebel Angels, by whose aid aspiring
To set himself in Glory above his Peers,
He trusted to have equall'd the most High,
If he oppos'd; and with ambitious aim
Against the Throne and Monarchy of God
Rais'd impious War in Heav'n and Battle proud
With vain attempt. Him the Almighty Power
Hurl'd headlong flaming from th' Ethereal Sky
With hideous ruin and combustion down
To bottomless perdition, there to dwell
In Adamantine Chains and penal Fire,
Who durst defy th' Omnipotent to Arms.
(Book I, 34-49)

"the authority of his Messiah." In one sense, the defeat of Satan is an eschatological event. It occurs in its finality when

> "The kingdom of the world has become the kingdom of our Lord
> and of his Messiah." (11:15)

Yet John knows that, in essence, the defeat of Satan has already occurred. It took place on Calvary in the sacrificial death of Jesus. Satan was conquered "by the blood of the Lamb" (12:11; cf. 3:21; 5:5). The Lamb who was slain was the victorious Lamb who defeated all the powers of evil. John's soteriology is thoroughly christological. But how can John claim that the victory has already occurred and that Satan has already been defeated if evil continues to run rampant and "the devil has come down" (12:12) to earth to wreak havoc and persecute the people of God? [Devil] John is not naïve. He knows as well as, if not better than, anyone else that the forces of evil are still exercising their power in the world. In fact, he expects a fresh onslaught of persecution and violence to be unleashed against the church. [The Accuser] But John can sing the song of victory because he knows that the decisive battle in the great war has already been fought. It occurred on Calvary. The skirmishes still continue, but the outcome of the eternal struggle between good and evil has already been decided. For John, the coming assault against the church is nothing more than the futile, desperate last gasps of a dying Satan.

If John is really celebrating the defeat of Satan in the death and resurrection of Jesus, then how do we understand the heavenly contest between Michael and the dragon? The apocalyptic worldview conceived of earthly realities having heavenly counterparts. Thus in Daniel, the struggles between the people of Israel and their enemies are told in terms of the battles between Michael, the patron angel of Israel, and the patron angels of the other nations (10:10-21). The defeat of the dragon by Michael is not a separate event from Christ's victory on the cross. Rather, the story of Michael and the dragon is the story of the cross, cast in mythological language. Caird described it this way:

Devil

AΩ The word "devil" is derived from the Greek word *diabolos* (cf. "diabolical"). The Septuagint (Greek translation of the Hebrew Bible) used *diabolos* to translate the Hebrew word "Satan." The Greek word, like the Hebrew, basically means "accuser" or "adversary."

The Accuser

AΩ The description of the dragon in 12:10 as "the accuser of our comrades" is likely a play on the name Satan, which in Hebrew means "accuser" or "adversary." For John's contemporaries, faced with the possibility of being accused in a Roman law court with refusal to participate in emperor worship, the title "the accuser" would have had special significance.

Michael's victory is simply the heavenly and symbolic counterpart of the earthly reality of the Cross. Michael, in fact, is not the field officer who does the actual fighting, but the staff officer in the heavenly control room, who is able to remove Satan's flag from the heavenly map because the real victory has been won on Calvary.[6]

Verse 12 celebrates not only the victory of Christ, but the contribution of the martyrs as well. "By the word of their testimony" they have helped to defeat the forces of evil. The victory over Satan continues in the faithful witness of the martyrs who give their lives for the sake of God. John is giving meaning and significance to the suffering and death of the faithful. Their sacrifices have not been wasted, nor are they trivial. Rather, in their faithful witnessing the martyrs have contributed to the overthrow of Satan. To the world (and even to the church), the deaths of the martyrs may have appeared to be defeat, but John knows otherwise. He holds the martyrs up as heroes who have become joint conquerors with Christ. Martyrdom "is a positive achievement which helps forward Christ's victory."[7] [Defeat of Satan]

Defeat of Satan
Luke 10:18 reports that upon hearing of the success of the seventy people who had been sent out on mission, Jesus proclaimed, "I watched Satan fall from heaven like a flash of lightning." Like John of Patmos, Jesus attributes the defeat of Satan to the faithful witness of God's people.

One should note that the martyrs conquer not by their testimony alone, but first of all "by the blood of the Lamb" (12:11). Their witness, even their deaths, has no meaning apart from Christ. Swete stated this well: "The Blood of the Lamb is here . . . the Sacrifice of the Cross, which is regarded as the primary cause . . . of the martyrs' victory; His conquest of Satan rendered conquest possible for them."[8]

The Pursuit of the Woman, 12:13-18

In 12:13-18, the conflict between the dragon and the woman is resumed. This section picks up and elaborates on 12:6, which described the fleeing of the woman to the wilderness. Thrown out of heaven, the dragon pursues the woman, who receives divine assistance to allow her to escape his assault. The imagery of the woman's flight to the wilderness for safety (with "the two wings of the great eagle") is reminiscent of the exodus tradition. [Escape to the Wilderness] Pursued by Pharaoh, the Hebrew people escaped his clutches by fleeing into the wilderness of the Sinai. In Exodus

Escape to the Wilderness
Rev 12:6, 14 mention the escape of the woman to the wilderness for safety. Some scholars have suggested that this might be an allusion by John to the escape by the Christians of Jerusalem to the city of Pella (across the Jordan River) at the beginning of the first Jewish-Roman war in AD 66.

The Woman Clothed in the Sun

The figure of the "woman clothed in the sun" in ch. 12 has been interpreted in some rather bizarre ways throughout history. During the 18th century, Ann Lee Stanley, who immigrated to the United States from England with several followers, was proclaimed by her followers to be the woman of Rev 12. After being given the two wings of the great eagle, she "flew away into the desert of America, where she was kept by God until she might bring forth children of the gospel." Stanley, known to her followers as Mother Ann Lee, was the founder of the religious group known as the Shakers. Shaker theology claimed that Christ's second coming had already occurred, this time in the form of a woman, and that Ann Lee was that woman. She was the feminine incarnation of God, as Jesus was the masculine incarnation.

Warren Lewis, "What to Do after the Messiah Has Come Again and Gone: Shaker 'Premillennial' Eschatology and Its Spiritual Aftereffects," in *The Coming Kingdom: Essays in American Millennialism and Eschatology*, ed. M. Darrol Bryant and Donald W. Dayton (Barrytown NY: International Religious Foundation, Inc., 1983), 76.

19:4, God speaks to the people about this experience, saying, "I bore you on eagles' wings and brought you to myself." In the wilderness, the woman is nourished, just as God nourished the Hebrew people through quail and manna. [The Woman Clothed in the Sun] The duration of her time in the wilderness is "for one thousand two hundred sixty days" (12:6), which is the same as "a time, and times, and half a time" (12:14), that is, three and a half years. John has previously used this same time span (borrowed from Dan 7:25; 12:7) as a symbol for the period of persecution against the church. The assault of the serpent is relentless, but unsuccessful, for even the earth comes to the aid of the woman. The spewing out of water at the woman and the earth swallowing it up are likely images borrowed from ancient mythology, for in some of the combat myths, the chaos monster is a water monster. Beasley-Murray provided an insightful additional view. He stated, "For John, however, with the Exodus typology in mind, the story could not but be reminiscent of the Israelites being confronted by the waters of the Red Sea, which were dried up to enable them to pass through."[9] Such divine protection of the woman is assurance that the people of God will never be destroyed by Satan. In spite of persecution and attack, God will preserve the faithful.

Who or what does the woman represent in this chapter? [Early Church Interpretations of the Woman] We have noted already that the source for this imagery is at least partially the ancient, international

Early Church Interpretations of the Woman

Commentators in the early centuries of the church offered some interesting suggestions for the identification of the woman of ch. 12. Victorinus, bishop of Pettau (d. c. AD 304), said that the woman represented the church, and the sun in which she is clothed is the hope of resurrection and the promise of glory. Oecumenius, whose 6th-century commentary is the oldest extant Greek commentary on Revelation, said, in the words of Arthur Wainwright,

The woman is Mary; the dragon's attempt to destroy her child is Satan's activity in leading Herod the Great to plot against the infant Jesus; and her flight into the wilderness is Mary's journey with Jesus and Joseph into Egypt.

Arthur W. Wainwright, *Mysterious Apocalypse: Interpreting the Book of Revelation* (Nashville: Abingdon, 1993), 28, 45.

combat myth. Jewish tradition had apparently modified the myth so that the woman represented the nation of Israel, that is, the people from whom the Messiah was born. In her conflict with the serpent she is also reminiscent of Eve (cf. Gen 3). Christian readers are likely to be quick to identify her with Mary, the mother of Jesus, "whose divine child is saved from wicked Herod by divine intervention (Matt 2:1-15)."[10] [Mary, the Mother of Jesus] Yet in her role as the one who is pursued by Satan, the woman brings to mind the church. Even though scholars have made arguments for each of these identifications, attempts to pin down precisely what the woman symbolizes have not succeeded. In a general sense, the woman symbolizes the faithful people of God of all time—Israel and the church, and even Mary, a specific example of one who was receptive and faithful to the claims of God. John's image of the woman is polyvalent; that is, it carries several meanings at the same time. Such richness in meaning is intrinsic to mythological imagery and is part of the reason for the power of John's vision.

After failing to conquer the woman, the dragon goes off "to make war on the rest of her children, those who keep the commandments of God and hold the testimony of Jesus" (12:17). The children of the woman (literally, her "seed"; cf. Gen 3:15) are faithful Christians, the "brothers and sisters of Christ." Even though Satan is unsuccessful in defeating the people of God, he is relentless in his attack. He has come down to earth "with great wrath, because he knows that his time is short!" (12:12). Like an angry and wounded animal who lashes out at those around him, the dragon strikes out at Christians, intensifying the persecution against them. For John,

Mary, the Mother of Jesus

Chapter 12 of Revelation has left its mark on artistic representations of Mary. Painters have often shown Mary with a crown of twelve stars and the moon under her feet, drawn from Rev 12. The frequent depiction of Mary enthroned as the Queen of Heaven is at least partially dependent on this scene as well.

Giambattista Tiepolo. *Immaculate Conception*. 1696–1670. Museo Civico. Vicenza, Italy. (Credit: Alinari/Art Resource, NY)

the attack of the dragon is specifically embodied in Rome's persecution of the faithful, which he describes in more detail in chapter 13.

The closing words of this chapter are rather ominous: "Then the dragon took his stand on the sand of the seashore." [He Stood] John may know the dragon is mortally wounded, but the dragon has not given up. He is making plans to continue his attack on God's people. He stands on the edge of the sea, the great reservoir of evil, the place from which monstrous beasts arise (cf. Dan 7). Unfortunately for the people of God, the dragon stands on the shore not in order to leave the land and return like Leviathan to his watery lair, but he stands awaiting the arrival of reinforcements, the beasts who will carry out the assault on the church.

He Stood

AΩ In 12:18, some ancient manuscripts contain the wording, "And I stood on the sand of the sea," in place of "And he stood on the sand of the sea." The majority of textual critics accept the latter reading as the most likely one. The former reading, followed by the KJV and other translations, likely arose from copyists making the verb in 12:18 agree with the first person singular verb of 13:1.

CONNECTIONS

Many modern readers may feel somewhat uneasy with this chapter. In some circles, any talk of the reality of evil is considered naïve and unsophisticated. As Walter Wink has observed, "Our culture resolutely refuses to believe in the real existence of evil, preferring to regard it as a kind of systems breakdown that can be fixed with enough tinkering."[11] This aversion to speaking about evil is particularly true if one speaks of evil in terms of a Satan figure. But this chapter, indeed all of Revelation, forces us to face squarely the problem of evil in our world. Whether we choose to retain the traditional imagery of Satan and demons to speak of the presence of evil in the world, or to demythologize the language of evil and recast our understanding in more modern terminology, we cannot remain true to the biblical witness if we do not recognize that evil is a reality, indeed a force, that threatens to overwhelm us. What is important is not the imagery we choose to depict evil, but rather the resolve to resist evil and align ourselves with God.

Attributing evil to Satan or the devil is not widespread in the Hebrew Bible. Christians are often surprised to learn that Satan is not a part of the garden of Eden story in Genesis. [Fall of Satan] The protagonist in that account is not Satan, but the serpent, a cunning creature who opposes the purposes of God. The major appearance of Satan in the Hebrew Bible is in the book of Job, where Satan tests the faithfulness of the righteous Job. Even here, however,

Fall of Satan

AΩ Biblical literature knows of no primordial fall of Satan. The story fragment in Gen 6:1-4 that tells of "the sons of God" (supernatural beings?) having sexual intercourse with human women was expanded in later Jewish literature into a story about the fall of sinful angels, led by Semyaza or Azazel (variant traditions), who are eternally punished by God for their wickedness (see *1 En.* 6–36). Isa 14, often misunderstood as a reference to the fall of Satan, adapts a Canaanite myth to celebrate the death of a Babylonian king. The original myth told of the attempt of a Canaanite god, Day Star, to usurp the place of El, the chief god. Day Star was not successful, however, and was thrown from the heavens to Sheol. Because the Vulgate, followed by the KJV, translated the word for Day Star as "Lucifer," the Isaiah passage was erroneously interpreted as describing the primeval fall of Satan.

Satan is not the evil figure of later Jewish and Christian tradition. In Job, the word "Satan" is not a proper noun. It is descriptive rather than nominative. In Hebrew, "satan" means "the adversary" or "the accuser." In Job, "the satan" plays the role of the heavenly informer and tester of people's faithfulness to God. In later Jewish tradition, the idea develops that "Satan" is the Evil One, the leader of the forces of evil, who tempts and leads astray the world. He becomes an independent evil power who is the ruler of the underworld and the demons. As such, he is the archenemy of God. Jewish literature uses various names, in addition to Satan, for this malevolent being—Belial (or Beliar), Semyaza (or Shemihazah), Azazel, Asmodeus, Mastema, the Devil. Later Jewish tradition, as well as the book of Revelation, identified the serpent who tempted Eve as Satan. The New Testament writers, including John of Patmos, shared in this understanding of Satan as the leader of the forces arrayed against God.

The concept of a Satan figure apparently arose as an attempt to explain the existence of evil. [History of Satan] If God is an all-powerful and benevolent creator, then how could evil exist? Rather than attribute evil to God, blame was shifted to a "Satan." Is such language still viable today? Is there room in the postmodern world for a Satan figure? Several positive results may accrue from speaking of evil in terms of Satan. First is that such language may lead us to take seriously the pervasive, alluring, and powerful influence of evil in the world. To connect evil to a malevolent, powerful figure may help us remember that evil is not to be taken lightly. Evil does not

History of Satan

The following works provide a history of the development of the concept of Satan:

Hamilton, Victor P. "Satan." Pages 985-89 in vol. 5 of *The Anchor Bible Dictionary*. Edited by David Noel Freedman. 6 vols. New York: Doubleday & Co., 1992.

Russell, Jeffrey Burton. *The Devil: Perceptions of Evil from Antiquity to Primitive Christianity*. Ithaca: Cornell University Press, 1977.

_____. *Lucifer: The Devil in the Middle Ages*. Ithaca: Cornell University Press, 1984.

_____. *Mephistopheles: The Devil in the Modern World*. Ithaca: Cornell University Press, 1986.

_____. *The Prince of Darkness: Radical Evil and the Power of Good in History*. Ithaca: Cornell University Press, 1988.

_____. *Satan: The Early Christian Tradition*. Ithaca: Cornell University Press, 1981.

result simply from the failure to "think good thoughts." Drug abuse, violence, sexual abuse, poverty, greed, hatred, racism—these, along with many other negative elements of our world, are concrete manifestations of evil. The first step in dealing with evil is the recognition that it exists and that it is powerful.

Second, to use "Satan" language is to speak of the extrahuman dimension of evil. Evil is more than individual acts or even the sum of a host of evil deeds. Evil seems to take on a life of its own. It pervades our world, infecting not only individuals, but also institutions, systems, organizations, and even nations. A part of the difficulty encountered by people concerned with correcting social ills is that evil seems to reside not only in the individuals involved, but in the very systems, whether social, political, or religious, that allow and foster the problems of society. John's image of Satan as a many-headed dragon is appropriate. When one head of evil is chopped off, another is always there to mangle and devour. To attribute evil to Satan may help us realize the enormity of evil. The author of Ephesians expressed this concept of the supernatural dimension of evil when he wrote, "For our struggle is not against enemies of blood and flesh, but against the rulers, against the authorities, against the cosmic powers of this present darkness, against the spiritual forces of evil in the heavenly places" (6:12). [Evil and the Modern World]

> **Evil and the Modern World**
> The following trilogy offers thoughtful reflection on evil and terminology for evil in the modern world:
>
> Wink, Walter. *Engaging the Powers: Discernment and Resistance in a World of Domination*. Minneapolis: Fortress, 1992.
> ____. *Naming the Powers: The Language of Power in the New Testament*. Philadelphia: Fortress, 1984.
> ____. *Unmasking the Powers: The Invisible Powers That Determine Human Existence*. Philadelphia: Fortress, 1986.

On the other hand, the notion of Satan, at least as it is popularly held, carries with it several risks. First, the belief in a powerful supernatural being of evil verges on being a denial of the oneness of God. Biblical religion is monotheistic; it proclaims the uniqueness of God. As popularly expressed, belief in Satan produces an alternative to God, an evil god. For all practical purposes, such belief systems end up being theologically dualistic, rather than monotheistic. (Such is the case with the Persian religion of Zoroastrianism in which the good god, Ahura Mazda, is in a cosmic struggle with the evil god, Aingra Mainyu. The development in Judaism of the concept of Satan was possibly influenced strongly by these Zoroastrian ideas.) The Christian faith has no room for any competing deities. One of the major themes of Revelation is that there is no god but God alone. All other pretenders—whether they be Rome, angelic messengers, or even the notion of Satan—are to be rejected.

A second and more pervasive danger of speaking of evil in terms of a Satan figure is that such patterns of thought can easily lead to a failure to recognize our own responsibility for evil. Several years ago the comedian Flip Wilson created a character named Geraldine whose trademark line was, "The Devil made me do it." Denial of personal responsibility may be funny as a comedy routine, but it is inadequate as a way of dealing with sin and evil. Biblical faith teaches us that we must take responsibility for our own failures and sinfulness. One of the most poignant aspects of the temptation story of Adam and Eve is when they both deny responsibility for their actions. "The woman whom you gave to be with me, she gave me fruit from the tree," said Adam, when God confronted him with his disobedience. "The serpent tricked me," said Eve, pointing the finger of blame elsewhere. To blame another person, our past, our society, or Satan for the evil that we do is an indication of our own moral weakness and sinfulness. Satan becomes our scapegoat, and we can rationalize our failures by locating the blame outside ourselves. If Satan is the cause, then we do not have to change. The same holds true for evil beyond our individual sins—our corporate, societal, and institutional sins. If we can blame Satan for the problems that ravage our world, we do not have to take responsibility for trying to challenge and correct them. We feel no compulsion to confront corporate executives, politicians, and board members. After all, people are not responsible, we tell ourselves; Satan is to blame.

Another possible problem with Satan language is that its use may lead us to "satanize" any person or institution that seems to operate contrary to the ways of God. Once we have identified the person or institution as being in league with Satan, we can more easily rationalize our hatred and opposition to them. Why should I be compassionate or concerned about someone who is a manifestation of Satan? I can feel self-righteous in my attempts to discredit, malign, or destroy such an individual. An extreme case of such "satanization" is cited by Dean Peerman. General Rios Montt, the former fundamentalist dictator of Guatemala, once excused the massacre of children by claiming, "I'm not killing the people. The devil has entered into the people. I'm killing the devil."[12] Such extreme demonization of our enemies may be beyond our experiences, but the temptation to view our opponents as manifestations of evil is strong. If we believe in a personal Satan who directs the lives of individuals, then we may be even more likely to demonize our enemies, to see them as pawns of Satan.

Michael Defeating the Dragon

The archangel Michael is seen defeating the dragon with sword raised. Raphael Santi (1483–1520) is often considered the great assimilator of the Italian Renaissance style. This painting was commissioned by Duke Guidobaldo I of Urbino sometime c. 1504. Raphael worked as a court painter in his hometown of Urbino until moving to Florence in 1504. The beauty of Michael's facial features and the grace of his stance (even as he stands on a ferocious dragon) are typical of the style of Raphael. The wings are fully extended to exaggerate the movement of the triumphant figure.

Raphael (1483–1520). *Saint Michael.* 1504. Wood. Louvre. Paris, France. (Credit: Erich Lessing/Art Resource, NY)

A fourth danger of using the concept of Satan to explain evil is that eventually we may fail to recognize the human face of evil. If we can convince ourselves that evil is something outside of us, a separate entity, then we can more easily ignore it. On the other hand, if we recognize the visage of evil every time we look in the mirror, then we are apt to be more likely to confront the problem. Chapter 12 of Revelation has been the source of inspiration for many painters. The woman clothed in the sun, the great red dragon, and the archangel Michael have been represented in a variety of ways. In one of his paintings, Raphael depicted the dragon as a relatively small beast who seems to be easily conquered by the heroic Michael. [Michael Defeating the Dragon] Herrad von Landsperg, a twelfth-century abbess, made the woman the centerpiece of her work, with the dragon a rather small and not too ferocious character. [The Woman Clothed with the Sun] William Blake, on the other hand, in one of his watercolors, fills the canvas with the image of the dragon. The woman, stretched horizontally across the bottom of the scene is easily overlooked, so overpowering is the dragon creature. Blake's dragon is the embodiment of power and brute force, a terrifying figure of evil. Yet what makes Blake's painting so riveting is the human form of the dragon. The dragon looks more like a muscle-bound human than a scaly dragon or a horned Satan. In viewing Blake's dragon, one recognizes that evil comes in human form. [The Dragon]

The Woman Clothed with the Sun
This illustration, based on a copy of the 12th-century *Hortus deliciarum* by Herrad von Landsperg, shows the woman clothed with the sun being attacked by the great red dragon.

(Credit: Barclay Burns)

A final point to be made about the danger of casting evil in the disguise of Satan is that, contrary to what was noted above, such an approach may actually lead to the trivialization of evil rather than to the recognition of its power. The comic image of Satan as a pitchfork-toting, red-suited, horned figure with a pointed tail is not a threat. This popular conceptualization of Satan turns evil into a cartoonish boogeyman. If that is all Satan—and evil—is, then we do not have to take it too seriously.

If continuing to speak of evil in terms of Satan helps one to realize and confront the reality of rebelliousness, corruption, and failure in the world, then Satan language has a place for the

The Dragon

William Blake (1757–1827).
The Great Red Dragon and the
Woman Clothed with the Sun.
c. 1803–05. Watercolor on
paper. 21½"x17". Brooklyn
Museum of Art, Gift of William
Augustus White. 15.368.
Brooklyn, New York. (Credit: The
Brooklyn Museum of Art)

modern Christian. On the other hand, if one finds such language
repugnant and not useful, then one should find other images and
concepts that communicate the reality that Satan language was
intended to express. Belief in a personal, metaphysical being called
Satan is not a required doctrine of the Christian faith. John's purpose in Revelation in talking about Satan was not to argue about
the origin of evil or the existence of Satan. In fact, John's use of
Satan imagery is rather subdued, compared to what one finds in
other Jewish and Christian writings. John exhibits no concern
about the origin of Satan or Satan's role in tempting people or leading them astray. He does not present Satan as the commander of a
force of demons who torment and wreak havoc on the earth.
Instead, John uses the figure of Satan as a shorthand way to talk
about the seductive and destructive power of evil. John knows from

personal experience that evil was real. He has seen it incarnated in people, churches, and the empire. He has seen the works of Satan in the churches' acculturation to the standards of their society, in the demands for emperor worship, and in the persecution and martyrdom of the faithful. John speaks about Satan in order to alert his hearers/readers to the dangers of evil in their world.

His purpose is not simply to make them aware of evil, however, but to remind them that they have an important role to play in the ongoing struggle against evil. [Resistance to Evil] By "the word of their testimony"—a testimony sometimes given in blood—they will help to defeat Satan and his forces. The people of God, in our time as well as in the first century, are called to resist the forces of evil. The particular manifestations of evil in our world may be different than they were in first-century Asia Minor, but the responsibilities of God's people are the same. We are engaged in a cosmic conflict with evil. Allan Boesak has noted, "There is a war on; there is a struggle. There is a fight for justice, peace, freedom, and reconciliation. These are not things that come to us on the wheels of inevitability. They must be fought for."[13] We are called to be "conquerors," as the messages to the seven churches remind us. We conquer, however, not by violence, but by faithfulness to the witness of Jesus, which means being faithful to his sacrificial, self-giving lifestyle.

Perhaps the most important thing to notice about John's use of Satan imagery is that even though John presents Satan as a powerful, dangerous force, he adamantly declares that Satan is ultimately doomed. Satan may (and certainly will) continue to inflict damage on the church and the world, but his efforts will eventually fail. John declares that Satan has already been conquered (12:11) and that "his time is short" (12:12). Such encouragement and assurance that evil was already defeated would have been welcomed words to the Christians in Asia Minor who were struggling not only against oppression from the state but also against accommodation to their larger society. John's words are also welcomed words

---

Resistance to Evil

In discussing the responsibility of Christians to struggle against the forces of evil, Allan Boesak has written,

In his book *Ah, But Your Land Is Beautiful* (pp. 66-67) Alan Paton introduces a cautious middle-class black man who belatedly joins the struggle. To his bemused white friend he explains, "When I go up there, which is my intention, the Big Judge [in heaven] will say to me, Where are your wounds? and if I say I haven't any, he will say, Was there nothing to fight for?"

Allan A. Boesak, *Comfort and Protest: Reflections on the Apocalypse of John of Patmos* (Philadelphia: Westminster, 1987), 89.

to modern believers who need to be reminded that in spite of how dominant and pervasive evil may appear, evil carries with it a mortal wound.

NOTES

[1] Christopher C. Rowland, "The Book of Revelation: Introduction, Commentary, and Reflections," *The New Interpreter's Bible*, 12 vols. (Nashville: Abingdon, 1998), 12:648.

[2] Jürgen Roloff, *The Revelation of John: A Continental Commentary*, Continental Commentaries, trans. John E. Alsup (Minneapolis: Fortress, 1993), 139.

[3] George R. Beasley-Murray, *The Book of Revelation*, New Century Bible (Greenwood SC: Attic, 1974), 231.

[4] Raymond E. Brown, *An Introduction to the New Testament* (New York: Doubleday & Co., 1997), 779.

[5] M. Eugene Boring, *Revelation*, Interpretation: A Bible Commentary for Teaching and Preaching (Louisville: John Knox, 1989), 151.

[6] G. B. Caird, *The Revelation of St. John the Divine*, Harper's New Testament Commentaries (New York: Harper & Row, 1966), 154.

[7] E. F. Scott, *The Book of Revelation* (New York: Charles Scribner's Sons, 1940), 127.

[8] Henry Barclay Swete, *The Apocalypse of St. John: The Greek Text with Introduction, Notes and Indices* (3rd ed.; London: Macmillan & Co., 1911), 156.

[9] Beasley-Murray, *Revelation*, 205-206.

[10] Boring, *Revelation*, 152.

[11] Walter Wink, *Unmasking the Powers: The Invisible Forces That Determine Human Existence* (Philadelphia: Fortress, 1986), 9.

[12] Dean Peerman, "What Ever Happened to Rios Montt?" *The Christian Century* 102 (September 25, 1985): 819; cited by Walter Wink, *Engaging the Powers: Discernment and Resistance in a World of Domination* (Minneapolis: Fortress, 1992), 334.

[13] Allan A. Boesak, *Comfort and Protest: Reflections on the Apocalypse of John of Patmos* (Philadelphia: Fortress, 1987), 88.

THE TWO BEASTS

13:1-18

Chapter 13 of Revelation provides some of the most memorable and powerful images of John's entire visionary account—the beast from the sea, the beast from the land, 666, the mark of the beast, the antichrist (although the term "antichrist" is never used in Revelation). By means of these images, John portrays the earthly struggles between the forces of evil and the church. Chapter 13 flows smoothly from the preceding chapter, with its vision of the heavenly battle between Michael and the dragon. The heavenly voice in chapter 12 has warned that the dragon, after his expulsion from heaven, was then going to vent his wrath on the people of earth. Chapter 13 presents that earthly struggle, in which the work of the dragon is carried out by his two lieutenants, the beast from the sea and the beast from the land. While the events in chapter 13 follow the events in chapter 12—the dragon shifts his focus to earth after being cast out of heaven—in another sense the events of chapter 13 represent the same struggle that is depicted in chapter 12, only seen from a different perspective. Chapter 12 presents the heavenly battle against evil; chapter 13 portrays its earthly counterpart. At its core, the struggle in chapter 13 is a struggle over authority and loyalty. Who is ultimately in charge of the world—Satan and his cohorts or God? To whom does one owe allegiance?

COMMENTARY

The Beast from the Sea, 13:1-10

As the curtain falls on the scene from the preceding chapter, we are left with an ominous, haunting sight—the angry, vengeful dragon standing alone on the shore of the sea. But he does not remain alone for very long, for John sees a terrifying beast rising from the sea. The description of this beast makes clear his alignment with the dragon: they both have ten horns and seven heads adorned with crowns. These similarities are John's way of saying that the beast from the sea is a manifestation of the dragon. Leviathan, the mythological sea

The Beast from the Sea

AΩ   John's readers would have likely seen, in addition
to the mythic significance of the beast's arising
from the sea, another meaning in its coming from the sea
to the land. To the inhabitants of Asia Minor, the Roman
troops that occupied their land came "out of the sea" as
they arrived by ship from Rome.

monster, has provided the imagery for
both the dragon and the beast. John has
also borrowed his description of the beast
from the sea from Daniel 7. In Daniel's
vision, four separate beasts—like a lion, a
bear, a leopard, and one with ten horns—
come up from the great sea. John has
modified the Danielic vision and com-
bined all the characteristics of all four creatures into one terrifying
beast from the deep. [The Beast from the Sea]

As will become clear throughout this chapter and in chapter 17,
this beast from the sea represents the Roman Empire and specifically the empire as embodied in its emperors. That identification
helps explain the statement that "on its heads were blasphemous
names" (13:1), likely a reference to divine titles that were sometimes given to the emperors, or even demanded by them—such
titles as "savior," "lord," "god," or "son of god." Since such titles
and the allegiance they represent rightly belong to God and God
alone, any attribution of them to anyone else is blasphemy. The
most revealing comment that John makes in his description of the
beast is the statement that "the dragon gave it his power and his
throne and great authority" (13:2). In essence, John is unmasking
the empire and its pretensions to dominance and authority. John
wants his readers to recognize the real power behind the empire.
The emperors may claim to be divine, but their real power comes
from Satan. They are demonic rather than divine, and the empire
over which they rule is a tool of Satan.

This beast from the sea is presented as a parody of God and
Christ. The beast supposedly is divine; in reality, he is a pawn of
Satan. The only power and authority the beast has is that which
comes from Satan. In John's understanding, such authority is only
pseudoauthority. Furthermore, the beast
"seemed to have a death-blow, but its
mortal wound had been healed" (13:3).
This description is suggestive in two ways.
First, this fatal wound that had been
healed is likely a parody of the "Lamb
standing as if it had been slaughtered"
(5:6). [The Beast's Wound] The beast is an
antitype of the Messiah. Second, this
description likely has a historical signifi-
cance for John, recalling for his readers/hearers the Nero *redivivus*
myth that claimed that Nero would come back once again and

The Beast's Wound

AΩ   The parallelism between the beast and the Lamb
is even more evident in the Greek text. The
statement that one of the beast's heads "seemed to have
received a death-blow" reads literally that one of its
heads was "as slaughtered (*hōs esphagmenēn*) unto
death." The same Greek words are used to describe the
Lamb standing "as if it had been slaughtered" (*hōs
esphagmenēn*).

reclaim his throne (cf. 13:14, "the beast that had been wounded by the sword and yet lived"). Ancient writers have given at least two versions of this myth. In one, the report that Nero was dead (he supposedly committed suicide in AD 68 by stabbing himself in the throat) was considered a false report. The people feared that Nero was in hiding and waiting for the chance to retake the throne. The other version of the myth claimed that Nero had died, but that he would come back to life and resume his cruel reign. The latter version of the myth seems to be the one upon which John is drawing. John does not really believe that Nero is still alive or that he will be brought back from the dead. Rather, John is warning his readers that the evil that was incarnate in Nero is not finished yet. In the figure of a future ruler (17:10), a particularly malevolent one, "Nero" will return once more to wreak havoc on the people of God. In a more general sense, John saw that in all the emperors who claimed divine status, including the present one (likely Domitian), the spirit of Nero was at still at work.

John's use of the Nero *redivivus* myth was a powerful means of speaking of evil incarnated in the office of the emperor. Nero held a special place of infamy in the minds of Christians because he was responsible for the gruesome execution of Christians in Rome in AD 64. To identify the emperor as a Nero figure would have had an effect on Christians (and many others in Rome) somewhat similar to calling someone today "another Hitler." Such designation is a shorthand way of evoking feelings of dread, terror, and anxiety. John wants his audience to understand clearly—the emperor with his claims to divinity is no benign figure. He is a beast, another Nero and, even worse, the agent of Satan. The world is easily duped by such pretensions to power: "In amazement the whole earth followed the beast" (13:3). John, however, sees what others are not able to see. He recognizes the face of evil behind the empire and attempts to make that realization evident to the churches.

Verse 4 is apparently a reference to the imperial cult, which was particularly strong in Asia Minor. [Suggested Reading on the Roman Imperial Cult] Leonard

Suggested Reading on the Roman Imperial Cult

Cuss, Dominique. *Imperial Cult and Honorary Terms in the New Testament*. Fribourg: University Press, 1974.

Ferguson, John. *The Religions of the Roman Empire*. Ithaca: Cornell University Press, 1970.

Jones, Donald L. "Roman Imperial Cult." Pages 806-809 in vol. 5 of *The Anchor Bible Dictionary*. Edited by David Noel Freedman. 6 vols. New York: Doubleday & Co., 1992.

Kraybill, J. N. *Imperial Cult and Commerce in John's Apocalypse*. JSNTSup 132. Sheffield: Sheffield Academic Press, 1966.

Magie, David. *Roman Rule in Asia Minor*. Princeton: Princeton University Press, 1950.

Millar, F. *The Emperor in the Roman World*. Ithaca: Cornell University Press, 1977.

Price, S. R. F. *Rituals and Power: The Roman Imperial Cult in Asia Minor*. Cambridge: Cambridge University Press, 1984.

Scherrer, Steven J. "Signs and Wonders in the Imperial Cult: A New Look at a Roman Religious Institution in the Light of Rev 13:13-15." *Journal of Biblical Literature* 103/4 (1984): 599-610.

Taylor, L. R. *The Divinity of the Roman Emperor*. Middletown CT: American Philological Association, 1931.

Thompson has noted, "The churches of the Book of Revelation were located geographically, organizationally, and culturally where the imperial cult was most heavily distributed."[1] Of the seven cities addressed in chapters 2 and 3 of Revelation, "five of the seven cities had imperial altars (all but Philadelphia and Laodicea), six had imperial temples (all but Thyatira), and five had imperial priests (all but Philadelphia and Laodicea)."[2] The imperial cult could not be easily avoided in the urban areas of Asia Minor. Statues of the emperors were prevalent in the cities; large, impressive temples to the emperors dominated the cities; coins sometimes depicted the emperors as divine figures. In addition, festivals were held to honor the emperors on their birthdays, to celebrate victories, or to commemorate important events in the life of the emperor or his family. These festivals, which could last for several days, involved feasts, athletic contests, processionals, and sacrifices to the gods. To be a part of the civic life of the cities of Asia Minor meant being involved in the imperial cult. [Imperial Cult in the Seven Cities of Revelation]

Imperial Cult in the Seven Cities of Revelation

X indicates literary or archaeological evidence of temple, altar, or priest during the 1st–4th centuries AD. Some cities contained more than one of the indicated cultic items. Ephesus, for example, boasted of five imperial temples.

City	Imperial Temple	Imperial Altar	Imperial Priest
Ephesus	X	X	X
Laodicea	X		
Pergamum	X	X	X
Philadelphia	X		
Sardis	X	X	X
Smyrna	X	X	X
Thyatira	X	X	X

The question that confronted the Christians of Asia Minor was, "To what extent can we be involved in the imperial cult ceremonies and still be true to our Christian convictions?" Apparently some people in the churches of Asia Minor were taking a rather lax approach to the issue, finding ways to justify their accommodation to the demands of society. They likely were able to participate in varying degrees in the imperial cult and even in the worship of the state gods, justifying their behavior as nothing more than a matter of civic responsibility. Similar to the "stronger" Christians in Corinth, they may have reasoned, "We know that 'no idol in the world really exists,' and that 'there is no God but one' " (1 Cor 8:4). On that basis, they could participate with a clear conscience in the activities of the imperial cult, convincing themselves that such practice was acceptable since they knew that the emperor was really no god. John, however, sees no room for compromise on this issue. Emperor worship, no matter how it is explained or rationalized, is a denial of the sole sovereignty of God. To participate in the

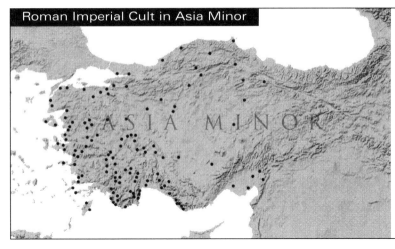

Roman Imperial Cult in Asia Minor

Map of Asia Minor indicating cities that contained one or more imperial altars, temples, and/or priests during the 1st–4th centuries AD.

Adapted from S. R. F. Price, *Rituals and Power: The Roman Imperial Cult in Asia Minor* (Cambridge: Cambridge University Press, 1984), xxv.

imperial cult is to render to a human being the worship and allegiance that is due solely to God. Even worse, John says, worshiping the beast (the emperor) is in reality worshiping the dragon (Satan), the archenemy of God, because the dragon is the real source of the beast's authority. [Map: Roman Imperial Cult in Asia Minor]

The acclamation of the people—"Who is like the beast, and who can fight against it?"—is a parody of the praise rendered to God in the Hebrew Bible (Exod 15:11; Pss 89:6; 113:5; Isa 40:25; Mic 7:18). This statement should not be understood as a word of fear or resignation by the people. They are not proclaiming their helplessness in the face of the overwhelming power of the beast. Rather, their words are a song of praise to the beast, extolling his greatness over all the earth. The accolades of the people offered to the beast, along with his own blasphemous claims (13:5-6), are reminiscent of the boastful claims of King Nebuchadnezzar in Daniel 4, who after surveying his mighty kingdom proclaimed, "Is this not magnificent Babylon, which I have built as a royal capital by my mighty power and for my glorious majesty?" (4:30). Immediately after uttering those words, Nebuchadnezzar was struck down by God because of his arrogance. Even more, the blasphemies of the beast are similar to the blasphemies and boasts of the haughty and wicked ruler in Daniel 7:8, 20, 25, who is Antiochus IV (see also 11:36). John knows that such blasphemous arrogance, promoted and encouraged by the imperial cult, would also lead to disastrous effects, as he will describe in chapters 17–19.

Blasphemies against God

AΩ In v. 6, some ancient manuscripts insert the word "and" before the last clause, thus indicating three objects of blasphemy: the name, the dwelling, and the inhabitants of heaven. (The KJV follows this inferior textual tradition.) This reading is almost certainly not to be preferred because it does not appear in the best ancient manuscripts of Revelation, and it is an "easier" reading, explained as an attempt by copyists to smooth out a more difficult reading.

The blasphemy of the beast is directed against God ("his name") and "his dwelling, that is, those who dwell in heaven" (13:6). [Blasphemies against God] Blasphemy against God is clear, but what is meant by blasphemy against those who dwell in heaven? Some commentators have interpreted this to mean angels or other members of the heavenly host. Yet, as Caird wryly observed, "It is very hard to imagine what would be involved in blaspheming angels."[3] A more attractive interpretation is to view those blasphemed by the beast as the martyrs, whom John has described as being under the altar in heaven (6:9). God's "dwelling" or "presence" is especially strong with those who are the most faithful, the martyrs. In venting his arrogance and rage on the martyrs and taking their life, the beast is blaspheming God, the source of all life.

The authority of the beast "over every tribe and people and language and nation" is a parody of the universal authority of God and Christ (cf. Phil 2:9-11). To John's audience this description of universal authority would have sounded like the Roman Empire with its domination over much of the known world. Throughout vv. 5-8, John describes this power and authority of the beast as that which "was given" (13:5, 7) or "was allowed" (13:7) to the beast. Although earlier John stated that the dragon gave the beast "his power and his throne and great authority" (13:2), a different agent is in mind here. These passive verbs are examples of the use of "divine passives," a way of referring to the activity of God. Even though John does not ascribe evil to God, his strong commitment to the ultimate sovereignty of God leads him to claim that even the work of Satan and his cohorts falls under God's control. We should not press John here for a fully developed theodicy. To claim that even the forces of evil must answer to God is one way in which John assures his readers that God is supreme over all the universe. Even though John utilizes the Jewish-Christian mythology of Satan as the leader of the forces of evil, John never slips into theological dualism in which Satan is an equal adversary to God. For John, the outcome is already decided. Satan continues his assault against the church only because God allows it. But even that activity of Satan will soon come to a decisive end. Satan and his beasts may be able to "make war on the saints and to conquer them," but such conquest is illusory. The true victors are the faithful followers of the Lamb whose very deaths help assure Satan's defeat (12:11).

The power and influence of the beast will be so great that those "whose name has not been written from the foundation of the world in the book of life of the Lamb that was slaughtered" (13:8) will worship the beast. Those who are truly God's people, whose names are in the Lamb's Book of Life (see comments on 3:5), will refuse to yield allegiance and homage to this false god. A translation difficulty appears in this verse. Some translators, likely influenced by the parallel passage in 17:8, attach the phrase "from the foundation of the world" to the writing of the names in the Book of Life. Other translators, following the actual grammatical structure of the Greek sentence, associate the phrase with the slaughtering of the Lamb. Theologically, either idea is compatible with the thought of the book of Revelation. Both readings affirm that the course of history has always been in God's hands. In spite of the parallel wording in 17:8, the better choice is likely to follow the natural reading of the Greek syntax and hear John attesting to God's eternal plan of redemption for the world through the sacrificial death of Christ (cf. 1 Pet 1:18-20). Beasley-Murray commented, "The sacrifice of the Lamb of God lay hidden in the heart of God from all eternity, and expresses the very nature of God."[4]

John prefaces the message in v. 10 with a declaration in v. 9: "Let anyone who has an ear listen." This admonition is John's way of saying that the following statement is important. A colloquial translation might be "Pay attention" or "Listen to this." John has used this admonition at the close of the messages in chapters 2 and 3 to exhort his readers/hearers to be conquerors, that is, faithful followers.

Verse 10 is a reformulation of Jeremiah 15:2 and 43:11, which declare the inevitability of God's punishment. Unfortunately, the textual tradition of Revelation 13:10 is very uncertain. The last part of the verse is particularly difficult. One early and often reliable manuscript reads, "If anyone is to be killed with the sword, with the sword he will be killed," a reading in keeping with the Jeremiah texts. This reading would form a good parallel with the first couplet of v. 10. Together the two couplets emphasize endurance and fulfillment of God's will, as well as the inevitability of persecution and martyrdom for the church. The Christian is to accept whatever persecution brings, whether it be imprisonment or death. The main variant reading, discussed below, is then explained as a scribal assimilation to the words of Jesus in Matthew 26:52. Although this first reading occurs in only one manuscript, codex Alexandrinus from the fifth century, this witness is considered one of the most reliable for the book of Revelation.

Other early manuscripts of Revelation read, "If anyone kills with the sword, with the sword he must be killed," a saying that is similar to Matthew 26:52. If this reading is accepted, two interpretations

Nonviolence

Martin Luther King Jr. was one of the most eloquent practitioners of nonviolence. He knew that suffering and nonviolence could function as effective means of active resistance against evil. In one of his sermons he said,

To our most bitter opponents we say: "We shall match your capacity to inflict suffering by our capacity to endure suffering. We shall meet your physical force with soul force. Do to us what you will, and we shall continue to love you. We cannot in all good conscience obey your unjust laws, because noncooperation with evil is as much a moral obligation as is cooperation with good. Throw us in jail, and we shall still love you. Bomb our homes and threaten our children, and we shall still love you. Send your hooded perpetrators of violence into our community at the midnight hour and beat us and leave us half dead, and we shall still love you. But be ye assured that we will wear you down by our capacity to suffer. One day we shall win freedom, but not only for ourselves. We shall so appeal to your heart and conscience that we shall win *you* in the process, and our victory will be a double victory."

Martin Luther King Jr., "Loving Your Enemies," *Strength to Love* (New York: Harper & Row, 1963), 40.

---

are still possible. Either John is assuring the Christians that their enemies who kill them will themselves be killed, or he is exhorting the faithful not to resist persecution by force, warning them of the dangers of such action. Of these two meanings, the first seems disconnected with the earlier part of v. 10. The first couplet is concerned with the faithful believers. The second couplet likely refers to them also.

As for which of the two variant readings is to be accepted, a decision must be given with caution. Both readings can be adequately explained, and both suit the context well. On the basis of better textual support, most English translations (including the NRSV) accept the second reading given above. The message to John's readers, then, is that they prove themselves faithful witnesses, not by armed resistance and violence, but by suffering for the gospel when necessary. [Nonviolence] This reading is also consistent with John's image of the Lamb, who conquers not by force but by his sacrificial death.

Endurance

AΩ "The early church began [the transformation of society and persons] from the pole of steadfastness in prayer and the refusal of idolatry, manifesting that *hypomonē* which the Book of Revelation regards as the highest Christian virtue. It is usually somewhat limply rendered 'patient endurance,' but it is in fact closer to 'absolute intransigence,' 'unbending determination,' 'an iron will,' 'the capacity to endure persecution, torture, and death without yielding one's faith.' It is one of the fundamental attributes of nonviolent resistance."

Walter Wink, *Naming the Powers: The Language of Power in the New Testament* (Philadelphia: Fortress, 1984), 127-28.

The closing line of v. 10 is appropriate, regardless of which of the two readings for the first part of the verse is accepted. Verse 10b is a refrain that reverberates throughout the Apocalypse: "Here is a call for the endurance and faith of the saints" (cf. 1:9; 2:2, 3, 19; 3:10; 14:12). In the intensification of conflict and persecution that John expects will soon engulf the church, the task of the people of God will be to remain loyal and faithful in their commitment to God. [Endurance]

Leviathan and Behemoth

AΩ "Then you kept in existence two living creatures: the one you called Behemoth and the name of the other Leviathan. And you separated one from the other, for the seventh part where the water had been gathered together could not hold them both. And you gave Behemoth one of the parts that had been dried up on the third day, to live in it, where there are a thousand mountains; but to Leviathan you gave the seventh part, the watery part; and you have kept them to be eaten by whom you wish, and when you wish." (2 Esd 6:49-52)

"On that day, two monsters will be parted—one monster, a female named Leviathan, in order to dwell in the abyss of the ocean over the fountains of water; and (the other), a male called Behemoth, which holds his chest in an invisible desert whose name is Dundayin, east of the garden of Eden, wherein the elect and the righteous ones dwell. . . . Then I asked the second angel in order that he may show me (how) strong these monsters are, how they were separated on this day and were cast, the one into the abysses of the ocean, and the other into the dry desert. . . . And the angel of peace who was with me said to me, 'These two monsters are prepared for the great day of the Lord (when) they shall turn into food.' " (*1 En.* 60:7-9, 24)

"And it will happen that when all that which should come to pass in these parts has been accomplished, the Anointed One will begin to be revealed. And Behemoth will reveal itself from its place, and Leviathan will come from the sea, the two great monsters which I created on the fifth day of creation and which I shall have kept until that time. And they will be nourishment for all who are left." (*2 Bar.* 29:3-4)

The Beast from the Earth, 13:11-18

The latter half of chapter 13 introduces the second beast, the beast from the earth. If the first beast is an adaptation of the ancient mythological sea monster Leviathan, the second beast is modeled after another primeval monster—Behemoth, the monster on the land. In Jewish legend, Leviathan and Behemoth were primordial monsters who would be killed in the end time when the messiah comes. Their carcasses would be food for the people left on the earth. [Leviathan and Behemoth] This second beast, like the first, is a parody of Christ: it has horns "like a lamb." Its speech betrays its true identity, however. In contrast to Christ, who speaks the word of God, this beast speaks "like a dragon" (Satan). The role of the second beast is to exercise the authority of the first beast and to enforce worship of the first beast. [Predestination] The description of the second beast is reminiscent of the prophets who also performed "great signs" (13:13), such as causing fire to come down (cf. Elijah, 1 Kgs 18:20-40), and encouraged worship. Accordingly, John later refers to the second beast as "the false prophet" (16:13; 19:20; 20:10). The signs of this beast are false signs by which it deceives the people and fosters the worship of the first beast. It

Predestination

"We must not read more into John's doctrine of predestination than he intends. He is not saying that 'the inhabitants of earth will worship' the monster because they have no choice, because this is the fate to which they have been destined from all eternity. His doctrine springs from the thoroughly biblical idea that salvation is from start to finish the unmerited act of God. But he constantly qualifies it with an equally strong statement of human responsibility."

G. B. Caird, *A Commentary on the Revelation of St. John the Divine,* Harper's New Testament Commentaries (New York: Harper & Row, 1966), 168.

◄ Imperial Statues

Statues of Roman emperors were prominent and numerous in the cities of Asia Minor. Statues were placed in the temples, in public buildings (including theaters and gymnasiums), along the streets, in the marketplaces, in fountains, and on gates. In order to evoke divine associations, statues of the emperors were sometimes designed to resemble traditional representations of the gods. Some of the imperial statues were monumental. Shown here is a statue of Emperor Trajan (98–117) portrayed in richly decorated armor, wearing a wreath on his head to symbolize his victory over Dacia.

Trajan. 2d C. Marble. Antalya Museum. Antalya, Turkey. (Credit: Mitchell Reddish)

Imperial Priest ➤

Statue of an imperial priest from Perge in modern Turkey, 2d C. AD. Imperial priests helped maintain the system of emperor worship.

Imperial Priest. 2d C. Marble. Antalya Museum. Antalya, Turkey. (Credit: Mitchell Reddish)

causes the people to make an image (statue) of the first beast and even causes this image to speak. [Imperial Statues]

If the first beast represents the empire and particularly the emperors, what does the second beast symbolize? Specifically, it represents everyone who encourages and fosters emperor worship (local magistrates, imperial priests, provincial councils). In the provinces, an elaborate system supported the imperial cult, involving priests, sacrifices, festivals, statues, and temples. [Imperial Priest] Making an offering to the emperor was sometimes used as a test of loyalty. All of this supporting network of political-religious promotion of the imperial cult is subsumed under the image of the second beast. This identification, however, as correct as it likely is, unnecessarily limits the meaning of John's symbol. Eugene Boring has correctly pointed to a broader meaning in the symbol of the second beast: "All who support and promote the cultural religion, in or out of the church, however Lamb-like they may appear, are agents of the beast. All propaganda that entices humanity to idolize human empire is an expression of this beastly power that wants to appear Lamb-like."[5]

Commentators have frequently compared the second beast's use of signs by which to deceive the people, including his making the image of the first beast speak, to magical tricks and charades performed in the ancient world. For example, R. H. Charles stated,

Talking Statues

Ancient writers mention several examples of "talk-ing" statues used to deceive worshipers in pagan cults. One of the most interesting is Lucian's description of the statue of Asclepius, the god of healing, that was created and manipulated by the 2d-century "prophet" Alexander, whom Lucian considered a charlatan. The snake was a sym-bol for Asclepius, so Alexander made a canvas statue like a snake. According to Lucian, the statue "would open and close its mouth by means of horsehairs, and a forked black tongue like a snake's, also controlled by horsehairs, would dart out" (*Alexander the False Prophet* 12). In order to make the serpent's head (which looked like a human head) talk, Alexander was able to "fasten crane's windpipes together and pass them through the head, which he had so fashioned as to be lifelike. Then he answered the questions through someone else, who spoke into the tube from the outside, so that the voice issued from his canvas Asclepius" (*Alex.* 26).

"Most oriental cults had recourse to magic and trickery, and that the imperial cult availed itself of their help, as our text states, there is no just ground for doubting."[6] Hippolytus (AD 170–236), in *The Refutation of All Heresies* (8.28-42), explained in detail how several of the deceptions practiced by sorcerers and religious figures were carried out. He explained, for instance, how thunder was pro-duced, or the sensation of an earthquake was created, or a skull was made to speak. The specific example of trickery that John men-tions, a speaking statue, is mentioned in several ancient sources. Through ventriloquism, through a person hiding in a hollow statue, or through some mechanical device, statues could appear animated and be made to talk. [Talking Statues]

While the use of deceptive "signs" and "miracles" was prevalent in ancient society, and perhaps even in the imperial cult, John may not have had such specific instances in mind. The idea that the time immediately preceding the end would be filled with false prophets or other evil figures working their signs and miracles was widespread in Jewish and Christian apocalyptic literature. *Sibylline Oracles* 3:63-67 describes the eschatological arrival of Beliar:

> Then Beliar will come from the *Sebastēnoi*
> and he will raise up the height of mountains, he will raise up the sea,
> the great fiery sun and shining moon,
> and he will raise up the dead, and perform many signs
> for men.

Mark 13:22 says, "False messiahs and false prophets will appear and produce signs and omens, to lead astray, if possible, the elect" (cf. 2 Thess 2:9; *Ascen. Isa.* 4:10).

The authority of the second beast is great, for it causes "those who would not worship the image of the beast to be killed" (13:15). [Bust of Domitian] There is no evidence to support any massive execution of people who refused to participate in the imperial cult.

Yet John knows of isolated cases in which Christians had been martyred, perhaps for their refusal to pay homage to the emperor. The letter of Pliny to Trajan in the early second century indicates that making an offering to the emperor was sometimes used as a test of loyalty against Christians. Those who refused were put to death. From such sporadic incidents, John imagines a full-scale persecution breaking out against the church because of the refusal of faithful Christians to bow down to the emperor. The massive outbreak of martyrdom, as well as the economic boycott described in vv. 16-17 ("no one can buy or sell" who does not participate in the worship of the image), derives more from John's creative imagination than from present reality. John envisions how bad the situation could become as a means of warning his audience about the seriousness of the imperial claims.

Bust of Domitian

A statue of Domitian in Ephesus, the head, left forearm, and some smaller pieces of which have been discovered, probably originally stood twenty to twenty-five feet high. Some scholars have suggested that this colossal cult statue of Domitian is the background for "the image of the beast" in Rev 13. (Other scholars believe that this statue may be of Titus, the previous emperor and the brother of Domitian.)

Statue of Domitian. 1st C. Marble. Ephesus Museum. Selçuk, Turkey. (Credit: Mitchell Reddish)

The mark that is given to those who refuse to participate in the imperial cult is a parody of the mark given to the servants of God (7:1-8). As God's people are sealed with a mark to indicate that they belong to God, so the followers of the beast are also marked as an indication to whom their loyalties belong. For John there is no room for compromise. Either one belongs to God or one belongs to the beast (and thus to Satan). The idea for such a mark on the right hand or the forehead may have been the practice of branding or tattooing runaway slaves or prisoners of war in the Roman world. Worshipers of particular gods and goddesses were sometimes branded or tattooed to indicate their loyalty, such as the devotees of Dionysus being branded with an ivy-leaf symbol (3 Macc 2:29-30).[7] John's point, however, is not that people will be divided into two groups on the basis of actual marks placed upon them, the mark of God or the mark of the beast. Rather, John is saying that those (including people in the church) who participate in the worship of the emperor have, in so doing, "marked" themselves as belonging to Satan.

The identity of this mark of the beast has "bedeviled" readers of the book since antiquity. John says that the mark is "the name of the beast or the number of its name" (13:17) and that it is "the number of a person" (13:18). Specifically, the number is six hundred sixty-six. By saying that "this calls for wisdom" (13:18), John is indicating that the proper understanding of this mysterious

Gematria

Examples of gematria from the ancient world cited by Adolf Deissmann include:

1. From graffiti written on walls at Pompeii (destroyed by the eruption of Mount Vesuvius in AD 79):

"I love her whose number is 545."

"Amerimnus thought upon his lady Harmonia for good. The number of her honorable name is 45 (or 1035)."

2. Gematria in the *Sib. Or.* 5:1-25:

There will be the first prince who will sum up twice
   ten

with his initial letter. . . . [a]

He will have his first letter of ten,[b] so that after him

will reign whoever obtained as initial the first of the

   alphabet. . . . [c]

After a long time he will hand over sovereignty to

   another,

who will present a first letter of three hundred,[d]

and the beloved name of a river. . . .

Then whoever obtained an initial of three will rule [e].

Next, a prince who will have twice ten on his first

   letter [f].

One who has fifty as an initial will be commander....[g]

[a] Kaisar (Caesar); K=20 in the Greek alphabet
[b] Iulius (Julius); I=10
[c] Augustus; A=1
[d] Tiberius; T = 300; the river is the Tiber
[e] Gaios (Caligula); G=3
[f] Klaudios (Claudius); K=20
[g] Nero; N=50

Adolf Deissmann, *Light from the Ancient East: The New Testament Illustrated by Recently Discovered Texts of the Graeco-Roman World*, trans. Lionel R. M. Strachan, rev. ed. (New York: Harper & Brothers, 1927), 277.

The translation, as well as the identifications in the footnotes, comes from John J. Collins, trans., "The Sibylline Oracles," *The Old Testament Pseudepigrapha*, ed. James H. Charlesworth, 2 vols. (Garden City NY: Doubleday & Co., 1993), 1:393.

---

symbol will require a discerning mind. Among the various suggestions that have been made, the most likely explanation for 666 is that it is an example of the practice of gematria, a numerical riddle in which words or names are coded as numbers. [Gematria] In the ancient world, letters of the alphabet functioned as numbers also. Thus, for example, in our alphabet A=1, B=2, C=3, etc. Accordingly, any word or name could have a numerical value based on the sum of the individual numbers in the word. Enough examples of gematria are known from the ancient world to indicate that the practice was widely known. Establishing the numerical value for a given word is easy; the difficulty occurs in trying to go in the opposite direction and determine what word or name is represented by a certain number. Numerous words could have the same numerical value. For that reason, one must assume that the identity of the person represented by 666 must have already been known to John's readers.

Who then did 666 stand for? The most likely suggestion is that it represents the emperor Nero. When the Greek words for Caesar Nero are transliterated into Hebrew letters their numerical value is 666. [666] Support for this interpretation comes from a variant reading in some manuscripts that has 616 instead. In Latin, the numerical value of Caesar Nero is 616. Jürgen Roloff has made another interesting observation about the significance of 666 for Nero: "The numerical value

666

AΩ The Greek spelling of Nero Caesar, transliterated into Hebrew letters, is נרון קסר. The numerical values of these letters would be:

נ = 50
ר = 200
ו = 6
נ = 50
ק = 100
ס = 60
ר = 200
666

of the Greek word *thērion* (=the beast), written in Hebrew letters, also produces 666. From this fact the statement in v. 18, that the number of the *beast* (=666) is a human number, can receive an additional symbolic weight."8

Commentators have also suggested another symbolic meaning for 666. Since seven is considered the number for perfection or completeness, six would represent incompleteness, imperfection, or even evil, since it is one less than seven. Accordingly, 666 would be triple evil, a fitting symbolic number for the beast that is the puppet of Satan. Somewhat along these same lines, Beasley-Murray pointed out that in *Sibylline Oracles* 1.324-29, the numerical value of the name of Christ in Greek is recognized as 888. The 666 of the beast could then be seen as an intentional contrast to the number of Christ. This satanic beast "falls as far short of being the true deliverer of mankind as the Christ of God exceeds all the hopes of man for a redeemer."9 Although this understanding of the symbolic meaning of the number six is appealing, as well as appropriate, one should be cautious. Adela Yarbro Collins has pointed out that the number six does not function with that meaning anywhere else in Revelation and that the Jewish writer Philo considered the number six to be a perfect number.10

If the number of the beast is indeed a reference to Nero, why is John concerned with Nero, who was already dead? Domitian is the current emperor. As mentioned above, Nero is a fitting symbol for evil because Nero is remembered as the first persecutor of the church. Now, in Domitian, John is saying that the cruelty and oppression of Nero is appearing all over again. Even though John may have expected another emperor to appear after Domitian (see 17:10) who would be more fully a reincarnation of Nero, any ruler, including Domitian, who demanded worship and persecuted the people of God is in part a reappearance of Nero. By branding the entire imperial system with the mark of Nero, John is warning his readers to avoid involvement in the emperor cult.

CONNECTIONS

1. In the cult of the emperor in John's day, religion, politics, and nationalism were all intermixed. In offering incense or sacrifice to the emperor (or to the gods on behalf of the emperor), the participant was expressing loyalty to the emperor and to the empire, as well as currying the favor of the gods. The entire system of emperor worship, as well as the state-supported cults devoted to the

traditional gods and goddesses, was a system of religion in the service of the state. The situation of modern readers of the Apocalypse may appear totally unrelated to John's context. After all, not too many people are tempted to bow down in worship before the political leaders of today's world. Enough examples can be found, however, to demonstrate that modern Christians and religious institutions have too often rendered to Caesar that which belonged to God. One of the most notorious examples is the support that many German Christians and churches gave to Hitler in his efforts to unify Germany and strengthen it as a world power, even at the expense of Jews, gypsies, homosexuals, and other "undesirables." Anything for the Fatherland! In South Africa, the white Dutch Reformed Church was a staunch supporter of the government's racist apartheid policy, twisting biblical texts to provide justification for a system that oppressed and terrorized the non-white segment of the population. In Nicaragua, the hierarchy of the Roman Catholic Church continued to support the Somoza regime until the late 1960s, in spite of its atrocities and human rights violations.[11]

In modern America, the church has often become an instrument, if at times unwittingly, of the policies and programs of the state. During times of war, from World War I to the recent Gulf War, many churches and church leaders have rallied around the military, demonizing our national enemies and portraying them as godless subhumans that deserve to be annihilated. In times of peace, churches hold patriotic rallies, particularly on the Fourth of July weekend, with much flag waving and singing of patriotic songs. During such celebrations—even during Sunday morning worship—churches are literally, as well as figuratively, wrapped in red, white, and blue, thus intertwining so closely God and country that it is difficult to tell where one starts and the other ends. Even more subtle, but perhaps more dangerous, is the practice of placing American flags in our churches and teaching our children to pledge allegiance to the United States flag as a part of Vacation Bible School activities. Caesar demands to be worshiped, and too readily the church obeys. The church becomes a servant of the state, making "the earth and its inhabitants worship the first beast."

[Temple of Domitian]

American Christianity is particularly in danger of "worshiping the beast," of replacing God with country. The entire history of our nation is infused with biblical idealism, with the notion that this country is God's special land. The settlement of this country was seen as a part of the divine plan—perhaps this was the place where

Temple of Domitian
The ruins of the temple of the Flavian Sebastoi in Ephesus, built near the end of the 1st century during the reign of Domitian. (The temple is often called the temple of Domitian. The three Flavian emperors, or *sebastoi*, were Vespasian, Titus, and Domitian.) (Credit: Mitchell Reddish)

God's new kingdom would be located. This land was the "New World" filled with a New England, a New York, and a New Hampshire. This new world was where God would create a new heaven and a new earth.

The language may have changed, but the idea still persists among certain Christian groups—America is God's country, and Christians are called to support the government in all its endeavors, even when the nation becomes involved in deception, oppression, cover-ups, and warfare. America is seen as God's instrument of righteousness and justice in the world. Dale Aukerman perceptively described this situation when he wrote,

In the common American view, widespread among church people, the United States is looked to as having the world role quite similar to that which the Hebrews recognized as God's: Stability, liberty, justice, peace, and prosperity around the world depend chiefly on the exercise of U. S. power. This outlook has shaped much of American history. John Adams in a letter to Thomas Jefferson on November 13, 1813, expressed it in characteristically messianic terms: "Our pure, virtuous, public spirited, federative republic will last forever, govern the globe, and introduce the perfection of man." Though such optimism as to what the United States can bring about globally is mostly gone, there remains the dogged certainty that the United

States must be the world guarantor for everything that has to be pre-served and promoted.[12]

In his classic critique of American society (based on his reading of the Apocalypse), *An Ethic for Christians and Other Aliens in a Strange Land*, William Stringfellow offered a similar analysis:

The American vanity as a nation has, since the origins of America, been Babylonian—boasting, through Presidents, often through phar-isees within the churches, through folk religion, and in other ways, that America is Jerusalem. This is neither an innocuous nor benign claim; it is the essence of the doctrine of the Antichrist. [13]

2. Revelation 13 is a reminder that no person or institution deserves our ultimate allegiance. For all of us, life is filled with rela-tionships, organizations, jobs, and institutions to which we owe various commitments. We are committed to our spouses, to our children, to our friends. We are loyal to our alma maters, to our civic organizations, to our nation. We live out our lives in a web of allegiances and loyalties. Such commitments are an important and necessary part of life in modern society. The problem arises when we allow any of these loyalties to become the ultimate loyalty in our lives, when a commitment to job, family, or nation takes prior-ity over all over commitments, including our commitment to God. Every individual or group that lays claim to our allegiance has within it the potential to become "the great beast" that demands to be worshiped and kills those who refuse.

A careful reading of Revelation should cause us to question where our loyalties lie and, even more, how much allegiance is due to any-one or anything but God. In Judaism of the first century, this question was raised concerning loyalty to the Roman Empire, specifically participation in the emperor cult. Judaism's commit-ment to monotheism certainly meant that no sacrifices or worship could be offered to the emperor. As a compromise, the Jewish people, by means of the high priest, offered a sacrifice to God *on behalf of* the emperor. By so doing they satisfied the Roman test of loyalty to the empire, but also remained true to their ultimate allegiance to God.

Where do we draw the line? When does patriotism slide over into idolatrous allegiance? At what point do our jobs or our civic commitments become so consuming of our time and resources that they have usurped the place of God in our lives? No easy answers can be given to such questions. Those questions must be answered on an individual basis as we assess our own lives and ask if "the beast," in whatever form it may have arisen, has entered our lives and demanded our worship and our loyalties.

3. The majority viewpoint of the New Testament toward the state is a positive, or at least neutral, assessment. The most well-known passage dealing with Christians and the government is Romans 13:1-7. Paul wrote, "Let every person be subject to the governing authorities; for there is no authority except from God, and those authorities that exist have been instituted by God. Therefore whoever resists authority resists what God has appointed, and those who resist will incur judgment." The author of 1 Peter 2:13-14 likewise urged submission to governmental authorities, whereas the author of 1 Timothy counseled Christians to pray for "kings and all who are in high positions" (2:1-2). Frequently these teachings have been presented as the "correct" Christian approach to the state, with the explanation that faithful Christians must always be supportive of the government. Interpreted along these lines, these verses have been used to support blind allegiance to the state and to condemn any acts of civil disobedience. The passage from Romans 13, in particular, was the basis for many German Christians' support of the evil regime of Hitler. In American churches, these verses have been used to castigate draft dodgers and antiwar demonstrators during the Vietnam War years, to condemn participants in the Civil Rights marches and protests, and to criticize anyone who would actively challenge the government's authority.

Any use of these texts, however, to foster unqualified support of any and all government activities is a misuse of the texts. While recognizing the legitimate role of governmental authority, these texts do not call for uncritical submission to the state. They stop short of that idolatry. Even if such an interpretation could be legitimately argued from these texts, Revelation 13 still stands as a forceful declaration that, in the name of God, idolatrous power must be resisted, not obeyed. Revelation 13 calls for civil disobedience. John unmasks the powers that claim illegitimate authority. Such powers are not divine, but are beastly, demonic powers. Resistance to the state has a rich history in biblical and Christian tradition. Daniel and his three friends risked their lives rather than bow to the king. Peter and the apostles, when ordered to stop spreading their Christian message, declared that they "must obey God rather than any human authority" (Acts 5:29). Martin Luther King Jr. defied the segregation laws to struggle for justice.

At times the most Christian response, as John knows well, is to resist the demands of the state, to fight the beast who demands allegiance that does not belong to him. [Resistance to Emperor Worship] John does not sanction violence, however. His call is for nonviolent civil disobedience, for he knows that violence only breeds more violence—"If you kill with the sword, with the sword you must be killed" (Rev 13:10). Resistance to the beast can be costly, even deadly. Those who resist the beast in any manner, especially in public acts of civil disobedience, must be willing to suffer the punishment meted out by the beast. Imprisonment, fines, public humiliation, and even assassination have been the wounds inflicted by the beast when people have failed to obey it. Nelson Mandela, Philip and Daniel Berrigan, Dorothy Day, Dietrich Bonhoeffer—these and many others have felt the wrath of the beast for their resistance to his claims. Too often, we choose the easy way and rationalize our cooperation with the beast, rather than face the consequences of resistance. John knows too well the dangers of such accommodation with the beastly powers. All around him he sees Christians in the cities of Asia Minor who are willing to offer incense to the image of the emperor or to join in the public feasts and eat the meat sacrificed to the gods or to the emperor. They can justify their behavior by saying it means nothing to them or that such practices are expected if they want to be successful, both financially and socially. John knows otherwise, however. Such practices are not benign. They are idolatrous, rendering to Caesar the allegiance that belongs only to God.

Between Romans 13 and Revelation 13, where does the modern Christian stand? Is submission to the state or civil disobedience the path which the follower of Christ should walk? In truth, at different times both responses may be appropriate. When the state works for peace, justice, equality, and the dignity of all humanity (including the citizens of other countries), the state deserves our support. On the other hand, when the state becomes an instrument of oppression, greed, or injustice—when it confuses its role with that of God and demands ultimate allegiance or when it demands from its citizens actions that are immoral or idolatrous—the state needs to be challenged and even opposed.

Walter Wink described the appropriate Christian response to the state when he wrote,

Resistance to Emperor Worship

Polycarp (c. 69–c. 155), bishop of Smyrna, was one of the early Christians who faced a martyr's death. Brought before the proconsul, Polycarp was given a choice: deny his allegiance to Christ or be killed. Polycarp refused. The ancient account of his martyrdom states,

The Proconsul continued insisting and saying, "Swear, and I release you; curse Christ." And Polycarp said, "Eighty-six years have I served Him, and He has done me no wrong: how then can I blaspheme my King who saved me?"

The Proconsul continued to persist and to say, "Swear by the genius of Caesar"; he answered, "If you vainly imagine that I would 'swear by the genius of Caesar', as you say, pretending that you are ignorant who I am, hear plainly that I am a Christian. And if you are willing to learn the doctrine of Christianity, appoint a day, and listen." (*Mart. Pol.* 9.3–10.1)

Antichrist

AΩ Both of the beasts of ch. 13, particularly the first beast, function as antichrist figures, even though John never uses the title "antichrist" for either of them. The term "antichrist" appears in the New Testament only in 1 John (2:18, 22; 4:3) and in 2 John (7). In 2 Thessalonians (2:3, 8, 9), the phrase "the lawless one" is used to describe an antichrist figure, that is, one who appears in the last days as the epitome of evil and who leads a campaign of deception against the people of God. For John of Patmos, the Roman Empire has become a fitting candidate for the title. The Letters of 1 and 2 John enlarge the concept of the antichrist, claiming that many "antichrists" exist. The writer(s) of these letters shifted the antichrist from an eschatological figure to a present-day reality. Since an antichrist is basically anyone opposed to Christ, then anyone who does not follow Christ is an antichrist:

"Many deceivers have gone out into the world, those who do not confess that Jesus Christ has come in the flesh; any such person is the deceiver and the antichrist!" (2 John 7)

I love my country passionately; that is why I want to see it do right. There is a valid place for a sensible patriotism. But from a Christian point of view, true patriotism acknowledges God's sovereignty over all the nations, and holds a healthy respect for God's judgments on the pretensions of any power that seeks to impose its will on others. There is a place for a sense of destiny as a nation. But it can be authentically embraced and pursued only if we separate ourselves from the legacy of the combat myth and "enter a long twilight struggle against what is dark within ourselves." There is a divine vocation for the United States (and every other nation) to perform in human affairs. But it can perform that task, paradoxically, only by abandoning its messianic zeal and accepting a more limited role within the family of nations.[14]

4. Throughout the history of the church, various attempts have been made to decipher the code of the beast. Who is the beast, the antichrist, about whom John warns? [Antichrist] The list of alleged "antichrists" is lengthy: Muhammad, the Roman Catholic Church, the papacy, individual popes (John XV, Gregory VII, John XXII, Innocent IV, Boniface VII, Benedict XI, Leo X, Clement XIV, John Paul II), Emperor Frederick II Hohenstaufen, Martin Luther, Napoleon Bonaparte, Napoleon III, Benito Mussolini, Mikhail Gorbachev, Henry Kissinger, Ronald Wilson Reagan (note that each of the three parts of his name has six letters—666), Anwar Sadat, Muammar Gadhafi, and Saddam Hussein. In recent years, some of the more bizarre interpretations of the "mark of the beast" have identified it with Social Security numbers, the Universal Product Code (UPC) bar codes on merchandise, credit cards, and computers and computer chips. All such attempts to name the antichrist or to decode the mark of the beast

Antichrists

"Each person ought to question his own conscience, whether he be an antichrist. For antichrist in our tongue means, contrary to Christ."

Augustine, *Tract. ep. Jo.* 3.4 (*NPNF*[1] 7:476-77).

are misguided and sometimes even dangerous. Literalistic interpretations of these symbols rob them of their power to engage the imagination and their ability to unmask the many forms and varieties of evil that threaten our world. [Antichrists]

The "antichrist" is a symbol for evil, for all that stands in opposition to God. John was correct in identifying the Roman emperors as the antichrist. But then so have been countless other interpreters who have identified the antichrist as various religious or political figures. The antichrist continues to reappear throughout history in many forms and many disguises. To look for the appearance of one antichrist is to miss the appearance of many antichrists all around us, including the presence of the antichrist within our own lives. As John recognized, one of the primary tactics of the antichrist is that it "deceives the inhabitants of the earth" (13:14), leading them to worship false gods and accept hollow promises. Sometimes we deceive ourselves, setting up our own false gods, making ourselves into antichrists. [The Antichrist Legend]

Bernard McGinn has concluded his excellent survey of the antichrist legend with these words:

> From its origins, the Antichrist legend has had a collective dimension—the *pseudochristoi* of the Synoptic Apocalypse and the *antichristoi* of the Johannine Letters. While it has been easy for many Christians over the centuries to identify these multiple opponents of Christ in a purely external fashion with some easily identifiable group of opponents—heretics, Jews, or others—their original character was that of the enemy *within* the community of believers. Furthermore, from the early centuries, through the writings of such thinkers as Origen, Augustine, Gregory the Great, and others, the image of Antichrist has often been personally internalized by insisting, as Augustine put it, that "everyone must question his own conscience whether he be such." It is this recognition of the Antichrist within, both within Christianity and in each Christian, that needs renewed emphasis today. . . .
>
> It may no longer be possible for most of us to believe in the legendary figure of a coming individual who will sum up all human evil at the end of time. But at the end of this millennium we can still reflect on deception both within and without each of us and in our world at large as the most insidious malice—that which is most contrary to what Christians believe was and still is the meaning of Christ.[15] [Suggested Reading on the Antichrist]

The Antichrist Legend

"The history of the [Antichrist] legend certainly gives more attention to dramatically portrayed accounts of Antichrist conceived of as an identifiable external foe, either individual or collective. Yet biblical texts, such as the First Epistle of John (which contains the earliest appearance of the word "Antichrist"), and major Christian thinkers—from Origen, Augustine, and Gregory the Great among the ancients, through medieval poets like William Langland and Reformation radicals, down to modern novelists and psychologists who have used Antichrist motifs—all have insisted that the true meaning of Antichrist is to be found within, that is, in the spirit that resists Christ present in the hearts of believers."

Bernard McGinn, *Antichrist: Two Thousand Years of the Human Fascination with Evil* (San Francisco: HarperSanFrancisco, 1994), 4.

Suggested Reading on the Antichrist

Bousset, Wilhelm. *The Antichrist Legend: A Chapter in Christian and Jewish Folklore*. Translated by A. H. Keane. London: Hutchinson, 1896.
Fuller, Robert. *Naming the Antichrist: The History of an American Obsession*. New York: Oxford University Press, 1995.
McGinn, Bernard. *Antichrist: Two Thousand Years of the Human Fascination with Evil*. San Francisco: HarperSanFrancisco, 1994.

NOTES

[1] Leonard L. Thompson, *The Book of Revelation: Apocalypse and Empire* (New York: Oxford University Press, 1990), 160.

[2] Ibid., 159. Thompson has drawn heavily here from the work of S. R. F. Price (*Rituals and Power: The Roman Imperial Cult in Asia Minor* [Cambridge: Cambridge University Press, 1984]).

[3] G. B. Caird, *A Commentary on the Revelation of St. John the Divine*, Harper's New Testament Commentaries (New York: Harper & Row, 1966), 166.

[4] George R. Beasley-Murray, *The Book of Revelation*, New Century Bible (Greenwood SC: Attic, 1974), 214.

[5] M. Eugene Boring, *Revelation*, Interpretation: A Bible Commentary for Teaching and Preaching (Louisville: John Knox, 1989), 157.

[6] R. H. Charles, *A Critical and Exegetical Commentary on the Revelation of St. John*, The International Critical Commentary, 2 vols. (Edinburgh: T. & T. Clark, 1920), 1:361.

[7] See Robert H. Mounce (*The Book of Revelation*, The New International Commentary on the New Testament, rev. ed. [Grand Rapids: Eerdmans, 1998], 259) for a discussion of other suggested sources for this imagery.

[8] Jürgen Roloff, *The Revelation of John: A Continental Commentary*, Continental Commentaries, trans. John E. Alsup (Minneapolis: Fortress, 1993), 166.

[9] Beasley-Murray, *Revelation*, 221.

[10] Adela Yarbro Collins, "Numerical Symbolism in Jewish and Early Christian Apocalyptic Literature," *Aufstieg und Niedergang der römischen Welt*, ed. Hildegard Temporini and Wolfgang Haase (Berlin: Walter de Gruyter, 1984), II.21.2:1271-72.

[11] John M. Kirk, *Politics and the Catholic Church in Nicaragua* (Gainesville: University of Florida Press, 1992), 33-57; Philip J. Williams, *The Catholic Church and Politics in Nicaragua and Costa Rica* (Pittsburgh: University of Pittsburgh Press, 1989), 13-41.

[12] Dale Aukerman, *Reckoning with Apocalypse: Terminal Politics and Christian Hope* (New York: Crossroad, 1993), 38.

[13] William Stringfellow, *An Ethic for Christians and Other Aliens in a Strange Land* (Waco: Word Books, 1973), 114.

[14] Walter Wink, *Engaging the Powers: Discernment and Resistance in a World of Domination* (Minneapolis: Fortress, 1992), 30-31.

[15] Bernard McGinn, *Antichrist: Two Thousand Years of the Human Fascination with Evil* (San Francisco: HarperSanFrancisco, 1994), 279-80.

INTERLUDE

14:1-20

Chapter 14 contains three loosely connected scenes (each beginning with *kai eidon*, "then I saw") that together form an interlude in John's eschatological drama. As with the other interludes (7:1-17 and 10:1–11:14), this interlude functions partially to offer reassurance to the faithful after the previous scenes of suffering and persecution. [Outline of 14:1-20] If the coming days will be filled with as much suffering and death as depicted in chapters 12 and 13, what comfort is there for the faithful? If Satan and his cohorts are able to wreak such havoc on God's people, is there any hope? Chapter 14 answers those questions through visions of reward for God's people and punishment on the wicked. [Structure]

> **Outline of 14:1-20**
> 1. The 144,000 with the Lamb—14:1-5
>   a. The Vision—14:1
>   b. The Audition—14:2-3
>   c. The Explanation—14:5
> 2. The Messages of the Three Angels—14:6-13
>   a. The Message of the First Angel—14:6-7
>   b. The Message of the Second Angel—14:8
>   c. The Message of the Third Angel—14:9-11
>   d. Call for Endurance—14:12
>   e. Benediction—14:13
> 3. The Harvests of the Earth—14:14-20
>   a. The Grain Harvest—14:14-16
>   b. The Vintage Harvest—14:17-20

Structure

Scholars have offered several suggestions for the structure of ch. 14 and its relation to the rest of the Apocalypse. Charles Talbert has divided the chapter into an opening vision (14:1-5), followed by seven announcements of judgment: vv. 6-7, 8, 9-11, 12, 13, 14-16, 17-20. Beasley-Murray found a slightly different seven-fold pattern: vv. 1-5, 6-7,8, 9-12, 13, 14-16, 17-20. Adela Yarbro Collins has divided ch. 14 into three parts (14:1-5, 6-13, 14-20) and saw these as three visions that help comprise a cycle of seven unnumbered visions in 12:1–15:4.

All such attempts to find an unmarked seven-fold pattern either in ch. 14 alone or in the central section of the Apocalypse likely owe more to the imagination of the interpreter than to John's own design.

Elisabeth Schüssler Fiorenza's comment is pertinent: "One can assume that the author would have been capable of writing another series of seven [such as the seven messages, seven seals, seven trumpets, and seven bowls] in clear and explicit fashion if that had been his intention."

Charles H. Talbert, *The Apocalypse: A Reading of the Revelation of John* (Louisville: Westminster/John Knox, 1994), 59-68.

George R. Beasley-Murray, *The Book of Revelation*, New Century Bible (Greenwood SC: Attic, 1974), 221.

Adela Yarbro Collins, *The Apocalypse*, New Testament Message 22 (Wilmington DE: Michael Glazier, 1979), 80-107.

Elisabeth Schüssler Fiorenza, *Revelation: Vision of a Just World*, Proclamation Commentaries (Minneapolis: Fortress, 1991), 73.

Mount Zion
The Old City of Jerusalem. In biblical times, Mount Zion was the name of the hill upon which the temple was built. Atop this area today is the Dome of the Rock Mosque. (Today the name "Mount Zion" is given to a hill to the west of the temple mount.) (Credit: Mitchell Reddish)

COMMENTARY

The 144,000 with the Lamb, 14:1-5

Throughout the Apocalypse, John has conveyed his eschatological drama not solely through visual imagery, but also by describing sounds, tastes (8:11; 10:8-10), smells (8:3-4; 9:17-18), and touch (1:17; 3:15-16; 9:5). Visual and auditory descriptions dominate the work. This opening scene of chapter 14 contains a vision (14:1), an audition (14:2-3), and an explanation (14:4-5). In his vision, John sees the Lamb standing on Mount Zion with the 144,000. [Mount Zion] Clearly this is the slain Lamb (Jesus) that John has seen earlier in chapters 5–8. The 144,000 are the same people that chapter 7 introduced, the ones who have been marked with the seal of God for protection. They are also the victims of the dragon and beasts in chapters 12 and 13. The preceding scenes have ended with the apparent defeat of God's people. The assault of the dragon on the church appears successful as the beast has been able to kill all those who have not bowed down in worship. The scene on Mount Zion reverses that judgment, depicting the faithful not as defeated but as triumphant. This scene is a proleptic vision of God's faithful (here, specifically the martyrs) sharing in the triumph of the Lamb. Mount Zion is used frequently in the biblical tradition as a synonym for Jerusalem, believed to be God's special

Zion

AΩ Prior to the conquest of the area by David, Zion was the name of a fortress in the area of Jerusalem, the "stronghold of Zion" (2 Sam 5:7; 1 Chr 11:5). The name was later applied to the ridge in Jerusalem that ran between the Kidron Valley and the Tyropeon Valley, the southern area of which was the location of David's city. Solomon built his temple and palace to the north of David's city on the highest elevation of this ridge, an area that came to be known as Mount Zion. "Zion" became synonymous with the temple and with the city of Jerusalem itself. Zion was thought of as the dwelling place of God (Pss 9:11; 76:2; 132:13-18; 135:21). As the people of God, Israel could also be called "Zion." In Jewish eschatological thought, Zion would play a special role once more as God's city, the place where God's people would be gathered and the messiah would appear (cf. Isa 24: 23; Mic 4:7; *Jub.* 1:28; 2 Esd 13:33-38). In some Jewish traditions, the new Jerusalem "is thought of as a

pre-existent city which is built by God in heaven and which comes down to earth with the dawn of a new world" [Eduard Lohse, "Σιών κτλ," *TDNT*, ed. Gerhard Kittel and Gerhard Friedrich; trans. Geoffrey W. Bromiley, 10 vols. (Grand Rapids: Eerdmans, 1971), 7:325; cf. *2 Bar.* 4:1-7; 2 Esd 7:26]. New Testament writers borrowed from Judaism this idea of a heavenly counterpart to the earthly Zion, a new Jerusalem, that would appear at the end of time (cf. Gal 4:26; Heb 11:13-16; 12:22; Rev 21–22). The idea of Zion or the new Jerusalem as the heavenly home of the people of God is particularly strong in Christian hymnody. Note, for instance, the words of "We're Marching to Zion":

> We're marching to Zion,
> Beautiful, beautiful Zion;
> We're marching upward to Zion,
> The beautiful city of God.

---

city and the place where God was especially present. Zion comes to be used metaphorically for the eschatological kingdom of God and thus a symbol for security, protection, and the presence of God. When John locates the 144,000 with the Lamb on Mount Zion, the significance is not geographical, but metaphorical. The redeemed stand with Christ, safe and victorious. [Zion]

From the heavenly throne room John hears the sound of music—harps being played and voices singing. [Voice from Heaven] The song is the "new song" of 5:9, a song celebrating God's salvation of the people. In chapter 5, the singers are the angelic chorus. Here, the singers are not identified. Likely they are the 144,000, who now join in singing praise to God for the deliverance of the people. Only the 144,000 could learn this song. Those who worship the beast perhaps sing their songs of praise to the beast, but only the faithful followers of God can join in this heavenly anthem.

The description of the followers of the Lamb as those "who have not defiled themselves with women, for they are virgins" (14:4) has sparked much discussion by commentators. R. H. Charles understood this characteristic of the 144,000 literally, but rejected vv. 4-5 as a later addition to the text made by a "monkish interpolator" who

Voice from Heaven

AΩ The NRSV translates 14:2-3a as,

And I heard a voice from heaven like the sound of many waters and like the sound of loud thunder; the voice I heard was like the sound of harpists playing on their harps, and they sing a new song.

The Greek word *phōnē*, which occurs four times in 14:2, can be translated as "voice" or "sound." Even though John has heard a voice from heaven earlier (4:1; 5:2, 11; 6:7; 10:4, 8; 12:10; see also 11:12), in 14:2 "sound" seems to be a better rendering of what is meant. John hears the sound of harps and singing.

wanted to stress the superiority of the celibate life.[1] Adela Yarbro Collins has also argued for a literal understanding of the reference to virginity, suggesting that the background for this idea was in the Israelite traditions of holy war and the priesthood, both of which demanded temporary sexual abstinence. Since John views the church as engaged in a "holy war" with Rome and sees all believers as priests (1:6), he expects sexual abstinence on the part of all believers.[2]

In a work as highly symbolic as the book of Revelation, a literal reading of 14:4 is unwarranted. (A literal reading would exclude not only sexually active men, but would categorically exclude all women from God's new world!) John has earlier used sexual imagery to symbolize religious unfaithfulness (2:14, 20-22); those who follow false teachings and those who yield to the demands of the larger culture are guilty of "fornication" against God. Here in 14:4, John again uses sexual imagery figuratively, this time to denote moral and religious purity. The 144,000 have not been defiled by idolatry and the enticements of the great whore of Babylon (ch. 17). They have resisted impure relationships with the Roman world, whether that means participation in the imperial cult, eating food offered to the pagan gods, or violation of Christian moral standards. Because John uses military imagery quite often in the Apocalypse, the ancient regulation for holy war that demanded sexual abstinence prior to battle (cf. Deut 23:9-10; 1 Sam 21:4-5) likely contributed to John's use of this metaphor. The 144,000 comprise the army of God, which is engaged in a fierce battle with the dragon and the beasts. Needless to say, John's imagery is not intended to exclude females. Since only males were soldiers in Israel's army, masculine terminology is used here in the call for sexual purity. The 144,000 who are "virgins" represent the faithful people of God—male and female—who refused to worship the beast and wear his "mark."

The 144,000 "follow the Lamb wherever he goes" (14:4). [Following the Lamb] If the 144,000 specifically refers to the martyrs, those who were killed because they refused to bow down to the beast (see comments on 7:1-8), then this description has special application to those who follow Jesus even to death. Caird stated,

Following the Lamb

"Within John's horizons, *martyr* is not a technical term for those unfortunate individuals who happen to be killed. Rather, it defines the very nature and existence of the church. The recognition of this should put to rest the claims of some scholars that the Revelation is a *triumphalist* book. Victory is indeed a major theme, but victory comes . . . through suffering and death. What counts in the end is not simply believing in Jesus, but in 'following the Lamb wherever he went' (14:4)—the path of discipleship, suffering, and death. No one can teach, preach, or even seriously study the Revelation without recognizing how deeply it contradicts all our dominant cultural values of wealth, success, and power."

J. Ramsey Michaels, *Interpreting the Book of Revelation*, Guides to New Testament Exegesis (Grand Rapids: Baker Book House, 1992), 137.

"The best commentary on this verse is the saying of Jesus to Peter in the Fourth Gospel: 'Where I am going you cannot follow me now, but later you shall follow' (John 13:36)."[3] The martyrs have followed Christ in suffering and in death; now they are at his side in the eschatological kingdom. [The Lamb on Mount Zion]

John also describes the 144,000 as having been "redeemed from mankind as first fruits for God and the Lamb." The sacrificial language here is appropriate as a description of the martyrs. They have given their lives sacrificially in their faithfulness to God. A fuller use of this sacrificial motif has been seen in 6:9-11 where the souls of the sacrificed martyrs were under the altar. The "first fruits" signified the first part of the crop or livestock that was offered to God. The first fruits would be first in time and possibly in quality. The 144,000 are the first fruits, the first of the offerings to God. The rest of the redeemed will complete the offering. [First Fruits]

Verse 5 further characterizes the 144,000: "In their mouth no lie was found, for they are blameless." The martyrs have maintained their witness even under persecution, refusing to proclaim Caesar as lord. They have proclaimed only the truth—Jesus is Lord. The claim that the emperor holds ultimate control over the lives of people and demanded worship and homage has been the "big lie" that has been perpetrated on the people. A major task of John's Apocalypse is the unmasking of that deception. The martyrs have not succumbed to the false claims of the empire. They have kept themselves "blameless," or "unblemished," a word with sacrificial overtones. Animals that were offered as sacrifices had to be unblemished, free from any defects. By refusing to yield to the demands of the imperial cult, the martyr victims present themselves as unblemished sacrifices to God. In this regard they model Christ, who "offered himself without blemish to God" (Heb 9:14). [The Gathering on Mount Zion]

The Lamb on Mount Zion

G. B. Caird suggested that in 14:1-5, as well as in 11:18 and 12:5, John "is engaged in an exposition of Psalm 2 as Christian scripture."

G. B. Caird, *A Commentary on the Revelation of St. John the Divine,* Harper's New Testament Commentaries (New York: Harper & Row), 178.

First Fruits

AΩ In ancient Israel, the first of the crops (vegetables, grains, fruits) to ripen were to be given as an offering to God (Exod 23:19; Lev 23:9-14; Deut 26:1-11). The first of the wine and oil produced, as well as the first born of the livestock, were also to be offered to God (Deut 18:4). These offerings given to the priests represented a "tithe" of the worshiper's harvest and new livestock. By offering the first fruits to God, one gave thanks for the harvest and encouraged God to bless the remainder of the crops. Thus the first fruits were, in part, a token of the coming abundant harvest. The New Testament uses "first fruits" metaphorically to symbolize the idea of something that is the first in sequence and the harbinger of more to come (cf. Rom 8:23; 11:16; 1 Cor 15:20, 23; 16:15; Jas 1:18).

The Gathering on Mount Zion

An interesting parallel to John's scene of the Lamb and the 144,000 on Mount Zion is found in 2 Esd 2:42-48. The first two chapters of 2 Esdras (which by themselves are sometimes known as 5 Ezra) are a separate Christian work possibly from the 2d century. This scene in 2 Esdras was likely influenced heavily by Rev 7 and 14. The words of 2 Esd 2:42-48 are as follows:

I, Ezra, saw on Mount Zion a great multitude that I could not number, and they all were praising the Lord with songs. In their midst was a young man of great stature, taller than any of the others, and on the head of each of them he placed a crown, but he was more exalted than they. And I was held spellbound. Then I asked an angel, "Who are these, my lord?" He answered and said to me, "These are they who have put off mortal clothing and have put on the immortal, and have confessed the name of God. Now they are being crowned, and receive palms." Then I said to the angel, "Who is that young man who is placing crowns on them and putting palms in their hands?" He answered and said to me, "He is the Son of God, whom they confessed in the world." So I began to praise those who had stood valiantly for the name of the Lord. Then the angel said to me, "Go, tell my people how great and how many are the wonders of the Lord God that you have seen."

The Messages of the Three Angels, 14:6-13

The second vision of chapter 14 consists of messages from three different angels, each proclaiming the coming judgment of God. By calling the angel of v. 6 "another angel," John distinguishes this angel from the angels that have appeared previously in the book. The angel flies in midheaven in order to broadcast its message far and wide. Accordingly, it speaks "in a loud voice." The proclamation of the angel is a universal message, intended for "every nation and tribe and language and people" (14:6). The angel calls on the people of the earth to repent, to turn from their worship of false gods or caesars; rather, they are to worship the true God, the one "who made heaven and earth, the sea and the springs of water" (14:7). They are to "fear God," that is, to submit to God with reverence and obedience. The message of the angel is filled with urgency, for the time of God's judgment upon the earth is near ("has come"). The time for decision is now; it should not be postponed.

If the angel's message is a proclamation of God's judgment, in what sense can John call this angelic announcement "gospel" or "good news"? The message is good news because God's judgment means an end to Satan and his dominance over the people of the world. The dragon and his cohorts, the beasts, will be destroyed. Evil will be wiped out and will no longer threaten God's creation. To those who respond in repentance to this call, this

Good News

AΩ The message of the angel in v. 6 is described as "good news" (*euangelion*). An inscription from Priene in Asia Minor in 9 BC celebrates the reign of Augustus with the same word, claiming that "since the birthday of the god Augustus was the beginning for the world of the good tidings [*euangelion*] that came by reason of him." Whether John had such imperial claims in mind or not, the "good news" contained in his revelation is the true good news because it is "an eternal gospel" that comes from God.

Cited in *Hellenistic Commentary to the New Testament*, ed. M. Eugene Boring, Klaus Berger, and Carsten Colpe (Nashville: Abingdon, 1995), 169.

indeed is good news, for they will share in God's new kingdom.
[Good News]

The message of the second angel continues the announcement of the judgment of God. The angel's cry is proleptic—it announces the future destruction of Babylon as if it had already occurred. "Fallen, fallen is Babylon" is borrowed from Isaiah 21:9 (cf. Jer 51:8). "Babylon the great" is John's designation for the city of Rome (cf. 1 Pet 5:13). Babylon is an apt symbol for Rome. In 587 BC, Babylon conquered Jerusalem, destroying the city and its temple and carrying a large portion of the people away into exile. For the Jewish people Babylon became a symbol of evil, the destroyers and persecutors of God's people. In AD 70, Rome took over the role of Babylon when it destroyed the city of Jerusalem, including the temple. Even more significant for John, the emperor is a new Nebuchadnezzar, demanding that the people worship the image that he has constructed (cf. Dan 3). Rome has become the terrible persecutor of God's people, the new Babylon, that is, the archenemy of God.

When John states that Rome "has made all nations drink of the wine of the wrath of her fornication" (14:8), he is adapting imagery from Jeremiah's denunciation of Babylon. Jeremiah stated,

> Babylon was a golden cup in the LORD's hand,
> making all the earth drunken;
> the nations drank of her wine,
> and so the nations went mad. (51:7)

John has combined this with Jeremiah 25:15 in which the prophet reported that God told him to take from God's hand the "cup of the wine of wrath, and make all the nations to whom I send you drink it." John has reworked these texts into "the wine of the wrath of her fornication." Babylon (Rome) entices the people with her power, her idolatry, and her riches. Her allures are intoxicating; yielding to them renders one guilty of "fornication," for one has then committed unfaithfulness to God. Those who are intoxicated by Rome are the nations of the world. In view here are the imperial claims to universal sovereignty. Rome's authority is great, and its power is seductive. The nations and rulers of the world bow in obeisance to this mighty empire (cf. 17:2). Not only is this cup the cup of fornication, but it is also the cup of wrath, meaning the wrath of God. Drinking from the cup of Rome has dire consequences, for it brings the nations under the threat of divine judgment. John's imagery of Rome as seductive Babylon, which leads people and nations into fornication and drunkenness, as well

Potent Wine

AΩ The word translated in the NRSV as "poured" normally means "mixed." Translated in this way, the phrase in 14:10 would read, "the wine of God's wrath mixed unmixed in the cup of his anger." As noted, "unmixed" likely means not diluted with water; that is, the wine is full strength. If *kekerasmenou* is translated "mixed," the idea would be that spices were mixed with the wine, which was commonly done to strengthen the effects of the wine. Thus the "wine of God's wrath" is particularly potent because not only is it full strength, but it has been enhanced by being mixed with spices. Compare Ps 75:8:

For in the hand of the LORD there is a cup
    with foaming wine, well mixed;
he will pour a draught from it,
    and all the wicked of the earth
    shall drain it down to the dregs.

as his depiction of God's judgment against the city, will be expanded in chapters 17 and 18.

Whereas the announcement of the second angel told of Babylon's downfall and warned of the nation's immoral involvement with Rome, the announcement of the third angel speaks of the people's scandalous affair with Rome. Such unfaithfulness is in direct contrast to the 144,000, who have remained "virgins" and have not violated their commitment to God. Chapter 13 has described the imperial punishment that will fall on those who refuse to worship the beast and are not marked with the mark of the beast. Now the third angel announces the divine punishment that will fall on those who do worship the beast and wear its mark. As several commentators have noted, the warning should be understood as directed at those who *continue* to worship the beast after being called to repentance. Verse 7 extends a call to repent to all the people of the earth. Those who persist in their rebellion against God will suffer dire consequences. They will drink "the wine of God's wrath, poured unmixed into the cup of his anger" (14:10). Wine was mixed (or diluted) with water to make it weaker. The punishment, however, on the followers of the beast will be full strength! [Potent Wine]

What will "the wrath of God" entail? John describes it in imagery borrowed from God's judgment upon Sodom and Gomorrah (Gen 19:24). The worshipers of the beast will be tormented with fire and sulfur (brimstone). Fire serves as a common instrument of divine punishment in Jewish apocalyptic writings (cf. *1 En.* 10:13-14; 21:1-10; 90:22-27; *Sib. Or.* 2:196-213, 252-310) as well as in the writings from other cultures and religions. By this point in the Apocalypse, the reader should be well aware that John's language here is metaphorical. Divine punishment will no more be actual fire and sulfur than Christ will literally be a lamb. The angel declares that God's punishment on the wicked will not be short-lived, but will be forever and ever. Furthermore, the torment will be continuous, from which there will be "no rest day or night." [No Rest for the Wicked]

The rhetorical purpose of John's depiction of the punishment of the wicked is to call the church to faithful endurance, to impress upon his readers the serious consequences of rejecting God. Eugene Boring has commented:

> John's language does not deliver a doctrine about the fate of outsiders; it functions to warn insiders, who ponder the question "Is it such a terrible thing to participate in the Roman worship?" John regards this worship as making a this-worldly substitute for the one Creator and Lord and answers, "more terrible than you can imagine!"[4]

In response to the announcements of judgment by the angels, John adds the call to faithfulness in v. 12 (cf. 13:10). Beasley-Murray labeled this verse the "punch line" for the words of judgment in the preceding verses.[5] John is saying to his readers that if these punishments await those who yield to the demands of emperor worship, then in order to avoid such torment Christians need to "keep the commandments of God and hold fast to the faith of Jesus" (14:12).

This section of chapter 14 concludes with a voice from heaven instructing John to write down a beatitude: "Blessed are the dead who from now on die in the Lord." This statement is one of seven beatitudes in Revelation for the people of God (1:3; 14:13; 16:15; 19:9; 20:6; 22:7, 14). The one here in 14:13, like the one in 20:6, is specifically for martyrs. The phrase "from now on" indicates that John specifically has in mind the faithful believers who will die in the impending persecution by the beast (cf. 13:15). Those who die in the service of Christ will not be abandoned by God. Their faithfulness will be rewarded by a period of rest. [Eschatological Rest] After death, they will no longer have to endure trials and persecution. This period of rest that the martyrs will enjoy is in direct contrast to the lack of rest imposed on those who worship the beast (14:11). The faithful are assured of this reward because "their deeds follow them." This statement should not be understood as a declaration of works-righteousness, that is, that the martyrs have earned their way into God's favor. Rather, to say that their deeds follow them is another way of saying that God takes note of their faithfulness. Their deeds indicate their true allegiance, their true selves. In Jesus' parable of the Last Judgment (Matt 25:31-46), what people say is not as important as what they do.

No Rest for the Wicked

John envisions the lack of any rest or relief to be an aspect of God's punishment on the wicked. In the 3rd- or 4th-century AD work known as the *Apocalypse of Paul*, Jesus, in response to the prayers of Paul and the archangel Michael, mercifully grants to the wicked one day and night each week of respite from their torments.

Eschatological Rest

In the hymn, "For All the Saints," the author William W. How adapted Rev 14:13 for the opening line of the hymn:

For all the saints who from their labors rest,
Who thee by faith before the world confessed,
Thy name, O Jesus, be forever blest.
Alleluia! Alleluia!

Their Deeds Follow Them

On a plaque at the base of a statue of Wang Zhiming in Wuding, China, are the words, "As Scripture says of the Saints, 'They will rest from their labours for their deeds follow them' (Rev 14:13)." These 1st-century words addressed to martyrs are a fitting tribute to this 20th-century Christian martyr. Wang Zhiming was a Christian leader and pastor who refused to renounce his Christian faith when pressured by the Communist government of China. An opponent of the local Red Guard unit, Wang Zhiming was publicly executed because of his religious commitment on 29 December 1973. The martyr witness of Wang Zhiming strengthened the faith of the other Christians in the area and became a catalyst for the growth of the church.

Philip L. Wickeri, "The Abolition of Religion in Yunnan: Wang Zhiming," *The Terrible Alternative: Christian Martyrdom in the Twentieth Century*, ed. Andrew Chandler (London: Cassell, 1998), 128-58.

Their real loyalties are indicated by their actions. Thus their actions, their deeds, go with them to the Last Judgment as testimony for or against them. Similarly, John assures the martyrs that their ultimate sacrifice on behalf of God will not go unnoticed. It will accompany them before the throne of God. [Their Deeds Follow Them]

The Harvests of the Earth, 14:14-20

This section presents two scenes, both depicting the judgment of God upon the earth in imagery drawn from Joel 3:13, which reads,

> Put in the sickle,
>   for the harvest is ripe.
> Go in, tread,
>   for the wine press is full.
> The vats overflow,
>   for their wickedness is great.

One of the major interpretive difficulties with these two scenes in Revelation 14:14-20 is whether they both portray God's punishment against the wicked, or alternately one is punishment on the wicked, while the other depicts the ingathering of the righteous. In Joel, both the harvesting and the pressing of the grapes are images of punishment against the wicked.

In Revelation, the latter scene (14:17-20) is almost certainly a picture of divine judgment against the wicked.[6] The real question concerns the first scene. The details of this harvest are sparse. Who is "harvested," the righteous, the wicked, or both? Those who argue for this scene as the ingathering of the righteous point to other texts in the New Testament in which the harvest motif refers to an ingathering of God's people (cf. Luke 10:2; John 4:35-38). Also in Mark 13:26-27 the Son of Man comes on the clouds to gather his

One Like a Son of Man

AΩ The identity of the figure in 14:14 is not clear. The NRSV reading, "one like the Son of Man," obscures the uncertainty of the text. (Capitalization is due to the English translator; it is not represented in the ancient Greek manuscripts.) The Greek text actually reads "one like a son of man" (*homoion huion anthrōpou*). This phrase, along with the coming of this figure on a cloud, is adapted from Dan 7:13. In Daniel, "one like a son of man" simply means "in human form," a description that is applied elsewhere to an angel (10:18). Is this "son of man" figure in Rev 14:14 an angel, or is it Christ, who is described in 1:13 as "one like a son of man"? The statement in 14:15 that "another angel" appears implies that the former figure is also to be understood as an angel. Furthermore, this angel who comes from the temple issues an order to "one like a son of man," which some commentators have argued is inappropriate if the "one like a son of man" is Christ.

On the other hand, the similarity between this passage and the coming of the Son of Man in clouds in Mark 13:26-27 argues for the figure in 14:14 to be a reference to Christ. Furthermore, the phrase "another angel" in 14:15 does not necessarily contrast the angel in v. 15 with the "Son of Man" figure in v. 14. "Another angel" may be in contrast to the three angels of 14:6-9. Also, while it is true that the angel who comes from the temple does issue a command to the "Son of Man" figure, the coming of the angel from the heavenly temple indicates that the command originates from God. For God to issue the command to begin the eschatological "harvest" is appropriate since "about that day or hour no one knows, neither the angels in heaven, nor the Son, but only the Father" (Mark 13:32). While the identity of the "Son of Man" with Christ is likely, John's text is ambiguous enough to make identification uncertain.

elect. On the other hand, the parallel with the Joel text argues for the first scene being a vision of punishment on the wicked. John gives no clear indication that he is using the Joel imagery in a different way. But perhaps we are demanding too much precision from John's imagery. The value of symbols is that they carry a variety of meanings. As a symbol for God's judgment, this harvesting may connote both negative and positive meanings. The judgment of God will be a time of ingathering for the faithful, while at the same moment a time of punishment for the wicked (cf. Matt 13:41-43).

The one who performs the harvesting is "one like the Son of Man," the same description used of Christ in 1:13. [One Like a Son of Man] This figure is likely, though not certainly, to be understood as Christ. He waits for the command from God to begin reaping, a command that is delivered by the angel who comes from the heavenly temple. In surprisingly sparing language, John states the results of the harvest: "The one who sat on the cloud swung his sickle over the earth, and the earth was reaped" (14:16).

In the second scene, another angel appears from the temple of heaven, sickle in hand. Upon receiving instructions from an angel from the heavenly altar (cf. 8:1-5), he swings his sickle and gathers in the grapes, the "vintage of the earth" (14:19). [The Angel Who Has Authority over Fire] In describing the grapes as being thrown into "the great wine press of the wrath of God," John is borrowing another biblical image for God's judgment. (In addition to Joel 3:13, cf. Isa 63:3; Lam 1:15. Revelation uses this imagery again in 19:15.)

The Angel Who Has Authority over Fire

In Jewish tradition, various angels were assigned specific tasks. For example, *Jub.* 2:2 lists angels of sanctification, angels of the spirit of fire, angels of the spirit of the winds, angels of the spirit of the clouds and darkness and snow and hail and frost, angels of resoundings and thunder and lightning, and angels of the spirits of cold and heat and winter and springtime and harvest and summer. In speaking of "the angel who has authority over fire" (14:18), John may have a similar tradition in mind. A more likely connection, however, can be made with the angel who appears in 8:3-5. Both the angel in 8:3-5 and the angel in 14:18 are associated with the heavenly altar. The angel "who has authority over fire" probably refers to the angel's duties in relationship to the heavenly altar. In 8:3-5, the angel takes fire from the altar and throws it on the earth, unleashing God's judgments on the earth. In 14:18, the role of the angel is similar. The angel gives the command that inaugurates God's punishments on the wicked.

Wine Press

An ancient wine press from Capernaum in Israel.

(Credit: Mitchell Reddish)

Grapes were usually pressed by being treaded by foot on a flat, hard surface or in a vat or trough. As the grapes were mashed, the juice ran through a channel into a reservoir from which it was collected and stored. Red juice from the grapes would be appropriate imagery for the flowing of blood. For John the crushing of the grapes represents God's wrath, that is, God's defeat and punishment of the wicked. [Wine Press]

John places the treading of the wine press "outside the city," without specifying what city is meant. Perhaps the location is a general, rather than a specific reference, in the sense that outside a city's walls would be the normal place for executions to take place. Some commentators have suggested that Jerusalem is meant, pointing to examples from Jewish tradition that expected the defeat of God's enemies in the valleys near Jerusalem (cf. Joel 3:12-14; *1 En.* 53:1). Readers familiar with the story of Jesus' crucifixion can hardly fail to hear an allusion here to his death, which took place "outside the city" (John 19:20; Heb 13:12). Perhaps this is poetic justice: the "world" that put Jesus to death "outside the city" now faces its own destruction "outside the city." Or maybe it is John's way of insinuating "that the judgment of the world was achieved on the cross."[7] [Harvest of the Grapes]

The extent of God's judgment is overwhelming— "blood flowed from the wine press, as high as a horse's bridle, for a distance of about two hundred miles" (14:20). This gruesome description is certainly not to be taken literally. Various suggestions have been offered for the distance John cites: "about two hundred miles," which in the Greek text actually reads "sixteen hundred stadia." (One stade equals 185 meters, which was the standard length of a Greek stadium in which foot races and other athletic contests were held.) Some have suggested that 1,600 is significant because it is the square of forty, a number that sometimes designates the length of punishment in biblical traditions (Israel was in the wilderness forty years; the flood lasted forty days and nights).[8] Other interpreters have suggested that since 1,600 results from multiplying the

Harvest of the Grapes

The 17th-century French Catholic preacher and bishop, Jacques Bénigne Bossuet, wrote in his commentary that the harvest of the grapes in 14:19 alludes to the invasions by Attila the Hun.

Arthur W. Wainwright, *Mysterious Apocalypse: Interpreting the Book of Revelation* (Nashville: Abingdon, 1993), 64.

square of ten (a number for completeness) by the square of four (which denotes the wholeness of the world, as in four compass directions, four corners of the world), "the meaning would then be that the destruction encompasses the entire world in all its regions."[9] Both suggestions seem rather strained. We should perhaps simply admit that we have no clue to the significance, if any, that the number held for John.

CONNECTIONS

1. The scene of the 144,000 on Mount Zion, in 14:1-5, is intended to function as a word of comfort and assurance: those who are faithful followers of the Lamb, even when they follow him in a martyr's death, will share in Christ's eschatological kingdom. Some readers, however, may have a hard time hearing the words of 14:1-5 as good news because of some of the imagery used in this passage. Specifically, the words of v. 4 may be troubling: "It is these who have not defiled themselves with women, for they are virgins; these follow the Lamb wherever he goes." Some readers have heard these words as being degrading, even abusive of women. Tina Pippin has commented,

> Women are most noticeably absent in the Apocalypse in 14:4. . . . The 144,000 represent the whole number of the faithful, and they are all men. Women's bodies are seen as negative and capable of defiling the men. . . . For the candidates for heaven to remain "spotless"—indeed for heaven itself to remain spotless—women are displaced.[10]

It is easy to dismiss such comments and attribute them to someone who is perhaps being overly sensitive. Such is particularly the case for male readers/hearers of the text who do not come to the text with the same experiences that women readers do, experiences of being abused, ignored, silenced, or treated as inferior. While certain responses to the text may not be our own responses, that does not make them invalid responses. The language of the text may convey a multiplicity of meanings, some intended by the author, others unintended but just as real. Those "who have ears to hear" often hear different messages.

In dealing with John's imagery, the teacher/preacher has a responsibility to be sensitive to the way the text sounds to the modern audience. We can correctly point out that John is writing from a male perspective, as a first-century male in a male-dominated culture. Such explanations are correct and necessary. But for the sensitive teacher or preacher these explanations are not enough. One must ask how John's imagery is heard in today's world. Do the right words (that is, verbatim quotations from the text) convey the wrong message? This issue is larger than this passage, for throughout Revelation, feminine imagery, and especially feminine sexual imagery, is frequently used in a negative way. The false teacher at Thyatira is described as a Jezebel figure who causes people to "commit adultery with her" (2:20-23). The faithful 144,000 are those "who have not defiled themselves with women" (14:4). Rome is a drunken whore, who leads others to "commit fornication" with her (17:1-18). Do these images perpetuate and reinforce negative portrayals of women or feminine sexuality, even if that is not their intent? Are the negative messages of these images offset by the more positive portrayals of women, such as the woman of chapter 12 or the faithful as the bride of Christ (19:6-8)?[11]

Susan Garrett has described the dilemma faced by many women readers of Revelation who are bothered by the portrayal of women in the Apocalypse. She has written:

> The woman reader is thus divided: she wants to identify with the good but is reluctant to do so because the images deny female self-determination; she hesitates to identify with the bad but may endorse the defiance of the "whores" against those who would control or destroy them. John's feminine imagery is dangerous because (whether intentionally or not) it promotes an ethos in which women are not allowed to control their own bodies and their own destinies and in which violence against women is—at least in some cases—condoned.[12]

What can be done to lessen the damage of these negative images of women? At the very least, teachers and preachers should be sensitive to the negative implications these images may have on their audiences. An approach that ignores the damaging potential of these texts simply because "that's not what's intended" or "that's not what they mean to me" is not only misinformed but also inconsistent with a model of leadership patterned after Jesus. In sermons and in classes in which these texts are used, the leader should explain the purpose of the imagery and the background out of which it came. In a classroom or other context in which these passages are being studied, it will be important for the leader to invite dialogue about the messages, especially negative ones, that these texts communicate to the students. Particularly in worship settings, when opportunity for discussion and clarification is not readily available, the worship leader should exercise care in picking texts for public reading. All biblical texts may not be suitable for isolated readings in public worship. [Offensive Language] When potentially sensitive texts are used, the worship leader should look for translations that, while maintaining the integrity of the text, use language that may be more appropriate for a public setting. For example, the Contemporary English Version translates the first part of Revelation 14:4 as, "All of these are pure virgins," omitting the statement that "they have not defiled themselves with women." This translation still captures the meaning of the text but does so in an inoffensive manner. Finally, the task of the biblical interpreter always is to find new images and new vehicles for old ideas. The preacher or teacher should seek to translate John's message into metaphors that are less offensive to modern readers.

Offensive Language

"This line [14:4a] sounds horrible to our ears today, and, however it might be explained, it still sounds horrible. Hence it should be eliminated from new translations, and a different reading should be put in its place, one that faithfully expresses the meaning of the original text."

Pablo Richard, *Apocalypse: A People's Commentary on the Book of Revelation* (Maryknoll NY: Orbis Books, 1995), 119.

A second way in which Revelation 14:4 may fail to function as "good news" for its readers/hearers is if the imagery of sexuality is taken literally. Sexual relations are described as being defiling and are to be avoided. As noted in the earlier comments on this verse, the background for this imagery of 144,000 virgins is the Israelite holy war concept that required soldiers to abstain from sexual activity prior to participating in battle. The text should not be heard as a denigration of human sexuality or as a call to an ascetic lifestyle. Such beliefs did become strong in certain groups in the church from the fourth century onwards, groups and individuals for whom "such practices were regarded as a way for people to advance their spiritual lives, and even to regain the innocence of paradise."13 Whereas celibacy can be a viable choice for certain individuals, even for religious reasons, repudiation of the physical dimension of life, including sexuality, is inconsistent with the biblical tradition. The Bible celebrates sexuality as a part of the human experience (cf. Song of Solomon). Even Paul, who believed that celibacy was beneficial, recognized the value and importance of human sexual relations and encouraged husbands and wives to share themselves sexually with each other on a regular basis. For him, celibacy was a gift that only certain people possessed; celibacy was not a choice that everyone was expected to make (cf. 1 Cor 7).

2. No passage in the Apocalypse presents as gruesome and vengeful a picture of the punishment of the wicked as does 14:9-20. Other passages contain similar ideas, but the images of violence and torment are especially concentrated in chapter 14. In 20:10, the devil, the beast, and the false prophet are thrown into the lake of fire and sulfur where "they will be tormented day and night forever and ever." A few verses later, John states that "anyone whose name was not found written in the book of life" will also be thrown into the lake of fire (20:15). In chapter 14, statements about the eternal torment of the damned are joined by the vivid imagery of the wicked being crushed in the wine press of the wrath of God. [Grapes of Wrath]

Grapes of Wrath

The biblical imagery of the crushing of the grapes representing the wrath of God has been preserved in the title of John Steinbeck's novel, *The Grapes of Wrath*, and in the words of Julia Ward Howe's "Battle Hymn of the Republic": "He is trampling out the vintage where the grapes of wrath are stored."

John's description of the punishment on those who worship the beast is extremely harsh, even sub-Christian, some would claim. As terrible as John's depiction of the torment is, it is not as repulsive as that described in some other early Christian or Jewish apocalypses. The author of 2 Esdras implies that the righteous will be able to view the torment of the wicked (7:36-38, 88-93) as a part of their eternal reward. This idea is explicit in *1 Enoch* 27:3. In the *Apocalypse of Peter*, people who have been killed will be allowed to watch the eschatological torment of those who killed them (chs. 7–8). John avoids such sadistic rewards for the righteous. The punishment of the worshipers of the beast occurs only in the presence of the angels and the Lamb.

The horror of John's imagery is lessened somewhat when one bears in mind that John is not depicting literal events. [Language of Hatred] This is not descriptive language intended to give the readers an actual description of what God's punishment on the wicked will be like. Rather this is rhetorical speech intended to shock complacent hearers/readers into action. John is particularly concerned to awaken half-hearted or lackadaisical Christians (his work is addressed to Christians, not to outsiders) who might join in the imperial cult. He presents a graphic portrayal of divine judgment as a warning shot across the bow of those who might be tempted to

Language of Hatred

"What does language so heavily laden with hatred mean? John . . . intends to warn his hearers to resist this idolatrous integration into the Roman empire. John may also be reflecting the accumulated hatred of the holy ones who are excluded by the empire, who cannot buy and sell and are persecuted and murdered. Why does he reflect such hatred? One possibility might be catharsis. Like the Greek tragedies, Revelation would then be an exercise of catharsis, that is reading it within the community would serve as a kind of inner purging, so that by listening the people might be freed of hatred."

Pablo Richard, *Apocalypse: A People's Commentary on the Book of Revelation* (Maryknoll NY: Orbis Books, 1995), 124.

take cultural accommodation too lightly. John's imagery is a warning against apostasy and a call to repentance. As J. P. M. Sweet has noted, "John uses pictures, as Jesus used parables (cf. Matt 18:32-34; 25:41-46), to ram home the unimaginable disaster of rejecting God, and the unimaginable blessedness of union with God, while there is still time to do something about it."[14]

NOTES

[1] R. H. Charles, *A Critical and Exegetical Commentary on the Revelation of St. John*, The International Critical Commentary, 2 vols. (Edinburgh: T. & T. Clark, 1920), 2:8-11.

[2] Adela Yarbro Collins, *Crisis and Catharsis: The Power of the Apocalypse* (Philadelphia: Westminster, 1984), 127-31.

[3] G. B. Caird, *A Commentary on the Revelation of St. John the Divine*, Harper's New Testament Commentaries (New York: Harper & Row, 1966), 118.

[4] M. Eugene Boring, *Revelation*, Interpretation: A Bible Commentary for Teaching and Preaching (Louisville: John Knox, 1989), 170.

[5] George R. Beasley-Murray, *The Book of Revelation*, New Century Bible (Greenwood SC: Attic, 1974), 226.

[6] *Contra* Caird (*Revelation*, 189-195), who argued that "by the gory vintage [John] meant to portray the death of the martyrs."

[7] Wilfrid J. Harrington, *Revelation*, Sacra Pagina (Collegeville MN: Michael Glazier, 1993).

[8] Beasley-Murray (*Revelation*, 230) cited this as a plausible meaning.

[9] Jürgen Roloff, *The Revelation of John: A Continental Commentary*, Continental Commentaries, trans. John E. Alsup (Minneapolis: Fortress, 1993), 178.

[10] Tina Pippin, *Death and Desire: The Rhetoric of Gender in the Apocalypse of John*, Literary Currents in Biblical Interpretation (Louisville: Westminster/John Knox, 1992), 70-71.

[11] Pippin (*Death and Desire*, 69-86) has argued that even these images are negative portrayals of women because all of them present women as "victims; they are objects of desire and violence" (72).

[12] Susan R. Garrett, "Revelation," *The Women's Bible Commentary*, ed. Carol A. Newsom and Sharon H. Ringe (Louisville: Westminster/John Knox, 1992), 382.

[13] Deidre J. Good, "Early Extracanonical Writings," *The Women's Bible Commentary*, ed. Carol A. Newsom and Sharon H. Ringe (Louisville: Westminster/John Knox, 1992), 382.

[14] J. P. M. Sweet, *Revelation*, Westminster Pelican Commentaries (Philadelphia: Westminster, 1979), 228.

SEVEN ANGELS
WITH SEVEN BOWLS

15:1-8

The Seven Bowl Plagues, 15:1–16:21

In the visions of the seven seals (6:1–8:5) and the seven trumpet plagues (8:6–11:19), John has presented images of the eschatological judgments upon the earth. Now, after the lengthy insertion that has portrayed the conflict between the church and the powers of evil (12:1–14:20), he returns to the theme of the final woes, this time depicting them in a new seven-fold series, the seven bowl plagues. This new series does not present a different judgment of God, but the same judgment captured in new images. We should not try to conceive of John's organization of this material linearly, but spatially. In a sense, all three judgment scenes are taking place on different parts of the stage, simultaneously. As we shift our attention from one scene to another, we gain a richer understanding of John's revelation.

Structurally, this last judgment series follows the pattern of the seven trumpet plagues. [Outline of 15:1–16:21] After announcing the new series, John delays the beginning of the judgment scenes in order to present a preparatory heavenly throne room scene (8:3-5; 15:2-8). These scenes of the heavenly throne room connect this part of John's revelation to the throne room vision of chapters 4–5. They serve to remind the hearers/readers that the events on earth cannot be divorced from the realm of God. All that happens, whether it be the sufferings of the faithful or the activities of the enemies of God, occurs under the watchful eye of the one who is both Alpha and Omega, the creator and redeemer of the entire universe.

> **Outline of 15:1–16:21**
> 1. Introduction of the Seven Angels—15:1
> 2. The Martyrs on the Heavenly Shore—15:2-4
> 3. The Seven Angels and the Tent of Witness—15:5-8
> 4. The Seven Bowl Plagues—16:1-21

COMMENTARY

Introduction of the Seven Angels, 15:1

Verse 1 introduces not only the opening scene in this chapter, but the entire bowl plague series. This verse serves "as a kind of superscription over all that follows in chapters 15–16."[1] Twice before (12:1, 3), John has described the events that he sees as a "portent," or sign. Here, the portent is the appearance of the seven angels who will pour out the seven plagues on the earth. [Seven Plagues] John tells us that these plagues will be the last ones to strike the earth, "for with them the wrath of God is ended" (15:1). As mentioned above, these plagues are a recasting of the eschatological woes that John has already shown in the seven seals and the seven trumpets. The bowl plagues are "last," not in the sense that they follow chronologically the other disasters, but because they are the last depiction of the final woes that John will offer us. Furthermore, they are "last" because after them will come the final judgment and the consummation of God's kingdom. The reader familiar with the remainder of Revelation may question John's statement that these are the last plagues because in chapters 17 and 18 the destruction of "Babylon" is still going on. The solution to this problem lies in the recognition that chapters 17 and 18 give the details of what is already announced in the last bowl plague, the fall of mighty Babylon. Chapters 17 and 18, then, do not present a new scene after the final plagues; rather, they offer an elaboration and development of the seventh plague.

Seven Plagues

AΩ In Lev 26:21, God warned the Israelites, "If you continue hostile to me, and will not obey me, I will continue to plague you sevenfold for your sins."

The Martyrs on the Heavenly Shore, 15:2-4

Prior to revealing the contents of the seven bowl plagues, John describes another scene, this one a heavenly throne scene. In the initial throne room scene in chapter 4, John has mentioned that in front of the throne was "something like a sea of glass, like crystal" (4:6). In chapter 4, the sea represented the cosmic sea, perhaps also connoting the chaotic, untamed part of creation. Here in this new vision, the sea acquires additional meaning. It functions as a part of the exodus imagery of this scene. [Exodus Imagery] As

Exodus Imagery

📖 John has reworked several items from the exodus narrative for this chapter. Among these are the plagues, the song of Moses, the crossing of the sea, and the tent of witness.

the ancient Israelites crossed through the Red Sea (or "Sea of Reeds"), so the faithful followers of the Lamb cross through the sea of glass. The sea is "mixed with fire" (15:2), a description that has frequently been interpreted as a reference to the wrath or judgment of God that is to be unleashed on the world. The faithful arrive safely through the sea, but the sea becomes God's judgment on the world, similar to the exodus narrative when the sea closed in on Pharaoh's army as God's act of deliverance for the Israelites and destruction for their enemies. Another possibility is that the fire that is mingled with the sea is to be interpreted martyrologically. H. B. Swete commented, "The crystal light of the Sea of Glass is reddened as by fire. . . . The red glow on the Sea spoke of the fire through which the Martyrs passed."[2]

> **Beside the Sea**
>
> AΩ Since the Greek preposition *epi* normally means "on" or "upon," 15:2 could be translated to mean that the group of conquerors was standing on the sea, with the idea that the sea of glass was a solid surface (cf. KJV). The parallel with the exodus story, however, in which the Israelites gathered beside the sea, makes "beside the sea" the better translation in 15:2.

Who are those gathered beside this heavenly sea? [Beside the Sea] They are the ones who resisted "the beast and its image and the number of its name" (15:2). They refused to be marked with the mark of the beast, choosing rather to identify themselves as the followers of the Lamb and to receive "his name and his Father's name written on their foreheads" (14:1). Specifically, they are martyrs, for John stated that any who refused to yield to the beast were killed (13:15). In reality, these martyrs are not victims, in spite of earthly appearances and the claims of the beast and the false prophet. The martyrs are the true conquerors, for they have remained faithful to God, who has brought them safely through their "Red Sea" experience. They stand on the shore of the sea of glass, holding harps in their hands in order that they might join in the heavenly orchestra that breaks forth in praise to God (cf. 5:8; 14:2).

The song that these heavenly pilgrims sing is particularly appropriate. They sing "the song of Moses, the servant of God, and the song of the Lamb" (15:3). [Moses, the Servant of God] The exodus motif is strong throughout this section of the Apocalypse. As already noted, the seven bowl plagues are modeled after the plagues on Egypt. Furthermore, the faithful have

---

Moses, the Servant of God

AΩ "The servant of God" is a frequent description applied to Moses in the Hebrew Bible. The many instances include Exod 4:10; 14:31; Num 12:7; Deut 34:5; Josh 1:1, 2, 7, 13, 15; 8:31, 33; 9:24; 11:12, 15; 12:6; 13:8; 14:7; 18:7; 22:2, 4, 5; 1 Kgs 8:53, 56; 2 Kgs 18:12; 21:8; 1 Chr 6:49; 2 Chr 1:3; Neh 1:7, 8; 9:14; 10:29; Ps 105:26; Dan 9:11; and Mal 4:4.

passed safely through their own Red Sea and stand on the shore, singing praises to the God who delivered them. As God saved the Israelites from the oppression of Pharaoh, now God has delivered the faithful from the persecution of the Roman Empire. They have been rescued, not from physical harm (they have endured martyrdom), but from spiritual harm. They have found safety in the presence of God.

Function of the Hymn

Speaking of 15:3-4, Elisabeth Schüssler Fiorenza has written, "Like the chorus in a Greek drama, this hymn interprets the meaning and intention of the preceding and following visions of cruel judgment. Their goal is justice and salvation."

Elisabeth Schüssler Fiorenza, *Revelation: Vision of a Just World*, Proclamation Commentaries (Minneapolis: Fortress, 1991), 92.

Exodus 15:1-18 contains a song that Moses and the people sang in praise and thanksgiving to God as they stood by the Red Sea after God had brought them safely through to the other side. Likewise, the victorious martyrs now sing a new "song of Moses," which is also "the song of the Lamb." [Function of the Hymn] Whereas Moses had been the leader of the Israelites who guided them safely through the Red Sea, the wilderness, and to the promised land, for the faithful of John's vision, Christ is the one who has led the way, "the pioneer and perfecter of our faith" (Heb 12:2). His death has made their victory possible. They have followed "the Lamb wherever he goes" (14:4), through martyrdom and on to victory; so now they join together to celebrate the God who has delivered them.

Although the song of the martyrs is intended to recall the song of Moses in Exodus 15, the contents of the song in Revelation 15 are only generally similar to the celebration of victory sung by Moses and the Israelites. [Song of Moses] The

Song of Moses

Two passages in the Hebrew Bible contain a song sung by Moses, Exod 15:1-18 and Deut 32:1-43. The former is sung after the Israelites' successful crossing of the Red Sea; the latter is sung by Moses shortly before his death. Although the fact that John places the singing of this new "song of Moses" on the shore of the sea suggests that Exod 15 is in mind, the contents of the song draw more from Deut 32.

song of Moses recounted the Israelites' safe passage through the Red Sea and the destruction of Pharaoh's army as they tried to cross through. The song gloated over and celebrated the defeat of the enemies of the Israelites. In Revelation 15, the song speaks in more general terms of God's redemptive activity in history. The song of praise sung by the martyrs is a patchwork of texts borrowed from the Hebrew Bible that celebrates the greatness and justice of God. [The Song of Moses and the Song of the Lamb]

One of the major themes of the victory song of the martyrs is the universal sovereignty of God, "the King of the nations" (15:4). The question of v. 4, "Lord, who will not fear and

> **The Song of Moses and the Song of the Lamb**
> The song in 15:3-4 is a composite drawn from several texts in the Hebrew Bible. The following chart shows the parallels between this passage and texts from the Hebrew Bible.
>
> | Revelation 15:3-4 | Parallels in the Hebrew Bible |
> |---|---|
> | "Great and amazing are your deeds" | Pss 92:5; 98:1; 111:2; 139:14 |
> | "Lord God the Almighty" | Amos 3:13 LXX; 4:13 LXX |
> | "Just and true are your ways" | Deut 32:4; Ps 145:17 |
> | "King of the nations" | Jer 10:7 |
> | "Lord, who will not fear and glorify your name" | Jer 10:7; Pss 86:9, 12; 99:3; Mal 1:11 |
> | "For you alone are holy" | 1 Sam 2:2; Pss 99:3; 111:9 |
> | "All nations will come and worship before you" | Ps 86:9; Isa 2:2; 66:23; Jer 16:19 |
> | "for your judgments have been revealed" | Ps 98:2 |

glorify your name?" expects the answer "no one." The justice and majesty of God will be so compelling that John envisions all people will bow in reverence and worship before God. This song reveals the ultimate purpose behind God's acts of judgment. These are not vengeful acts of a vindictive God. Rather, they are punishments designed to elicit repentance and worship. This is the reason why God's "judgments have been revealed" (15:4). Although previously John has reported the failure of the people to repent in the face of the judgments of God (9:20), now he holds out hope that the final plagues will have their intended effect and "all nations will come and worship" (15:4; cf. 11:13; 21:24-26; 22:2).

For John's readers, the emphasis in vv. 3-4 on the universal sovereignty of God would have been especially significant. The Roman Empire claimed dominion over all other nations. In the opinion of many people in John's day, the "King of the nations" was the emperor. [King of the Nations] Yet John knows that such claims are false. The only true king is the "Lord God, the Almighty." Only this king is worthy of reverence and worship.

The Seven Angels with Bowls, 15:5-8

Beginning with v. 5, John describes a new vision that appears in heaven. John sees the heavenly sanctuary, out of which come seven angels. John calls this sanctuary the "temple of the tent of witness."

> **King of the Nations**
> Instead of "King of the nations" some manuscripts read "King of the ages." The latter reading is accepted by, among others, the RSV, NIV, and the REB. The NRSV, NAB, and CEV follow the first reading. The committee that produced the United Bible Society's 3rd edition of the Greek New Testament chose the first reading as more likely, even though both readings have about equal support in ancient manuscripts. Their reasons were that "King of the ages" was probably introduced from 1 Tim 1:17, and "King of the nations" fits the context better. The wording of the KJV, "King of saints," should certainly be rejected. It has extremely weak manuscript support and apparently arose from confusion of similar Latin words.
>
> Bruce M. Metzger, *A Textual Commentary on the Greek New Testament* (United Bible Societies, 1971), 455-56.

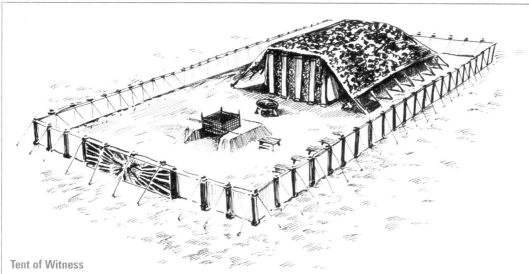

Tent of Witness

AΩ The tent of witness, also called the tent of meeting, is described in Exod 33:7-11. It was a portable shrine carried by the Israelites during their wilderness wanderings and later placed in Canaan at Shiloh (1 Sam 2:22), at Gibeon (2 Chr 1:3), and finally inside Solomon's temple (1 Kgs 8:4). The tent of meeting was the place for receiving divine oracles, thus its name "tent of meeting" because there Moses met with God to receive divine instructions. Another tradition in the Hebrew Bible speaks of a tabernacle (or "dwelling place") that served as the Israelites' central worship shrine during this period. Exod 25–30 gives detailed instructions concerning the building of this tabernacle, whereas its actual construction is described in Exod 35–40. The tabernacle, as described in these accounts, was a large (approximately 75 by 150 feet), elaborate structure made of wood, gold, silver, and fine linen. Scholars are divided over the relationship between the tabernacle and the tent of meeting. Some would see the terms as being used interchangeably to describe the same structure. Most see the tent of meeting as an earlier, simpler structure. The real question concerns the historicity of the tabernacle account. As it stands, the biblical account of the tabernacle raises several questions: Where would the Israelites have obtained all the materials necessary to build the tabernacle as described? Would they have had the requisite skills to construct such a structure? How could such a structure have been carried with them and assembled and disassembled as they moved from place to place? Because of these and other problems, the tabernacle as described in the biblical narrative probably reflects a retrojection of the Solomonic temple into the wilderness period. The tent of meeting was likely a simple tent that the Israelites carried with them and eventually constructed at certain sacred sites when they settled in Canaan.

In the New Testament, the author of Hebrews spoke of a heavenly tabernacle that was the prototype after which the earthly tabernacle was patterned (8:2, 5; 9:1-22). The earthly tabernacle was only "a sketch and shadow of the heavenly one" (8:5). In Rev 15:5-8, John draws upon this idea of a heavenly tabernacle.

(Illustration credit: Barclay Burns)

[Tent of Witness] This imagery continues the exodus motif that is so prominent in this section of the Apocalypse. The tent of witness was the portable place of worship that the Israelites carried with them during their wilderness wanderings and into the land of Canaan. It was a place of sacrifice, communication with God, and revelation from God. [Temple of the Tent of Witness] Now from this heavenly prototype of the earthly tent of meeting comes a new revelation from God, the seven bowl plagues.

The description of the seven angels—"robed in pure bright linen, with golden sashes across their chests" (15:6)—is similar to the description of the angelic figure that appeared to Daniel: "clothed in linen, with a belt of gold from Uphaz around his waist" (Dan 10:5; cf. the Son of Man figure in 1:13). [Linen] Since the angels come out of the heavenly tabernacle, their linen robes may also designate the priestly functions of these angels, for linen was the fabric from which the priests' vestments were to be made (Exod 28:39). One of the four living creatures (cf. 4:6-11; 6:1-8) gives to each of the seven angels a golden bowl "full of the wrath of God" (15:7). The four living creatures have played a pivotal role in the unleashing of the calamities of the first four seals (6:1-8); once more they serve to inaugurate God's judgment upon the earth.

The imagery of the bowls held by the angels combines two different ideas from the Hebrew Bible. [Bowls] First, these bowls probably represent cultic utensils, objects used in the sacrificial worship. Bronze basins or bowls were used by the priests to carry away ashes from the altar after sacrifices were burned (Exod 27:3; 38:3; Num 4:14). In Revelation 5:8, the angels at the altar hold golden bowls filled with incense, "which are the prayers of the saints." In taking the bowls they have brought from the altar and pouring them out on the earth, the angels in chapter 15 function in a manner similar to that of the angel in 8:5 who fills a censer with fire from the altar and throws it on the earth. Second, the bowls given to the angels are "full of the wrath of God" (15:7). Several passages in the Hebrew Bible speak of the cup of God's wrath (Ps 75:8; Isa 51:17; Jer 25:15-29; 49:12) that God's enemies must drink, symbolizing God's punishments on them. John has used this metaphor for divine punishment already in the previous chapter (14:8, 10).

After the angels receive their bowls full of wrath and are prepared to pour them on the earth to initiate the final plagues, John sees the heavenly temple fill "with smoke from the glory of God and from his power" (15:8). This scene is a typical

Temple of the Tent of Witness

ΑΩ The phrase "the temple of the tent of witness" in 15:5 should probably be understood grammatically as a genitive of apposition and translated as "the temple, that is, the tent of witness."

Linen

ΑΩ John describes the angels in 15:6 as dressed in linen (*linon*). Some ancient manuscripts say they were dressed in stone (*lithon*). Some scholars have argued for the latter as the correct reading, based on a parallel with Ezek 28:13. *Lithon*, however, makes little sense in 15:6 and likely is simply a scribal error.

Bowls

ΑΩ The Greek word *phialē* refers to a flat, shallow cup or bowl, not a vial (as in KJV) or flask. Such bowls were commonly used for drinking or for drink offerings for the gods.

Results of Worship

"What is about to transpire originates in the presence of God. That it follows the worship of the conquerors implies (as in 8:2-5) that what follows flows from Christian worship. Again, from John's point of view, the most significant thing Christians can do to change the world is to worship God and to pray. Why? It is because just and lasting change in the world ultimately is God's doing."

Charles H. Talbert, *The Apocalypse: A Reading of the Revelation of John* (Louisville: Westminster/John Knox, 1994), 69-70.

theophany scene from the Bible. In the Hebrew Bible, smoke or clouds frequently represent the presence of God. During the Israelite's wilderness wandering, a pillar of cloud went in front of them by day and a pillar of fire by night, guiding their journey and signifying the presence of God with them (Exod 13:21). Later, when Moses ascended Mount Sinai to meet with God, the cloud descended upon the mountain. When the tabernacle was completed, "then the cloud covered the tent of meeting, and the glory of the LORD filled the tabernacle. Moses was not able to enter the tent of meeting because the cloud settled upon it, and the glory of the LORD filled the tabernacle" (Exod 40:34-35; cf. 1 Kgs 8:10-11). In Isaiah's vision in which he was called to be a prophet, he saw God enthroned in the temple and the temple filled with smoke (Isa 6:4). [Results of Worship]

Once God's presence fills the temple, John says that "no one could enter the temple until the seven plagues of the seven angels were ended" (15:8). Moses was not able to enter the tent of meeting because of the cloud and the glory of the LORD (Exod 40:35). Likewise, when Solomon built the temple in Jerusalem and a cloud filled the temple, the priests "could not stand to minister because of the cloud; for the glory of the LORD filled the house of the LORD" (1 Kgs 10:11). Why does John mention that no one could enter the temple? Is he simply following the traditions in the texts cited? Or is there special significance to this statement for John? At the very least, this is John's way of emphasizing that the judgments that occur in the bowl plagues have their origin with God. No one else is in control of the events that occur; rather, "God himself is present in his majesty and glory to perform that action which will execute his judgments and establish his kingdom in power."[3] Some commentators have suggested a further meaning: The denial of access to the temple indicates that the time for intercession and mercy is past; now is the time for judgment. As R. H. Charles explained, "None could avert by prayer the doom about to befall the earth through these plagues."4

CONNECTIONS

Few biblical metaphors are as powerful as that of crossing through the Red Sea. The story of the Hebrew people escaping from Egypt through God's miraculous parting of the waters is a story that connects with our own experiences in many ways. This is a story that begins with a people in bondage, in slavery to an oppressive pharaoh. It tells of relief and excitement at the anticipated freedom from that bondage. Yet those hopes were dashed as that freedom, looming on the other side of the waters, seemed to be a cruel joke when Pharaoh's army was bearing down on the fleeing crowd. Cries of anger, frustration, and fear, mixed with prayers for deliverance, rang out as the people felt crushed between two seemingly insurmountable instruments of destruction. As the waters parted and the journey began, hope returned. Finally, safe on the other side, with the waters overwhelming the enemy, joy and celebration broke forth, for the people were saved; death was cheated. From the throes of death and despair, life was reborn. ["I Will Sing the Wondrous Story"]

"I Will Sing the Wondrous Story"
The scene of the faithful gathered on the shore of the sea, singing their song of victory, was preserved in the last line of the hymn "I Will Sing the Wondrous Story," whose words were written by Francis H. Rowley:

Yes, I'll sing the wondrous story
Of the Christ who died for me,
Sing it with the saints in glory,
Gathered by the crystal sea.

In choosing to reuse this ancient story of liberation, John knows that this story has the ability to speak once again to a different people who are enslaved by a new Pharaoh. This story is so powerful for John because he sees it being reenacted in the lives of the faithful Christians of his day. They are living in a world that is not theirs, a culture that is alien to them. The worldview of the larger society saw a world that was controlled by a variety of gods and goddesses—Aphrodite, Artemis, Poseidon, Dionysus, Cybele, Demeter, and many others. Along with this pantheon was the emperor himself who was given divine status and was expected to be worshiped. Daily life was filled with reminders of the deities and the emperors. Temples and statues of the emperors and the gods and goddesses were prominent, being located in every major city in Asia Minor. Social, economic, and political activities were conducted under

Song of Victory

 "For Christians under the stress of a militant emperor-cult, anticipating a struggle to the death with an idolatry claiming the allegiance of all mankind, this song affords great encouragement. The last word of history is not with Satan and his Antichrist, but with the Lord and his Christ."

George R. Beasley-Murray, *The Book of Revelation*, New Century Bible (Greenwood SC: Attic, 1974), 236-37.

the *aegis* of the gods and goddesses. John and the Christians who share his viewpoint would have felt estranged from such a society. Along with this social alienation, physical persecution and even martyrdom are possibilities for those Christians who resist the claims of the imperial cult and refuse to participate. Such pressures and dangers are the "Pharaoh's army" and the "Red Sea" of John's day that are threatening destruction of God's people.

In that perilous situation, is there any hope? John says, "Yes." There is another shore on the other side of this "Red Sea." Those who are faithful and have "conquered the beast and its image and the number of its name" (15:2) will find safety and comfort in the presence of God. [Song of Victory]

The task of the preacher and teacher of this text is to help modern readers hear their own story reflected in these verses. The "easy" message to gain from this text is to hear it simply as a future hope, an eschatological promise: if we are faithful to God in this life, we will be rewarded in the next. This story is more powerful than that, however. It is a text that gives hope not only for the future, but for the present as well. It is a text that empowers an embattled and despairing people to experience life now, in the presence of God. [Worship in Anticipation]

The song that the martyrs sing standing on the shore of the sea is a song of celebration, a song of victory. While in John's vision it is an eschatological song, in the real world of John's day this was a song that was already being sung. The victory that was in the future was being anticipated in the present. Robert Mounce has pointed out that "the structure of the hymn suggests that it may have been used in the liturgy of the early church."[5] This song has the characteristics of an actual hymn that was sung in Christian worship. If that was the case, then this song from the heavens was already being

Worship in Anticipation

"The juxtaposition of songs of celebration with scenes of terrible judgment is thus not gleeful gloating, but neither is it merely a promise of future celebration. The message is not that 'now is the time of trouble, someday we will be able to celebrate.' Rather, Christian worship anticipates the eschatological victory and celebrates it in the present."

M. Eugene Boring, *Revelation*, Interpretation: A Bible Commentary for Teaching and Preaching (Louisville: John Knox, 1989), 174.

sung by the churches of John's day. They knew victory already. Even though to all outward appearances their lives—and especially their deaths—may have looked like defeat, John knew that they were experiencing the initial signs of victory. That is the empowering force of this heavenly vision of the martyrs standing on the seashore. This vision affirms once more that evil will not succeed; it will be defeated. In fact, it is already in the process of being defeated. That is cause for celebration. The God who brought the waters of the sea crashing down on Pharaoh's army, the God who will bring the faithful through to stand in victory on the heavenly shore is the same God who is already at work bringing evil to an end in our world.

In a sermon based on the Red Sea experience of the children of Israel, Martin Luther King Jr. said,

> We must be reminded anew that God is at work in his universe. He is not outside the world looking on with a sort of cold indifference. Here on all the roads of life, he is striving in our striving. Like an ever-loving Father, he is working through history for the salvation of his children. As we struggle to defeat the forces of evil, the God of the universe struggles with us. Evil dies on the seashore, not merely because of man's endless struggle against it, but because of God's power to defeat it.[6]

King made those statements in the midst of the Civil Rights struggle, a time when many faithful people were being beaten, imprisoned, and even killed. In many ways, the situation for Martin Luther King Jr. and the other participants in the Civil Rights movement was analogous to the situation faced by John and his readers. Like John, King knew the power of the story of God's rescue of the people at the Red Sea, "a story not only about ancient Israel, but also about 'us too, the living.' As a story about both the past and the present, it images the human condition and God's relationship to us in all times."[7] Both in Exodus and in Revelation, the song at the sea is a song of victory because it is a song that celebrates the power of God to overcome evil and even to transform evil into good. It is a song about a God whose deeds are indeed "great and amazing" (15:3), about a God who does not abandon God's people, but hears their cries because God's ways are "just and true" (15:3). In singing this song, the church today celebrates the continued presence of that God in our lives and in our own stories. [The Song of the Lamb]

The Song of the Lamb

Daniel Berrigan, the activist Jesuit priest, has written a book titled *Beside the Sea of Glass: The Song of the Lamb* while in prison after an antinuclear demonstration outside the Pentagon. Based on his reading of Rev 15:2-4, Berrigan's work is a thought-provoking political reading of "the song of the Lamb" in a modern American context. Berrigan introduced his book with the following words:

In February of 1977 a group of us were in the Alexandrian (Va.) city jail, meditating and discussing the book of Revelation. It dawned on me that ours was a perfect setting for such an enterprise. After all, hadn't many early Christians ended up in just such places, for just such offenses against law and order? Hadn't they been forbidden to preach in the name of the Risen One—forbidden, that is, by the civil authorities, to whom that name and that event were understood as a mortal danger?

We had undertaken something not very different from that offense, saying nothing more momentous than this: the State has no right to build and maintain an arsenal of nuclear weapons that threaten the life of the planet. To underscore our resistance to this grotesque program, we had poured our own blood on the pillars of the building and chained ourselves to its doors. For this, we were of course jailed. We had expected nothing else. It was not the first time; nor would it be the last.

So, Alexandria, here we were.

I thought it might be a good thing, especially for myself and those who were in jail with me and possibly our friends "outside," if I were to set down these reflections concerning a prayer that unexpectedly moved us all, a prayer virtually unknown to us up to that time. (One, indeed, that I think will be equally unfamiliar to others.) It is a prayer that one passes by easily, its language at once unfamiliar and overfamiliar, phrases that trip easily off the tongue, having to do with things beyond our ken or indeed our interest. Nevertheless, the prayer stopped us short. It seemed, perhaps due to our circumstance, charged with a terrible energy and beauty; a prayer almost like an instrument of torture, stretching us, adding inches to our moral understanding—if only given the chance, given some reflection.

Daniel Berrigan, *Beside the Sea of Glass: The Song of the Lamb* (New York: Seabury, 1978), 9, 11.

Walter Wink has captured the confidence and celebration of this vision:

The Book of Revelation may be gory, surrealistic, unnerving, even terrifying. But it contains not a single note of despair. Powerful as the Dragon of the abyss may appear, he has been stripped of real heavenly power. Those still in the clutches of the Enemy may not yet experience it, but the decisive battle has already been won. The struggle continues, but the issue is no longer in doubt. The far-off strains of a victory song already reach our ears, and we are invited to join the chorus. This is the rock on which we stand: the absolute certainty of the triumph of God in the world.

That is why the celebration of the divine victory does not take place at the end of the Book of Revelation, after the struggle is over. Rather, it breaks out all along the way (1:4-8, 17-18; 4:8-11;

5:5, 9-14; 7:1-17; 11:15-19; 12:10-12; 14:1-8; 15:2-4; 16:5-7; 18; 19:1-9). We have here no sober pilgrims grimly ascending the mount of tears, but singers *enjoying* the struggle because it confirms their freedom. Even in the midst of conflict, suffering, or imprisonment, suddenly a hymn pierces the gloom, the heavenly hosts thunder in a mighty chorus, and our hearts grow lighter.[8]

NOTES

[1] George R. Beasley-Murray, *The Book of Revelation*, New Century Bible (Greenwood SC: Attic, 1974), 234. Beasley-Murray credited Wilhelm Bousset for this insight.

[2] Henry Barclay Swete, *Commentary on Revelation* (1911; reprint, Grand Rapids: Kregel Publications, 1977), 194. Morris Ashcraft ("Revelation," *The Broadman Bible Commentary*, 12 vols. [Nashville: Broadman, 1972], 12:322) explained, "The red color suggests the fire through which the martyrs had come, or the blood shed in martyrdom."

[3] Beasley-Murray, *Revelation*, 238.

[4] R. H. Charles, *A Critical and Exegetical Commentary on the Revelation of St. John*, The International Critical Commentary, 2 vols. (Edinburgh: T. & T. Clark, 1920), 2:40.

[5] Robert H. Mounce, *The Book of Revelation*, The New International Commentary on the New Testament, rev. ed. (Grand Rapids: Eerdmans, 1998), 286.

[6] Martin Luther King Jr., "The Death of Evil upon the Seashore," *Strength to Love* (New York: Harper & Row, 1963), 64.

[7] Marcus J. Borg, *Meeting Jesus Again for the First Time: The Historical Jesus and the Heart of Contemporary Faith* (San Francisco: HarperSanFrancisco, 1994), 123.

[8] Walter Wink, *Engaging the Powers: Discernment and Resistance in a World of Domination* (Minneapolis: Fortress, 1992), 321.

THE POURING OF
THE SEVEN BOWLS

16:1-21

COMMENTARY

The Pouring of the Seven Bowls, 16:1-21

All is now ready for the final series of eschatological judgments. John has assured the faithful that they will be safe by showing the vision of the martyrs on the heavenly shore. The angels have received their bowls of wrath and stand poised to pour them out on the earth. John hears an unidentified voice from the heavenly temple that issues the command for the bowl plagues to begin. If the statement in 15:8 that "no one could enter the temple until the seven plagues of the seven angels were ended" is pressed, then the voice must be that of God. Since the voice comes from the temple, the implication is certainly that the ultimate source of the command is God. [Outline of 16:1-21]

> **Outline of 16:1-21**
> 1. Divine Command—16:1
> 2. First Bowl—16:2
> 3. Second Bowl—16:3
> 4. Third Bowl—16:4-7
> 5. Fourth Bowl—16:8-9
> 6. Fifth Bowl—16:10-11
> 7. Sixth Bowl—16:12-16
> 8. Seventh Bowl—16:17-21

The plague associated with the first bowl—"a foul and painful sore" (16:2)—is reminiscent of the sixth plague on the Egyptians, in which the people were afflicted with festering boils (Exod 9:8-12). The ones who are affected by this first bowl plague are "those who had the mark of the beast and who worshiped its image" (16:2). This punishment is a form of ironic justice: those who have the "mark of the beast" now have a new "mark"—an affliction of painful sores all over their bodies.

The second plague is modeled after the first plague in Exodus 7:14-25 that turned the Nile River to blood (cf. the second trumpet plague in 8:8-9). John divides the Egyptian plague of turning water to blood into two bowl plagues. The first one (16:3) affects the sea, whereas the second one (16:4-7) affects fresh water (rivers and springs). John graphically depicts the results of this plague: The sea becomes like the blood of a dead person; or as Beckwith described it, "The sea is changed to the coagulated and decaying blood of the

Angel of the Waters

AΩ In 14:18, John has mentioned "the angel who has authority over fire." Here in 16:5, he refers to "the angel of the waters." In certain Jewish traditions, specific angels were given authority over various elements of nature (cf. *1 En.* 60:11-25). The author of *1 En.* 66 speaks of angels of punishment who "were in charge of the forces of the waters." Rev 16:5 may be reflecting a similar idea of an angel in charge of the waters.

Who Are and Were

AΩ The description of God as "You . . . who are and were" is a truncated form of the phrase in 1:4, 8: the one "who is and who was and who is to come." As in 11:17, the description omits the future element, "who is to come." The final events have already begun with this series of plagues. The future coming of God is already taking place.

dead."[1] Not surprisingly, all the living things in the sea die when the water becomes blood. This result is an intensification of the result of the second trumpet plague in 8:8-9. The second trumpet plague has turned a third of the sea into blood and has killed a third of the living creatures of the sea. Here, the entire sea becomes blood and all living things are killed. This intensification adds to the dramatic tension of the work: The end is getting nearer; the effect of the woes is becoming more extensive.

The third angel goes and pours his bowl into the rivers and springs of the earth, turning them into blood (16:4). [Angel of the Waters] As in the third trumpet plague, this plague affects the fresh water. Again, the effect of the plague is complete, for all the waters become blood, not simply a third of them (cf. 8:11). After the pouring of the third bowl, John hears a doxological hymn praising God's justice in dealing with God's opponents. [Who Are and Were]

The theme of this hymn is similar to that of the song sung by the martyrs in 15:3-4. By means of this liturgical insertion, John interprets the significance of the third bowl plague, and indeed of all the bowl plagues. These plagues are God's means of bringing judgment against those who oppose God's plans and inflict suffering and death on God's people. [Justice Hymn]

The major point that is made in this hymn is that God is just in dealing with the earth. Those who are punished have received nothing less than what they deserve. The punishment of those who killed God's people is a fitting punishment. Because they have shed the blood of God's servants, now

Justice Hymn

The following parallel columns illustrate the similarities between the "hymn" to God's justice in 16:4-6 and the song of Moses and the Lamb in 15:2-4:

16:4-6	15:2-4
"You are just"	"Just and true are your ways"
"Who are and were"	"King of the ages" (textual variant)
"O Holy One"	"For you alone are holy"
"For you have judged these things"	"For your judgments have been revealed"

Adapted from Robert H. Mounce, *The Book of Revelation*, The New International Commentary on the New Testament, rev. ed. (Grand Rapids: Eerdmans, 1998), 294.

Measure-for-Measure Punishment

AΩ Measure-for-measure punishment is found in several apocalyptic writings. Two major examples are the *Apocalypse of Peter* and the *Apocalypse of Paul*. Both of these are Christian apocalypses. The former contains a vision revealed to Peter in which he sees the gruesome punishments of the wicked in hell. Their punishments are frequently measure-for-measure punishments in which the punishments match the sins which they have committed: Blasphemers are hung by their tongues; men guilty of fornication are hung up by their thighs (likely a euphemism for genitals); women who have committed abortion or infanticide are tortured by beasts formed from congealed milk flowing from the mothers' breasts; liars have their lips cut off. The *Apocalypse of Paul* likewise contains a section describing punishments of the wicked that are appropriate to their sins. In this writing, Paul is supposedly taken by an angel to the place of punishment of the wicked where he sees agonizing penalties imposed on the godless. Many of these punishments relate specifically to their transgressions. Examples include men and women who "committed the iniquity of Sodom and Gomorrah" (39) placed in a pit of tar and brimstone; men and women guilty of adultery are suspended by their eyebrows and hair (hair was considered sexually seductive); and men and women guilty of throwing their infants out to be eaten by dogs or trampled by pigs are themselves torn apart by wild animals.

they are forced to drink blood when all their water supplies have been turned into blood. This is "measure-for-measure" punishment; that is, the punishment meted out to them is appropriate to their offense. [Measure-for-Measure Punishment] Similarly, in v. 2, those who received the mark of the beast are given painful sores as marks. This punishment follows the pattern expressed in the Wisdom of Solomon 11:16: "one is punished by the very things by which one sins."

In response to the angel's hymn of praise, the heavenly altar cries out,

"Yes, O Lord God, the Almighty,
    your judgments are true and just!" (16:7)

Whose voice is that represented by the personification of the altar? Unquestionably this is the voice of the martyrs themselves, those whose blood had been spilt and who are now vindicated by God's punishments on their enemies. The voice from the altar is the collective voice of the martyrs from underneath the altar in 6:9-11. Their cry of "How long will it be before you judge and avenge our blood on the inhabitants of the earth?" has now been answered. The martyrs join in the praise of God, affirming that God indeed deals justly with the people of the earth.

In action parallel to that of the fourth trumpet plague, the fourth angel pours his bowl on the sun. Although the sun is affected in both plagues, the results are different. Whereas the fourth trumpet plague brings about darkness when the sun is struck, the fourth bowl plague causes an intensification of the sun's heat. John is still borrowing from the Egyptian plague story, although his dependence on that tradition is not as obvious with the fourth bowl plague. The ninth Egyptian plague was a plague of darkness (as in John's fourth trumpet plague). With the fourth bowl plague, the sun (the source of light) is affected, but John modifies the exodus tradition so that a different result occurs—scorching heat, instead of darkness. This punishment on the enemies of God is the antithesis of God's protection of the faithful, who are assured that "the sun will not strike them, nor any scorching heat" (Rev 7:16; cf. Ps 121:6; Isa 4:6; 25:4-5; 49:10).

Even after being burned by the scorching heat, the people refuse to repent and give glory to God. Instead they curse ("blaspheme") the name of God. Their blasphemy of God means that in their agony they clearly recognize the source of their punishment yet refuse to give up their idolatrous and rebellious ways. Their blasphemy is an active cursing of God for bringing such punishments on them. John sees that "they are so deeply entangled in their hostility toward God that even now, in view of the destruction, they are not prepared to repent and give him the honor (cf. 9:20). Instead, they remain in their cult of the hostile, demonic power and thus in the blasphemy of the true God (cf. at 13:5)."[2] Their eyes are still blinded to the true God. Their continuation in the worship of the beast is itself an act of blasphemy, for they are giving to Caesar the homage and glory that belong to God alone. They have "exchanged the glory of the immortal God for images resembling a mortal human being" and have "exchanged the truth about God for a lie and worshiped and served the creature rather than the Creator" (Rom 1:23, 25). These people are the persistently obstinate ones, those who continue to resist God in spite of numerous warnings and punishments. The plagues have both a retributive and penitential purpose. Sadly, these individuals reap only the retributive aspect of the plagues. In this regard they are the opposite of

---

⌂ The Bowl Plagues and the Plagues in Exodus

Bowl Plagues	Plagues in Exodus
1st plague—Painful sores (16:2)	6th plague—Boils (9:8-12)
2d plague—Sea turned to blood (16:3)	1st plague—Nile River turned to blood (7:14-25)
3rd plague—Fresh water turned to blood (16:4-7)	1st plague—Nile River turned to blood (7:14-25)
4th plague—Scorching heat of the sun (16:8-9)	9th plague?—Darkness throughout the land (10:21-29)
5th plague—Darkness (16:10-11)	9th plague—Darkness throughout the land (10:21-29)
6th plague—Euphrates River dried up; three foul spirits like frogs (16:12-16)	2d plague—Frogs (8:1-15)
7th plague—Lightning, thunder, earthquake, and hail (16:17-21)	7th plague—Thunder and hail (9:13-35)

the people in 11:13 who "gave glory to the God of heaven" after seeing the devastating judgment of the great earthquake.

The fifth bowl plague also draws upon the Egyptian plague of darkness. [The Bowl Plagues and the Plagues in Exodus] The angel pours his bowl not upon the entire earth, but directly on the center of the earth's opposition to God, that is, "on the throne of the beast" (16:10), which is Rome. As in ancient Egypt, so now throughout the kingdom the land is plunged into darkness. This is no ordinary darkness, however; this is a fearsome, supernatural darkness that causes the people to gnaw their tongues in agony. The horror of a plague of darkness is described by the author of the Wisdom of Solomon, who elaborated on the Egyptian plague of darkness, describing the psychological terrors it inflicted on the people (ch. 17). Like John, the author of the Wisdom of Solomon saw this as no ordinary darkness; indeed in Wisdom 17:14, the darkness is said to have come "upon them from the recesses of powerless Hades." In addition to the darkness, the agonies of the previous plagues continue to torment the wicked, for John states that they cursed God "because of their pains and sores," a reminder of the "painful sore" that came upon the worshipers of the beast as a result of the first plague (16:2).

The fifth bowl plague is no more effective than the fourth in bringing about repentance. The people continue to curse God and refuse to repent from their rebellion against God. The darkness that engulfs this kingdom is metaphorical as well as literal: in their continued opposition and antagonism to God, the people remain in spiritual darkness. The failure of the people to repent and turn to God demonstrates the obstinacy and defiance of a portion of humanity who recognize the power and authority of God but refuse to submit to God. [Cursing God] Their hearts, like that of the ancient Pharaoh, have been hardened. While the plague of darkness is clearly an adaptation of the Egyptian plague, Caird suggested that the chaos of the Roman Empire following the death of Nero perhaps served for John as a vivid model for this plague. Caird wrote, "The doubts, suspicions, terrors, and hysteria which had ended with the accession of Vespasian had given a foretaste of what might happen if ever the lights went out all over the empire."3

Whereas the fifth bowl was poured on the throne of the beast, the sixth bowl is poured on the river Euphrates, causing the river to

Cursing God

Concerning the unrepentant in v. 11, Beasley-Murray said, "These, therefore, who curse God for his judgments are the obdurate. The mark of the beast on their bodies has penetrated their souls, instilling in them the hostility towards God and his holiness which is characteristic of the beast himself."

George R. Beasley-Murray, *The Book of Revelation*, New Century Bible (Greenwood SC: Attic, 1974), 243.

dry up. The purpose for the drying up of the river is to make possible the crossing of the river by the "kings from the east," likely in order that they might attack Rome. This event recalls the parting of the Red Sea in the exodus story, except that the parting of the sea allowed the Israelites to escape to safety, whereas the drying up of the Euphrates allows the foreign armies to invade and bring destruction. Two additional biblical texts that refer to God's miraculous drying up of water may also have contributed to this imagery. In Joshua 3:14-17, God caused the Jordan River to cease flowing in order that the Israelites might cross over into the land of Canaan. In Jeremiah 50:38, the prophet declared that God would dry up the waters of Babylon as punishment against the city (cf. 51:36). The significance of the Euphrates is that it was traditionally the boundary between the Roman and the Parthian Empires. Parthia was the dreaded enemy of the Romans (cf. 9:13-19). The "kings of the East," then, is a reference to the Parthian rulers.

The sixth bowl plague and the sixth trumpet plague are similar in their expectation of a military invasion from the east, specifically from the area of the Euphrates River. These similarities suggest that the two plagues are variations of the same eschatological disaster, a massive military invasion of armies from the east. The association of these invading armies with the Euphrates not only may reflect the fear that the Romans had of the Parthians, but may also be a reference to the Nero *redivivus* myth (see commentary on 13:1-10) because one version of that myth claimed that Nero would eventually return with an invading Parthian army to conquer and regain the Roman throne.

John then sees "three foul spirits like frogs coming from the mouth of the dragon, from the mouth of the beast, and from the mouth of the false prophet" (16:13). The dragon and the beast are familiar to John's hearers/readers by now. They have been amply described in chapters 12 and 13. But what about the "false prophet"? He, too, has already appeared, although not by that name. The false prophet is the second beast of chapter 13, the beast from the earth. He is a false prophet because he "deceives the inhabitants of earth" (13:14), leading the people astray to worship the first beast. A true prophet is one who speaks the word of God truthfully and leads the people to obedient and faithful worship of God. Modern readers are likely to be tempted to see in this evil triumvirate a parody of the church's doctrine of the Trinity. Such an interpretation is hardly intended by John, however, since the church at the end of the first century had no firmly developed doctrine of the Trinity.

Three Foul Spirits Like Frogs

In this illustration from the *Apocalypse of Angers*, John sees "three foul spirits like frogs coming from the mouth of the dragon, from the mouth of the beast, and from the mouth of the false prophet" (Rev 16:13).

Nicolas Bataille. *Dragons Vomiting Frogs* from the *Apocalypse of Angers*. 1373–1387. Mussee des Tapisseries. Angers, France. (Credit: Erich Lessing/Art Resource, NY)

The foul spirits that proceed from the mouths of this unholy threesome are described as being like frogs. That description seems strange. In describing these evil spirits, why did John picture them as frogs? A hideous, loathsome, or dangerous creature would seem more appropriate than a frog to depict these servants of evil. In answer to that question, some scholars have pointed to the association of frogs with certain gods or goddesses in the ancient world. [Three Foul Spirits Like Frogs] R. H. Charles, for example, noted that frogs were the source of plagues and death in the Zend religion and that frogs were also considered the agents of the evil spirit Ahriman in Zoroastrianism.[4] Other scholars have suggested that these foul (or "unclean") spirits are pictured as frogs because frogs were considered ritually unclean in Judaism on the basis of Leviticus 11:10, which states that "anything in the seas or the streams that does not have fins and scales" is detestable and an unclean animal. Whereas both of these ideas may have contributed to John's use of frogs to represent the foul spirits, the most likely reason for the use of frogs here is that John is still drawing upon the motif of the Egyptian

Dead Sea Scrolls

The Jewish group that produced the Dead Sea Scrolls was an apocalyptically minded group. Like John, they spoke of a final battle that would take place between good and evil. The *War Scroll* describes this final battle in which "the sons of light" will fight against "the sons of darkness." The latter will be led by Belial, one of the names in Jewish tradition for the leader over the forces of evil. The *War Scroll* states:

[The Rule] of War on the unleashing of the attack of the sons of light against the company of the sons of darkness, the army of Belial: against the band of Edom, Moab, and the sons of Ammon, and [against the army of the sons of the East and] the Philistines, and against the bands of the Kittim of Assyria and their allies the ungodly of the Covenant. . . .

This shall be a time of salvation for the people of God, an age of dominion for all the members of His company, and of everlasting destruction for all the company of Belial. . . .

On the day when the Kittim fall, there shall be battle and terrible carnage before the God of Israel, for that shall be the day appointed from ancient times for the battle of destruction of the sons of darkness. At that time, the assembly of gods and the hosts of men shall battle, causing great carnage; on the day of calamity, the sons of light shall battle with the company of darkness amid the shouts of a mighty multitude and the clamour of gods and men to (make manifest) the might of God. And it shall be a time of [great] tribulation for the people which God shall redeem; of all its afflictions none shall be as this, from its sudden beginning until its end in eternal redemption. (1.1-2, 5, 9-12)

Geza Vermes, *The Complete Dead Sea Scrolls in English* (New York: Penguin, 1997), 163-64.

---

plagues. The second plague upon Egypt was an infestation of frogs throughout the land (Exod 8:1-15). John has adapted that tradition, changing the swarm of frogs into three frog-like foul spirits.

In describing the foul spirits as proceeding from the mouths of the dragon, beast, and false prophet, John indicates their role: they are promoters of lies and propaganda in order to deceive the people and lead them to destruction. As with the second beast (false prophet) in 13:11-18, their false words will be reinforced by the deceptive signs that they perform. The specific task of the lying frog-like spirits is to rouse the kings throughout the world and assemble them for the final battle against God. [Dead Sea Scrolls] The kings from throughout the world are not the same people as "the kings from the East" (16:12). The kings from the east appear to be a threat to the Roman Empire and are poised to attack and destroy Rome. The kings from throughout the world are a larger group. They will join forces to wage war against the forces of God. The relationship of these two groups (as well as their relationship to the ten kings of 17:12-18) is not clear. Some commentators have supposed that both groups are gathered together as allies for the final battle against God, a battle that will take place only after these united forces have turned against Rome and destroyed the once mighty power. Others have seen the "kings of the whole world" as allies of Rome who will fight against "the kings from the East." Perhaps, as R. H. Charles noted, "the uprising of the kings of the East against Rome is only the preparatory step to their conflict with the Lamb, as we see in 17:12-17. Hence their combination here

(16:12) with the kings of the whole earth (17:14) to resist the Lamb."[5] We will return to this issue as we examine chapter 17.

Part of the problem in understanding the details of this section is that John has combined two different traditions here. As a result, the presentation of the material is not entirely clear. In 16:12, the picture is of an invasion of armies whose purpose is apparently to overthrow Rome. These invading armies, which, as noted, are likely an adaptation of the Nero *redivivus* myth, become instruments of God's destruction and punishment on the evil Roman Empire. In chapter 16, John does not describe their attack on Rome and its subsequent destruction. The destruction of Rome will be given in detail in chapters 17 and 18.

In 16:14-15, John is drawing upon a tradition in the Hebrew Bible that envisions God gathering all the nations of the world for divine judgment (cf. Joel 3:2; Zeph 3:8; cf. Ezek 38–39, a text that John will make use of in 19:11-21). A variation of this idea that has even more similarities with John's description occurs in Zechariah 14. This text describes God gathering all the nations of the earth for an eschatological battle against Jerusalem. God will defeat the other nations and will become the king over all the earth. John has modified this tradition, making the instigator of this gathering of the nations not God, but the evil triumvirate. Since, as noted earlier, Psalm 2 was a favorite text for John, that psalm likely was in his thoughts here also. Psalm 2:1-2 could easily be adapted to fit the idea of a final assault of the wicked nations against God:

> Why do the nations conspire,
>   and the peoples plot in vain?
> The kings of the earth set themselves,
>   and the rulers take counsel together,
>   against the LORD and his anointed.

The insertion of 16:15 seems at first glance out of place. [The Beatitude of 16:15] In fact, some scholars have argued that this verse does not belong here, but is a misplaced verse or was a later addition to the text.[6] While that is possible, no textual evidence supports the transposition or removal of this verse. Furthermore, even though the verse interrupts the flow of the sixth bowl plague, its message is appropriate for its current location in the text. This verse is the third of seven beatitudes in the Apocalypse. It promises a blessing for those who are faithful to God,

The Beatitude of 16:15

This beatitude "is John's way of reminding his hearer-readers that the visions are not to provide speculative information about the future but are a challenge from the living Christ for them to orient their lives in the present toward the coming eschatological reality."

M. Eugene Boring, *Revelation*, Interpretation: A Bible Commentary for Teaching and Preaching (Louisville: John Knox, 1989), 178.

Beatitude

In 16:15, "John suddenly steps out of his role as storyteller to address his readers directly. Being ready to face the Lord's judgment is more important than knowing in detail how it will be administered."

Adela Yarbro Collins, *The Apocalypse,* New Testament Message 22 (Wilmington DE: Michael Glazier, 1979), 115.

Words of Jesus

Because of the similarity between the beatitude of 16:15 and the words of Jesus in the Gospels, Charles Talbert has suggested that for people "who have heard the gospels in worship, these words in the Apocalypse have the effect of reinforcing the identity of the pre-Easter Jesus and the risen Christ."

Charles H. Talbert, *The Apocalypse: A Reading of the Revelation of John* (Louisville: Westminster/John Knox, 1994), 76.

who remain loyal even in the midst of the coming crisis. [Beatitude] The end time will be a period of severe crisis. The people of God must remain alert and not waver in their commitment to God. Otherwise, their fate will be the same as those who are being gathered for the final battle against God. This beatitude, then, serves as a warning that Christians must be prepared. The coming of Christ, associated with the downfall of Rome and the rebellion of the nations against God, will occur quickly and unexpectedly. The faithful should not be caught unaware and unprepared ("naked and exposed to shame"). [Words of Jesus]

The place where the kings of the world will be gathered for the final battle is called "Harmagedon" (or "Armageddon," 16:16). [Armageddon] The popular intrigue with Armageddon has grown totally out of proportion to the importance that John places on this term. This verse is the only place in all the Bible where the term occurs. The meaning of the word itself is not clear. The most widely followed suggestion explains the word etymologically as a combination of the two Hebrew words *har měgiddôn*, meaning "mountain of Megiddo." Megiddo was an ancient city that guarded the pass through the Central Highlands at the Jezreel Valley. Because of its strategic location, Megiddo was an important military site. Occupied perhaps as early as 4000 BC, the place later served as a fortified city for the Canaanites and then the Israelites. Near Megiddo was where Deborah and Barak defeated the armies of Jabin, a Canaanite king (Judg 5:19). When King Ahaziah of Judah was attacked by Jehu, he fled, wounded, to Megiddo where he died (2 Kgs 9:27). Megiddo was also the place where Josiah, king of Judah, was killed in battle against Pharaoh Neco of Egypt (2 Kgs 23:29). Megiddo, then, was associated in biblical thought with

Armageddon

AΩ   Several variations of the word "Armageddon" occur in ancient texts. Some ancient texts read "Harmagedon"; others have "Armagedon." Some texts have a single "d"; others spell the word with a double "d." A few texts lack Har (or Ar) and have only "Maged(d)on." The NRSV and several other modern English translations follow the spelling accepted now by most critical scholars, "Harmagedon." The KJV, as well as a variety of other versions, has accepted "Armageddon," the reading that is popularly used today.

Megiddo
Archaeological excavations at the site of ancient Megiddo have revealed the remains of several settlements here, each built on top of the ruins of previous settlements. The numerous layers of civilizations testify to the geographical and military importance of this site. (Credit: Mitchell Reddish)

warfare and military battles. The problem with "Mount Megiddo," if that is the correct understanding of Armageddon, is that no such mountain exists. The city of Megiddo was situated in the Jezreel Valley, not on a mountain. Visitors to the site today are aware that the present ruins sit atop a tell, an archaeological mound, because the city was continually rebuilt after it was destroyed. After being destroyed and rebuilt several times, the elevation of the city increased. Even so, Megiddo still could not be considered a mountain. Robert Mounce has noted that in John's day the tell was only around seventy feet in height.[7] [Megiddo]

H. B. Swete explained the designation of Megiddo as Mount Megiddo based on John's desire "to bring the final conflict into connexion with Ezekiel 29:2, 4," a text that describes the eschatological battle against Gog of the land of Magog as a battle that will occur in "the mountains of Israel."[8] This suggestion is plausible since John will make use of the Gog traditions later in the Apocalypse (20:8). Other commentators have suggested that *har mĕgiddôn* is a variation of *har-môʿēd*, meaning "mount of assembly," the mythical mountain of the gods in Isaiah 14:13 that the king of

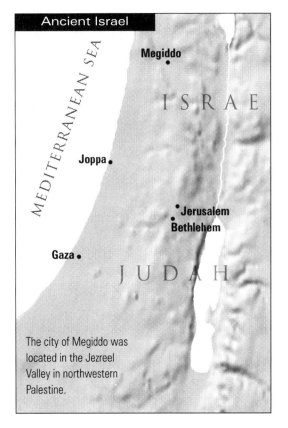

Ancient Israel

MEDITERRANEAN SEA

Megiddo

ISRAE

Joppa

Jerusalem
Bethlehem

Gaza

JUDAH

The city of Megiddo was
located in the Jezreel
Valley in northwestern
Palestine.

Babylon boasted he would climb in order to exalt himself. As Beasley-Murray commented, however, this "notion is interesting, but no one has satisfactorily explained why *Har Mo'ed* should become corrupted to *Har-Megiddo*, and so the speculation must be viewed as dubious."9

Whereas "Mount Megiddo" is the most plausible understanding of "Armageddon," John is certainly not predicting an actual battle that would occur on the plains of Megiddo. Like so much else in John's Apocalypse, Armageddon is symbolic language. It is John's name for the final conflict between good and evil.

[Map: Ancient Israel]

When the seventh angel pours out his bowl, this time into the air, John hears a voice from the temple declaring, "It is done!" (16:17). Finally, the judgments and punishments that comprise the eschatological woes have been completed. After the voice speaks, a cataclysmic earthquake strikes the earth destroying the cities of the nations that are opposed to God. The "great city" Babylon, John's code name for Rome, is singled out as the recipient of severe destruction, being "split into three parts." In the following chapters, John will present in detail the punishment and downfall of Rome for its role in the persecution of God's servants and its idolatrous and blasphemous claims. The phenomena that accompany the great earthquake ("flashes of lightning, rumblings, and peals of thunder") are typical events associated with the presence of God (cf. 4:5; Exod 19:16; Ps 18:7-19). Their occurrence here is a reminder that the punishment that befalls Rome and the other nations comes from God. The fleeing of the islands and mountains is John's poetic way of depicting the magnitude of God's judgment upon mighty Rome and its cohorts. The islands and mountains flee before such awesome and terrible devastation.

The last part of this final bowl plague is a barrage of huge hailstones that falls upon the people. The hail recalls the seventh plague in Exodus when heavy hail fell throughout the land of Egypt (Exod 9:13-26). The people who are struck by the hundred pound hailstones in Revelation are the ones who throughout John's story have refused to acknowledge the authority and power of God. Even after this punishing hailstorm, the people refuse to acknowledge the sovereignty of God. The results are the same as after the fourth and fifth bowl plagues: they curse God and refuse to repent.

CONNECTIONS

1. This series of seven bowl plagues, we are told, is the last of the plagues. After all the destruction, devastation, and pain that have been inflicted upon the earth by the seven seals, the seven trumpets, and now the seven bowls, we are ready to shout, "Thank God; it's finally over!" The intensity and horror of the scenes of punishment in the Apocalypse have been numbing. Even to a generation raised on a steady diet of violence on television, in movies, and on our streets, the destruction described in the Apocalypse is shocking. What makes these scenes of the wrath of God even more unpalatable is that the righteous characters in the story (whether human or supernatural) applaud and revel in the scenes of God's punishment on the world. "You are just, O Holy One," an angel cries as the plagues afflict the wicked. "It is what they deserve." There is something unsettling about this celebration of divine vengeance. We are uneasy with the attitudes of acceptance and even joy that accompany these plagues. This response to God's judgment seems inappropriate, as inappropriate and barbaric as the cries of waiting spectators gathered outside a Death Row prison who burst into applause and celebration when the execution of an inmate is announced. Thomas Long has clearly described this scene in chapter 16:

> It is an account of the wrath of God in all of its sea-boiling, thunder-rolling, earthquake-rattling fury. Here we see the very kitchens of heaven serving up brimming bowlfuls of God's wrath to be poured by angels upon the face of the earth. And what we read is not just a *description* of the wrath of God; it is a hand-clapping, hallelujah-shouting *celebration* of its coming.[10]

The Bowl Plagues

"The bowls do not describe events which follow and complete the events of the trumpets. Rather, the visions of the bowls express more fully the absolute accountability of humanity, its thorough-going subjection to the divine forces of judgment."

Adela Yarbro Collins, *The Apocalypse,* New Testament Message 22 (Wilmington DE: Michael Glazier, 1979), 111.

What do we do with these scenes in the Apocalypse? [The Bowl Plagues] How do we incorporate these images into our understanding of God as one who loves and cares for all of creation? The first thing to notice is that the

Beatitudes of the Apocalypse

The seven beatitudes of the Apocalypse are as follows:

1:3—"Blessed is the one who reads aloud the words of the prophecy, and blessed are those who hear and who keep what is written in it; for the time is near."

14:13—"Blessed are the dead who from now on die in the Lord."

16:15—"Blessed is the one who stays awake and is clothed, not going about naked and exposed to shame."

19:9—"Blessed are those who are invited to the marriage supper of the Lamb."

20:6—"Blessed and holy are those who share in the first resurrection."

22:7—"Blessed is the one who keeps the words of the prophecy of this book."

22:14—"Blessed are those who wash their robes, so that they will have the right to the tree of life and may enter the city by the gates."

series of calamities that strike the earth does not arise from the vindictiveness of God. A refrain that runs throughout the series of plagues, and which is most prominent in the bowl plagues, is that the purpose of these punishments is to bring people to repentance, to lead them to acknowledge the one who is both creator and redeemer. God seeks the wholeness, the salvation, of all people. Otherwise, why keep drawing the reader/hearer's attention to the failure of people to repent and acknowledge God? [Beatitudes of the Apocalypse]

Our reaction to John's emphasis on the justice of God is likely to be ambivalent. On the one hand, we yearn for justice in a world in which just and fair treatment often seems illusive. When we think about the victims of the Holocaust, when we encounter children who have been perversely violated and abused, when we hear of people who have been mercilessly tortured, raped, or slaughtered, then we yearn for and even demand justice, not only legal justice, but divine justice. If we are sensitive to racial discrimination, economic disparity, or social outcasts, then we want to join with the prophet Amos in crying, "Let justice roll down like waters." These situations, along with other less severe instances of injustice or mistreatment, especially if the victims are our friends, our family, or even ourselves, make us clamor for God to bring justice to our world. It is that same yearning for justice that stands behind the various plagues directed against an evil world in Revelation. John recognized that a God whose ways are indeed "true and just" (16:7) must eventually bring justice to a world that is wrecked by hatred, cruelty, pain, and suffering. The God who heard the cries of the Hebrew slaves in Israel and set them free must one day act to set the rest of the world free from its bondage to injustice. [The Seven Bowl Plagues]

Thomas Long, in the sermon cited earlier, has stated:

To speak of God's wrath is to speak of God's liberating and redemptive love pitted against all that opposes it, all that would keep humanity captive and in slavery. God's wrath is that expression of God's love that will not allow victims to suffer everlastingly without hope, that will not forever abandon the helpless, that will not allow the forces that destroy and demean human life to speak the last word. . . .

But the word from the seer of Revelation is that God, who is not bound by the walls of history, will not leave the helpless forever

The Seven Bowl Plagues

Giusto de Menabuoi (1349–c.1390) was a painter born in Florence but trained in northern Italy. He became a successful and progressive painter due to his exposure to the work of the artists Giotto and Maso di Banco in Padua. Giusto became a Paduan citizen in April 1375 and shortly thereafter began the fresco decoration of the Romanesque baptistery in that city. The patron was Fina Buzzacarina, wife of the ruler of Padua, Francesco I da Carrara. The couple hoped to be, and were, buried in the baptistry. The overall plan of the interior decoration was complex, including scenes of the *Pantokrator*, *Creation*, the *Evangelists*, the *Life of St. John the Baptist,* and the *Life of the Passion of Christ*. The Apocalypse scenes are located on the walls. Giusto depicts a single angel holding the seven bowls of the plague. The angel has not yet distributed the bowls to other angels as is written in Rev 16 or begun to pour them. Instead, he stands majestically, balancing four in one hand and three in the other, in a seemingly timeless position. Giusto de Menabuoi. *Angel with the Seven Bowls.* 1375. Fresco. Baptistry, Padua, Italy. (Credit: Alinari/Art Resource, NY)

---

alone. The prayers of all the hopeless have been heard, and neither death, nor principalities, nor things present, nor things to come, nor powers, nor height, nor depth, nor anything else in all creation can stay the hand of God's redemption. The Red Sea boils again, the earthquake shakes Golgotha once more, the heavenly courts are stirring, and Death itself, with all its arrogant allies, will be made to drink from the bowls of the wrath of God.

So, if you hunger for righteousness, hear this word of the wrath of God poured out on all evil. If you cry out in hopeless pain, hear this word of the wrath of God poured out on all foul disease and cruelty. If you cannot read the newspaper without weeping for children who are abused and war widows who grieve without consolation and people who starve with knots of grass in their stomachs, hear this word of the wrath of God poured out upon injustice. And pray—pray to God that it's true.[11]

And yet as valid and true as this understanding of God's justice is, we must never forget that pure justice is not what we want

Divine Justice

 In regard to John's depiction of divine justice in ch. 16, Elisabeth Schüssler Fiorenza has written,

Such justice is inflicted neither from the outside nor with despotic arbitrariness. Justice is not an alien imposition by some external authority. Rather, justice is understood as the conviction that each act brings about consequences which must be faced responsibly. It is God who has the power to make sure that all people have to bear the consequences of their actions. All receive what is their due. The Greek text does not speak of punishments but about judgment and justice. Not the desire to inflict punitive torments but the values of equity and vindication motivate and direct God's wrath and judgment.

Elisabeth Schüssler Fiorenza, *Revelation: Vision of a Just World*, Proclamation Commentaries (Minneapolis: Fortress, 1991), 95.

---

either. [Divine Justice] We want justice tempered by mercy—justice for others, perhaps, but mercy for ourselves! If God were to give us only what we deserved, the punishment would be more than we could bear. Perhaps that is part of our discomfort with the many scenes of God's judgment in the Apocalypse. We are afraid that if we ask too loudly and too persistently for justice, then that may be exactly what we get!

Is mercy compatible with justice? Is there room in God's love for wrath? John's answer is "yes." In fact, God's wrath is a part of God's love. It is God's wrath, God's justice, that responds to the cries of the martyrs under the altar in 6:9-11. It is God's wrath that hears and responds to the prayers of God's people in 8:3-5. God's love for creation and the people God created means that God cannot ignore the cries of the people of the earth nor the whole creation that has been groaning for redemption (Rom 8:18-25). For John, the wrath of God is the wrath of the Lamb—the Lamb, John never lets us forget, who was slain; the Lamb who conquered by his own death. That self-sacrificial death is a part of God's response to a world that cries for justice. So when we look for the justice of God, we should not be surprised if that justice is tempered by—even comes in the form of—mercy (cf. the parable of the laborers in the vineyard in Matt 20:1-16).

The various plagues in Revelation are John's pictorial way of saying that God has not abandoned creation nor ignored the pain, suffering, and evil that have taken root in that creation. Ultimately, God will act to bring justice to God's broken world.

2. The teacher or preacher dealing with chapter 16 must inevitably respond to his/her audience's questions about Armageddon, a term that is used frequently today to refer to any kind of major catastrophe or cataclysmic event. Popular purveyors of apocalyptic

scenarios frequently claim on the basis of this text that a literal battle will take place on the plains of Megiddo. There in northern Israel, the returning Messiah will defeat the antichrist, who will lead all the armies of the wicked nations of the world. Or in some schemes, Armageddon will be the final battle between the wicked forces, who will defeat each other, after which Christ will return. On the basis of a perverse reading of the sixth trumpet plague and the sixth bowl plague, apocalyptic preachers proclaim that one of the armies involved in this final battle will be two hundred million Chinese cavalry ("from the East"). Until the collapse of the Soviet Union in the 1990s such preachers were certain that they could find proof in biblical texts that one of the combatants at Armageddon would be the Russians. [Final Battle]

It should be clear to anyone who values the Bible that these approaches to the text of Revelation, contrary to the claims of their proponents, do not take the text seriously. Rather, they turn the Apocalypse, and indeed the rest of the Scriptures, into a deck of religious Tarot cards whereby the "spiritually enlightened" can "predict" specific events that will occur in the world. Armageddon in Revelation 16:16 does not refer to a literal battle that will occur. This scene in Revelation is another example of John's creative use of symbolic language. No seven-headed beast will occur at the end of time; no various colored horses will gallop across the world; no swarm of mutant locust-horses will attack the world; and no actual battle will occur at Megiddo. Armageddon symbolizes the final desperate struggle of evil against the overwhelming power and goodness of God. If the generally accepted meaning of Armageddon as Mount Megiddo is correct, then John likely chose that name for the final battle because of Megiddo's association with military conquests. If John were writing today for an American audience, then he might locate the "final battle" at Gettysburg or Bunker Hill, places that would connote war to modern readers.

One is tempted to dismiss and ignore these literalistic interpretations of Armageddon as not only foolish, but also benign. Unfortunately, in some cases such views are not only misguided, but potentially dangerous. Because of the identification of Megiddo as the site for this eschatological conflict, any disturbances in the Middle East take on immense significance. "Are these

Final Battle

"The conception of the last great battle between good and evil was part of the traditional Jewish belief about the Last Things. It is a profound myth, witnessing to the reality of good and the seriousness of evil. Hebrew belief in God's nature was such that it was not content to look on life as an unending conflict between good and bad as in Persian religion. Because God was both righteous and almighty he must eventually overcome evil."

Ronald H. Preston and Anthony T. Hanson, *The Revelation of Saint John the Divine* (London: SCM, 1949), 108-109.

conflicts the prelude to Armageddon?" the apocalyptic peddlers ask. "Are the 'evil nations' of the world beginning their assault on Israel?" Israel is viewed as an innocent victim, and all Arab nations are seen as evil instruments of Satan. Such interpretations frequently degenerate into racial and ethnic hatred: Arabs are demonized and must be annihilated. Plus, Middle East politics are volatile enough without pouring more fuel on the fire. Teachers and preachers should help their audiences understand that while these symbols of the Apocalypse are serious attempts to describe the struggle between good and evil, they are not predictions that will come true in any detailed or literal manner. To read the Apocalypse as foretelling actual events that will occur, as if John were some religious fortune-teller, is to distort and demean this powerful vision of God's sovereignty, justice, and triumph.

NOTES

[1] Isbon T. Beckwith, *The Apocalypse of John: Studies in Introduction with a Critical and Exegetical Commentary* (Macmillan, 1919; reprint, Grand Rapids: Baker Book House, 1979), 680.

[2] Jürgen Roloff, *The Revelation of John: A Continental Commentary*, Continental Commentaries, trans. John E. Alsup (Minneapolis: Fortress, 1993), 189.

[3] G. B. Caird, *A Commentary on the Revelation of St. John the Divine*, Harper's New Testament Commentaries (New York: Harper & Row, 1966), 204-205.

[4] R. H. Charles, *A Critical and Exegetical Commentary on the Revelation of St. John*, The International Critical Commentary, 2 vols. (Edinburgh: T. & T. Clark, 1920), 2:47.

[5] Ibid.

[6] Charles (*Revelation*, 2:49), for example, argued that the verse originally belonged between 3:3a and 3:3b.

[7] Robert H. Mounce, *The Book of Revelation*, The New International Commentary on the New Testament, rev. ed. (Grand Rapids: Eerdmans, 1998), 301.

[8] Henry Barclay Swete, *Commentary on Revelation* (1911; reprint, Grand Rapids: Kregel Publications, 1977), 209.

[9] George R. Beasley-Murray, *The Book of Revelation*, New Century Bible (Greenwood SC: Attic, 1974), 245.

[10] Thomas G. Long, "Praying for the Wrath of God," *Preaching Through the Apocalypse: Sermons from Revelation*, ed. Cornish R. Rogers and Joseph R. Jeter Jr. (St. Louis: Chalice, 1992), 134.

[11] Ibid., 138-39.

THE GREAT WHORE

17:1-18

The Fall of Babylon, 17:1–19:10

The contents of 17:1–19:10 develop further the seventh bowl plague of chapter 16. John is not presenting a new event but is presenting more fully the same destruction of "Babylon" that was passed over quickly in 16:17-21. Jürgen Roloff described 17:1–19:10 as "an enlargement photograph" of the seventh bowl plague.[1] Or to use imagery from the computer world, 17:1–19:10 functions as a hypertext, a "window" that can be opened to provide the reader more details about the events in the main body of the text (16:17-21). At the outset, John cues the hearer/reader to this connection between the bowl plagues and the events of 17:1–19:10 by identifying the angel of 17:1 as "one of the seven angels who had the seven bowls."

COMMENTARY

The Great Whore, 17:1-18

Chapter 17 falls into three parts: an introduction (17:1-2), the vision of the great whore on the scarlet beast (17:3-6), and the interpretation of the vision (17:7-18). The introduction in vv. 1-2 serves to introduce the entire section of 17:1–19:10, rather than only the vision of chapter 17, for the entire section is concerned with "the judgment of the great whore" (17:1). The technique of presenting a vision followed by its interpretation is common in apocalyptic tradition as is found, for example, in Daniel 7–12. Often, as here in Revelation, the interpretation is given by an angel guide. John does not utilize the interpreting angel as fully as other apocalyptic writers often do. In 2 Esdras, for example, the angel Uriel repeatedly appears to Ezra to interpret his dreams and answer his questions. In Revelation, John has mentioned in the opening verse of the book that an angel has been sent to him to make known God's message, but an interpreting angel does not actually appear until chapter 17. Later, in 22:6, John will state again that an angel has been sent to reveal God's message to him.

The Great Whore on the Beast

Nicolas Bataille. *The Great Whore Riding on the Seven-Headed Beast* from the *Apocalypse of Angers*. 1375–1380. Musee de Tapisseries. Angers, France. (Credit: Erich Lessing/Art Resource, NY)

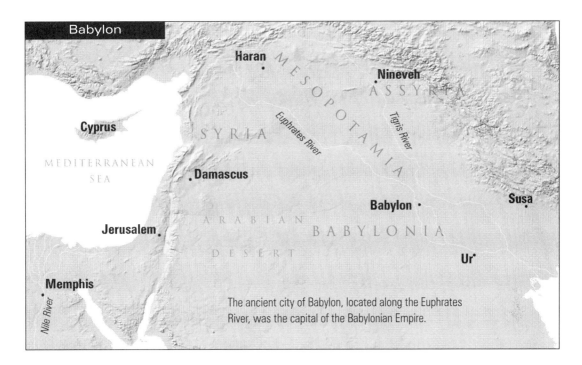

The ancient city of Babylon, located along the Euphrates River, was the capital of the Babylonian Empire.

The words of the angel introduce the figure who dominates this section of John's vision, the "great whore" (17:1). [The Great Whore on the Beast] Yet even though the great whore is on center stage, this scene is not her shining moment, for as John tells us, the purpose of this scene is to present God's judgment of the whore (17:1). As the hearer/reader of Revelation should expect by now, John's imagery of a prostitute represents something other than what it seems. This woman is called "Babylon" (17:5), John's name for Rome (cf. 14:8; 16:19). [Map: Babylon] A fuller description and iden- tification of the woman is given in the verses that follow. The use of sexual imagery to describe unfaithfulness to God has a rich biblical history (see commentary on 2:12-17). John himself has already used sexual language to describe religious infidelity when he accused the woman, "Jezebel," in the church at Thyatira of "prac- ticing fornication" and her followers of committing "adultery with her" (2:20-22). In John's eyes, Rome deserves to be called a whore because of her arrogant claims of universal sovereignty, power, and authority—claims that John sees as false claims. Furthermore, as chapter 18 will elaborate, the luxury and greed of the city are a major part of her "fornication." In addition, the imperial cult and the many gods and goddesses of the empire contribute to the city's sin of "fornication." [The Role of Rome]

Much of John's description of Rome as Babylon, the "great whore," is borrowed from Jeremiah 51, which declares God's judg- ment and destruction of Babylon (cf. Nah 3, which describes the

The Role of Rome

"In Revelation, Rome's relationship to the kings of the earth and the inhabitants of the earth is a prostituted (i.e., idolatrous) relationship. The upshot is that Rome becomes a subject, an absolute and divine subject, and all its kings and vassals become objects bought and sold. Imperial Rome is fetishized, as expressed in the veneration of Rome as a goddess. This fetishization turns the whole empire into one huge *porneia*, that is, into massive harlotry, an orgy of idolatry."

Pablo Richard, *Apocalypse: A People's Commentary on the Book of Revelation* (Maryknoll NY: Orbis Books, 1995), 130.

city of Nineveh as a drunken prostitute "who enslaves nations through her debaucheries"). Such is the case with the statement that she is "seated on many waters" (17:1; cf. Jer 51:13), originally a reference to the Euphrates River and the many canals around ancient Babylon that dispersed the water to the surrounding areas. Also borrowed from Jeremiah 51 is the statement that others have become drunk from her wine (17:2; cf. Jer 51:7). As with Babylon, Rome's wealth, power, and influence are too alluring for many kings and nations to resist. They have entered into political and commercial alliances with Rome. They drink from her cup and become intoxicated and thus share in her guilt.

[Map: The Roman Empire]

The Roman Empire at the beginning of the 2d C. AD.

In 17:3, John declares that the angel "carried me away in the spirit into a wilderness." Four times in the Apocalypse, John states that he "was in the spirit" or "carried away in the spirit" (1:10; 4:2; 17:3; 21:10), meaning he was in a trance or a state of ecstasy. During this revelatory experience John envisions himself being carried to a wilderness. In biblical tradition, the wilderness is often the place of divine revelation. It is also the place of divine rescue or salvation. On the other hand, the wilderness is also a place of disobedience, temptation, or evil. It is the haunt of demons. The negative connotation seems to be at work here.

Verses 3-6 present John's description of the woman and the beast on which she rides. The beast—with ten horns, seven heads, and covered with blasphemous names—we recognize already. He has appeared in chapter 13 as the beast from the sea, John's symbol for the Roman Empire. His scarlet color (as well as the ten horns and seven heads) reminds us of another beast, the dragon of chapter 12.

He is scarlet in color because he is the agent of the great red dragon, Satan. The blasphemous names that cover the beast are likely allusions to the application of divine titles to the Roman emperors, such titles as "lord," "god," "savior," "almighty."

The portrait John paints of the woman depicts her in luxuriant, even ostentatious, attire. She is arrayed in purple (the color of royalty) and scarlet. [Purple] Both of these colors were symbols of the high status of the wealthy. Not only her clothing but also her accessories (gold, jewels, and pearls) denote wealth and extravagance. She is a symbol of status, power, and affluence. At least that is the way that she sees herself and was viewed by almost everyone else. She is attractive, rich, and powerful. No wonder she has enticed the world to follow after her! For John, however, the attire of the woman is perhaps better understood as an expression of excess and wantonness. She is not a symbol of beauty to be admired, but a representation of gaudiness and debauchery that is to be abhorred. David Aune has pointed out that the dress of the woman has much in common with the stereotypical dress of courtesans or wealthy prostitutes.[2]

The golden cup in the woman's hand is likely John's adaptation of Jeremiah 51:7:

> Babylon was a golden cup in the LORD's hand,
>   making all the earth drunken.

For Jeremiah, Babylon was the cup in God's hand. John modifies the image, making the woman the bearer of the cup. Her cup is not filled with wine, but with "abominations and the impurities of her fornication" (17:4). The term "abominations" (*bdelygmatōn*) can mean anything that is abhorrent or detestable. In the Hebrew Bible, the comparable word (*šiqqûṣ*) was often applied to idols and idolatrous practices. The best-known example is in Daniel 9:27, which describes the profanation of the Jerusalem temple when Antiochus IV turned the temple into a temple for Zeus ("an abomination that desolates"; cf. Mark 13:14, "desolating sacrilege" [*bdelygma tēs erēmōseōs*]). In Revelation, "abominations and the impurities of her fornications" likely refer to the idolatrous beliefs and practices associated with the imperial cult. [The Great Whore and Jezebel]

Purple

The color purple was highly prized in the ancient world and was a symbol of status and wealth. Although not restricted to use by royalty alone, it was often associated with kings, queens, and other powerful rulers. The best purple dye was made from various genera and species of marine snails, especially from *Murex brandaris*. Dye made from this particular snail was deep blue violet in color and was colorfast. Such dye was very expensive, "for it is estimated that 12,000 *Murex brandaris* would have been needed to produce 1.4 grams of crude dye."

Frederick W. Danker, "Purple," *The Anchor Bible Dictionary*, ed. David Noel Freedman, 6 vols. (New York: Doubleday & Co., 1992), 5:557-60.

The Great Whore and Jezebel

The woman of ch. 17 and the Jezebel figure of 2:20-23 have several characteristics in common. Both are accused of fornication; both have followers whom they have seduced; both are doomed, along with their followers, to punishment. In essence, both figures are manifestations of the same sin: they encourage people to worship other gods, either through participation in the religious aspects of pagan culture or through the imperial cult.

Written across the forehead of this jewel-bedecked woman astride the scarlet beast is her name, "Babylon the great, mother of whores and of earth's abominations." Some commentators have suggested that the placement of the name on the forehead is drawn from the supposed practice of Roman prostitutes of wearing their names on their headbands. While this is possible, the evidence for such a practice is questionable.[3] Previously John has used the motif of an identifying mark stamped on an individual's forehead (7:3; 9:4; 13:16; 14:1; see also 3:12; 19:12; 22:4). Here, the woman is identified by the name on her forehead: "Babylon the great, mother of whores and of earth's abominations." Not only is Rome guilty of idolatry and seduction herself, but she is the source of such evil throughout the world. Worship of the emperor reached well beyond the boundaries of Rome and seduced people throughout the empire into participating in its idolatry. [Dea Roma]

Rome's guilt includes more than idolatry, however. She has also persecuted and killed the faithful people of God. This reference to the "blood of the saints and the blood of the witnesses to Jesus" (17:6) could include not only the martyrdoms of Antipas (2:13) and others in Asia Minor whom John has known who were killed on account of their Christian faith, but might also refer to the infamous persecution under Nero that resulted in the horrendous deaths of several Christians in Rome.

Dea Roma

Statue of a seated *Dea Roma*, the goddess of Rome.

Dea Roma. 2d C. AD. Marble. Palazzo dei Conservatori, Capitoline Museums. Rome, Italy. (Credit: Mitchell Reddish)

This scene is an unmasking of the identity of Rome in which the description of the great whore serves as a parody of Dea Roma, the patron goddess of Rome. [Rome] Instead of Rome, the great goddess, John reveals what Rome is really like. She is a gaudy, drunken whore who persecutes and slaughters the people of God. Instead of an attractive goddess, she is a repulsive drunk whose cup is filled with the blood of her victims.

John's statement that "when I saw her, I was greatly amazed" (17:6) is a literary device that prepares the way for the interpreting angel to explain the meaning of what John has seen. Even though

Rome
Ruins of the Roman Forum, the political and administrative center of ancient Rome. (Credit: Mitchell Reddish)

the angel promises to explain both the woman and the beast, the latter receives the major attention, while the former is almost forgotten until 17:18. The angel describes the beast as one "who was, and is not, and is about to ascend from the bottomless pit and go to destruction" (17:8). The reader/hearer should recognize this statement immediately as a parody of the words applied to God: the one "who is and who was and who is to come" (1:4, 8; 4:8; cf. 11:17; 16:5). The beast is the antithesis of God. Whereas God is the eternal one who is the source of all life, the beast is headed for destruction and will carry his supporters to destruction as well. This statement about the beast is connected with the Nero *redivivus* myth (see 13:3). The beast who "was and is not" refers to Nero, who has already died. Yet he "is about to ascend from the bottomless pit," meaning that the menace of Nero will appear once more. John would not have intended this literally, as if Nero would be reborn or reincarnated. Rather, John is saying that in the future the horrors of Nero will be visited on the empire again. Even this frightening message has a word of hope, however. The forces of "Nero" will not last, but will be destroyed. [Nero]

A shift has taken place in the symbolism in v. 8. Earlier in chapter 17 the beast symbolizes the Roman Empire. In v. 8, the beast represents an individual, the emperor. The reader/hearer should not be overly concerned with this seeming inconsistency. Symbols, particularly in apocalyptic literature, are often fluid. Furthermore, the emperor is an embodiment of the empire and its evils.

Verses 9-14 provide the angel's interpretation for the seven heads and ten horns of the beast. Two interpretations are given for the seven heads. The first interpretation is clear: "the seven heads are seven mountains on which the woman is seated." Rome was known as the city of seven hills. This statement is a clear indication that the woman and the beast represent Rome and the empire. Unfortunately, the second meaning given for the seven heads is not as evident. The angel says the seven heads "are seven kings, of whom five have fallen, one is living, and the other has not yet come" (17:9-10). Clearly the seven heads represent Roman emperors. [John's Critique of the Empire] The problem arises in trying to determine which seven emperors John had in mind. Scholars have proposed numerous solutions to this problem, none completely satisfactory. Depending upon with which emperor one chooses to

Nero

A bust of the young Nero, emperor of Rome from AD 54–68.

Bust of Nero. AD 54–68. Marble. Ancient Corinth Archaeological Museum. Corinth, Greece. (Credit: Mitchell Reddish)

start the numbering, different emperors appear on the list. Does one start with Augustus, whose reign is usually considered the beginning of the empire? Or does one begin with Julius Caesar (who ended the Roman Republic) as the first emperor, a practice followed by some ancient writers? Some commentators have suggested beginning with Tiberius, who was the emperor when Jesus was crucified, on the basis that, for Christians, the death of Jesus began a new era. For a similar reason, some have suggested starting with Gaius (Caligula), who followed Tiberius and thus was the first emperor of the new age that began with the death of Jesus. Other commentators have proposed starting the numbering with Nero, the first emperor to persecute the church, or even with Galba, with whom the Roman historian Tacitus began his *Histories*. In addition to the problem of determining where to start the numbering, a question arises about the three emperors whose reigns were from

---

John's Critique of the Empire

Although John's imagery of the multiheaded beast emphasizes the role of the emperors, Steven Friesen has persuasively argued that John's primary target was the provincial administration and society that fostered emperor worship. He has written,

John's critique was therefore directed more at local enemies than at the distant emperor. Outmoded views of imperial cults that focused on the role of the emperor resulted in a misinterpretation of Revelation. Certainly John railed against the emperor, but was the emperor his primary audience or even his primary opponent? In the late first century in Asia, a denunciation of imperial cults constituted a denunciation of city efforts to define themselves, a rejection of proper legal decisions of the *koinon* [provincial assembly], and a sarcastic commentary on the public religious activities of the wealthy and of many others. John not only prophesied against imperial power; he also declared illegitimate the presuppositions of the local élite's claim to authority and condemned the general population for their compliance. If the author's trip to Patmos was punishment, it occurred because John was a nuisance to the province rather than the empire.

The Book of Revelation must be understood in its local setting as part of a clash of religious ideologies, for it represents an assault on fundamental issues of social organization in late first-century Asia. The text was seditious not because it attacked the emperor, but because it indicted the emerging social order in Asia as a blasphemous force that deceived all people and spilled the blood of the saints.

Steven Friesen, "The Cult of the Roman Emperors in Ephesos: Temple Wardens, City Titles, and the Interpretation of the Revelation of John," *Ephesos: Metropolis of Asia,* ed. Helmut Koester (Valley Forge PA: Trinity, 1995), 250.

AD 68–69. Should they be counted in the list since some ancient writers considered their reigns insignificant?

These uncertainties highlight the problems in trying to decipher John's enigmatic seven heads of the beast. Because seven is a favorite number for John in Revelation, seven probably carries more symbolic than historic value in the enumeration of the emperors. We have already seen in chapter 12 that a seven-headed monster is part of the imagery that John has borrowed from the world of mythology. Furthermore, Rome was traditionally said to have had seven kings from its founding in 753 BC until its last Etruscan king in 508 BC.[4] Thus to spend time trying to determine exactly which Roman emperors make up the seven heads is likely an exercise in futility. John does not intend to enumerate specific rulers. Rather, the five who "have fallen" (17:10) represent all the rulers up to his time. The one who "is living" is the current emperor, likely Domitian. After him another ruler will arise whose reign will be brief. He will be followed by the final ruler, one who will be a "rebirth" of the spirit of Nero, the last great figure of evil, the antichrist. Thus the eighth "belongs to the seven" (17:11) because it is Nero all over again. [Roman Emperors]

Roman Emperors

The following chart gives the Roman emperors up to Domitian (including Julius Caesar, who actually bore the official title *dictator*, not *imperator*) and various attempts by scholars to number them on the basis of Rev 17:9-11.

Emperor										
Julius Caesar (d. 44 BC)	1	1	1							
Augustus (27 BC–AD 14)	2	2	2	1	1					
Tiberius (14–37)	3	3		2	2	1				
Gaius (Caligula) (37–41)	4	4		3	3	2	1	1		
Claudius (41–54)	5	5	3	4	4	3	2	2		
Nero (54–68)	6	6		5	5	4	3	3	1	
Galba (June 68–January 69)	7			6		5	4		2	1
Otho (69)	8			7		6	5		3	2
Vitellius (69)				8		7	6		4	3
Vespasian (69–79)		7	4		6	8	7	4	5	4
Titus (79–81)		8	5		7		8	5	6	5
Domitian (81–96)			6		8			6	7	6

Reasons for beginning the list with different emperors:

Julius Caesar—Brought the Roman Republic to an end

Augustus—First official emperor

Tiberius—Emperor during death of Jesus; beginning of "new age" according to Christian thought

Gaius—First emperor after death of Jesus and the beginning of "new age"; also infamous for his mistreatment of Jews and attempt to place his statue in Jerusalem temple.

Nero—First persecutor of Christians

Galba—Roman historian Tacitus begins his *Histories* with the reign of Galba

- The third column numbers the emperors who were deified by the Roman Senate, plus Domitian who claimed divine status for himself.
- The last column begins with Gaius since he was the first emperor (not counting Julius Caesar) who was killed ("have fallen" in 17:10 is understood as referring to violent death); remainder in list also died violently.
- Some columns omit Galba, Otho, and Vitellius whose reigns were so brief.

Adapted from David E. Aune, *Revelation 17–22,* Word Biblical Commentary (Nashville: Thomas Nelson, 1988), 947.

By placing the contemporary ruler as the sixth out of seven (or eight), John is following typical apocalyptic practice of claiming that time is running out and the current point in history is near the end. After the present ruler, another will arise who will last only a short while before the final ruler appears. For beleaguered readers/hearers who were tempted to give up on their faith, the implicit message is, "Hold out a short while longer. The end is near" (cf. 1:1, 3). Even though an eighth ruler will arise, he "goes to destruction" (17:11).

The angel identifies the ten horns of the beast as "ten kings who have not yet received a kingdom, but they are to receive authority as kings for one hour, together with the beast" (17:12). The imagery of ten horns on the beast comes from the fourth beast of

Daniel 7. As with the number of heads on the beast, the number of horns is borrowed from tradition and does not denote a definite, fixed amount. These ten rulers join with the beast to attack the Lamb. Whether they are the same as the "kings of the whole world" in 16:14 or are a separate group is not clear. Some commentators have argued that because the ten are not kings yet, but in the future will "receive authority," as well as because they are a part of the beast (they are his "horns"), they are distinct from "the kings of the whole world" of 16:14. If this argument is valid, then they likely represent provincial governors or other local rulers. On the other hand, they play the same role as the kings of 16:14, joining forces with the beast to wage war against the forces of God.

The final battle between the allies of the beast and the forces of God has been mentioned already in the preceding chapter when John described the assembling of the armies at Harmagedon "for battle on the great day of God the Almighty" (16:14). Neither in chapter 16 nor here does John give any details about this eschatological battle, which will culminate in the defeat of the beast and his forces. Further details will have to wait until John returns to this theme in 19:11-21. Here in chapter 17, John assures us that Christ will be victorious—"the Lamb will conquer them" (17:14). [Defeat of the Beast] The assault by the forces of evil will be brief, for the ten horns will receive authority "for one hour" only (17:12). In declaring the Lamb to be "Lord of lords and King of kings" (17:14; cf. 19:16), John applies to Jesus titles that are used elsewhere in biblical tradition for God (cf. Deut 10:17; Ps 136:3; Dan 2:47; 2 Macc 13:4; 1 Tim 6:15). This practice is consistent with John's exalted Christology, evident throughout the Apocalypse. Even though Christ is distinct from God, he functions on God's behalf and is so closely identified with God that the same titles can be applied to both.

The conquering Lamb is accompanied by those who "are called and chosen and faithful" (17:14). These are the faithful followers of the Lamb described in 14:1-5, the ones who have conquered "by the blood of the Lamb and by the word of their testimony" (12:11). Is their presence with Christ a passive role only? Not likely, for John sees the faithful as contributing to the overthrow of evil. The attack of the beast is directed against God's people. Those who validate their calling by remaining "faithful and true witnesses"

Defeat of the Beast

"In 17:12-14 the beast who appears at the end is directly defeated by the Lamb, along with the 'ten kings' who are his cohorts in the last days. This is John's pictorial, not historical, affirmation that evil, however it is imagined, will finally be defeated by the power of God already manifest in the victory of the Lamb who by his cross has conquered (5:1-14). Evil is doomed because it is already defeated by God's act in Christ."

M. Eugene Boring, *Revelation*, Interpretation: A Bible Commentary for Teaching and Preaching (Louisville: John Knox, 1989), 184.

help bring about the defeat of the beast and his cohorts. These are the ones who "have fought the good fight . . . and have kept the faith" (2 Tim 4:7), even if their faithfulness cost them their lives.

The Roman Empire of John's day stretched throughout much of the known world. Accordingly the angel interprets the waters upon which the woman is seated (cf. Jer 51:13) as representing "peoples and multitudes and nations and languages" (17:15). All is not well for this woman riding the beast, however. In a surprising twist, the angel interpreter declares that the powers represented by the ten horns will join forces with the beast and turn against the whore. In gruesome imagery, the angel describes their attack on mother Rome: "they will make her desolate and naked; they will devour her flesh and burn her up with fire" (17:16). [They Will Devour Her Flesh] Mighty Rome, which ruled the seas and the land and was the center of power and wealth, is now humiliated and destroyed. The Nero *redivivus* myth expected Nero to return from the East with an army of Parthian soldiers and attack Rome. The destruction of the whore by the beast and the ten kings is, in part, John's adaptation of the Nero *redivivus* myth. John is also dependent here on imagery from the Hebrew Bible. The details of the assault on Rome, the whore, likely are modeled after Ezekiel 23, in which Ezekiel portrayed the cities of Samaria and Jerusalem as sibling whores, Oholah and Oholibah, whose lovers eventually turn on them and destroy them (cf. Ezek 16). The descriptions in Ezekiel are even more graphic than John's portrayal of the whore's defeat. Ezekiel said that the Assyrians turned on Oholah (Samaria) and "uncovered her nakedness; they seized her sons and her daughters; and they killed her with the sword" (23:10). The fury against Oholibah (Jerusalem) is even worse. Her former lovers "shall cut off your nose and your ears, and your survivors shall fall by the sword. They shall seize your sons and your daughters, and your survivors shall be devoured by fire. They shall also strip you of your clothes and take away your fine jewels. . . . They shall deal with you in hatred, and take away all the fruit of your labor, and leave you naked and bare" (23:25-29).

This scene in Revelation 17 depicts the self-destructiveness of evil. Eventually the allies of Rome turn on the city and destroy it. Caird stated, "The savaging of the whore by the monster and its horns is John's most vivid symbol for the self-destroying power of evil."[5] Greed, power, and violence may succeed for a while.

They Will Devour Her Flesh

The statement that the ten kings and the beast will turn on the woman and devour her flesh (17:16) is reminiscent of the fate of Jezebel, an archetype for the whore of Babylon. In 2 Kgs 9:30-37, after being thrown from the window, Jezebel was devoured by dogs so that "when they went to bury her, they found no more of her than the skull and the feet and the palms of her hands" (17:35).

Empires may even be built based on them. Yet, ultimately, such forces turn on their own leaders and devour them. Rome may look all-powerful and unassailable, but John knows better. Its days are numbered. The loyalty of its subjects is a false and fickle loyalty. Given the chance, they will bring mighty Rome to ruin. John wants his readers/hearers to see Rome as he sees it—not invincible and eternal, but vulnerable and doomed. As J. P. M. Sweet commented, "His purpose is to warn Christians infatuated or overawed by Rome of the fragility of the *dominion* she exercises over *the kings of the earth* (17:18)."[6]

The coup against Rome by its allies serves the ultimate purposes of God. It demonstrates how God uses the forces of evil to bring about God's plans. Even though the mighty armies and nations of the world may think they are in control, John believes otherwise. Even the destructiveness of the ten kings and the beast serves the will of God by bringing about the end of Rome. The idea that God uses even God's enemies to carry out divine purposes is commonplace in the Hebrew Bible (cf. Isa 5:25-30; 7:17-25; 9:8-12; 10:5-11; 13:17-22; 21:1-10; Jer 5:10-17; 25:8-14; Ezek 16:35-43; 23:9-10, 22-35; Hab 1:5-11).

Several commentators have noted the awkwardness of John's arrangement of his material in the latter half of chapter 17. Verses 12-14 describe the war waged by the beast and the ten horns against the Lamb, who conquers them. Yet in the following verses, 15-17, the beast and ten horns attack Rome and destroy the city. Logically, the destruction of Rome should precede the defeat of the beast and his cohorts. As elsewhere in John's visions, logical or chronological consistency should not be pressed. John is presenting images of the overthrow of evil, not actual historical events that will occur. For John, the defeat of Rome and the final overthrow of evil are closely related.

CONNECTIONS

1. In spite of the amount of time often spent trying to decode the numbers in chapter 17, the purpose of this chapter is not to provide clues to the identity of political figures in the ancient (or modern) world. This text is no parlor game or mathematical puzzle. John's readers/hearers likely could not name the previous five emperors, in the same way that modern readers would probably have a hard time naming in order all the presidents of the United States in the last seventy-five years.[7] Even though John's

It Goes to Destruction

Allan Boesak, writing while South Africa was still in the grips of apartheid, has proclaimed with the voice of a prophet,

The political observers count tanks and missiles, soldiers and guns. They analyze the "strength" of Pretoria and count the threats and the dead bodies on the streets, and they smile paternalistically at the witness of the church. They ask us for the reasons for our "optimism." They do not understand the faith of the church, neither do they understand the continuity of the biblical tradition. When they see guns and more guns, they see power. The church sees a growing powerlessness: "it goes to perdition" (17:11). They scrutinize a new law that gives even more frightening powers to the Minister of Law and Order and to his "security forces." They see power. The church knows: "it goes to perdition." They look at the long lists of names of detainees,

lists smuggled out of the country contrary to the laws of the state of emergency, and they see power. The church prays for those people, calls their names before the throne of God, and knows that "it goes to perdition," this beast. For the key here is not who the beast is; the church knows that. Neither is the key whether we begin counting from D. F. Malan, or H. F. Verwoerd or P. W. Botha, from 1910 or from 1948. The key here is the understanding of the mystery: this beast, this powerful, merciless, violent beast, was and is not and goes to perdition. "The beast that you saw was, and is not, and is to ascend from the bottomless pit and go to perdition" (17:8). It has no life and no future. It goes from hell to hell.

Allan A. Boesak, *Comfort and Protest: Reflections on the Apocalypse of John of Patmos* (Philadelphia: Westminster, 1987), 115-16.

---

readers/hearers know who the current emperor is, John is concerned that they do not understand the true nature of the emperor and the empire over which he rules. Some have been seduced by the wealth and extravagance of mighty Rome. Others are thinking they can be involved with Rome and its activities without any compromise to their faith. John knows that is not the case, however. As alluring as Rome may seem, she is not a benign and benevolent figure. John portrays the "divine Roma" for what she really is— a drunken, murderous whore who is the enemy of the people of God. Supporting the woman is a terrible beast, the beast that rises from the bottomless pit. By portraying the true nature of the beast in such stark terms, John lays before his audience a choice—they must be loyal either to the Lamb or to the beast. They cannot serve both. [It Goes to Destruction]

As explained in the commentary on 17:5, the woman "Babylon" is John's depiction of Rome. Yet to identify the woman as Rome does not exhaust the meaning of this symbolism. The woman is Rome, but she is much more. The woman (and the beast) represents any system (political, economic, religious) or institution that tries to usurp the role and authority of God or that oppresses and abuses people. As Eugene Boring has rightly noted, "It is arrogant human empire as such that is here condemned, not just its embodiment in Rome in John's time."[8] The use of sexual imagery is appropriate, for power, prestige, and wealth are alluring. One can easily be seduced by them.

🔍 **The Women of Chapters 12 and 17**

The woman of ch. 17 contrasts with the woman in ch. 12. The woman of ch. 12 represents faithfulness to God as opposed to the woman of ch. 17, who represents rebellion against God.

Woman of Chapter 12

- Clothed with the sun (v. 1)
- Attacked by great red dragon with seven heads and ten horns (v. 3)
- Dragon attempts to *devour* her child (v. 4)
- Woman is pursued by the dragon who tries to harm her (vv. 13-17)
- Mother of a son who is to rule all nations (v. 5)
- Fled into the wilderness (v. 14)
- Threatened by water like a river (v. 15)
- Protected by God from the dragon (vv. 6, 14-16)

Woman of Chapter 17

- Clothed in purple and scarlet, adorned with gold and jewels and pearls (v. 4)
- Rides on a scarlet beast with seven heads and ten horns (v. 3)
- Woman is *devoured* by the beast (v. 16)
- Woman is killed by the beast and his cohorts (v. 16)
- Mother of whores (v. 5)
- Woman is in the wilderness (v. 3)
- Seated on many waters (v. 1)
- Killed by the beast according to the purposes of God (vv. 16-17)

The challenge for the believer is to learn to see the world as John saw it, to ask where in our modern world seductive "Babylon" is present. American readers have been quick to point to other countries and powers as modern manifestations of Babylon. Nazi Germany, the Soviet Union, and the government of Saddam Hussein of Iraq are candidates that come quickly to mind. To the degree that these powers demand ultimate allegiance, then indeed they are "Babylon" in new dress. But what about our own culture, our own government? It is more difficult to recognize and confess the adulterous nature of our nation. We are too accustomed to viewing America as the defender of freedom and justice throughout the world, to calling America a "Christian nation." Yet if John were writing in our time, might his image be "lady liberty," in place of Dea Roma, who is the drunken whore dressed in jewels and fine clothing on the back of the beast? [The Women of Chapters 12 and 17]

In a work published in 1973, *An Ethic for Christians and Other Aliens in a Strange Land*, William Stringfellow argued that modern America is Babylon. American political, social, and economic institutions and powers dehumanize, oppress, and exploit people. In other words, they have become demonic, instruments of the beast in Revelation—what Stringfellow called "the power of death." He wrote,

A nation, or any other principality, may be such a dehumanizing influence with respect to human life in society, may be of such antihuman purpose and policy, may pursue such a course which so demeans human life and so profits death that it must be said, analytically as well as metaphorically, that that nation or other principality is in truth governed by the power of death.[9]

In whatever form or guise "Babylon" and the beast manifest themselves, the task of the Christian is to resist them, not to be tempted or deceived by their allures. We have been "called and chosen." Now we must remain faithful (17:14). To allow ourselves to be seduced by the beast is to move from the domain of life to the domain of death, for John warns us that the beast "goes to destruction" (17:11).

2. One of the most troubling aspects of this text for many readers is John's use of the whore imagery and especially his graphic depiction of violence against this female figure. The city of Rome is pictured as a gaudy, drunken whore. Eventually she is hated, stripped naked, burned, and her flesh devoured. The imagery is shocking in its brutality and its excess. Granted, one can explain the imagery as one of the traditional ways in which the writers of the Hebrew Bible depicted the punishment of God's cities. Furthermore, one can point out that this is metaphorical language; it does not describe an actual assault on a real woman. Yet those responses do not remove the horror and even the danger of these images. The symbols we use do matter. As telling racist, sexist, or ethnic jokes can contribute to prejudice and discrimination, the use of inappropriate symbols can degrade certain individuals or categories of people. At the least, such symbols can desensitize us to the feelings of others, while contributing to the offended person's loss of self-respect and esteem. At the worst, such violent metaphors may unintentionally sanction violence against certain individuals or groups.

Susan R. Garrett has affirmed the message intended by this text, which is that all perpetrators of evil "will one day be called to account for their deeds." She decried the language in which the message is cast, however, when she wrote,

> One can only regret the misogynist imagery that the author has used to convey this important message. To be sure, the book's imagery is violent from beginning to end; both the people of God and the enemies of God suffer harsh fates. But the author seems especially to delight in describing the gory destruction of the woman Babylon (see, e.g., 17:16). The objection that "Babylon" is only a metaphor, a symbol, does not eliminate the problem that the text creates for women readers. The author's exultation over the mutilation, burning,

and eating of a woman—even a figurative one—tragically implies that women are sometimes deserving of such violence.[10]

We live in a world in which violence is an everyday occurrence. The amount of domestic violence that takes place is appalling. [Violence against Women] Women often serve as punching bags for abusive, domineering husbands. Black eyes, broken ribs, cracked skulls, and even death are often the outcome. In some cultures, women are still considered the property of the dominant male (whether that be father or husband, or even other male relatives). Women who bring dishonor to the family are beaten and even killed. The danger of imagery such as that used in Revelation 17 is that it may be heard by some (certainly erroneously) to condone violence against women, particularly "evil" women. What makes this text even more difficult is that the violence against the woman seems divinely sanctioned, "for God has put it into their hearts" (17:17). The more authority a person or community grants to the Bible as "the word of God," the greater the possibility that the Bible might be seen as condoning such actions.

> **Violence against Women**
> Commenting on Rev 17:16, David Barr has written,
>
> Contemporary men can justify their mistreatment of women by such ancient texts; contemporary women draw self-images from such stories. No one can be allowed to feel that what happens to John's whore in this story could ever be justified for any woman. It is dangerous that John used a human image here. We must challenge the text at this point (as we must challenge its comfort with violence generally).
>
> David L. Barr, "Towards an Ethical Reading of the Apocalypse: Reflections on John's Use of Power, Violence, and Misogyny," paper read at the 1997 Annual Meeting of the Society of Biblical Literature, 5.

How does the church today use such texts? At one extreme would be readers who say that a text such as Revelation 17 is so violent and degrading that it should not be used at all. In essence, they would remove it from the canon. At the other extreme would be those who claim that such concerns are pointless, even silly. They would argue that only people who are hypersensitive or uninformed about the source and meaning of John's symbolism would be offended by the use of this text. Neither of these extremes is acceptable. The book of Revelation, with all of its images, is a part of the Christian canon. As such, it needs to be heard and wrestled with. On the other hand, the concerns about misogynist and violent imagery are legitimate concerns. They are not simply an attempt to be "politically correct" or to split linguistic or theological hairs. Language is important. It is more than simply the vehicle for one's message. The language itself becomes a part of the message. For some readers, in the case of Revelation 17, the medium prevents them from hearing the message of the text. [The Woman on the Beast]

The Woman on the Beast
Sonnet XIII by Edmund Spenser

I saw a woman sitting on a beast
Before mine eyes, of orange color hue:
Horror and dreadful name of blasphemy
Filled her with pride. And seven heads I saw,
Ten horns also the stately beast did bear.
She seemed with glory of the scarlet fair,
And with fine pearl and gold puffed up in heart.
The wine of whoredom in a cup she bare.
The name of Mystery writ in her face.
The blood of martyrs dear were her delight.
Most fierce and fell this woman seemed to me.
An angel then descending down from Heaven,
With thundering voice cried out aloud, and said,
Now for a truth great Babylon is fallen.

Robert Atwan and Laurance Wieder, eds., *Chapters into Verse: Poetry in English Inspired by the Bible* (Oxford: Oxford University Press, 1993), 2:355.

To acknowledge and respect this text as a part of the canon, however, does not mean that its use is always appropriate. In certain settings and with certain groups, this text is perhaps best left unheard, particularly if the situation does not allow critical comment or discussion. At the very least, the teacher and preacher who would use this text must help the audience understand that John is drawing on traditional imagery. Such explanations will not neutralize the harsh language of the text but will perhaps render it more understandable. In addition, one should acknowledge the potentially damaging nature of this imagery and invite reflection and dialogue on the problem of language of hatred and violence. Finally, we can heed the advice of Elisabeth Schüssler Fiorenza, who has argued that in our present situation in which we have become more sensitive to the rhetorical power of symbols to promote prejudice and injustice, the feminine images in Revelation must be translated into appropriate modern symbols and images.[11] (See also comments on 14:4.)

NOTES

[1] Jürgen Roloff, *The Revelation of John: A Continental Commentary,* Continental Commentaries, trans. John E. Alsup (Minneapolis: Fortress, 1993), 193.

[2] David E. Aune, *Revelation 17–22*, Word Biblical Commentary (Nashville: Thomas Nelson, 1998), 935.

[3] See J. Massyngberde Ford, *Revelation*, The Anchor Bible (Garden City NY: Doubleday & Co., 1975), 279.

[4] See Aune, *Revelation 17–22*, 948.

[5] G. B. Caird, *A Commentary on the Revelation of St. John the Divine*, Harper's New Testament Commentaries (New York: Harper & Row, 1966), 221.

[6] J. P. M. Sweet, *Revelation*, Westminster Pelican Commentaries (Philadelphia: Westminster, 1979), 260-61.

[7] Ibid., 257.

[8] M. Eugene Boring, *Revelation*, Interpretation: A Bible Commentary for Teaching and Preaching (Louisville: John Knox, 1989), 184.

[9] William Stringfellow, *An Ethic for Christians and Other Aliens in a Strange Land* (Waco: Word, 1973), 32.

[10] Susan R. Garrett, "Revelation," *The Women's Bible Commentary* (Louisville: Westminster/John Knox, 1992), 381.

[11] Elisabeth Schüssler Fiorenza, *The Book of Revelation: Justice and Judgment* (Philadelphia: Fortress, 1985), 199.

LAMENTS ON EARTH

18:1-24

COMMENTARY

Laments on Earth, 18:1-24

Chapter 17 described the great city "Babylon," ending with a prediction of its destruction by the beast and his cohorts, the ten kings. John does not give details about the actual downfall of the city. Rather, in chapter 18 he moves to describe the aftermath of the once powerful city's destruction. This chapter functions as a pronouncement of judgment and a lament over the fallen city. Five major sections comprise the chapter: angelic taunt song, vv. 1-3; summons to flee the city, vv. 4-8; laments over the fallen city, vv. 9-19; call to rejoice, v. 20; and pronouncement of the city's destruction, vv. 21-24. The reaction to the city's demise continues in 19:1-10, but with major differences. In chapter 18, the scene is primarily on earth, and the major response (at least in vv. 9-19) is sorrow and lamentation. In chapter 19, the scene shifts to heaven, and the response is celebration and praise. [Outline of 18:1-24]

The angel that John sees in 18:1 is not the same as the interpreting angel of chapter 17, for this is "another angel." Three aspects of John's description emphasize the power of this angel: he has "great authority" (18:1), makes the earth "bright with his splendor" (18:1), and speaks "with a mighty voice" (18:2).

The words of the angel are similar to prophetic taunt songs, such as are found in Isaiah 23–24; 47; Jeremiah 50–51; and Ezekiel 26–27. These songs, which announce with mockery the downfall or death of an enemy, "have no fixed form but are characterized by derision and joy over the (past, present, or future) misfortunes and shortcomings of others."[1] The time references in this chapter are difficult to nail down. Verses 2-3 speak of the fall of Babylon in the

---

Outline of 18:1-24

past tense, whereas in vv. 4-24 the destruction is future. The opening verses of chapter 19 celebrate the destruction of the city as a *fait accompli*. As elsewhere in Revelation, John is not presenting a chronological chart. His concern is not with *chronos* but with *kairos*, that is, not with "clock time" or measurable time but with the "right time." At the appropriate time, God's time, the fall of Babylon will take place. John is so certain that evil, as epitomized in "Babylon," will be defeated by God that he can announce the city's destruction in vv. 2-3 as if it had already occurred. John sees with the eyes of faith what his contemporaries cannot see or will not see.

In language borrowed from the books of Isaiah and Jeremiah, v. 2 describes the fate of Rome. Like ancient Babylon, it will become a desolate city, inhabited only by wild animals. John paints a scene of a deserted city, a ghost town, that is devoid of any human life or activity. The NRSV translation "haunt" captures the mood of the text, although (strictly speaking) *phylakē* means a place that is watched or guarded, thus a preserve or a prison (cf. 2:10; 20:7).

According to ancient belief, demons lived in deserted and uninhabited areas. Their presence signifies the desolation of the city. The beasts and birds are called "unclean" (NRSV: "foul") because they are the animals that attack or scavenge a dying population, such birds and beasts as hawks, ravens, vultures, and jackals. All such animals, according to the Hebrew Bible, were considered ritually unclean and forbidden for human consumption (cf. Lev 11:1-47). Rome, once bustling with activity and filled with people from all over the world, will eventually lie silent and empty.

Leaving the City

The command to come out of the city before it is destroyed is reminiscent of the command to Lot and his family to flee the city of Sodom:

"Up, get out of this place; for the LORD is about to destroy the city." (Gen 19:14)

Verse 3 basically repeats the charges against Rome that were stated in 17:2—the great city is guilty of committing fornication and leading others to join in her acts. [Leaving the City] Through emperor worship, the cults of various gods and goddesses, and simply through her claims to ultimate authority and allegiance, Rome has seduced people and nations to pay homage to false powers and deities. Furthermore, the city is condemned for its extravagance and wealth—"the merchants of the earth have grown rich from the power of her luxury" (18:3). The guilt of Rome, particularly its excessive wealth and greed, will be delineated further in the laments of those who shared in the city's power and wealth—the kings, the merchants, and the sailors (18:9-19).

Sources of John's Imagery

As an example of John's reuse of texts from the Hebrew Bible, compare Rev 18:2 with the texts that are quoted from Isaiah and Jeremiah.

Revelation	*Isaiah and Jeremiah*
"Fallen, fallen is Babylon the great!"	"Fallen, fallen is Babylon." (Isa 21:9) Suddenly Babylon has fallen and is shattered. (Jer 51:8)

"It has become a dwelling place of demons, a haunt of every foul and hateful beast."	It [Babylon] will never be inhabited
	   or lived in for all generations;
	Arabs will not pitch their tents there,
	   shepherds will not make their flocks lie down there.
	But wild animals will lie down there,
	   and its houses will be full of howling creatures;
	there ostriches will live,
	   and there goat-demons will dance.
	Hyenas will cry in its towers,
	   and jackals in the pleasant palaces;
	its time is close at hand
	   and its days will not be prolonged. (Isa 13:20-22)
	
	From generation to generation it shall lie waste;
	   no one shall pass through it forever and ever.
	But the hawk and the hedgehog shall possess it;
	   the owl and the raven shall live in it. (Isa 34:10b-11)
	
	Therefore wild animals shall live with hyenas in Babylon, and ostriches shall inhabit her;
	   she shall never again be peopled, or inhabited for all generations. (Jer 50:39)
	
	And Babylon shall become a heap of ruins,
	   a den of jackals. (Jer 51:37)

In vv. 4-8, "another voice from heaven" speaks. The speaker is unidentified, but almost certainly is to be understood as an angel who urges the faithful ("my people," v. 4) to leave the city so that they will not participate in Rome's sinfulness and thus share in her punishment. [Sources of John's Imagery] John has modeled this section after passages from Isaiah (48:20; 52:11) and Jeremiah (50:8; 51:6, 9, 45) that called for the people to flee from ancient Babylon because of God's impending destruction of that city (cf. the warnings to flee in Mark 13:14-23; Matt 24:15-28). This call is more figurative than literal. The people of God are to leave the city by separating themselves from its lifestyle of greed, indulgence, and idolatry. It is a call to resist conforming to those aspects of culture that are antithetical to God. As Eugene Boring has noted, "The call to 'come out' is not a matter of geographical relocation but of inner reorientation."[2]

Rome's Colosseum
One of the major buildings in Rome during the imperial period was the Colosseum, built from AD 72 to 96. This amphitheater seated 50,000 spectators who came to watch gladiatorial contests with contestants fighting each other to the death, animals (lions, tigers, and bears) attacking and killing one another, or gladiators fighting against wild animals. Contrary to popular belief, there is little evidence to support the notion that Christians were thrown to the lions in the Colosseum. (Credit: Mitchell Reddish)

Rome cannot claim that its guilt is inconsequential or that its sins are insignificant, for the angel declares that its "sins are heaped high as heaven" (18:5; cf. Jer 51:9). As a result, "God has remembered her iniquities" and brought judgment against the city. To say that God "has remembered" Rome's sins does not imply that God is forgetful or has had a mental lapse. In biblical parlance, God's remembering is frequently a way of saying that God is mindful of someone or something and acts accordingly.[3] John assures his hearers/readers that God takes notice of Rome's sinfulness. Those Christians in Asia Minor who have been suffering from persecution related to emperor worship or who have been victims of Rome's greed and economic policies likely echoed the cries of the martyrs under the altar in 6:10, "How long will it be before you judge and avenge our blood on the inhabitants of the earth?" The statement of the angel that God has remembered Rome's iniquities would serve as a strong word of encouragement and reassurance. God does not ignore the evil in the world but will act to bring justice to a hurting world. [Rome's Colosseum]

In v. 6, turning from the faithful who are addressed in vv. 4-5, the angel speaks to the agents of destruction, calling on them to bring punishment upon the city. These agents are either the kings and the beast of 17:15-17 who unwittingly carry out the purposes of God, or angels of punishment who do God's bidding. Even though, grammatically, the ones addressed appear to be the same ones spoken to in vv. 4-5, that is, the people of God, such an identification of the addressees is out of keeping with the remainder of the Apocalypse. Nowhere else does John envision the people of God being the agents of God's punishment on the wicked.[4]

The angel calls for Rome to receive punishment appropriate to her sins (cf. Jer 50:15, 29). In fact, she is to receive "double for her deeds" (cf. Isa 40:2; Jer 16:18; 17:18). In a form of ironic justice, Rome will have to drink a double dose of the pain, terror, and persecution that she inflicted on others. The cup from which she drinks is the cup that held "the blood of the saints and the blood of the witnesses to Jesus" (17:6). Now her cup has become "the wine-cup of the fury of [God's] wrath" (16:19). Since Rome has destroyed the people of God, the city itself will now be destroyed. Persecution of God's people, luxuriant living, and arrogance are singled out in the angel's remarks as the sins of the city for which it deserves punishment. The words attributed to Rome—"I rule as a queen; I am no widow, and I will never see grief" (18:7)—epitomize the pride and haughtiness of the city that thought it ruled the world and could not be defeated. [Widows] Like Nebuchadnezzar in Daniel, whose arrogant boasting led to his downfall (Dan 4), the arrogant city will discover that

> Pride goes before destruction,
>   and a haughty spirit before a fall. (Prov 16:18)

The destruction of Rome will come swiftly—"in a single day" (18:8)—and will be complete. (Both the image of Rome as an arrogant braggart and the statement that its fall will come in one day are adapted from Isa 47:8-9.) The plagues (pestilence, mourning, and famine) and fire are frequent accompaniments of warfare. Powerful Rome may think that it is invincible and supreme, but it will soon learn that "mighty is the Lord God who judges her" (18:8). [Attitude toward Rome]

The third section of this chapter, vv. 9-19, contains laments over the fallen city by those who have collaborated with and profited from the city. In describing the response

Widows

The woman "Babylon" brags, "I rule as a queen; I am no widow" (18:7). Widows in the ancient world were often powerless, poor, and at the mercy of family or friends. Babylon's claim not to be a widow is an assertion of her power, wealth, and independence.

Attitude toward Rome

The attitude toward Rome expressed in Revelation is exactly opposite that expressed by a 2d-century AD writer Aelius Aristides, who in his *Oration to Rome* 109 wrote,

> Let all the gods and the children of the gods be invoked to grant that this empire and this city flourish forever and never cease until stones [float] upon the sea and trees cease to put forth shoots in spring, and that the great governor and his sons be preserved and obtain blessings for all.

Quoted in Erich S. Gruen, ed., *The Image of Rome* (Englewood Cliffs NJ: Prentice-Hall, 1969), 149.

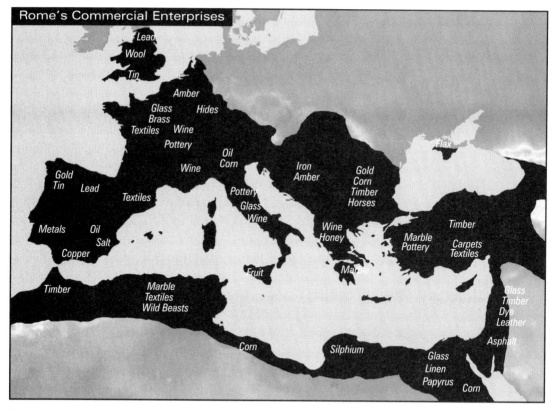

Rome's Commercial Enterprises

This map shows the major products produced in the Roman Empire during the 1st and 2d centuries AD.

Adapted from M. Cary and H. H. Scullard, *A History of Rome down to the Reign of Constantine*, 3rd ed. (New York: St. Martin's, 1975), 455.

of the people to the fall of Rome, John has adapted Ezekiel's portrayal of the lamentations over the fall of Tyre (Ezek 26–28). John singles out three groups of people who have shared in Rome's political and economic success—the kings of the earth, the merchants, and the seafarers—and who now bemoan the fall of the once great city. Each of them weeps, and wails, and mourns the loss. Their lamentations are likely derived more from their own sense of loss than from grief over Rome's demise. Rome was the source of their power and wealth. With the city's downfall, all the benefits which they enjoyed from their alliance with Rome were lost. All of Rome's former partners "stand far off, in fear of her torment" (18:10, 15, 17). They do not come to her assistance or seek to offer solace, for such actions are too late. They are paralyzed by fear, in shock that such a huge and powerful city was reduced to rubble.

The kings of the earth have "committed fornication and lived in luxury" with Rome (18:9). They represent the various nations, client kingdoms, and provincial governors who have joined forces with Rome, yielding their support and allegiance to the empire (not the kings of 17:12-17). They are "in bed together," having become willing partners in Rome's conquests and domination. Rome is their master, not God. City after city in the Roman world vied for the privilege of building temples to the various emperors, demonstrating their loyalty to Rome through promulgation of emperor worship. The rulers of such territories, "the kings of the earth," will gaze in horror and shock at the destruction of their former benefactor and protector, "the great city . . . the mighty city" whose end will come swiftly ("in one hour," 18:10; cf. 17:12).

John devotes greater space to describing the reactions of the merchants to Rome's demise than he does to the reactions of the kings. The list of their merchandise indicates the wealth and extravagance of Rome. [Map: Rome's Commercial Enterprises] Their commercial success is based on the sale of luxury items, rather than on necessities: gold, silver, jewels, ivory, scented wood, fine linen, and spices. Even some of the food products that might be considered staples are the finest available—"choice flour and wheat." The merchants have made their wealth by taking advantage of and pandering to the greed and opulence of Rome. [Vanity Fair] The last item in the list of v. 13 is rather jarring and indicates the depth of Rome's depravity: "slaves—that is, human lives."5 Slaves are simply another commodity to be bought and sold, lumped together with "cattle and sheep, horses and chariots." Slaves were brought from all over the world to serve the needs of Roman society, a society that depended so heavily on slaves that its economy could be considered a "slave economy."6 [Slaves]

John delivers a scathing critique of Roman society in v. 14:

"The fruit for which your soul longed
    has gone from you,
and all your dainties and your splendor
    are lost to you,
    never to be found again!"

Vanity Fair

John's description of the wealth and wares of Babylon is reminiscent of John Bunyan's description of Vanity Fair in *Pilgrim's Progress*. At Vanity Fair was sold "all sorts of Vanity," including:

Houses, Lands, Trades, Places, Honors, Preferments, Titles, Countries, Kingdoms, Lusts, Pleasures and Delights of all sorts, as Whores, Bawds, Wives, Husbands, Children, Masters, Servants, Lives, Blood, Bodies, Souls, Silver, Gold, Pearls, Precious Stones, and what not.

John Bunyan, *The Pilgrim's Progress* (London: Oxford University Press, 1904), 107-108.

Slaves

According to one estimate, during the 1st century AD slaves comprised a third of the population of most urban centers in the Greco-Roman world. Prisoners of war and people kidnapped by pirates were two sources of slaves in the ancient world, although the latter had diminished by the time of the New Testament. Children born of women slaves constituted a large portion of the slave population. People could also become slaves by being sold into slavery by their creditors to whom they were in debt, or people could sell themselves into slavery in order to raise money.

S. Scott Bartchy, "Slavery (Greco-Roman)," *The Anchor Bible Dictionary*, ed. David Noel Freedman, 6 vols. (New York: Doubleday & Co., 1992), 6:66-67.

Roman Opulence

The 2d-century Roman writer Aelius Aristides (*To Rome* 11–13) described the bounty of Rome in these terms:

Around [the Mediterranean] lie the continents far and wide, pouring an endless flow of goods to [Rome]. There is brought from every land and sea whatever is brought forth by the seasons and is produced by all countries, rivers, lakes, and the skills of Greeks and foreigners. So that anyone who wants to behold all these products must either journey through the whole world to see them or else come to this city. For whatever is raised or manufactured by each people is assuredly always here to overflowing. So many merchantmen arrive here with cargoes from all over, at every season, and with each return of the harvest, that the city seems like a common warehouse of the world. One can see so many cargoes from India, or if you wish from Arabia Felix, that one may surmise that the trees there have been left permanently bare, and that those people must come here to beg for their own goods whenever they need anything. Clothing from Babylonia and the luxuries from the barbarian lands beyond arrive in much greater volume and more easily than if one had to sail from Naxos or Cythnos to Athens, transporting any of their products. Egypt, Sicily, and the civilized part of Africa are [Rome's] farms. The arrival and departure of ships never ceases, so that it is astounding that the sea—not to mention the harbor—suffices for the merchantmen . . . and all things converge here, trade, seafaring, agriculture, metallurgy, all the skills which exist and have existed, anything that is begotten and grows. Whatever cannot be seen here belongs completely to the category of nonexistent things.

Quoted in Robert B. Kebric, *Roman People*, 2d ed. (Mountain View CA: Mayfield Publishing, 1997), 2.

Roman society, according to John, is not characterized by a pursuit for justice, compassion, human well-being, or any other noble ideal. Rather, what it longs for are "dainties" and "splendor." The Greek word *lipara* ("dainties") means costly items or luxuries; the word *lampra* ("splendor") means things that glitter or shine. John portrays Roman society as being mainly interested in flashy, expensive luxuries, even if the procuring of those items comes at the cost of human lives. [Roman Opulence]

Whereas the "kings of the earth" see a "mighty city" that has fallen when they look at God's judgment against Rome (18:10), the merchants view the world in economic rather than political terms. They see not a once powerful city, but an expensively dressed city (cf. 17:4) that has lost all its wealth. The self-interest of the merchants is evident in their cry: "For in one hour all this wealth has been laid waste!" (18:17). They mourn the loss of their revenue and trade, not the loss of the city for its own sake.

The third group that bewails the fall of the great city is composed of "shipmasters and seafarers, sailors and all whose trade is on the sea" (18:17). [Mourning] As with the merchants, their relationship with Rome is an economic relationship. They represent those who profited from maritime operations. Being an inland city, Rome was not itself a seaport. The city of Ostia, located about twelve miles away, near the mouth of the Tiber River, was Rome's primary port

Mourning

AΩ The mariners "threw dust on their heads" as they wept and mourned over Babylon (18:19). Throwing dust on one's head was an act of mourning or contrition (Josh 7:6; Job 2:12; Lam 2:10; Ezek 27:30).

Luxury Items

"The demand for luxury items greatly increased during the imperial period, with most of the imports going to Rome. . . . Primary import items included perfumes, ointments, precious stones, incense, spices, and silk. Exotic animals were brought from central Africa and India, amber from the Baltic countries. Such trade, handled by independent merchants and middlemen, was very lucrative, while trade in mass-consumption goods became so unprofitable that the emperors had to provide subsidies and management."

Helmut Koester, *Introduction to the New Testament,* 2d ed. (New York: Walter de Gruyter, 1995), vol. 1, *History, Culture and Religion of the Hellenistic Age,* 313.

city. Yet, as the capital of the empire, Rome was the center of the empire's trade and commerce. During the late first and early second centuries,

> The expansion of foreign commerce . . . attained its quickest pace, yet it could not keep up with the increase of internal trade in the Roman Empire. Of this traffic Rome still retained the lion's share. The mere magnitude of the capital city, and the presence of the court and of an ever-growing body of officials, ensured its continued supremacy among the Mediterranean markets."7

Because of this tremendous commercial activity, "all who had ships at sea grew rich by her wealth" (18:19). Now with the fall of Rome those opportunities are lost, gone up in smoke with the city itself.

[Luxury Items]

Verse 20 issues a call for heaven and the people of God ("saints and apostles and prophets") to rejoice over the fall of the city. As Swete noted, this is "the reverse of the picture drawn in 11:10," where the people of the earth gloat and celebrate over the deaths of God's two witnesses.8 Now it is time to celebrate God's triumph over evil. The identity of the speaker who issues this call to rejoice is unclear. The punctuation of the NRSV includes the summons as a part of the speech of the mariners. Understood in that way, the summons is a bitter cry by the mariners, addressed to those they see as partially responsible for Rome's demise. The shift from lamentation to a spiteful call for celebration, as well as the change of addressees (from wailing to themselves to speaking to the faithful), however, is rather jarring. Another possibility is that the speaker is the angel of vv. 4-8, who calls for the people to rejoice that God's justice has been achieved. Yet the failure to mention the angel in the intervening verses (18:9-19) renders less likely the possibility that the voice is that of the angel. A third option is to understand the voice as that of John himself. The author breaks into the scene to call for celebration because the epitome of evil has been

The Millstone
An angel brings the millstone, symbolizing Babylon, and throws it into the sea while John (seated on the right) watches.

Opening of the Fifth Seal from the *Douce Apocalypse.* Original c. 1270. Manuscript on Vellum. MS Douce 180, p. 17. Bodleian Library. Oxford, England. (Credit: The Bodleian Library, University of Oxford)

overthrown. Although this option also requires an abrupt change in speaker, there is precedent in Revelation for John to address his readers/hearers in such a manner (cf. 9:12; 11:14; 13:9-10, 18; 14:12).

In the final scene of this chapter, vv. 21-24, a mighty angel appears and casts a huge millstone into the sea, symbolizing the destruction of Rome. [The Millstone] Almost this entire section is an adaptation of passages from the book of Jeremiah. The symbol of the stone cast into the sea and the accompanying words of v. 21 are borrowed from Jeremiah 51:63-64, where the prophet wrote in a scroll the disasters that would befall Babylon. Giving the scroll to one of the people of Judah being carried away into exile, he said, "When you finish reading this scroll, tie a stone to it, and throw it into the middle of the Euphrates, and say, 'Thus shall Babylon sink, to rise no more, because of the disasters that I am bringing on her.' " (Cf. the saying of Jesus, "If any of you put a stumbling block before one of these little ones who believe in me, it would be better for you if a great millstone were hung around your neck and you were thrown into the sea" [Mark 9:42].)

The devastation of Rome will be complete: No music will be heard; no artisans will be found; no sounds of millstones or bridal parties will be heard; and no light will shine any longer (cf. Isa 24:8; Jer 25:10; Ezek 26:13). The words "no more" reverberate from the angel's pronouncement, emphasizing the finality of God's judgment against the once proud city.

The end of the angel's speech gives three reasons for Rome's punishment: (1) Rome had made possible the rise of powerful merchants who controlled the economy of the empire. They were the "magnates" (literally, "great ones"), who had become rich and powerful through their catering to the luxury and opulence of Roman society. The economic success of "the great ones" likely was built on the exploitation of "the little ones" of the empire, including the slaves mentioned in their list of cargo (18:13). (2) Rome had deceived the nations by its sorcery (cf. the accusation against Babylon in Isa 47:12). [Sorcery] The word *pharmakeia* refers to potions or spells used in sorcery or magic, a practice that was common in the ancient world. Magic involved the use of ritual actions or the recitation of formulas in order to affect the course of present or future events. The ancient world also had its charlatans, people who used trickery to deceive the people into thinking that their prayers, healings, or magical actions were successful. John is likely not accusing Rome of actually practicing magic on the world, but claiming that Rome is guilty of deceiving the world through its claims to sovereignty and divine status. It has "cast a spell" on the whole empire. David Aune has written, "The mention of magical spells at this point suggests that the power and success of Rome in conquering and dominating the Mediterranean world, like that of ancient Babylon, was such that it could only be attributed to magic."[9] (3) Rome had put to death the faithful people of God. From the martyrdoms by Nero in Rome to the death of Antipas in Pergamum, Rome had on its hands "the blood of prophets and of saints." In fact, John could claim that in Rome was found the blood "of all who have been slaughtered on earth" (18:24) because, for John, Rome was the example *par excellence* of power gone awry that destroys rather than sustains life (cf. Matt 23:34-35 and Luke

Sorcery

AΩ John's accusation against Babylon that "all nations were deceived by your sorcery" (18:23) is perhaps an adaptation of the prophet Nahum's attack on the Assyrian capital Nineveh in which the city is portrayed as a prostitute that is guilty of sorcery. Nah 3:4 explains that God's judgment is against Nineveh,

Because of the countless debaucheries of the prostitute,
gracefully alluring, mistress of sorcery,
who enslaves nations through her debaucheries,
and peoples through her sorcery.

**Lamentations
over the Fallen City**

In this scene, based on a copy
of the 12th-century *Hortus
deliciarum*, the great whore
astride the beast is cast into
the lake of fire while the merchants and kings and others
bewail her downfall.

(Credit: Barclay Burns)

11:47-51 for a similar attribution of guilt to Jerusalem for all who
have been killed). [Lamentations over the Fallen City]

John's broadening of Rome's guilt to include all who have been
slaughtered on the earth is an indication that even though Rome is
uppermost in John's mind, his condemnation of evil goes well
beyond the Rome of his day. As Babylon is a symbol for Rome, it is
also a symbol for all people, institutions, and systems that oppress
and persecute people and deceive them into rendering ultimate loyalty to anything other than God. For all such "Babylons," the
judgment of God is certain.

CONNECTIONS

1. The condemnation of "Babylon" in chapter 18 is based largely
on the political and economic situation of the Roman Empire.
John depicts a nation that exerts tremendous political and economic control over the peoples of the world, while at the same time
living in grand style, enjoying the luxury goods that others cannot
afford. For modern readers it is hard to read John's description of
Rome and not think of the situation in the modern world in which
the so-called first-world countries dominate global politics and economics. America, along with other Western nations, enjoys a
standard of living far greater than that of the majority of the world

population. We spend more, consume more, waste more, and exploit more. What we often consider "necessities," the rest of the world considers luxuries. [Overindulgence] Consider the figures:

> People in the industrial world account for only about 21 percent of the global population, and that share is decreasing, given the faster rate of population growth in the developing world. But industrial countries consume about 86 percent of the globe's aluminum, 81 percent of its paper, 80 percent of its iron and steel, 75 percent of its energy, and 61 percent of its meat. So they are responsible for the vast majority of the hazardous wastes created by the mining and smelting of aluminum and iron ores, the clear-cutting of forests done for the sake of paper production, the air pollution and buildup of greenhouse gases caused by fossil fuel burning, and the severe soil erosion found on grazing lands.[10]

Overindulgence

"We live today in a nutritionally divided world, one where some people eat too much and others too little. Both are forms of malnutrition. Ironically, those who are overfed and overweight and those who are underfed and underweight face similar health problems. And the health effects are the same—increased susceptibility to illness, reduced life expectancy, and reduced productivity.

Worldwide, the number of overweight people could total 600 million. In the United States, the world's largest industrial country, 97 million adults now fall into this category, representing 55 percent of those 20 years of age or older."

Lester R. Brown, "Feeding Nine Billion," *State of the World 1999: A Worldwatch Institute Report on Progress Toward a Sustainable Society,* ed. Lester R. Brown, et al. (New York: W. W. Norton & Co., 1999), 117.

Because our economies are so massive and powerful, we in the first world dominate the world market. Multinational corporations (the new "merchants" who are the "magnates of the earth"), driven by the desire for more and more profits, seek cheaper ways to produce more goods and more successful ways of marketing them to consumers. Factories are built in third-world countries where cheap labor (slave labor?) is available, often without the health and safety standards that must be met in more developed nations. The natural environment is exploited and dangerously abused in order to reap more profits. Too often, the controlling criterion in world economic matters is not what is best for all the people of the world, and certainly not what is best for the poor and disenfranchised, but what is best for the few who already possess and control the most. So the rich get richer while the poor not only get poorer, but starve to death as well. [Consumption]

Economics and politics are often inextricably intertwined. The U.S. government has been guilty of supporting political factions and regimes in other countries on the basis of whether those parties were in the best economic interests of the United States, despite records of serious civil and human rights abuses. In such instances, the United States, along with "Babylon," must bear the guilt of

Consumption

Alan Durning described an ad campaign by a Canadian foundation aimed at convincing North Americans of their inequitable consumption of the earth's resources. He wrote,

The premier spot in their High on the Hog campaign shows a gigantic animated pig frolicking on a map of North America while a narrator intones: "Five percent of the people in the world consume *one-third* of the planet's resources . . . those people are us." The pig belches.

Alan Durning, "Asking How Much Is Enough," *State of the World 1991: A Worldwatch Institute Report on Progress Toward a Sustainable Society,* ed. Lester R. Brown, et al. (New York: W. W. Norton & Co., 1991), 168.

innocent blood that is spilled. We who by the standards of most of the world's population are wealthy, we who are citizens of the most powerful nation on earth, we whose higher standard of living has contributed to a lower standard of living for people in our own country as well as throughout the world, we who live in a society that is marked by violence and bloodshed and that promotes and exports that violence throughout the world must see ourselves in the great whore of Babylon. We may prefer to see ourselves and our nation as the "city set on a hill," the savior and protector of the world. In the eyes of many oppressed people in the world, however, we may look more like an intoxicated whore on whom is found the blood of countless victims. If we hear the message of Revelation clearly, we are forced at times to admit, to paraphrase the comic strip character Pogo, "We have met the beast, and he is us." [Income Gap]

Ernesto Cardenal, a Nicaraguan priest and poet, is an astute interpreter of Revelation who has seen the parallels between the beastly evils described by John and our present world. Paraphrasing the book of Revelation, he recast it as a critique on our modern society that is ruled by technology, oppression, and money. One section of his poem "Apocalypse" reads,

And the Angel carried me away into the wilderness
        and the wilderness blossomed with laboratories
    and there the Devil carried out his atomic tests
    and I beheld the Great Whore riding on the Beast

Income Gap

"In 1991, the richest 20 percent of the world's people earned 61 times more income than the poorest 20 percent, according to the United Nations Development Programme (UNDP). Not only is this gap wide, it has been growing. Thirty years ago, the richest 20 percent received 30 times more than the poorest 20 percent—half as wide a gap as today. Since then, the poorest one fifth saw their share of global income drop from 2.3 to 1.4 percent, while that of the richest group rose from 70 to 85 percent. . . .

The average income for the top 20 percent of U.S. households grew to $105,945 in 1994 from $73,754 in 1968, a jump of 44 percent after being adjusted for inflation. In contrast, the bottom 20 percent of households saw their income go up in constant dollars from $7,202 to $7,762, a 7 percent increase during the same period."

Hal Kane, "Gap in Income Distribution Widening," *Vital Signs 1997: The Environmental Trends That Are Shaping Our Future,* ed. Lester R. Brown, et al. (New York: W. W. Norton & Co., 1997), 116.

(the Beast was a technological Beast all slogan-bedecked)
and the Whore came clutching all manner of checks and bonds
and shares and commercial documents
her harlot's voice sang drunkenly as in a night club
in her left hand she bore a cup of blood
and she was drunk with the blood of all those tortured
all those purged all those condemned by military courts
all those sent to the wall
and of whoever had resisted upon earth
        with all the martyrs of Jesus
and she laughed with her gold teeth
        the lipstick on her lips was blood.[11]

Seldom does the Apocalypse speak with such force in our churches today. We have "ears to hear, but we do not hear." If the book of Revelation is allowed to speak at all, typically its message is first neutered and domesticated. If we interpret the symbols of Revelation as static symbols, referring only to specific events, individuals, or institutions in the first century, then Revelation becomes a "safe" text, one that does not address us or make demands on us. Similarly, if we view the text as John's literal forecast of end-time events, it becomes little more than a checkout stand tabloid, complete with outlandish stories and predictions of the future. However, if we are able and willing to recognize the polyvalent nature of John's symbolism and allow the imagery of the Apocalypse to speak not only to John's original audience but also to us, then perhaps the words of this text can function as words of judgment and words of redemption for us in the church today.

2. The purpose of chapter 18 is not only to announce the downfall of "Babylon" because of its flagrant sinfulness, but also to summon the people of God to leave the city. The voice from heaven entreats:

"Come out of her, my people,
   so that you do not take part in her sins,
and so that you do not share in her plagues." (18:4)

How do we "come out of the city"? [Discerning Babylon] How do we live faithfully in a world whose values are often vastly different from those of God? From the Qumran community that produced the Dead Sea Scrolls to hermit monks, from the Amish communities to the Branch Davidians, religious individuals have sought ways literally to remove themselves from what they perceived to be society's evil and dangerous influences. John's call to leave the city is

Discerning Babylon

📖 "Only when disciples recognize where and what Babylon is can they depart from it. In any century disciples are to struggle for discernment of what constitutes Babylon, the beast, and the imperial image, lest they be drawn into that insurgency against God."

Dale Aukerman, *Reckoning with Apocalypse: Terminal Politics and Christian Hope* (New York: Crossroad, 1993), 107.

not to be taken literally, however. The summons to "come out" is a call to separate oneself from the idolatry, oppression, and greed of the larger society. The prayer of Jesus in John 17 reflects this same idea: "I am not asking you to take them out of the world, but I ask you to protect them from the evil one. They do not belong to the world, just as I do not belong to the world" (17:15-16). The faithful people of God may physically live "in the city," but they do not belong to the city.

We "come out of the city" when we do not allow consumerism and greed to control our lives. We "come out of the city" when we donate our money and our time to God's causes, partially as a demonstration that we still control our money and our time rather than allowing them to control us. We "come out of the city" when we refuse to accept the belief that coercion and violence are acceptable means of achieving our goals, either individual or national goals. We "come out of the city" when we refuse to succumb to the idea that the ultimate meaning in life is found in materialism. We "come out of the city" when we adopt a simpler lifestyle in which we do not consume a disproportionate share of the earth's resources. [The Whore of Babylon]

3. John viewed the "city" as being so corrupt that there was no hope for it. One could only flee the city so as not to suffer its fate. Because of his apocalyptic view that the events of the end would occur soon, John was not concerned with trying to change society and its values, in perhaps salvaging the "city." We do not live with that same sense of end-time urgency today. Two thousand years after Christ, we realize that in spite of the early church's expectation, the world has not come to an end. In addition to "coming out of the city" by living by a different set of values, the task of the Christian includes trying to change "the city," attempting to make it a place more in keeping with the standards of God. Options for making a positive impact on our society are available to us that were not available to John and other early Christians. We may become involved in the political arena, through holding political office, voting, participating in election campaigns, or pushing for the adoption of particular legislation. We may work for better housing for the poor, find ways to help feed the hungry, or provide relief for the sick. We may work for equal and fair treatment for all people, regardless of racial, ethnic, gender, or sexual differences.

The Whore of Babylon

Miles Coverdale, who produced the first complete, printed translation of the entire Bible in English in 1535, correctly recognized that "Babylon" was not limited to Rome of the 1st century. In his poem, "Let Go the Whore of Babylon," he echoed the call of Rev 18 for the people of God to come out of the city.

Let go the whore of Babylon,
    Her kingdom falleth sore
Her merchants begin to make
        their moan
    The Lord be praised therefore.
Their ware is naught / it will not
        be bought
Great falsehood is found therein.
Let go the whore of Babylon
    The mother of all sin.

No man will drink her wine any
        more
    The poison is come to light,
That maketh her merchants to
        weep so sore
    The blind have gotten their
        sight
For now we see / gods grace
        seely
Is Christ offered us so fair
Let go the whore of Babylon
    And buy no more her ware.

Of Christian blood so much she
        shed
    That she was drunken withal
But now Gods word hath broken
        her head
    And she hath gotten a fall
God hath raised / some men in
        deed
To utter her great wickedness
Let go the whore of Babylon
    And her ungodliness.

Ye hypocrites what can ye say?
    Woe be unto you all
Ye have beguiled us many a day

Heretics ye did us call
For loving the word / of Christ the
    Lord
Whom ye do always resist
Let go the whore of Babylon
    That rideth upon the beast.

Ye proud and cruel Egyptians
    That did us so great wrong
The lord hath sent us deliverance
    Though ye have troubled us
        long
Your Pharaoh / with other mo
He drowned in the Reed Sea
Let go the whore of Babylon
    With her captivity.

Ye Canaanites ye enemies all
    Though ye were many in deed
Yet hath the lord given you a fall
    And us delivered
Even in your land / do we now
        stand
Our lord god hath brought us in
Let go the whore of Babylon
    And flee from all her sin.

Dagon Dagon that false idol
    The Philistine's god
Which hath deceived many a soul
    In such honor he stood
But now the lord / with his sweet
        word
    Hath broken him down before
        the ark
Let go the whore of Babylon
    And forsake the beastës mark.

Balaam Balaam thou false
        prophet
    Thou hast cursed us right sore
Yet into a blessing hath god
        turned it
    No thank to thee therefore
For thy belly / thou wouldest lie
    Though God make thee to say
        the sooth
Let go the whore of Babylon
    And turn you to the truth.

Thy God be praised o Daniel
    For his goodness so great
The greedy priests of the Idol Bel
    Were wont too much to eat
And that privily / no man did see
But now the king hath spied their
        cast
Let go the whore of Babylon
    For Bel is destroyed at the last.

O glorious God full of mercy
    We thank thee evermore
Thou hast showed us thy verity
    Thy name be praised therefore
For thy sweet word / O gracious
        Lord
Let us be ever thankful to thee
And send the whore of Babylon
    Into captivity.

Rejoice with me thou heaven
        above
    And ye Apostles all
Be glad ye people for Christ's
        love
    That the whore hath gotten a
        fall
Be thankful now / I require you
Amend your lives while ye have
        space
Let go the whore of Babylon
    And thank God of his grace.

Robert Atwan and Laurance Wieder, eds., *Chapters into Verse: Poetry in English Inspired by the Bible* (Oxford: Oxford University Press, 1993), 2:356-58.

Because our situation is different from that of first-century Christians, we must not allow John's call to "come out" to be an excuse for us to turn our backs to the problems of the world and to refuse to be involved in trying to correct those problems. [Engendering Hope]

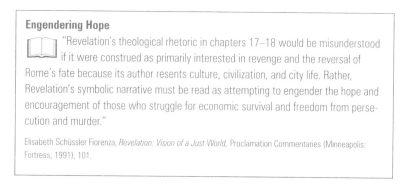

Engendering Hope

"Revelation's theological rhetoric in chapters 17–18 would be misunderstood if it were construed as primarily interested in revenge and the reversal of Rome's fate because its author resents culture, civilization, and city life. Rather, Revelation's symbolic narrative must be read as attempting to engender the hope and encouragement of those who struggle for economic survival and freedom from persecution and murder."

Elisabeth Schüssler Fiorenza, *Revelation: Vision of a Just World*, Proclamation Commentaries (Minneapolis: Fortress, 1991), 101.

NOTES

[1] David E. Aune, *Revelation 17–22*, Word Biblical Commentary (Nashville: Thomas Nelson, 1998), 976.

[2] M. Eugene Boring, *Revelation*, Interpretation: A Bible Commentary for Teaching and Preaching (Louisville: John Knox, 1989), 189.

[3] H. Eising, "*zākhar*," *Theological Dictionary of the Old Testament*, ed. G. Johannes Botterweck and Helmer Ringgren, trans. David E. Green, 12 vols. (Grand Rapids: Eerdmans, 1980), 4:64-82.

[4] *Contra* Aune, *Revelation 17–22*, 993-94.

[5] NRSV translation: "slaves—and human lives." The Greek word *kai* should be understood epexegetically, indicating that the following words further define what precedes. Thus a better translation here for *kai* is "namely" or "that is," rather than "and." The words "slaves—that is, human lives" indicate one item on the list, not two. Isbon T. Beckwith (*The Apocalypse of John* [Macmillan, 1919; reprint, Grand Rapids: Baker Book House, 1979], 717) commented, "Neither here nor elsewhere is there anything to indicate a difference between the two terms, as denoting different classes of slaves. Numerous suggestions of a distinction have been made, but they are arbitrary, without foundation in our passage or in the use of the terms elsewhere."

[6] S. Scott Bartchy, "Slavery (Greco-Roman)," *The Anchor Bible Dictionary*, ed. David Noel Freedman, 6 vols. (New York: Doubleday & Co., 1992), 6:66.

[7] M. Cary and H. H. Scullard, *A History of Rome down to the Reign of Constantine* (3rd ed.; New York: St. Martin's, 1975), 458.

8 Henry Barclay Swete, *Commentary on Revelation* (1911; reprint, Grand Rapids: Kregel Publications, 1977), 238.

9 Aune, *Revelation 17–22*, 1010.

10 Aaron Sachs, "Upholding Human Rights and Environmental Justice," *State of the World 1996: A Worldwatch Institute Report on Progress Toward a Sustainable Society*, ed. Lester R. Brown, et al. (New York: W. W. Norton & Co., 1996), 144.

11 Ernesto Cardenal, "Apocalypse," *Apocalypse and Other Poems* (New York: New Directions, 1971), 36.

CELEBRATION IN HEAVEN AND THE TRIUMPHANT CHRIST

19:1-21

COMMENTARY

Celebration in Heaven, 19:1-10

The great city has fallen; the people of God have been summoned to leave; and the funeral dirge has been sung as the various groups of mourners have wailed and lamented the fall of mighty Babylon. Now the focus shifts to the heavenly response to the news of Babylon's fall. The first part (19:1-8) of this section is more auditory than visionary: John hears rather than sees the celebration that takes place over the announcement of the fall of Babylon (although in v. 4 he does see action occurring around the throne). Two major

> **Outline of 19:1-10**
> 1. Heaven's Songs of Celebration—19:1-4
>   a. First Song from the Chorus of Angels—19:1-2
>   b. Second Song from the Chorus of Angels—19:3
>   c. Response from the Elders and Living Creatures—19:4
> 2. The Faithful on Earth Join the Celebration—19:5-8
>   a. Summons to Praise—19:5
>   b. Song Celebrating the Marriage of the Lamb—19:6-8
> 3. Exchange between John and the Angel—19:9-10

auditions comprise this first part, although whether v. 5 should be seen as completing the first audition or beginning the second is unclear. Since the hymn in 6-8 seems to be a direct response to the summons to praise in v. 5, it is perhaps better to include v. 5 with vv. 6-8.[1] In vv. 1-4, John hears a hymn of rejoicing sung by a great multitude in heaven. In vv. 6-8, a second song of rejoicing breaks out. Verses 9-10 complete this section with an interaction between John and the interpreting angel. [Outline of 19:1-10]

The phrase "after these things" or "after this" has occurred several times in Revelation to indicate a new vision or audition (cf. 4:1; 7:1, 9; 15:5; 18:1). John uses it in 19:1 as the scene shifts from the destruction of Babylon to the reaction of the heavenly multitude. (All the other instances of "after these things" or "after this" are followed by "I saw" rather than, as in 19:1, "I heard.") The "loud voice of a

Singing Hallelujah

The *Apocalypse of Paul*, likely written around the end of the 4th century AD, contains the following interesting discussion in ch. 30 about singing "Hallelujah":

And I said to the angel: Sir, what is "Hallelujah"? And he answered and said to me: You search and inquire into everything. And he said to me: Hallelujah is a word in Hebrew, the language of God and angels. And the meaning of Hallelujah is this: tecel. cat. marith. macha. And I said: Sir, what is tecel. cat. marith. macha? And the angel answered and said to me: Tecel. cat. marith. macha is this: Let us bless him all together. I asked the angel and said: Sir, do all who say "Hallelujah" bless the Lord? And the angel answered and said to me: That is so; and again, if anyone should sing Hallelujah and there are some present who do not sing (it) at the same time, they commit sin because they do not join in the singing. And I said: Sir, does someone who is doting or very old sin in the same way? And the angel answered and said to me: No, but whoever is able, and does not join in the singing, you know that he is a despiser of the word. And it would be proud and discreditable that he should not bless the Lord God his maker.

Translation by Hugo Duensing and Aurelio de Santos Otero, *Apocalypse of Paul* in Edgar Hennecke, *New Testament Apocrypha*, ed. Wilhelm Schneemelcher, English trans. ed. R. McL. Wilson, rev. ed., 2 vols. (Louisville: Westminster/John Knox, 1992), 2:729-30.

great multitude in heaven" is not identified. Some scholars have interpreted the group to be the angelic choir that breaks out in praise to God, as at 5:11-12 and 7:11-12. Others have argued, on the basis of the similarity to 7:9, that the jubilant voices belong to the great throng of the redeemed, whom John has seen standing before the throne in his anticipatory vision of 7:9-17. John does not provide enough details for a firm solution to the identity of this group. If, as will be argued below, the group in vv. 6-8 is composed of the faithful on earth, then the group in vv. 1-3 is likely the chorus of angelic beings.

The arrangement of 19:1-8, then, is similar to the structure of 5:6-14, in which first the heavenly beings (angels, the four living creatures, and the twenty-four elders) and then the inhabitants of earth sing their praises of God. These verses depict first the heavenly beings "in a series of concentric circles, commencing in verses 1-3 with the 'myriads of myriads and thousands of thousands' of angels about the throne (5:11), passing to the twenty-four elders and the four living creatures (19:4), and finally to the voice from the throne (19:5). At the bidding of that voice the worship of the redeemed follows (19:6-8a)."[2]

The hymn of the heavenly multitude begins with the word of praise, "Hallelujah," a term that is repeated three more times in the hymns of 19:1-8. "Hallelujah" is a transliteration of the Hebrew *halēlû-yah* meaning "praise Yah(weh)." Originally a call to others to join in praise to God, the word itself became an exclamation of praise. [Singing Hallelujah] Surprisingly, these four instances of "hallelujah" in chapter 19 are the only occurrences of this word in the New Testament. The hymn is a victory celebration, praising God for the downfall of Babylon. David Aune has referred to it as a "judgment doxology," that is, an ascription of praise to God for God's judgment.[3] "Salvation and glory and power to our God" (19:1) is a triumphal shout in recognition of what God has done in bringing down once mighty Babylon. ("Salvation" [Greek: *sōtēria*] in this instance carries more the meaning of "victory.") Three specific reasons for praising God are given in v. 2: because God is just, because God has judged "the great whore," and because God has avenged the blood of the martyrs.

In a second outburst of praise, the same heavenly chorus once again sings "Hallelujah," followed by a restatement of the reason for their rejoicing: "The smoke goes up from her forever and ever" (19:3). Mighty Babylon lies in ruins, a smoldering heap that will forever be destroyed (cf. Isa 34:10 where the same fate awaits the land of Edom).

In response to the angel's song, the twenty-four elders and the four living creatures worship God and voice their agreement with the celebration of God's triumph over Babylon, saying "Amen. Hallelujah!" [Hallelujah] All of heaven celebrates and ratifies God's actions in bringing judgment upon the rebellious and wicked city.

One of the heavenly beings (unidentified, but certainly not God), a voice "from the throne" (19:5), summons all God's faithful, that is, "all who fear him, small and great" to join in the worship and praise of God. The use of the word *kai* (NRSV: "and") here is epexegetical; that is, it explains who "his servants" are. Thus "his servants" and "those who fear him" are not two different groups. As 18:20 called on heaven and the people of God to celebrate the destruction of Babylon, 19:1-5 summons the heavenly beings and God's people on earth to join in praise and celebration over what God has done. "Praise our God" (*aineite tō theō hēmōn*) is virtually equivalent to "hallelujah."

> **Hallelujah**
>
> AΩ The invitation to praise God, "hallelujah," appears at the beginning and/or end of several psalms in the Psalter (104–106; 111–113; 115–117; 135; 146–150). With the exception of Pss 104–106, all these psalms belong to Book V of the Psalter (Pss 107–150). These are the only occurrences of the specific form "hallelujah" in the Hebrew Bible, although there are similar expressions that call on the people to praise God. "Hallelujah" developed as a set expression of praise in Hellenistic Judaism, as evidenced by its occurrence in Tob 13:17 and in 3 Macc 7:13. Early Christians adopted the practice of singing "hallelujah" or using it as a congregational response.
>
> Henry Barclay Swete, *Commentary on Revelation* (Grand Rapids: Kregel, 1977; reprint of the 3rd ed. published by Macmillan, London, 1911, under the title, *The Apocalypse of St. John*), 242.

As noted above, v. 5 can be understood as concluding vv. 1-4 or introducing vv. 6-8. Since vv. 6-8 appear to be a response to the call to praise God, we have opted to include v. 5 as a part of that section. In reality, v. 5 serves as a connective between the two hymnic sections.

Once more John hears "what seemed to be the voice of a great multitude" (19:6). Whereas some commentators view this group as the same as the "great multitude" that bursts forth in praise in vv. 1-3, this is likely a different group. This group appears to be the ones addressed in v. 5, the servants of God. As such, they are the people of God on earth, whereas the "great multitude" of vv. 1-4 is the angelic chorus. The great chorus of vv. 6-8 may include the angelic chorus along with the faithful servants of God since this is a tremendous chorus: "like the sound of many waters and like the sound of mighty thunderpeals" (19:6). Rather than getting mired in the details, the reader should be overwhelmed by the majestic strains of the songs of celebration. Heaven and earth are united in glorious peals of praise to God as "Hallelujahs" reverberate throughout all creation.

The other hallelujah songs of this chapter have offered praise for the judgment and destruction of Rome. This last song of praise calls for celebration for two reasons: because God reigns supreme and because the marriage of the Lamb has occurred. From the perspective of John's world (as also from ours), God's sovereignty is not obvious. Granted, on the one hand God already reigns supreme since God as creator is the one who holds sway over the entire universe. God is Alpha and Omega, the one who holds the beginning and the end of space and time together. Yet parts of that creation are in rebellion against God so that the sovereignty of God appears to be in doubt. John is convinced that at the appropriate time, in the mythic language of the Apocalypse, God will defeat the beasts of chaos and evil and bring creation under his control. To proclaim in the midst of a world seemingly dominated by the forces of the Roman Empire that "the Lord our God the Almighty reigns" is the ultimate statement of faith on John's part. He knows that Rome's power was temporary and fragile. The true "Lord and God" is the creator and sustainer of the universe whom John worships, not some Roman emperor who lays claim to divine status and world control. [The Lord Our God]

In addition to celebrating God's sovereignty, the hymn in vv. 6-8 also rejoices over the marriage of the Lamb. The imagery of the people of God as God's bride has a rich history in the Hebrew Bible (cf. Isa 54:1-8; Jer 31:32; Ezek 16:8-14; Hos 1–3). According to the Gospels (Mark 2:18-20; Matt 25:1-12; John 3:29), Jesus

---

The Lord Our God

AΩ The opening words of the hymn of praise in vv. 6-8 may have been heard by John's hearers/readers as an intentional polemical jab at the Roman emperors. John has the redeemed proclaim, "For the Lord our God the Almighty reigns." The Roman writer Suetonius (*Dom.* 13.2 [Rolfe, LCL]) stated that Emperor Domitian sent out a letter in the name of his procurators which began "Our Master and our god bids that this be done."

Dio Cassius (*Hist. rom.* 67.4.7 [Cary, LCL]) supported Suetonius' description of Domitian's claim to divinity. He wrote, "For he even insisted upon being regarded as a god and took vast pride in being called 'master' and 'god.'"

Marriage Supper of the Lamb

This detail from a 16th-century Brussels tapestry (one of eight large tapestries representing the Apocalypse) shows the marriage supper of the Lamb.

Willem de Pannemaker. *Marriage Supper of the Lamb,* detail from tapestry number 5 from Palacio Real, woven at Brussells. 1540–1553. Palacio de San Ildefonso. Madrid, Spain. (Credit: ©Patrimonio National)

applies the metaphor of a bridegroom to himself. New Testament writers adapts the bride and bridegroom imagery to the church as the bride of Christ (cf. 2 Cor 11:2; Eph 5:25-33). In Revelation, the marriage of the bride (the church) to Christ is an eschatological event, as it apparently is in 2 Corinthians 11:2 where Paul tells the Corinthians, "I promised you in marriage to one husband, to present you as a chaste virgin to Christ." At the end time, Paul will present the church to Christ in marriage. During the interim, the church is betrothed to Christ, awaiting the marriage that is yet to come. (That is likely the idea in Eph 5 as well.)

The bride is ready for the marriage ceremony, clothed in "fine linen, bright and pure" (19:8). John, as narrator, intrudes into the scene to explain that the fine linen garments of the bride are "the righteous deeds of the saints." Even though "it has been granted" to the church by God to become the bride of Christ, the church must demonstrate its readiness by its faithful living. Here is the paradox of God's salvation as both gift and demand. [Marriage Supper of the Lamb]

The contrast between the church and Rome is unmistakable. Rome is the great whore of Babylon, dressed in purple and scarlet. The church is the bride of Christ, clothed in fine linen, bright and pure. The former is destroyed and her flesh devoured (17:16); the latter has a wedding feast held in her honor.

After the last notes of the "Hallelujah Chorus" have faded, John is instructed to write down the fourth of seven blessings or beatitudes of the Apocalypse. The person speaking to John is not identified. ("The angel" is supplied by the NRSV; in the Greek text, the subject is not stated.) The similarity with 22:8-9 suggests that the speaker is an angel, likely the interpreting angel of 17:1 who is apparently still present with John. The blessing is directed at the faithful people of God, who are the ones "invited to the marriage supper of the Lamb" (19:9). How can the church be both the bride and the wedding guests? One cannot press John's imagery for consistency. His language and imagery are fluid. This is poetic, imaginative language, not analytical or scientific language. In John's creative presentation, the church can be both the bride and the wedding guests. These two images of the church—bride and banquet guests—draw from different biblical traditions, which John has combined here. The former has already been noted; the latter is represented in texts that speak of an eschatological banquet for the people of God (Isa 25:6-8; Matt 8:11-12; 26:29; Mark 14:25; Luke 13:29; 22:18) or that use the metaphor of a wedding banquet for the kingdom of God (Matt 22:1-14; 25:1-13). The imagery of a wedding and a wedding feast convey the mood of the kingdom of God. God's kingdom is filled with joy and celebration, happiness and intimacy.

In response to all that he has seen and heard, John falls prostrate before the feet of the angel. Taken aback by John's actions, the angel responds quickly and decisively, "You must not do that! I am a fellow servant with you and your comrades who hold the testimony of Jesus. Worship God!" [Worship in the Apocalypse] The admonitory words of the angel are actually intended for John's audience as much as for John. These words are a reminder that nothing or no one is deserving of worship

Worship in the Apocalypse

Elisabeth Schüssler Fiorenza correctly described the purpose of John's call to worship when she wrote,

Revelation's call to worship would be misconstrued if it were merely understood in a spiritualized, liturgical, or pietistic sense. . . .

Although the prophetic rhetoric of Revelation is replete with cultic language and imagery, its social location and theological goal are not liturgical but political. Worship and praise in Revelation serve political ends and ethical decisions. John's prophetic-apocalyptic rhetoric . . . [is] not for the sake of persuading his audience to participate in the daily or weekly liturgy. Rather, he utilizes such cultic language . . . for the sake of moving the audience to political resistance. He seeks to motivate them either to give obeisance to the power and empire of God and the Lamb or to the dominion of Babylon/Rome.

Elisabeth Schüssler Fiorenza, *Revelation: Vision of a Just World,* Proclamation Commentaries (Minneapolis: Fortress, 1991), 103.

but God alone. The worship of angels was a problem in some areas in early Christianity, according to Colossians 2:18. This text, the only other reference in the New Testament outside of Revelation to the worship of angels, is in a work addressed to Christians living in the same area as the intended readers/hearers of Revelation. It is feasible, then, that the prohibition in 19:10 is intended to address an actual problem of angel cults in Asia Minor.

The words of the angel were appropriate words for John's audience in another way, as well. Tempted to compromise their faith and participate in emperor worship, they would hear these words as a warning against yielding ultimate allegiance to the cult of Caesar. No one, not even the angels and certainly not the arrogant and idolatrous emperor, is worthy of worship. Worship belongs to God alone.[4]

The angel places himself on the same level with John and all those who "hold the testimony of Jesus." Scholars debate whether this construction, which occurs six times in Revelation (1:2, 9; 12:17; 19:10 [twice]; 20:4), should be understood as an objective or a subjective genitive. If objective, then the testimony is a testimony about Jesus. If subjective, the phrase refers to the witness that Jesus himself gave. The grammatical distinction should perhaps not be pressed. In Revelation, the witness that the people of God bear when they are faithful to God is the same faithfulness that Jesus attested in his life and in his death. They testify about Jesus most clearly when their faithfulness approximates that of Jesus. The final statement of v. 10 is rather enigmatic. It perhaps means that those who truly have the spirit of prophecy will give evidence of it by their faithfulness to the testimony of Jesus or, conversely, that "witness to or about Jesus is confirmed by the return of the gift of prophecy."[5]

The Final Victory, 19:11–20:15

The struggle between God and evil is at the heart of the Apocalypse. The final defeat of evil is the goal toward which the entire work has been moving. Several times John has intimated or directly stated that the victory over evil, at least partially, has been accomplished (11:15; 12:10-11; 14:8; 16:17-21; 18:1-24; 19:1-8). In many cases, those have been only anticipatory announcements of the overthrow of evil which is yet to come. In this section of the Apocalypse, John presents his final and most complete portrayal of the defeat of all the forces aligned against God. The fall of Babylon is a part of God's victory over evil, but it is only a part. The dragon and the two beasts and the kings of the earth who are aligned with them, still exert their influence and control over the world. In 19:11–20:15, these forces will meet their final destiny as well. [Outline of 19:11–20:15]

Elisabeth Schüssler Fiorenza has presented an interesting suggestion for John's arrangement of his material dealing with the overthrow of evil.[6] She has noted that the evil forces are defeated in the reverse order in which they appear. The dragon first appears in chapter 12, the two beasts in chapter 13, and Babylon/Rome in chapter 16. When the destruction of evil takes place, it begins with Babylon/Rome (ch. 18), followed by the two beasts (ch. 19), and finally the dragon (ch. 20).

This section of the Apocalypse also presents the millennial kingdom, the eschatological resurrection of all people, and the final judgment. As elsewhere in the Apocalypse, the scenes here are not literal predictions of coming events, arranged in chronological order. Instead, John presents powerful images of judgment, punishment, and the righteousness of God.

The Triumphant Christ, 19:11-21

Since the time of the earliest church, the followers of Jesus have expressed their belief in the final consummation of God's work in the world in terms of the return of Christ. New Testament writers speak of the return of Jesus at the end of time in order to bring judgment, punishment, and salvation. In the last half of chapter 19, John paints his picture of this scene of the returning, conquering Christ who comes as judge and warrior. This section contains two units: 19:11-16 that describes Christ as the divine warrior, and 19:17-21 that portrays the defeat of the two beasts and their followers.

The Rider on the White Horse, 19:11-16

In his vision, when John sees heaven opened, there is a rider on a white horse. Contrary to the arguments of some interpreters, this figure is not the same rider on the white horse that appeared when the first scroll seal was opened (6:2). The rider in chapter 6 represented military victory and was one of the plagues upon the earth. This rider is Christ, as John's description makes clear. He is called "Faithful and True," reminiscent of the words applied to Christ in

3:14—"the faithful and true witness." Also borrowed from the description of the Christ/Son of Man figure in chapters 1–3 is the statement that "his eyes are like a flame of fire" (cf. 1:14; 2:18).

The diadems on Christ's head are symbols of his royalty; he wears many diadems because he is "King of kings and Lord of lords" (19:16). They also contrast with the seven diadems of the dragon (12:3) and the ten diadems of the beast (13:1). The statement that he has "a name inscribed that no one knows but himself" (19:12) is surprising, in light of the names he bears in vv. 11, 13, and 16. His bearing this secretive name is a way of claiming that there is a mystery about Christ that is beyond human comprehension. The belief was widespread in the ancient world that divine beings had secret or unknown names. To know the name of a god or a demon gave a person some control or power over them. When magicians and sorcerers uttered their incantations, they often piled name upon name of every god or goddess they could imagine in order to gain control over all the powers of the universe for the purpose of achieving their desired goal. Christ has a name that is unknowable because he is beyond human control and beyond full human understanding.

This entire scene has been shaped by Isaiah 63:1-6, which portrays God as a warrior returning victoriously from his battle against the Edomites. One of the most obvious borrowings is the statement that he wears "a robe dipped in blood" (19:13). [Dipped in Blood] This imagery of the bloodstained robe has intrigued many commentators. Most interpret the blood as that of Christ's enemies, based on the Isaiah text in which the blood sprinkled on the robe of the divine warrior is that of his enemies. Yet John has exhibited creative license throughout the Apocalypse when he borrows texts from the Hebrew Bible. He does not simply borrow ideas and images; he adapts them for his purposes. In the scene in the Apocalypse, in contrast to the Isaiah text, the blood is on the warrior's robe *before* he engages in battle, thus lessening the likelihood that it is the blood of his enemies. A better understanding is to view the blood as Christ's own blood. The bloodstained garment is a reminder of the cross. Like the repeated description of the Lamb who was slaughtered (5:6, 9, 12; 13:8; see also 7:14; 12:11), the bloodstains serve as a reminder to the readers/hearers that the conquering Christ is also the suffering Christ, the Christ of

Dipped in Blood

AΩ Instead of Christ's robe having been "dipped in blood," some ancient Greek manuscripts read "sprinkled with blood" (accepted by the older Douay Version of the Bible). John's imagery is clearly borrowed from Isa 63:3 where the garments were sprinkled with the blood of God's enemies. If the original reading in Revelation was "sprinkled," it is difficult to explain why the wording would have been changed to "dipped." If the original wording was "dipped," it is easy to imagine a copyist changing the Revelation text so that it would agree with "sprinkled" in the Isaiah text. Accordingly, "dipped" is likely the correct reading of the text.

the cross. Ronald Preston and A. T. Hanson have correctly observed that in the difference between the use of this imagery in Isaiah and its use in Revelation "lies the whole Christian gospel."[7] In the Apocalypse, Christ conquers not by shedding the blood of his enemies, but by shedding his own blood for his enemies.

The name of this mighty warrior figure is "The Word of God" (19:13). Obviously this name must be different from the secret name of v. 12 that no one knows but Christ himself. For most modern readers the designation "The Word of God" is likely to suggest the *Logos* ("word") hymn of John 1:1-18 (cf. 1 John 1:1). A closer parallel, however, to John's picture of the "The Word of God" is Wisdom of Solomon 18:15-16a, which reads,

> Your all-powerful word leaped from
>   heaven, from the royal throne,
> into the midst of the land that was doomed,
> a stern warrior
> carrying the sharp sword of your
>   authentic command.

As "The Word of God," Christ acts as the agent of God, carrying out God's judgment on the earth. This name for the mighty warrior fits well with the statement that "from his mouth comes a sharp sword with which to strike down the nations" (19:15; cf. 1:16; 2:12). He defeats the nations not by actual physical violence, but by declaring God's judgment against them. John knows what the author of Hebrews declared: "The word of God is living and active, sharper than any two-edged sword" (4:12).

Although some commentators understand the armies of heaven who accompany Christ (19:14) on white horses to be composed of angels, they are perhaps identical with the 144,000 who stand with the Lamb on Mount Zion in 14:1-5 and the "called and chosen and faithful" of 17:14 who are present with Christ when he does battle with the beast and his cohorts. They are the martyrs, who have proven their faithfulness to God and have already helped defeat evil by "the word of their testimony" (12:11). They do not

Armies of Heaven

AΩ In Rev 19, the heavenly armies who accompany the divine warrior do not participate in the eschatological battle. In the *War Scroll* from the Dead Sea Scrolls, the final battle will involve "the sons of light against the company of the sons of darkness, the army of Belial" (1.1). The "sons of light" is the term used in the Dead Sea Scrolls to refer to the religious community at Qumran that produced and preserved the scrolls, whereas the "sons of darkness" refers to their enemies. The sons of light will be victorious when God sends the archangel Michael to their aid.

Translation from Geza Vermes, *The Complete Dead Sea Scrolls in English* (London: Penguin, 1997), 163.

engage in actual combat (notice they wear festal garb, not battle vestments), but they accompany Christ to share in his victory. [Armies of Heaven]

Three images describe how Christ executes divine judgment against God's enemies. The first image, discussed above, portrays Christ wielding a sharp sword from his mouth (cf. Isa 11:3-5). The second image, drawn from Psalm 2:8-9 (cf. Rev 2:26-27; 12:5), describes Christ ruling with a rod of iron, a symbol of destruction. The third image, like the robe dipped in blood in v. 13, comes from Isaiah 63:1-6 where God said, "I have trodden the wine press alone. . . . I trod them in my anger and trampled them in my wrath" (63:3). John has used this same imagery already to describe God's judgment against the wicked (14:17-20). Obviously all three of these images are metaphors drawn from the biblical tradition and are not literal in any sense.

The name inscribed on the warrior Messiah—"King of kings and Lord of lords"—we have encountered already at 17:14 (although, there, the order of the titles is reversed). The puzzling aspect of this name is where it is located: on his robe and on his thigh. The first location creates no difficulty, but what does John mean by saying that the name was on his thigh? Two major possibilities have been proposed: (1) John means that the name was written on his robe at the point where his robe covers his thigh; thus the name only appears once. (2) John is reflecting the custom mentioned in some ancient inscriptions of statues that have on the thigh of the person the name of the individual represented. Whatever the solution to this minor enigma, the purpose of this name that he bears is to serve as a reminder that this warrior Messiah exercises, as God's representative, supreme authority and power over the earth. [Images of Jesus in Revelation]

The Defeat of God's Enemies, 19:17-21

The heavenly warrior has appeared with his armies; the stage is now set for the final confrontation. Prior to the battle, John sees an angel who calls for the birds to gather for "the great supper of God, to eat the flesh of kings, the flesh of captains, the flesh of the mighty, the flesh of horses and their riders—flesh of all, both free and slave, both small and great" (19:17-18). The birds are summoned in anticipation of the great slaughter that will occur when Christ defeats the wicked. This grisly scene is a parody of the "marriage supper of the Lamb" (19:9). Like the redeemed who are invited to the marriage supper of the Lamb, the wicked of the earth

Images of Jesus in Revelation	
The faithful witness	1:5; 3:14
The firstborn of the dead	1:5
The ruler of the kings of the earth	1:5
The one who will come with the clouds	1:7
The Son of Man	1:13-20; chs. 2–3; 14:14
The Son of God	2:18
The holy one, the true one	3:7
The Amen	3:14
The origin of God's creation	3:14
The Lion of the tribe of Judah	5:5
The Root of David	5:5; 22:16
The (slain) Lamb	5:6, 8, 12, 13; 6:1, 16; 7:9-10, 14, 17; 12:11; 13:8; 14:1-5, 10; 15:3; 17:14; 19:7, 9; 21:9, 14, 22-23, 27; 22:1, 3
The Messiah (Christ)	1:1, 2, 5; 11:15; 12:10; 20:4, 6
The Lord of lords and King of kings	17:14; 19:16
Warrior	17:14; 19:11-21
Judge	19:11
Faithful and True	19:11
The Word of God	19:13
The bridegroom	19:7, 9
Alpha and Omega	22:13
The first and the last	2:8; 22:13
The beginning and the end	22:13
The bright morning star	22:16
The Lord	11:8; 14:13; 22:20, 21

will also participate in a great feast. The difference is that they will be the main course! (As sickening as this scene is, it does not quite match the gruesomeness of Ezek 39:17-20, upon which it based.)

This final battle, for which John sees "the beast and the kings of the earth with their armies gathered to make war against the rider on the horse and against his army" (19:19), is the same battle John labeled earlier as Harmagedon (16:16; the battle is also mentioned in 17:14). Neither in chapter 16 nor here, however, does John describe a battle scene. The battle is apparently over before it gets started. The beast and the false prophet (the second beast, the beast from the land in 13:11-18) are captured and thrown alive into "the lake of fire" (19:20; cf. 14:10-11). The lake of fire is gehenna, the place of torment for the wicked. In 20:10, the devil is thrown into this lake of fire and sulfur; and in 20:14-15, Death and Hades are cast in, along with "anyone whose name was not found written in the book of life." [The Rider on the White Horse]

Surprisingly, the rest of Christ's opponents (the kings who are allied with the beast in 17:9-18) are not thrown into the lake of fire along with the beast and false prophet but are killed and become food for the ravenous birds. What does John mean that they were killed by "the sword that came from his mouth"? This is a figurative way of saying that the word of God is decisive and effective. Christ does not actually engage in a physical destruction of God's enemies. Rather, he pronounces God's judgment against them. This "picture is a symbolic portrayal of what is essentially a judicial procedure."[8] The identification of Christ's weapon as the sword of his mouth (i.e., the word of God) should be a caution to anyone who is tempted to interpret the battle imagery of Revelation literally.

The Rider on the White Horse

Benjamin West, a frontiersman born in Pennsylvania, traveled to Italy and England and became one of the most famous Neoclassicists. West visited England, intending to stay only a short while in 1763, but his work caught the eye of the British art world and King George III. He remained in England, married, had two sons, and became history painter to the King. West executed religious paintings based on scriptural narrative and history paintings.

As is common for Neoclassical paintings, the artist combined contemporary ideas with subjects and images from the antique world of Greece and Rome. This work, with its Christ figure dressed in Roman combat attire, was painted during the period that West served as President of the Royal Academy, a group which he aided in founding several years earlier with Joshua Reynolds. This is also the period of the American Revolution (1775–1883) and Britain's war with France. The beast and false prophet may be interpreted in light of Britian's enemies—France and America.

Benjamin West (1738–1820). *Destruction of the Beast and the False Prophet.* 1804. Oil on panel. The Minneapolis Institute of Arts. Minneapolis, Minnesota. (Credit: The Minneapolis Institute of Arts)

CONNECTIONS

1. This portion of the Apocalypse is the "hallelujah" section, the only place in the New Testament where the word "hallelujah" occurs. The text of Handel's famous "Hallelujah Chorus" from his oratorio *Messiah* is composed of portions of two verses from this chapter (19:6b, 16b), along with part of a verse from an earlier chapter (11:15b). The choirs of heaven burst forth with "hallelujahs" in celebration of the downfall of evil Babylon (Rome). The redeemed on earth join in the celebration, offering their "hallelujahs" because the marriage of the Lamb, symbolizing Christ's complete union with his followers, has taken place.

Celebration and Praise

"The worship services in Revelation are all the more remarkable given the circumstances of the churches of Asia Minor. Common sense and observation would say that those Christians would be without a song; a dirge or lament, perhaps, but certainly no hallelujahs. Yet praise never ceases, in heaven, on earth, and under the earth. . . . Those who praise God then and now find their reason for doing so not in themselves nor in their circumstances, but in God. All sing of what they know—the redeeming strength of God, for there are two classes of persons who know an experience—those who have tasted it and those who want it so bad they can taste it. They praise God because they see through what is going on to what is really going on."

Fred B. Craddock, "Preaching the Book of Revelation," *Interpretation* 40/3 (July 1986): 278.

Singing is an important activity in the Apocalypse. We hear melodic strains wafting from the heavenly throne room; we hear all creation joining their voices in praise to God and the Lamb; we hear the oppressed and persecuted sounding forth notes of hope and confidence. In a work that is often popularly characterized as grim, terrifying, and pessimistic, the presence of so much joyful and confident music might be surprising. [Celebration and Praise]

Music functions in several ways in Revelation, ways that are not mutually exclusive. The music in the Apocalypse is a vital part of the worship scenes in the book, providing a way for both the heavenly creatures and the people of earth to offer their praise and thanksgiving to God. Music, whether in the form of hymns or instrumental music (5:8; 14:2; 15:2), functions as a part of Revelation's liturgy. The word "liturgy" is derived from two Greek words, *leitos* and *ergon*, meaning "the work of the people," "a public work." Through its liturgy—Scripture readings, prayers, responses, litanies, choral music, and congregational singing—the gathered people of God offer not only their words, but themselves to God. Because music plays such an important role in the church's worship, it should be chosen with great care, with attention given to both the message of the text and the appropriateness of the music. Hymns and instrumental music should be chosen on the basis of their ability to help the congregation offer itself to God, not on the basis of their emotional appeal or entertainment value. [Music in Revelation]

Music in Revelation

"Music plays a larger role in the book of Revelation than in any other book of the New Testament, and few books in all of Scripture have spawned more hymns sung in Christian worship today."

Craig R. Koester, "The Distant Triumph Song: Music and the Book of Revelation," *Word and World* 12/3 (Summer 1992): 243.

The hymns of the Apocalypse also serve as expressions of confidence and courage in the face of adversity. Confronted by a world that seemed dominated by evil and injustice, whose power structures appeared invincible and all-powerful, John does not lose hope. Rather, through the songs sung by the heavenly choirs and the redeemed on earth, he declares his belief that the God whose "judgments are true and just" will prevail over the forces of evil. Regardless of present appearances, John can declare, "The kingdom of the world has become the kingdom of our Lord and of his Messiah."

Not to be overlooked is the way in which the songs of the Apocalypse function as songs of resistance. The songs of Revelation are the protest songs of a persecuted and alienated minority who refuse to accept the claims and values of a culture that diminishes and even excludes God. The imperial cult attributed power and salvation to the emperor; the hymns of Revelation proclaim, "Salvation and glory and power to our God." The emperor claimed dominion over the empire; the music of Revelation responds, "The Lord our God the Almighty reigns." The culture of John encouraged and enticed the people to offer their allegiance to "the great whore" and "the beast"; the songs of the Apocalypse answer defiantly, "Let us rejoice and exult and give God the glory." Like the popular song of the Civil Rights movement of the 1960s, "We Shall Overcome," these songs in Revelation confidently declare that the present power structures will one day crumble, and truth and righteousness will prevail. [Songs of Protest]

Songs of Protest

The power of music to inspire, motivate, and serve as an instrument of protest against oppressive powers was experienced during the Civil Rights movement in the 1960s. Taylor Branch, describing the volatile situation in Albany, Georgia, during the most violent days of the movement, has written:

The spirit of the songs could sweep up the crowd, and the young leaders realized that through song they could induce humble people to say and feel things that otherwise were beyond them. Into the defiant spiritual "Ain't Gonna Let Nobody Turn Me Around," Sherrod and Reagon called out verses of "Ain't gonna let Chief Pritchett turn me around." It amazed them to see people who had inched tentatively into the church take up the verse in full voice, setting themselves against feared authority.

Taylor Branch, *Parting the Waters: America in the King Years 1954–63* (New York: Simon & Schuster, 1988), 532.

2. D. H. Lawrence, who considered the Apocalypse "a rather repulsive work,"[9] decried the book's celebration over the fall of Babylon. He wrote,

> The great whore of Babylon rises rather splendid, sitting in her purple and scarlet upon her scarlet beast. . . . Splendid she sits, and splendid is her Babylon. How the late apocalyptists love mouthing out all about the gold and silver and cinnamon of evil Babylon. How they *want* them all! How they *envy* Babylon her splendour, envy, envy! How they love destroying it all. The harlot sits magnificent with her golden cup of the wine of sensual pleasure in her hand. How the apocalyptists would have loved to drink out of her cup! And since they couldn't, how they loved smashing it![10]

If Lawrence is correct that the victory songs of chapter 19 are primarily expressions of personal revenge and envy, then his assessment of the book has merit—Revelation is a rather repulsive work. But these "hallelujah" songs are not jealous gloats over a fallen enemy. Rather, they are celebrations of divine justice finally being realized. Revelation does not promote personal vengeance or individual vendettas. John's vision is much larger than that. He recognizes that a cosmic struggle is underway between God and evil, a struggle that manifests itself in people, yes, but even more in institutions, systems, and worldviews. The hymns call for rejoicing because a system of oppression and persecution has been overthrown and destroyed. The fall of Babylon declares that all systems and institutions that pervert God's world, promote injustice, treat people inhumanely, and attempt to thwart God's rule will finally fall. Evil and God cannot and will not co-exist in God's ultimate design. That is good news worth celebrating!

3. The last half of chapter 19 portrays what has been called the Parousia of Christ. The Greek word *parousia* means "presence" or "coming." The belief in the second coming of Christ, as the return of Christ is popularly called, is widespread in the New Testament.[11] After Jesus' death, the early church expected him to return to bring to completion the work he had begun and to bring the present age or world to an end. The Gospel of Mark describes the return of the Son of Man in terms borrowed from the book of Daniel: "Then they will see 'the Son of Man coming in clouds' with great power and glory. Then he will send out the angels, and gather his elect from the four winds, from the ends of the earth to the ends of heaven" (Mark 13:26-27). Paul envisioned that Christ, accompanied by the call of the archangel and the sounding of the trumpet, "will descend from heaven, and the dead in Christ will rise first. Then we who are alive, who are left, will be caught up in the clouds together with them to meet the Lord in the air; and so we will be with the Lord forever" (1 Thess 4:16-17). Other New Testament texts that mention the belief in the return of Christ include Matthew 16:28; 24–25; 26:64; Mark 14:62; Luke 12:40; 17:22-37; 21:25-36; John 14:3; 1 Corinthians 1:7-8; 15:20-28; 2 Corinthians 1:14; Philippians 1:6, 10; 2:16; 3:20; 2 Thessalonians 2:1-12; Hebrews 9:28; James 5:7-8; 1 Peter 1:7; and 2 Peter 3:1-15.

An examination of these texts, along with the various passages in Revelation that speak of the coming of Christ, reveals no uniform and consistent picture of this eschatological event that the followers of Christ awaited. In some passages the emphasis is on the redeemed and the rewards that they will receive (resurrection and enthronement with Jesus); other texts highlight the negative aspect of Christ's coming (judgment and punishment for the wicked). Christ is portrayed in these texts in various ways, as redeemer, judge, and warrior. The diversity of eschatological beliefs in the New Testament, including beliefs about the return of Christ, should serve as a caution about taking any one eschatological view as definitive or attempting to cut and paste all the texts in order to create one homogenized end-time scenario. [Interpreting the Second Coming]

Interpreting the Second Coming

"Some Christians see the Second Coming of Christ as a literal event, to happen at some specific moment in the future. Other Christians see the Second Coming as a metaphor, a symbolic statement of the pervasive force of the constant inbreaking of God's kingdom into history, working toward the betterment of the social structures of this world. However the poetic images be interpreted, the irreducible minimum of the doctrine of the Second Coming is that just as the beginning of this world, of this history, and of our lives was in the hands of God, so too is the end of this world, of this history, and of our lives. It imbues the living of our lives and the conduct of our history with a seriousness that can come from no other ground than the faith that decisions made here are of eternal import."

Roger A. Bullard, *Messiah: The Gospel According to Handel's Oratorio* (Grand Rapids: Eerdmans, 1993), 136.

Notice that, contrary to some popular notions today, John's presentation of the return of Christ in chapter 19 contains no "rapture," wherein faithful believers are whisked away to heavenly safety. In fact, nowhere in Revelation can the idea of a "rapture" be found.[12] Also missing from John's picture of the return of Christ in chapter 19 is the accompanying salvation of the faithful and the resurrection of believers, while the idea of Christ serving as a judge is minimal (19:11).

In chapter 19, as is true throughout the Apocalypse, John speaks in the language of myth and metaphor, not in the language of objective reality. Christopher Rowland reminded us of the nature of John's language in chapter 19 when he wrote,

The reader is reminded at the start of the vision of the Rider on the White Horse that discourse of a very different kind is being used here. The reference to the open heaven is a sign that we have to do with attempts to evoke rather than to describe exhaustively what is to come. It is about what is beyond in the sense that it is both future and different from the patterns of society currently offered. To speak of it, therefore, demands a language which is both less precise and yet more potent and suggestive, a language which after all is what is appropriate when one sets out to speak of that which is still to come.[13]

The idea of the second coming of Christ has been interpreted in various ways throughout the history of the church. Some believers have looked forward to an actual, visible return of Jesus to earth at some point in the future. Others have understood the concept

The Parousia

"In pop apocalypticism the end of the world comes when the insuperable Good Guy wipes out the bad guys—by violence, in the nick of time, for rescue of the innocent, almost as in all those television dramas. A facile reading of certain passages, especially Revelation 19:11-21, may give apparent support to that picture.

Such an understanding divorces the Parousia from the cross. The Parousia, however, will be the unveiling of the resurrection, the Appearing of the Lamb that was slain. In raising Jesus from death, the might of God's gracious love triumphed over all that was set against it. Still largely hidden, that victory will burst into view in the Parousia, and his love will have its way. The glory of the Parousia will be the glory of that life and that death—the glory of God's coming to suffer with and for humankind."

Dale Aukerman, *Reckoning with Apocalypse: Terminal Politics and Christian Hope* (New York: Crossroad, 1993), 220.

more symbolically, expressing the idea of Christ's presence with believers throughout history (cf. John 14–17 in which the Paraclete, or Advocate, at times seems to fulfill Christ's promised return) or the idea that God, who is sovereign over the world, will one day act to bring the world into conformity to God's purposes. Regardless of which approach one takes to the concept of Christ's return, the fundamental teaching of this idea is the belief that the God who is creator of the universe is also its redeemer; the God who was present at the beginning will also be present at the end, when the powers of chaos and evil are finally subdued. As God declares in Revelation, "I am the Alpha and the Omega, the beginning and the end" (21:6). [The Parousia]

4. Once more, John's use of violent imagery is likely to be disturbing for modern readers. The rider on the white horse, wearing a robe dipped in blood, defeats his enemies, throws some alive into the lake of fire and sulfur, and slays the others. The latter group becomes food for the birds, who are "gorged with their flesh" (19:21). In order to help their audience deal with these texts, the teacher and preacher can note several points: (a) John is using traditional imagery in chapter 19. Virtually every aspect of his description of the rider on the white horse, the feasting of the birds, and the destruction of the enemies is taken from texts from the Hebrew Bible. (b) The purpose of the scene is not to predict actual events that will occur, but to portray, symbolically, God's triumph over evil. (c) The scene does not sanction human violence or vengeance. Judgment is carried out solely by God—through Christ as God's representative—not by human agency. The heavenly army that accompanies the divine warrior does not participate in the battle. (d) Christ slays his enemies not by an actual sword, but by the sword of his mouth, which symbolizes the word of God. Furthermore, even though Christ is a warrior in 19:11-21, he is a warrior who conquers by his own death. "The *Lamb* is the controlling image throughout. The Messiah is still clothed in the bloody garments (19:13) of the eschatological victory, but the blood is his own (1:5)."[14] [Conquering Christ]

Conquering Christ

Misuse of John's imagery of the conquering Christ, as exemplified in this illustration of Christ leading the soldiers during the Crusades, has resulted in numerous atrocities in the name of religious zeal. John's depiction of the warrior Christ is symbolic, not literal. The book of Revelation should not be used to justify violence of any kind.

Christ Leading the Crusades. (ROY.19.B VX f37). British Library. London, England. (Credit: By Permission of The British Library)

NOTES

[1] A strong argument, on the other hand, for including v. 5 with vv. 1-4 instead of with vv. 6-8 has been given by Adela Yarbro Collins ("The Apocalypse [Revelation]," *The New Jerome Biblical Commentary* [Englewood Cliffs NJ: Prentice Hall, 1990], 1013). She has written, "The close verbal parallels between v. 1 and v. 6 suggest that a new unit begins in v. 6."

[2] George R. Beasley-Murray, *The Book of Revelation*, New Century Bible (Greenwood SC: Attic, 1974), 270.

[3] David E. Aune, *Revelation 17–22*, Word Biblical Commentary (Nashville: Thomas Nelson, 1998), 1022.

[4] Aune (*Revelation 17–22*, 1035-36) has cautioned that "the motif of the angel who refuses worship from a seer in the context of an angelic revelation (as in Rev 19:10 and 22:9) is a *literary* motif with many parallels in apocalyptic literature." He, thus, has been wary of finding any local significance to this episode.

[5] J. Massyngberde Ford, *Revelation*, The Anchor Bible (Garden City NY: Doubleday & Co., 1975), 312.

[6] Elisabeth Schüssler Fiorenza, *Revelation: Vision of a Just World*, Proclamation Commentaries (Minneapolis: Fortress, 1991), 103-104.

[7] Ronald H. Preston and Anthony T. Hanson, *The Revelation of Saint John the Divine: Introduction and Commentary* (London: SCM, 1949), 120.

[8] Beasley-Murray, *Revelation*, 284.

[9] D. H. Lawrence, *Apocalypse*, in *Apocalypse and the Writings on Revelation*, ed. Mara Kalnins (Cambridge: Cambridge University Press, 1980), 143.

[10] Ibid., 121.

[11] The phrase "the second coming" never occurs in the New Testament to describe Christ's return. The closest biblical expression to "the second coming" is in Heb 9:28.

[12] The classic proof-text for the idea of a "rapture" of believers is 1 Thess 4:17. It is not clear, however, that even this text supports the idea of a rapture. The text does not say that those who are "caught up in the clouds . . . to meet the Lord in the air" continue to ascend to heaven, as is popularly imagined. It is possible, perhaps even likely, that what Paul envisioned was believers going to meet Christ in order to accompany him back to earth for an earthly reign, as city officials would go out to the city limits to welcome a visiting dignitary and escort the dignitary back to the city.

[13] Christopher C. Rowland, "Parousia," *The Anchor Bible Dictionary*, ed. David Noel Freedman, 6 vols. (New York: Doubleday & Co., 1992), 5:169.

[14] M. Eugene Boring, *Revelation*, Interpretation: A Bible Commentary for Teaching and Preaching (Louisville: John Knox, 1989), 118.

THE MILLENNIAL REIGN
AND THE DEFEAT OF SATAN

20:1-15

COMMENTARY

The Millennial Reign and the Defeat of Satan, 20:1-10

The beast, the false prophet, and the kings of the earth have all been defeated. Yet one enemy of God still remains—the dragon, or Satan, the most formidable foe of all. The conquest of Satan occurs in two stages: he is first imprisoned, then let loose, following which time he mounts a final assault against God's people before finally being permanently vanquished. During the time that Satan is imprisoned for a thousand years, a special reward is given to the martyrs: they are resurrected to reign with Christ. Structurally, the description of the millennial reign is "sandwiched" between the two stages of Satan's defeat. [Outline of 20:1-15]

> **Outline of 20:1-15**
> 1. The Millennial Reign and the Defeat of Satan—20:1-10
>   a. The Imprisonment of Satan—20:1-3
>   b. The Millennial Reign—20:4-6
>   c. The Final Conflict—20:7-10
> 2. The Last Judgment—20:11-15

The Imprisonment of Satan, 20:1-3

In 12:7-12, Satan and his evil angels have been thrown out of heaven and down to the earth where they waged war on God's people. The results of Satan's work on earth have been described in the following chapters. Now Satan's opposition to God will finally be brought to an end as God acts to subdue the forces of evil. As in chapter 12, John is using the ancient combat myth here in depicting God's defeat of the dragon.

The descent of the angel with the key to the bottomless pit (Greek: the "abyss") is reminiscent of the events following the blowing of the fifth trumpet in chapter 9. There, an angel ("a star," 9:1) who has fallen from heaven is given the key to the bottomless pit with which he opens the pit to release the angel of the pit and his demonic army. In 20:1-3, the opposite occurs: evil is bound rather than released. As Leonard Thompson has commented, in 20:1-3 an angel "moves

Sealing the Pit

"The purpose of sealing the entrance to a prison was to prevent any attempt at escape or rescue passing unobserved."

Henry Barclay Swete, *Commentary on Revelation* (Grand Rapids: Kregel, 1977; reprint of the 3rd ed. published by Macmillan, London, 1911, under the title, *The Apocalypse of St. John*), 261.

down the *axis mundi*, to reverse the action of the fallen star at 9:1-3."[1] Equipped with a great chain, the angel captures the dragon, binds him with the chain, locks him in the pit, and seals the door behind him. [Sealing the Pit] The triple binding of the dragon—he is chained, locked, and sealed—indicates the certainty of his imprisonment. During the time of his captivity he will no longer be able to thwart the purposes of God, that is, to "deceive the nations" (20:3). In order that there be no mistake about the identity of the dragon, John reiterates what he said in chapter 12: The dragon is the "ancient serpent, who is the Devil and Satan." [The Dragon Locked in the Pit]

Several ancient parallels to the idea of binding or imprisoning evil forces can be found. The clearest parallel in the Hebrew Bible is Isaiah 24:21-22, which portrays God's judgment against rebellious heavenly and earthly beings. The text reads:

On that day the LORD will punish
 the host of heaven in heaven,
 and on earth the kings of the earth.
They will be gathered together
 like prisoners in a pit;
they will be shut up in a prison,
 and after many days they will be punished.

In *1 Enoch* 10:4-6, God told the angel Raphael to bind Azazel (the leader of the evil angels) by his hands and feet, throw him into darkness, and cover him with stones. There he would stay until the great day of judgment when he would be hurled into the fire. In another version of the story, God sent Michael to tell Semyaza (another name for the leader of the evil angels) and his cohorts that they would be bound for seventy generations under the hills of the earth. At the day of judgment they would be cast into the abyss of fire, where they would be imprisoned in torment forever (*1 En.* 10:11-14). Other Jewish parallels include *1 Enoch* 13:1; 14:5; 18:12-16; 21:1-10; 54:1-6; *2 Baruch* 40; 56:13; *Testament of Levi* 18:12; *Jubilees* 5:6; 10:4-14. New Testament writers also were familiar with this idea (cf. Jude 6; 2 Pet 2:4).[2] [Binding of Satan]

The Dragon Locked in the Pit

This woodcut by Albrecht Dürer shows the angel with the key to the bottomless pit locking Satan (the dragon) in the pit. At the top right, another angel shows John the new Jerusalem.

Albrect Dürer (1471–1528). *The Angel with the Key Hurls the Dragon Into the Abyss.* 16th C. Woodcut. (Credit: Dover Pictorial Archive Series)

Binding of Satan

Augustine understood the binding of Satan at the beginning of the millennium in light of Jesus' words in Matt 12:29: "How can one enter a strong man's house and plunder his property, without first tying up the strong man?" According to Augustine,

> This binding of the Devil was not only effected at the time when the Church began to spread beyond the land of Judaea into other nations, at various times; it is happening even now, and will continue to happen until the end of the age.

The binding of Satan occurs "in the case of every man who is snatched away from him."

Civ. 20.8, trans. Henry Bettenson; ed. David Knowles (New York: Penguin, 1972), 912.

The Millennial Reign, 20:4-6

Satan's captivity will last only for a thousand years, after which time he will be released and will gather an army to do battle once more. John describes the events following Satan's release in vv. 7-10. Prior to revealing that scene, John pauses to show what else takes place during the thousand-year period. John reports that he saw thrones, and seated upon the thrones were individuals to whom judgment was given. Who the occupants of the thrones are is not entirely clear. The Greek text itself is somewhat obscure. Translated literally, the text reads,

> And I saw thrones, and they sat upon them, and judgment was given to them, and [I saw] the souls of the ones who had been beheaded on account of the testimony of Jesus and on account of the word of God, and who did not worship the beast nor its image and did not receive the mark upon their forehead and upon their hand. [Function of 20:4-6]

The first difficulty is with the phrase beginning "and [I saw] the souls." The word "and" (Greek: *kai*) is best understood as an epexegetic or explanatory use of *kai*; that is, the souls of the ones beheaded are the ones he saw seated on the thrones. The remainder of this sentence poses another problem. Is John describing two groups or only one? The first clause that modifies "the souls" undeniably describes martyrs—"those who had been beheaded on account of the testimony of Jesus and on account of the word of God." The problem arises with the

Function of 20:4-6

According to Elisabeth Schüssler Fiorenza, 20:4-6 "has a similar rhetorical function to that of the vision about the sealing of the 144,000 (7:1-8) and the injunction to measure the temple of the true worshipers (11:1-2). It aims to assure the audience of the protection and salvation of the elect."

Elisabeth Schüssler Fiorenza, *Revelation: Vision of a Just World*, Proclamation Commentaries (Minneapolis: Fortress, 1991), 108.

next clause, introduced by "and who did not worship." Does the second clause describe a second group of the faithful, those who had not been faced with the ultimate test of loyalty—martyrdom? Or does this clause further specify who the martyrs are—are they the ones who were killed because they refused to participate in emperor worship? Whereas the Greek text could be translated to support either viewpoint, most likely John has only one group in mind here—the martyrs. David Aune has noted,

Interpreting the Millennium

In discussing John's imagery of the millennium as a reward for the martyrs, Henry Barclay Swete gave some cogent advice for modern interpreters who try to provide details about the millennium. Swete wrote,

When, under what circumstance, or by what means this happy result [the millennium] should be attained, St. John does not foresee, and has not attempted to explain. It might have been well if students of his book had always followed the example of this wise reserve.

Henry Barclay Swete, *Commentary on Revelation* (Grand Rapids: Kregel, 1977; reprint of the 3rd ed. published by Macmillan, London, 1911, under the title, *The Apocalypse of St. John*), 266-67.

It is more natural to construe the text as referring to a single group of martyrs, who had been executed for both positive reasons (v 4b: their obedience to the commands of God and their witness to Jesus) and negative reasons (v 4c: their refusal to worship the beast or its image and to receive its brand on their foreheads and right hands).³

This scene is based on Daniel 7:9-27, in which Daniel saw a vision in which "thrones were set in place and an Ancient One took his throne. . . . The court sat in judgment." In the New Testament, reference is made to the disciples (Matt 19:28; Luke 22:30) and to the saints (1 Cor 6:2) being involved in the judging process. In Revelation, however, those seated on the throne are the martyrs only. Those who sealed their witness with their lives are resurrected at the beginning of the millennium to share in Christ's millennial reign. During this thousand-year period "they will be priests of God and of Christ" (20:6). This interim period is a special reward for those who have given their lives for the sake of God's kingdom. Martin Rist contended that part of John's purpose in assigning special rewards to the martyrs was to make martyrdom so attractive "that his readers would quite willingly accept death as martyrs rather than be disloyal to Almighty God and his Christ by worshiping Roma and the emperors."⁴ [Interpreting the Millennium]

John calls the resurrection of the martyrs "the first resurrection." Only they are resurrected at that time. The rest of the dead (righteous and unrighteous) must wait before the millennium has ended before they will be raised. The first resurrection is only for those who have paid the ultimate price for their witness. They are the *first fruits* (14:4) of the harvest. The remainder of the faithful will be united with them after the second resurrection. [Martyrs Receiving Their Crowns]

The millennial reign of Christ and the martyrs is an interim reign that is temporary. The concept of an interim earthly rule prior to the consummation of the kingdom of God arises from the merger of two distinct traditions in Judaism. One tradition in Judaism conceived of the messianic kingdom as an earthly kingdom, realized within the course of world history. One day God would establish Jerusalem as a world center with a Davidic king on the throne of Israel. Israel's enemies would be defeated; the faithful would be rewarded; and the wicked would be punished. This period would be a "golden era" of peace and prosperity for Israel. Another tradition developed within apocalyptic thought expected a cataclysmic end to the present world and the creation of a new world—a new heaven and earth. Hope was shifted from this world and this age to another world and another age. The interim reign of the messiah, followed by the coming of a new heaven and earth, preserves both concepts.

An interim kingdom is found in at least three Jewish writings— 2 Esdras 7:26-44; 12:31-34; *1 Enoch* 91:11-17; *2 Baruch* 29:1–30:5; 40:1-4; 72:2–74:3. In two of these three writings— 2 Esdras and *2 Baruch*—the messiah plays a role during the interim kingdom. [Interim Messianic Reign] No messiah is present during the temporary kingdom in *1 Enoch* 91. The length of the messianic kingdom varies in Jewish tradition. In 2 Esdras, it lasts 400 years; in *2 Baruch*, it is an indefinite period. Later rabbinic literature

Martyrs Receiving Their Crowns. Fresco. St. John the Divine. Patmos. (Credit: Mitchell Reddish)

Martyrs Receiving Their Crowns

This scene from a fresco on a wall of the main church at the Monastery of St. John the Divine on the island of Patmos depicts the Forty Martyrs of Sebaste receiving their crowns, reminiscent of the martyrs in Rev 20:4 who reign with Christ. According to early tradition, during the early years of the 4th century a group of forty Roman soldiers who refused to renounce their Christian faith were condemned to stand naked on a frozen lake near Sebaste in Armenia on a bitterly cold night. Forced to remain on the lake until they would deny their faith, all but one of the men remained steadfast in their commitment to Christ and died from exposure that night. Although one of the forty abandoned his comrades and went ashore, another soldier (impressed by the commitment of the Christians) stripped off his clothes and went onto the lake to join the thirty-nine and become one of the martyrs.

"Sebaste, the Forty Martyrs of," *The Oxford Dictionary of the Christian Church*, ed. F. L. Cross; 3rd ed. ed. E. A. Livingstone (3rd.; New York: Oxford University Press, 1997), 1476-77.

Interim Messianic Reign

An interesting parallel to John's vision of the millennial reign of Christ is found in 2 Esd 7:26-33, a work written c. AD 100, thus contemporaneous with Revelation. In 2 Esdras, the interim messianic kingdom lasts only 400 years, at the end of which the Messiah dies. The description in 2 Esdras is as follows:

"For indeed the time will come, when the signs that I have foretold to you will come to pass, that the city that now is not seen shall appear, and the land that now is hidden shall be disclosed. Everyone who has been delivered from the evils that I have foretold shall see my wonders. For my son the Messiah shall be revealed with those who are with him, and those who remain shall rejoice four hundred years. After those years my son the Messiah shall die, and all who draw human breath. Then the world shall be turned back to primeval silence for seven days, as it was at the first beginnings, so that no one shall be left. After seven days the world that is not yet awake shall be roused, and that which is corruptible shall perish. The earth shall give up those who are asleep in it, and the dust those who rest there in silence; and the chambers shall give up the souls that have been committed to them. The Most High shall be revealed on the seat of judgment, and compassion shall pass away, and patience shall be withdrawn."

indicates that various Jewish teachers assigned the messianic kingdom a length of 40 years; 60 years; 70 years; 354 years; 365 years; 600 years; 2,000 years; 4,000 years; 7,000 years; or even 365,000 years.[5] The idea of a messianic kingdom of 1,000 years is apparently original with John. The length of time of this kingdom is not to be taken literally. A thousand years symbolizes "a lengthy yet limited period of time."[6]

The Final Conflict, 20:7-10

At the end of the millennium, Satan is released from his imprisonment. True to his nature, he immediately begins "to deceive the nations" (20:8). John does not indicate why Satan is let loose, other than to say that "he must be let out for a while" (20:3). "Must" indicates divine imperative. In typical apocalyptic understanding, all that happens occurs within the ultimate purposes of God. Even the release of Satan is a part of God's plan. Perhaps the resurgence of Satan is John's way of emphasizing the formidable power of evil. Even when it appears that evil has been contained and is no longer a threat, it has the capacity to rebound and wreak havoc in one's life. A more mundane reason for having Satan released is so John could introduce one more image in his apocalyptic drama, the figures of Gog and Magog. [The Loosing of Satan]

The Loosing of Satan

"The repeated rebellions of Satan impress on the reader that irrepressible character of the forces of evil and chaos. The implication is that creation and order, peace and justice are quite fragile and partial states and that they are in constant tension with their opposites. The definitive defeat of Satan implies that even though chaos is irrepressible it is less powerful, less real than creative order."

Adela Yarbro Collins, *The Apocalypse,* New Testament Message (Wilmington DE: Michael Glazier, 1979), 141.

Gog and Magog symbolize for John the nations who are deceived by Satan and join with him in his assault on "the beloved city." Clearly they do not represent two specific nations or peoples, for John locates them "at the four corners of the earth" and says "they are as numerous as the sands of the sea" (20:8). John is dependent upon Ezekiel 38–39 for Gog and Magog. In Ezekiel, Gog is the leader of the land of Magog, an unspecified place in the north. God said to Ezekiel,

> Therefore, mortal, prophesy, and say to Gog: Thus says the Lord GOD: On that day when my people Israel are living securely, you will rouse yourself and come from your place out of the remotest parts of the north, you and many peoples with you, all of them riding on horses, a great horde, a mighty army; you will come up against my people Israel, like a cloud covering the earth. In the latter days I will bring you against my land, so that the nations may know me, when through you O Gog, I display my holiness before their eyes. (Ezek 38:14-16)

God will fight against Gog, killing him and destroying the land of Magog with fire. Through this defeat of Gog, the world will know that God is the supreme ruler. God declared: "My holy name I will make known among my people Israel; and I will not let my holy name be profaned any more; and the nations shall know that I am the LORD, the Holy One in Israel" (Ezek 39:7).

John has borrowed the Gog and Magog tradition and adapted it. Whereas in Ezekiel, Gog is a person and Magog is the land over which he rules, in Revelation both Gog and Magog have become the names of evil nations. In Ezekiel, even though Gog has taken on mythical proportions, he is still a localized threat, the foe from the North. In Revelation, Gog and Magog are all-embracing symbols for all the nations or peoples who are in rebellion against God.[7] [Gog and Magog]

Exactly who comprises "Gog and Magog" in John's scenario? The natural understanding of 19:21 is that all the rebellious forces had been killed. So from where do these people who are "as numerous as the sands of the sea" come? This is an example of the problem of pressing John's imagery too hard and of expecting logical consistency. (Likewise, one could ask who are the saints and the population of the "beloved city" in 20:9. Consistency would dictate

Gog and Magog

During the 17th century when many important scientific discoveries were being made, some interpreters gave "scientific" explanations for some of Revelation's imagery. Thomas Burnet, for instance, explained that Gog and Magog, who would arise at the end of the millennium to wage war on the righteous, would be a horde of fearsome creatures who would be "generated from the slime of the ground."

Thomas Burnet, *The Sacred Theory of the Earth* (London: Centaur, 1965), 82, 146-47; quoted by Arthur W. Wainwright, *Mysterious Apocalypse: Interpreting the Book of Revelation* (Nashville: Abingdon, 1993), 74.

that they are strictly the martyrs of 20:4-6.) John is combining variant Jewish traditions to portray God's final defeat of the forces of
evil. One should not be concerned that in piecing the traditions
together, the pieces do not always fit well and that sometimes the
"seams" are rough and uneven.

Satan and his forces surround "the camp of the saints and the
beloved city" (20:9). The "beloved city" is Jerusalem (Pss 78:68;
87:2), but not the actual earthly city. John uses it here as a symbol
for God's people. As was the case in 19:17-21, no battle is
described. Apparently, before the armies of evil are able to attack,
God destroys the armies of "Gog and Magog" with fire. The fire
that comes down from heaven (that is, from God) is reminiscent of
God's sending "fire on Magog and on those who live securely in the
coastlands" in Ezekiel 39:6. Satan is not consumed by the fire but is
cast into the lake of fire to join the beast and the false prophet.

The Last Judgment, 20:11-15

Evil has finally been completely apprehended and eliminated.
Those who have rebelled against God and have attempted to usurp
his sovereignty have failed. Now all must come before God's presence to face judgment. John describes the throne from which
judgment is dispensed as "a great white throne" (20:11). Its size
indicates the importance and power of the one who occupies it,
whereas its brilliant color symbolizes God's glory. John sees who is
seated on the throne, but he does not describe the Judge.
Obviously, this is the throne of God (ch. 4). Before the awesome
majesty and judgment of God, earth and heaven flee. This is poetic
language that portrays the created world's response before the overwhelming holiness and righteousness of the Creator. It is also John's
way of saying that the old order, the old way of rebellion, sin, and
chaos—the old heaven and earth—is a thing of the past. With the
consummation of God's kingdom, something new is taking place.
"No place was found" for the old heaven and earth, for God is creating a new heaven and a new earth (cf. 21:1).

All the dead are called before the throne to face judgment. The
judgment is inclusive—the "great and small," the important and
unimportant—all stand before the Supreme Judge. In John's vision,
"No one is so important as to be immune from judgment, and no
one is so unimportant as to make judgment inappropriate."[8] Even
though John does not refer to the events of 20:12-13 as the second
resurrection, that is what it is. Nowhere else in the Bible does the
concept of two resurrections appear. [The Last Judgment]

The Last Judgment

Giotto's version of the Last Judgment is frescoed on the entrance wall to the Arena Chapel in Padua. The decoration of the chapel was commissioned by Enrico Scrovegni. It is documented that Giotto and his workshop executed this painting in 193 days. Christ is seated in the center surrounded by the heads of angels, each conveying a unique expression. These emotional angels are characteristic of Giotto's style. Archangels positioned on either side of the window roll away the sun, the moon, and the heavens like a scroll (Isa 34:4; Rev 6:14), revealing the gates of Paradise. At the base of the cross and to the left, we see Giotto's rendering of Scrovegni kneeling and holding a replica of the chapel in which the fresco appears. Scrovegni hoped that by immortalizing himself in the fresco, he could secure his own entrance into Paradise.

Giotto di Bondone. *The Last Judgment.* 1305. Fresco. Arena Chapel. Padua, Italy. (Credit: Alinari/Art Resource, NY)

The events of v. 13 actually precede the action of v. 12; that is, the resurrection of the dead occurs before they must face the judgment of God. Sailors and others who died at sea were not buried on land; thus "the sea gave up the dead that were in it" (20:13). Likewise, Death and Hades (the place of the dead; see comments on 1:18) yield up their dead. Death and Hades represent the realm of the dead, the place where all people go after burial, with the apparent exception of those who die at sea.[9] By saying that the sea, Death, and Hades give up their dead, John indicates the universal scope of this resurrection. All the dead are raised to face the final judgment.

Judgment is based on two types of books. First, John speaks of books that contain the works that each person has done. This heavenly record of each person's actions serves as the criterion by which one is judged by God. The idea of such heavenly record books was widespread in the ancient Near Eastern world, including in Jewish literature (biblical and nonbiblical sources; cf. Dan 7:10; Mal 3:16; 2 Esd 6:20; *1 En.* 47:3; 81:1-4; 89:61-77; 90:17, 20; 98:7-8; *2 Bar.* 24:1). Second, John speaks of a "book of life," a heavenly registry of the redeemed, that is, the people of God (cf. Exod 32:32-33; Ps 69:28; Dan 12:1; Luke 10:20; Phil 4:3; Heb 12:23; Rev 3:5; 13:8; 17:8; 20:12, 15; 21:27; see comments on Rev 3:5).

The imagery here of these two types of books appears to be in conflict. If one's name is in the Book of Life, how can one also be judged by works? If one's name is not in the Book of Life, can one be saved on the basis of one's deeds that are recorded in the books? The resolution of this tension lies in the creative juxtaposition of these two images. The concept of the Book of Life of the Lamb is a reminder that salvation is a matter of God's grace, not human achievement. On the other hand, one's actions do matter. They are an indication of the seriousness of one's commitment to God. Grace and works are held together in this scene in creative tension. This same grace/works understanding of God's salvation is present throughout the New Testament. Frank Stagg has correctly noted,

Grace and Responsibility

"All judgment scenes regard human responsibility as crucial (=judged by what they had done, 20:12b), but the book of life says that the ones who endured do so only because of God's grace. This is a paradox that can be resolved only when one goes back to one's own experience with God and finds divine grace and human responsibility bound together in an indissoluble union."

Charles H. Talbert, *The Apocalypse: A Reading of the Revelation of John* (Louisville: Westminster/John Knox, 1994), 98.

> Of the many paradoxes in the New Testament, one of the more striking and persistent is that of salvation as God's gift and God's demand. . . . [I]t is God's free gift; . . . yet on the other hand it requires everything of us, placing us under most radical demand. It is free and costs everything![10] [Grace and Responsibility]

Even Death and Hades do not escape the judgment of God. They are thrown into the lake of fire, there to join the dragon, the beast, and the false prophet. Death and its companion Hades are under the control of God, for Christ himself holds "the keys of Death and of Hades" (1:18). Christ's resurrection had dealt a "death blow" to Death itself. What was inevitable since Easter morning, has now become reality—"Death has been swallowed up in victory" (1 Cor 15:54; cf. 1 Cor 15:26 where death is the last enemy destroyed). God's new world has no place for the pain and anguish caused by Death, so Death and Hades must be eliminated.

The final action in this judgment scene is the carrying out of the sentence that has been pronounced against the unrighteous, that is, those whose names were "not found written in the book of life" (20:15). The punishment for such individuals is that they, too, are cast into the lake of fire, which John calls "the second death" (20:14). Although fire figures prominently in apocalyptic writings as a form of punishment for the wicked, the image of "a lake of fire" is apparently unprecedented. Does being thrown into the lake of fire mean eternal destruction or eternal punishment? John's imagery is ambiguous. On the one hand, to equate the lake of fire with "the second death" implies that what John envisions is destruction or annihilation. On the other hand, in 14:10-11 he has stated that the worshipers of the beast "will be tormented with fire and sulfur. . . . And the smoke of their torment goes up forever and ever. There is no rest day or night for those who worship the beast." This text in chapter 14 suggests that eternal punishment, not destruction or annihilation, is in mind. John does not answer all the questions that modern readers of Revelation might ask. He is not concerned with presenting a detailed scenario of events beyond time and space. The lake of fire is a symbol of God's justice that demands that evil, though present now, shall not always exist to corrupt and harm God's creation. John is extremely restrained in his portrayal of the punishment of the wicked. Modern readers would do well to follow his example.

CONNECTIONS

1. With the amount of attention that is sometimes given to the idea of "the millennium," one would think that this concept is a major motif of the Bible. In actuality, the only place in the entire Bible that "the millennium" occurs is in Revelation 20:1-7. The

Views on the Millennium

Amillennialism	*Historic Premillennialism*	*Dispensational Premillennialism*	*Postmillennialism*
Believes there is no future millennial reign	Believes Christ will return before the millennium.	Believes Christ will return before the millennium.	Believes Christ will return after the millennium.
Christ's reign is a spiritual reign.	Christ will return for a literal, personal reign over an earthly kingdom.	Christ will return for a literal, personal reign over an earthly kingdom.	Christ will reign from heaven through his church during the thousand-year period.
The millennium has already occurred in the ministry of Jesus, or is occurring now through the church, or is occurring now through the reign of the souls of deceased believers in heaven with Christ.	The millennium has yet to occur; will be momentous event.	The millennium has yet to occur; will be momentous event.	The millennium has yet to appear; may merge imperceptibly with the present age.
The world continues to be a mixture of good and evil.	The world is getting progressively worse.	The world is getting progressively worse.	The world is getting better and better.
The conflict between good and evil will intensify as the church continues to spread the gospel.	The seven-year great tribulation period occurs on earth during which time the antichrist rules.	Christ will return to raise the faithful dead and "rapture" them and the living faithful to heaven.	At some point in the future, the influence of the gospel in the world defeats evil, and the millennium is ushered in. Satan is "bound" and as a result the millennium will be a thousand-year reign of peace and righteousness by the faithful on the earth.
The "great tribulation" began at Christ's first coming as he was engaged in a spiritual warfare with the forces of evil. Satan has continued this attack on the church.	At the end of the tribulation period, Christ will return to earth. The righteous dead will be raised and along with the living saints will be "raptured" to meet Christ in the air to accompany him back to earth to rule with him in the millennium.	The antichrist appears on earth to rule the world during a seven-year tribulation period. Jerusalem temple is rebuilt by Jews. Jewish evangelists will preach to people to prepare for the coming of the Messiah.	
The antichrist will arise, who will lead a major persecution of the church.	The antichrist will be judged; the righteous will be resurrected; and Satan will be bound.	At end of tribulation period, the battle of Armageddon will occur in Israel. Jesus returns with the saints. God's enemies are destroyed; Satan is bound; and the Jews are converted to Christianity.	The "first resurrection" of Rev 20:4-6 is not a literal, physical resurrection but figuratively refers to the rebirth of the spirit of the martyrs, a spirit of faithfulness and commitment that will occur at the beginning of the millennium.
Christ will return; the antichrist, as well as Satan, will be defeated.	The millennium will occur, a period of peace and righteousness during which time Christ will be physically present on earth to rule.		At the end of the millennium, Satan will be loosed and will lead a brief, unsuccessful rebellion against God. This rebellion will be ended by the return of Christ, when Satan is completely and finally defeated.
A general resurrection will occur, followed by the Last Judgment.	At the end of the thousand-year period, Satan will be loosed and will lead a brief, unsuccessful rebellion against God. Following Satan's defeat, the general resurrection will occur, followed by the Last Judgment.	The thousand-year reign of peace and righteousness on earth begins, with Christ ruling from Jerusalem. Israel and the Jewish people will be particularly blessed and prominent during this period.	After Christ's return at the end of the millennium, a general resurrection will occur, then the Last Judgment.
		At the end of the millennium Satan is loosed, gathers the unbelieving nations, and attacks Christ's kingdom. He and his forces are defeated.	
		Then come the general resurrection and the Last Judgment.	

The view taken in this commentary, and held by most critical scholars, is that none of these views on the millennium is the best approach. Rather, the millennium is a part of John's creative imagery and is not to be taken as reality.

only other New Testament passage that possibly speaks of an interim messianic kingdom is 1 Corinthians 15:24-28. In spite of some attempts to understand this passage from Paul as referring to Christ's interim kingdom after his Parousia, that is almost certainly not the meaning of the text. For Paul, Christ's enthronement and rule began with his resurrection. Christ's reign, when he will destroy "every ruler and every authority and power," is between his resurrection and his return. Paul does not seem to know any other interim messianic reign. We are left, then, with only the Revelation text for any New Testament belief in a millennial reign of Christ.

During the first three centuries of the church, John's concept of the millennium was mainly understood literally. This interpretation of Revelation 20 is often known as millenarianism or chiliasm (*chilias* is the Greek word for "thousand"). Such important figures in the church as Justin Martyr, Irenaeus, Tertullian, Hippolytus, and Lactantius held to this view, expecting Christ to return to earth to inaugurate a literal thousand-year reign on earth. [Views on the Millennium]

Augustine's Millennium

Jürgen Roloff has described the importance of Augustine and his view on the millennium:

In his book *The City of God* he [Augustine] advocated a church historical interpretation of Revelation 20 that held wide influence for centuries. According to it, the thousand-year kingdom would encompass the time from the first appearance of Christ on earth until his return—that is, the time of the church. This interpretation, which strongly de-eschatologizes the text, was extraordinarily momentous; it formed the fertile soil for the empire ideology of the medieval emperors as well as for the worldly claim of dominion of the papacy. The panic of the decline of the world that seized all of Europe around the year AD 1000 also goes back to it.

Jürgen Roloff, *The Revelation of John: A Continental Commentary*, Continental Commentaries, trans. John E. Alsup (Minneapolis: Fortress, 1993), 223.

The millennial belief held sway until the fourth century when certain church leaders rejected the idea of an actual earthly reign of Christ and argued that the millennium referred to the spiritual reign of Christ, beginning either at his birth, death, or resurrection, and lasting until his return. The thousand-year period was not to be taken literally. This view (sometimes called amillennialism) holds that there will be no actual millennial reign at the end of history. The church is already experiencing "the millennium." One of the earliest known proponents of this nonmillenarian interpretation was Tyconius (d. c. 400), whose views were primarily responsible for persuading Augustine to understand Revelation 20 in this manner. Augustine was the most influential holder of this nonliteral, spiritual view of the millennium. During the fourth century, this view became the dominant approach to the idea of a millennium. This spiritual understanding of the millennium dominated the church, at least officially, for most of the succeeding centuries. [Augustine's Millennium]

During the late twelfth century, the teachings of Joachim of Fiore revived interest in millenarianism through his interpretation of

Revelation that treated the book as a detailed prediction of the events of history. Later, during the seventeenth century, millennial interests were heightened once again, primarily in Protestant circles, as various interpreters argued that the millennium was a literal event that would occur and would likely occur soon. Such millennial beliefs were a prominent part of the views of many of the early European settlers of the western hemisphere, who viewed the "New World" as perhaps the place where the millennial kingdom or its successor would be located.

Two millenarian approaches arose within Protestantism. One, known as postmillennialism, believed that Christ would return after the millennium. A "golden era" of peace and righteousness would occur on earth, which would be a time of growth and prosperity for the churches. As the world got better and better, more in line with God's expectations, the millennium would be ushered in, after which Christ would appear. Although popular in the nineteenth century, postmillennialism declined in the twentieth century as the terrible events of the century (two world wars, the Holocaust) left little hope that the world was actually on the verge of a golden era.

The second strand of millenarian thought was premillennialism, the view that Christ would return at the beginning of the millennium to inaugurate his reign on earth. The most prevalent form of premillennialism today, particularly among evangelical and fundamentalist Christians, is known as dispensational premillennialism, a system that was popularized in the 1800s by John Darby. In the 1900s, C. I. Scofield, through the notes in his Scofield Bible, widely disseminated dispensationalist views. Dispensationalism is characterized by the practice of interpreting events occurring in the world today as literal fulfillments of events mentioned in Revelation and other biblical texts. These "prophecies" are seen as proof that the current generation is living in the last days. A time of great tribulation will occur soon, followed by the return of Christ to inaugurate his millennial reign on earth. Before, after, or during the tribulation (according to whether one holds to the pre-tribulation dispensationalist view, the posttribulation view, or the

Bibliography on the Millennium

Clouse, Robert G., ed. *The Meaning of the Millennium: Four Views*. Downers Grove IL: InterVarsity, 1977.

Cohn, Norman. *The Pursuit of the Millennium: Revolutionary Millenarians and Mystical Anarchists of the Middle Ages*. Rev. and exp. ed. New York: Oxford University Press, 1970.

Ford, J. Massyngberde. "Millennium." Pages 832-34 in vol. 6 of *The Anchor Bible Dictionary*. Edited by David Noel Freedman. 6 vols. New York: Doubleday & Co., 1992.

Grenz, Stanley J. *The Millennial Maze: Sorting Out Evangelical Options*. Downers Grove IL: InterVarsity, 1992.

Soards, Marion L. "Millennium." In *Mercer Dictionary of the Bible*, Watson E. Mills, gen. ed., 576-77. Macon GA: Mercer University Press, 1990.

Wainwright, Arthur W. *Mysterious Apocalypse: Interpreting the Book of Revelation*. Nashville: Abingdon, 1993.

Millennium

"To understand the millennium only as a segment in a chronological series of events that may be plotted on a calendar or chart is to miss the theological message communicated by its own pictorial medium."

M. Eugene Boring, *Revelation,* Interpretation: A Bible Commentary for Teaching and Preaching (Louisville: John Knox, 1989), 205.

midtribulation view), the rapture will occur, in which true believers will be taken from the earth. [Bibliography on the Millennium]

One of the problems with all of these views in their many convolutions is that they place too much emphasis on what is a minor concept in the Bible. This emphasis on and concern about the millennium is grossly out of proportion to its relative insignificance in the Bible. Another problem with these approaches—even some of the nonmillennial views—is that they attempt to understand historically what is figurative language to John. To try to understand when the millennium has begun or will begin is as pointless as asking if the "good Samaritan" in Jesus' parable was ever reimbursed for his expenses. Both queries fail to recognize the nature of the language and symbolism being used. Finally, all attempts to understand the millennium literally ultimately flounder on the inconsistencies contained within John's various views of the end. During the millennium, whom do the martyrs judge? According to 19:21, everyone has been killed already; the general resurrection does not occur until after the millennium. Do the martyrs sit around judging themselves? Furthermore, if the martyrs of the millennium are the same as the 144,000 of 14:1-5, a literal reading of the two passages requires that one understand that the only ones who participate in the millennium are male virgins who have died for their faith by being beheaded! There certainly will not be many thrones needed for the millennial reign! Obviously such a reading of John's text is ludicrous. But when one begins reading symbolic texts literally, such convoluted results occur. [Millennium]

In dealing with this passage, pastors and teachers need to help their audiences place this scene in the larger perspective of John's Apocalypse, rather than allowing them to get bogged down in minutiae. John's scene of the millennium is a way of assuring the martyrs that God has not forgotten them. Divine justice will prevail, even though at the time of their persecution such justice is not visible. This is a scene of role reversals. The martyrs have had to stand before the imperial throne (at least figuratively) and receive the sentence of death. Now they are the ones who are seated on the thrones and deliver judgment. This passage promises the persecuted believers that circumstances will not remain as they now

---

Millennium Fever

Throughout the history of the Christian church, various individuals and groups have believed that their task was to help usher in the millennial reign of Christ on earth. One of the most interesting and tragic of such attempts was that which took place in the city of Münster in Germany. The Dutch Anabaptist leader Jan Matthys taught that the righteous must prepare the world for the millennium by killing all the godless people. He sent out preachers to other Anabaptist communities to share his message with them, including the Anabaptists in Münster. Matthys's ideas took hold quickly in Münster, with many of the townspeople joining with the Anabaptists.

One of his converts was Jan Bockelson (also known as John of Leyden), who led an armed uprising in the town in February of 1534. Many of the wealthy Lutherans (who were the majority in the town) fled, leaving behind an Anabaptist majority who took control, led by Bockelson and Matthys (who had recently arrived in Münster). These Anabaptist leaders announced that Münster was to be the new Jerusalem, whereas the rest of the earth was soon to be destroyed. They urged Anabaptists from other communities to join them in Münster. Any remaining Lutherans or Roman Catholics in the town were cruelly driven out or were rebaptized as Anabaptists.

What was supposed to be an idealistic community of shared property and equal distribution of goods soon turned into a cruel dictatorship with Matthys and then Bockelson in charge. Town discipline was strictly enforced, often by execution. Bockelson claimed, on the basis of divine revelation, that polygamy was to be practiced in the town. All women of a certain age had to be married. In these and all other matters, Bockelson terrorized any dissenters. Later, on the basis of a revelation from an outside prophet, Bockelson was proclaimed king of the new Jerusalem. He, his family, and his "royal" retinue lived in luxurious style, while he imposed on the citizens a strict and meager lifestyle, even rationing clothes and bedding.

Bockelson's oppressive rule grew worse and his claims more extravagant. Christ would return soon, Bockelson said, to exterminate the godless. Already he had established his kingdom in the town of Münster, with Bockelson as the new Davidic king. The task of the people was, by means of the sword, to help rid the world of the unrighteous, which basically meant any who were not Anabaptists. Conditions eventually became so bad in the city, which had been placed under siege by the Roman Catholic bishop, that many of the people died from starvation. Finally, in June of 1535 the bishop was able to capture the city and bring the "new Jerusalem" to an end.

For this episode, as well as other medieval millennial movements, see Norman Cohn, *The Pursuit of the Millennium: Revolutionary Millenarians and Mystical Anarchists of the Middle Ages* (rev. and exp. ed.; New York: Oxford University Press, 1970), 252-80.

---

appear. God will have the last word. Those who have been judged and condemned in an earthly law court will in the millennium become the judges. They, not the emperor and his cohorts, will reign. In 20:4-6, special rewards are promised to the martyrs—participation in the first resurrection and the millennial reign and escape from the second death. The millennium is John's way of offering encouragement to the martyrs. Those who have paid the greatest price receive the greatest reward. [Millennium Fever]

Perhaps the best approach to take regarding the millennium is the view advocated by the wag who claimed to be "panmillennialist," explaining, "It will all pan out in the end." As flippant as that remark may sound, it seems more in keeping with John's view than any of the standard views on the millennium discussed above.

2. Even though the term "hell" (Greek: *gehenna*) is not a part of the vocabulary of the Apocalypse, a place of punishment for the wicked is present, what John calls the "lake of fire." John's scene of

The Bottomless Pit

John Milton, in his epic work *Paradise Lost*, described the bottomless pit into which Satan and his evil angels are cast. In *Paradise Lost*, however, Satan is cast into the pit prior to the creation of humanity. This pit is hell, where Satan must reside and suffer punishment. Milton wrote,

A Dungeon horrible, on all sides round
As one great Furnace flam'd, yet from those flames
No light, but rather darkness visible
Serv'd only to discover sights of woe,
Regions of sorrow, doleful shades, where peace
And rest can never dwell, hope never comes
That comes to all; but torture without end
Still urges, and a fiery Deluge, fed
With ever-burning Sulphur unconsumed.
(Book I, 61-69)

judgment and the ensuing punishment of the wicked (20:11-15), in spite of its restraint, is still a scene of judgment and punishment. [The Bottomless Pit] How does this understanding of the nature and workings of God cohere with the idea of God as a God of mercy and grace? How can a God of love permit a place of eternal torment? The following points may be helpful in thinking theologically about the idea of eternal punishment for the wicked, especially as it appears in Revelation:

• Like other New Testament writers, John utilizes concepts and terminology borrowed from apocalyptic Judaism to depict eschatological punishment on the wicked. At times, those borrowed ideas and terms may not be perfect matches for the message John is trying to convey. The use of traditional imagery may sometimes miscommunicate rather than communicate.

• Later Christian writers (examples would include the authors of the *Apocalypse of Peter* and the *Apocalypse of Paul*) present vivid and gory scenes of the punishments of the wicked in hell. John does not. God's judgment against and punishment of the wicked are not reasons to gloat or to celebrate. (There are celebrations over the fall of Babylon, but not over the punishment of people.)

• Like other aspects of John's eschatological vision, the "lake of fire" is a symbol, rather than an actual entity. The lake of fire (or hell) expresses a theological truth, not a geographical reality. Being cast into the lake of fire symbolizes being cut off from the presence of God. If sharing in the new Jerusalem represents experiencing life in full community with God, then hell or the lake of fire represents experiencing the complete absence of God. It makes no more sense to argue that hell is literally a fiery place of torment than it does to argue that Christ is literally a lamb with seven horns and seven eyes.

• The biblical tradition about eschatological judgment and punishment is a way of affirming the justice of God. Pain, misery,
cruelty, oppression, injustice, and even death are a part of the present state of creation, much of which is the result of intentional
human actions. A just and loving God must act to remove evil
from creation. The notion of the final judgment and resulting
punishment affirms that God will correct the ills of the created
order.

• The idea of hell says that God honors human choice. If people
choose to exist apart from God, then God honors that choice.
God does not force anyone to accept God's offer of grace and salvation. G. B. Caird wrote, "The lake of fire stands at the end of
the world's story as a proof of the dignity of man, whom God will
never reduce to the status of puppet by robbing him of his freedom of choice."[11]

• The biblical notion of the final judgment should serve as a warning to all people not to presume upon the mercy of God. True,
the biblical witness affirms that God is a God of love and grace.
Yet it also indicates that God is a God of righteousness, who
places demands of right living upon all people. We are ultimately
accountable to God's judgment for how we live our lives, particularly how we respond to the needs of others around us (cf. Matt
25:31-46).

• Eternal punishment or separation seems inconsistent with a God
of love. Is it possible that God's love eventually overcomes
humanity's rebellion and resistance, that God's love ultimately
becomes irresistible? Is universal salvation a possible outcome of
God's dealings with the world? Certain biblical texts, including
some in Revelation (5:13; 11:13; 15:4; 21:3, 24-26; 22:2), seem
to point in that direction, or at least to leave the possibility open.
While sincere Christians have differed over this question, of one
thing we can be certain: God will always act in mercy and love,
far beyond anything we can imagine. Even hell must submit to
the sovereignty of God.

Judgment and Punishment

Scenes of the Last Judgment and the punishment of hell have been favorites for painters. Often the imagination of the artist runs wild in depicting the torments and agonies of hell, contrary to the extremely subdued imagery in Revelation of the punishment of the wicked. This painting of hell by the Limbourg brothers is an illustration from the early 15th-century book, *Les Trés Riches Heures du Duc de Berry*. Note the grotesque tortures being inflicted on the damned.

Limbourg Brothers. *Hell* from *Les Tres Riches Heures du Duc de Berry.* 15th C. Manuscript on Vellum. Musée Condé. Chantilly, France. (Credit: Giraudon/Art Resouce, NY)

At the end of his examination of the idea of hell, the theologian Hans Küng summarized the major conclusions of his study. [Judgment and Punishment] They are worth repeating here in their entirety, for they provide a good synopsis of a responsible, thoughtful approach to the notion of eschatological divine punishment. Küng has written:

- Hell in any case is not to be understood mythologically as a place in the upper- or underworld, but theologically as an exclusion from the fellowship of the living God, described in a variety of images but nevertheless unimaginable, as the absolutely final possibility of distance from God, which man cannot of himself *a priori* exclude. Man can miss the meaning of his life, he can shut himself out of God's fellowship.

- The New Testament statements about hell are not meant to supply information about a hereafter to satisfy curiosity and fantasy. They are meant to bring vividly before us here and now the absolute seriousness of God's claim and the urgency of conversion in the present life. This life is the emergency we have to face.

- Anyone who fails to perceive the seriousness of the biblical warnings of the possibility of eternal failure judges himself. Anyone who is inclined to despair in face of the possibility of such a failure can gain hope from the New Testament statements about God's universal mercy.

- The eternity of the "punishment of hell" (of the "fire"), asserted in some New Testament metaphorical expressions, remains subject to God and to his will. Individual New Testament texts, which are not balanced by others, suggest the consummation of a salvation of all, an all-embracing mercy.[12]

NOTES

[1] Leonard L. Thompson, *Revelation*, Abingdon New Testament Commentaries (Nashville: Abingdon, 1998), 177.

[2] David E. Aune (*Revelation 17–22*, Word Biblical Commentary [Nashville: Thomas Nelson, 1998], 1078-1081) has mentioned some similar motifs in ancient Greek literature that may have been the source for the traditions in Jewish literature.

[3] Ibid., 1088.

[4] Martin Rist, "The Revelation of St. John the Divine," *The Interpreter's Bible*, ed. George Arthur Buttrick, 12 vols. (New York: Abingdon, 1957), 12:354.

[5] See George R. Beasley-Murray, *The Book of Revelation*, New Century Bible (Greenwood SC: Attic, 1974), 288-89; and Aune, *Revelation 17–22*, 1107-8.

[6] Aune, *Revelation 17–22*, 1108.

[7] These adaptations are not necessarily original to John. Already in Jewish tradition Gog and Magog were used as the names of two rulers or two kingdoms. See, for example, *Sib. Or.* 3:319, 512.

[8] Robert H. Mounce, *The Book of Revelation*, The New International Commentary on the New Testament, rev. ed. (Grand Rapids: Eerdmans, 1998), 376.

[9] Aune (*Revelation 17–22*, 1103) has cited Achilles Tatius 5.16.2 as support for "the popular belief that the souls of those who died at sea did not enter Hades but remained where they died in the water."

[10] Frank Stagg, *Polarities of Man's Existence in Biblical Perspective* (Philadelphia: Westminster, 1973), 164.

[11] G. B. Caird, *A Commentary on the Revelation of St. John the Divine*, Harper's New Testament Commentaries (New York: Harper & Row, 1966), 297.

[12] Hans Küng, *Eternal Life?: Life after Death as a Medical, Philosophical, and Theological Problem,* trans. Edward Quinn (Garden City NY: Doubleday & Co., 1984), 141-42.

NEW HEAVEN AND NEW EARTH AND THE HOLY CITY

21:1-27

The New Jerusalem, 21:1–22:5

The entire Apocalypse has been moving toward this grand finale that depicts God's ultimate plan for the world—a new creation in which evil and rebellion have no place. The eschatological woes, the punishments, the scenes of destruction, the Last Judgment—all are left in the shadows of this final spectacular scene of God's glorious kingdom. Using the imagery of the new Jerusalem, the new heaven, and the new earth, John depicts the people of God living in intimate communion with God and the Lamb.

COMMENTARY

New Heaven and New Earth, 21:1-8

In a new vision ("Then I saw"), John sees "a new heaven and a new earth" (21:1). John has already stated that the earth and heaven had fled and "no place was found for them" (20:11). He reiterates their demise at the end of 21:1 and adds a new element—"the sea was no more." This is the sea that was before the throne of God in heaven (4:6). The sea represents chaos and rebellion; it is the untamed part of creation. In ancient Israelite mythology, the sea was the place where the monstrous power of chaos lived, Leviathan or Rahab (see comments on 4:6). In the old order, the sea was still present, both on the earth and even in heaven. In the new heaven and earth, no place exists for the sea because chaos, rebellion, and evil have all been eliminated. To say that "the sea was no more" is to portray in different imagery the same thing John has proclaimed in saying that Satan, the beast, and the false prophet have been thrown into the lake of fire. In the new creation, God's ultimate design for God's people, evil has been defeated and removed.

The idea of a new heaven and new earth echoes the words of Isaiah 65:17-18 (cf. 66:22):

> For I am about to create new heavens
>   and a new earth;
> the former things shall not be remembered
>   or come to mind.
> But be glad and rejoice forever
>   in what I am creating;
> for I am about to create Jerusalem as a joy,
>   and its people as a delight.

That which the postexilic prophet who penned these words could only hope for, John declares will be a reality in the new age that is to come (cf. *1 En.* 91:16; 2 Pet 3:10-13).

The centerpiece of the new heaven and earth is the new Jerusalem that John sees descending from heaven. [The New Jerusalem Comes from God] As in Isaiah 65, John links the new heaven and new earth with a new Jerusalem. Obviously John is not talking about the rebuilding of the earthly city of Jerusalem. This is a *new* Jerusalem that he sees. [The New Jerusalem as Fulfillment] It is qualitatively different from the old Jerusalem. In the Hebrew Bible, Jerusalem is God's special city, the place where God dwells with God's people. In seeing a new Jerusalem, John envisions a new community, a new way in which God dwells among God's people (cf. Ezek 37:26-27). [People or Peoples]

The unidentified voice from the heavenly throne declares in vv. 3-4 the meaning and significance of the imagery of a new Jerusalem. The primary focus is relational—God's home will be

The New Jerusalem Comes from God

"This city comes from heaven. It is not at all a human realization: it is the opposite of Babel whose tower mounted up from earth toward heaven."

Jacques Ellul, *Apocalypse: The Book of Revelation* (New York: Seabury, 1977), 221.

The New Jerusalem as Fulfillment

"By calling the city *New* Jerusalem, John does not abolish the old, but fulfills it. God the Eschatological Renewer does not 'make all new things,' but 'makes all things new.' All that was worthwhile and salvageable in the old city of human striving is taken up into eternity and redeemed."

M. Eugene Boring, "Revelation 19–21: End without Closure," *The Princeton Seminary Bulletin* Supplement 3 (1994): 74-75.

People or Peoples

AΩ Ancient Greek manuscripts differ concerning the wording of 21:3. Some ancient manuscripts read "and they will be his peoples." Other manuscripts, almost equally as old and reliable, contain the wording "and they will be his people." Although a decision is far from certain, the original wording was likely "peoples." Some later scribe in copying the text of Revelation changed "peoples" to "people" to make it conform to the wording in Lev 26:11-12 and Ezek 37:27, upon which the Revelation text is based. Assuming that "peoples" is the correct reading in Revelation and that John intentionally changed the wording in his sources, we have here further indication of John's universal understanding of the kingdom of God. In the new Jerusalem, God will have not one "people," but many "peoples."

made among God's people (cf. Ezek 37:27). God will "pitch God's tent" among us. (The Greek word *skēnoō* comes from the word for "tent.") In the prologue to the Gospel of John, the writer claimed that in Jesus of Nazareth "the Word became flesh and lived among us" (1:14; the same Greek word *skēnoō* is used here as in Rev 21:3). The presence of Jesus among his followers was a foretaste of the eschatological presence of God with God's people. In the history of Israel, various leaders had acted as God's representative, God's surrogate with the people—Moses, David, the priests, the kings. In the new Jerusalem, no one will come between the people and God for "God himself will be with them" (21:3). Pain, death, and mourning will have no place in the new Jerusalem. Like a compassionate parent, God will "wipe away every tear" (cf. 7:17; Isa 25:8). Nothing will separate the people from their God, not physical distance, not emotional anguish, not physical pain.

The new Jerusalem is not so much a place as it is a people—the people of God. This is clear from the statement that the city is "prepared as a bride adorned for her husband" (21:2). In 19:7-10, John has already used the metaphor of the bride as the people of God. Here, the new Jerusalem and the bride are equated (cf. 21:9-10). Interpreters must not be overly concerned about the lack of consistency in the city/bride imagery. On a literal level, obviously a city cannot be a bride. Furthermore, if the new Jerusalem is the people themselves, then how can they enter the city and live there? One must remember that John's Apocalypse draws from the world of imagination and creativity. John's imagery is fluid. The new Jerusalem is the community in which the people of God will dwell, but even more, it represents the people themselves. [Church Architecture and the New Jerusalem]

In 21:5-8, for only the second time in the Apocalypse (see 1:8), God speaks directly, affirming what the heavenly voice in 21:1-4 has already made known—"See, I am making all things new" (cf. Isa 43:19). John can write down the divine message with complete assurance that what it says will come to pass, for God's words "are trustworthy and true" (21:5). With the declaration "It is done!" God announces that the goal of creation has been accomplished:

Church Architecture and the New Jerusalem

The great cathedrals of medieval Europe, particularly those built in the Gothic architectural style, were often interpreted and even designed to evoke the majesty and grandeur of the new Jerusalem of Rev 21. In designing the cathedrals, the architects "sought to represent the splendor of the city that, according to the Book of Revelation, was of 'pure gold, like to clear glass.' " Some of the ways in which the architects sought to create the feeling of the celestial city were by the use of arches, vaults, and bays to create the sense of the infinite vastness of heaven and the extensive use of windows to represent the divine light of the city as well the "gold, transparent as glass" (Rev 21:21). The interpretation of the cathedrals as images of the new Jerusalem is seen in the dedication rite for new cathedrals, in which the Epistle reading for the liturgy was Rev 21:2-5.

Otto von Simson, *The Gothic Cathedral: Origins of Gothic Architecture and the Medieval Concept of Order*, 2d ed. (New York: Pantheon Books, 1962), 8, 11.

All things have now been transformed by the power of God. The
one who started the process of creation ("the Alpha") is the same
one ("the Omega") who has now brought creation to its consummation. The claim that God is Alpha and Omega, the beginning
and the end, is not a vacuous or marginal statement for John.
Indeed, this assertion is the major theological underpinning of
John's entire Apocalypse. The book of Revelation is about sovereignty and power. Who is really in control of the universe? Is Satan
the master of the world? Is evil the dominant power? Are the
Roman emperors the true rulers of the earth? The resounding
answer of John's visionary work is that "power and might [belong]
to our God forever and ever!" (7:12). Because God is the initiator
of the world, God is also its consummator.

All the promised blessings of the new Jerusalem, including the
gift of "the water of life" (see comments on 7:17), God will grant to
those who conquer, that is, those who are the faithful believers.
God wills that all people be a part of the new Jerusalem, that all
will be God's children (21:7). Those, however, who through their
actions and their lifestyles choose to follow the way of the beast
rather than the way of the Lamb will find themselves excluded
from the new Jerusalem. Instead, "their place will be in the lake of
fire . . . the second death" (21:8).

While the list of those excluded may be indebted to traditional
vice lists (cf. Rev 9:20-21; 22:15; Rom 1:29-31; 1 Cor 5:9-11;
6:9-10; Gal 5:19-20; 1 Tim 1:9-10), several of the sinful actions
included in this list would have had particular relevance for John's
situation. Leading the list of those who will not be a part of the
new Jerusalem are the cowardly and the faithless. Throughout the
book of Revelation, John has called for endurance and faithfulness
on the part of the beleaguered Christians. The rewards of God are
for those who do not yield to the charms and threats of the beast.
(In this context, the "faithless" or "unbelieving" likely refers not to
non-Christians, but to Christians who renounce their faith by worshiping the beast.) Likewise, the "polluted" have rendered
themselves unclean through their unfaithfulness; they have "soiled
their clothes" (3:4). The fornicators have committed religious adultery by offering worship to the emperor; they are "the idolaters"
(21:8). The sorcerers have tricked others into joining them in following the beast (see comments on 18:23). The liars are likely not
people who spread untruths generally, but those who are participants in the "Big Lie," the notion that someone or something other
than God is deserving of ultimate allegiance. In sharing in this lie,
they are true followers of Satan, "the deceiver of the whole world"

(12:9). The purpose of this list was to serve as a pastoral warning to the members of the churches of Asia Minor. If they want to be a part of the new Jerusalem, they must persevere in faithfulness.

The Holy City, 21:9-27

The next scene sets up a deliberate contrast between "the bride, the holy city Jerusalem" and "the whore, Babylon, the mighty city." [The Two Cities] The introductory words of this scene closely parallel the opening words of the vision of Babylon (cf. 17:1-3). Each scene begins with one of the seven angels of the bowl plagues telling John to come and he will show him the city. In both instances, John says that he was carried away "in the spirit." Whereas in chapter 17 John is carried away to the wilderness, in chapter 21 he is carried to "a great, high mountain." The two settings serve symbolic purposes, not geographic ones. In the biblical tradition, the wilderness is often the place of temptation, disobedience, and evil (cf. Exod 16:1-3; Num 14:1-35; Deut 9:7; Pss 78:40; 95:8; 106:14; Matt 4:1-11; Mark 1:12-13; Luke 4:1-13). Mountains, on the other hand, are places associated with God or divine revelation (cf. Gen 22:1-14; Exod 3:1, 12; 19:1–34:35; 1 Kgs 19:1-18; Matt 5–7). The setting on a mountain is likely drawn also from Ezekiel (40:2),

The Two Cities

John has drawn an intentional contrast between the city of "Babylon" and the new Jerusalem. A comparison of the details of the cities illustrates the opposing natures of these two cities.

Babylon
- Its "sins are heaped high as heaven" (18:5)
- Located in the wilderness (17:3)
- The great prostitute (17:1)
- Clothed in purple and scarlet (17:4)
- Adorned with gold and jewels and pearls (17:4)

- Full of abominations and impurities (17:4)

- A dwelling place of demons (18:2)
- God's people told to "come out" of the city (18:4)
- A city of death—filled "with the blood of the saints and the blood of the witnesses to Jesus" (17:6)
- The kings of the earth commit fornication with the city (17:2)
- God will give the city torment and grief (18:7)
- The light of a lamp will shine in it no more (18: 23)

- Deceives the nations by its sorcery (18:23)
- The city will be destroyed (ch. 18)

The New Jerusalem
- The holy city (21:2)
- Located on a mountain (21:10)
- A bride (21:9)
- "Prepared as bride adorned for her husband" (21:2)
- Adorned with precious jewels, gates of pearls, street of gold (21:18-21)
- Uncleanness, abomination, and falsehood are excluded (21:27)
- The dwelling place of God (21:3)
- God's people will enter the city (22:14)
- In the city death will be no more (21:4)

- The kings of the earth bring their glory into the city (21:24)
- "Mourning and crying and pain will be no more" (21:4)
- God is its light, the Lamb is its lamp; there will be no night there (21:23, 25)
- Leaves of its tree are for the healing of the nations (22:2)
- The redeemed will live in the city forever and ever (22:5)

from which John has borrowed many of the elements of this scene. The mountain is the idealized Mount Zion. John is taken to the mountain, not in order to have a good vantage point from which to view the city, but because the mountain is the place to which the city descends. The city "has the glory of God" because God is the source of the new Jerusalem; it comes "down out of heaven from God" (21:10; cf. Ezek 43:1-5 where the glory of the LORD enters the new temple and fills it). John describes the brilliance of God's glory as like the brilliance of a crystal-clear jasper (cf. 4:3 where God is described like jasper; thus the city, which reflects God's brilliance, is also like jasper).

Measuring the City

The motif of measuring the new Jerusalem functions differently than the measuring of the temple in 11:1-2. In the latter instance, the act of measuring the inner courts was a symbol of protection for the people of God. In ch. 21, the measuring of the new Jerusalem is simply a literary technique by the writer to make the huge measurements of the city known to the hearers/readers of the text.

The city's surrounding wall, symbolizing the security of the city, has twelve gates and twelve foundations. The twelve gates are engraved with the names of the twelve tribes of Israel; the twelve foundations bear the names of the twelve apostles. Here, in picturesque language, John portrays the city as being all-inclusive—it contains all the people of God, those from the old covenant and those from the new covenant.

The angel guide uses a measuring rod to measure the city (cf. Ezek 40:5). [Measuring the City] It is a perfect cube: twelve thousand stadia in length, width, and height. The NRSV translation "fifteen hundred miles," while correct mathematically, obscures the symbolism in the city's measurement. Twelve symbolizes completeness and wholeness, which is seen also in the height of the wall—one hundred forty-four cubits, a multiple of twelve. The huge size of the city not only is awe-inspiring, but also symbolizes the enormity and completeness of the kingdom of God that comprises "a great multitude that no one could count, from every nation, from all tribes and peoples and languages" (7:9). The jasper wall, which John describes as "a great, high wall" (21:12) is actually, in comparison to the city, ludicrously puny if the measurement given is the wall's height and not its width. (The city is fifteen hundred miles high, while the wall is only seventy-five yards high.) [Measurement of the Wall]

John's description of the city—pure gold, clear as glass; foundations of precious jewels; twelve gates of a single pearl each; street of transparent gold—is John's attempt to overwhelm the hearers/readers with the splendor and majesty of the new Jerusalem. His imagery here is traditional. The idea of the new Jerusalem being made of precious stones is almost certainly derived from Isaiah 54:11-12, which reads:

> O afflicted one, storm-tossed, and not
>   comforted,
>   I am about to set your stones in antimony,
>   and lay your foundations with sapphires.
> I will make your pinnacles of rubies,
>   your gates of jewels,
>   and all your wall of precious stones.

The New Jerusalem in Tobit

ΑΩ Tobit's hymn of praise in ch. 13 contains a prediction of the city of Jerusalem being rebuilt in glorious style. His description (13:16) states:

> The gates of Jerusalem will be built with sapphire
>   and emerald,
>   and all your walls with precious stones.
> The towers of Jerusalem will be built with gold,
>   and their battlements with pure gold.
> The streets of Jerusalem will be paved
>   with ruby and with stones of Ophir.

The author of Tobit expanded on this tradition in his description of the future Jerusalem (13:16). [The New Jerusalem in Tobit] Several fragmentary copies of a "new Jerusalem" text have been discovered at Qumran. Inspired by Ezekiel 40–48 (as is John's vision), the fragments tell of an angel guide who measures the new Jerusalem and all its contents. Some of the fragments describe aspects of the city being made of gold, sapphire, rubies, alabaster, and onyx.

The specific list of twelve precious stones that adorn the foundations of the city is possibly drawn, directly or indirectly, from Exodus 28:17-21 and 39:10-14, texts that describe the breastpiece

---

Measurement of the Wall

In 21:17, John does not specifically say that the *height* of the wall is one hundred and forty-four cubits, but that the *wall* is one hundred forty-four cubits. This measurement, if referring to the wall's height, would mean the wall would be ridiculously small in comparison to the height of the city it surrounds. In order to solve this problem, some scholars have suggested that instead of the height of the wall, the measurement refers to the wall's thickness. David Aune, for instance, has understood that the wall's width is meant, pointing out that in Ezek 40 both the height and width of the temple wall are measured and that in ancient cities the thickness of the walls was often emphasized (because thick walls would have been difficult for an enemy to break through). The most normal reading, however, is that the wall's height is being given.

Other interpreters have tried to resolve the problem by suggesting that the cubit (traditionally the distance between a person's elbow and the end of the forefinger, or approximately eighteen inches) refers not to a human cubit, but to an angel's cubit, since the angel is the one measuring. Angels were often considered to be enormous creatures.

Thus an "angel's cubit" would be much larger than a human cubit. Accordingly, we have no idea how high a wall would be that measured one hundred forty-four angel's cubits. Against this view, however, is that the last part of v. 17 (which is somewhat ambiguous in Greek) seems to mean that the measurement used by the angel was the normal "human" measurement. Furthermore, to give a measurement that has no point of reference (how big is an angel's forearm?) negates the whole purpose in measuring.

Perhaps, as some commentators have suggested, the relatively low height of the wall indicates that the new Jerusalem does not need a massive wall for protection since all God's enemies have been defeated. All such concerns, however, arise from taking too literal an approach to John's imagery. The wall is, as John says, a "great, high wall" (21:12)—it is seventy-five feet high. The specific measurement has more symbolic significance, though, than literal. The one hundred forty-four symbolizes completeness or perfection—the wall is perfect as it stands!

David E. Aune, *Revelation 17–22*, Word Biblical Commentary (Nashville: Thomas Nelson, 1998), 1162.

that was worn by the high priest. (John says the foundations "are adorned with" the jewels; the description of the foundations, however, seems to imply that each foundation is composed of one large precious stone.) On the high priest's breastpiece were twelve stones, each inscribed with the name of one of the twelve tribes of Israel.

The list of stones is very similar to the list given in Revelation 21:19-20. The difference in the order of the stones listed, as well as some variation in the names of the stones, renders tenuous any decision about John's use of the exodus tradition. If he is consciously drawing upon the tradition of the priest's breastpiece, then perhaps the presence of the jewels supports the claim made earlier in Revelation that the people of God are a priestly people (1:6; 5:10; 20:6). Note that whereas in Exodus the stones are inscribed with the names of the twelve tribes of Israel, in Revelation they are inscribed with the names of the twelve apostles (21:14). [Jewels]

Jewels

The identification of many of the jewels that John names as a part of the new Jerusalem is uncertain. The focus for the reader should not be on trying to identify individual gemstones, but on appreciating the overall effect John was trying to create. He was attempting to portray a city of overwhelming brilliance, beauty, and worth—a city worthy to be the dwelling place of God and God's people.

In Ezekiel's vision of the restored Jerusalem, the centerpiece of the city is the temple. (In fact, in Ezekiel the temple dominates almost the entire description.) John makes a major change in this tradition. In his vision of the new Jerusalem, there is no temple. The purpose of the earthly temple had been to serve as a connection between the people and God. The temple was where God dwelled and where the people gave their offerings and sacrifices to God. In the new Jerusalem, God and the Lamb dwell directly with the people. The glory and presence of God fill the entire city, similar to Ezekiel's vision when the glory of God filled the new temple (Ezek 43:4-5). As there is no need for a temple, there is also no need for the sun or moon, for God and the Lamb will provide the light. This statement is a clear adaptation of Isaiah 60:19 (cf. 60:1-2):

> The sun shall no longer be
>   your light by day,
> nor for brightness shall the moon
>   give light to you by night;
> but the LORD will be your everlasting light,
>   and your God will be your glory.

New Testament writers also made use of the imagery of light, proclaiming that "God is light and in him there is no darkness at all" (1 John 1:5). Jesus is the true "light of the world" (John 8:12). The author of 1 John recognized that where the love of God is present in the world, "the darkness is passing away and the true light is already shining" (2:8). What is experienced now only in part will be experienced in its fullness in the new Jerusalem. The light of God and the Lamb, which at present often seems dim and flickering, will shine in overwhelming brilliance in the new age.

In 21:24-27, John once more adapts Isaiah 60. The postexilic prophet of this section of Isaiah looked forward to the renewed and rebuilt Jerusalem. He wrote,

> Foreigners shall build up your walls,
>   and their kings shall minister to you;
> . . . .
> Your gates shall always be open;
>   day and night they shall not be shut,
> so that nations shall bring you their wealth,
>   with their kings led in procession. (60:10-11; see also 60:3-5).

Likewise, John says of the new Jerusalem that "the kings of the earth will bring their glory into it. . . . People will bring into it the glory and the honor of the nations" (21:24-26). [The Kings of the Earth] This is one of the most astounding passages in the Apocalypse. The "kings of the earth" and "the nations" have throughout the book of Revelation been those who have resisted the claims of God on their lives and have instead followed after the beast. Although John has recorded the destruction of the kings of the earth (19:17-21) and the nations (20:7-9), now they too enter the holy city to "bring their glory into it."

Several passages in the Hebrew Bible (including Isa 60; see also Dan 7:14; Zech 2:11; 8:23) express confidence that in the glorious future when Israel is a mighty kingdom with Jerusalem as its magnificent capital, then the Gentiles (the nations) will come to the city and pay homage and reverence to the city and its God. John is clearly following that tradition here. The difficulty arises in trying to determine what John intends to say by his use of this tradition. Some interpreters see here a clear indication of John's belief in universal salvation—ultimately all people will enter the new Jerusalem and be a part of God's people.

The Kings of the Earth

Speaking of John's vision of the kings bringing their glory into the new Jerusalem, Beasley-Murray commented,

The encouragement which this expectation would afford the original readers of the Revelation, and its pertinence to their situation, should not be overlooked. It indicates that their opponents, whose hostility is to grow to murderous proportions, are yet to render up their sword to God and the Lamb and offer him the tribute of their adoration. It suggests more. The nations who once offered their riches to the city of the Antichrist will yield them instead to the city of God and the Lamb (vv. 24, 26), and that implies a sanctification of the whole order of this created world and its products.

George R. Beasley-Murray, *The Book of Revelation*, New Century Bible (Greenwood SC: Attic, 1974), 328-29.

Other interpreters argue strongly that such a reading misstates John's intention, claiming that to understand this passage as supporting universal salvation is to read "far too much theology into incidental references that are more easily explained in another way."[1] John does not really expect any nonbelievers to be on the renewed earth at this time. Thus "the kings" and "the nations" are simply a part of the tradition John is adapting. The terms do not have the same meaning they do elsewhere in Revelation. Here, they represent the people of God. Jürgen Roloff has explained, "The fulfillment of the promise of the end-time pilgrimage of nations serves him [John] merely as a symbol of the universal unity, free from distance and fear, of human beings in the light of the presence of God."[2] [The New Jerusalem]

Both of these views—exclusive and universal salvation—are overstatements in regard to the book of Revelation. On the one hand, John does hold out hope for all people to become a part of the kingdom of God. That seems to be the message of 21:24-26 (cf. 5:13; 11:13; 15:4; 21:3; 22:2). Yet John also warns (even in this scene; see 21:27) that certain actions and practices are not consistent with the God revealed in Jesus Christ. Those who persist in rejecting God and living apart from God face God's judgment. These two views are held in tension in Revelation—promise and warning. Can all people and nations be saved? Definitely. Can some people be excluded—exclude themselves—from God's presence? John knows that possibility as well. At the very least, John's passages that seem to speak of the salvation of all people "express hope that the truth embodied in the church

The New Jerusalem
This painting of *The Elect*, which is the left panel of Hans Memling's work *The Last Judgment* shows the redeemed receiving their robes and entering the new Jerusalem.

Hans Memling (1433–1494). *Reception of the Righteous into Heaven.* Left panel of *The Last Judgment* triptych. 1467–1471. Narodowe Museum. Gdansk, Poland. (Credit: Erich Lessing/Art Resource, NY)

will one day be recognized by the whole world."[3] Recognizing that God's judgment falls upon human sinfulness and rebellion, we can still hope that ultimately God's grace and mercy will overcome even human resistance.

In trying to fathom John's position on human judgment and salvation, George R. Beasley-Murray exhibited an admirable mix of insight and humility when he wrote,

> Candour compels us to state that John has given no clear indication of any such teaching [that all will be a part of the new Jerusalem]. He simply presents stark alternatives before mankind of life for or against God in the here and now, and its consequences in the age to come. With his eye on the impending climax of history in the life and death struggle of the forces of Christ and the Antichrist among the nations, and its issue in the judgments of God within and beyond this world, John was not worried by the problems which perplex us in our more detached reflections on time and eternity. Without doubt John would have affirmed as readily as any that the last word on the ultimate destiny of man remains with God, who has revealed himself in our Lord Jesus Christ, and whose grace and truth are equally present in his judgment of man as they were united in judgment of the cross. When we have stated all our arguments, we too finally have to rest in that acknowledgement.[4]

Because all nations will freely enter the city and embrace it as their own, the gates of the city will no longer need to be closed (21:25). Walls and gates around ancient cities were for protection from the city's enemies. [Pearly Gates] The perpetually open gates symbolize the safety and inclusiveness of the new Jerusalem. The righteousness and holiness of God demand that all that is spiritually unclean remain outside God's city. Thus "nothing unclean will enter it, nor anyone who practices abomination or falsehood" (21:27). Abomination and

Pearly Gates

The popular image of heaven's "pearly gates" comes from Rev 21:21. Note that in John's vision each gate is one massive pearl, not gates overlaid with pearls.

falsehood are characteristics of Babylon (17:4-5; 18:23). Those who belong to Babylon and follow its ways cannot be a part of the new Jerusalem. A radical choice is demanded—either one lives in Babylon or one lives in Jerusalem; either one joins the whore or one joins the bride. This verse serves "as a pastoral warning to John's hearers. The new Jerusalem—the kingdom of God—is a reality of a new world wholly free of evil. Christians must, here and now, prepare for citizenship. They must begin to root out of their lives whatever is incompatible with life in this new realm of God."[5]

[A Tale of Two Cities]

A Tale of Two Cities

"The Revelation as a whole may be characterized as *A Tale of Two Cities*, with the sub-title, *The Harlot and the Bride*. 21:9 is written in order to make that theme crystal clear. The harlot-city reposes on the beast from hell—she partakes of the character of the devil, and the bride-city descends from heaven—she is the creation of God. But one thing they have in common. They stand alike on the earth, and invite humanity to come to them."

George R. Beasley-Murray, *The Book of Revelation*, New Century Bible (Greenwood SC: Attic, 1974), 315.

CONNECTIONS

1. John's vision of a new Jerusalem is often referred to as the heavenly Jerusalem. This description is correct in one sense: The new Jerusalem comes down from heaven, from God. It is not simply a rebuilt Jerusalem, a renovated and repaired former system. Rather, this is a *new* Jerusalem, located on the new earth. God has transformed the old into something new. As "new wine is not for old wineskins," God's new kingdom does not fit old structures and old patterns. To be a part of this new Jerusalem requires new ways of thinking and acting on our part. Life with God is not life as usual. Paul recognized this when he wrote, "So if anyone is in Christ, there is a new creation: everything old has passed away; see, everything has become new!" (2 Cor 5:17). [The City of God]

In another sense, however, to call the new Jerusalem the heavenly Jerusalem is to misunderstand John's imagery. This new Jerusalem originates in heaven, but it descends to earth. John pictures eternal life with God not as some ethereal existence in the clouds or in some celestial realm. Rather, John places the new Jerusalem on a renewed earth. Instead of the people of God ascending to heaven to be with God, in John's vision God descends to a renewed earth to make God's home with people. John's description of the new Jerusalem is very physical—a wall, gates, foundations of jewels, streets of gold, a river, a fruit-bearing tree. The original world that God created, that humanity has misused and abused, is transformed in God's future. Obviously John does not intend these details to be taken literally. They are imaginative descriptions of a glorious existence with God. Yet if John is comfortable using the imagery of a renewed

The City of God

In a sermon on John's vision of the new Jerusalem, David Buttrick said,

Well, now do you see why the Holy City must come down from God? The city must come from God because we can't build it on our own. And do you understand why the book of Revelation hears a great voice from heaven shouting, "See, I make all things new!"? Left to ourselves all we can do is remake the old, trade in the stone ax for the B-2 bomber (Whatever good it will do!). Left to our own devices we'll dream a Holy City and build Babel every time. But, "See," cries the voice of God, "I make things new!" Well, God better, because we can't. God must shape a new heart for loving and a new will for living, and a whole new humankind.

David G. Buttrick, "Poetry of Hope," *Preaching Through the Apocalypse: Sermons from Revelation*, ed. Cornish R. Rogers and Joseph R. Jeter Jr. (St. Louis: Chalice, 1992), 162-63.

physical world to describe eschatological existence with God, this indicates that John has no Gnostic disparagement of the material world. The world that God created and of which God said "That's good" is here redeemed and renewed. This insight has implications for how we live our lives in the present. It means God's creation is to be enjoyed, celebrated, respected, and affirmed. [Augustine]

> **Augustine**
>
> Augustine commented that the new Jerusalem "has been coming down from heaven since its beginning" in the lives of people who by grace have become children of God. After the Last Judgment, the city will be revealed in its fullness when "the splendour of that City will be made apparent."
>
> *Civ.* 20.17, trans. Henry Bettenson; ed. David Knowles (New York: Penguin, 1972), 928.

2. The words from the heavenly throne in 21:3-4 are some of the most powerful and moving words in the Apocalypse. It is not surprising that this text has become a frequently read text at funerals and graveside services. The text functions to offer comfort that life as it is currently experienced—full of pain, mourning, and death—is not how life is experienced in God's eschatological kingdom. The text assures us that suffering and death, which presently wreak havoc not only on humanity but on all of God's creation, will have no place in the new heaven and earth.

This text reminds us of something about the nature of God also, which is that the God revealed in the Scriptures is opposed to suffering and pain. Well-meaning but ill-informed people frequently respond to suffering with words such as, "It was God's will" or "God has a reason for everything," as if pain and suffering were a part of God's design. This text assures us that such is not the case. A theology that presents God as intentionally and willingly inflicting suffering and pain on creation is bad theology. Along with John of Patmos, "Christians must proclaim emphatically *that* the God of Scripture is not a sadist; *that* he hates suffering in his good creation; and *that* suffering is fundamentally alien to his coming kingdom."[6]

The hope expressed in this text is not simply an "otherworldly" hope, a yearning for future bliss that is meaningless in the present. Rather, this eschatological hope can help sustain us during the painful and agonizing experiences of suffering, mourning, and death. The experience of countless sufferers who have been overcome by the tragedies of life is that eschatological hope does sustain and support the believer when life seems to come crashing down. J. Christiaan Beker, reflecting on the biblical hope that is grounded in eschatology, has written,

> A biblical theology of hope views the present power of death in terms of its empty future and in the knowledge of its, not God's sure defeat. It can tolerate, therefore, the agonizing presence of the power of

death as "on the way out," and be confident that evil will not have
the final say over God's creation. . . .

   And so the biblical vision still offers a promissory word in the face
of suffering due to the power of death. That promise instills in us the
hope of God's triumph in the face of the agonizing burden of suffering which so many of us carry. Although the awesome "not yet" of
God's final triumph over suffering and death all too often fills us with
agony and despair, the promise of the gospel continues to evoke in us
the prayerful cry: "Come, Lord Jesus" (Rev 22:20).[7]

3. Ultimately, Christian hope resides in God, not in a place. In
popular idiom, eternal life—or eschatological salvation—means
"going to heaven." Such language is acceptable only when we recognize that "heaven" is metaphorical language for the dwelling of
God. To "go to heaven" means to live in complete community with
God. As noted earlier, John locates the new Jerusalem on earth, not
in heaven, because God has come down to dwell with people.
Whether, as did John, we locate existence with God on a transformed earth or we continue to use the language of heaven, the
substance of our hope is relational—eternal bliss is knowing and
being known by God. [Hymns]

   In this regard, John's use of a city as a metaphor for eternal life is
instructive. To be a part of a city is to be engaged with other people, to be involved in relationships with other people. Eternal life is
relational not only in that we are in community with God, but we
are also in community with the people of God. John does not present eschatological salvation in terms of isolated individuals, living
in a pristine wilderness apart from society. Salvation is communal.
As Eugene Boring has noted, "The goal of history is not an individualistic and anticultural 'back to nature,' but community, life
together; not self-contained monads, but Theopolis."[8] If a foretaste
of eschatological glory is to be found in the present life, then we
find it also in community, and not in isolation. "Individual" salvation is almost an oxymoron. We are saved into a community. We
become a part of the people of God, both now and forever.

4. The book of Revelation has been accused of fostering an escapist
mentality among Christians because it holds out a hope for life
beyond the present existence. It has been blamed for creating a
sense of apathy or nonresponsibility toward the world and its problems: "This world is not my home; I'm just a-passin' through."
While John's visions can be read that way (and often are), such an
understanding of the Apocalypse is both misguided and unfair to
John. The eschatological orientation of the Apocalypse does not

---

Hymns

📖 John's vision of the heavenly Jerusalem has inspired many poets and hymn writers. The following verses from various hymns are only a few of the many examples that could be provided:

Lamb of God, the heavens adore you; let saints and angels sing before you,
as harps and cymbals swell the sound.
Twelve great pearls, the city's portals: through them we stream to join the immortals
as we with joy your throne surround.
No eye has known the sight, no ear heard such delight:
Alleluia!
Therefore we sing to greet our King; for ever let our praises ring.

From: "Sleepers, Wake!" words by Philipp Nicolai, 16th C.; trans. Carl P. Daw Jr.

....

In the heavenly country bright, need they no created light;
thou its light, its joy, its crown, thou its sun which goes not down:
there for ever may we sing alleluias to our King.

From: "As with Gladness Men of Old," words by William Chatterton Dix, 19th C.

....

Jerusalem the golden, with milk and honey blest,
beneath thy contemplation sink heart and voice oppressed:
I know not, oh, I know not, what joys await us there;
what radiancy of glory, what bliss beyond compare!

From: "Jerusalem the Golden," words by Bernard of Cluny, 12th C.; trans. John Mason Neale.

....

Jerusalem, my happy home, When shall I come to thee?
When shall my sorrows have an end? Thy joys, when shall I see?
Thy saints are crowned with glory great; They see God face to face;
They triumph still, they still rejoice; Most happy is their case.
There David stands with harp in hand As master of the choir;
Ten thousand times that man were blest That might this music hear.
Jerusalem, Jerusalem, God grant that I may see
Thine endless joy, and of the same, Partaker ever be!

From: "Jerusalem, My Happy Home," words by Joseph Bromehead, 18th or 19th C.

---

justify a lack of concern for the current world order. Contrary to the way the book is often perceived, John's visions of the future are not calls to abandon the present. The book of Revelation, like many other apocalypses, is (at its core) protest literature. It is resistance literature. It calls on its readers not to accept the world as it is. They are to stand firm in their commitment to an alternative worldview. By holding before its readers an eschatological vision of a new heaven and earth, the Apocalypse declares that the world as

The New Jerusalem as Catalyst

Walter Russell Bowie (1882–1969), rector of Grace Episcopal Church in New York and writer of the text for the hymn "O Holy City, Seen of John," recognized that the imagery of the new Jerusalem should serve as a catalyst for social action in the present. While guilty of attributing the "building of the kingdom" to human efforts, the hymn still correctly understands John's vision as a call to action and not simply a word of comfort. The words of the hymn are as follows:

O holy city, seen of John, where Christ, the Lamb, doth reign,
within whose foursquare walls shall come no night, nor need, nor pain,
and where the tears are wiped from eyes that shall not weep again!

O shame to us who rest content while lust and greed for gain
in street and shop and tenement wring gold from human pain,
and bitter lips in blind despair, cry, "Christ hath died in vain!"

Give us, O God, the strength to build the city that hath stood
too long a dream, whose laws are love, whose crown is servanthood,
and where the sun that shineth is God's grace for human good.

Already in the mind of God that city riseth fair:
lo, how its splendor challenges the souls that greatly dare—
yea, bids us seize the whole of life and build its glory there.

it now exists is not the way that God intends it to be. This vision of a world of freedom, dignity, justice, and reconciliation should serve as a catalyst to motivate the people of God to be at work trying to bring that vision into reality. [The New Jerusalem as Catalyst]

The book of Revelation does not present a picture of a God who has given up on the world and is ready to discard it. The message of Revelation is that God is the creator of the world. This world is God's "baby," God's creation. Rather than discard it, God seeks to save it, to rid it of its beasts and its monstrous evils, to drive out its dragons, to purge it of its impurities. The climactic finale of the book is God's creation of a new heaven and a new earth, transforming the old into something new. "See, I am making all things new" (21:5).

If we are God's children, we are called to participate with God in that transformative process. This view is no egotistical or arrogant "Let's build the kingdom of God" understanding. It is not another self-help program, like the many that line the bookstore shelves. From the Oneida Community to the Branch Davidians (to name only American examples), history is littered with failed attempts by individuals and groups who thought that their actions were capable of ushering in God's kingdom. The new heaven and new earth are ultimately all God's doings. (Remember, the new Jerusalem comes down "out of heaven from God.") It is God who "makes all things new." We are simply called to be partners with God in that work. Adela Yarbro Collins has expressed this conviction well: "The destiny of the world and even of the church is beyond human control. But people can discern the outlines of that destiny and ally themselves with it. They can avoid working against it. And they can embody its values in witness to the world."[9]

5. John does not let us become so enamored with the vision of the heavenly Jerusalem that we become complacent or self-assured. Twice in this vision of the new Jerusalem, he stops to remind us who will *not* be participants in God's new kingdom (21:8, 27). Since the book of Revelation is addressed to people in the churches of Asia Minor, these warnings likewise are addressed to those who think that they are a part of God's people. [A Call to Repentance] Yet from his knowledge of those churches, John knows that that perception is not always reality. Some people "have a name of being alive, but . . . are dead" (3:1). He warns that it is possible to have one's name blotted out of the Book of Life (3:5) and thus be excluded from sharing in the new Jerusalem. Those of us in the church today should hear these verses as an exhortation to live our lives in accordance with the will of God and as a warning that some people who think they are "insiders" in regard to the kingdom of God may in reality be "outsiders." As Jesus says in Matthew 7:21, "Not everyone who says to me, 'Lord, Lord,' will enter the kingdom of heaven, but only the one who does the will of my Father in heaven."

A Call to Repentance

"The vision [of ch. 21] confronts us not so much with relief that everything will turn out well in the end but with the reality that things, here and now, are profoundly *un*well and that repentance and change of life are required. Disease is present in a society where there is so much plenty, but there is inadequate provision for the sick and dying. The promise of a new heaven and a new earth is a vision of judgment on Babylon and its culture of death, where money and privilege can buy success, health, and care, and the dignity and well-being of people, young and old, are subordinated to the demands of economic accounting and ability to pay."

Christopher C. Rowland, "The Book of Revelation: Introduction, Commentary, and Reflections," *The New Interpreter's Bible*, 12 vols. (Nashville: Abingdon, 1998), 12:730.

NOTES

[1] Robert H. Mounce, *The Book of Revelation*, The New International Commentary on the New Testament, rev. ed. (Grand Rapids: Eerdmans, 1998), 397.

[2] Jürgen Roloff, *The Revelation of John: A Continental Commentary*, Continental Commentaries, trans. John E. Alsup (Minneapolis: Fortress, 1993), 245.

[3] Adela Yarbro Collins, *The Apocalypse*, New Testament Message: A Biblical-Theological Commentary (Wilmington DE: Michael Glazier, 1979), 150.

[4] George R. Beasley-Murray, *The Book of Revelation*, New Century Bible (Greenwood SC: Attic, 1974), 304.

[5] Wilfrid J. Harrington, *Revelation*, Sacra Pagina (Collegeville MN: Liturgical, 1993), 218.

[6] J. Christiaan Beker, *Suffering and Hope: The Biblical Vision and the Human Predicament* (Grand Rapids: Eerdmans, 1994), 96.

[7] Ibid., 121-23.

[8] M. Eugene Boring, "Revelation 19–21: End without Closure," *The Princeton Seminary Bulletin* Supplement 3 (1994): 74.

[9] Collins, *Apocalypse*, 150.

THE RIVER OF LIFE
AND EPILOGUE

22:1-21

COMMENTARY

The River of Life, 22:1-5

This section continues John's description of the new Jerusalem. The preceding section flows into this section with hardly a break. The chapter division in modern Bibles makes too harsh a separation between these verses and the preceding section. Only a minor shift occurs as the angel shows John another aspect of his final vision. John's dependence on the book of Ezekiel is clearly evident in this passage. In Ezekiel 47, the prophet saw a river flowing from beneath the temple in the restored Jerusalem. On both sides of the river "grow all kinds of trees for food" whose "leaves [are] for healing" (47:12). This river has life-giving properties, nourishing the trees on its banks and turning the lifeless, foul waters of the Dead Sea into waters teeming with fish. [The River of Life]

In Ezekiel's vision, as is true in several apocalyptic texts, hope for the future is expressed in terms of a renewed garden of Eden or paradise. Ezekiel's river is a part of that paradise motif. Genesis 2:10 speaks of a river flowing out of Eden to water the garden. John includes the river in his vision also, but he goes even further with the Eden imagery than did Ezekiel. John changes Ezekiel's trees on the sides of the river into the tree of life, an obvious reference to the tree of life in the midst of the garden of Eden (Gen 2:9). In Genesis, Adam and Eve were forbidden to eat from the tree of life. To do so would have meant that they would live forever (Gen 3:22). Now in the new Jerusalem, where the redeemed will live forever, the presence of the tree of life is appropriate. It is no longer forbidden for food, but rather it produces twelve kinds of fruit each month, apparently for the enjoyment of the city's inhabitants. The fruit from the tree is the fulfillment of the promise made to the faithful in Revelation 2:7.

The leaves of the trees are "for the healing of the nations" (22:2). Although the idea that the leaves will be for healing is drawn from

The River of Life

William Blake's pen and ink and watercolor work interprets Rev 22:1-2. According to the text, the river of life flows from the throne of God and to the tree of life. Blake placed Christ in the river holding the hands of two children. He leads them toward the light, symbolic of God. The traditional reading of this signed work on paper is that the left bank represents Innocence, and the right bank symbolizes Experience.

William Blake (1757–1827). *The River of Life.* 1805. Tate Gallery. London, England. (Credit: Tate Gallery/Art Resource, NY)

Ezekiel, John has made the interesting addition "of the nations." The nations are those mentioned in 21:24, 26. They represent those people who had been opponents of God. David Aune regarded the addition of this phrase as "simply mechanical, however, since there is no real place in the eschatological scheme of Revelation for the 'healing of the nations' construed as their conversion."[1] That explanation is unconvincing. Why would John have altered his source by this addition if it had no meaning for him? At the least, the healing of the nations is an indication that "the population of the new Jerusalem will be made up of every ethnic and national identity."[2] The phrase possibly has a broader meaning, however. As we have seen already, John leaves open the possibility that God's mercy is wider than we might expect or even imagine. The leaves that are for the "healing of the nations" is perhaps another of John's pointers in the direction of God's surprising and overwhelming grace.

John's reference to the tree of life is somewhat confusing. Does he mean only one tree ("the tree of life") or does he intend to describe an avenue of trees that are life-giving? [Location of the Tree of Life] The Greek word used here—*xylon*—is singular in form, but it is sometimes used in the singular to refer to several trees ("a forest"). Apparently John has borrowed the idea of many trees from Ezekiel and combined it with the singular tree of life from Genesis. Even though he likely envisions a

Location of the Tree of Life

AΩ Exactly how John pictures the trees in relation to the street in the city and the river is not clear. If a period is placed after "city" in v. 2 (as in the NRSV; ancient Greek manuscripts had no punctuation marks), then the text indicates that the river flows down the middle of the street, and the trees are on each side of the river. If, however, a period is placed after "Lamb," then the sentence would read, "In the midst of its street and on each side of the river is the tree of life," perhaps meaning that the street and the river run parallel to each other, with the trees in between them.

whole avenue of trees, he retains the singular to reinforce the reference to the primeval tree of life. The eschatological "garden" is vastly superior, then, to the first garden of Eden. The latter had only one tree of life; in the new Jerusalem, the street is lined with trees of life.

Whereas Ezekiel placed the source of the river at the temple, John's new Jerusalem has no temple. In John's vision, the river of life flows "from the throne of God and of the Lamb" (22:1). God and the Lamb are the source of life and blessings for the inhabitants of the new Jerusalem. Their throne in the midst of the city's garden symbolizes that they do not reign from afar, but they live in the midst of the people. John's exalted Christology is evident once more in his statement that the throne is that "of God and of the Lamb." God shares sovereignty with Christ, who is worthy "to receive power and wealth and wisdom and might and honor and glory and blessing" (5:12), because he was the faithful witness, the Lamb that was slaughtered.

The statement in v. 3 that "nothing accursed will be found there any more" can be heard both as a warning and as a word of assurance. It serves as a warning that if one's lifestyle is "accursed"—in rebellion against God—then one will have no place in this new paradise setting. It offers comfort by reassuring the readers/hearers that the new Jerusalem will be free from any evil and unsettling influence. If, as some commentators suggest, the allusion is to the "curses" pronounced on Adam, Eve, and the serpent in Genesis 3:14-19, then the statement promises a reversal of the garden of Eden scenario. In the eschatological garden will be no death, no pain, no difficult struggle for food (since the trees produce bountiful fruit year round). The new garden is a place of eternal life, joy, and fertile abundance.

Beatific Vision

One characteristic of life in the new Jerusalem is that the people of God "will see his face" (22:4). Paul expressed the same idea when he wrote, "For now we see in a mirror, dimly, but then we will see face to face. Now I know only in part; then I will know fully, even as I have been fully known" (1 Cor 13:12). This experience of finally seeing God, of knowing God intimately and fully, is what is sometimes known as the Beatific Vision. The subject of the Beatific Vision was much discussed and debated during the Middle Ages. The traditional view is that the Beatific Vision can only be attained by the redeemed after death. Some theologians, however, argued that "the vision is bestowed in exceptional circumstances for brief periods in this life; for example, St. Thomas Aquinas held that it was granted to Moses (Exod 34:28-35) and St. Paul (2 Cor 12:2-4)."

"The Beatific Vision," in *The Oxford Dictionary of the Christian Church*, ed. F. L. Cross; 3rd ed. ed. E. A. Livingstone (Oxford: Oxford University Press, 1997), 174.

Worship, which has been a major emphasis in the Apocalypse and which has sustained John and his hearers/readers throughout their trying times, will also be an important component of life in the new Jerusalem. Since worship draws people closer to God, it is appropriate that worship should continue now that God is with them and the throne of God and the Lamb is in their midst. The God whom they worshiped from a distance can now be celebrated and praised face to face. The most revealing characteristic of life in the new Jerusalem is that the people of God "will see his face" (22:4). This claim is particularly intimate and personal. [Beatific Vision] Elsewhere in the Bible, God, even at the most accessible moments, always remains somewhat aloof or hidden. Humans are not allowed to see God or sometimes even to hear him directly (Exod 3:6; 20:19; 33:20-23; John 1:18; 1 Tim 6:15-16; 1 John 4:12). To see God—which means to have a full and intimate experience of God—is an eschatological promise that John sees as being fulfilled (cf. Matt 5:8; 1 Cor 13:12).

The faithful in the vision of 7:1-8 have been marked for protection with the seal of God on their foreheads (note also 9:4; 14:1). In 3:12, the promise given to the conquerors at Philadelphia is that they will have written on them "the name of my God, and the name of the city of my God, the new Jerusalem that comes down from my God out of heaven, and my (Christ's) own new name." Once more John refers to the redeemed being "marked" as a sign of their belonging to God (22:4). Being inscribed with the name of God is a picturesque way of saying that they are God's people, a privilege they will enjoy "forever and ever" as they reign with God and the Lamb (22:5).

Epilogue, 22:6-21

The epilogue of the book, which contains warnings, exhortations, and assurances, is more than simply a collection of loosely connected closing statements. These final verses function in at least three important ways. First, they serve as an epistolary ending to the work, bringing the writing to a close in a manner consistent with the epistolary greeting with which John began the Apocalypse (1:4-6). Paul's letters in the New Testament frequently conclude with a section of exhortations or ethical injunctions, followed by a final greeting or blessing. Second, the epilogue has several clear connections with the opening chapter of Revelation (which will be identified in the comments below). [Epilogue and Prologue] These connections serve to tie the two chapters together, allowing them to function structurally as an *inclusio* for the entire book. Third, these verses reiterate some of the major emphases of John's revelation, reminding the readers/hearers of the important elements of the message of the book.

Throughout this section, the identity of the speakers is not always clear. In vv. 7, 12-13, 16, and 20a, the speaker is Christ. In v. 9, the speaker is identified as an angel. Verses 8 and 20b-21 are clearly from John. Verses 6 and 10-11 may be from Christ or an angel. Verses 14-15 and 18-19 may be from Christ or John. (Modern readers should keep in mind that quotation marks, as well as other punctuation marks, are not present in ancient Greek

---

Epilogue and Prologue

This chart lists some of the similarities between the prologue (1:1-8) and the epilogue (22:6-21) of Revelation.

Prologue	*Epilogue*
"The revelation of Jesus Christ, which God gave him; . . . he made it known by sending his angel to his servant John" (1:1)	"The Lord, the God of the spirits of the prophets, has sent his angel to show his servants what must soon take place" (22:6)
	"It is I, Jesus, who sent my angel to you" (22:16)
"John, who testified to the word of God and to the testimony of Jesus Christ" (1:1-2)	"The one who testifies to these things" (22:20)
"John, who testified . . . to all that he saw" (1:2)	"I, John, am the one who heard and saw these things" (22:8)
"Blessed is the one who reads aloud the words of the prophecy, and blessed are those who hear and who keep what is written in it" (1:3)	"Blessed is the one who keeps the words of the prophecy of this book" (22:7)
	"Those who keep the words of this book" (22:9)
	"The words of the prophecy of this book" (22:10)
"For the time is near" (1:3)	"For the time is near" (22:10)
"To the seven churches that are in Asia" (1:4)	"This testimony for the churches" (22:16)
"Look! He is coming with the clouds" (1:7)	"See, I am coming soon!" (22:7)
	"See, I am coming soon" (22:12)
	"Surely I am coming soon" (22:20)
"I am the Alpha and the Omega," says the Lord God, who is and who was and who is to come, the Almighty (1:8)	"I am the Alpha and the Omega, the first and the last, the beginning and the end" (22:13)

manuscripts.) The approach taken in this commentary as to the identity of the speakers is as follows:

> v. 6—Angel
> v. 7—Christ
> v. 8—John
> vv. 9-11—Angel
> vv. 12-16—Christ
> vv. 17-19—John
> v. 20a—Christ
> vv. 20b-21—John

Trustworthy and True

AΩ In 22:6, the angel declares the words to be "trustworthy and true" (*pistoi kai alēthinoi*). This phrase is the same one used to describe Christ, the rider on the white horse in 19:11, who is "faithful and true" (*pistos kai alēthinos*). The words of the angel are "faithful and true" because they have their origin in the one who is himself "faithful and true," the one who sent the angel to declare the message (22:16).

The speaker in v. 6 is likely an angel, apparently the same one who showed John the vision of the heavenly Jerusalem in 21:9–22:5. The angel authenticates the revelation that has been given to John. [Trustworthy and True] "These words" is best understood as referring to the entire contents of the book and not only to the previous vision. [These Words] The angel reaffirms what was announced at the beginning of the book (cf. 1:1-2), which is that the message John delivers is one that has been given to him by an angel sent from God. The ultimate source of John's revelation is "the God of the spirits of the prophets." [The God of the Spirits of the Prophets] Even though he does not explicitly call himself a prophet, John almost certainly includes himself among the prophets (cf. 1:3; 22:9). The revelation is not only for John, but for God's "servants" (plural), that is, all God's people. As in 1:1, 3, John is convinced that the end is near, for he believes that these events he has described "must soon take place."

The exalted Christ speaks in v. 7, reinforcing the expectation that the end is near. His "coming" here should not be generalized so that it refers to the coming of Christ into the lives of believers throughout history. The "coming of Christ" in 22:7 is the future, eschatological return of Christ to inaugurate the consummation of the final events John has described in his Revelation. The early Christians lived in the expectancy of that event happening soon. John shares in that belief. The latter part of v. 7 presents the sixth beatitude of Revelation, which is a reminder that simply hearing the message proclaimed by

These Words

The angel's declaration that "these words are trustworthy and true" could refer simply to the preceding vision of the new Jerusalem that has been shown to John; or "these words" could refer to what is about to be stated; or, more likely, "these words" refers to the entire revelation that has been given to John.

The God of the Spirits of the Prophets

In the phrase, "the God of the spirits of the prophets" (22:6; cf. 19:10; 1 Cor 14:32), "spirits" refers to the "highest faculty of human beings" (Aune, *Revelation 17–22*, 1182). This phrase identifies God as the source of the prophets' inspired messages. The same God who inspired earlier prophets is now the source behind the revelation given to John. Beckwith has explained,

> The purpose of this sentence is to authenticate the book as a genuine work of prophecy; God who controls the inspiration of the prophets has inspired his angel and the Apocalyptist to show his servants what must shortly come to pass.

Isbon T. Beckwith, *The Apocalypse of John* (Macmillan, 1919. Reprint. Grand Rapids: Baker, 1979), 772-73.

John is not enough. One must "keep," that is, be obedient to, the words of John's message.

John speaks in v. 8 to legitimate further the contents of his writing. What is contained herein is what John "heard and saw." This statement is his own stamp of approval, his imprimatur, his signature attesting to the authenticity of this work. In a scene almost identical to 19:10, John again falls down to worship the angel who has been the mediator of the revelation. Once more, John is chastised for offering homage and worship to one other than God. Only God—not angels (nor emperors)—is worthy of ultimate human allegiance.

The statement of the angel in v. 10 is the reverse of the command given to Daniel in 8:26; 12:4, 9. Daniel was told to "keep the words secret and the book sealed until the time of the end" (12:4). The book of Daniel was written pseudonymously; that is, claiming to have come from the sixth-century BC figure Daniel, in actuality it was written during the second century BC. The command to seal the book explained to readers in the second century why they had not known about this purportedly four hundred-year-old writing before—it had been sealed up and kept secret. Furthermore, its being revealed indicated that "the time of the end" was now at hand. John writes in his own name, however, not in the name of some venerable figure from the past. His message is directed at his contemporaries. There is no need to seal up the message until the end time, for already "the time is near" (22:10).

The saying in v. 11, based on Daniel 12:10, is difficult. After being told to seal the scroll until the time of the end, Daniel was informed that "many shall be purified, cleansed, and refined, but the wicked shall continue to act wickedly." In Daniel, this verse serves to describe the interim period until the end—some people would be "purified," but the wicked would continue their wickedness. Some commentators have understood Revelation 22:11 in a

Jesus, the Alpha and Omega

On this wall painting from a 4th-century tomb near Thessaloniki, Greece, Christ is represented by the superimposed *chi* (X) and *rho* (P), the first two letters in Χριστός (Christ). On either side are the letters alpha (A) and omega (ω).

Museum of Byzantine Culture. Thessaloniki, Greece. (Credit: Mitchell Reddish)

deterministic sense: The end is so near that no time is left for anyone to change. Repentance is no longer possible. Certainly John believes the time is short before the end arrives, but that does not justify such a fatalistic reading of 22:11. A "softened" version of this interpretation is only slightly less pessimistic: "Since the time is short, the author holds out little hope that sinners will repent."[3] Another interpretation is possible, however. The statement in 22:11 is an imperative, not a declarative sentence. It functions both as warning and exhortation. The thought of the sentence could perhaps be paraphrased as follows: "Let those who are wicked continue in their wickedness if that is what they choose; but they must pay the consequences. On the other hand, let those who are righteous continue to do what is right because that is what God expects and demands from them."

Jesus speaks again in v. 12, reiterating the imminence of his coming (cf. 22:7). When he comes, he will come in judgment, bringing his reward with him (cf. Isa 40:10) "to repay according to everyone's work" (cf. Prov 24:12). As in 2:23, Christ will serve as the eschatological judge who "will give to each of you as your works deserve." This declaration by the exalted Christ is both warning and promise, depending upon the nature of one's works. In 20:11-15, God (the one seated on the "great white throne") is the one who renders the final judgment on people "according to what they had done" (20:13). Here, Christ is the eschatological judge. The seeming contradiction causes no problem for John, for throughout Revelation the exalted Christ has been closely identified with God. He is God's agent. What God does, Christ does.

This exalted Christology of the Apocalypse is evident once more when, in 22:13, John has Christ apply to himself the same titles that have been applied previously to God. Christ is "the Alpha and the Omega" (cf. 1:8; 21:6); [Jesus, the Alpha and Omega] he is "the first and the last" (cf. Isa 41:4; 44:6; 48:12; Rev 1:17; 2:8); he is "the beginning and the end" (21:6). J. P. M. Sweet has noted, "The end is not an event but a person, from whom the world devolves and to whom it moves; he has shared his throne and his title with Jesus."[4]

The final beatitude of the book occurs in v. 14, declaring blessed "those who wash their robes, so that they will have the right to the tree of life and may enter the city by the gates." [Wash Their Robes] The rewards— the right to the tree of life and entrance into the city—are metaphors of salvation or eternal life. The idea of clean robes has appeared twice earlier in Revelation. The closest parallel to 22:14 is 7:14, which describes the faithful as those who "have washed their robes and made them white in the blood of the Lamb." To wash one's robe means to be redeemed by the atoning death of Jesus, to be a recipient of the grace of God made effective through the self-sacrifice of the Lamb who was slain. The other reference to clean robes is in 3:4 where Christ says that in Sardis are still a few people "who have not soiled their clothes; they will walk with me, dressed in white, for they are worthy." Both of these ideas of clean robes are perhaps combined in 22:14. The faithful "wash their robes" when they accept God's offer of forgiveness and mercy and become a part of the people of God. They keep their robes clean by their faithfulness to God.

Whereas the faithful will experience life in God's eternal community, those who have refused to "wash their robes" will not be able to enter the eternal city. They will remain outsiders, having cut themselves off from God by their stubborn resistance to God. The list of those excluded from God's kingdom is similar to the lists in 21:8, 27. Unique to the list in 22:15 is the mention of "dogs" as among the outsiders. The term "dog" was used as a term of contempt, both in Judaism and in early Christianity. (The word can still have that connotation today.) Here in Revelation 22:15, "dogs" refers generally to the wicked, that is, to all who by their actions and lifestyle live as enemies of God.[5] [Dogs]

In 22:6, God is said to be the one who sent the angel with the message. In 22:16 (as well as in 1:1), Jesus is the one who sent the angel. God and Jesus act in consort throughout the Apocalypse. According to the "chain of command" in 1:1, one could say that God was the primary source and Jesus was the secondary source for the sending of the angelic messenger. Jesus applies to himself in 22:16 two titles: he is "the root and the descendant of David," and he is "the bright morning star." The first title has already been

Wash Their Robes

AΩ Instead of "wash their robes" (*plynontes tas stolas autōn*) in 22:14, some Greek manuscripts and versions (whose text was accepted by the KJV) read "do his commandments" (*poiountes tas entolas autou*). Either reading makes sense and fits the context. Perhaps the variant reading arose accidentally due to the two readings looking and sounding somewhat similar. The first reading is probably the original since it is found in the earlier and better Greek manuscripts. Furthermore, in the two places in Revelation (12:17 and 14:12) where adherence to the commandments is mentioned, the phrase that is used is "keeping the commandments," not "doing the commandments."

Dogs

AΩ Whereas dogs were used in Palestine to herd livestock (cf. Job 30:1) and some seem to have been "house dogs" (cf. Matt 15:26-27; Mark 7:27-28), dogs were generally despised. In the Hebrew Bible, dogs are disparaged as those who eat their own vomit (Prov 26:11). They ate the corpses and drank the blood of people who were slain (1 Kgs 14:11; 16:4; 21:19, 23-24; 22:38; 2 Kgs 9:10; 9:36; Ps 68:23). To be surrounded by dogs is a metaphor for being encircled by evildoers (Ps 22:16). A dog was considered one of the lowest forms of animal life (2 Kgs 8:13; Eccl 9:4); a dead dog, then, was a metaphor for "less than nothing" (1 Sam 24:14; 2 Sam 9:8; 16:9). Their scavenging habits also contributed to the feelings of contempt and disgust toward them.

In the New Testament, also, the word "dog" has a negative connotation. The statement in Matthew 7:6 not to "give what is holy to dogs," although originally drawn from a prohibition against giving sacrificial meat or bones to dogs, came to be used as an injunction against giving anything sacred or valuable to the wicked. Paul warned the Christians in Philippi to "beware of the dogs" (3:2), referring to individuals whom he viewed as dangerous heretics. The author of 2 Peter applied the imagery of dogs and swine to false teachers who were leading others astray (2:22). In the *Didache*, an early church manual (possibly 2d century), the Matthean prohibition, "Give not that which is holy to the dogs," is applied to any unbaptized persons as ones who are to be excluded from participation in the Eucharist (9.5).

---

applied to Jesus in 5:5. "The root and descendant of David" (drawn from Isa 11:1, 10) is a messianic designation. Jesus is the one who fulfills the expectations of a messianic Davidic king. The application of the title "bright morning star" is unique to John in the New Testament. This title is likely an allusion to Numbers 24:17, which describes the rise of a future ruler who will defeat the enemies of God's people:

"A star shall come out of Jacob,
   and a scepter shall rise out of Israel."

This text from Numbers was interpreted messianically within Judaism (cf. *T. Levi* 18:3; *T. Jud.* 24:1; and the Qumran documents CD 7.18-21; 1QM 11.6-7; 4QTest 9-13; the Jewish messianic pretender Simon bar Kosiba, who led an unsuccessful revolt against the Romans from AD 132–135, was referred to as Bar Kokhba, meaning "son of the star," apparently an allusion to Num 24:17). Here in Revelation 22:16, as well, the title is likely a messianic designation. The title "bright morning star" is appropriate also in another way for Christ, the "light of the world" (John 8:12) and the one who is the "lamp" for the new Jerusalem (21:23).

In response to Christ's promise that he is coming soon (22:7, 12), the Spirit and the bride (the church) issue their own invitation for Christ to come. Some interpreters have suggested that the invitation is directed not at Christ, but at nonbelievers, inviting them to become a part of the people of God. In support of the invitation being addressed to Christ is that the Greek verb *erchou* ("come") is singular in form, not plural. The Spirit and the bride urge Christ to come in order to complete the work that he has begun, to bring to fulfillment the kingdom of God. Their invitation is also a sympathetic response to the cries of the martyrs under the altar in 6:9-11, who are waiting for divine justice to be enacted. Next, "everyone who hears" is invited to join in urging Christ to come. "Everyone who hears" may refer in general to the hearers/readers of John's work and to all who hear the message from them. More specifically, those who hear are those who "keep the words of this book" (22:9). To those who hear but refuse to obey this divine message, the coming of Christ is not something to desire, for it will involve punishment, not reward.

The next invitation, in v. 17, is composed of two parts that repeat the same thought. Structurally, this is an example of synonymous parallelism in which the second line reiterates in different words the idea of the first line.

> And let everyone who is thirsty come.
> Let anyone who wishes take the water of life as a gift.

In contrast to the first two invitations that are issued to Christ, this invitation is addressed to people to come and partake of God's offer of salvation. This invitation is reminiscent of Jesus' invitation in John 7:37-38: "Let anyone who is thirsty come to me, and let the one who believes in me drink." The text also recalls Isaiah 55:1:

> Ho, everyone who thirsts,
>   come to the waters;
> and you that have no money,
>   come, buy and eat!

These words are an "evangelistic invitation" to everyone who thirsts for God to come and be satisfied. The water of life that provides salvation, wholeness, and healing is God's gift to creation.

The next section of this chapter, vv. 18-19, contains a curse formula intended to safeguard the accuracy and authenticity of the work. (Commentators are divided over whether to attribute the words to Jesus or to John.) Such formulas, found in several ancient writings, were added to the end of manuscripts by the author in an attempt to keep future copyists from intentionally altering the message contained in the work. The best-known example from antiquity is the warning in the *Letter of Aristeas*, a letter probably originating in Alexandria, Egypt, during the second–first centuries BC. At the close of the letter, which describes the circumstances surrounding the translation of the Septuagint (the Greek version of the Hebrew Scriptures), the writer included a curse that was

Letter of Aristeas on the Curse

AΩ In the *Letter of Aristeas*, the writer described the curse that was pronounced on anyone who would in any way change the newly completed translation of the Jewish Scriptures into Greek. He stated,

> As the books were read, the priests stood up, with the elders from among the translators and from the representatives of the "Community," and with the leaders of the people, and said, "Since this version has been made rightly and reverently, and in every respect accurately, it is good that this should remain exactly so, and that there should be no revision." There was general approval of what they said, and they commanded that a curse should be laid, as was their custom, on anyone who should alter the version by any addition or change to any part of the written text, or any deletion either. This was a good step taken to ensure that the words were preserved completely and permanently in perpetuity. (310-311)

Letter of Aristeas, trans. R. J. H. Shutt, in *The Old Testament Pseudepigrapha*, ed. James H. Charlesworth, 2 vols. (Garden City NY: Doubleday & Co., 1985), 2:33.

pronounced upon anyone who dared alter the newly completed translation of the Hebrew Scriptures (cf. Deut 4:2; 12:32). [*Letter of Aristeas* on the Curse] The curse formula in Revelation serves somewhat like a copyright statement, putting the reader on notice not to tamper with the contents of the work. Contrary to the way this warning is often popularly understood, this statement does not apply to the entire Bible. Furthermore, it is not directed at changes by text critics or translators! The addition by John of this curse formula to his work indicates that he believes his message is a true word from God, whose integrity needs to be preserved. John addresses this warning to "everyone who hears the words of the prophecy of this book" (22:18). They are to read the words and heed them, but not change them in any way. Note the balanced (and almost playful) phrasing of the formula: If anyone adds to the book, God will add plagues to that person; if anyone takes away from the book, God will take away his or her eschatological reward. [Irenaeus]

For the third time in this chapter, Christ declares that he is coming soon (22:20). He is the one "who testifies to these things" (22:20). John's message is not his message, but a message from God, a message that has been authenticated by Christ, who bears witness that John's words are true. In response to the promise of Christ's coming, John answers in words that are both a shout of jubilation and a prayer for fulfillment: "Amen. Come, Lord Jesus!" This entreaty is basically a translation of the Aramaic phrase that Paul used in 1 Corinthians 16:22, *marana tha* (Our Lord, come). [*Marana tha*] Paul did not translate the phrase, but simply transliterated

Irenaeus

Similar to John's warning in 22:18 is the charge to later copyists that Irenaeus (2d century AD) added at the end of his work *On the Ogdoad*. Irenaeus wrote,

> I adjure you who shall copy this book, by our Lord Jesus Christ and by his glorious coming, when he comes to judge the living and the dead, to compare what you transcribe and correct it carefully in accordance with this copy from which you transcribe; and likewise transcribe and put this oath in the copy.

Cited by Eusebius, *Hist. eccl.* 5.20.2 (author's translation).

Marana tha

AΩ The Greek phrase *marana tha*, a transliteration of the Aramaic phrase meaning "Our Lord, come," appears in three different forms in ancient Greek manuscripts of 1 Cor 16:22. (In Rev 22:20, the phrase is translated into Greek, not simply transliterated.) Some manuscripts have *marana tha* ("Our Lord, come"); some have *maran atha* ("Our Lord has come" or "Our Lord is coming"); and some have the two words combined into one, *maranatha*. The contexts in 1 Corinthians, Revelation, and the *Didache* point toward an eschatological usage of the phrase; thus, *marana tha* ("Our Lord, come) is likely the correct transliteration.

---

the Aramaic into Greek letters. (Modern English versions usually translate the Greek transliteration into English.) The same Aramaic expression (transliterated into Greek as *maran atha*) appears in the *Didache* (10.6). *Marana tha* was apparently a liturgical phrase widely used by the early church to express its hopes for the consummation of God's kingdom. For John, the phrase is more than simply a set formula to be repeated in worship. This earnest prayer encapsulates the theological focus of the entire book, for the narrative movement of John's Apocalypse, from the opening words of chapter 1 to the grand vision of the new Jerusalem, has been advancing toward this climax. Three times in this final chapter, Christ has promised that he is coming. Now, in these words that are both a confession of faith and a powerful entreaty, John prays for Christ to come so that he might see and experience in totality what he has known proleptically through his visions. If we as hearers/readers of Revelation have been caught up in this spiritual experience with John, then we too must exclaim with John, "Amen. Come, Lord Jesus!"

The last verse of the Apocalypse is an epistolary conclusion, similar to the endings in Paul's letters. As John began the work with a greeting formula common to New Testament letters (1:4-6), so he ends the work with a conclusion that was a typical feature of the letters. This conclusion is in the form of a benediction, bestowing upon the people the grace of God that comes through Jesus. "Grace" (Greek: *charis*) is not a common word in the Apocalypse; in fact, it occurs only twice—here and in the greeting in 1:4. One would be tempted, therefore, to see John's use of "grace" here as nothing more than a formulaic conclusion. Yet this benediction of grace is an appropriate closing to the Apocalypse, for even though John does not use the word "grace" other than in the opening and closing, the concept underlies his entire understanding of God's dealings with the world, seen most clearly in John's image of the Lamb who was slain "from the foundation of the world."

[Textual Variants]

Textual Variants

 The final verse in the book of Revelation appears in various forms in ancient manuscripts. Three major variants occur in several combinations:

1. Lord Jesus
    Lord
    Lord Jesus Christ
    our Lord Jesus Christ
    our Lord Jesus

(A couple of manuscripts completely omit this phrase because the scribes accidentally skipped from "Lord Jesus" in v. 20 to the same phrase in v. 21.)

"Lord Jesus" is almost certainly the correct reading. The others arose from scribal expansion. The appearance of "Lord" alone in one manuscript probably occurred because of an accidental scribal omission.

2. with all
    with all of you
    with all of us
    with the saints
    with your saints
    with all the saints
    with all his saints

The two readings with the highest probability of being original are "with the saints" and "with all." Scholars are divided over which of these two is most likely. The other readings are expansions or conflations of these two readings, with the exception of "with all of you"(accepted by the KJV), which probably arose from the influence of 2 Cor 13:13 and 2 Thess 3:18.

3. The majority of manuscripts end the verse with "amen." Several manuscripts, including an early, important one, do not have "amen."

CONNECTIONS

1. In 22:1-5, John completes his description of the new Jerusalem. John's portrayal of the new Jerusalem, coupled with his visions of the heavenly throne room, has been the basis for the popular image of heaven—a walled city, streets of gold, pearly gates, the river of life, the tree of life, a garden-like setting, a place of perpetual light, and angels singing to the accompaniment of their harps. [Popular Image of Heaven] Chapter 19 adds to this bank of images with its depiction of the marriage supper of the Lamb, a version of the idea of an eschatological banquet. Obviously these are not literal descriptions, but metaphorical attempts to describe the indescribable. These images connote protection, security, beauty, peace, abundance, joy, community, and celebration. John's picture of eschatological bliss speaks of an existence lived in intimate communion with God and with each other, an existence in which we will have a fuller understanding of God (we "will see his face," 22:4).

Christians today are sometimes hesitant to use these biblical metaphors for heaven because they are often misunderstood as

Popular Image of Heaven

Mark Twain humorously satirized the popular conception of heaven in his work *Letters from the Earth*, letters supposedly written from earth by Satan to the archangels Michael and Gabriel. In one of those letters, "Satan" describes humans' imagination of what heaven must be like. He wrote:

In man's heaven *everybody sings!* The man who did not sing on earth sings there; the man who could not sing on earth is able to do it there. This universal singing is not casual, not occasional, not relieved by intervals of quiet; it goes on, all day long, and every day, during a stretch of twelve hours. And *everybody stays;* whereas in the earth the place would be empty in two hours. The singing is of hymns alone. Nay, it is of *one* hymn alone. The words are always the same, in number they are only about a dozen, there is no rhyme, there is no poetry: "Hosannah, hosannah, hosannah, Lord God of Sabaoth, 'rah! 'rah! 'rah! Siss!—boom! . . . a-a-ah!"

Meantime, every person is playing on a harp—those millions and millions!—whereas not more than twenty in the thousand of them could play an instrument in the earth, or ever wanted to. . . .

. . . Now then, in the earth these people cannot stand much church—an hour and a quarter is the limit, and they draw the line at once a week. That is to say, Sunday. One day in seven; and even then they do not look forward to it with longing. And so—consider what their heaven provides for them: "church" that lasts forever, and Sabbath that has no end!

Mark Twain, *Letters from the Earth*, ed. Bernard DeVoto (New York: Harper & Row, 1962), 10-12.

---

crass, materialistic expectations. We are often more comfortable trying to explain in theological terms the ideas John is attempting to convey. Certainly explanations are helpful and sometimes even necessary. Yet teachers and preachers must not forget the power of symbols and visual imagery to express theological truth. John's metaphors have survived and prospered because they successfully convey humanity's deepest yearnings and aspirations. [Heaven as the End]

2. John began his work by saying that it was an *apokalypsis*, a revelation or unveiling. The revelation that John discloses is not primarily about end-time events but about the one who controls the end—God, the Alpha and Omega, the beginning and the end. When the last strains of the angels' hallelujahs have died away and the vision of the new Jerusalem has faded, we are left not with places and happenings for which to yearn, but with a God in whom to trust. At the end of John's vision we do not know any more about the details of the future than we did before we began reading the Apocalypse. All attempts to create charts and timetables of the end times, to describe in literal terms what the words "hell" and "heaven" symbolize, and to predict events or forecast scenarios of the last days are useless flights of fancy. The advice

Heaven as the End

"Heaven is not a reward that gets added on to the life of faith, hope, and love, but it is simply the end of that life, that is to say, the working out of the life that is oriented by these principles. . . . The symbol stands for fullness of being; it is the fruition toward which the existent advances as he is brought into 'eternal life.' Since this fruition is an increasing closeness to Being, so that the individual being converges upon Being and is taken up into Being, heaven is rightly identified with the 'beatific vision,' that direct indubitable awareness of the immediate presence of God which may be contrasted with the attitude of faith where, in this ambiguous world, we 'see in a mirror dimly.' "

John Macquarrie, *Principles of Christian Theology*, 2d ed. (New York: Charles Scribner's Sons, 1977), 365-66.

of Reinhold Niebuhr is pertinent: "It is unwise for Christians to claim any knowledge of either the furniture of heaven or the temperature of hell, or to be too certain about any details of the Kingdom of God in which history is consummated."6

We do a grave disservice to John's visionary genius, as well as to his deep Christian insight, if we reduce the book of Revelation to a collection of end-time riddles or futuristic schemes. The rhetorical purpose of the Apocalypse is not to inform as much as it is to warn, to exhort, and to comfort. John writes to warn believers of the dangers of cultural and social accommodation, including the danger of yielding ultimate allegiance to any person or institution. He writes to exhort Christians to remain steadfast in their commitment to God and to live by a different value system than that of the social and political world of their day. He writes also to comfort those people of God who have been crushed and overwhelmed by evil and suffering, who are on the brink of despair, and who need to be assured that "the Lord our God the Almighty reigns." [The Right Time]

3. Commentators have frequently detected eucharistic overtones in 22:17, understanding the invitation to the thirsty as an invitation to the Lord's table to share communion. Properly understood, the celebration of the Lord's Supper is not only a remembrance of Christ's sacrificial death, but also an anticipation of his future coming to complete the work he began. Accordingly, Paul said, "For as often as you eat this bread and drink the cup, you proclaim the Lord's death until he comes" (1 Cor 11:26). In the *Didache* (10.6), the eucharistic service ends with the words *maran atha*, the Aramaic expression meaning, "Our Lord, come." Since the entire book of Revelation has a strong liturgical flavoring, the invitation in 22:17 may indeed serve as an invitation to the Lord's Supper. If this interpretation is correct, then the comment of Jürgen Roloff is fitting: "Where the church gathers around the table of the Lord, there it receives the gift of salvation that God desires to give to his own. Thus, John is not content with pointing to a temporally imminent future dawning of salvation (cf. 1:3; 22:10); rather, he indicates where salvation can be discovered and experienced in the present."7

The Right Time

"Revelation teaches us to live the *present* time as a *kairos*, as an opportune and decisive moment, in the light of eschatology realized in the resurrection of Christ. Revelation teaches us also to live the *past* as a history of salvation and to ask how that history is taking place today. But most important is to interpret Revelation so that we can correctly confront the *future* and so overcome all the manipulation that creates anguish, fear, and terror. Revelation teaches us to imagine the present and final eschatology with a sense of joy and hope. It also helps us to rebuild the transcendent utopia of the reign of God on earth and of the new creation. It teaches us to rethink the judgment of God now and in the present time and the final judgments in the future with a sense of exodus and hope."

Pablo Richard, *Apocalypse: A People's Commentary on the Book of Revelation* (Maryknoll NY: Orbis Books, 1995), 172-73.

4. Three times in 22:6-21 John reports Jesus saying that he is coming soon. For the modern reader of the Apocalypse, the expectation of the imminent end of the world and the consummation of God's kingdom (which is what the metaphor of the Parousia symbolizes) may be hard to maintain. After all, nineteen hundred years have passed since the early Christians voiced their belief that Christ would return soon. G. B. Caird, as well as other commentators, interpreted the expectation of Christ's soon return in Revelation in terms of realized eschatology—Christ has already come (and continues to come) into the lives of believers. Caird wrote,

> John's book begins on the Lord's day and ends in eucharistic worship; and it is in the setting of worship that his eschatology is to be understood. He and his fellow Christians had no difficulty in believing that the end [that is, Jesus] could come to meet them in the midst of time. For week by week their prayer *Maranatha*, Come, Lord Jesus, was answered as they kept their tryst with him who was Alpha and Omega, the beginning and the end.[8]

Certainly John and the early church experienced the presence of Christ not only in their worship, but also as they faced the difficulty of remaining steadfast and loyal witnesses. Yet to reduce Revelation's statements about the return of Christ to nothing more than the believers' experiences with Christ in the present is to misinterpret John's eschatological expectations. As did other apocalyptic writers, John believed that the end was literally at hand. He expected that the prevailing political and social institutions of his day, particularly the Roman imperial system, would soon be brought to an end by God and that God would establish "a new heaven and new earth," a new community, something better than anyone could imagine. [Advent]

Advent

The season of the church year called Advent (from the Latin word meaning "arrival" or "coming"), which in western Christianity is the period covering the four Sundays prior to Christmas, usually focuses on preparation for the celebration of the birth of Jesus. In addition, Advent is intended to be a time of preparation for the eschatological coming of Christ as Judge and Redeemer.

In dealing with John's expectation of the imminence of Christ's Parousia and the end of the world, we must be forthright and recognize that in terms of chronology, John was mistaken. The world did not end as he expected. In attempting to appropriate the message involved in the early church's belief in the soon return of Christ, we cannot simply continue to say, "The end is near." Nearly two millennia of waiting has deadened that refrain. To continue to say that Jesus is coming soon renders illogical any meaning for the word "soon." J. Christiaan Beker addressed this issue in the writings of Paul when he said, "Christians today can no longer expect with Paul the imminent arrival of the kingdom, in the same manner, because 'the appointed time'—which for Paul 'has grown very short' (1 Cor 7:29)—has for us grown 'very long.' "[9] For the church today, the statement that Christ is coming soon functions not as a chronological prediction, but as a call for readiness, for righteous living, so that whenever the end occurs—cosmically or for us individually—we will be prepared to enter into a new existence with God.

Even though we may not be able to believe in the imminence of Christ's return in the same way in which the early church did, we can still join with them in praying, *Marana tha*, Our Lord, come! To pray for the coming of Christ is to pray for God's triumph over sin, evil, and death. To pray for the Parousia is to pray for a world of compassion, nonviolence, love, joy, and justice. To pray for the coming of God's kingdom is to pray that God's world will be healed and renewed. We need to be clear, also, that to pray such prayers is a political act on our part, for in so praying we align ourselves against all systems, institutions, people, and worldviews that are opposed to the kingdom of God. Thus let us raise our voices to say, "Our Lord, come," but let us not do so glibly or simply in rote imitation. Properly understood, the prayer *Marana tha* is one of the deepest and most powerful prayers we can utter. "Amen. Come, Lord Jesus!" [God as the Creator and Finisher]

God as the Creator and Finisher

"The biblical testimony of faith sees the end essentially as the *completion of God's work* on his creation. Both at the beginning of the world and at its end, there is not nothing, but God."

Hans Küng, *Eternal Life?: Life after Death as a Medical, Philosophical, and Theological Problem* (Garden City NY: Doubleday & Co., 1984), 210.

5. Liturgical elements abound in 22:7-21. Verses 8-9 emphasize the proper focus of Christian worship; verses 7, 14, and 21 contain benedictions that could be used in worship; verse 20 is a prayer that was commonly used in early Christian worship. Furthermore, as mentioned above, some commentators have suggested that this section reflects the wording and pattern of early Christian eucharistic services. Wilfrid Harrington has even suggested that v. 17 could serve as a liturgical dialogue, with portions spoken by the leader and responses given by the people. He has offered the following pattern, which could easily be used for a litany in worship today:

And the Spirit and the Bride say:	"Come."
And let one who hears say:	"Come."
And let one who thirsts:	Come.
Whoever will:	Take the water of life, freely.[10]

As we have noted throughout this examination of the Apocalypse, worship is central to John and to his visionary work. In chapter 1, John falls down in awe and reverence before the exalted Christ. The major visions of the heavenly throne room that begin in chapter 4 are scenes of heavenly worship. That same heavenly worship is in the background throughout the remainder of the book as the prayers of the people are received by the angels in heaven and offered up on the heavenly altar to God. Periodically in the Apocalypse we hear the heavenly songs of celebration and worship break forth. Worship is important in Revelation because John realizes that worship is important for the church. Through worship, the church expresses and renews its commitment to God. Through worship, the church confesses its allegiance to God above all people, institutions, or value systems that may lay claim upon us. In that regard, the act of worship is a political act on our part. Worship is also a way of establishing and nurturing community—with God and with fellow believers. Through worship, we experience now a foretaste of the eschatological kingdom of God, the new Jerusalem, when God will dwell fully and intimately with us. [The Act of Worship]

> **The Act of Worship**
>
> "This emphasis on worship has programmatic significance for the theology of Revelation. Worship is the place where the church experiences the presence of the One who is coming, where again and again it subordinates itself to his dominion; at the same time it is also the place of departure for a refusal of obedience to the cult of humanity, who celebrates one's own power over the world. Revelation is both an eminently political book and an eminently liturgical book."
>
> Jürgen Roloff, *The Revelation of John: A Continental Commentary,* Continental Commentaries, trans. John E. Alsup (Minneapolis: Fortress, 1993), 254.

Worship is such an important component of Revelation that the book cannot be fully comprehended or appreciated outside the context of a worshiping community. The visions of John originated in a worship setting (he was "in the spirit on the Lord's day," 1:10); they were sent to churches to be read during worship; and they fulfill their purpose when they successfully call us to join together in worship. Revelation can be studied in a classroom; it can be read and studied in private; it can be analyzed and commented upon by scholars. As insightful and meaningful as those experiences with the Apocalypse may be, they still fall short of the potential power and value of the book. Revelation invites us to join in worshiping the God "who is and who was and who is to come, the Almighty." It encourages us to join our "hallelujahs" with those of the heavenly chorus, to offer our praise and thanksgiving to God. The Apocalypse calls on us to unite our voices in prayer, to pray together the early church's prayer, *Marana tha,* "Our Lord, come."

This call to gather to worship is not an escape from the world. Rather, true worship that directs us to God also causes us to see the world as God sees it—a world that still experiences "mourning and crying and pain," a world still ruled by the power of sin and death. As Christians we can never be content with such a world. Worship draws us closer to God and to the community of believers, but it also propels us back into the hurting world to share the love and grace of God.

NOTES

[1] David E. Aune, *Revelation 17–22*, Word Biblical Commentary (Nashville: Thomas Nelson, 1998), 1178.

[2] Frederick J. Murphy, *Fallen Is Babylon: The Revelation of John* (Valley Forge PA: Trinity Press International, 1998), 429.

[3] Ibid., 437.

[4] J. P. M. Sweet, *Revelation*, Westminster Pelican Commentaries (Philadelphia: Westminster, 1979), 316.

[5] Some commentators have argued that because "dogs" is used in Deut 23:18, possibly as a term for male prostitutes, it has a similar meaning in Rev 22:15 (see Aune, *Revelation 17–22*, 1222-23). Given the use of the term "dogs" elsewhere in early Christianity as a general term for "outsiders" or "enemies," the specialized (and uncertain) meaning of the term as a reference to male prostitutes is highly unlikely in Revelation.

[6] Reinhold Niebuhr, *Human Destiny,* vol. 2 of *The Nature and Destiny of Man* (New York: Charles Scribner's Sons, 1964), 294.

[7] Jürgen Roloff, *The Revelation of John: A Continental Commentary*, Continental Commentaries, trans. John E. Alsup (Minneapolis: Fortress, 1993), 253.

[8] G. B. Caird, *A Commentary on the Revelation of St. John the Divine*, Harper's New Testament Commentaries (New York: Harper & Row, 1966), 301.

[9] J. Christiaan Beker, *Paul's Apocalyptic Gospel: The Coming Triumph of God* (Philadelphia: Fortress, 1982), 115.

[10] Wilfrid J. Harrington, *Revelation*, Sacra Pagina (Collegeville MN: Liturgical, 1993), 223.

BIBLIOGRAPHY

Anderson, Bernhard W. *Out of the Depths: The Psalms Speak for Us Today.* Philadelphia: Westminster, 1983.

Ashcraft, Morris. "Revelation." Pages 240-361 in vol. 12 of *The Broadman Bible Commentary.* Edited by Clifton J. Allen. 12 vols. Nashville: Broadman, 1972.

Atwan, Robert and Laurance Wieder, editors. *Chapters into Verse: Poetry in English Inspired by the Bible.* Volume 2. Oxford: Oxford University Press, 1993.

Aukerman, Dale. *Reckoning with Apocalypse: Terminal Politics and Christian Hope.* New York: Crossroad, 1993.

Aune, David E. "The Influence of Roman Imperial Court Ceremonial on the Apocalypse of John." *Biblical Research* 28 (1983): 5-26.

_____. *The New Testament in Its Literary Environment.* Philadelphia: Westminster, 1987.

_____. *Revelation 1–5.* Word Biblical Commentary. Dallas: Word Books, 1997.

_____. *Revelation 6–16.* Word Biblical Commentary. Dallas: Word Books, 1998.

_____. *Revelation 17–22.* Word Biblical Commentary. Nashville: Thomas Nelson, 1998.

Barclay, William. *Letters to the Seven Churches.* Philadelphia: Westminster, 1957.

Bartchy, S. Scott. "Slavery (Greco-Roman)." Pages 65-73 in vol. 6 of *The Anchor Bible Dictionary.* Edited by David Noel Freedman. 6 vols. New York: Doubleday & Co., 1992.

Barr, David L. "Towards an Ethical Reading of the Apocalypse: Reflections on John's Use of Power, Violence, and Misogyny." Paper presented at the annual meeting of the Society of Biblical Literature, 1997.

Bauckham, Richard. *The Theology of the Book of Revelation.* New Testament Theology. Cambridge: Cambridge University Press, 1993.

Bauer, Walter, William F. Arndt, F. Wilbur Gingrich, and Frederick W. Danker. *A Greek-English Lexicon of the New Testament and Other Early Christian Literature.* 2d ed. Chicago: University of Chicago Press, 1979.

Beale, G. K. *The Book of Revelation: A Commentary on the Greek Text.* New International Greek Testament Commentary. Grand Rapids: Eerdmans, 1998.

Beasley-Murray, George R. *The Book of Revelation.* New Century Bible. Greenwood SC: Attic, 1974.

"The Beatific Vision." Page 174 in *The Oxford Dictionary of the Christian Church.* Edited by F. L. Cross; 3rd ed. edited by E. A. Livingstone. Oxford: Oxford University Press, 1997.

Beckwith, Isbon T. *The Apocalypse of John.* Macmillan, 1919. Reprint. Grand Rapids: Baker, 1979.

Beker, J. Christiaan. *Paul's Apocalyptic Gospel: The Coming Triumph of God*. Philadelphia: Fortress, 1982.

_____. *Suffering & Hope: The Biblical Vision and the Human Predicament*. Grand Rapids: Eerdmans, 1994.

Berrigan, Daniel. *Beside the Sea of Glass: The Song of the Lamb*. New York: Seabury, 1978.

Blevins, James L. *Revelation*. Knox Preaching Guides. Atlanta: John Knox, 1984.

_____. *Revelation as Drama*. Nashville: Broadman, 1984.

Boesak, Allan A. *Comfort and Protest: Reflections on the Apocalypse of John of Patmos*. Philadelphia: Westminster, 1987.

Borg, Marcus J. *Meeting Jesus Again for the First Time: The Historical Jesus and the Heart of Contemporary Faith*. San Francisco: HarperSanFrancisco, 1994.

Boring, M. Eugene. "Everything Is Going to Be All Right." Pages 75-82 in *Preaching Through the Apocalypse: Sermons from Revelation*. Edited by Cornish R. Rogers and Joseph R. Jeter Jr. St. Louis: Chalice, 1992.

_____. "The Gospel of Matthew: Introduction, Commentary, and Reflections." Pages 87-505 in vol. 8 of *The New Interpreter's Bible*. Edited by Leander E. Keck. 12 vols. Nashville: Abingdon, 1995.

_____. *Revelation*. Interpretation. A Bible Commentary for Teaching and Preaching. Louisville: John Knox, 1989.

_____. "Revelation 19-21: End without Closure." *The Princeton Seminary Bulletin* Supplement 3 (1994) 57-84.

Boring, M. Eugene, Klaus Berger, and Carsten Colpe, editors. *Hellenistic Commentary to the New Testament*. Nashville: Abingdon, 1995.

Bousset, Wilhelm. *The Antichrist Legend: A Chapter in Christian and Jewish Folklore*. Translated by A. H. Keane. London: Hutchinson, 1896.

Bowman, John Wick. *The First Christian Drama*. Philadelphia: Westminster, 1955.

Branch, Taylor. *Parting the Waters: America in the King Years 1954–63*. New York: Simon & Schuster, 1988.

Brown, Lester R. "Feeding Nine Billion." Pages 115-32 in *State of the World 1999: A Worldwatch Institute Report on Progress Toward a Sustainable Society*. Edited by Lester R. Brown et al. New York: W. W. Norton & Co., 1999.

Brown, Raymond E. *An Introduction to the New Testament*. New York: Doubleday & Co., 1997.

Bruce, F. F. "Travel and Communication (NT World)." Pages 648-53 in vol. 6 of *The Anchor Bible Dictionary*. Edited by David Noel Freedman. 6 vols. New York: Doubleday & Co., 1992.

Brueggemann, Walter. *The Message of the Psalms*. Augsburg Old Testament Studies. Minneapolis: Augsburg, 1984.

Buechner, Frederick. *Telling Secrets*. San Francisco: HarperSanFrancisco, 1991.

Bullard, Roger A. *Messiah: The Gospel According to Handel's Oratorio*. Grand Rapids: Eerdmans, 1993.

Bunyan, John. *The Pilgrim's Progress*. London: Oxford University Press, 1904.

Buttrick, David G. "Poetry of Hope." Pages 159-64 in *Preaching Through the Apocalypse: Sermons from Revelation*. Edited by Cornish R. Rogers and Joseph R. Jeter Jr. St. Louis: Chalice, 1992.

Caird, G. B. *A Commentary on the Revelation of St. John the Divine.* Harper's New
Testament Commentaries. New York: Harper & Row, 1966.

Cardenal, Ernesto. "Apocalypse." Pages 33-37 in *Apocalypse and Other Poems.* New York:
New Directions, 1971.

Cary, M. and H. H. Scullard. *A History of Rome down to the Reign of Constantine.* 3rd ed.
New York: St. Martin's, 1975.

Chandler, Andrew, editor. *The Terrible Alternative: Christian Martyrdom in the Twentieth
Century.* London: Cassell, 1998.

Charles, R. H., editor. *The Apocrypha and Pseudepigrapha of the Old Testament.* 2 vols.
Oxford: Clarendon, 1913

____. *A Critical and Exegetical Commentary on the Revelation of St. John.* 2 vols. The
International Critical Commentary. Edinburgh: T. & T. Clark, 1920.

Charlesworth, James H., editor. *The Old Testament Pseudepigrapha.* Vol. 1: *Apocalyptic
Literature and Testaments.* Garden City NY: Doubleday & Co., 1983.

Clouse, Robert G., editor. *The Meaning of the Millennium: Four Views.* Downers Grove IL:
InterVarsity, 1977.

Cohn, Norman. *The Pursuit of the Millennium: Revolutionary Millenarians and Mystical
Anarchists of the Middle Ages.* Rev. and exp. ed. New York: Oxford University Press,
1970.

Collins, Adela Yarbro. *The Apocalypse.* New Testament Message. Wilmington DE: Michael
Glazier, 1979.

____. "The Apocalypse (Revelation)." Pages 996-1016 in *The New Jerome Biblical
Commentary.* Edited by Raymond E. Brown, Joseph A. Fitzmyer, and Roland E.
Murphy. Englewood Cliffs NJ: Prentice Hall, 1990.

____. *Crisis & Catharsis: The Power of the Apocalypse.* Philadelphia: Westminster, 1984.

____. "Numerical Symbolism in Jewish and Early Christian Apocalyptic Literature."
Aufstieg und Niedergang der römischen Welt. 21.2: 1221-87. Part 2, *Principat,* 21.2.
Edited by Hildegard Temporini and Wolfgang Haase. Berlin: Walter de Gruyter, 1984.

____. "Reading the Book of Revelation in the Twentieth Century." *Interpretation: A
Journal of Bible and Theology* 40/3 (July 1986): 229-42.

____, editor. *Early Christian Apocalypticism: Genre and Social Setting. Semiea* 36 (1986).

____, editor. "'What the Spirit Says to the Churches': Preaching the Apocalypse."
Quarterly Review 4/3 (Fall 1984): 69-84.

Collins, John J., editor. *Apocalypse: The Morphology of a Genre. Semeia* 14 (1979).

____. *The Apocalyptic Imagination: An Introduction to the Jewish Matrix of Christianity.*
New York: Crossroad, 1984.

____. "Introduction: Towards the Morphology of a Genre." *Apocalypse: The Morphology of
Genre.* Edited by John J. Collins. *Semeia* 14 (1979): 1-20.

Comby, Jean. *How to Read Church History.* New York: Crossroad, 1989.

Craddock, Fred B. "Preaching the Book of Revelation." *Interpretation* 40/3 (July 1986):
270-82.

Culpepper, R. Alan. *John, the Son of Zebedee: The Life of a Legend.* Columbia SC:
University of South Carolina Press, 1994.

Cuss, Dominique. *Imperial Cult and Honorary Terms in the New Testament.* Fribourg:
University Press, 1974.

Danker, Frederick W. "Purple." Pages 557-60 in vol. 5 of *The Anchor Bible Dictionary*. Edited by David Noel Freedman. 6 vols. New York: Doubleday & Co., 1992.

Deissmann, Adolf. *Light from the Ancient East: The New Testament Illustrated by Recently Discovered Texts of the Graeco-Roman World*. Translated by Lionel R. M. Strachan. Rev. ed. New York: Harper & Brothers, 1927.

Durning, Alan. "Asking How Much Is Enough." Pages 153-69 in *State of the World 1991: A Worldwatch Institute Report on Progress Toward a Sustainable Society*. Edited by Lester R. Brown et al. New York: W. W. Norton & Co., 1991.

Ellul, Jacques. *Apocalypse: The Book of Revelation*. New York: Seabury, 1977.

Fant, Clyde E. *Preaching for Today*. Rev. ed. San Francisco: Harper & Row, 1987.

Farrer, Austin M. *A Rebirth of Images*. Boston: Beacon, 1949.

Ferguson, Everett. *Backgrounds of Early Christianity*. 2d ed. Grand Rapids: Eerdmans, 1993.

Ferguson, John. *The Religions of the Roman Empire*. Ithaca: Cornell University Press, 1970.

Fiorenza, Elisabeth Schüssler. *The Book of Revelation: Justice and Judgment*. Philadelphia: Fortress, 1985.

_____. *Invitation to the Book of Revelation*. Garden City NY: Image Books, 1981.

_____. *Revelation: Vision of a Just World*. Proclamation Commentaries. Minneapolis: Fortress, 1991.

Ford, J. Massyngberde. "Millennium." Pages 832-34 in vol. 6 of *The Anchor Bible Dictionary*. Edited by David Noel Freedman. 6 vols. New York: Doubleday & Co., 1992.

_____. *Revelation*. Anchor Bible. Garden City NY: Doubleday & Co., 1975.

Friberg, Jöran. "Numbers and Counting." Pages 1139-45 in vol. 4 of *The Anchor Bible Dictionary*. Edited by David Noel Freedman. 6 vols. New York: Doubleday & Co., 1992.

Friesen, Steven. "The Cult of the Roman Emperors in Ephesos: Temple Wardens, City Titles, and the Interpretation of the Revelation of John." Pages 229-50 in *Ephesos: Metropolis of Asia*. Edited by Helmut Koester. Valley Forge PA: Trinity, 1995.

Fuller, R. H. *Preaching the New Lectionary: The Word of God for the Church Today*. Collegeville MN: Liturgical, 1974.

Fuller, Robert. *Naming the Antichrist: The History of an American Obsession*. New York: Oxford University Press, 1995.

Garrett, Susan R. "Revelation." Pages 377-82 in *The Women's Bible Commentary*. Edited by Carol A. Newsom and Sharon H. Ringe. Louisville: Westminster/John Knox, 1992.

Glasson, T. F. *The Revelation of John*. The Cambridge Bible Commentary on the New English Bible. Cambridge: Cambridge University Press, 1965.

González, Catherine Gunsalus and Justo L. González. *Revelation*. Westminster Bible Companion. Louisville: Westminster/John Knox, 1997.

Good, Deidre J. "Early Extracanonical Writings." Pages 383-89 in *The Women's Bible Commentary*. Edited by Carol A. Newsom and Sharon H. Ringe. Louisville: Westminster/John Knox, 1992.

Grenz, Stanley J. *The Millennial Maze: Sorting Out Evangelical Options*. Downers Grove IL: InterVarsity, 1992.

Gruen, Erich S., editor. *The Image of Rome.* Englewood Cliffs NJ: Prentice-Hall, 1969.

Hamilton, Victor P. "Satan." Pages 985-89 in vol. 5 of *The Anchor Bible Dictionary.* Edited by David Noel Freedman. 6 vols. New York: Doubleday & Co., 1992.

Hanson, Paul D. *The Dawn of Apocalyptic.* Rev. ed. Philadelphia: Fortress, 1979.

_____. *Old Testament Apocalyptic.* Interpreting Biblical Texts. Nashville: Abingdon, 1987.

Harrington, Wilfrid J. *Revelation.* Sacra Pagina. Collegeville MN: Liturgical, 1993.

Hennecke, Edgar. *New Testament Apocrypha.* Vol. 2: *Writings Relating to the Apostles; Apocalypses and Related Subjects.* Edited by Wilhelm Schneemelcher. English translation edited by R. McL. Wilson. Rev. ed. Louisville: Westminster/John Knox, 1992.

Hersey, John. "The Revelation of Saint John the Divine." Pages 346-55 in *Incarnation: Contemporary Writers on the New Testament.* Edited by Alfred Corn. New York: Viking, 1990.

Jeske, Richard. "The Book of Revelation in the Parish." *Word and World* 15/2 (Spring 1995): 182-94.

_____. *Revelation for Today: Images of Hope.* Philadelphia: Fortress, 1983.

Jeter, Joseph R. Jr. "I Have This Against You." Pages 69-74 in *Preaching Through the Apocalypse: Sermons from Revelation.* Edited by Cornish R. Rogers and Joseph R. Jeter Jr. St. Louis: Chalice, 1992.

Jones, Brian W. "Domitian." Pages 221-22 in vol. 2 of *The Anchor Bible Dictionary.* Edited by David Noel Freedman. 6 vols. New York: Doubleday & Co., 1992.

Jones, Donald L. "Roman Imperial Cult." Pages 806-809 in vol. 5 of *The Anchor Bible Dictionary.* Edited by David Noel Freedman. 6 vols. New York: Doubleday & Co., 1992.

Kane, Hal. "Gap in Income Distribution Widening." Pages 116-17 in *Vital Signs 1997: The Environmental Trends That Are Shaping Our Future.* Edited by Lester R. Brown et al. New York: W. W. Norton & Co., 1997.

Kebric, Robert B. *Roman People.* 2d ed. Mountain View CA: Mayfield Publishing, 1997.

King, Martin Luther Jr. *Strength to Love.* New York: Harper & Row, 1963.

King, Philip J. "Jerusalem." Pages 747-66 in vol. 3 of *The Anchor Bible Dictionary.* Edited by David Noel Freedman. 6 vols. New York: Doubleday & Co., 1992.

Kirk, John M. *Politics and the Catholic Church in Nicaragua.* Gainesville: University of Florida Press, 1992.

Kittel, Gerhard and Gerhard Friedrich, editors. *Theological Dictionary of the New Testament.* Translated by Geoffrey W. Bromiley. 10 vols. Grand Rapids: Eerdmans, 1964–1976.

Koester, Craig R. "The Distant Triumph Song: Music and the Book of Revelation." *Word and World* 12/3 (Summer 1992): 243-49.

Koester, Helmut. *History, Culture and Religion of the Hellenistic Age.* Vol. 1 of *Introduction to the New Testament.* 2d ed. New York: Walter de Gruyter, 1995.

Kraybill, J. N. *Imperial Cult and Commerce in John's Apocalypse.* JSNT Sup 132. Sheffield: Sheffield Academic Press, 1966.

Krentz, Edgar and Arthur A. Vogel. *Proclamation 2: Aids for Interpreting the Church Year, Easter, Series C.* Edited by Elizabeth Achtemeier, Gerhard Krodel, and Charles P. Price. Philadelphia: Fortress, 1980.

Küng, Hans. *The Church.* Translated by Ray and Rosaleen Ockenden. New York: Sheed and Ward, 1967.

_____. *Eternal Life?: Life after Death as a Medical, Philosophical, and Theological Problem.* Translated by Edward Quinn. Garden City NY: Doubleday & Co., 1984.

Ladd, George Eldon. *A Commentary on the Revelation of John.* Grand Rapids: Eerdmans, 1972.

Lawrence, D. H. *Apocalypse.* Pages 57-149 in *Apocalypse and the Writings on Revelation.* The Cambridge Edition of D. H. Lawrence. Edited by Mara Kalnins. Cambridge: Cambridge University Press, 1980.

Lewis, Warren. "What to Do after the Messiah Has Come Again and Gone: Shaker 'Premillennial' Eschatology and Its Spiritual Aftereffects." Pages 71-109 in *The Coming Kingdom: Essays in American Millennialism and Eschatology.* Edited by M. Darrol Bryant and Donald W. Dayton. Barrytown NY: International Religious Foundation, Inc., 1983.

Long, Thomas G. "Praying for the Wrath of God." Pages 133-39 in *Preaching Through the Apocalypse: Sermons from Revelation.* Edited by Cornish R. Rogers and Joseph R. Jeter Jr. St. Louis: Chalice, 1992.

Macquarrie, John. *Principles of Christian Theology.* 2d ed. New York: Charles Scribner's Sons, 1977.

Magie, David. *Roman Rule in Asia Minor.* Princeton: Princeton University Press, 1950.

Maier, Walter A. III. "Hadad." Page 11 in vol. 3 of *The Anchor Bible Dictionary.* Edited by David Noel Freedman. 6 vols. New York: Doubleday & Co., 1992.

Malina, Bruce J. and Richard L. Rohrbaugh. *Social-Science Commentary on the Synoptic Gospels.* Minneapolis: Fortress, 1992.

Marty, Martin E. "M.E.M.O.: A Revelation." *The Christian Century* 114/16 (14 May 1997): 495.

McGinn, Bernard. *Antichrist: Two Thousand Years of the Human Fascination with Evil.* San Francisco: HarperSanFrancisco, 1994.

_____. "Revelation." Pages 523-41 in *A Literary Companion to the Bible.* Edited by Robert Alter and Frank Kermode. Cambridge MA: Belknap, 1987.

McGinn, Bernard, Stephen J. Stein, and John J. Collins. *The Encyclopedia of Apocalypticism.* 3 vols. New York: Continuum, 1998.

McManners, John, editor. *The Oxford Illustrated History of Christianity.* New York: Oxford University Press, 1990.

Metzger, Bruce M. *A Textual Commentary on the Greek New Testament.* United Bible Societies, 1971.

Michaels, J. Ramsey. *Interpreting the Book of Revelation.* Guides to New Testament Exegesis. Grand Rapids: Baker, 1992.

Millar, F. *The Emperor in the Roman World.* Ithaca: Cornell University Press, 1977.

Minear, Paul. *New Testament Apocalyptic.* Nashville: Abingdon, 1981.

Morris, Leon. *Apocalyptic.* Grand Rapids: Eerdmans, 1972.

Mounce, Robert H. *The Book of Revelation.* The New International Commentary on the New Testament. Rev. ed. Grand Rapids: Eerdmans, 1998.

Murphy, Frederick J. *Fallen Is Babylon: The Revelation to John.* The New Testament in Context. Harrisburg PA: Trinity, 1998.

Newman, Barclay. *Rediscovering the Book of Revelation.* Valley Forge PA: Judson, 1968.

Newsom, Carol and Duane F. Watson. "Angels." Pages 248-55 in vol. 1 of *The Anchor Bible Dictionary.* Edited by David Noel Freedman. 6 vols. New York: Doubleday & Co., 1992.

Niebuhr, H. Richard. *Christ and Culture.* New York: Harper & Row, 1951.

Niebuhr, Reinhold. *Human Destiny.* Vol. 2 of *The Nature and Destiny of Man.* New York: Charles Scribner's Sons, 1964.

Nielsen, Kjeld. "Incense." Pages 404-409 in vol. 3 of *The Anchor Bible Dictionary.* Edited by David Noel Freedman. 6 vols. New York: Doubleday & Co., 1992.

Palmoni, Yaaqov. "Locust." Pages 144-48 in vol. 3 of *The Interpreter's Dictionary of the Bible.* Edited by George Arthur Buttrick. 4 vols. Nashville: Abingdon, 1962.

Pippin, Tina. *Death and Desire: The Rhetoric of Gender in the Apocalypse of John.* Literary Currents in Biblical Interpretation. Louisville: Westminster/John Knox, 1992.

Pope, M. H. "Seven, Seventh, Seventy." Pages 294-95 in vol. 4 of *The Interpreter's Dictionary of the Bible.* Edited by George Arthur Buttrick. 4 vols. Nashville: Abingdon, 1962.

Preston, Ronald H. and Anthony T. Hanson. *The Revelation of Saint John the Divine.* London: SCM, 1949.

Price, S. R. F. *Rituals and Power: The Roman Imperial Cult in Asia Minor.* Cambridge: Cambridge University Press, 1984.

Ramsay, W. M. *The Letters to the Seven Churches.* Edited by Mark W. Wilson. Updated edition. Peabody MA: Hendrickson, 1994.

Reddish, Mitchell G., editor. *Apocalyptic Literature: A Reader.* Nashville: Abingdon, 1990. Reprint. Peabody MA: Hendrickson, 1995.

Richard, Pablo. *Apocalypse: A People's Commentary on the Book of Revelation.* Maryknoll NY: Orbis Books, 1995.

Rist, Martin. "The Revelation of St. John the Divine." Pages 345-613 in vol. 12 of *The Interpreter's Bible.* Edited by George Arthur Buttrick. 12 vols. New York: Abingdon, 1957.

Rogers, Cornish R. and Joseph R. Jeter Jr., editors. *Preaching Through the Apocalypse: Sermons from Revelation.* St. Louis: Chalice, 1992.

Roloff, Jürgen. *The Revelation of John: A Continental Commentary.* Continental Commentaries. Translated by John E. Alsup. Minneapolis: Fortress, 1993.

Rowland, Christopher C. "The Book of Revelation: Introduction, Commentary, and Reflections." Pages 501-736 in vol. 12 of *The New Interpreter's Bible.* Edited by Leander E. Keck. 12 vols. Nashville: Abingdon, 1998.

____. *The Open Heaven: A Study of Apocalyptic in Judaism and Early Christianity.* New York: Crossroad, 1982.

____. "Parousia." Pages 166-70 in vol. 5 of *The Anchor Bible Dictionary.* Edited by David Noel Freedman. 6 vols. New York: Doubleday & Co., 1992.

Russell, D. S. *Apocalyptic: Ancient and Modern.* Philadelphia: Fortress, 1978.

____. *Divine Disclosure: An Introduction to Jewish Apocalyptic.* Minneapolis: Fortress, 1992.

____. *The Method and Message of Jewish Apocalyptic, 200 BC–AD 100.* Philadelphia: Westminster, 1964.

_____. *Prophecy and the Apocalyptic Dream: Protest and Promise*. Peabody MA: Hendrickson, 1994.

Russell, Jeffrey Burton. *The Devil: Perceptions of Evil from Antiquity to Primitive Christianity*. Ithaca: Cornell University Press, 1977.

_____. *Lucifer: The Devil in the Middle Ages*. Ithaca: Cornell University Press, 1984.

_____. *Mephistopheles: The Devil in the Modern World*. Ithaca: Cornell University Press, 1986.

_____. *The Prince of Darkness: Radical Evil and the Power of Good in History*. Ithaca: Cornell University Press, 1988.

_____. *Satan: The Early Christian Tradition*. Ithaca: Cornell University Press, 1981.

Sachs, Aaron. "Upholding Human Rights and Environmental Justice." Pages 133-51 in *State of the World 1996: A Worldwatch Institute Report on Progress toward a Sustainable Society*. Edited by Lester R. Brown et al. New York: W. W. Norton & Co., 1996.

Scherrer, Steven J. "Signs and Wonders in the Imperial Cult: A New Look at a Roman Religious Institution in the Light of Rev 13:13-15." *Journal of Biblical Literature* 103/4 (1984): 599-610.

Scott, C. Anderson. *Revelation*. The Century Bible. New York: Henry Frowde, n.d.

Scott, E. F. *The Book of Revelation*. New York: Charles Scribner's Sons, 1940.

Scott, Kenneth. *The Imperial Cult under the Flavians*. New York: Arno, 1975.

Select Papyri. Vol. 1: *Non-Literary Papyri, Private Affairs*. Translated by A. S. Hunt and C. C. Edgar. Loeb Classical Library. Cambridge MA: Harvard University Press, 1932.

Simson, Otto von. *The Gothic Cathedral: Origins of Gothic Architecture and the Medieval Concept of Order*. 2d ed. New York: Pantheon Books, 1962.

Soards, Marion L. "Millennium." Pages 576-77 in *Mercer Dictionary of the Bible*. Edited by Watson E. Mills. Macon GA: Mercer University Press, 1990.

Sparks, H. F. D., editor. *The Apocryphal Old Testament*. Oxford: Clarendon, 1984.

Stagg, Frank. *Polarities of Man's Existence in Biblical Perspective*. Philadelphia: Westminster, 1973.

Stringfellow, William. *An Ethic for Christians and Other Aliens in a Strange Land*. Waco: Word Books, 1973.

Summers, Ray. *Worthy Is the Lamb*. Nashville: Broadman, 1951.

Sweet, J. P. M. *Revelation*. Westminster Pelican Commentaries. Philadelphia: Westminster, 1979.

Swete, Henry Barclay. *Commentary on Revelation*. Grand Rapids: Kregel, 1977; reprint of the 3rd ed. published by Macmillan, London, 1911, under the title, *The Apocalypse of St. John*.

Talbert, Charles H. *The Apocalypse: A Reading of the Revelation of John*. Westminster/John Knox, 1994.

Taylor, Barbara Brown. "Faith Matters: The Great Tribulation." *The Christian Century* 115/22 (12-19 August 1998): 758.

Taylor, L. R. *The Divinity of the Roman Emperor*. Middletown CT: American Philological Association, 1931.

Thompson, Leonard L. *The Book of Revelation: Apocalypse and Empire*. New York: Oxford University Press, 1990.

____. *Revelation*. Abingdon New Testament Commentaries. Nashville: Abingdon, 1998.

Thurman, Howard. *With Head and Heart: The Autobiography of Howard Thurman*. San Diego: Harcourt Brace & Co., 1979.

Tillich, Paul. *Systematic Theology*. Vol. 1. Chicago: University of Chicago Press, 1951.

Trites, Allison A. *The New Testament Concept of Witness*. New York: Cambridge University Press, 1977.

Turner, Nigel. *Christian Words*. Nashville: Thomas Nelson, 1981.

Tutu, Desmond. *Hope and Suffering*. Grand Rapids: Eerdmans, 1984.

Twain, Mark. *Letters from the Earth*. Edited by Bernard DeVoto. New York: Harper & Row, 1962.

Vermes, Geza. *The Complete Dead Sea Scrolls in English*. London: Penguin, 1997.

Wainwright, Arthur W. *Mysterious Apocalypse: Interpreting the Book of Revelation*. Nashville: Abingdon, 1993.

Williams, Philip J. *The Catholic Church and Politics in Nicaragua and Costa Rica*. Pittsburgh: University of Pittsburgh Press, 1989.

Willimon, William H. *Word, Water, Wine and Bread*. Valley Forge PA: Judson, 1980.

Wink, Walter. *Engaging the Powers: Discernment and Resistance in a World of Domination*. Minneapolis: Fortress, 1992.

____. *Naming the Powers: The Language of Power in the New Testament*. Philadelphia: Fortress, 1984.

____. *Unmasking the Powers: The Invisible Powers That Determine Human Existence*. Philadelphia: Fortress, 1986.

Yamauchi, Edwin M. *New Testament Cities in Asia Minor*. Grand Rapids: Baker, 1980.

INDEX OF MODERN AUTHORS

INDEX OF SIDEBARS

Illustration Sidebars

INDEX OF SCRIPTURES

INDEX OF TOPICS